Introductory Programming with

Simple Games

Using Java and the Freely Available Networked Game Engine

Dr. Brian C. Ladd
Dr. Jam Jenkins

WILEY
Publishers Since 1807

ACQUISITIONS EDITOR	Beth Golub
MARKETING MANAGER	Chris Ruel
COVER DESIGN	Wendy Lai
COVER PHOTO	Front: Michael Klatt, Rachel Mitchell and Michael Hogan
	Back: Brian C. Ladd
MEDIA EDITOR	Lauren Sapira
PRODUCTION MANAGER	Micheline Frederick

This book was designed by the author and typeset using LaTeX and the Gentium Book Basic font. It was printed and bound by Courier Westford. The cover was printed by Courier Westford.

This book is printed on acid free paper.

Library of Congress Cataloging in Publication Data:

978-0470-21284-4

Printed in the United States of America

10 9 8 7 6 5 4 3 2 1

Contents

Acknowledgments

We would especially like to thank Robert Duvall of Duke University for making valuable contributions to the FANG engine and early versions of the textbook.

We would like to thank the following Paul Barton, Daniel Fernandez, and Blair Sanders, students at Georgia Gwinnett College, helped us review early versions of the textbook and provided valuable feedback.

Our thanks go to our editor at Wiley, Beth Golub. She knew just how hard certain academics need to be motivated with a boot. Without her effort on our behalf, this book would not exist. Her assistant, Michael Berlin, handled every "Make it so" with aplomb and made sure everything went as smoothly as possible. Micheline Fredrick, the production editor, also worked very hard to make sure that what we visualized could become what you hold in your hands.

Finally, our thanks to all of the FOSS designers, authors, contributors, testers, and document writers who developed the software behind the development of this book: LaTeX, emacs, Inkscape, GIMP, Linux, Shutter, ImageMagik, and the *Gentium Book Basic* font.

Thanks to my wife, Maegan Bos, and my son, Nicholas J. Bos-Ladd. They were both long suffering, one wondering when I might cook dinner again, the other wondering why we weren't playing *Fallout 3*. I would never have made it without them.

Dr. John B. Smith at UNC Chapel Hill, for helping me realize that the random ideas I had about introductory programming texts were aspects of an event-driven introduction to programming. Also, for being my academic and thesis advisor.

Lynn Andrea Stein's *Rethinking CS101* project for starting a discussion (in my head) about what expectations in introductory programming books should be.

Kim B. Bruce and the *Java: An Eventful Approach* gang at Williams College for reviving my interest in an event-driven introduction to computer programming. — Dr. Brian C. Ladd

A special thanks goes out to all of the former students at the Duke University Talent Identification Program for pushing the limits of what the FANG engine could do, for all of the valuable testing, and for inspiring me to work so hard.

Thanks to Dietolf Ramm for all his guidance and mentoring in computer science education, and for team teaching with me as part of my first college teaching experience (using a very early version of the FANG engine).

Thanks to my wife, Christine Clay, for her patience during the many long days of intense work on this textbook. — Dr. Jam Jenkins

Forward

So, you want to be a game developer?

You're part way there, by buying this book. The next step is the most important one you can take.

Make some games.

There's nothing that proves you want to do something more than doing it. Believe me, I get thousands of resumes from kids who want to make video games. A recent survey showed that more than half of the students entering an undergraduate computer science program had the goal of working in computer games. These guys work hard in school, volunteer in their community, and letter in two varsity sports . . . but so often, they never found time to just *make some games*. And when we see that, the resume is an immediate no-hire. Honestly, I'd rather hire someone who dropped out of school and worked passionately on games, than sat in a classroom doing the minimum, waiting for a games career to come to him.

But you do need to distinguish yourself from the pack. The first step, really, is to *make some games*. But the next step is to be better than everyone else. You'll need a solid background in math, and physics, and the theory and basis of computer science. You'll need the experience of working as part of a team, which you'll get during more advanced software project courses. So maybe, staying in school is the right idea. And you never know who you'll meet while you're taking classes in a field you enjoy.

I met the lead author, Brian Ladd, when we were in graduate school at the University of North Carolina at Chapel Hill. We both enjoyed playing games, but neither of us had any plans to work with them. We both initially followed the pure academic route, completing our doctorate degrees and joining university faculty. Soon after, however, our paths diverged.

I joined the faculty at a military postgraduate school. My students were officers, and our emphasis was on simulations, virtual reality, and training systems. My colleagues and I definitely saw the benefit of games in improving interest in training programs; just like students, soldiers were more willing to spend extra time with training software when it was designed around a game. We eventually built *America's Army*, which we released publicly in hopes of improving recruiting for the U.S. Army. That game was a major success, and the success was attributed to the fact that it was *fun*. Players knew they were learning about the Army, and they didn't mind, because it was fun.

It didn't take long for me to realize that I was a much better game designer/producer than I was a researcher. That led me to start a games company, which I later merged with Epic Games, makers of *Unreal Tournament* and *Gears of War*. We also make the Unreal Engine, which is being used in hundreds of game titles worldwide. And it led me to beg and plead with Brian to leave academia for a little while, to be a game developer at Epic. Brian was very successful at Epic, but it was clear his true passion was with teaching, and he left a year later to return to a teaching university in New York. He loved teaching first-year computer science classes, so he could introduce students to the field, and possibly infect them with his enthusiasm. Most of his students were majoring in another subject, using the programming course to fulfill a science elective. For him, the challenge was engaging his students, and he saw the best response and interest in games-based assignments. With his practical experience learned with us at Epic Games, Brian refined that games-focused curriculum over the years, which of course was the genesis of this textbook.

Flipping through the table of contents for this book, you might be wondering what a flu epidemic simulator, or a text adventure game, has to do with making blockbuster franchise games like *Grand Theft Auto* or *Gears of War*. To me, that's a great test for whether the games industry is the right place for you. I hope you look at that epidemic simulator and want to build it — mostly so you can figure out how to take it apart! I admit, when I saw that program, that's what I did. Then, I wanted to make a game out of it, in which the goal was to determine the ideal place to start an infection. (Whether "ideal" was the quickest route to wiping out the population, or maximizing survivors, was left as an exercise.) If you, like me, began mentally breaking down that program, you're probably cut out for the games industry. As the book explains, playing games is just problem solving, approached with a fun attitude. Fun is what makes them so powerful — they can be used to motivate students, keep trainees focused longer, and even teach gamers about the Army. That power doesn't come for free. Games are simple, but making fun games can be deceptively complex.

Take a racing game, for example. One might guess at the effort that goes into the physics to make the cars behave in a realistic manner as they move around the track. Imagine a five-lap race against a computer opponent, in which the player accidentally hits the brake button instead of the gas button at the start of the race. If the computer opponent drives effectively, the player can never catch up—which means they'll get frustrated, and they'll give up. So, you need a way for the computer driver to make occasional mistakes, to give the human player a reason to stay in the race. But those mistakes can't be too obvious, or else the player will realize what's happening, realize there's no real challenge, and stop playing. That delicate balance is an integral piece in creating fun, and, as a game programmer, that will be your job. At first, it'll probably be your job to write the version that's no fun because of the good driver, the bad driver, the bad physics, the bad racetrack design . . . but eventually, you'll get it right, and that's the fun version.

The authors of *Simple Games* call computer science an art, and I agree wholeheartedly. Cliff Bleszinski, the well-known Design Director at Epic Games, doesn't write program code. Instead, he works with the design team on an idea, like a new kind of grenade that's thrown like a bolo, and then he hands it to a programmer. The programmer isn't simply deciding what data structure to use; she is also deciding how the animations will work, how the damage will occur in what area, whether it should bounce before exploding, when to trigger the sound, etc. There's so much "last mile design" that goes into making games, and that usually rests on the programming team.

And speaking of teams — every game programmer works on a team at some time in his or her career. Since you're just learning how to program, some of the best advice I can give is to learn now to make your programs easy to read. Reading programs is often much more difficult than writing them. This book will give you a number of tips on commenting and readability — believe them! Live by them! So many people learn to program by writing small exercises in a day or two, so they never see the inevitable problem that arises from unreadable code. Undecipherable, uncommented code will hurt team productivity. It'll also hurt your personal productivity; inevitably, you'll come back to that grenade code weeks after you wrote it, to figure out why it's not bouncing enough. If you didn't think about readability, you'll waste time trying to decipher your own work. Once you're near the end of this book, give it a try; go find one of your programs from the middle of the book, and make some minor changes. Writing readable code isn't any harder; it just takes a little practice. I promise it's worth it.

That's not the only valuable lesson hidden between the lines in this book. The majority of games are made with a resuable engine, which handles many of the problems that are shared between multiple games, like graphics, physics, networking, sound, and so forth. Your time with the FANG engine will help you there, and you've got a guide to help you along the way. After that, think about spending some time with one of the modifiable commercial engines. Whether it's our Unreal Engine 3, the Quake engine, or something else entirely, get some experience with modding. I can't say it enough: if you want a job in this industry, show your passion for creating games by creating them. The secret to making games is that there isn't a secret. Getting started with games isn't hard. Sure, it can be a little intimidating to dive right in and create a modification to *Unreal Tournament*, or make a flash game to sell online. But you've got an edge, because *Simple Games* has everything you need to get started. By the time you're done, you'll be ready to start experimenting with your own games.

Please do. We need all the fun we can get!

Dr. Mike Capps
President, Epic Games

Preface

Introductory Programming with Simple Games grew out of a love for computer games and a recognition that the field of computer games contains *every* hard problem in software development and most hard theory problems as well. It was also informed by the observation that most fascinating discoveries come in the overlap between two disciplines. Computer games, just growing into an academic field on their own, represent a frontier where computer science, storytelling, art, and play all come together. Students are introduced to this area full of ideas where different views are used to teach them introductory computer programming.

Motivation

When this project started, too many moons ago, Dr. Ladd had been using computer games as final projects in an introductory course for almost a decade. He had also just taken a year off of teaching to go develop games at Epic Games. The return to teaching had him reexamining everything he did in the classroom to see if he could do it better.

At about the same time, in another classroom far, far away, Dr. Jenkins was developing a pedagogical game engine to support introductory students in programming games. He, too, had used games as ad hoc assignments for a while and wanted to rethink how CS1 could harness games. From this work sprang the Freely Available Networked Game (FANG) engine.

The point, for both authors, at that time was how to use computer games to motivate students. Successful computer scientists *play* with their code; the then current crop of undergraduates seemed less interested in experimenting with the code, making changes just to see what happened. Yet many of them played video games, learning complex button sequences for special moves, memorizing maps, and maximizing return on investment for various game resources. The same spirit of play was needed in the classroom.

The goal of this book is modest: to teach introductory computer science *using* computer games as the problem domain. Traditional outcomes such as familiarity with sequence, selection, iteration, delegation, and abstraction, the ability to read files, and experience declaring, filling, and traversing arrays (or `ArrayLists`) are expected even though the problems are not strictly traditional.

When Dr. Ladd and Dr. Jenkins met at a computer science education conference (for the third time in as many years) and found themselves discussing the need for students to play with their code, to make small changes to see what happened, they both brought up games in CS1. Mutual interest in games and respect of what the other had already done led to collaboration on *Introductory Programming with Simple Games*.

Mining the Past for the Future

Much of this book is standard: chapters introduce new topics, each section ends with some reading review questions, and each chapter has a series of review *and* programming projects at the end. Some is less standard: each chapter develops a single computer game to motivate the new concepts, the `main` method is introduced very late, and, perhaps strangest of all, loop constructs don't appear until the second half of the book. This section puts the unconventional choices in context.

Focus on a single computer game.   After the first two chapters, each chapter begins with the high-level design of a computer game. The games are simple two-dimensional arcade games, owing a great debt to the golden age of the arcade in the early 1980s (when the authors misspent both their youth and their allowances in video game parlors and tinkering with early home computers).

The new game presents new challenges by designing features that are difficult or impossible with the Java programming learned in previous chapters. This motivates the need for reading from data files (Chapter 12), creating and using single- and multidimensional `ArrayList` structures (Chapters 8 and 9, respectively), and even the use of the `if` statement (Chapter 4). In addition to motivation, the game design also provides an intellectual framework for students, into which they can place the new Java constructs they are learning. It is something like "Just-in-time Java," providing the student with just the constructs they need, just as they need them.

The games themselves explore some of the all-time great arcade games of the past. There are clones of *Tetris*, *Space Invaders*, and, of course, *Pong*. There is a flu pandemic simulator[1] to introduce serious uses of games and the building of an interactive fiction (text adventure game) engine that can be modified to play multiple different games. Students and teachers using this book are encouraged to use these games as jumping off points to explore the history of computer hardware, computer game studies, and even the ethics of computer games.

Delayed introduction of the `main` method.   One driving force behind writing a textbook was the desire to vanquish the magic incantation, presented on day one in every CS1 classroom using Java: "You type in **public static void** main inside each and every program you write. No, we will not be explaining any of those terms for several weeks." The FANG engine, using code based on the ACM's Java Task Force's `acm` package,[2] does not require students to have their own `main` method. This means that both applications and applets (programs running on *your* computer or programs served up inside a Web browser) can be written without any **static** methods.

Learning to program with a toolkit can be a trade-off: the more powerful the toolkit, the more interesting the programs a beginner can produce, but the more powerful the toolkit, the more the student learns to program the toolkit and *not* the underlying programming language. FANG was designed with this firmly in mind. Every design decision was made in the service of teaching introductory computer science. Thus the book does introduce `main` and non-FANG programming (three chapters use no FANG at all). The book also exposes as much of the engine as possible so that beginners can understand what is happening inside of the FANG engine.

Iteration deferred until the second half of the book.   You might ask how a student can learn "traditional" computer science from a book that delays the introduction of count-controlled and sentinel-controlled loops so long. The answer lies in FANG and the game loop.

At the heart of every interactive computer game (and every interactive computer program, for that matter) is a loop that runs over and over until the game is finished. At its most general, the game loop is

```
while (game is not done)
   show the game state
   read user input
   advance game state using input and previous state
```

The game state is the current configuration of the game, user input is whatever mechanism the game expects the user to use to interact with it, and advancing the game state permits the configuration to evolve over time in response to the players' choices.

---

[1]Written well before the N1H1 "swine" flu scare of 2009.
[2]And code developed, independently, by Dr. Ladd.

This loop is at the heart of *every* FANG game. Students write their own advance method. That means the student is in charge of updating the game state in response to the players' choices. It also means that the student's code is called over and over and over again (approximately 20 times per second) so they can *effectively* iterate by executing a command once each time advance is called.

Consider adding 100 elements to the screen. It would be possible to put a Java for loop into advance to do that once during the first frame. Alternatively, the student could program a counter and each time through advance test if the count is less than 100. If it is, add an element, increment the counter, and move on. After five seconds the counter will count the 100 elements on the screen.

The *idea* of iteration is introduced much earlier than the Java iteration constructs are introduced. The Java for loop is introduced with traversal of ArrayLists and the while loop is introduced with end-of-file controlled loops and Scanner objects.

Getting and Using FANG

The Freely Available Networked Game Engine is exactly that

- **Freely Available** — the most current version of FANG is always available from www.fangengine.org. The code is *open source* so you can download, study, and modify the engine to your heart's content.

  Also available at www.fangengine.org are tutorials on integrating FANG in most modern integrated development environments. If you want to play with FANG without downloading it, you can surf over to www.javawide.org, the home of the Java Web IDE. FANG is already installed there and all the source code from this book is available to play with. The JavaWIDE environment permits you to edit Java code in Web pages and then run the results right there in your browser.

- **Networked** — FANG programs can work together across the network. Look at Chapter 7 or surf over to www.fangengine.org and look at the multiplayer tutorials. As with all games in this book, JavaWIDE has the code and can run multiplayer games right inside your browser.

- **Game Engine** — FANG was developed to support students in introductory courses writing games from day one. The first chapter of this book contains two variations on the venerable *Asteroids* game each with less than a page of Java code. Sample student projects (such as those used for cover images) are also available at the FANG Website. They cover the spectrum of two-dimensional games from platformers to role-playing games.

Instructor information on *Introductory Programming with Simple Games* including additional chapter review questions, programming projects, and some pointers on teaching a game-based CS1 are available at the book's site, www.simplecomputergames.com and the Wiley Website, www.wiley.com.

How to Read Syntax Templates

Computer languages are artificial languages designed to eliminate as much ambiguity as possible. Because they are designed to be processed by computers, the structure of the language can be formally expressed.

The Extended Backus-Naur Form (EBNF) is a mathematically formal way of expressing the syntax (structure) of a programming language. The notation was developed by John Backus and enhanced by Peter Naur more than forty years ago.

We will use an EBNF notation to describe templates for various language constructs. The notation will use <somename> to indicated named *non-terminal* symbols, that is, symbols that stand for other templates defined somewhere else. Symbols outside of the angle brackets, except for those special characters defined here, stand for themselves.

The special symbols are:

:=	Defined as: the symbol to the left of this symbol is defined by the template on the right of the symbol.
[...]	Group the elements between into one expression for application of the various repeat and optional markers.
|	Selection between the prior and following expressions. One or the other can appear.
?	Optional: the item this follows can appear zero or one time.
+	Optional repeat: the item this follows can appear one or more times.
*	Repeat: the item this follows can appear zero or more times.

So, as an example, a floating point number, a number with an optional decimal part, could be written with the rules:

```
<floatingPoint> := -? <digit>+ [. <digit>+]?
<digit> := 0 | 1 | 2 | 3 | 4 | 5 | 6 | 7 | 8 | 9
```

This says that a floating point number has at least one digit to the left of the decimal point (thus .1 is *not* valid according to this template) and if there is a decimal point, there must be at least one digit to the right of the decimal point. The decimal point (and any following digits) are optional. The negative sign is optional and, by this definition, a leading plus sign is not valid.

The point of using these templates is that they are unambiguous and show exactly what is valid when declaring some particular Java language structure.

One note is that we will use simplified templates early in the book, templates that do not include all of the complexities permitted in a given structure. As we make use of the complex features we will repeat the template with the more complex parts. Thus the *last* template presented in the book is the most complete. To aid in studying, the templates presented in each chapter are repeated at the end of the chapter in the summary, and the most complete templates are collected in Appendix C on page 497.

Getting Started: What's in a Game?

While some computer scientists are sometimes loath to hear it, creating a computer program is as much art as it is science. Converting an **idea** for a computer program into a **programmable description** of that idea is a *design task*; in fact, that phase of development is called the *design phase* by developers. Designers of all types have rules that they apply, yet there remains an *aesthetic* dimension which cannot be learned from a book; it is learned only through practice.

This is actually a very wonderful thing: computer programming, from scratch to running code, involves both *creative* and *analytic* capabilities. It uses all the parts of the programmer's brain that can be brought to bear.

Learning the aesthetic component of a design skill requires *practice* and evaluation of the results. One of the most important parts of the practice is to play with the elements, trying different combinations and trying for different effects. This book uses computer games as a programming area to teach introductory computer programming. The preface discusses the approach in detail, but there are two primary reasons for this: computer games encompass all of the hard problems in computer science, and making computer games tricks you into playing with the computer programs.

Playing the computer games in this book motivates you to improve them; some improvements are suggested in the text or exercises, but you are sure to come up with other, better changes on your own. To tweak what happens in the computer *game* you have to tweak what happens in the computer *program*.

This chapter begins with an overview of how this book is designed. It then examines the parallels between a game and a computer program, starting by looking for a usable definition of a game. The following chapters begin giving you the tools to build your own game using the Freely Available Networked Game (FANG) engine and the Java programming language.

1.1 Learning rom *Simple Computer Games*

This book is about computer programming. Specifically, it is an introduction to computer programming for students with little or no experience with computer programming. It is important to keep that in mind as you read the book, because there is a lot of talk about games. It might seem, superficially, that the book is *about* games; this section explains how that is not the case.

Structure

The book begins, in this chapter, with a definition of what a *game* is. That definition is then tied to the definition of a *computer program*. At the end of the chapter the code for an *Asteroids*-clone, *Meteors*, is presented. You are given the game and only a brief explanation so that you can play with the code. You only learn design skills and programming skills by practicing them.

The program given in this chapter is also an instance of the spiral approach taken by the text. New features of the programming language, the game engine, and computer science are presented as soon as you could possibly *use* them. Later sections and chapters revisit the same topics so that you learn why they work the way they do and, more importantly, how to design and build them yourself.

In this first chapter you see a Java program and receive a recipe for compiling and running the program. The terms "compile" and "run" are both given a sentence of definition, and the structure of the program is presented in three paragraphs.

If you have limited programming experience, this is not enough for you to understand what is going on. It should be enough for you to compile and run one program. With some guidance from end-of-section and end-of-chapter questions, you can then modify it. At this point, if anything goes wrong, you do not know enough to fix it.

Chapter 2 again presents the overall structure of a Java program with five times as much explanation. Now some of the "magic incantations" used in making the program run are explained.

The book uses a game engine/learning library called FANG. FANG provides a lot of support for beginning students for writing games. It is, initially, another collection of magic incantations, protecting the student from the sharp corners inside of Java. As you gain familiarity with Java concepts while using FANG, some of the pieces of FANG are peeled back. Three of the last four chapters of the book involve writing game programs that do not use FANG at all.

The first two chapters are atypical: they present new concepts in a very broad context. This is because you need to learn a little bit about how computers work in order to understand the commands you type into the machine.

The remaining chapters begin by setting a much more limited context: they begin by describing a particular game. The game in each chapter requires some new aspect of programming. You begin using objects defined in FANG and controlled by rules defined in FANG. One game requires defining your own rules for FANG objects. Another has a large number of similar objects, motivating the development of object containers. In each case, the game design discussion at the beginning of the chapter leads to a program design discussion and a realization of what we have not yet learned to do. This gives you a place to hang the new programming concepts and Java techniques.

This book is *about* the programming concepts first, about Java programming skills second, and finally about simple computer games. The *simple* is there so that you can focus on the underlying structure, the introductory computer science, that makes the games possible. The *computer games* are there to give you feedback as you learn the computer science concepts.

1.2   What's in a Game?

Consider for a moment the seemingly simple question: What is a *game*? Do *you* know what a game is? Everyone I have ever asked that question answers, "Yes," yet almost everyone balks when I follow up with the obvious, "Well, what is it?" Before we can compare games and programs, we need a working definition of each term.

Definitions

Before proceeding, we should examine that last statement above: *do* we need a definition of a game? Is it true? In *The Art of Game Design* [Sch08], Jesse Schell spends almost two pages talking about academics, game researchers who demand detailed game definitions, definitions that do not interest practicing game designers.

The rant stung as the authors both are academics who study and teach with games. As Schell worked through the next dozen pages, he found some merit in the struggle to define games: a definition provides a mental framework for holding the pieces we learn about game design and programming. Having a working definition of a game also makes it easier to exploit parallels between game and program design and implementation; it lets us analogize from one field to the other.

Dictionary Definitions

The *Oxford English Dictionary* provides an interesting starting place with "**4. a.** a diversion of the nature of a contest, played according to rules, and displaying in the result the superiority either in skill, strength, or good fortune of the winner or winners." [OED71] Alternatively, "**8. c.** the apparatus for playing particular games." [OED89] Each of these definitions provides useful pieces: a game has *rules* and is played with *apparatus* of some sort. If you think about a simple computer game, the game has virtual apparatus of some kind and some sort of rules.

Other dictionaries have the same general definition though the *American Heritage Dictionary* is one non-specialized dictionary providing a mathematical definition: "A model of a competitive situation that identifies interested parties and stipulates rules governing all aspects of the competition, used in game theory to determine the optimal course of action for an interested party". [AHD00] Again we see rules but these rules apply to the party *playing* the game rather than to the apparatus *in* the game. This definition might be useful when developing *strategies*, ways of playing games, particularly when constructing computer opponents.

The current popularity of game design in general and the study of video games in particular means that there is a considerable specialized literature on games and play. Perhaps their definitions are better suited to our need.

Literature Definitions

Salen and Zimmerman, in *Rule of Play*, relate *play* and *game* by noting that not all languages have two different words for the two concepts. Further, they note that, "Games are a subset of play," and "Play is a component of games." [SZ04] Of all the play we do, only some of it is games (the first statement), yet when we use a game, we play it (the second statement). This permits us to look at definitions of play as well as games.

Johan Huizinga, a Dutch anthropologist, published his *Homo Ludens* ("Man the Game Player") in 1938, offering one of the first and broadest academic definitions of play:

> [Play is] a free activity standing quite consciously outside "ordinary" life as being "not serious," but at the same time absorbing the player intensely and utterly. It is an activity connected with no material interest, and no profit can be gained by it. It proceeds within its own proper boundaries of time and space according to fixed rules and in an orderly manner. It promotes the formation of social groupings, which tend to surround themselves with secrecy and to stress their difference from the common world by disguise or other means. [Hui55]

What does this have that our dictionary definitions lack? It talks about play as being outside of ordinary life, bounded in time and space; he goes on to talk about the "magic circle" that people enter when they begin a game, the magic circle containing the rules that apply while the players are in it. The magic is further reflected in the total absorption of players while the game lacks seriousness or real-world consequences.

David Parlett, a game historian, offers a definition of *formal* games in the *The Oxford History of Board Games*:

> A formal game has a twofold structure based on *ends* and *means*:

> Ends. It is a contest to achieve an objective. (The Greek for game is agôn, meaning contest.) Only one of the contenders, be they individuals or teams, can achieve it, since achieving it ends the game. To achieve that object is to win. Hence a formal game, by definition, has a winner; and winning is the "end" of the game in both senses of the word, as termination and as object.

Means. It has an agreed set of equipment and of procedural "rules" by which the equipment is manipulated to produce a winning situation. [Par99]

This definition captures the idea of challenge or competition in a game as well as explicitly mentioning both the game rules and the game equipment.

There are literally dozens of attempts to define game and play in the emerging game studies literature as well as in game design guides, books that are less academic but more focused on helping budding game designers learn the skill of game design.

Jesse Schell, in *The Art of Game Design*, examines a number of definitions before settling on our final and shortest definition of play and games:

Play is manipulation that satisfies curiosity. . . . A game is a problem-solving activity, approached with a playful attitude. [Sch08]

This is of particular resonance for a computer programmer because computer science is, fundamentally, problem solving. *All* a computer program is is a formal description of how to solve a problem. This definition does not go into detail about the rules and equipment, but that is what the rest of Schell's book is about.

Game Studies

Game studies is a fairly young field of academic study, having grown up in parallel with the rise of the video game industry. Prior to the 1980s, only a handful of historians and anthropologists studied games and play and their definition. Johan Huizinga, in his 1938 *Homo Ludens* (quoted in the chapter), offered a book-length examination of games across cultures and across history.

Several different approaches to the study of games have emerged. Anthropologists remain interested in the meaning of games to the people who play them. Sociologists and economists study how people interact with games as systems. New media scholars study games as artistic constructs, examining how they communicate their different messages. Computer scientists, game designers, and other technologists focus on how games are made and on the industry that makes them. In the following descriptions of specific research, notice how interconnected the different approaches are.

Study of the meaning and impact of games on players includes looking at games as learning tools, games as simulations, and how games change their players. The military has been interested in games in the first two senses here since before World War II with the use of flight simulators. As early as the 1940s *analog computers* were used to calculate the outcomes of the settings of flight controls.

Learning with games has begun moving into the mainstream with Gee's *What Videogames Have to Teach Us About Learning and Literacy* [Gee03] being a recent attempt to look at **what** players learn from the games they play and how that experience can be used to reach modern students. The negative impact of games is also a focus of this approach. *Grand Theft Childhood: The Surprising Truth About Violent Video Games* [KO08] by Kutner and Olson is a popular press book surveying this research. This research impacted the games presented in this book in that there is a conscious effort to limit the amount of violence in any of the game designs. This is a personal, designer-specific decision, but the book attempts to create games with playable mechanics without a violent veneer.

Sociologists look at the social constructs surrounding games. Some study massively multiplayer online games (MMOs) and the societies that arise within them. Others look at the "mod communities," the groups that form around different games to modify and extend them. Mia Consalvo's *Cheating: Gaining Advantage in Videogames* [Con07] looks at players who subvert the social contract in multiplayer games. Another interesting approach to examining MMOs is taken by economist Edward Castranova in *Synthetic Worlds: The Business and Culture of Online Games* [Cas05] which looks at online games' internal economies as models of the real world.

Media studies looks at the message being sent by the game designer. This is closely related to what/how games teach their players. Many in this field, such as Ian Bogost (*Persuasive Games* [Bog07]), look at the

---

Game Studies

"accidental" messages contained in some early and commercial video games and look for ways to use the same methods to actively communicate a particular message.

The book in your hands is a result of the computer science approach to game studies: looking at how games are made exposed the deep computer science problems in video games, which was then brought back to the introductory classroom. Others, including Rudy Rucker in *Software Engineering and Computer Games* [Ruc02], have had similar insights.

This approach also includes the massive number of game design books. Chris Crawford's *The Art Of Computer Game Design: Reflections Of A Master Game Designer* [Cra84] is a seminal work in this field. Salen and Zimmerman's *Rules of Play: Game Design Fundamentals* [SZ04] is a more recent, incredibly comprehensive take on game and, in particular, video game design.

A recent, readable overview of the state of video game studies as a whole is James Newman's *Videogames* [New04]. The fledgling field of game studies has only recently begun having its own academic journals and conferences; the continuing popularity of video games indicates that the field continues to grow apace.

A Working Definition

Looking at these sample definitions, we can extract our own more general and more detailed definition:

> A *game* is a collection of components that interact according to a set of rules presenting the player with a meaningful choices to make in determining the outcome of a struggle with the environment or another player.[1]

The "meaningful choices" is an attempt to capture the problem solving in Schell's definition; these are also where the absorption of Huizinga's definition emerges. The "outcome" of the game reflects the contest elements in Parlett's definition and implies we need ways of keeping score.

This definition gives us names for the parts of a game, a way to talk about how a game is built. It also gives us names for the parts of a *computer game*.

The remainder of this section explores components and rules as they appear in games. Following sections explore how they apply to computer programs and computer games.

This chapter talks about computer programs but includes only one. Do not use that as an excuse to skip it. It is not that long, and the insight you gain from this parallel presentation will help you explore the computer programs presented in all of the following chapters.

Things: Components

Figure 1.1: Components of Checkers

---

[1]This definition fails to address the "entertaining" and "amusing" portions of the dictionary definitions; these dimensions are subjective and difficult to quantify. This book uses games to teach software design and development; while some mention is made of "fun," the player experience is more properly the domain of game design. Interested students are referred to the references at the end of the book.

Components are the *things* used to play a game. A traditional game of checkers, for example, has sixty-four squares in two colors arranged in an 8×8 alternating square, that is, a checkerboard, and twenty-four checkers, also in two colors.

There are two flavors of components: *passive* components (like those in checkers) and *active* components which move on their own (due to physics) or add something new to an ongoing game.

Passive Components

Passive components are placeholders, used to keep track of the game's progress. The checkers and board in Figure 1.1, the playing cards in bridge or poker, or the peg board in cribbage are all examples of passive components. The players of the game manipulate the passive components according to the rules of the game.

Active Components

Active components are components that "make decisions" about how to contribute to the game. The "decision maker" differs for different components: dice and marbles move according to the laws of physics (interacting with the table, gravity, one another, and friction); collectible cards have their automatic actions enumerated on them or listed in the rules for the game.

Cubic dice, when rolled, bounce and rub on the surface to provide the players with a random number, something that was not there before. Other games' active components include the marbles in Milton Bradley's *Hungry Hungry Hippos* or the creature cards in the various collectible card games (Wizards of the Coast's *Magic: The Gathering* or Nintendo's *Pokémon*).

Actions: Rules

Figure 1.2: Checkers Opening Position

Rules determine how the components of the game interact: the starting configuration of components, legal moves to change the configuration, how the configuration is evaluated for scoring, and how to know when the game ends. The rules also determine the winning player, and even if there *is* a winning player.

Consider traditional checkers again. The rules specify the opening configuration shown in Figure 1.2. Players then alternate moving one checker at a time diagonally onto an adjacent, unoccupied square. Initially, all checkers may move only toward the opponent's rear rank; checker pieces are *promoted* when they reach the opponent's rear rank and as *kings* can move in any diagonal direction. Checkers may *jump* an opposing checker if they are adjacent to it and there is an unoccupied square just past it in a direction that the checker could normally move. The game ends when one player loses his last checker or cannot make a legal move; the player unable to move loses the game. The rules prescribe each player's goal within the game as well as how checkers and board squares interact.

A set of rules can be applied to different components without changing the game: for example, chess can be played on a pocket board, with life-sized pieces, or even on a piece of paper by mail. The components differ in scale but not in kind; the same set of rules means the *same* game.

Figure 1.3: Playing Cards

The same is not true of games sharing only components. Both bridge and "Go Fish!" use a deck of 52 cards divided into four suits with thirteen values each. The *relationship* between the components, embodied in the rules, is different. The initial configuration, sets of legal moves, and even each player's goals differ. This is a different game.

Review 1.2

(a) You are trying to create your own game to play with two six-sided dice and two or more players. The game is made up of rounds. The first round begins by each player rolling the dice and marking down the number that is the sum of the two dice. This number is the starting score. After everyone has had a chance to roll the dice, the first round ends. During each successive round, the player with the lowest score rolls first and then the player with the next lowest score rolls next, and so on until all players have rolled during the round. After each roll, the sum of the die rolls is added to the previous sum. The first player to reach or exceed 100 wins the game. According to our definition, is this a game? Why or why not?

(b) Chris Crawford, in *The Art of Game Design* [Cra84], differentiates between a *puzzle* and a *game*: a puzzle presents the player with a configuration and rules for changing the configuration, but the configuration is fixed and to be *solved*. A game has *interactivity* in that the configuration changes over time with or without intervention of the player. Does our definition capture this difference? Or would our definition admit a puzzle as a game? Is such a difference important?

(c) Can you name three games played primarily with a pair of six-sided dice? Describe the rules of each. How are *turns* different between the games? How are *winning conditions* different between the games? Could any of the rules work with twelve-sided dice instead of six-sided?

1.3 Active and Passive: Rule Followers

The rules provide the users with the choices they make in their struggle to win the game. How are rules followed for active and passive components? Can we reconcile the two different kinds of components?

Who Follows the Rules?

In a turn-based game with only passive components, who follows the rules? As a practical question, how are the rules being interpreted, and how are game configurations modified so that only legal configurations are used?

Consider players **A** and **B** playing a game of checkers. As they alternate turns, each follows the rules as part of making his or her turn. When player **A** makes his move, he considers the rules of the checkers; he is, of course, also considering how he is going to win. He follows the rules of checkers in making a legal move and the rules of his strategy by picking his "best" move from those available. After player **A** moves, player **B** takes over, following the rules of checkers and her own strategy for the duration of her turn. Thus **A** and **B** together provide the rule follower for their game.

What if we add a new active component, a *moderator* who mediates the players' interactions with the passive components. The players limit their interaction to the moderator, and the moderator, following the rules of the game, interacts with the remaining components.

The Moderator

Instead of moving components on their own, the checkers players in a game with a moderator take turns submitting their moves to the moderator. The moderator then follows the rules of checkers.

To keep the moderator as simple as possible, we enhance the checkers: each checker indicates all currently legal moves and, when moved, which opposing checkers (if any) are to be removed and whether or not the moving checker should be promoted. The movement rules of checkers are embedded in the checkers themselves; they are followed by the moderator.

The moderator's rules are simple and generic:

```
while current player has at least one legal move
  ask current player to pick a checker
  if checker is not legal
    back to top of loop
  else
    ask player to pick move
    if move is not legal
      back to top of loop
    else
      make move
      change current player


current player loses/other player wins
```

Though the moderator's rules say "checker," if that is changed to "component" then these rules are completely generic. They do not depend on what game is being played: the moderator follows the *game loop*.

The Game Loop

The game loop is at the heart of any moderator proctoring a game; it is also at the heart of any computer game or other interactive computer program you have ever run. At its most general, the game loop is:

```
while (not game over)
  show the game state
  get input from the user
  advance game state
```

The *game state* is the current configuration of the game: where all the pieces are, whose turn it is, what all previous moves were (if that is significant), what the goal of the game is (though that might be intrinsically part of the game definition). The state captures all of the *changeable* things in the game.

How does that match the loop above? The moderator, an example of a *rule follower*, does not actively show the state of the game (players look at the board) but otherwise follows the above loop directly.

The only thing the moderator knows about checkers is that players alternate making legal moves and that a player loses when he or she has no more legal moves. This is because we have placed all of the complicated movement rules inside the components that are moved. A turn-based game such as checkers, one with no active components other than the moderator, can be played with a single rule follower. The moderator asks each player in turn for his action, waiting and doing nothing while he thinks about the move. The moderator then follows the game loop rules (and those embedded in the checkers) according to the current player's request. Players concentrate on their personal *strategies* or rules for *winning* the game (more on strategies in the next section); the moderator concentrates on enforcing the rules to *play* the game. It is important to note the distinction between the rules of the game (which are inherent in checkers) and the strategy each player employs.

Note that each active component in a game has its own rule follower. In *Hungry Hungry Hippos*, every marble is moving according to the rules of physics *at the same time*. Each hippo waits for a player to tell it to move (by pressing her control button), but any player can tell her hippo to move at any moment and the hippo responds by biting into the arena. The marbles respond to gravity (and being hit by hippos), so the laws of physics determine their motion; each of these components moves independently and has, for our purposes, its own rule follower.

Rule followers are event-driven. That means that they act in response to things that happen. The moderator asks a question and then waits for an answer, continuing with his work only when an answer is given. The hippos are similar. The marbles, too, are waiting for things to happen to them (being hit by another marble, being swallowed by a hippo), but rather than sitting still while waiting, the marbles also move around on the board. So the two patterns of action we see with the rule followers here are waiting, doing nothing, for some trigger event to set off a sequence of rules or the continuous following of rules. In either case, each independent active component in the game has its own rule follower.

This section defined a game as a collection of components and a collection of rules that determine how the components interact, presenting the player with meaningful choices influencing the outcome of the game. Players (in this section) are outside of the game and interact with the components either one at a time or simultaneously. Components are either active or passive. Active components have rule followers that permit them to act simultaneously and they react to certain events. Central control for a game can be either manifest in a particular component or provided by the players collectively. What players choose to do is guided by their strategies, the rules they use to try to win the game.

Retrogaming

Retrogaming, also known as *old-school gaming* or *classic gaming*, is the hobby (or obsession) of playing games designed for a bygone era of gaming hardware. Some play, as does one of the authors, because they fondly recall when *Space Invaders* and *PacMan* took over their lives. Some play to experience some of the best-crafted games ever designed. Some play to explore specific designers' work. And, finally, some play because retrogames have been introduced on modern game platforms, bringing the Golden Age of arcade games alive for a new generation.

Retrogames are played in three ways, each providing a different take on the original experience: on retro hardware, in emulation, and in ports. Retro hardware is the purist's choice: find an original game system, arcade game, or console, restore it to working order, and play your heart out just as the game was designed.

Considering games from the early 1970s, it is important to remember that game machines were *not* general-purpose computers that happened to play games. They were custom-built, special-purpose computers that *only* played a specific game. This was true of the quarter-draining machines in the local arcade (a market niche virtually created by *Space Invaders* and *PacMan*), and it was true of the first generation of home game consoles.

From 1972 to 1976 home game systems such as Magnivox's **Odyssey** and Atari's **Pong** had one to five games hardwired into them; hardwired in this case to be taken literally because the circuit boards and custom logic chips really were wired to play only a few different games. In 1976 Fairchild Electronics introduced the **Channel F**, the first home game console with a computer at its heart. Games were bought on cartridges which plugged in and provided the program for the computer to run. It was also the first home console to have enough memory to provide computer-controlled opponents for games.

Retrogaming

The following year Atari introduced the **Atari 2600** (also known as the **Video Computer System (VCS)**). The **2600** was a runaway best seller, creating the real market for video game consoles and spawning hundreds of game titles from dozens of publishers.

Generations of consoles are referred to by the number of bits the computer processes at one time; more bits means more power. The 8-bit generation included the **VCS**, Mattel's **Intellivison**, and, after the Video Game Crash of 1984, the original **Nintendo Entertainment System (NES)**. The **Super NES** and the Sony **Playstation** (redubbed the **PSone** in 2000) were 16-bit winners. While the bit-size wars have ended, the computing and graphics power of consoles has continued to grow in each successive generation.

Retrogamers, longing to play the good old games but unable to find or afford the original hardware, sometimes play the original software on a console *emulator*. An emulator is a program, on a general-purpose computer, that "behaves like" the original hardware. The original game software instructs the emulator just as it would the console, and the emulator drives the modern hardware to make it play a game like the original. The idea of hardware *virtualization* is very similar to emulation. In virtualization the machine software behaves as if it were a complete computer of the *same type* as the one it is actually running on; emulation is used when the two types of computer are different.

The Multiple Arcade Machine Emulator (MAME) [MAM09] is an emulator that can play retrogames from the 8-bit through the modern eras on current PCs. As a legal note, the game software for the original system is, quite probably, under copyright and is not free to download and share.

Retrogames are also available as *ports*. A port is when a computer program written for one type of computer is translated into a program for a different computer; what the program *does* remains the same though how it does it is changed. Games are ported to gain revenue from popular titles. It is also done to make use of games designed for limited hardware: these games are well suited to the computing power now available in mobile devices. Ports are also popular on Internet distribution channels such as the **Xbox Arcade** and the **PlayStation Network**; the titles are inexpensive and appeal to a casual gamer demographic.

The games in this book owe a great debt[2] to the Golden Age (1977–1983, approximately), the 8-bit generation. Tight constraints on graphics and computing, like the linguistic limitations when writing haiku, drove designers to create masterpieces of minimalist beauty. The games here pay homage to the designers of that era but the limitations are used to keep the focus on computer programming. You, the reader, still get to create fun, playable games while you learn the fundamentals of computer programming.

Review 1.3

(a) Many sports games have referees. What is the role of a referee in a game such as baseball or basketball (or some other sport)? How is the role of the referee similar to that of the moderator described in this section?

1.4   Running a Game

This book is supported by the FANG engine. FANG is a library used by the Java programming language. FANG *is* a game moderator. A game is a collection of *objects* (software "components") of types FANG knows; FANG runs its game loop over and over, updating the state of the game according to the rules in the objects.

This section, in an effort to whet your appetite, presents the code for a simple game along with the commands you would type at the command line to run the game. The goal is to make a game run rather than for you to understand how the game works; the rest of the book covers the same ground with detailed explanations.

A *Java program* is a description of rules written in the Java programming language. The Java programming language is written in words, some of which are special *keywords*, or words defined and required by the language, and some of which are *identifiers* or names for things which the programmer can choose.

To read a Java program, we know that the code that comes after a `//` on a line or between `/*` and `*/` is a *comment*. A comment is ignored by Java (it is there only for us humans). In this book, comments are typeset in *italics*:

```
// this is a single line comment - next line is a blank line

/* <- that symbol (both characters together) starts a comment.
   The comment is treated as blank lines by Java (content ignored).
   The comment ends with that symbol -> */
```

In this book, Java keywords are typeset in **boldface**. Identifiers and all of the punctuation are typeset in a normal face. The following listing shows two keywords, an identifier and a *block*: a block is any section of the program enclosed inside of curly braces, { and }. When to use a block is explained in the next chapter.

```
public class DemonstrationClass {

}
```

```
1  // package default
2
3  import spacesprites.*; // get all space sprites
4  import fang2.core.Game;
5
6  /** Asteroids-clone game */
7  public class Meteors
8    extends Game {
9    private Ship playersShip; // Ship = component type for game
10   private Meteor rock; // Meteor = component type for game
11
12   //Called (automatically) by FANG before the game starts
13   @Override
14   public void setup() {
15     playersShip = new Ship(this); // get new component from system
16     playersShip.setColor(getColor("SCG Red"));
17     playersShip.setLocation(0.2, 0.8); // id.command(parameters)
18     // what to shoot, what to run into
19     playersShip.setTarget(Meteor.class);
20     playersShip.addCollision(Meteor.class);
21     // show the score and remaining life counter
22     playersShip.showLives();
23     playersShip.showScore();
24     addSprite(playersShip); // add ship to game
25
26     rock = new Meteor(this); // get new component
27     rock.setLocation(0.8, 0.8); // position
28     addSprite(rock); // add rock to game
29   }
30 }
```

Listing 1.1: `Meteors.java`

A complete Java listing using the Game type defined in FANG along with two spacesprites types, the Ship and the Meteor, is given above in Listing 1.1.

Important things to notice: the name after the keyword **class** in line 7 matches the name of the file where the code is stored (without the .java at the end); there are two nested blocks, the outer one running from the end of line 8 all the way to line 30 and the inner one running from the end of line 14 to line 29; and an identifier can be asked to perform an action (of which it is capable) by having the name of the identifier, a dot, the action, and any information needed by the action in parentheses.

Running a human-readable Java program is a two-step process: first you must *compile* (translate) the Java program into a simpler form and then you must *execute* (start) the simpler form with the java program. The following commands assume that you have a *command prompt*, a computer shell program where you can type commands. In the following, the *prompt*, the characters printed by the computer to tell you it is ready for a command, appears in italics; what you type is shown in normal type.

The prompt shows the folder where you are; the tilde, ~, is the current user's home directory (folder), so the source code for the class was installed directly below the home directory of the user of the code. The -classpath parameter includes a dot, a colon, and then the p*path* (folder location) of the fang2.jar file where the FANG library code is provided.

```
~/Chapter01% javac -classpath .:/usr/lib/jvm/fang2.jar Meteors.java

~/Chapter01% java -classpath .:/usr/lib/jvm/fang2.jar Meteors
```

Assuming all goes well with typing in the classpath (where Java looks for library information used by the program), the first command results in a slight pause (while the javac program, the Java *compiler*, translates the code we see in the listing above into a simpler language which is machine-friendly) and the prompt is printed again. No news is good news.

The second line runs the java (not javac) program. When the program runs, then you should see a window similar to that in Figure 1.4.

In FANG, everything above the four buttons at the bottom of the window is the game canvas; FANG game objects such as ship and rock are drawn on the game canvas. The triangle in the lower-left of the window is ship. Looking at the code in Listing 1.1, we note that the location of ship, set in line 17, is (0.2, 0.8).

FANG objects are located by their center point. The center of ship is one-fifth of the window width from the left edge of the window (0.2) and four-fifths of the window height from the top edge (0.8). The width and height of the canvas are *always* treated by FANG as 1.0 and 1.0, no matter what size the window actually is. (0.0, 0.0) is the upper-left corner of the window and (1.0, 1.0) is the lower-right corner (the y-axis is *inverted*; values get bigger the farther down the screen you go).

A FANG game is started by clicking on the **Start** button just below the game canvas on the left. When Meteors begins, the meteor begins moving (its speed and direction are randomly selected). The ship is controlled by the keyboard with left and right arrows turning it, the up arrow applying thrust in the current direction, and the space bar shooting little blue lazer balls that shatter meteors into smaller and smaller pieces.

The two numbers at the top of the screen are a count of the number of lives remaining for your ship (upper-left corner) and the score (one point per hit on a meteor). The game keeps going even after all meteors are destroyed or the ship is destroyed. Detecting the end of game and doing something reasonable in that circumstance takes more code.

Listing 1.2 on page 14 shows a meteor shower game with three meteors of varying sizes.

The three lines calling **new** to construct a meteor are the same as they were in the previous listing but for the sizes of rockA and rockB: the rock in the last game (and rockC in this game) started at size 3; they broke in half three times. Sending in 2 or 4 (as in lines 27 or 31) changes the starting size and the number of levels of splitting.

Lines 32 and 37 show a new command which Meteor supports (all screen objects in FANG support it; you can try changing the color of playersShip if you like) is setColor. All FANG Game-extending programs have the getColor command which can convert the name of a color into a Java representation of the color. The color

Figure 1.4: Meteors: A running FANG game

is passed to the setColor method to change the color of the object on the screen. Figure 1.5 on the following page shows the result of a few moments' play, with all the meteors scooting around.

This section is just a hint at what you can do with FANG. One of the goals of the text is to get you started with all of the eye candy and support in FANG, to get you playing with Java. The important thing to do is to start *playing* with the code.

Review 1.4

(a) Looking at Listing 1.2, what line number would you change to have the playerShip start in the upper-left rather than the lower-left corner? What would be an appropriate change?

(b) What do you think you would change in Meteors.java to change the gameplay so that the meteor does not collide with the player's ship?

(c) Assume you wanted to make major modifications in Meteors.java, so major that the result would really be a different game. Assume you copy the Java file to NewSpaceGame.java. What is the very first change you would have to make so that the program could compile?

Figure 1.5: MeteorShower: Game in progress

```
1   // package default
2
3   import spacesprites.*; // get all space sprites
4   import fang2.core.Game;
5
6   /** Asteroids-clone game */
7   public class MeteorShower
8     extends Game {
9     private Ship playersShip; // Ship = component type for game
10    private Meteor rockA; // Meteor = component type for game
11    private Meteor rockB; // Meteor = component type for game
12    private Meteor rockC; // Meteor = component type for game
13
14    //Called (automatically) by FANG before the game starts
15    @Override
16    public void setup() {
```

```
17    playersShip = new Ship(this); // get new component from system
18    playersShip.setLocation(0.2, 0.8); // id.command(parameters)
19    // what to shoot, what to run into
20    playersShip.setTarget(Meteor.class);
21    playersShip.addCollision(Meteor.class);
22    // show the score and remaining life counter
23    playersShip.showLives();
24    playersShip.showScore();
25    addSprite(playersShip); // add ship to game
26
27    rockA = new Meteor(this, 4); // get new component
28    rockA.setLocation(0.8, 0.2); // position
29    addSprite(rockA); // add rock to game
30
31    rockB = new Meteor(this, 2); // get new component
32    rockB.setColor(getColor("yellow"));
33    rockB.setLocation(0.2, 0.2); // position
34    addSprite(rockB); // add rock to game
35
36    rockC = new Meteor(this); // get new component
37    rockC.setColor(getColor("misty rose"));
38    rockC.setLocation(0.8, 0.8); // position
39    addSprite(rockC); // add rock to game
40  }
41 }
```

Listing 1.2: `MeteorShower.java`

1.5   Strategies: Winning a Game

A strategy is a manner of playing a game. Just as a game has components and rules, a strategy has a game and a set of rules. The rules here are not the rules for *playing* the game but rather the rules for *winning*[3] the game.

Systems: *All* of the Components

If we take a step back from the game and consider the game plus all of its players, we have a system where each player is an active component (and a rule follower), following their own rules amd looking to win the game. The rules for a strategy are probably more complex than the rules for the game they play[4] because they likely include the rules of the game. A winning strategy in checkers must reflect a knowledge of what constitutes a legal move in a given situation as well as a sense of what constitutes a *good* legal move in a given situation.

Abstraction: Different Levels

In a game-mastered checkers game and its players, there are three active components and thus three rule followers: the moderator follows the rules of the game and the players each follow the rules of their individual strategy. As anyone who has mastered any nontrivial game can attest, developing a winning strategy is

---

[3]There are valid goals in playing a game other than winning: having a good time, socializing, killing time, etc. A strategy could be devised to support any of these goals; in this section we assume a strategy is selected to win the game.

[4]Exceptions such as "Pick any legal move at random" are unlikely to produce very *good* winning strategies.

exceedingly difficult. While we define strategies here, this book does not get to computerizing them. This section expanded our view of a game system to include players and consider them as active components following a set of their own rules.

Review 1.5

(a)   Tic-tac-toe is a simple game with some basic strategies. Using your own personal experience or some Internet research, describe two strategies you can use to help you win at tic-tac-toe.

1.6   What Is in a Computer Program?

A computer program is a collection of data or information stored in the computer and the instructions that tell a computer "what to do." It consists of components and rules which together interact with the user to permit them to accomplish something. This definition depends on understanding what a computer *can* do and how it can be instructed. We must take a moment and define what a computer is. This definition of a computer is going to be abstract, leaving more detailed discussions until they are necessary.

What Is in a Computer?

At a minimum, a computer consists of a memory and a processor. In order to communicate with the outside world, the computer also needs some form of input/output (I/O) devices such as keyboards, mice, joysticks, and a video monitor.

General Purpose Computers

Modern computing machines are *electronic digital binary* computers. "Electronic" means that the processing is done with electrical signals sent through wires from component to component. The signals represent discrete numbers rather than a smooth range of values; this is the "digital" part. Everything inside the computer is encoded as numbers. The numbers inside a modern computer are represented in base 2, "binary." A single *binary digit* is either 0 or 1. Binary digit is condensed to *bit*. Each bit can represent only two different values (just as a decimal digit can represent only 10 values); groups of bits can represent a greater number of values. A *byte* is a group of 8 bits (the 8 bits of early video game generations).

If everything inside the computer is a number, how can computers play video games? Or run word processors? The key is that a number in the computer can be *interpreted* in various ways. A byte containing the value 01000001 in binary can be interpreted as the letter 'A' (it is, in fact, interpreted that way if a word processor expects that memory location to hold a character). It could, alternatively, represent the decimal number 65 (the decimal equivalent of the binary number). Or, on a particular computer, it might represent an instruction to the computer to add the following location in memory to a counter.

The memory of a computer does *not* differentiate these interpretations. Any given location can be interpreted in any of these ways (and many more besides). This gives the computer its general purpose capabilities: it can behave like a DVD player by loading instructions which interpret the content of the optical disk as encoded video data, it can behave like a game machine by loading and executing rules which draw pretty pictures on the screen, and it can behave like a dedicated word processor by loading rules (a program) that treat memory contents like a text document with fonts and margins.

The important thing to note is that for each different function the computer loaded a new set of rules, a new program. The program which is running, the instructions which are being loaded and executed, determines how different parts of memory are interpreted and therefore what the computer is capable of. We return to this description in greater detail in the next chapter.

Rules and Components: Memory

The memory of the computer can be random access memory (RAM), a CD/DVD or optical drive, a hard drive, or a memory card. The main differences between the memory types are speed, cost, and size. Faster memory such as RAM is more expensive per unit amount and tends to be smaller, while slower memory such as a hard drive is cheaper per unit and tends to be much, much larger. Other differences include volatility: RAM memory contents last only as long as the computer is on; hard disk and memory card contents are nonvolatile and last even after power is turned off.

A typical computer advertisement mentions the computer having between 1 GB and 4 GB of RAM and a hard disk drive of from 80 GB to some much higher number. What is a "GB"? A gigabyte is a GB. Computer scientists and computer advertisers disagree on what a GB is. Advertisers use powers of ten, making the giga- prefix mean one billion or 10^9 bytes. Computer scientists use powers of two, making the giga- prefix mean 1024 cubed (1024 = 2^{10}) or $2^{30} = 1073741824$ bytes. A single Western European alphabetic character takes up a single byte.

What do these various memories remember? The memory of a computer is used to store computer programs and the data that the computer programs operate on. The memory contains the program that runs *Quake* as well as the description of your character, the other characters and objects in the level, and the current level. The memory contains rules and components.

Rule Follower: The Central Processing Unit

With rules and components represented in the computer's memory, the only thing missing from our earlier game system description is some rule follower to handle any active components represented in the computer. The processor or central processing unit (CPU) is a rule follower.

The CPU is advertised with the number of *cores* or complete processors that are on the chip at the center of the computer as well as the clock speed of each core. The clock speed or clock of the core is approximately the number of instructions the core can execute per second.

Different kinds of CPU chips use different instructions (thus the machine instructions for an **XBox 360** are different than those on an Intel-based PC, even if the two might run the "same" game). The exact structure of the instructions is beyond the scope of this book, though we return to computer instructions in the next chapter when we talk about what a computer can possibly do for us.

Modern CPUs run at a given speed, the gigahertz of the computer. During each time step or *clock cycle*, the CPU runs one iteration of its own fetch-execute-store loop.

The Central Loop

One way the RAM can be interpreted is as instructions for the CPU. Each clock cycle the CPU fetches an instruction from the RAM, decodes what instruction it is, executes the instruction (which may require fetching data from the RAM), and stores the result somewhere in memory. This fetch-execute-store loop is the central loop in the computer. No matter what program you are running, this is what is happening hundreds of millions or billions of times per second.

The above is a simplified view: fetching information from secondary storage takes much more than one clock, and fetching information from RAM often takes more than one clock; some CPUs can execute more than one instruction per clock cycle. We stick with the simplified view because it is sufficiently close to the real thing to give us insight into how the computer works.

What instruction does the CPU fetch *next*? Normally the CPU fetches the instruction directly following the current instruction in memory. One of the amazing powers of the modern computer is that the CPU can change the address of the next instruction to any valid RAM address. The next instruction can be determined by the result of some calculation. On any given clock cycle, the computer can interpret *any* memory location as an instruction. Selection of what to do next, high-speed execution, and the ability to interpret numbers in memory in multiple ways combine to make modern computers general-purpose information processors (and decent game platforms!).

Talking to the World: Input and Output

The minimal computer described above is also lacking interaction with the real world—input from and output to the player of the game. Output is presented on a computer screen and through computer speakers. The computer and peripherals communicate through the computer's memory. Some I/O devices are computers in their own right, having processors and memory to present pretty pictures and music.

The keyboard, mouse, and even a joystick can provide input to the computer, input that the CPU can react to. The input devices provide events that the CPU can react to.

Software: Rules and Components

A computer program is a collection of components stored in a computer's memory. Those components interact according to rules also stored in the computer's memory. The rules are followed by the computer's CPU, and each rule can result in changes in the state of components stored in memory.

Multitasking

Interestingly, a computer program can have multiple rules being followed at the same time even if the computer has only a single CPU. How? Consider our game-mastered checkers game again. Imagine that rather than two players playing checkers, there are eight players who wish to play checkers. How could one moderator satisfy all of the players?

The moderator could line up the players and play a game for the first pair and then, when that game is done, play a game for the second pair, and then help the third and fourth pairs. By serving each pair *sequentially*, the moderator has helped four pairs play checkers. Unfortunately, though, it takes four times as long as playing one game to finish all four (assuming, for the moment, that all checkers games last the same amount of time).

An alternative scheme would be for the moderator to phone three other moderators, inviting them down so that all four games could be played, in *parallel*, using four identical sets of components. This approach requires only the amount of time it takes to play one game to finish all four games; it is quite costly in terms of checkers, boards, and moderators.

Consider a hybrid approach: have four sets of checkers components (pieces, boards) but only one moderator. The four sets of checkers represent the four games and the four pairs can play simultaneously but the moderator divides his time among the four games. He can ask the player in game one for his move and then, while waiting for the answer, he can make a pending move in game two, announce a victory in game three, check that the player in game four has made a legal choice of checker, and then return to listening for a move in game one.

This division of attention takes advantage of the fact that in the original game, the moderator spent most of his time waiting for things to happen. Using what in one game was waiting time to service a different game means that four simultaneous games take only a little bit longer than a single game. This is an example of *multitasking*, working on multiple tasks by using down time in one task to take care of another task.

Multitasking is not getting something for nothing. Imagine very fast players selecting moves as quickly as the moderator can make them. This would take all of the moderator's time just to service *one* game. If all four pairs were that fast, multitasking would actually take *longer* than running the four games in sequence. Multitasking might still be a good idea as the last pair in line would get to start their game sooner than if they had to wait for the three other games to finish.

Similarly, a single CPU can multitask, providing a computer program with multiple parallel rule followers, each getting a slice of the attention of the CPU. This is important because a single computer program might need multiple active components. Imagine a program that reads from the keyboard and receives information from the network at the same time; each of these activities should have its own rule follower so that no input is missed.

A rule follower in a computer program is also known as a thread of control. Will a program with multiple threads of control run many times slower than one with a single thread of control? Yes and no. If all of the threads of control have very complex sequences of rules that work on very small components, then it is possible that each thread of control is trying to use the full capacity of the CPU. Such threads are *processor-bound*, and this situation is equivalent to the players making moves as fast as or faster than the moderator.

Most programs spend at least some of their time waiting for events that occur slowly, in terms of CPU speeds: waiting for data read from the network, a hard drive, or an optical drive, waiting for a human being to press a key. Human reaction speed is hundreds of millions of times slower than the time it takes the CPU to follow a single rule; a lot of work can be provided to a ready thread while another thread waits for an event.

Multiple threads of control do not execute as fast as if the machine were truly parallel (a CPU per thread of control) but all threads (after the first) are started much sooner than if each thread of control were executed from beginning to end, sequentially. It also has the advantage that the different threads of control can communicate and cooperate to provide the user with a compelling experience.

Levels of Abstraction

A computer game is both a game and a computer program. A computer game is two *different* collections of components and rules. It has components and rules at two different *levels*.

Designing a computer game is really two different design tasks: designing a game and then translating the components and rules of the game into virtual components and rules in a particular computer programming language.

Translation typically involves moving from a very high level of abstraction to a more concrete level by specifying more details. This section introduces some of the general techniques for specifying rules and components in computer games (and other computer programs, too). The remainder of the book can be read as the continued expansion of techniques mentioned here.

Designing a game requires defining the components and the rules. It is possible to enumerate the components.[5] Rules, however, are more difficult to define. A first thought might be to list all of the configurations of the components and how to get from one to another. Unfortunately, the number of configurations for even a small number of components can grow astronomically: with a 3×3 grid, each empty or containing an "X" or an "O," there are almost twenty thousand component configurations.[6] Some of the configurations are illegal in play (the board containing nine "X"s is counted though you could never see it in play), but the exponential growth in configurations means that rules must be expressed more compactly.

Instead of exhaustively listing all game configurations, simple rules are typically built up into more complex rules. The rules for combining rules can be considered *problem-solving techniques*.[7] Very simple rules (i.e., pick a checker, capture a piece, roll two dice) are combined into more useful rules using five simple techniques: sequence, selection, iteration, delegation, and abstraction.

For example, in Listing 1.3, on page 8, the rule follower asks a player to select a checker and then a spot to move the checker, and then the checker is moved. This simplification is an example of the simplest rule writing technique: sequence. Do this *and then* do this other thing *and then* do that. This is the simplest mechanism for combining simple rules into more complex rules.

The previous example is an oversimplification of the original processing done by the moderator. A player selects a checker and the moderator determines if it is legal or not. If it *is*, then the moderator asks for a target square; if it is not, the game master asks again for a checker to move. This illustrates the second rule combining mechanism: selection. Two rules can be combined with some condition that can be tested, and one or the other of the rules is executed, but not both.

The moderator's complete program actually repeats a sequence of two selection statements and a smaller sequence multiple times. Such repetition combines rules using the iteration rule-writing technique: a rule can be combined with some sort of condition and the rule is repeated until the condition is met (or so long as the condition is met; these two are logically indistinguishable).

---

[5] *Infinite* games are beyond the scope of this book.

[6] $3^9 = 19683$

[7] These problem-solving techniques are based on Nell Dale's problem-solving techniques from the Turbo Pascal days (see [DW92]).

The additional rule-writing techniques were not used in the game master's "program." Delegation is the creation of a new named rule. It would be possible to use the following definition:

```
define move for player
  ask player to pick a checker
  if checker is not legal fail
  ask player to pick move
  if move is not legal fail
  make move
  succeed
```

This defines a new rule for the moderator, a rule called move. That rule can be applied to any player and is applied to each player in turn:

```
while game not done
  if move for current player succeeds
    change current player
```

This new rule shortens the moderator's main routine at the cost of defining the move command. When you learn to name new commands in Java there is discussion of when it makes sense to use delegation and when it makes sense to include code directly *inline*.

The final rule-combining technique, abstraction, is the packaging of an entire game, a "minigame," as a component in another game. Examples of this are provided as we study how to define our own types in Java.

The earlier description of checkers components brings up one possible problem in describing a game's components: scale. Is the checkerboard a component that is divided into squares (the squares are part of a component), or are the squares components that are assembled into a checkerboard (the board is a collection of components rather than a component itself). The answer to the question is one of scale, and picking the right scale to examine a game (or a computer program) is something of an art rather than a science; both of the above views are valid, and it might be nice to be able to switch between them at various moments (when moving a given checker, it seems the squares are important; when selecting a checker to move, the checkerboard's configuration is most important).

Interpreting Memory

The RAM contains both instructions (fetched by the CPU in the fetch-execute-store loop) and data (loaded in the execute phase and then replaced in the store phase). How can you tell what a given location in the RAM *means*? The answer is that you can't. That is, a given value in a given place in the RAM has a particular meaning only if you know the context in which it should be interpreted.

The need to know how to interpret a memory location has implications in how we write computer programs: when we set aside memory to hold data, we must tell Java what *type* of component we put in that location. That way when we read or write the actual values stored there, we know the context in which it should be interpreted. We return to this when we begin assigning types to memory locations.

A computer program is a collection of virtual components that reside in the computer's memory and interact according to a collection of rules also stored in the computer's memory. The rules are followed (active components are executed) by the computer's processor. A single processor can be shared between many active components (threads of control) because most active components have pauses built into their rules sequence (waiting for input from the user or reading from one of the slower components in the memory), and those pauses can be used to overlap execution of multiple active components. Active components' sequencing can be modified by events that the computer detects. For game purposes the primary events of interest come from input devices such as keyboards and mice or from other computers connected to the network.

Review 1.6

(a) Between RAM and hard drives, which tends to have a larger capacity? Which tends to be more expensive per gigabyte (GB)?

(b) Consider eating at a small restaurant with only 4 tables and 16 chairs. Is it necessary to hire 16 waiters to serve each patron individually? Why not? About how many waiters would be required? How does a restaurant with fewer than 16 waiters serve all 16 customers who may be in the restaurant at the same time?

(c) Do some Internet research to find out how much memory a computer uses for gaming needs. Cite at least two sources in coming up with your answer.

(d) Describe how to draw the letter A using a combination of only the following instructions (where X can be replaced by a number):

```
put pen down
lift pen up
move pen forward X cm
turn pen X degrees
```

Assume the pen starts up, and that after drawing the letter, the pen should finish up.

(e) Take your answer to the previous question and randomly reorder the instructions, then follow them. Do you get an A? Why not?

Randomly reordering the correct set of instructions for a computer program is unlikely to produce the right order. When debugging a program you should make sure you understand *why* moving a given line should make the code do the right thing.

1.7   Summary

In this chapter we developed a simple definition for a game: a *game* is a collection of components that interact according to a set of rules. Components are the *things* used to play a game. Rules describe how the components of the game *interact*.

Rules specify the starting configuration of components, legal moves to change the configuration, how the configuration is evaluated for scoring, how to know when the game ends, and how to determine the winner.

The same game can be played with different components: whether you use poker chips, different denominations of coins, painted manhole covers, or bottle caps, the movement and capture rules make the game checkers. Alternatively, multiple games can be played with the same components interacting according to different rules: solitaire, poker, go fish, or rummy are all played with the same deck of cards but they are very different games because their specified rules are different.

A *rule follower* (moderator) can automate the rules of a game. The rules for playing the game are distinct from a *strategy* for winning the game. A rule follower knows only the rules of the game and how to move it forward. Each active component can be considered to have a rule follower assigned to it (even rule followers which just follow the laws of physics).

A *computer program* is a collection of components that interact according to a set of rules. Both components and rules are stored in the computer's memory (RAM). Rules are followed by the computer's processor (CPU). Rule followers in a computer program are called *threads of control*. A single processor can simulate multiple threads of control by rapidly switching from one thread of control to another, giving each a tiny slice of its attention. The result is *multitasking*, which can make use of otherwise wasted CPU time.

Rules, whether for a game or a computer program, are almost always built up. Simple single-action rules are combined using the five problem-solving techniques: sequence, selection, iteration, delegation, and abstraction. Sequence is doing one thing after another. Selection is evaluating some condition and doing one thing or another depending on the condition's value. Iteration is repeatedly doing something until some condition is met. Delegation is naming a part of a program to make a new command. Abstraction is the creation of a new component, a component that encapsulates its own rules into a sort of minigame within a game.

1.8   Chapter Review Exercises

Review Exercise 1.1 Describe the components and rules of Tic-Tac-Toe.

Review Exercise 1.2 Describe the components and rules of Chinese Checkers.

Review Exercise 1.3 Describe the components and rules of Go Fish!

Review Exercise 1.4 Describe the components and rules of poker.

Review Exercise 1.5 Compare the components and rules from the previous two questions.

Review Exercise 1.6 Ignoring whether a position is legal or not, and assuming an unlimited number of both colors of checkers, how many board positions are possible on a checker board?

Review Exercise 1.7 Consider the game Tic-Tac-Toe. Describe what a rule follower (moderator) would do to supervise a game between two players.

Review Exercise 1.8 Consider the game *Battleship*.[8] Each player begins with a 10×10 grid of squares and a fleet of five ships of varying lengths (lengths appear after each ship's name): aircraft carrier (5), battleship (4), cruiser (3), submarine (3), and destroyer (2). To set up the game, each player secretly places her fleet in her grid, each ship placed horizontally or vertically across the given number of squares.

The player then takes turns selecting squares in her opponent's grid, shooting at any ship occupying the square. Each player's goal is to sink her enemy's fleet before her own is sunk.

Formally describe the components and rules for this game.

Review Exercise 1.9 How would you add a rule follower to *Battleship*?

Review Exercise 1.10 If the ships and the grid are the components of *Battleship*, consider modifying the rules:
Describe how you would modify the rules to make the game more difficult.
Describe how you would modify the rules to make the game easier.
How would you modify the rules to permit players of different skill levels to compete evenly (be sure to note your definition of even).
How could you use the same components to play a completely different game?

Review Exercise 1.11 For *Battleship*, it is possible to vary the components while keeping approximately the same rules.
Describe how you would modify the components to make the game harder.
Describe how you would modify the components to make the game easier.
Can you make the game work between opponents of differing skill levels by modifying just the components?

Review Exercise 1.12 You have been asked to stage a game of checkers during the half-time of a football game in a large outdoor stadium. Describe the components you would use. Would there be any need to modify the rules of the game?

---

[8] A version of *Battleship* is produced by Hasbro Games, but the game predates the Milton Bradley Games (now Hasbro) 1967 release by at least 50 years.

Designing Your First Program

A game is a collection of components with associated rules governing their interaction and providing the player with meaningful choices to solve the problem present by the opposition, be it the game environment or an opposing player. Computers can process only numbers, but components, rules, environments, and even opposing players' strategies can be encoded, modeled, and executed in the memory of a modern computer.

This chapter introduces the Java programming language, discussing the *structure* of Java computer programs and *object-oriented* programming practices. The simple computer games in this book are supported by the Freely Available Networked Game (FANG) engine. FANG provides types of objects representing games, players, screen objects, and even behaviors for the screen objects. This chapter focuses on the structure of a handful of games using only a few of FANG's features. The next chapter looks at a much broader selection of game objects leading, in Chapter 4, to writing a game with all behavior explicitly programmed.

2.1 BasketBall

A game, whether on a computer or not, begins with an idea. Similarly, a computer program, whether a game or not, begins with an idea. The idea is translated into a design, a description of what the game or program should do and look like. The translation of a *finished* design into a concrete product depends on technique rather than design skills.

Most chapters in this book begin by introducing a game design, an idea for a simple computer game. The game components and rules are explained so that the reader and the author have, generally, the same game in their mind. The design is followed by an inventory of concepts required to *implement* the game with special attention paid to new, unfamiliar concepts.

"To implement" means to accomplish, to make real. Implementing a game design is making the parts and writing the rules; implementing a computer program is writing the code that makes the design work. Implementation of a video game design is actually another layer of design: a computer program must be designed to play the given game before the program can be implemented. The remainder of each chapter introduces the computer science and Java techniques that are new with that chapter's game. The chapter ends with a finished game program.

The `Meteors` game in Chapter 1 is less than a page in length, yet it had a zooming spaceship, laser blasts, and meteors which split in half when shot. FANG provides high-level tools for building a game by expressing connections between behaviors and screen objects. This chapter again uses these highly abstract building blocks to build a game with mouse input, a bouncing ball, and even a target on the screen, all in less than seven pages of code[1].

The game we are designing is *BasketBall*, a take on the carnival game of making a free throw to win a prize. Design diagrams using a "handwritten" font to emphasize the conceptual nature of the work accompany most game designs. The final game looks more or less like the drawing.

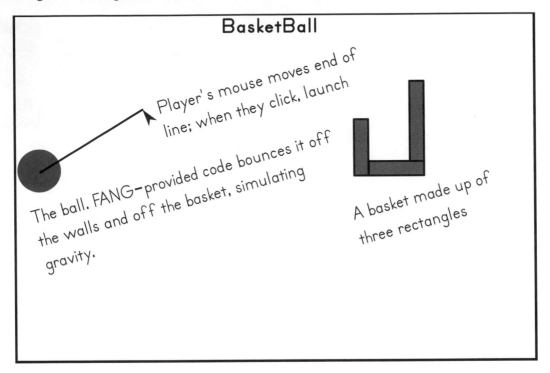

Figure 2.1: `BasketBall` game design diagram

Looking at Figure 2.1, notice that most of the writing on the drawing is done at an angle. That indicates comments rather than text, which is part of the game. The title at the top is also, typically, not part of the game itself but appears as the title in screen shots of the window decorations around the game.

`BasketBall` has three components: the basket, the ball, and the "launcher." When the game starts, the player has control of one end of the line representing the launcher. It indicates the direction and force with which the ball is being launched. When the player clicks, the game launches the ball with the appropriate initial velocity.

As mentioned in the design comments, the ball is also influenced by a constant acceleration due to gravity (toward the bottom of the screen) and it bounces off of the basket and the edges of the screen.

What do you need to know how to do to implement `BasketBall` using the FANG engine? You have seen one Java program using FANG but were not supposed to look too closely at it. This time around you examine the structure of a Java program first with a minimal program that just draws a square on the screen and then one that draws the basket. Placing the basket on the screen requires understanding FANG screen coordinates.

The chapter code provides two *classes*, types of components defined for inclusion in a Java program, `BasketBallLauncherSprite` and `BasketBallSprite`. A *sprite* is the name, in the FANG library, for elements visible on the screen. This chapter explains how to include them in a game and how to modify their associated behaviors.

---

[1]Not to worry: we are looking, in detail, at about two pages of code, including two simpler programs along the way to making our game.

One interesting thing about computer games is that you can model things that you cannot experience in real life. If we want to see how much fun the free-throwing on Jupiter would be, we can increase the gravity. And if we would rather make the game more like billiards, we can turn gravity off completely. But first, on to Java.

Review 2.1

(a) What does it mean when the writing on a design diagram is slanted?

(b) In your own words define *implementation*. How would you implement bridge (or poker or any other familiar card game) given a description of its rules. This implementation is in the real world, not the computer.

(c) When you look at the description of what the `BasketBallSprite` does in the game, bounce and fall, is there anything you think is missing? If so, what?

2.2 Java

Java is an example of an *object-oriented* programming language. What that means, in a nutshell, is that every rule in a program is associated with some *object*; an object is, in computer science terms, what we have been calling a component in a game. The remainder of the book endeavors to use component when talking about games and object when talking about objects inside a computer program. Since we are designing computer games, there may be some grey areas; we err on the side of calling them objects.

Every object is of some particular type. In Java an object type is a *class*. The rules followed by *all* objects of a give class are defined once in the definition of the class.

This is analogous to the idea of a *Pawn* type of component for a game of chess. The rules of moving any pawn are part of the definition of the *type*, whereas the color, starting location, and current location of any given *Pawn* is specific to that pawn. The *Pawn* type is analogous to a class in Java and each of the sixteen pawns in the game are analogous to objects, each of the type *Pawn*.

One powerful feature of object-oriented languages such as Java is support for programmer-defined classes. Java has many classes built into the language and it ships with a staggering number of standard libraries, packages of class definitions which can be included into user programs. This book also uses the FANG engine. FANG provides classes for components such as game, player, and screen objects.

A program written in Java is not in a form that a computer can directly execute. The Java program must be translated into a more computer-friendly (and human-unfriendly) form by a program called a *compiler*. The compiler can process Java because it has an artificial grammar that was designed to be processed by a computer program.

Syntax

Java is an artificial, yet to you, a foreign language. Learning a new language requires learning a grammar, how concepts are strung together, and a vocabulary, a collection of the words used to express the concepts. Computer scientists make this split at a finer level, talking about the *syntax* or structural rules and the *semantics* or meaning of the resulting program. Syntax is the rules for what constitutes a well-formed program. A program is well-formed if it has no *structural* errors; a well-formed program may or may not *mean*, or do, anything at all.

Getting started with Java requires learning about the syntax, how to write a well-formed computer program. That means having a language to talk about language. The next section introduces the overall structure of a Java program along with the Java templates used to describe Java syntax.

A General Class Template

A *Java template* is a text diagram summarizing the form a given Java language feature must take. The template begins with the name of the feature and a "defined as" symbol. We are learning how to define a class; the feature is named `<classDeclaration>`. The beginning of the template is:

```
<classDeclaration> :=
```

The name of the feature is in angle brackets so that we, readers of the template, can tell the difference between words that are actually *part* of the template and words that represent other syntactic structures. The := symbol is read "is defined as". The first line of a class definition shows both literal words and syntactic structures used in a definition:

```
<classDeclaration> := public class <className>
```

The two words ''`public`'' and ''`class`'' are part of the definition of the class, *keywords* that form part of the vocabulary (they are set aside in the language definition) and the grammar (their position tells the Java translator program that this is the beginning of a class definition) of the Java language. The `<className>` represents another template value, an item that has some specified structure with a value that can be different every time the `<classDeclaration>` template is used.

Before finishing the class definition template, we examine the template for `<className>`. It illustrates how we can specify a variable length structure.

```
<className> := <identifier>

<identifier> := <letterOrUnderscore><letterOrDigitOrUnderscore>*
```

Notice how `<className>` is really just an alias, a different name, for an `<identifier>`. Identifiers are user-chosen names and appear in a lot of different places in Java; we use more descriptive names for them, identifying what it is that they name, in most of our templates.

The two templates inside our definition, `<letterOrUnderscore>` and `<letterOrDigitOrUnderscore>`, represent single characters chosen from the named sets of characters. A `<letterOrUnderscore>` could be the '`_`', the '`A`', the '`p`', or the '`Z`' character, among others.

Notice that we used single quotes, ', around individual characters. The single quotes are *not* part of the character itself. They serve to focus our eyes on the character and make clear what we are talking about. The two template names are touching; this is significant because identifiers cannot contain spaces.

What is the star at the end of the template? It means "zero or more of the preceding item." An identifier begins with a letter or an underscore followed by any number (including zero) of letters, digits, or underscores. `<letterOrDigitOrUnderscore>*` means "zero or more items from the template called `<letterOrDigitOrUnderscore>`."

A class definition is

```
<parentClassName> := <identifier>

<classDefinition> := <classDeclaration>
                     <classBody>

<classDeclaration> := public class <className>
                      extends <parentClassName>

<classBody> := {
                   <definition>*
               }
```

```
<definition> := <fieldDeclaration> |
                <methodDefinition>
```

This template says that a `<classDeclaration>` is defined to be the two words **public** and **class** followed by an identifier naming the class, followed by the word **extends**, followed by another identifier naming a "parent" class (whatever that relationship means in Java). After the parent class name comes a block of definitions enclosed in curly braces.

`<definition>*` is a list of zero or more `<definition>`s where a `<definition>` is a `<fieldDeclaration>` or a `<methodDefintion>`. The | is a template character meaning *or*. Declaration/definition of whatever constitutes a field or a method is the meat of the next four chapters.

The spacing and indenting in the template is permitted by Java and expected by the author of this book. Java is free-form in that it tends to ignore extra spaces. The space between **public** and **class** is *not* extra; without the space, Java would see the word publicclass, a word it does not understand and therefore it signals an error. Because Java is free-form, the two words *could* appear fifteen spaces apart or even on separate lines.[2] The spacing and indentation shown is that employed when using the template in Java.

This is a lot of syntax just to be able to talk about syntax. Templates define language constructs by naming the construct (name inside angle brackets) and use the := symbol to begin the definition. The definition is composed of literal characters and other templates (which are replaced by something matching their definition). Literal characters or words match exactly what they say. There are two characters that are neither literal nor a template name: '|' and '*'. '|' is a template symbol meaning the template matches one or another item. '*' is a template symbol that means zero or more of the preceding item.

These syntax templates use an Extended Backus-Naur Form (EBNF) . The form is named for John Backus and Peter Naur and has been used to describe programming language syntax since the 1950s.

A Whole Program

Listing 2.1 is a very short example program. You can see that lines 7–16 match the `<classDeclaration>` template (lines 9–15 match `<definitions>` as explained later).

```java
 1  // package default
 2
 3  import fang2.core.Game;
 4  import fang2.sprites.RectangleSprite;
 5
 6  // FANG Demonstration program: RectangleSprite
 7  public class Square
 8    extends Game {
 9    // Called before game loop: create named rectangle and add
10    @Override
11    public void setup() {
12      RectangleSprite rectangle = new RectangleSprite(0.5, 0.5);
13      rectangle.setLocation(0.5, 0.5);
14      addSprite(rectangle);
15    }
16  }
```

Listing 2.1: `Square.java`: A complete program

---

[2]The term "spaces" is used to mean "whitespace" or characters whose printed form just moves where the next character prints. The space, ' ', the tab (no good way to write it now), and the end-of-line character are all whitespace.

Java class files are named for the **public class** they contain: the class Square *must be* in a file named Square.java. Notice that Java is *case-sensitive*, so uppercase and lowercase letters are different. The names must match exactly.

Lines 1, 6, and 9 begin with //. The // characters begin an *end-of-line* comment. A comment is treated as whitespace by Java. An end-of-line comment marks everything from the // through the end of the current line as a comment; in this book, comments are typeset using an *italic* typeface. The comment lines are, as far as Java is concerned, empty. The comments are there for humans reading the code. They serve as guideposts for other programmers; there is much more on comments later.

Listing 2.1 as a whole matches the Java template for a *<classFile>*:

```
<classFile> := <imports>
               <classDefinition>

<imports> := <import>*

<import> := import <importClassPath>;
```

The contents of a .java file are zero or more **import** lines (*<imports>* is a list of zero or more of the *<import>* template; the import template is a line importing one library or library class) followed by the definition of the **public class**.

The **import** statements begin with the obvious keyword and end with a semicolon (you will see a lot of semicolons in Java). The *<importClassPath>* is the name of the class or library to import. Line 3, **import** fang2.core.Game; imports the Game class (the last name, before the semicolon, is a class name) from the core library which is part of the fang library. The name is read backwards.

By using **import**, we have access to two classes in our program, Game and RectangleSprite. The Game class is the *parent class* (or *base class*) for our Square game. That comes from the naming of the identifier after **extends** in the *<classDeclaration>* template. What *is* a base class?

A base class is a type which the class being defined is extending. Think about it in terms of board games. *Battleship* is a game. *Electronic Battleship* extends the standard *Battleship* game; everything you can do with *Battleship* (play, clean up, lose pieces) you can also do with *Electronic Battleship* except that the new game might do some things better. Or at least differently. Rather than calling out a shot location and the other player answering "Hit" or "Miss," putting the shot marker on your board tests whether or not it is a hit and plays an appropriate sound effect. The rules for *Electronic Battleship* could mostly consist of "See *Battleship* rules for this section."

The same thing, to an extent, is true in Java when one class **extends** another. The *child class* automatically gets all of the rules defined for the parent class. So, since Game can be translated and run on the computer, so can Square.

The results of compiling and running Square are in Figure 2.2. The screenshot is in grey scale; the actual square is in a color referred to as FANG Blue.

Structure of a FANG Program

So, Square is a Game because it **extends** the Game class. What happens when a Game is run?

The heart of any interactive program or computer game was introduced in Section 1.3: the game loop. While the game loop directly models what happens *during* play, there is usually a setup phase before the game actually starts while players pick sides, set up their pieces and all the like:

```
define setup
  create/gather playing components
  set initial configuration
```

Figure 2.2: Running Square

```
define advance
  update game state

call setup
while (not game over)
  show game state
  get input from user
  call advance

indicate winner (or tie)
```

A *method*, sometimes called a *procedure* or *subroutine*, is a new command. The language used by our moderator is pretty close to English but there is an attempt to keep each instruction simple. A method is a *named* definition of a new instruction composed of multiple simpler instructions. By giving the new instruction a name we can use it as a "regular" instruction in the description of the game loop below.

When the moderator is following the instructions, he begins at the top and executes them one after the other, in sequence. Sometimes, it is useful to interrupt that order and execute a different sequence of instructions, returning to the point of interruption after the different sequence is finished. Consider a World War II wargame such as *PanzerBlitz*. The rules include the following for the German player's turn:

> 1. German player resolves any Minefield attacks against Russian units.
>
> 2. German player announces which of his units are attacking which Russian units, and what attack techniques are being used.
>
> 3. German player resolves all Normal combat, rolls the die once for each attack. German player flips face-down all firing units, as they are fired, to signify that they may not move.
>
> 4. ...(Steps 4–8 omitted) [Pan70]

This turn sequence, taken from page 11 of the rules, specifies what happens each time through the game loop. In particular, the first actions for the German player are listed in phases 1–3 here. In step 3 the player "resolves all Normal combat." That is a reference to page 5 (and following) where the resolution of normal combat is explained. The sequential following of the rules on page 11 is interrupted to do combat resolution; the player keeps track of where they were, though, and returns to page 11 when the combat is over to continue with step 4. The interruption of the flow on page 11 is *calling* the rule defined on page 5, the method previously defined.

The new setup method is called exactly once before the game starts. Once the game starts, advance is called over and over to advance the game toward its conclusion. While simplified, this loop matches the internal operation of a FANG game almost exactly. The Game class defines two *empty* methods, setup and advance. We must provide new, non-empty redefinitions if we want our game to do anything.

Setting up the Game

Looking at lines 10–15 in Listing 2.1, we see a definition for the setup method:

```
10   @Override
11   public void setup() {
12       RectangleSprite rectangle = new RectangleSprite(0.5, 0.5);
13       rectangle.setLocation(0.5, 0.5);
14       addSprite(rectangle);
15   }
```

Listing 2.2: Square.java: setup

The first line in the listing, @Override, tells the Java compiler that this method redefines an already defined version of the program in the parent class (Game). The compiler checks that there is such a method and throws an error if we say we are overriding and there is no method to override. This helps protect us from typographic errors in the name or parameter list of the method.

The second line is the *method header*. The method header consists of the access level (the keyword **public**), the return type (the keyword **void**), the name (setup), and the list of parameters (() — an empty parameter list; more below on just what parameters are). Detailed presentation of method definition is left for Chapter 6. For now, we just define the four parts of the function header that appear here:

public is a Java keyword used to indicate that the thing so labeled is visible and usable outside of the current class. Since the game loop sketched above runs somewhere inside of FANG, the setup method must be publicly available.

Methods can behave like mathematical functions, returning calculated values. Methods returning a value must specify the type of object they return; `void` is a special type indicating that the method does not return any value at all.[3]

The name is a valid Java identifier (no spaces, case-sensitive). To override an existing method, the name and parameter list must match the previous definition exactly.

The parameter list is between the parentheses; in this case there is nothing between the parentheses, so there are no parameters. Parameters are values passed into a method to permit it to behave differently each time it is called. Parameters are discussed in detail over the next four chapters.

The *body* of a method comes between the curly braces (opening and closing on lines 11 and 15, respectively). The curly braces serve as a container for the code they enclose. `setup` is called by FANG once, before the game begins running. The center of the rectangle is moved to the center of the screen, creating the image seen in Figure 2.2.

Screen Coordinates

Two-dimensional coordinates are typically expressed as a pair of distances: the distance along the x-axis from the origin to the coordinate point and the distance along the y-axis from the origin. Each point on the plane has coordinates of the form (x, y) and every pair of numbers refers to a specific point.

Given a point, (x, y), there are several questions that must be answered to find the point it corresponds to: What is the origin (where is (0, 0))? What is the unit of measure in each dimension (they need not be identical)? What are the unit vectors of the two dimensions (where do the axes point)?

FANG adopts standards from computer graphics in expressing game locations: The origin is the upper-left corner of the visible game-play area; the x-axis points from left to right (values increase from left to right); the y-axis points down the screen (values increase as you move from top to bottom of the screen).

What units of length are available? It would be possible to use the tiniest *picture elements* or pixels as a unit of measure, except that no two screens are likely to have exactly the same pixel size. It would also be possible, by querying the computer, to figure out what size pixels it has in some more traditional measure of length and then convert all screen distances to millimeters or inches.

Both of these *absolute* measurement systems have a similar problem: the size of the game (and the coordinates of all locations) change when the game window is resized. On modern computers, most windows have "resizing handles" and can, at any time, be used to resized the window. If the square is a given number of millimeters down from the top, if the window is the given size the square is centered; a window resized to twice the height would have the square near the top rather than centered.

Instead of absolute units defined outside the game, x and y dimensions are measured *relative* to the current size of the screen. That means that the upper-left corner, the origin, has the coordinates (0.0, 0.0); the decimal point in each number reminds us that we are using fractions to express screen locations. The lower-right corner is (1.0, 1.0) (one screen width to the right of the origin and one screen height below the origin).

Figure 2.3 shows the coordinates of the origin and the bottom-right corner. It also shows two long, thin rectangles crossing at the center of the screen, (0.5, 0.5).

Looking back at Listing 2.1, the coordinate parameters make sense.

```
12   RectangleSprite rectangle = new RectangleSprite(0.5, 0.5);
13   rectangle.setLocation(0.5, 0.5);
```

Listing 2.3: `Square.java`: a new `RectangleSprite`

In line 12 the keyword `new` tells the system to make a new object, the type of which is determined by the type name following `new`. The line `new RectangleSprite...` *constructs* a new `RectangleSprite`, whatever that

---

[3]This is the *empty type* or the type with no values, not to be confused with the term `null`, the value meaning *no value provided*. `null` plays an important part in Java and is discussed later.

Figure 2.3: FANG Game Coordinates

is. Notice that we **import**ed the type from `fang2.sprites` at the beginning of the Java file (line 4). The two parameters passed along with the type are the width and height of the rectangle in screens. The parameters (`0.5, 0.5`) on line 12 means the rectangle is a square half a screen wide and half a screen high.

FANG screen objects, sprites, are located by their centers. When you create a new `RectangleSprite`, it is located at the origin. The *center* of the rectangle is at the origin of the screen. We want it centered on the screen so we must set its location. `rectangle.setLocation(0.5, 0.5)` in line 13 calls a method defined for `rectangle`, a method called `setLocation`. The two parameters are the x-coordinate and the y-coordinate where the rectangle should be located. The center of the rectangle is moved to the center of the screen, creating the image seen in Figure 2.2.

Review 2.2

(a) Write the Java/FANG code to construct a `RectangleSprite` as wide as the screen and 75% as high as the screen.

(b) What is the purpose of the `//` characters in a Java program?

(c) What does the annotation `@Override` indicate?

(d) What symbols are used to indicate the start and end of a method body?

2.3 Creating Executable Programs

How can a human being create a program that a computer can execute? Remember that a computer stores only numbers. Those numbers can be interpreted as instructions, characters, numbers, or even screen objects. So how could a human being create a computer program a computer could *directly* execute?

One way would be to store the numeric value for each instruction directly into the various locations of the computer's memory and then command the CPU to begin interpreting them as instructions. Figure 2.4 shows an IMSAI 8800 microcomputer from the middle 1970s; notice the two sets of eight switches. Since a byte is a collection of eight bits, eight switches can express each of the eight 0 or 1 values.

Figure 2.4: Gandalf IMSAI 8800 at the Computer History Museum (1976 microcomputer) [IMS76]

The programmer would enter the desired byte value for a given memory location on one set of switches and the corresponding address of the byte on the other. Pressing the **write** switch, one of the control switches on the far right, made the computer copy the byte value into the given memory location. The programmer could then add one to the address, enter the value for the *next* byte, and again press **write**. After entering the whole program (and any data required), the programmer could press the **run** switch and begin program execution, hoping there were no mistakes.

Even assuming we could get the CPU on your personal computer to execute instructions we entered this way, this approach to writing a computer program is daunting: a modern game program may take upwards of a megabyte (about a million bytes) for the executable; the rest of the DVD or downloaded package is typically art and sounds (data) in various formats. Keying in a million bytes' worth of instructions would take a long time (at one byte per second it would take just over eleven and a half days). The IMSAI and its cousins had no hard drives or CD/DVD readers, so keying in the data (measured in gigabytes or billions of bytes) takes a thousand times longer.

Rather than write programs in the *machine code*, the numbers where one entry is one encoded instruction for the CPU, it would make more sense to write in a language at a *higher level* of abstraction. Each statement in the higher-level language would express some larger number of simple machine instructions. The higher-level language could be translated into machine codes which could then be entered into the computer. This is similar to outlining a paper before writing it: the outline permits you to solve problems with overall structure and the presentation of your argument without the distraction of overwhelming detail. Once your outline is correct, you can translate it into paragraphs, sentences, and individual words.

The high-level programming language used in this book is *Java*. Java, designed by Sun Microsystems in the 1990s, is an artificial programming language designed specifically to eliminate ambiguity. No ambiguity means that the translation from Java to machine language is by rote: a given sequence of instructions in Java always translates into the same sequence of machine instructions. A major step in computer history was the realization that a computer program could do this translation. (Admiral Grace Murray Hopper, mentioned in a sidebar on page 35, was among the first to realize this.) A *compiler* is a program that takes a high-level program as input and translates it into a lower-level program which does the same thing; lower level means closer to the machine language.

Different CPUs are found at the center of different computing devices (game consoles, PCs, PDAs, cell phones, etc.) and different CPUs have different machine languages. As was said before, the contents of memory must be understood in context; the same sequence of values means something completely different in a different machine language. An advantage to a high-level language is that different compilers can be written, each of which translates the *same* high-level program into a *different* machine code file, each specialized for a particular CPU and machine language.

Once a high-level program is translated into a computer's machine language, that machine code can be loaded into the computer's memory and executed by the *operating system*. Operating systems (such as Microsoft's Windows Vista, the open source Linux, and Apple's OSX) are an important field of study in computer science. For our purposes, they are programs that run on the computer that can start, stop, and manage *other* computer programs. Operating systems also permit programs to create directories (or folders), read and write files, and use the network. The operating system provides an environment in which our programs run and can access the various resources of the computer and the Internet.

By analogy, compiling is similar to translating an entire book from one language to another. If we consider translating an encyclopedia, translating the entire thing is a lot of work. The user of the translated encyclopedia may not even be interested in the entire text, just the article she looks up along with those articles it leads her to. It might be more efficient to translate portions of the book only as they are needed. This would require an interpreter, fluent in both the source and target languages, alongside the reader, but the translation time would be minimized.

This same approach can be used in the computer: a program in a higher-level language can be *interpreted*, each part being translated just in time for it to be used. Parts that are never used are never translated. Note that the interpreter, here a program like the compiler, treats the higher-level program as input along with the actual input processed by the program.

Compiling has a speed advantage over interpretation **if** the program is run multiple times: the high-level representation of the program need be translated only once. Interpretation has a flexibility advantage if the program changes frequently: each time the interpreter is run, the most current version of the high-level representation is executed.

There is a hybrid approach where high-level programs are **compiled** into *bytecode*, a lower-level language that is not any computer's machine language, and the bytecode representation is then **interpreted** by a program that understands bytecode and runs in the local machine language. Each bytecode is interpreted each time it is executed and it is still possible to have bytecode files that are out-of-date (the higher-level program has changed but not yet been compiled).

While this approach appears to capture the worst of the other two approaches, there is a different flexibility advantage: a simple interpreter can be provided for each different machine language. This means the same bytecode file can be interpreted (executed) on multiple machines. Bytecode interpreters are both simpler to build and faster to run than high-level language interpreters. Much of the work of a standard interpreter is done in compiling into bytecode so that each bytecode executes very quickly.

The hybrid approach is analogous to the use of a particular human language for standard communication within a given field. The Medieval Church used Latin for scripture and communications across Europe because its clergy spoke a wide variety of languages. Rather than having to have an interpreter for every pair of languages (so that a Polish speaker could communicate with a Spanish speaker or a Frankish speaker could communicate with a Saxon), the Church could communicate with speakers of any language so long as there was an interpreter from Latin to the given vulgar tongue. Just as the cost of adding a new language to the Church's collection was minimized, the cost of adding a new computer to the list of machines where a given bytecode runs means implementing just a bytecode interpreter.

The hybrid compiler is simpler because it needs to know only one target language, the bytecode. The bytecode serves as the *lingua franca* for multiple CPUs, a language of exchange that they all, through their simple interpreters, can understand. This is very useful when computer programs are shared over the Internet to multiple, different kinds of computers.

Java is a successful example of a bytecode compiled language. In order to run a Java program which we write, we must go through a *write-compile-run* cycle: we must write and save the Java source code; we must provide the Java code to the `javac` Java compiler which translates it into bytecode; we then provide the bytecode file to `java`, the bytecode interpreter on our local machine. One thing to keep in mind is that there is no direct connection between the Java and bytecode files; you must remember to compile the program for any changes to appear in the interpreted program.

High-Level and Low-Level Languages

Two Audiences, One Text

A computer program is written for two different audiences: the computer and other programmers. For the computer you must adhere to the syntax of the programming language and make consistent use of names and labels. The compiler enforces many of these requirements.

For other programmers you are writing to tell them how you solved the problem at hand. Human readers of your code are familiar with the programming language, but not completely familiar with the problem you are solving; programmers are even less familiar with your thinking and the design decisions you made in designing the solution. Be aware that you will be such a programmer, unfamiliar with your own thinking, when you come back to your own code after a month or more away from it.

Comments are one way of providing information for the future human readers of your program. Since the Java compiler treats comments as if they were spaces, you are free to include as much context and information as you desire in program comments.

Java supports two kinds of comments: end-of-line comments and multiline comments.

End-of-line comments extend from a double slash, //, to the end of the current line. They are treated as if they are not there (the line effectively ends at the double slash). They are legal wherever a new line would be legal.

A multiline comment is one which begins with a /* symbol and extends until the first */ symbol. Each of these "symbols" is actually two characters long: they must appear directly next to each other in order to be interpreted properly by the compiler. A multiline comment is treated as a sequence of spaces taking up the same number of characters as the comment, so a multiline comment can appear anywhere that a space can appear.

The Java template for the two forms of comment is

```
<comment> := // <commentFromHereToEndOfLine>


<comment> := /*
             <anyNumberOfCommentLines>
             */
```

Admiral Grace Murray Hopper [1906–1992]

Grace Murray was born in New York, New York, graduating from Vassar in 1928 and receiving her PhD in mathematics from Yale in 1934. While in graduate school she married Vincent Hopper, an English professor.

Grace Hopper joined the Naval Reserves in 1943, serving on the Harvard Mark I electromechanical computer project as a programmer and operator. Her request to transfer to the active duty Navy at the end of World War II was denied because of her age; she remained in the reserves and worked at Harvard on new generations of computers.

Her work on the Harvard Mark II led to the discovery of the "first computer bug," an actual moth caught in a relay of the electromechanical

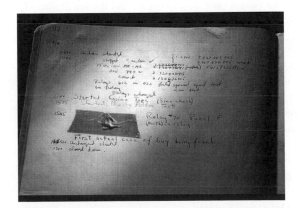

Figure 2.5: Smithsonian Image 92-13137: Grace Hopper's Computer Bug [Hop47]

Admiral Grace Murray Hopper [1906–1992]

computer (see Figure 2.5). She went on to work
on the UNIVAC computer line.

In 1952 she designed and built the world's first experimental compiler for the *A0* programming language. The term "compiler" comes from the idea of gathering up the pieces of the program and its libraries and putting them together in the right order, like compiling an anthology for publication. Grace Hopper was a member of the team that developed the *Common Business Oriented Language* (*COBOL*). For more than half a century, COBOL was used to write many government and business programs including payroll processing for the Defense Department and IRS check handling. It was one of the earliest high-level, compiled programming languages and it remained in common use past the year 2000.

Grace Hopper retired from the Navy in 1966; she was recalled to the active service in 1967 for a "six month tour," which turned into an indefinite appointment. Her expertise in both software and hardware made her indispensable to the government.

She retired again in 1971 and was again recalled in 1972; that same year she was promoted to Captain. Congress was required to exempt Grace Hopper from the mandatory retirement age for Naval officers. Before her final retirement from the Navy in 1986 as the oldest active duty officer in Navy history, she was promoted to Rear Admiral.

Admiral Grace Hopper spent the rest of her life as a lecturer on computer science around the world. She influenced a large number of computer designers by handing out 30-cm (approx. 12 in) wires which she referred to as "nanoseconds" since they were the distance that light could travel in one billionth of a second; this was the very farthest that components could be from one another if a computer was to run a billion clock cycles per second. Those wires are prized possessions among a certain group of computer scientists.

Since comments are treated as whitespace by the Java language processor (more on the processor in a moment), they are not part of the rules that a Java program follows. Instead, they are there solely for the programmers who come after you. There is more on writing good comments throughout the book. For the moment, keep in mind that your comments should document the *design decisions* you have made and guide the reader to how you thought about the program you wrote.

Basket

Listing 2.4 shows our first step toward making the BasketBall program. As for all FANG game programs, Basket **extends** fang2.core.Game; we can call it Game in line 10 because we imported the class in line 3. As we saw when looking at the enhance game loop in Section 2.2, FANG provides two empty methods, setup and advance, which we are expected to override in order to give our game rules that do something. Just as in Square, Basket only overrides the setup method.

```
 1  // package default
 2
 3  import fang2.core.Game;
 4  import fang2.sprites.RectangleSprite;
 5
 6  /**
 7   * Draw a basket (for "basketball") on the screen.
 8   */
 9  public class Basket
10    extends Game {
11    /**
12     * Setup the sprites (and anything else) necessary for our game.
```

```
13    * Use the new operator to construct three RectangleSprites. Each is
14    * sized and located in screens (screen is 0.0 to 1.0 from left to right
15    * across and 0.0 to 1.0 down from the top to bottom (y-axis is backward).
16    */
17    @Override
18    public void setup() {
19      // width, height (in screens); location is (x, y), in screens
20      RectangleSprite rectangleBottom = new RectangleSprite(0.25, 0.05);
21      rectangleBottom.setLocation(0.625, 0.475);
22      addSprite(rectangleBottom);
23
24      RectangleSprite rectangleBackboard = new RectangleSprite(0.05, 0.4);
25      rectangleBackboard.setLocation(0.75, 0.3);
26      addSprite(rectangleBackboard);
27
28      RectangleSprite rectangleFrontboard = new RectangleSprite(0.05, 0.2);
29      rectangleFrontboard.setLocation(0.50, 0.4);
30      addSprite(rectangleFrontboard);
31    }
32  }
```

Listing 2.4: `Basket.java`

`setup` is a **public** method (accessible from the rest of FANG), returning nothing (return type **void**) and having an empty parameter list. The method header on line 18 says all of this. The body of `setup` is everything inside the curly braces on lines 18 and 31; when `setup` is called by FANG, the lines in the body are executed in sequential order. The nine (non-blank, non-comment) lines in `setup` are grouped, for easy reading, into three sets of three.

Each block of three defines a label for a `RectangleSprite` and uses **new** to construct a new `RectangleSprite`. The one labeled `bottom` is wide and short, 0.25 screen wide and 0.05 screen high. The other two are thin and tall with `backboard` taller than `frontboard`. Each is then positioned on the screen. They all have their bottom at 0.5 screen down from the top. The front- and backboard overlap the bottom by a little bit to give them pretty location numbers.

How can we go from a Java, a high-level language, to bytecode, a lower-level language, and then have the bytecode interpreted? The next two sections address this.

Compiling

Remembering that Java uses a hybrid compiled/interpreted model we must

1. Type the program in an editor.

2. Save the program in a file named `Basket.java` (the name of the **public class** and the file must match).

3. Compile the `.java` (high-level) file to produce a `.class` (bytecode, low-level) file. `Basket.java` compiles into `Basket.class`.

4. Interpret the bytecode file.

This book demonstrates commands you would type at the command line on your computer. If you are running an integrated development environment such as *Eclipse*, *Netbeans*, or *IntelliJ*, you can do exactly the same thing by pressing a couple of buttons. If you are using the *JavaWIDE* online IDE, you need only save a newly created java page, and *JavaWIDE* compiles the program for you, returning a page with your program embedded right in it.[4]

Opening a command shell in the folder where we have saved .java, we run the Java compiler with the javac command:

```
~/Chapter02% javac -classpath .:/usr/lib/jvm/fang2.jar Basket.java
```

What is -classpath and the stuff after it? It is a parameter for the compiler, telling it where Java program and library files live. It is a colon-separated list of folder (directory) names. With two elements, this list tells the Java compiler to look in the current directory and in the fang2.jar Java archive file.[5] The fang2.jar archive was downloaded from www.fangengine.org; that Web site also contains instructions and tutorials for installing the FANG engine.

It is possible for the compiler to detect and report certain types of errors; we examine some of these in future chapters. For the moment, read the error message very carefully and examine the given line number and the ones just *before* it. A compiler works from the beginning of a file to the end and it may not be able to report an error until it has become completely confused. The reported location of the error is often after the actual location. Make sure that the contents of the file exactly match the code shown in Listing 2.4.

Running

After the javac command completes successfully, there is a new file in the current directory: Basket.class. This is the bytecode file generated by the compiler. The Java bytecode interpreter, java, is able to start any Java bytecode file which has a special main routine; one big thing provided by FANG is a default main routine that creates and runs a Game (or Game-derived) component. The interpreter expects the name of the component to run; it also requires a -classpath parameter to be able to find nonstandard Java libraries (such as FANG).

```
~/Chapter02% java -classpath .:/usr/lib/jvm/fang2.jar Basket
```

Figure 2.6 shows Basket running. The screen is divided into two parts: the top, black portion, the game field itself containing three FANG blue rectangles (which overlap and look like one big fishhook), and the row of buttons across the bottom of the screen.[6]

When a FANG Game-derived program is run in Java, FANG creates the screen spaces that you see, sets up the game , and then draws the game on the screen. The game does not actually begin until you press the **Start** button in the lower-left corner of the game window. Pressing **Start** for Basket has FANG update the game regularly but, because the update rules for the game are empty, nothing appears to happen.

In fact, when you press **Start**, the only change is the label on the button: it changes from **Start** to **Pause**. This happens whenever you start your game; this permits you to pause the game at any time you like.

The other three buttons permit you to turn on or off the **Sound**, display any **Help** for the current game, and **Quit** the current game, closing the window completely.

Review 2.3

(a) Programming languages such as C and C++ are compiled into machine code and do not need to be translated as they are executed. Other languages such as Javascript are translated as they are executed (called interpreted). Is the Java programming language compiled, interpreted, or both?

(b) What does it mean to compile a Java program? In your answer, properly use the terms "source code," "bytecode," and "compiler."

---

[4]Take a look at http://www.fangengine.org/ for step-by-step tutorials in setting up various environments. JavaWIDE, which has FANG already configured, can be used by pointing your browser at http://www.javawide.org/.

[5]In Windows, Linux, and OSX, the two folder names . and .. refer to the current folder (whatever folder you are currently in) and the parent folder of the current folder. By definition, the topmost folder is its own parent.

[6]Due to printing limitations in this book, screen shots appear primarily in shades of gray; on the screen the top portion is black and the buttons are maroon.

Figure 2.6: Basket running

(c) Type in the program in Listing 2.1, but leave out line 11. Compile and run the program. Describe what you see that is different and why you think this happens.

(d) Type in the program in Listing 2.1 but leave out line 12. Compile and run the program. Describe what you see that is different and why you think this happens.

(e) The messages your compiler gives you, as a new programmer, are hard to understand at first. One way to start understanding them better is to intentionally put errors in programs and see what the compiler says is wrong. In this way when you encounter the compiler message due to an unintentional error, you have a better chance at figuring out what went wrong.

Type in the program in Listing 2.4. Change a part of the program to cause a compiler error. Try to compile the program and see what message you get. Fix the error, note what you did to cause the error, and write down what message the compiler gives.c Repeat this two more times (try to get three different error messages).

2.4 Problem Solving

Computer science is problem solving. A program expresses *how* to solve a problem in a language that can be executed by a computer. Are there any restrictions on the solutions we can express?

A computer program is sometimes described as a concrete expression of an *algorithm*. An algorithm is a finite collection of well-defined rules for completing a task. The process of solving the problem is viewed as a set of *states*, the collection of everything you know about the problem and how far you are along the way to solving it. The rules move the problem solver from one state to the next; the well-defined part of the rules means that how to go from one state to another is perfectly clear. The rules also permit the problem solver to recognize when the *goal state*, the solution to the problem, has been reached.

Most people know a whole lot of algorithms even if they do not commonly use the word. Consider for a moment, how you would calculate the sum of 1259 and 3941. Assume you have to do it by hand. Further, as you do it (even if you just do it in your head), describe the steps you are following. The steps you are following, the ones you learned in the second grade, are an algorithm for adding multi-digit decimal numbers.

The finite length of the algorithm itself says nothing about how long it takes for the algorithm to do its work. It does say that the rules can all be read in a finite amount of time. There are slight variations among sources in the definition of algorithm. Some permit the algorithm to run forever on some problems (but they have to be problems that have no solution). Others require that an algorithm halt in a finite amount of time whether or not it can solve the problem; that means "cannot be solved" must be a valid result of the algorithm.

The meaning of what it means for something to be computable depends on the algorithms. The important takeaways from this short section are

- Algorithms are finite collections of rules.

- Algorithms are collections of well-defined rules so that a problem solver can follow them.

- If an algorithm can solve a problem, it halts with an answer in a finite amount of time.

- If an algorithm cannot solve a problem, it is possible that it just keeps on trying forever. Or it could halt and say there is no answer.

- Algorithms are fundamental to the theory of computation.

The five-problem solving techniques listed in the previous chapter, sequence, selection, iteration, delegation, and abstraction, are ways of combining simple, well-defined rules into more complex but still well-defined rules.

The programs we write are concrete expressions of algorithms: no program is infinitely long, and Java defines how different statements execute and move the computation from state to state.

Review 2.4

(a) An algorithm is finite. What does that mean?

(b) When *must* an algorithm halt under any definition? When might an algorithm *not* halt?

(c) What is a *goal state*? How does it relate to an algorithm?

2.5 FANG

FANG is the Freely Available Networked Game engine.[7] FANG is an educational game engine designed to support beginning students in writing simple computer games early in their careers.

This section discusses what an application framework is (game engines are a special kind of application framework) and why you would want to use one when learning Java. We then dissect the FANG name and see why it is a good choice for a beginning programming course.

---

[7]For up-to-the minute FANG developments, browse over to http://www.fangengine.org. The newest version of the engine, tutorials, and forums are available there.

What is a Framework?

An *application framework* is a combination of at least one programming language and a library which provides the infrastructure for building a particular type of application. Application frameworks are typically specialized for use in a particular environment, meaning for a particular computer family or operating system. Examples of application frameworks include Cocoa for the Machintosh's OSX operating system, the Mozilla Web browser framework, and the OpenOffice.org framework for building office applications. The important thing to note is that an application framework provides a higher level of abstraction than just a programming language, and, as discussed above in relation to high-level languages, computer programmers use abstraction to vanquish complexity.

Large + Flexible = Complex

Java is a large, flexible programming language designed to run on multiple, different computer platforms. That is why it uses the hybrid execution model of both compiling and interpreting. It is also why the language ships with close to two thousand different component types in the standard libraries. Java is flexible so that you can build games or instant messaging clients or Web servers or even complete social Web sites combining all three capabilities.

The flexibility of Java and the size of the documentation (Section 3.3) makes it difficult for beginners (and a fair number of "old hands") to know where to start when working in the language.

A Java "Tutorial Level"

Many modern video games are also large and complex. Consider *Half-Life 2* from Valve Software. Just as in its predecessor *Half Life*, the game begins with several simple levels where a voice in your ear or on the screen guides you through the various movements and attacks necessary to play the game.

Hand-holding during a tutorial level shows new players what to look for as well as familiarizes them with the available controls and the types of problems they have to solve. A *pedagogical application framework* such as *ObjectDraw*[8] or FANG is designed as a Java tutorial level: you learn the control structure and how to solve real problems while the framework supports you and lets you reach further than you could have without support. Like a tutorial level, FANG is designed to get out of your way as you learn how to tackle the real thing, writing programs from scratch in Java.

Freely Available Networked Game Engine

FANG is a collection of several Java *packages*; a package is a Java library of classes. `fang2.core` is a package as is `fang2.sprites`. This chapter presents three of the classes provided by FANG (`Game`, `RectangleSprite`, and, in `BasketBallSprite`, `OvalSprite`); more classes are presented in the next chapter, along with FANG and Java's documentation so you can find classes on your own.

What does the name *Freely Available Networked Game engine* mean?

Freely Available

FANG is an example of *open-source software* (OSS). Open-source means that programmers provide the high-level language representations of their programs along with compiled, low-level representations. The high-level source code, complete with comments, makes it easy for programmers to read, understand, and even modify open-source software.

Open-source software is in contrast to *closed-source* or *proprietary* software where the software vendor makes only the compiled or machine-language representation of the software available. Without the source

---

[8]See http://eventfuljava.cs.williams.edu/ for more information on *ObjectDraw*.

code, difficult reverse-engineering is required to enable modification of the software function, and many vendors require licensees to agree to not reverse-engineer their products before they can install them.

FANG is also an example of *free* software. The FANG software license[9] is designed so that you, the user, are free to use it as you wish. You can run it for any purpose (including figuring out how it works). You can modify it for your own purposes. You can freely distribute your changes to other people so that they can take advantage of your improvements. The only requirements on you are that you must acknowledge that your code includes or is based on FANG (just as FANG does, in particular in the `fang2.util` package where some amount of code is based on work done by the Association for Computer Machinery's Java Working Group on a different pedagogical toolkit).

Notice that the *free* in free software is freedom for you, the user, and how you choose to interact with the software. This is free as in "free speech": you are free to use speech as you see fit.

Free software is a subset of open-source software; you cannot exercise the freedoms the license promises unless you have access to the high-level language version of the software.

Free software has many benefits. Think back to the first computer game you played and really loved. Now, does that computer program run on modern hardware? If all you have is a DVD/CD[10] with the machine code for the game, you have to install it on the right kind of computer (machine code is specific to a particular CPU) and, perhaps, a particular version of an operating system. If you had the *source code* you could, potentially, compile it for your current machine and operating system. If it was free software, you would have the source *and* the freedom to compile it if you wanted to.

What if just recompiling the program failed to get it to work for you? The game might be tied to the speed of the processor or some particular type of graphics or networking hardware which is no longer available. With the source code, some knowledge, and a whole lot of patience, you could, at least potentially, fix the game and keep it running. When you have the source code and a free license, you can fix any bugs that come along and repurpose the software as you see fit.

Now, imagine if the software was a word processor rather than a game. What if all of your term papers were saved using version 1.0 of the software, and just before you apply to graduate school, the company ships version 2.0, revoking support for version 1.0? Further, what if version 2.0 could not read version 1.0 files? How can you assemble a portfolio of your term papers if you do not have a free license for the word processor? With open-source software and formats, you can do what you want with whatever version of the software you want to (as long as you follow the licensing requirements). With proprietary software you have only the options the vendor chose for you.

FANG is free and open-source software, freely available and free for you to modify.

Networked

Application frameworks provide infrastructure for particular types of applications. One thing they can provide is a communications infrastructure. FANG provides a network infrastructure that makes writing networked games, games with multiple players at multiple locations, almost as easy as writing single player games.

Game Engine

A *game engine* is a special kind of application framework. A game engine provides infrastructure for a particular genre of games. Commercial engines such as Valve's Source Engine or Epic Games' Unreal Engine provide sound, physics, graphics, lighting, networking, and other subsystems to licensees of the software.

FANG was designed as a teaching engine from the get go. It provides well-documented, clear source code. It also provides graphics, networking, and sound subsystems to support the creation of simple, 2-dimensional

---

[9]Gnu Public License v3.0.

[10]or, heaven forfend, a *floppy disk*.

arcade-style games. Because it is open source and flexible, it *is* possible to write different genres of games but it can be a lot more work than making a game in the genre the engine was built for.

Because FANG was designed as a teaching engine, as we progress through the book, we peel back some layers of the abstraction provided by FANG and peek "under the hood"; you get a chance to see how the concepts we use in our games are used inside the game engine as well. You can also extend the game engine. That is another benefit of open-source software: anyone in the community can contribute back to make the software better. As the saying goes, "Many hands make light work."

Review 2.5

(a) Define the term application framework and give three examples.

(b) Describe the flexibility present in using open-source software that is not present when using closed-source proprietary software.

(c) Is it possible to write multiplayer games using the FANG engine?

2.6   Finishing Up BasketBall

Finishing `BasketBall` requires adding a basket ball and a launcher to the `Basket` program. The ball and launcher *use* the `BasketBallSprite` and `BasketBallLauncherSprite` objects defined in the source code directory for this chapter. (What are the files defining the classes named?) We use the classes in the same way we use `RectangleSprite`, to make `BasketBall` work. Then we pull back the covers a bit to see where the behavior of the ball comes from.

To have the ball launched in the game, we just add a `BasketBallLauncherSprite` to our `Basket` game.

```
1  // package default
2
3  import fang2.core.Game;
4  import fang2.sprites.RectangleSprite;
5
6  /**
7   * Throw a basketball sprite. BasketBallLauncher knows about
8   * BasketBallSprite so we just add the launcher. When the mouse is
9   * clicked, the launcher launches a basket ball along the given line
10  * (gravity and bouncing change its course).
11  */
12 public class BasketBall
13   extends Game {
14   /**
15    * Setup the sprites (and anything else) necessary for our game.
16    */
17   @Override
18   public void setup() {
19     // width, height (in screens); location is (x, y), in screens
20     RectangleSprite rectangleBottom = new RectangleSprite(0.25, 0.05);
21     rectangleBottom.setLocation(0.625, 0.475);
22     addSprite(rectangleBottom);
23
24     RectangleSprite rectangleBackboard = new RectangleSprite(0.05, 0.4);
25     rectangleBackboard.setLocation(0.75, 0.3);
```

```
26        addSprite(rectangleBackboard);
27
28        RectangleSprite rectangleFrontboard = new RectangleSprite(0.05,
29            0.2);
30        rectangleFrontboard.setLocation(0.50, 0.4);
31        addSprite(rectangleFrontboard);
32
33        // location of the anchor point (launch point, too)
34        BasketBallLauncherSprite launcher = new BasketBallLauncherSprite(0.05, 0.5);
35        addSprite(launcher);
36    }
37 }
```

Listing 2.5: BasketBall.java

Lines 33–35 are the new code. Before finishing, setup adds a fourth sprite to the game, a BasketBallLauncherSprite. Line 34 calls the constructor for the new kind of sprite, specifying a location on the screen (0.05, 0.5) that is just off the left edge of the screen, halfway between the top and the bottom. A launcher is a "stretchy line," a line where one end is fixed (at the anchor point given to the constructor) and the other end tracks the mouse.

When the program is run, a small orange dot is visible at the given location until the player presses **Start**. When the player presses **Start**, the launcher begins keeping track of the player's mouse. An example moment during tracking is shown in Figure 2.7 on the next page.

The BasketBallLauncherSprite has something called a *transformer* attached to it. Transformers provide behaviors such as tracking where the mouse is (which is one of the transformers hooked to the launcher), detecting when the mouse is clicked, and things like that. More on playing with transformers below.

When the player finally decides to click the mouse, the BasketBallLauncherSprite creates a new BasketBallSprite and gives it an initial velocity based on the angle and length of the line that represented the launcher. The launcher also removes itself from the game so that the player gets to launch one ball and then watch it move around. A static figure, failing to capture the kinetic action of this little game, is shown in Figure 2.8 on page 47.

How can we change how this game works? All of the behavior is hidden inside of BasketBallSprite and BasketBallLauncherSprite. In the spirit of free software, we have the source code. We can look at it and modify it. BasketBallLauncherSprite has a method called mouseClickedAt. You could probably guess that this is the method called when the mouse is clicked and the launcher is in the game.

```
44    @Override
45    public void mouseClickedAt(Location2D location, int mouseButton) {
46        BasketBallSprite projectile = new BasketBallSprite();
47        // start the basketball at the anchor end of launcher
48        projectile.setLocation(getAnchor());
49        // launch velocity is double the length of the line
50        projectile.setVelocity(getVector().multiply(2.0));
51        // 270 degrees - straight down; 0.6 screens/second^2
52        projectile.setAcceleration(new Vector2D(270, 0.4));
53        // add new sprite to game
54        Game.getCurrentGame().addSprite(projectile);
55        // banish launcher
56        removeFromCanvas();
57    }
```

Listing 2.6: BasketBallLauncherSprite.java mouseClickedAt

Figure 2.7: BasketBall running, about to shoot

Notice that the mouseClickedAt method never uses its parameters. This is often a sign of bad design. In this case, line 44 indicates that the method overrides another definition; it must have the exact same formal parameter list whether or not it uses any of the parameters. The listing has a short comment before almost every line to explain what is going on.x

So, let's say we wanted to double the force of gravity. What line would we change? Well, setAcceleration on the ball sets the gravity field. So if we changed the 0.4 on line 52 to, say, 0.8, it would double the acceleration due to gravity. To turn gravity off, we could use 0.0 instead.

Notice that the last line of the method asks the game to remove the launcher (when a sprite wants to get out of a game, it should call removeFromCanvas). What if you commented out that line? A chance to have a million basketballs (which don't intersect with one another).

What if we wanted to change how hard the ball bounces off the basket or the edge (or, even, other basketballs)? We could look inside of BasketBallSprite. The method we are interested in is the *constructor*, the method called when new is used (in line 46 in the listing above). Inside the constructor three different transformers are built and hooked together.

```
42   public BasketBallSprite() {
43     super(DEFAULT_DIAMETER, DEFAULT_DIAMETER);
44     bouncer = new BounceInsideRectangleTransformer(
45         0.0, 0.0, 1.0, 1.0, // dimensions of screen
46         new VelocityTransformer(new Vector2D()));
47     // amount of bounce off edges
48     bouncer.setElasticity(0.66);
49     spriteBouncer = new BounceClassTransformer(this, bouncer);
50     spriteBouncer.add(RectangleSprite.class);
51     // amount of bounce off sprites
52     spriteBouncer.setElasticity(0.45);
53
54     gravity = new AccelerationTransformer(new Vector2D(), spriteBouncer);
55     addTransformer(gravity);
56     setColor(Game.getColor("misty rose"));
57   }
```

Listing 2.7: `BasketBallSprite.java` constructor

The three transformers of interest to us are assigned to the variable names `bouncer`, `spriteBouncer`, and `gravity`. The ball is very dead when it bounces off of the basket but pretty lively when it bounces off of the edges of the screen. Those two aspects of bouncing are determined by the elasticity of `spriteBouncer` (for bouncing off `RectangleSprites`) and `bouncer` (for bouncing off the edges of the screen). Right now the ball bounces off the top of the screen as well as the other edges. The four numbers passed to the `BounceInsideRectangleTransformer` on line 44 (and following) are the minimum x, minimum y, maximum x, and maximum y coordinates of the box inside which the ball bounces. So if you want the top to be above the screen, give it a negative value. You could also move the floor up or one of the walls in.[11]

So, you have now seen the insides of two classes that extend sprites. The next chapter goes into more depth about the available sprites and how you can use them.

Review 2.6

(a) Compile and run `BasketBall`. Try to launch the ball so that it ends up inside the basket.

(b) Starting with the `BasketBallLauncherSprite` as given, modify it so that the game has no gravity. Is the game more or less fun than the original? Can you try different levels, say between 0.0 and double the original gravity? Which one is most fun to you? (Note: Use a broad definition of "fun" for this exercise since the game is quite simple.)

(c) Modify `BasketBallLauncherSprite` so that you can launch more than one basketball.

(d) The `BasketBallSprite` is a Java class that **extends** `OvalSprite`. That is why it is round. What do you think would happen if you changed `OvalSprite` (in both the **import** line and in the **extends** line) to `RectangleSprite`? Try it and see.

2.7   Summary

Java

Java programs are written in *plain text*. Each *class* defines the rules for all *objects* of that type. A *class file* must have the same name as the **public class** defined inside the file. Java is *case-sensitive*, so uppercase and lowercase letters are considered different.

---

[11]Be careful moving the left wall in. If the ball starts outside of the defined rectangle, the physical modeling used breaks. The program runs but the behavior of the ball is not predictable.

Figure 2.8: BasketBall with BasketBallSprite bouncing

The name of a Java class can be any valid Java *identifier*. A valid identifier begins with a letter (or an underscore) which is followed by any number of letters or digits (or underscores). This is also shown below in a Java language template for *<identifier>*.

A Java class file begins with any required **import** statements. The next non-comment line is **public class** and the class name. A class is defined as *extending* some other class. This means that the *child class* can do anything the *parent class* can. A BasketBallSprite that extends OvalSprite can do anything an OvalSprite can do, including being added to the game and having its location set.

A *method* is a named group of instructions forming an effectively new instruction. The header of a method has four parts:

```
  public void setup() {
//^      ^    ^     ^ ^ - beginning of method body
//|      |    |     | - the parameter list
//|      |    | - the name of the method (an identifier)
//|      | - the return type of the method
//| - the access level of the method (public is all we know)
```

Java code is normally executed in *sequence*, the order in which it is written. The normal order is interrupted when a method name appears in the code: this is a method *call*. When a method is called, the method containing the call is suspended, and execution moves to the body of the method definition starting with the first line and normally continuing in sequence until the end of the method body. When execution finishes the body of the method, execution returns to the spot where the method was called and continues from there.

Levels of Abstraction and Languages

Computer program design requires working at multiple *levels of abstraction*. This idea of levels applies to programming languages: *high-level languages* are general and separated from the hardware level whereas *low-level languages* are typically closer to the hardware.

High-level languages have *source code*, the programs expressed in the high-level language, which can be *compiled* into a lower-level representation of the same program. The *compiler* translates the whole program at once. An *interpreter* runs the higher-level program more directly, interpreting each line and running the interpreter's routines to do what the line says.

Java is a high-level language which is compiled into *bytecode*, a machine language for a virtual computer. The bytecode is then interpreted so that the same bytecode can run on multiple computers without change.

Working from high to low levels of abstraction also works in designing programs, solving a given problem by expressing a solution as a combination of solutions to simpler problems. This same approach can then be applied at different levels as well.

FANG

The Freely Available Networked Game (FANG) engine is

- Free software.

  - You can study the source code.

  - You can modify the source code.

  - You can distribute the code with or without modification.

- Networked — It can build simple *multiplayer, multi-computer* games.

- A game engine — an application framework designed around making simple two-dimensional video games.

The `fang2.core.Game` class is the *parent class* for all FANG simple computer games. It provides two empty methods for games to *override*: `setup`, called once before the game is **Start**ed with the button on the FANG window, and `advance`, called once every time through the game loop.

FANG provides screen objects called *sprites* and behavior objects called *transformers*. The `BasketBall` game uses both to simulate a ball being shot, bouncing, and falling due to gravity.

2.8   Chapter Review Exercises

Review Exercise 2.1 What does the annotation `@Override` mean right before the header line of a method?

Review Exercise 2.2 What is the difference between *high-level* and *low-level* programming languages?

Java Templates

```
<identifier> := <letterOrUnderscore><letterOrDigitOrUnderscore>*

<className> := <identifier>

<parentClassName> := <identifier>

<classDefinition> := <classDeclaration>
                        <classBody>

<classDeclaration> := public class <className>
                            extends <parentClassName>

<classBody> := {
                    <definition>*
                  }

<definition> := <fieldDeclaration> |
                  <methodDefinition>
```

```
<classFile> := <imports>
                  <classDefinition>

<imports> := <import>*

<import> := import <importClassPath>;
```

```
<comment> := // <commentFromHereToEndOfLine>

<comment> := /*
                <anyNumberOfCommentLines>
                */
```

Review Exercise 2.3 What is a *compiler*?

Review Exercise 2.4 What is an *interpreter*?

Review Exercise 2.5 Define the following Java language terms:

   (a) `class`

   (b) `extends`

   (c) `import`

Review Exercise 2.6 When does FANG call each of the following methods (if you define one):

   (a) `setup`

   (b) `advance`

Review Exercise 2.7 What does the compiler do with comments? For whom are comments written?

Review Exercise 2.8 Explain why it is important to "document your intent" in comments rather than just describing the Java code.

Review Exercise 2.9 What is the screen coordinate for each of the following:

(a) the upper-right corner of the game screen?

(b) the middle of the left side of the game screen?

(c) the center of the screen?

Review Exercise 2.10 Where on the screen (what set of points) are the screen coordinates the same? Where on the screen are the x-coordinate and the y-coordinate equal?

Review Exercise 2.11 What are the screen coordinates of a point one-third from the left edge and two-thirds from the top of the screen?

2.9   Programming Problems

Programming Problem 2.1 Modify Square.java from this chapter so that instead of drawing a square it draws a *circle*. (Hint: Look at BasketBallSprite.)

Programming Problem 2.2 Modify BasketBall.java so that instead of launching from the middle of the left-hand side of the screen, the basketball launcher launches from very close to the bottom-left corner of the screen. You should be able to do this by changing just one line.

Programming Problem 2.3 Modify BasketBallSprite.java so that the right-hand edge of the "gym" (the bouncing rectangle) is one screen *past* the right edge of the screen. What happens when you miss the basket now?

Programming Problem 2.4 If you modified BasketBallLauncherSprite.java so that you can launch unlimited BasketBallSprites into the game, it would be nice to have them bounce off of each other. That requires changing BasketBallSprite's constructor.

(a) Find line 50 in BasketBallSprite.java. The line reads

```
50        spriteBouncer.add(RectangleSprite.class);
```

What happens if you comment the line out? Try it and see.

(b) Copy line 50 (so there are two calls to the add method). Change the second copy so that instead of saying RectangleSprite, it says BasketBallSprite (leave the .class part after the class name). Now see what happens with multiple BasketBallSprites.

Programming Problem 2.5 Start with BasketBall.java and try the following. Though it says to compile it only once, compile to test for typos in each of your changes as you go along.

(a) Copy BasketBall.java to a new .java file, BackwardBall.java.

(b) Compile and run BackwardBall.

(c) Move the BasketBallLauncherSprite from the left-hand to the right-hand side of the screen.

(d) Move the basket about half a screen to the left.

(e) Change the relative heights of the two vertical parts of the basket. This can be done by changing the locations of the two RectangleSprites *or* by changing the dimensions with which each is constructed.

Chapter

3

FANG: A Survey of Classes

The last two chapters presented short, simple game programs. They were simple because of the high level of abstraction at which you were able to work. Using a `Meteor` class or a `BasketBallLauncher` class is working with classes that have both an appearance and fairly complex behaviors already attached. It is time to start drilling down into lower levels of abstraction. This chapter surveys the *sprite* and *transformer* classes provided by FANG, presenting in the process a large collection of short *proto-games*, programs that are not games by our definition; most lack any problem to be solved or choices for the "player" to make. We drill down, way down, into how computers work and what, exactly, a digital, binary, general-purpose computer *is*. Finally, the chapter ends with a presentation of how to use the Java language's documentation (which also applies to the FANG documentation) to find the names of classes and methods.

3.1 How Computers Work

This section detours away from designing a game and translating our design into a program. It looks at what a computer is in more detail than we saw in Chapter 1. It then goes on to discuss how a computer program executes on the computer hardware and the exact mechanism of programming a computer.

Digital, General-Purpose Computers

The computer we program is a digital, binary, general-purpose computer. Digital means that the computer stores and operates on discrete rather than continuous values. Consider the difference between an old-fashioned, *analog*, needle speedometer (as in the left of Figure 3.1 on the next page) and a speedometer with a *digital* readout (as in the right of the figure). The needle can represent any speed between 0 and the maximum reading; if you speed up just a little bit, the needle rotates just a little bit clockwise, updating the reading of your current speed.

To emphasize the difference between digital and analog display, assume that the digital speedometer has the same range as the analog meter but that the ones digit is always "0." The digital speedometer shows speed to the nearest ten miles per hour. How many different values can the digital speedometer display? Assuming either speedometer is limited to the range 0–100, the digital speedometer can show only eleven different speeds. This limited number of discrete values is compared to the continuous resolution of the analog device.

Figure 3.1: Analog v. Digital Speedometers

Digital electronic signals (like those inside the computer) are more robust than analog signals. It is much simpler to build a circuit that can differentiate between the presence or absence of 3.3VDC than it is to build a circuit that can differentiate between all of the values between 0 and 3.3VDC. This also explains why modern digital computers are *binary* (using the base-2 number system; more on this later): it is easier to differentiate between 0 and 3.3VDC rather than tell 0 from 0.33 from 0.66 from 0.99 and so on up to eleven discrete values.

Although there have been analog computers, almost all modern computers are digital. Each memory location in the computer can hold a number of discrete states. You might ask how a machine, limited to holding entries from a small set of possible values, can be a general-purpose machine. The answer to that question comes in two parts: how many states can a sequence of discrete entries take on, and what do those states mean?

Note that you are holding a book in your hands, one written in the English language. Ignoring the pictures for the moment, how many different symbols can any given location in the book contain? Counting from the beginning of the book, what value might the one thousandth character in the text have? The ten thousandth? Any randomly selected location? There are only about 75 different values possible (a space, 26 lowercase letters, 26 uppercase letters, 10 digits, and a handful of punctuation characters; this is a computer science book, so the punctuation is more varied than in a book by Mary Shelley).

Yet, this sequence of alphabet characters, this *book*, purports to teach you about building simple computer games; no matter how simple the games are, the concept being taught is moderately complex. The sequence of characters, drawn from a fairly limited alphabet, conveys a great amount of information. And a different sequence drawn from the same limited alphabet might teach you how to bake fabulous desserts or tell you the story of *Frankenstein or the Modern Prometheus.*

The same thing happens inside the computer: its memory, composed of *bytes*[1] which each draw their value from one of 256 possible values, is arranged as a large sequence of bytes. Modern machines have main memories (RAM) measured in *gigabytes*[2] or billions of bytes. To put that in perspective, a page of this book contains about five thousand characters drawn from an alphabet about a quarter of the size of a byte's possible values. That means a page could be stored in just about a kilobyte (1024 bytes), which means that a computer with a one gigabyte memory could store almost a million pages in the RAM at one time.

Note that the memory inside the computer, the random access memory, is not fixed like the ink on this page. Instead, it can change over time. Thus it can store a *different* selection of a million pages at any given moment and, by following instructions, it can change any of those characters on any of those pages, changing what million pages are stored in a split second.

While each byte can be considered a number on the range 0–255, the interpretation or *meaning* of the contents of memory depends on what part of the computer is reading the value as well as on the current instructions being executed by the CPU. We now take a closer look at the parts of the computer.

Parts of a Computer

Figure 3.2 shows an abstract block diagram of a computer. The middle of the diagram is the central processing unit (CPU). The CPU is, literally, the rules follower for the computer. It follows a very simple cycle: fetch the contents of a location in the main memory, determine what the contents of that location mean in terms of the instructions the CPU knows how to follow, fetch any contents of memory that are needed by the instruction, and execute the instruction.

The main memory is *random access* in the sense that any byte can be accessed in the same amount of time. Individual bytes are addressed with their distance from the beginning of memory (memory location 0); no matter how large a byte's address, it can be accessed as quickly as the byte at location 0.

What would a non-random access memory look like? Consider a similar addressing scheme, where each chunk of data is labeled with its distance from the beginning of the memory but have it stored on a reel of magnetic tape. Let us compare a three-byte access pattern in the RAM and on our tape.

In the computer, the cost of accessing the byte at location 0 followed by the byte at location 1000000 followed by the byte at location 100 is three memory access times, all the same and all very quick.

Assuming the tape begins completely rewound, the same access sequence on the tape reel is very quick for byte 0 (the tape is positioned to read that location); then the tape must move 999999 memory locations past the read head and read the byte at location 1000000; finally, the tape must stop and rewind 9999001 locations to read the final byte. Even if moving the tape and not reading it is somewhat faster than reading each byte, moving forward and backward about two million locations certainly takes longer than it would to read locations 0, 1, and 2, one after another (or even 0, 100, and 1000). In RAM, all sequences are equally fast.[3]

The CPU can change the values stored in the RAM very quickly but the contents of the RAM are *volatile*: they go away when the power is turned off. Computers use *disk drives* to provide longer-term storage; disk storage includes optical (CD/DVD), magnetic (regular hard and floppy disks), and solid-state (memory stick, thumb drive) drives. These devices are slower but larger than the RAM. They are also *nonvolatile* meaning that changes to the content persist across power-off cycles.

On the right side of the drawing are several *input/output devices* (I/O). These include the screen, the keyboard, game controllers, and even the network interface. These devices can provide information for a running computer program or be driven to display information from the running program for the computer user.

---

[1]A byte is eight binary digits (or *bits*) wide; each bit can contain a 0 or a 1, so the total number of combinations that a byte can hold is $2 \times 2 \times 2 \times \ldots \times 2$ (eight times) or $2^8 = 256$. A byte directly encodes the numbers from 0 to 255 which can be interpreted in different ways.

[2]In computer science we use standard power of ten prefixes (i.e., giga-, mega-) to refer to the nearest power of two: a *kilobyte* is $2^{10} = 1024$ bytes; a *megabyte* is $2^{20} = 1048576$; a *gigabyte* = $2^{30} = 1073741824$.

[3]And then there was *cache*. Cache memory is a very, very fast memory that sits between the RAM and the CPU; the way it works changes the statement that *all* sequences are equally fast (close memory accesses are quicker, in general). Ignoring cache, the statement stands.

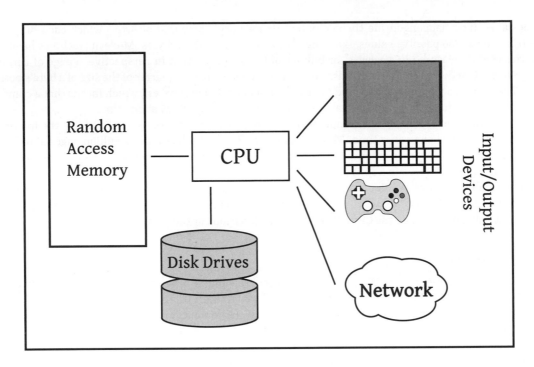

Figure 3.2: Abstract Structure of a Computer

The instructions executed by the CPU are **very** simple. They are things such as: get the value of a given memory address, add two numbers, store a result to a given memory address, and if the result of addition is negative, continue execution at a different address.

For example, the following sequence of instructions would load the contents of two memory locations and then put the larger of the two values into a different location in memory.[4] The number to the left of each line is the memory location where that instruction begins (each is assumed to take exactly 4 bytes).

```
1248    load contents of memory location 100 to x
1252    load contents of memory location 104 to y
1256    if x > y jump to memory location 1268
1260    store contents of y to memory location 108
1264    jump to memory location 1272
1268    store contents of x to memory location 108
1272    ...<more instructions here>...
```

This sequence of six instructions makes sure that the value stored at 108 is the larger of the values stored at 100 or 104. It takes six instructions to do something a human could do on inspection. A modern computer is powerful because it can execute these instructions billions of times per second. Simple arithmetic and decisions, done quickly enough, permit the computer to run any program from an operating system to a word processor to a real-time strategy game. It all depends on the contents of the computer's memory and what they mean.

---

[4]The numbers in the example are base 10 rather than binary; in the computer the instructions and memory locations would be encoded in binary numbers stored in the bytes of memory.

Interpretation of Computer Memory

The contents of the memory do not, of themselves, mean anything. They must be interpreted and the same contents can be interpreted differently depending on context. That is no different from the contents of a book: if this book said it were in Italian or German, the sequences of characters would be interpreted differently (and, in this case, incorrectly); when the book is read by an editor or your instructor, their interpretation of the material is different than yours, reading it as a student of computer science.

What makes the computer truly general-purpose is that the contents of the memory can be interpreted as *instructions* to the computer on how it should manipulate or interpret other parts of memory as *data*. The fact that the contents of the same memory can be interpreted in different ways and that the contents of memory can describe *how* the contents are to be interpreted is what permits a general-purpose computer to store a song (encoded using the MP3 or Ogg Vorbis coding scheme, for example), a program to *play* a song (a machine-language program for manipulating encoded songs and the computer's sound hardware), and an operating system to *start* the program that can play a song (a different program for manipulating *programs* as well as the computer's memory and other hardware).

Viewing a computer at multiple layers simultaneously, where what is a series of instructions at one level (the player program) is treated as data at another layer (the operating system), is what makes modern computers so powerfully general-purpose.

John von Neumann [1903-1957]

John von Neumann was a prodigious mathematician who contributed to the development of game theory and computer science. He was born in Budapest, Hungary, just after the turn of the twentieth century, received his PhD in mathematics by age 22, and emigrated to the United States in 1930.

In the United States, von Neumann was an original member of the Institute for Advanced Study at Princeton University, one of the first places in the world to build digital electromechanical and electronic computers. He also contributed to the computing power, mathematics, and physics of the Manhattan Project, the United States' World War II super secret initiative to develop the world's first atomic bomb.

While consulting on the Electronic Discrete Variable Automatic Computer (EDVAC), von Neumann wrote an incomplete but widely circulated report describing a computer architecture that used a unified memory to store both data and instructions. This contrasted with the so-called *Harvard* architecture, where the program and the data on which the program operated were segregated.

The von Neumann architecture is the fundamental architecture used in modern computers. A single, unified memory makes it possible for a computer program to treat itself (or another computer program) as data for input or output. This is just what the operating system described in this section or the compiler described in the next section does.

Von Neumann's report drew on but failed to acknowledge the work of J. Presper Eckert and John W. Mauchly; this led to some acrimony when it came time to allocate credit for the modern computer revolution.

Von Neumann's name comes up again when we examine game theory, a branch of economics that permits reasoning about strategies in competitive games.

Review 3.1

(a) Do the **Xbox 360, Playstation 3**, and **Wii** have operating systems? Do some Internet research to find the answer? Cite your sources when you answer this question.

(b) Take a look at the **Nintendo 64** game controller in Figure 3.3.

It has two directional controllers, the digital D-pad and the analog stick. How many directions are possible on the digital D-pad? the analog stick? Why is one called analog and the other called digital?

(c) Is a gaming console a computer? Why or why not?

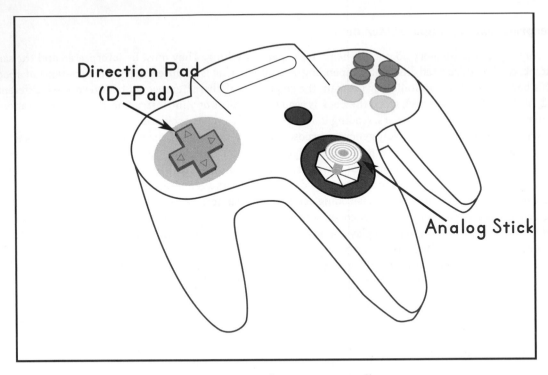

Figure 3.3: Nintendo 64 game controller

(d) When you type a term paper into your favorite word processor and then your cat turns the machine off, you lose what you typed. What kind of memory was the word processor using to store the contents of your paper? Where does the paper get moved when you select **File | Save**?

(e) How many bits are in one byte? What does *bit* mean?

(f) What does *binary* mean? How does it apply to your computer?

(g) Is the alphabet *analog* or *digital*?

(h) Can you give an example of information in real life where context determines how it is interpreted? Perhaps something that you and your teacher would both be able to read but which would mean something different to each of you.

3.2   FANG Basics

As we have seen in the games in the previous two chapters, FANG provides a class, fang2.core.Game, which represents an "empty" game, a game box, if you will, capable of holding any of a million different games. You must fill that box with the components necessary to make your specific game work. FANG also provides *sprites*, objects that represent elements on the screen, and *transformers*, objects that can be attached to different sprites and provide automatic behaviors. This section provides much deeper coverage of the features provided by each of these three FANG capabilities.

Note on Java syntax: sometimes it is important to be able to talk about a *specific* definition of a method, the definition of the method that appears inside a specific class. For example, many different sprites support the getX method. We might want to talk about the version defined in RectangleSprite as opposed to the version defined in OvalSprite. The Java notation for this is to use the name of the class, a dot, and then the name of the method. Thus `RectangleSprite.getX` is the version defined in `RectangleSprite`, and `OvalSprite.getX` is the version defined in the `OvalSprite` class. We use the name of the method without any class name whenever possible but must be more specific in some instances.

Creating Objects

Java objects have types and Java types are classes. The name of a class typically begins with a capital letter (more on naming in the next chapter). In order to use an object of a given type, you must create an *instance* of that object.

A high-level analogy of the relationship between classes and instances is the relationship between blueprints for a car and any given instance of that type of car. The blueprints describe the features every car has, the services it can provide such as "accelerate" and "open driver's door." Each car has a "level of gas" method, too; while all cars share the capability of reporting the contents of the gas tank, each reports its own specific level of gas.

An object constructor is a special method used by the Java system to create an object of a given type. A constructor is called by following the **new** operator with the name of the type you want to create. The following examples include calling constructors; in Chapter 6 and following, we define constructors for our own classes.

Naming an Instance

After a new object is created, it is important to be able to have that object *do* things. A rectangle might need to have its color set or a transformer might need to change the associated velocity. *What* a given object can do depends on the public methods it defines.

In Java a *local variable* is an identifier which can be associated with any object of a given type. A local variable is declared by stating the type to which it can refer and its name. The Java template for a local variable is

```
<typeName> := <identifier>

<variableName> := <identifier>

<variableDeclaration> := <typeName> <variableName>

<localVariableDefinition> := <variableDeclaration> [= <expression>];
```

This template introduces a little more EBNF notation: the [and] in the template are like the * notation for the template and are not representing themselves in the resulting Java code. Where * means zero or more copies of what comes before, the square brackets mean "what is inside is optional." There can be zero or one copy of the `= <expression>` part of the `<localVariableDefinition>` template.

A `<localVariableDefinition>` can appear inside the body of any method, between the curly braces following the method header for any method.

What is an `<expression>`? Along with `<statement>`, `<expression>` is one of the more complicated elements of a Java program. For the moment, we know of one definition:

```
<actualParameterList> := [<expression> [, <expression>]*]

<expression> := new <typeName>(<actualParameterList>)
```

What is an `<actualParameterList>`? It is empty (whole thing is optional) or it is an expression followed by any number of expressions, each separated by commas. So, it is a comma-separated list of zero or more expressions. So, we now know a couple of more definitions for `<expression>`: it could also be a number. How can we indicate that a template has more than one possible match? Again, | indicates that the template matches the stuff before the vertical bar or it matches the stuff after the vertical bar; read it as "or."

```
<expression> := <literal> |
                new <typeName>(<actualParameterList>)
```

This reads as "a <expression> is either a <literal> or it is the keyword **new** followed by a type and parameter list." A literal is a value directly typed into the source code: a number, a keyword literal, or a string.

An example of declaring a local variable inside of setup is

```
// inside of some Game-extending class
...
public void setup() {
  RectangleSprite sq = new RectangleSprite(1.0, 1.0);
  ...
}
```

The name of the local variable is sq. It can refer to RectangleSprite objects. The result of calling **new** refers to an object of the given type, so **new** RectangleSprite(1.0, 1.0) is an expression which has the type RectangleSprite (there is much more on expressions and their types in the following chapters). The = can be read as "is assigned the value of" or "refers to." So, the line declaring sq reads: "Create a local variable named sq which can refer to RectangleSprites *and* assign the value of a brand new RectangleSprite as big as the screen to it."

After the assignment, we can use the name sq to call *methods* defined in the RectangleSprite class. This chapter introduces some specific sprite methods; the final section describes how to figure out what methods and classes are available in both Java and FANG.

Calling a Method

An object has methods. An object's methods are the commands that it understands. Going back to our checkers game, a checkers piece knows how to move one square, how to jump, and how to be promoted. You can tell it what to do if you have a label for it. If one of my checkers is my favorite, I could ask it to move forward to the left (a square might have two squares "forward" and two squares "back," so left and right, from the player looking at their back row, disambiguates them) by saying favorite.move(forwardLeft). Here the name of the object is favorite, the name of the method is move, the parameter list has one entry, whatever forwardLeft is. The dot is how Java can tell where the identifier for the object and the identifier for the method name end and begin.

So, to set the color of the rectangle sprite we created in the previous example, we would use sq, a dot, and setColor. The parameter expected by setColor is a Color (more on this type at the end of the chapter). To get a color, Game provides a method, getColor, which takes a string naming the color we want. So, "red" is a string (notice the double quotes) naming the color red. So, to set the rectangle to red we use the following line:

```
sq.setColor(getColor("red"));
```

This line shows that we can call a method "on" another object by naming the object and using the dot and the method name. It also shows that we can call a method on the *current object*, the Game-extending class object where setup resides.

Games

Game or, more precisely, fang2.core.Game is a class provided by FANG. It is the standard starting point for creating a game because, after compiling, any Game-extending class can run as an application (or, if embedded in a Web page, as an applet; see http://www.javawide.org/ for free Web space where FANG programs can be automatically built). The Game class provides all of the code to put a window on the screen, put four buttons across the bottom, set up the game, and run a game loop.

The game is set up with a call to the setup method (full method header: **public void** setup()). Game defines setup, expecting classes that extend Game to override it.

To override is to provide a new, more specific definition of a method. When a Meteors game starts, FANG does all of the necessary construction of objects for the window and buttons and internal structures. Then it calls setup. Remember, *calling* a method means using the name of the method as a statement in another method, one which is running. When the method name is encountered, the running method, the *caller*, is interrupted but its place is remembered and the called method begins execution. When the called method finishes (when execution runs off the closing curly brace at the end of the method body), Java returns to the remembered location in the caller and continues execution.

What happens if there are more than one method with the same name? What if Meteors.setup and Game.setup both exist? Java looks at the actual type of the object on which the method is being called, the Meteors object constructed automatically calling by FANG, and checks to see if the method it needs is defined in that class, Meteors; if it is, that version is chosen.

Consider Meteors and the main game loop. In the loop, FANG calls the advance method every time through the loop (full method header: **public void** advance(**double** seconds)). Again, to find which advance method to actually call, Java begins looking for Meteors.advance. There is no such method (we never defined one back in Chapter 1). Java then, using the **extends** part of the class definition, looks for the method in the parent class, Game.advance. Game.advance is defined (and has an empty body so it does nothing), so Java calls that version every time through the game loop. If there had been no version in Game, Java would have looked at Game's parent class and then that class's parent class and so on until it reached the "root" class, Object. Object is the ultimate parent of all objects in Java; there is more to say about it in later chapters.

To create a FANG game we must

- extend fang2.core.Game.

- Override (redefine) setup if we want any new sprites added to the game.

- Override (redefine) advance if we want to do anything to update the game state each time through the game loop.

Some other features of Game objects are also presented along with sprites and transformers.

Sprites

In computer graphics, a sprite is a two-dimensional visual object that moves in front of the background of the screen. If you consider the game *Asteroids*, the basis for Meteors, the ship, the lasers, the rocks, and any power-ups used in the game are all sprites; they are visual objects that move in front of a background (empty in this case).

Historically, sprite was coined for an early 1980s video display controller from Texas Instruments [Whi92]. The sprite was named for flying pixies or fairies of that name because the generated image flew over the television picture. The sprite was a god-send for sportscasters everywhere.

In addition to movement, sprite hardware, which was common throughout the 1980s, also supported collision detection (it could tell whether or not two sprites overlapped). In the spirit of that "Golden Age of Gaming" technology, visual game components in FANG extend the fang2.sprite.Sprite class and have names ending in *Sprite*.

RectangleSprite

A RectangleSprite is constructed by calling **new**, naming the type of object (RectangleSprite) to construct, and specifying the width and height of the rectangle. We have also defined a *local variable*, a label, for referring to the new object *after* the line where it is constructed.

```
1   // package default
2
3   import fang2.core.Game;
4   import fang2.sprites.RectangleSprite;
5
6   // FANG Demonstration program: RectangleSprite
7   public class Square
8     extends Game {
9     // Called before game loop: create named rectangle and add
10    @Override
11    public void setup() {
12      RectangleSprite rectangle = new RectangleSprite(0.5, 0.5);
13      rectangle.setLocation(0.5, 0.5);
14      addSprite(rectangle);
15    }
16  }
```

Listing 3.1: Square.java

Recalling Square.java from the previous chapter, we see that line 12 begins with the words RectangleSprite rectangle. That is a type name followed by a variable name. rectangle is the label used to refer to the square made in line 12. It is necessary to have a label so that lines 13 and 14 can manipulate the rectangle (by changing its location) and add the square to the game.

Consider building a simple square "target" picture as shown in Figure 3.4. The picture is a series of alternating colored squares, centered on the screen, in blue and gold, each one a tenth of the screen smaller than the one around it.

Given that RectangleSprite has a setColor method, setting the color of a rectangle called rectangle to blue or to gold is simply

```
rectangle.setColor(getColor("gold");
// or
rectangle.setColor(getColor("blue"));
```

Before we go on and write the program, think about how you would specify each of the rectangles: What width and height do you send to each constructor? At what location is each square placed?

Layers and the Order of addSprite

Target01.java is our first attempt at implementing the "game" shown in the previous picture. The name is valid because a Java identifier must *begin* with a letter but can have any number of letters or digits for the rest of its name.[5]

```
1   // package default
2
3   import fang2.core.Game;
4   import fang2.sprites.RectangleSprite;
5
6   /** Good example of a bad example: one rectangle in 5 shows */
```

---

[5]Yes, "or underscore," should appear with "letter." We agree not to mention underscores except when naming constants, which is covered in Chapter 4. It is simpler to write letters and letters or digits, and we do not use many underscores in our naming.

Figure 3.4: Target03 screenshot

```
7   public class Target01
8     extends Game {
9     /**
10     * Create, color, and draw five rectangles centered at the center of
11     * the screen. Add to the game in largest to smallest order.
12     */
13     @Override
14     public void setup() {
15       RectangleSprite one = new RectangleSprite(0.1, 0.1);
16       one.setColor(getColor("gold"));
17       one.setLocation(0.5, 0.5);
18       addSprite(one);
19
20       RectangleSprite two = new RectangleSprite(0.2, 0.2);
21       two.setColor(getColor("blue"));
22       two.setLocation(0.5, 0.5);
```

```
23        addSprite(two);
24
25        RectangleSprite three = new RectangleSprite(0.3, 0.3);
26        three.setColor(getColor("gold"));
27        three.setLocation(0.5, 0.5);
28        addSprite(three);
29
30        RectangleSprite four = new RectangleSprite(0.4, 0.4);
31        four.setColor(getColor("blue"));
32        four.setLocation(0.5, 0.5);
33        addSprite(four);
34
35        RectangleSprite five = new RectangleSprite(0.5, 0.5);
36        five.setColor(getColor("gold"));
37        five.setLocation(0.5, 0.5);
38        addSprite(five);
39    }
40 }
```

Listing 3.2: `Target01.java`

Lines 15–18 declare a local variable, one, and set its value using a **new** expression to create a square 0.1 screen on a side. Then the square is colored gold, located at the center of the screen, and added to the game (addSprite adds the sprite to the list of sprites drawn during every iteration of the game loop). These four lines are common to all of the kinds of sprites presented in this chapter.

For this program, the following twenty or so lines do the same thing four more times. Each rectangle is a different size and every other one is given a different color.

Five squares of alternating colors are added to the game. Running the program, we see in Figure 3.5 on the facing page that there is only one gold rectangle visible. What happened?

Games are two-dimensional with an x-axis running from 0.0 to 1.0 from left to right and a y-axis running from 0.0 to 1.0 from top to bottom. This is also a *stacking* or *layering* order. Most drawing programs (*Inkscape*, *Adobe Illustrator*, *Adobe Photoshop*, etc.) have a similar ordering. Sometimes, this is referred to as at *z-ordering* because the layers stack along the z-axis running perpendicular to the surface of the computer screen.

The first sprite drawn on the screen is *behind* the second sprite which is behind the third and so on. You could imagine that sprites are made of construction paper and each is added to the scene covering up anything it overlaps. We were counting on this behavior when we designed the target using five squares. Each "ring" would need four rectangles without the overlap.

Look back at Listing 3.2. The lines in the setup method are executed in sequence, starting with line 15 and running through line 39. The addSprite lines, the lines that add a sprite to the scene, are executed in order from *smallest to largest.* Sprites are stacked in the order they are added to the scene. The other lines, where the sprites are colored, located, or even constructed, do not impact the stacking order. The addSprite lines execute in the reverse order from what we want: the big square covers up all of the rest.

The names one through five are arbitrary. Reversing chunks of code that construct, color, position, and add each sprite results in the following version of Target03 (only setup is shown; the rest is analogous to Target01).

```
14  public void setup() {
15        RectangleSprite five = new RectangleSprite(0.5, 0.5);
16        five.setColor(getColor("gold"));
17        five.setLocation(0.5, 0.5);
18        addSprite(five);
```

Figure 3.5: `Target01` screenshot

```
19
20      RectangleSprite four = new RectangleSprite(0.4, 0.4);
21      four.setColor(getColor("blue"));
22      four.setLocation(0.5, 0.5);
23      addSprite(four);
24
25      RectangleSprite three = new RectangleSprite(0.3, 0.3);
26      three.setColor(getColor("gold"));
27      three.setLocation(0.5, 0.5);
28      addSprite(three);
29
30      RectangleSprite two = new RectangleSprite(0.2, 0.2);
31      two.setColor(getColor("blue"));
32      two.setLocation(0.5, 0.5);
33      addSprite(two);
34
```

```
35    RectangleSprite one = new RectangleSprite(0.1, 0.1);
36    one.setColor(getColor("gold"));
37    one.setLocation(0.5, 0.5);
38    addSprite(one);
39  }
```

Listing 3.3: `Target03.java`: setup

Keep stacking order in mind when figuring out the order to add sprites to the screen. If you need to add a sprite *below* all of the other sprites already in the game, Game also has an addBottom method which works just like addSprite but adds the sprite to the bottom of the stacking order. Overlapping sprites can be used to create interesting pictures with very simple geometric objects.

Round: `OvalSprite`

An OvalSprite is specified like a RectangleSprite with its width and height. Thus CircleTarget03.java makes a circular target like Target03.java:

```
1  // package default
2
3  import fang2.core.Game;
4  import fang2.sprites.OvalSprite;
5
6  /** A sample program drawing five concentric circles. */
7  public class CircleTarget03
8    extends Game {
9    /**
10    * Create, color, and draw five circles centered at the center of
11    * the screen. Add to the game in largest to smallest order.
12    */
13   @Override
14   public void setup() {
15     OvalSprite five = new OvalSprite(0.5, 0.5);
16     five.setColor(getColor("gold"));
17     five.setLocation(0.5, 0.5);
18     addSprite(five);
19
20     OvalSprite four = new OvalSprite(0.4, 0.4);
21     four.setColor(getColor("blue"));
22     four.setLocation(0.5, 0.5);
23     addSprite(four);
24
25     OvalSprite three = new OvalSprite(0.3, 0.3);
26     three.setColor(getColor("gold"));
27     three.setLocation(0.5, 0.5);
28     addSprite(three);
29
30     OvalSprite two = new OvalSprite(0.2, 0.2);
31     two.setColor(getColor("blue"));
32     two.setLocation(0.5, 0.5);
33     addSprite(two);
```

```
34
35      OvalSprite one = new OvalSprite(0.1, 0.1);
36      one.setColor(getColor("gold"));
37      one.setLocation(0.5, 0.5);
38      addSprite(one);
39    }
40  }
```

Listing 3.4: CircleTarget03.java

The code (called `CircleTarget03` to match `Target03`; `CircleTarget` 01 and 02 are left as exercises for the interested reader) constructs five circles[6] in alternating colors. They are added to the scene from largest to smallest; thus they overlap the *right* way.

Figure 3.6: CircleTarget03 screenshot

What else can we do with layering? What if we draw some things in the *background color*? Those sprites would appear to erase any part of other sprites they overlapped. What would the following `setup` draw?

---

[6]A *circle* is a special case of an *oval*, one where both diameters are the same. A circle is to an oval as a square is to a rectangle.

```
13  public void setup() {
14      OvalSprite white = new OvalSprite(0.7, 0.2);
15      white.setColor(getColor("white"));
16      white.setLocation(0.5, 0.5);
17      addSprite(white);
18
19      OvalSprite black = new OvalSprite(0.7, 0.2);
20      black.setColor(getColor("black"));
21      black.setLocation(0.5, 0.4);
22      addSprite(black);
23
24      OvalSprite left = new OvalSprite(0.2, 0.2);
25      left.setColor(getColor("white"));
26      left.setLocation(0.25, 0.25);
27      addSprite(left);
28
29      OvalSprite right = new OvalSprite(0.2, 0.2);
30      right.setColor(getColor("white"));
31      right.setLocation(0.75, 0.25);
32      addSprite(right);
33  }
```

Listing 3.5: `Ovals.java` setup

(The rest of the program is just what you would expect, `import` for `Game` and `OvalSprite` and a **public class** named for the file `Oval`. Many of the following sprite examples just show the `setup` method, starting with the method header (just after the `@Override` line).)

Figure 3.7 shows the output: `left` and `right` are white circles, each centered half-way between the center and the obvious edge of the screen.

The `white` oval is wide and short, centered on the whole screen. Without `black`, the picture would be an oval centered and two circles above it. What does `black` do to the picture? It is *between* the layers with `white` and the circles. `left` and `right` stack above it (and are not modified). `white` is partially occluded by `black`. The edge of `black` touches the center of the screen (the center of the white oval). The bottom half of `white` is visible with a curved "bite" taken out of the top.

One useful skill is being able to read sprite coordinates and stacking order and picturing the results in your mind. Alternatively you can sketch a quick picture. It is helpful in designing complicated shapes out of simple geometries.

The next section takes a break from presenting sprites, instead looking at modifying rectangles and ovals with different transformers, objects that add animation behaviors to sprites. Then, the following section presents a mix of new sprites and new transformers to give you a broader pallet when working with FANG.

Transformers

Sprites represent screen objects. A given sprite can have any number of *transformers* associated with it. A transformer transforms the sprite in some way: some, like the `VelocityTransformer`, modify the sprite's location; others, like the `SpinTransformer`, change the rotation; some change the scale or the color, for example, `ScaleTransformer` and `ColorInterpolatorTransformer`; finally, some, like `KeyboardTransformer`, filter and modify when or how other transformers are applied.

Figure 3.7: Ovals screenshot

VelocityTransformer and WrapTransfomerNG

The first example program has a single sprite moving in a fixed direction at a fixed speed. When it goes off the screen on one side, it reappears at the corresponding point on the opposite side. One of the design goals in making the transformers was creating many small, single-purpose transformers that can be used together. Since moving and wrapping around are two different actions, this requires two transformers.

```
1  // package default
2
3  import fang2.core.Game;
4  import fang2.sprites.OvalSprite;
5  import fang2.transformers.VelocityTransformer;
6  import fang2.transformers.WrapTransformer;
7
8  // FANG Demonstration program: OvalSprite,
9  public class Circle
10    extends Game {
```

```
11   // Called before game loop: create named oval and add
12   @Override
13   public void setup() {
14     OvalSprite oval = new OvalSprite(0.2, 0.2);
15     oval.setColor(getColor("cornflower blue"));
16     oval.setLocation(0.5, 0.5);
17     addSprite(oval);
18
19     OvalSprite o2 = new OvalSprite(0.05, 0.05);
20     addSprite(o2);
21     // velocity is (facing in degrees, speed in screens/second);
22     // 0.0 degrees is positive x-axis, rotation goes counterclockwise
23     VelocityTransformer velocityTransformer =
24       new VelocityTransformer(25.0, 1.0);
25     oval.addTransformer(velocityTransformer);
26     o2.addTransformer(velocityTransformer);
27     // wrapping means wrapping from left to right or top to bottom
28     WrapTransformer wrapTransformer = new WrapTransformer();
29     oval.addTransformer(wrapTransformer);
30     o2.addTransformer(wrapTransformer);
31   }
32 }
```

Listing 3.6: `Circle.java`

Listing 3.6 creates a small `OvalSprite`, giving it the label `oval`, giving it the color `cornflower blue`, and positioning it at the middle of the screen. Then two transformers are constructed and added to the sprite. Notice that the transformer classes are in the `fang2.transformers` package.

Line 24 calls the `VelocityTransformer` constructor. The constructor needs a direction and a speed, the direction and speed with which associated sprites are moved. The direction 0.0 degree points to the right of the screen (along the positive x-axis) and rotation goes in the counterclockwise direction. So, 25.0 degrees is slightly up and to the right. The length of the velocity is screens per second. A transformer is added to a sprite with a call to `addTransformer`; line 25 adds the velocity transformer to `oval`.

What does it mean to have `velocityTransformer` added to `oval`? It means that once the game is started (by pressing the **Start** button), the transformer updates the location of the sprite, animating it with the given velocity.

A `WrapTransformer` wraps one edge of the screen around to the opposite side. When a sprite moves completely off the screen in one direction, the wrap transformer moves it to the corresponding point on the opposite side. Line 28 creates the `WrapTransformer`; it has no parameters since it always does the same thing. The sprite moves around the screen as if the screen were mapped onto a giant donut (technical term, *torus*).

There is no `Circle.java` screenshot: either the circle would be in the middle of the screen before the **Start** of the game *or* it would be shown at some other spot on the screen during the game. Neither image serves to improve understanding of these two transformers. Instead you should run the program and try changing the values passed in to the `VelocityTransformer` constructor to see if you can change how the circle moves. Several other animation programs lack screenshots for the same reason.

SpinTransformer

Most transformers can be applied to multiple sprites at the same time. So, if we wanted to take `Target03` and have all of the boxes spin together, one `SpinTransformer` added to all five of the `RectangleSprites` suffices. The following listing shows only `setup`; the only difference in the rest of the program from `Target03` is the addition of the appropriate **import** line.

```
16  public void setup() {
17    RectangleSprite five = new RectangleSprite(0.5, 0.5);
18    five.setColor(getColor("gold"));
19    five.setLocation(0.5, 0.5);
20    addSprite(five);
21
22    RectangleSprite four = new RectangleSprite(0.4, 0.4);
23    four.setColor(getColor("blue"));
24    four.setLocation(0.5, 0.5);
25    addSprite(four);
26
27    RectangleSprite three = new RectangleSprite(0.3, 0.3);
28    three.setColor(getColor("gold"));
29    three.setLocation(0.5, 0.5);
30    addSprite(three);
31
32    RectangleSprite two = new RectangleSprite(0.2, 0.2);
33    two.setColor(getColor("blue"));
34    two.setLocation(0.5, 0.5);
35    addSprite(two);
36
37    RectangleSprite one = new RectangleSprite(0.1, 0.1);
38    one.setColor(getColor("gold"));
39    one.setLocation(0.5, 0.5);
40    addSprite(one);
41
42    // SpinTransformer takes degrees/second of spin
43    SpinTransformer spinner = new SpinTransformer(90.0);
44    one.addTransformer(spinner);
45    two.addTransformer(spinner);
46    three.addTransformer(spinner);
47    four.addTransformer(spinner);
48    five.addTransformer(spinner);
49  }
```

Listing 3.7: SpinningTarget03.java

The new lines are at the end of setup, 42–48. Line 43 declares a local variable of type SpinTransformer having the name spinner; remember that a variable is declared with a type name (a **class** name, typically) followed by an identifier. We could call the variable groundhog, yodel, or just plain x. There is much more on naming in Chapter 4, but for now you can think of the names you choose as descriptions for human readers of your code. Choose a name that describes what the thing is *for*: spinner is a SpinTransformer, meant to spin all of the squares in the target.

spinner is assigned a value, the value returned from **new** when a SpinTransformer is constructed. The parameter passed to SpinTransformer is the number of degrees per second to rotate. As always, positive rotation is in the counterclockwise direction. The next five lines then add the new transformer to all five RectangleSprites.

This shows a feature of transformers: most of them are designed to work with multiple different sprites at the same time. This permits you to have an entire group of, say, lemmings, all using the same VelocityTransformer to move them all in the same direction. It is even possible to use a single WrapTransformer

Figure 3.8: SpinningTarget03 screenshot

to wrap every sprite on the screen. Figure 3.8 shows the target as it is spinning. Again, it is much more interesting to watch while it is running.

To use a transformer you must

- **import** the appropriate class.

- Construct one or more sprites and assign them to variables.

- Construct the transformer(s) you want, assigning them to variables, too.

- addTransformer to the sprite. That is done by calling the addTransformer method using the sprite variable:

  `<spriteVariableName>.addTransformer(<transformer-variableName>);`

The next section surveys sprites and transformers available in FANG, showing some different combinations.

More of Everything

Words: `StringSprite`

The `StringSprite` class is for displaying words, numbers, and anything else composed of characters on the screen. We use it for displaying things such as the score of a game or the number of seconds left in a level. `Hello.java` demonstrates how to create a `StringSprite`.

```java
1   // package default
2
3   import fang2.core.Game;
4   import fang2.sprites.StringSprite;
5
6   // FANG Demonstration program: StringSprite
7   public class Hello
8     extends Game {
9     // Called before game loop: Draws one string
10    @Override
11    public void setup() {
12      StringSprite string = new StringSprite("Hello");
13      string.setLineHeight(0.25);
14      string.setColor(getColor("misty rose"));
15      string.setLocation(0.5, 0.5);
16      addSprite(string);
17    }
18  }
```

Listing 3.8: `Hello.java`: A complete program

Line 12 constructs a `StringSprite`. The constructor takes a string, in double quotes, which is the text displayed by the sprite. The next line sets the *height* of a line of text in screens. The width of the sprite is determined by FANG which depends on the font and the text contents. It is also possible to set the width using `setWidth`, letting FANG set the appropriate line height.

`StringSprite` has a method, `setText`, which also takes a string as a parameter. It permits you to change the value displayed by the sprite. A string is a sequence of characters between double quotes, " characters. Inside the double quotes you may have any characters except for double quotes (it marks the end of the string) and new line characters (the quotes must be on the same line). We see how to encode these characters below.

Figure 3.9 shows what `Hello` looks like when run. As with other sprites, you can create any number of `StringSprites` and add them to the game. Inside a string you can use special character sequences: \n ("slash en") stands for a *new line* so that the string is broken across two lines; \" stands for the quote character. Both of these sequences have two characters in them but stand for only one character in the string.

```java
1   // package default
2
3   import fang2.core.Game;
4   import fang2.sprites.StringSprite;
5
6   /** Demonstration of StringSprite. Msg centered horizontally. */
7   public class Strings
8     extends Game {
9     /** Write the poem in four strings (6 lines).*/
10    @Override
```

Figure 3.9: `Hello` screenshot

```
11  public void setup() {
12      // '\n' sequence is the new line character (starts a new line)
13      StringSprite meddle = new StringSprite(
14          "Do not meddle in\nthe affairs of");
15      meddle.setLineHeight(0.10);
16      meddle.setColor(getColor("white"));
17      meddle.setLocation(0.5, 0.15);
18      addSprite(meddle);
19
20      StringSprite dragons = new StringSprite("DRAGONS");
21      dragons.setLineHeight(0.15);
22      dragons.setColor(getColor("green"));
23      dragons.setLocation(0.5, 0.4);
24      addSprite(dragons);
25
26      StringSprite thou = new StringSprite(
```

```
27          "for thou art crunchy\nand go well with");
28      thou.setLineHeight(0.10);
29      thou.setColor(getColor("white"));
30      thou.setLocation(0.5, 0.65);
31      addSprite(thou);
32
33      StringSprite ketchup = new StringSprite("ketchup");
34      ketchup.setLineHeight(0.20);
35      ketchup.setColor(getColor("SCG Red"));// red in the book
36      ketchup.setLocation(0.5, 0.85);
37      addSprite(ketchup);
38    }
39  }
```

Listing 3.9: `Strings.java`

The colors of the four sprites in `Strings.java` are different, drawing attention to the two colored lines (only one of which stands out in the book).[7] The text is also emphasized by increasing its size.

Finally, `ZoomingHello` shows the `ScaleTransformer` at work. It starts with a modified `Hello` program and adds a `ScaleTransformer` to the `StringSprite`.

The `StringSprite` scale value is different than it is for other sprites because the text being displayed can change, changing the relative width and height of the sprite. In an attempt to keep the appearance as similar as possible when the text changes, the scale of a `StringSprite` is the larger of the width or height dimension. The string "Hello" is *wider* than it is high, so line 14 sets the width to match the starting scale of the transformer.

The `ScaleTransformer` constructor takes three numeric parameters: the seconds the transformation takes, the starting scale in screens, and the ending scale in screens. The string starts very small (0.05 or a twentieth of the screen wide) and grows (or zooms) to fairly large (0.75 or three-quarters of the screen wide). There is no screenshot of the animation.

Additional features of `StringSprites` are introduced as we use them (see, in particular, Chapter 10 where we build a game of hangman).

```
1  // package default
2
3  import fang2.core.Game;
4  import fang2.sprites.StringSprite;
5  import fang2.transformers.ScaleTransformer;
6
7  // FANG Demonstration program: StringSprite, ScaleTransform
8  public class ZoomingHello
9    extends Game {
10    // Called before game loop: Draws one string
11    @Override
12    public void setup() {
13      StringSprite string = new StringSprite("Hello");
14      string.setWidth(0.05);
15      string.setColor(getColor("misty rose"));
16      string.setLocation(0.5, 0.5);
17      addSprite(string);
```

---

[7]This quote is an homage to J. R. R. Tolkien's "Do not meddle in the affairs of wizards, for they are subtle and quick to anger." [Tol54] The current author was unable to find any authoritative source for the dragon quote.

Figure 3.10: Strings screenshot

```
18
19    ScaleTransformer scale = new ScaleTransformer(15.0/*seconds */,
20        0.05/* start scale */, 0.75/* end scale */);
21    string.addTransformer(scale);
22  }
23 }
```

Listing 3.10: ZoomingHello.java: A complete program

Straight Lines: LineSprite and PolygonSprite

There are three sprites composed of straight lines. The LineSprite class is designed to hold a single line, so construction requires two end points. The PolygonSprite is designed to hold a closed collection of line segments such as a triangle or a hexagon; the constructor we use takes a number of sides and constructs a regular polygon with that number of sides. There is another constructor for PolygonSprite which takes a collection of screen coordinates and connects them with line segments, filling the whole thing in. Finally, there is a PolyLineSprite, similar to the point-constructed PolygonSprite, but it is never filled in.

```
1   // package default
2
3   import fang2.core.Game;
4   import fang2.sprites.LineSprite;
5   import fang2.sprites.PolygonSprite;
6
7   // FANG Demonstration program: PolygonSprite and LineSprite
8   public class HexAndLine
9     extends Game {
10    // Called before game loop: make hex and line over it and add
11    @Override
12    public void setup() {
13      PolygonSprite hex = new PolygonSprite(6);
14      hex.setScale(0.5);
15      hex.setLocation(0.5, 0.5);
16      hex.setColor(getColor("orange"));
17      addSprite(hex);
18
19      LineSprite line = new LineSprite(0.1, 0.9, 0.9, 0.1);
20      line.setColor(getColor("yellow green"));
21      addSprite(line);
22    }
23  }
```

Listing 3.11: HexAndLine.java

HexAndLine.java draws an orange hexagon centered on the screen and crosses it with a yellow green line. Line 14 in the listing calls the setScale method on the hexagon; this method takes a size, in screens, and scales the sprite to that size. *All* sprites support setScale, so we could have used it to set the scale of the RectangleSprite, OvalSprite, and StringSprite we created in other programs. We had to use it here because the regular polygon version of the PolygonSprite constructor does not have a scale parameter.

A VelocityTransformer can be modified by making it bounce. The reason bouncing is associated with a velocity, and wrapping is not, is that the velocity needs to be turned around when something is hit. So the BounceInsideRectangleTransformer takes a sprite, the sprite to check for hitting the edge, and a velocity transformer. Notice the use of lowercase: bouncing transformers work with any transformer that provides a velocity to a sprite, so VelocityTransformer, AccelerationTransformer, and other bounce transformers would also work.

Listing 3.12 shows a modified HexAndLine: at the end of setup, a VelocityTransformer is constructed and then modified by a BounceInsideRectangleTransformer. By default, the rectangle the sprite bounces in is bounded by 0.0 and 1.0 in the x and y dimensions: it matches the screen. Listing 2.7 at the end of the last chapter demonstrates how the minimum and maximum values can be included to have the sprite bounce inside a larger or smaller rectangle.

```
1   // package default
2
3   import fang2.core.Game;
4   import fang2.sprites.LineSprite;
5   import fang2.sprites.PolygonSprite;
6   import fang2.transformers.BounceInsideRectangleTransformer;
7   import fang2.transformers.KeyboardTransformer;
```

Figure 3.11: HexAndLine screenshot

```
8   import fang2.transformers.VelocityTransformer;
9
10  // FANG Demonstration program: PolygonSprite and LineSprite
11  public class BounceHex
12    extends Game {
13    // Called before game loop: make hex and line over it and add
14    @Override
15    public void setup() {
16      PolygonSprite hex = new PolygonSprite(6);
17      hex.setScale(0.5);
18      hex.setLocation(0.5, 0.5);
19      hex.setColor(getColor("orange"));
20      addSprite(hex);
21
22      LineSprite line = new LineSprite(0.1, 0.9, 0.9, 0.1);
23      line.setColor(getColor("yellow green"));
```

```
24      addSprite(line);
25
26      VelocityTransformer velocity = new VelocityTransformer(-45, 1.0);
27      BounceInsideRectangleTransformer bounce =
28        new BounceInsideRectangleTransformer(velocity);
29      hex.addTransformer(bounce);
30    }
31  }
```

Listing 3.12: BounceHex.java

The Java Color Class and FANG

Java provides a Color class (you import java.awt.Color to use it directly) that specifies color using four *channels*. A channel is any one of the additive primary colors, red, green, or blue, or it is how opaque the color is.

Red, green, and blue: primaries?   The computer projects light out of its screen and into your eye (just as a color television set does). Rather than using the subtractive primary colors, red, yellow, and blue, a system projecting rather than reflecting light uses a different set of primary colors. The subtractive primaries are called that because each subtracts some frequencies of light from what it reflects. When you mix all of them together you get black (or, with most paint sets, a dark, muddy brown). The red, green, and blue (RGB) additive primaries each add frequencies to what the screen is projecting and mix together to make white.

We have used different colors for our different examples, yet avoided including the Color class. That is because the Game class has a getColor method that returns a Color. We have used that method and passed its results to setColor for a sprite or setBackground for the game.

Colors can be specified by name (see Appendix D for a listing of all color names; the list includes those colors shown for the Web at http://www.w3schools.com/tags/ref_colornames.asp), by specifying the Web numeric value, or by specifying the numeric value for the RGB and, optionally, the opacity channel.

Rotation and Scaling

So far, whenever we create a rectangular sprite, the edges are parallel to the x and y axes of the game. This is not always what we want. Consider drawing the card suit of diamonds. A diamond is a square but rotated an eighth of a circle (or 45 degrees). Just as there is a setLocation method, there is also a setRotationDegrees method. Thus, to draw a single diamond at the center of the screen, the following setup method suffices:

```
19  public void setup() {
20    // make background white
21    setBackground(getColor("white"));
22
23    // create the diamond, set its color, position, and rotation
24    RectangleSprite diamond = new RectangleSprite(0.1, 0.1);
25    diamond.setColor(getColor("red"));
26    diamond.setLocation(0.5, 0.5);
27    diamond.rotateDegrees(45.0);
28    addSprite(diamond);
29  }
```

Listing 3.13: Diamond.java setup

Figure 3.12: `Diamond` screenshot

Outlining Sprites

One other feature supported by sprites is outlining their shapes. The following `setup` method creates two outlined ovals and rotates one of them 45 degrees. The outlines are different colors so that we can tell the original from the rotated oval in the screenshot.

```
15   public void setup() {
16       // Let the bee fly on a grassy background.
17       setBackground(getColor("green"));
18
19       OvalSprite originalWing = new OvalSprite(0.35, 0.7);
20       originalWing.setColor(getColor("Wheat", 128));
21       originalWing.setOutlineColor(getColor("white"));
22       originalWing.setOutlineThickness(0.01);
23       originalWing.showOutline();
24       originalWing.setLocation(0.36, 0.6);
25       addSprite(originalWing);
```

```
26
27    OvalSprite leftWing = new OvalSprite(0.35, 0.7);
28    leftWing.setColor(getColor("Wheat", 128));
29    leftWing.setOutlineColor(getColor("black"));
30    leftWing.setOutlineThickness(0.01);
31    leftWing.showOutline();
32    leftWing.rotateDegrees(+45.0);
33    leftWing.setLocation(0.36, 0.6);
34    addSprite(leftWing);
35    }
```

Listing 3.14: LeftWing.java setup

Lines 21–23 (and 29–31) demonstrate how to turn out outlining: you specify the outline color and the outline size (in screen widths), and, finally, tell the sprite to show the outline. After you specify an outline, scaling the sprite scales the thickness of the outline as well. This is consistent with the way many vector art programs handle scaling.

The screenshot for LeftWing.java shows the original oval, outlined in white, and the rotated oval, outlined in black. This indicates that positive rotation is *clockwise*. The screenshot also shows that the color used to fill the ovals is translucent.

Look at line 20. The color is created with the call getColor("Wheat", 128). The name, "Wheat", is one described in the appendix. The number, 128, specifies how opaque the color should be. If the value were 0, the wheat color would be completely transparent and if it were 255 the wheat color would be completely opaque. The higher the number, the more opaque the color. By default, no opaqueness setting means totally opaque or 255.

Review 3.2

(a) Does the order in which you add sprites matter? Why or why not?

(b) Name the sprite you use to create the following:

- (a) a circle
- (b) a square
- (c) some text
- (d) a pentagon
- (e) a diagonal line
- (f) an octogon

(c) Which of the following are NOT valid colors? (Hint: See the appendix on available colors)

- (a) Light Rose
- (b) Rose
- (c) Dark Brown
- (d) Dark Green
- (e) Mauve

(d) When you use the FANG engine, are you limited to the named colors? Why or why not?

(e) Try writing a program for Figure 3.4 *without* having any sprites overlap. (Hint: As mentioned in the text, all but the innermost ring require four rectangles.)

(f) What would happen if, in Circle.java, you commented out lines 28 and 29? How would the circle react when it went off of the screen?

(g) How would you modify SpinningTarget03.java so that just the center rectangle spun? Try it and see. Could you make the inner and outer rectangles rotate in *opposite* directions? How?

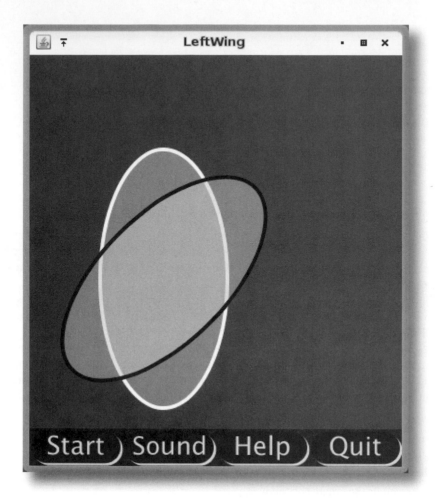

Figure 3.13: `LeftWing` screenshot

3.3   Examining a Public Protocol

Java was designed with a small core language (keywords, syntax, and built-in primitive types) and an extensive collection of standard libraries. With more than 2000 different standard library classes, Java programmers need an efficient way to find specific classes and the methods they provide.

This book adopts the term *public protocol* to mean the collection of all **public** methods of a class. The public protocol of `Sprite`, for example, includes the `setLocation`, `setRotation`, and `setScale` methods (as discussed above in Section 3.2). The public protocol of a child class extends the public protocol of its parent class.[8]

Java has extensive documentation for its standard libraries and tools for generating documentation for nonstandard libraries such as FANG. The Java documentation is provided as a collection of Web pages. These can be found at the Java Web site[9] or can be installed from Sun's download Web pages. The FANG documentation can be found online[10] or downloaded as well.

Figure 3.14 shows the first page of the documentation with three panes:

---

[8]Hence the keyword **extends**.
[9]`http://java.sun.com/javase/6/docs/api/`
[10]`http://www.fangengine.org/index.php/API`

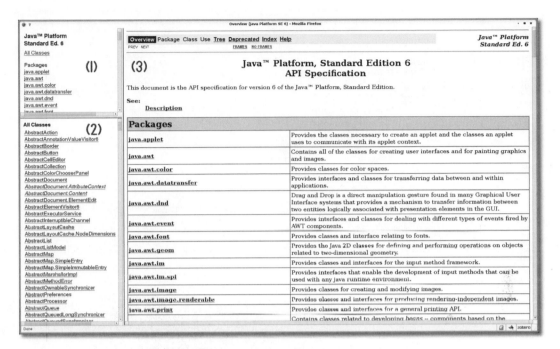

Figure 3.14: The initial Java documentation page

1. *Packages Pane:* Java collects classes into packages; this pane permits you to select a package to view. If you select a package, the classes in the *Classes Pane* are limited to only those classes in the selected package; *All Classes* returns to the all class view for the given library.

2. *Classes Pane:* An alphabetical listing of all of the classes in the currently selected package (or all of the classes in the whole library).

3. *Documentation Pane:* The documentation for the selected class or, if no class has yet been selected, a summary of the available packages.[11]

Finding Types and Public Protocols

FANG uses the same tools to produce its documentation, so Figure 3.15 shows the result of clicking on the Game entry in the *Classes Pane* of the FANG documentation. The documentation for the Game class appears in the *Documentation Pane*. Key to using the documentation is the small print above the Class Game headline: fang2.core tells us the package containing the class and what **import** line is required to import this class.

Also at the top of the page is a long, indented sequence of class names. This is the *inheritance hierarchy* or list of ancestor classes of Game. Game extends GameRedirection which extends GameLoop which ... and so on. Notice that the top of the hierarchy, the farthest back ancestor of Game is java.lang.Object; *all* classes in Java extend (through some number of intermediate classes) Object. Java makes such extensive use of the java.lang package that it is automatically imported into every Java program without an **import** line.

The text after the definition of the class describes how the Game class was intended to be used. This is a comment documenting the *intent* of the FANG programmers in making the class. Below the screen is a series of tables: the *Field Summary*, which lists any **public** fields; the *Constructor Summary*, which lists all **public** constructors; and the *Method Summary*, listing all of the **public** methods.

---

[11]The "API Specification" in the title of the page stands for *application programmer's interface*; this use of the word interface is similar to our use of protocol. The API is the collection of classes and methods provided by a library.

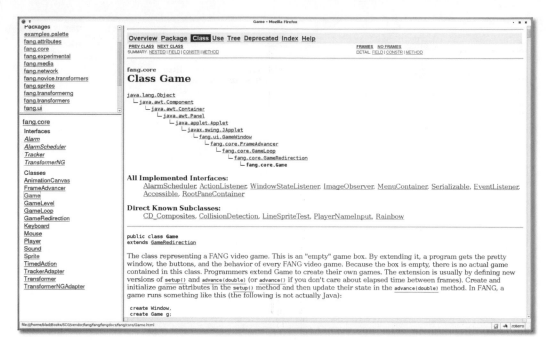

Figure 3.15: Top of the Game class documentation

Fields, as we discussed above, are labels for values stored in an object. All fields defined in sample programs have been **private**. Some classes have **public** fields which are listed in the *Field Summary*. Different access levels and how to set them is left for later chapters.

The *Constructor Summary* lists all of the forms that can follow **new** to construct a new object of the given class. Figure 3.16 shows the top of the Sprite class page. The *Constructor Summary* shows that a raw Sprite (the parent class of all sprites in FANG) can be created with an empty parameter list or a parameter list containing a Shape. Notice that Shape is a hyperlink, linked to the standard Java documentation (Shape happens to be in the java.awt package).

The *Method Summary* is similar to the *Constructor Summary* in that it lists the return type, name, and parameter list of every **public** method. Figure 3.17 shows the Sprite page farther down, in the middle of the *Method Summary*; this is where you can look up the parameter list of methods you might want to call. What if we wondered about how setColor is declared and what parameter(s) it expects?

In the middle of the figure you can see that the setColor method has a **void** return type, is named setColor (we knew that), and takes one parameter of type Color (which is called color; Java is case-sensitive so the two names are different. We discuss naming in detail in the next chapter). What is Color? Is it a FANG or a Java class? What would we import if we wanted to declare a Color field in our class? Again, notice that types are hyperlinked to the documentation for the **class**. Clicking on the link takes us to the page shown in Figure 3.18.

The setColor name is also hyperlinked (as is the name of every method). In the *Method Summary* is a one-line description of what the method does. If you need to know more, clicking on the name takes you to detailed documentation on that method. Below the *Method Summary* table all of the constructors and methods have detailed entries, and the name in the summary table is linked to the detail.

Figure 3.18 shows the documentation page for the Color type. The package containing the class appears right before the name of the class in the title. If this package is *not* java.lang, then you must import the class in order to use it in your program. When you look at this page, it is easy to see where the import line we use for Color comes from

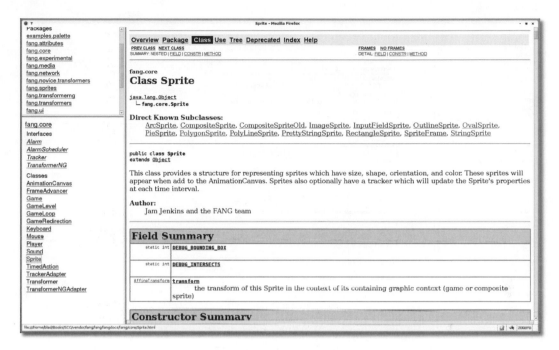

Figure 3.16: The methods of the `String` class

```
import java.awt.Color;
```

Java's documentation is very thorough and quite well linked (class names lead to the documentation page for that class). With upwards of 2000 classes, however, finding just the one you need can be daunting; reading package and class descriptions, even at random, can increase your grasp of these essential types.

JavaDoc: Two Audiences Again

When writing class and method header comments, you have probably wondered about some of the formatting. The template for a multiline comment specifies that it begins with /* and ends with */; yet all of the header comments in sample code begin with /**. And then there are a lot of @ signs peppered through the comments. What is all of that about?

That is all about *JavaDoc*, the Java Documentation. The Java development kit from Sun (and most other providers) includes javac, the Java compiler, java, the Java bytecode interpreter, and javadoc, the Java *documentation compiler*. The documentation presented in this section (and provided with FANG) was automatically generated from the source code of the library classes.

The complete features of javadoc are beyond the scope of this book. Suffice it to say that all comments beginning /** are processed by the Java documentation compiler, and the various @ names are directions to the documentation compiler of how to format and link the resulting code.

This means that header comments, rather than just being written for fellow humans, are also written for two audiences: the programmers who come after you in the source code *and* the javadoc program.

This section ends by evaluating a quote from Norm Schryer, an AT&T researcher and computer scientist, by way of an article called "Bumpersticker Computer Science" [Ben88]: "If the code and the comments disagree, then both are probably wrong." This is a great bumpersticker in that it is fairly short, pithy, and deeper than it seems.

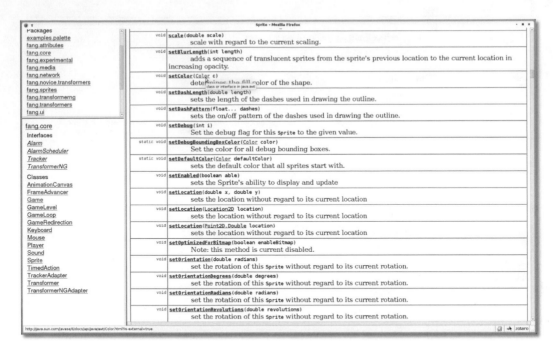

Figure 3.17: The Sprite *Method Summary*: setColor

The recommendation that you document your *intent* rather than your implementation makes it easier for the code to evolve without changing the commented behavior. Quality code requires constant vigilance against letting errors creep in.

Review 3.3

(a) Using the FANG documentation, what package contains the Location2D class?

(b) What opening and closing markers are used around a Java documentation comment in your code?

(c) How many classes are in the fang2.transformers package? What is the name of the last one alphabetically?

(d) Why should comments reflect *intent* rather than just restate what the code does?

3.4   Summary

How Computers Work

Today's computers are *digital*, *binary*, and *general-purpose*. Digital means they store discrete (rather than continuous) values. Binary means they use a base 2 numbering system with just 0 and 1 as digits and each position representing a power of 2. General-purpose refers to the ability to treat a binary, digital memory as encoding any type of data from a whole number to a formatted document to a DVD.

Computers have a *central processing unit* or CPU, the processor that follows rules stored in the computer. The CPU is connected to the system memory or *RAM* (random access memory). The contents of RAM must be interpreted in context: the same bit pattern in memory might represent the number 65, the letter 'A', or the beginning of Beethoven's Ninth Symphony.

RAM memory is random access in that accessing any given address is just as fast as accessing any other memory address. RAM is fairly expensive (per byte stored) and is volatile: it loses its value when power is

Figure 3.18: Documentation of the `Color` class in Java

turned off. Hard disk drives use magnetic storage to provide larger, cheaper (per byte stored), and nonvolatile storage. DVD/CD uses optical storage, and flash disks (USB thumb drives) use a nonvolatile memory technology.

Input/Output (I/O) is provided by keyboards, game controllers, microphones, monitors, network cards, and printers. The *operating system* is a program that interacts with the component parts of a computer and can control other computer programs, starting, stopping, monitoring, and, perhaps, pausing them.

CPU instructions are written in *machine language*, numbers encoding the specific instructions understood by a particular processor. Since instructions are numbers in memory, they can be manipulated by other instructions: computer memory contains both instructions and data for the instructions to process; any given memory content might be data to one program and instructions to another.

Memory is broken into addressable units which are collections of bits (binary digits). Eight bits grouped together are a *byte* and a byte can hold 256 different values. Computer memories are measured in binary *kilobytes*, *megabytes*, and *gigabytes*: 2^{10}, 2^{20}, and 2^{30}, respectively.

FANG

FANG is a collection of packages, all subordinate to the `fang2` package. `fang2.core` contains classes central to FANG's function such as `Game`. `fang2.sprites` contains all standard sprites; a sprite is a screen-visible object. `fang2.transformers` is home to all of the transformers provided by FANG; a transformer adds automatic behavior to a sprite or sprites.

Game

`fang2.core.Game` is the class a programmer *extends* to construct a FANG game. The class has two methods game programmers overload: `setup` and `advance`. It also has helper methods, a couple of which are summarized below.

Game	
Method	**Description**
addBottom(*<sprite>*)	Add the given sprite to the game. The stacking order is *below* all sprites already added to the game.
addSprite(*<sprite>*)	Add the given sprite to the game. The stacking order is *above* all sprites already added to the game.
getColor(*<colorName>*)	Get the color named in the string. The name must be a color that FANG understands. The string is checked in a case-insensitive manner (so "Misty Rose" and "misty rose" are the same color) and has all spaces squeezed out (so even "mIStyROse" is the same color as the other two).

Sprite Constructors	
Class Constructor	**Description**
RectangleSprite(*<width>*, *<height>*)	A rectangle on the screen. Values are decimal numbers in screens.
OvalSprite(*<width>*, *<height>*)	An oval on the screen. Values are decimal numbers in screens.
StringSprite(*<text>*, *<height>*)	A written value on the screen. *<text>* is a string and the height is a decimal number expressing line height in screens.
PolygonSprite(*<whole-number-of-sides>*)	A regular polygon on the screen. The number of sides cannot have a decimal point in it (hence the name). Scale automatically set to 1.0 (as big as the screen).
LineSprite(*<x1>*, *<y1>*, *<x2>*, *<y2>*)	Draw a line from (*<x1>*, *<y1>*) to (*<x2>*, *<y2>*). Coordinates in screens.

Sprites

Sprites are screen-visible, movable objects. FANG sprites have a location, measured from the upper-left corner of the screen to the center of the sprite, a scale in screens, and a rotation. Each different kind of sprite has different constructor parameters but all sprites support a certain standard set of methods. The next two tables list the sprites we saw in this chapter (with constructor parameters) and then the standard sprite methods.

Transformers

Transformers, extenders of fang2.core.Transformer, provide behaviors to sprites to which they are "attached." In general, one transformer can be associated with any number of sprites *and* any sprite can have any number of transformers. The following table lists different transformer classes with their constructor parameters.

Java Documentation *JavaDoc*

A *public protocol* is our term for all of the public *fields*, *constructors*, and other *methods* provided by a class. Any object of that class type (constructed with **new** followed by the class name and parameters) can be used to call the methods. A method call takes the form in the following template which extends the definition of *<expression>* again.

Sprite Methods	
Method	**Description**
setColor(*<color>*)	Set the color to the given color. Parameter is java.awt.Color; Game.getColor returns the right type.
setLocation(*<x>*, *<y>*)	Locate the sprite at the given location (coordinates in screens). Location is based on sprite center.
setScale(*<scale>*)	Set the scale of the sprite in screens. 1.0 means as big as the screen. On StringSprite, refers to the height of a line of text.
setRotationDegrees(*<degrees>*)	Set the rotation of the sprite to the given number of degrees counterclockwise.
addTransformer(*<transformer>*)	Add the given transformer to the group of transformers associated with the given sprite.
removeTransformer(*<transformer>*)	Remove the given transformer to the group of transformers associated with the given sprite. (We did not give examples in this chapter.)

Transformer Constructors	
Class Constructor	**Description**
VelocityTransformer(*<degrees>*, *<speed>*)	Add linear, constant velocity in the given direction (degrees off the positive x-axis) and speed in screens/second to the given sprite(s).
SpinTransformer(*<degrees>*)	Spin the sprite(s) at the given speed in degrees/second.
WrapTransformer()	Wrap the edges of the screen so it is treated as a torus.
ScaleTransformer(*<seconds>*, *<start>*, *<end>*)	Transform the scale of the given sprite, starting at start scale and ending with *<end>* scale after *<seconds>* seconds.
BounceInsideRectangleTransformer(*<sprite>*, *<velocity>*)	The *<sprite>* is bounced inside the screen boundaries (other coordinates can be provided; see documentation). *<velocity>* is the velocity used to bounce the sprite (bouncing requires moving, so the moving can be reversed). *This transformer is intended to be used with only one sprite at a time.*

```
<object> := <identifier> |
            <expression>


<methodName> := <identifier>


<methodCall> := [<object>.]<methodName>(<actualParameterList>)


<expression> := <literal> |
                new <typeName>(<actualParameterList>) |
                <methodCall>
```

Java and FANG provide extensive documentation. The documentation is generated from the comments inside the .java source files. It is provided in the form of hyperlinked pages listing all of the packages in a library, all of the classes in a package, and all of the methods in a class. It is the best way to find out what methods a given class supports. It provides links to the types used for parameters and comments from the programmer on how the method (or class) should be used.

At the top of a `class` documentation page is the **extends** list of all of the classes from `java.lang.Object` to the documented class. It also shows the package name that must be **import**ed to use the given class.

Java Templates

```
<typeName> := <identifier>


<variableName> := <identifier>


<variableDeclaration> := <typeName> <variableName>


<localVariableDefinition> := <variableDeclaration> [= <expression>];
```

```
<actualParameterList> := [<expression> [, <expression>]*]


<object> := <identifier> |
            <expression>


<methodName> := <identifier>


<methodCall> := [<object>.]<methodName>(<actualParameterList>)


<expression> := <literal> |
                new <typeName>(<actualParameterList>) |
                <methodCall>
```

3.5   Chapter Review Exercises

Review Exercise 3.1 Describe the function of each of the following parts of a modern computer
  (a) Central Processing Unit (CPU)
  (b) Random Access Memory (RAM)
  (c) Hard Disk/Solid-state Memory
  (d) Keyboard/Game-Controller
  (e) Screen/Printer

Review Exercise 3.2 What does *volatile* mean? How does it apply to computer memory?

Review Exercise 3.3 Why do hard drive manufacturers insist that KB, MB, and GB refer to 1,000, 1,000,000, and 1,000,000,000 bytes, respectively, rather than the values that computer scientists prefer?

Review Exercise 3.4 Modern machines are digital, binary computers.
  (a) What does `digital` mean?
  (b) What does `binary` mean?

Review Exercise 3.5 Define the following Java language terms:
  (a) `class`
  (b) `extends`
  (c) `import`

Review Exercise 3.6 How do you set the location of a Sprite extending class?

Review Exercise 3.7 What is a *sprite* in FANG?

Review Exercise 3.8 What is a *transformer* in FANG?

Review Exercise 3.9 What command would you use to create a LineSprite that ran from the upper-right corner down to the lower-left corner of the screen?

Review Exercise 3.10 How many different named shades of gray does FANG recognize.

Review Exercise 3.11 In the following line of code, what is the name of the object on which a method is being called, what is the name of the method, and what is the parameter list for the method?

```
someStringSprite.setText("Call me Ishmael.");
```

Review Exercise 3.12 When does FANG call each of the following methods (if you define one):

  (a) **public void** setup()

  (b) **public void** advance(**double** secondsSinceLastCall)

Review Exercise 3.13 What kind of transformer would you use to

  (a) Turn an OvalSprite into a billiard ball?

  (b) Turn a PolygonSprite around and around?

  (c) Make a moving sprite come back on the screen on the opposite side it moved off of?

  (d) Make a sprite get smaller and smaller?

Review Exercise 3.14 Look up the class TimeLimitedTransformer in the FANG documentation. What parameters does the constructor take? What does the import line for the class look like?

Review Exercise 3.15 Look up the class ColorTransformer in the FANG documentation. What is it for? What are the parameters to its constructor? What import line would you use to use ColorTransformer in your program?

3.6 Programming Problems

Programming Problem 3.1 Starting with Hello, create a program that displays your first name centered in the top half of the screen and your last name centered in the bottom half of the screen. Both names should be displayed in different colors.

Programming Problem 3.2 Using Target03.java as a starting point, make a program, TriangleTarget03, that displays five *triangles* with alternating colors, each about a tenth of a screen larger than the one within it. Pick two contrasting colors of your choice and have all of the triangles centered in the screen.

Programming Problem 3.3 Based on ZoomingHello.java, write a program that shows your name shrinking onto the screen. Your name should be written in green and should start up as tall as the screen. Then, over thirty seconds, it should shrink down to one percent of the screen high.

Programming Problem 3.4 Write a program, BilliardBalls, which adds two different colored OvalSprites to the game. Each sprite should move around the screen, bouncing off the edges. One should start moving up and to the right, the other should start moving up and to the left.

 To think about before programming: What kind of transformer(s) do you need? Can the sprites share transformer(s)?

Programming Problem 3.5 Write a program, Jet, which uses simple geometric shapes to draw a "jet" plane on the screen. The jet should be about a quarter of the screen in size. Animate the jet so that it flies around the screen, wrapping around from one side to the other.

 To think about before programming: What kind of transformer(s) do you need? How may sprites do you need? Can the sprites share transformer(s)?

Programming Problem 3.6 Look up the `TimeLimitedTransformer` in the FANG documentation.

Make a program with a sprite that displays your name. The sprite should be some shade of red and the name should be about a tenth of the screen high. Construct a `SpinTransformer` that spins a sprite one circle every two seconds. Use a `TimeLimitedTransformer` to attach it to the name so that it runs for twelve seconds and no more. What would happen if you changed it to eleven seconds?

Deciding What Happens: if

Our working definition of game is a collection of *components* and associated *rules* governing their interaction. Together the components and rules present the player with meaningful choices that shape the outcome of the game.

The last two chapters presented Java programs using FANG. We have seen the overall structure of a Java program, how to import FANG (and Java) libraries, and how to construct sprites and transformers.

To define our own game, we *override* the two methods setup and advance. In previous chapters we have constructed components and used predefined rules to make games; not many of our programs (except Meteors and, perhaps, Basketball) presented the player with meaningful choices. A big reason for that is we do not know how to have Java make a selection, choosing one set of rules or another based on some condition.

This chapter focuses on designing a simple game, as simple a game as possible. Designing the program to play the game requires examining the list of problem-solving techniques presented in the first chapter, sequence, selection, iteration, delegation, and abstraction.

4.1 A Simplest Game

By focusing on *simple* computer games, this book teaches traditional computer science topics. This chapter goes further, looking for a *simplest* complete game. This is interesting as an intellectual exercise, to test out our definition as well as be useful: this chapter uses no transformers. All sprite movement, interaction, and scoring is explicitly programmed in the resulting Game-extending class.

Why say "*a* simplest game" rather than "*the* simplest game"? The short answer is that there are any number of games with a minimal number of components and rules, different outcomes, and choices the player makes that influence those outcomes. Some different simplest games are suggested in the programming exercises at the end of the chapter.

Fewest Components and One Rule Follower

Simplicity dictates that we minimize the number of things in the game. We want the minimum number of players interacting with the minimum number of components, each with a minimum number of rules.

A single-player game has the fewest players possible. The computer controls the environment within the game and any opponents; the computer provides the rule followers for any elements of the environment or the opponents requiring them.

Computerized opponents require strategies; the program must have rules for both the *game* and *winning* the game. This violates our current goal of simplicity. A computer game where the computer enforces the rules is a form of solitaire. Note that many arcade games from the 1980s and 1990s (the Golden Age of video games to many) are solitaire games.

The minimum number of components is also one; it is difficult to imagine rules where a single component on the screen constitutes what we would consider a game. The fewest components in a viable *game* is two.

Now for the rules. We consider games where the player directly interacts with at least one of the components. One component in some way represents the player. The other component and the screen represent the "rest" of the game: the state of the game is communicated to the user through the single remaining component.

Many games are possible with just these simple components. Gameplay depends on many things: the computer component could move or remain stationary; the player could control the position, facing, speed, or size of his component; when moving, components might interact with each other or the edges of the screen in different ways.

If the computer component moves on its own, the player can be tasked either with catching it or avoiding it. Our first game, *NewtonsApple*, has the player catching the computer-controlled component.

In *NewtonsApple*, the player plays (moves) a component representing the famous physicist, Sir Issac Newton. The computer randomly "drops" apples by placing them along the top of the screen and moving them toward the bottom. While limited to moving from side to side, the player must move Sir Issac so that each apple falls on his head. *NewtonsApple*'s score is the ratio of the number of apples caught to the total number of apples dropped. Figure 4.1 draws a picture of the game play area.

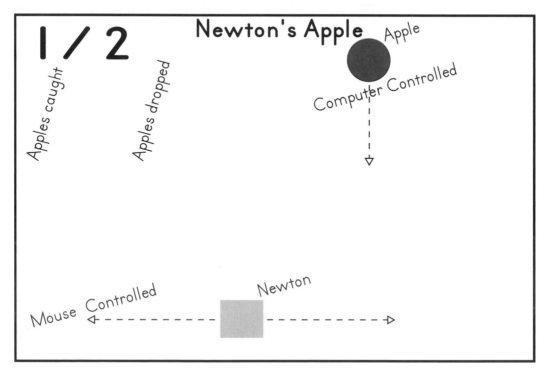

Figure 4.1: `NewtonsApple` game design diagram

There is a commonsense dictum that when you don't understand some problem, draw a picture. This holds particularly true in game and computer program design. This sort of diagram, a picture of the screen with components and some notes on their behavior, captures many of our design decisions more clearly and compactly than natural language. The design task is explicitly about taking a general idea and specifying it, understanding it well enough to be able to make the game or program. Deep understanding is also required to permit us to imagine how the game could be changed to make it more fun or how to translate it into a different medium.

Chapter 1 discussed the idea of differentiable outcomes, winning or losing. Differentiable outcomes imply some way of keeping score. In the text description of the game, this was mentioned as "the ratio of the number of apples caught to the total number of apples dropped." Our diagrams help us realize when important things are *missing*: we have added a third component, the score. When designing a game or a program, it is important to make everything explicit.

Scores are an important part of a game; players use them as feedback on how well they are doing and can compare them with other players for an indication of relative abilities. Our score tracks "trials" and "successes." This means that whenever an apple is dropped (the program selects a random spot for it to fall from) the number of trials is incremented; whenever an apple is caught, the number of successes is incremented. Different games use different scoring metrics in other chapters.

FANG and the Video Game Loop

The default program structure for the Game class is based around a video game loop and two methods that are intended to be *overridden*.

Framework authors provide methods they intend programmers using their framework to override. In FANG, setup and advance are two such methods, methods called in the core game loop as follows:

```
define setup
  do nothing

define advance
  do nothing

setup
while (not game over)
  displayGameState
  getUserInput
  advance
```

displayGameState is where FANG goes through the list of all sprites that have been added to the game and draws them on the screen.[1] The getUserInput step is done to see what has happened with the mouse or keyboard. The advance step is where, based on the current game state and the user's input, the new state of the game is calculated. The whole loop begins over again with displaying the new game state.

The *game state* is the current condition of the game. You could consider the game state for chess to be the current configuration of the board, the time on the chess clocks for each player, and, possibly, the list of moves that got us to this point. The state of a game of tennis is the score, who hit the ball last, the location and "state" of each player (tired, thirsty, distracted, etc.), and the location and state of the ball (velocity, bounciness, etc.).

Overriding

Figure 4.2 shows two classes that extend Game: NewtonsApple from this chapter and ZoomingHello from the last chapter. Each box represents a class (named at the top of the box); below it are listed the methods defined in

---

[1] FANG uses the *painter's algorithm*, drawing each sprite in order from the back to the front; this is why sprites added later overlap sprites added earlier. Note that it is possible to reset the ordering of the sprites.

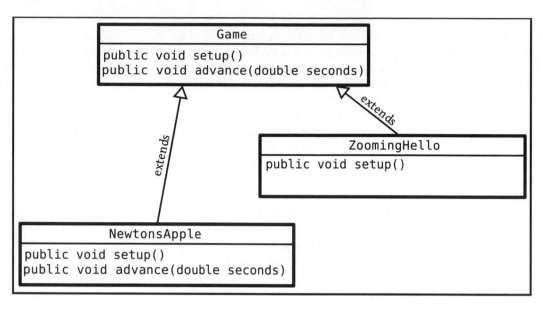

Figure 4.2: Overriding Methods

the class (not all of them but all of the ones we are interested in). The arrows, labeled **extends**, indicate that the class at the end of the arrow **extends** the class the arrow points to.

One key thing to keep in mind when looking at the core game loop description above is that setup and advance are Java methods, part of a Game object. In the last two chapters we saw that the Java syntax for calling a method is [*<objectName>*.]*<methodName>*(*<actualParameterList>*). So, somewhere inside of FANG lurks the following code:

```
Game currentGame = new /* MAGIC CONSTRUCTOR! */;
...
currentGame.setup();
...
/* we don't know the syntax for this yet */
while ... {
  ...
  currentGame.advance(timeSinceLastCall);
  ...
}
```

What is a *magic* constructor? It is one that constructs the Game-extending class which we are actually running. When the command line (leaving aside the -classpath) is java ZoomingHello, the magic constructor line becomes **new** ZoomingHello(), and when the command line reads java NewtonsApple, the magic constructor becomes **new** NewtonsApple().

When Java runs ZoomingHello, what happens when it calls currentGame.setup? Java begins at the bottom of the extends diagram with the *class that came after* **new**. Starting at ZoomingHello, Java seeks a definition of setup. Java sees one, ZoomingHello.setup, and calls that method (the version we wrote to add the StringSprite and ScaleTransformer to the game).

Inside the game loop, Java does the same thing with currentGame.advance. Starting at ZoomingHello and working up the **extends** arrows, it searches for the first (lowest) definition of the method advance. There is none in ZoomingHello, so the search continues with the class it extends, Game. There *is* a definition of advance in game so that each time through the FANG game loop, Game.advance is called. The advance method defined there does nothing.

The same discussion applies to NewtonsApple, the program we are writing in this chapter. currentGame is really a NewtonsApple, so the search starts at that class. Both methods are overridden in NewtonsApple. The lowest, most "extended" version of any overridden method is called.

The advance Method

The method header of the advance method is

```
public void advance(double secondsSinceLastCall)
```

It is **public** so that the FANG engine can call it. It returns **void** (or nothing at all). It is called advance and it has a single element in its parameter list. That value is a **double**, a number with a fractional part. Each element in a formal parameter list looks like a variable definition, a type name followed by an identifier. Instead of using an = to assign the parameter a value, the corresponding parameter in the call gives it a value. More on parameters getting values later.

secondsSinceLastCall is a long name but it is an attempt to say what the parameter means: FANG tries to call advance twenty times a second but there might be times when it does not hit that rate exactly. So, secondsSinceLastCall has a value very near 0.05 (second), but FANG calculates the actual time since the last call. The value is passed in to advance so that it can be used for calculating things such as how far the apple has fallen since the last time it was moved.

Before we fill in the body of the advance method, the next section discusses program (and game) design in light of different problem-solving techniques.

Review 4.1

(a) According to our definition, is *Newton's Apple* a game? Why or why not?

(b) Two methods of the Game class are typically overridden when a game is written. Chapter 2 covered simple programs overriding just the setup method.

This section describes the *other* method that is typically overridden. What is the name of that method? What is that method's *header*?

(c) What value does the parameter have when FANG calls **public void** advance(**double** secondsSinceLastCall)? What is the *meaning* of the floating point number which is passed?

(d) Approximately how frequently is the advance method called by the game engine?

(e) If a very complex advance method took 0.1 second to execute, could the game engine call the advance method at the normal rate?

4.2   Computer Program (Game) Design

It is possible to wander far and wide when introducing a section on software (or game) design. One of the first tasks is to track down a usable definition for design, and the reader recalls how long it took to do that for *game* back in Chapter 1; *design* is almost as ubiquitous as game and it is used "technically" by many different disciplines (some fun on the different meanings can be found in Spillers's design blog entry [Spi07]: "Yes, all 10 definitions!").

Computer program design is the creation of a program to solve a particular problem. It is the task *not* of solving the problem but rather of describing *how* the problem is solved. This is similar to being the author of a cookbook: you do not take a handful of fresh ingredients and create a fine meal; you describe how any competent cook could take a handful of fresh ingredients and create a fine meal.

What makes this design? What does it have in common with, for example, game design? It seems, when we look at the various design fields, that they all have the designer indirectly creating experiences. A graphic designer uses art and technique to create a poster (or computer interface or billboard or . . .), but the poster's purpose is to make the viewer want to purchase a particular brand of soft drink. Similarly, the computer programmer writes code that helps the user accomplish some task, solve some problem. There is a level of indirection in the thing being built.

So, what is a *game* designer building and what purpose does it have? In Jesse Schell's *The Art of Game Design* [Sch08], he claims that game designers build games in order to induce players to have a particular experience. He goes on to talk about the four basic elements of a game: aesthetics, story, mechanics, and technology. I mention these elements here because if we become good at software design, these same elements can be applied (perhaps giving short shrift to story).

Design Is Problem Solving

Design is problem solving at (at least) two different levels: describing how to solve a problem for the user requires you to understand how to solve the problem; describing the solution is, itself, a problem. Design involves moving between multiple levels of a problem and its solution multiple times.

How can programmers tame complexity? The answer is fundamental to all of computer science: work at multiple *independent* levels at the same time. This means working at multiple levels of *abstraction* simultaneously.

Abstraction is the process of reducing detail. A problem is generalized by folding specific details of the problem into sets or groups that can all be treated identically. What this really means is splitting the details up so that when focusing on a specific level of the solution, only one set of details is visible.

If you understand a problem very well, it is possible to solve it from the bottom up: design the most detailed parts of the solution, constructing building blocks where the *detailed problem* in each is solved, and combine those building blocks into another set of blocks abstracting away another level of detail, and so on until the original problem is solved. Thinking about this from a graphic designer point of view: first you pick the colors and the fonts, then you combine colors and text into poster components, and finally the components are placed on the poster, finishing the design. This requires that you understand the problem well.

A similar approach to game design would have you focusing on exactly how combat between individual units is resolved and how movement points are calculated. Having packaged the "combat" and "movement" bits, you could move up to combine those blocks into a turn, and turns are combined into a game or campaign. Bottom-up design is hard for beginners in any discipline because the small problems seem to be solved in a vacuum; this is not true because the experienced designer is guided by "instinct" to prefer good low-level solutions. What can we do if we don't yet have the right instincts?

Reverse the approach: start at the top, writing the solution to the main problem, naming and *pretending that you have* building blocks which hide the inappropriate details. Write a solution in terms of simpler subproblems: an action solving a subproblem is, by definition, simpler than the original, top-level problem. Once you have a top-level solution written using these deferred subproblem solvers, you can reapply the exact same approach to the subproblems. This is *top-down* design or *stepwise refinement*. This is the design approach we use throughout the book.

Very few successful programmers apply top-down *or* bottom-up approaches exclusively. With practice, it is possible to alternate between the two, thinking about the lowest-level commands that help solve the problem as well as decomposing the highest-level problems. Whichever way you move through the layers of abstraction, the importance of having independent layers, each only aware of the public protocols of the layer below it, is a tried and true way of taming complexity.

Problem-Solving Techniques

At any level of solution, the facilities provided by the next layer down can be combined in five basic ways (as introduced in Section 1.6): sequence, selection, iteration, delegation, and abstraction. Sequence is doing one thing and then another. Selection is deciding (based on some criteria) to do one thing or do another thing. Iteration is doing the same thing over and over until some criteria are met. Delegation is the use of named units of work, the creation of methods (or whatever you choose to call new commands). Finally, abstraction is the creation of a complete problem solver, a tool that can be used to solve part of a problem. Abstraction is the creation of classes of objects that can be constructed and used to solve the problem.

Using top-down design to tame complexity relies on the delegation and abstraction techniques because a given level depends solely on the public protocol of the next lower level, and a public protocol is the collection of public methods in a class; the next lower level might have more than one type of object, so we can imagine a public protocol combining the public protocols of multiple classes.

These techniques for combining simple rules into more complex rules are also used in game design. Consider the rules of *Monopoly*. Paraphrasing from the official rules the game proceeds like this:

```
PREPARATION (setup)
  put out board
  place Chance and Community Chest
  choose tokens
  hand out starting money (\$1500).
while (more than one player is not BANKRUPT)
  THE PLAY (advance)
    first player rolls and moves
    according to the space moved to: BUY/PAY RENT/GO/JAIL
    second player rolls and moves
    according to the space moved to: BUY/PAY RENT/GO/JAIL
    third player rolls and moves
    according to the space moved to: BUY/PAY RENT/GO/JAIL
    ...
```

The capitalized entries are from the sections of the rules [Dar35]. Notice that the setup is done *sequentially*. The body of the game loop is also done in sequence, each player taking her turn and then passing the dice to her left. As part of each player's turn, what she is able to do is *selected* according to the type of space her token landed on. The game loop *iterates* until only one player remains in the game. When a player performs an action on the square he landed on, how to do that is *delegated* to the appropriate section of the rules. This particular game does not have a good example of abstraction.

Notice that the delegation even has parameters:

> **BUYING PROPERTY**...Whenever you land on *an unowned property* you may buy *that property* from the Bank at *its* printed price. You receive *the Title Deed* card showing ownership; place it face up in front of you.

The emphasis was added. The whole buying procedure depends on *what* unowned property you land on. That property is the one that may be purchased, it is the one that determines the price, and it is the property that determines what title card the player receives.

This loop is also similar to the standard game loop. Players look at the board, roll dice to update their position on the board (state), and decide what to do on the landing square (input), leaving their token and title cards where the next player can see them when they go to move.

Notice that when you design a game, any game, you start with the general game you want to build, considering the four essential elements of aesthetics, story, mechanics, and technology, and then you describe how things work at that high level. Odds are, when considering the highest level of the game, you are not thinking about what color the dice should be or whether the attacker rolls first or second. Those decisions are farther down and would be part of defining how a player makes their move.

A hierarchical approach, where unimportant details are pushed down to a lower level, is a successful approach to game design as well as software design.

Review 4.2

(a) Designing a program and writing a program both involve problem solving, but at different levels. Which one is problem solving at a higher level (using instructions with less detail)?

(b) What is the difference between top-down and bottom-up design?

4.3   Sequence

Sequential execution of a computer program means following instructions in exactly the order in which they appear. In Java, the order in which the source code is written is the normal order for imposing sequence. Inside the body of a method, the statements are executed in the order written from the first one just inside the opening curly brace to the last one before the close. Look at the setup method from the Target03 program from the last chapter:

```java
14  public void setup() {
15    RectangleSprite five = new RectangleSprite(0.5, 0.5);
16    five.setColor(getColor("gold"));
17    five.setLocation(0.5, 0.5);
18    addSprite(five);
19
20    RectangleSprite four = new RectangleSprite(0.4, 0.4);
21    four.setColor(getColor("blue"));
22    four.setLocation(0.5, 0.5);
23    addSprite(four);
24
25    RectangleSprite three = new RectangleSprite(0.3, 0.3);
26    three.setColor(getColor("gold"));
27    three.setLocation(0.5, 0.5);
28    addSprite(three);
29
30    RectangleSprite two = new RectangleSprite(0.2, 0.2);
31    two.setColor(getColor("blue"));
32    two.setLocation(0.5, 0.5);
33    addSprite(two);
34
35    RectangleSprite one = new RectangleSprite(0.1, 0.1);
36    one.setColor(getColor("gold"));
37    one.setLocation(0.5, 0.5);
38    addSprite(one);
39  }
```

Listing 4.1: Target03 setup

Stacking order of sprites depends on the order in which they are passed as parameters to addSprite. What order are these sprites passed to addSprite? When FANG calls setup, whatever calling method is executing is suspended (but it remembers where it was), and execution moves to the first line of setup, line 15. After line 15 finishes, line 16 is executed, and then 17 and 18 and 19.[2] This is putting together a solution by specifying exactly what to do first, second, third, and so on.

So, in what order are the sprites added to the game? In line number order of the addSprite lines: lines 18, 23, 28, 33, and 38 in that order, or five, four, three, two, and one, largest to smallest.

The only difference between the setup methods of games in the previous chapter and NewtonsApple is that NewtonsApple does not define names for the objects inside of setup.

```
1   // package default
2
3   import fang2.core.Game;
4   import fang2.sprites.OvalSprite;
5   import fang2.sprites.RectangleSprite;
6   import fang2.sprites.StringSprite;
7
8   /** NewtonsApple pre-prototype */
9   public class NewtonsAppleSprites
10      extends Game {
11      // An OvalSprite field to name the apple
12      private OvalSprite apple;
13      // A RectangleSprite field to name newton
14      private RectangleSprite newton;
15
16      // First pass at defining the sprites for the game
17      @Override
18      public void setup() {
19          apple = new OvalSprite(0.10, 0.10);
20          apple.setColor(getColor("red"));
21          apple.setLocation(0.50, 0.00);
22
23          newton = new RectangleSprite(0.10, 0.10);
24          newton.setColor(getColor("green"));
25          newton.setLocation(0.50, 0.90);
26
27          addSprite(newton);
28          addSprite(apple);
29      }
30  }
```

Listing 4.2: NewtonsAppleSprites.java: a first pass

Lines 1 through 10 should be familiar from the previous chapters. The first two are a package comment, the next three import three types from FANG, line 8 is a comment, and 9 and 10 define the name of our class (which must match the name of the file in which it is defined) and what class this class extends. The end of line 10 is an opening curly brace, marking the beginning of the container which is the body of our class definition. The matching closing curly brace is on line 30.

---

[2]Okay, blank lines and comments are ignored by javac and never produce any bytecodes when compiled. For all intents and purposes, then, line 19 is skipped when the method is executed. Since a blank line would *do* nothing, it is safe (and more uniform) to talk about Java executing every line in sequence.

Lines 11 through 29 are *indented*. Because Java is free-form, Java does not require this though we have shown it in our Java templates. This aids the programmer in seeing the container relationship between the class and the lines within it.

Contained lines (inside a pair of curly braces) are normally indented one *indent level*, where indent level is some number of spaces. *Simple Games* uses two spaces for each indent level; it keeps the code from wrapping too much in the listings. You may choose to use a slightly greater indent if formatting the code that way makes the code structure more obvious to you.

Lines 12 and 14 are new. They look something like the definition of a local variable in the programs in the last chapter (e.g., lines 15, 20, 25, 30, and 35 in Listing 4.1 on page 98) but are not identical.

Lines 12 and 14 in Listing 4.2 on the preceding page each define a *field*. A field is a variable that belongs to an object rather than to a single method inside the object.

The *scope* of an identifier is where that identifier, that name, can be used in a program. There is much to be said about names and scope but the crux of the matter is that a variable can be used only while it is in scope, and it is in scope only inside the curly braces in which it is defined. The variable goes out of scope and cannot be used at all when the next unmatched closing curly brace is crossed.

A matched pair of curly braces and all of the code inside of them is called a *block* in Java. So a variable is only in scope inside the block in which it is defined.

There is a slight difference in scope for fields than for variables; we delay explaining it for a moment. The following is a simplified lie.

In Target03, the local variable five is in scope from the line where it is defined, 15, down to the closing of the block enclosing the body of setup on line 39.

In NewtonsAppleSprites, newton is in scope from line 14 where it is defined down to the closing of the block enclosing the *whole class definition* on line 30.

The important thing to note is that newton is available inside of setup, so line 19 refers to the field. newton is also in scope in any other method we define in the class. That means we can use the field in multiple methods, as a way of storing game information that lasts as long as the game does. Local variables go away when the called method returns (runs off the end); fields remain "alive" and keep their values as long as the *object* to which they belong is part of the Java program.

Defining a field includes an access level as well as a type and a name. The Java template is

```
<accessLevel> := public |
                 protected |
                 private

<fieldDeclaration> := <accessLevel> <variableDeclaration>;
```

The field definition takes an *access level*, like what we have said goes in a method header. Remember that in templates, | means "or." The access level is **public** or **protected** or **private**.[3]

The meaning of **public** is that any method with a reference to a NewtonsApple object can use a dot and the name and get or set the value.[4] **private** means that only methods defined in NewtonsApple can use the name. **protected** is somewhere in the middle between the two.

Rule of thumb: all *fields* are to be defined **private**.

The field definitions, just like the **import** lines above, each end with a semicolon. Definitions and statements in Java end with semicolons (unless they end with a curly brace). This is one of the important parts of the artificiality of Java: the semicolons make it much easier for the compiler to take a program apart into its constituent parts for translation to bytecode.

---

[3] There is an "empty" access level. We discuss it when we discuss Java packages in Chapter 13.

[4] The multiple versions of NewtonsApple defined in this chapter represent snapshots over time of the creation of the final game. While the complete name of the program is used in captions of the listings, the name NewtonsApple is used to refer to the current incarnation generally when no confusion results.

apple and newton are *fields* or parts of NewtonsApple. Each is a type of sprite, an instance of the class OvalSprite (or RectangleSprite). These objects are part of another object: this is an example of using levels of abstraction. The two sprite classes know all about things like setting the color and scaling; we don't need to think about those things except in order to use them to make our game work. An OvalSprite *is* an object and has a .java file and everything. Viewed in the context of NewtonsApple, however, the OvalSprite field named apple is just a part of the game.

Just as each component in a chess set has a type (the board, a black knight, a white queen, etc.), every object in Java has a type. The type of the object is the name of a type or **class**, either one provided by Java or FANG or one written by you, the programmer.

Field definitions appear within a class but outside of all methods. The field name is visible *everywhere* within the container of the class, including inside any and all methods.

The simplifying lie mentioned above is that the field is in scope from the line where it is defined to the end of the class. The truth is that a *field* and a *method*, defined within the body of a **class** definition, are in scope for the *entire body of the **class** definition*. A field is in scope inside methods defined before the field itself is defined. A local variable is only in scope from definition to the end of the block.

To avoid confusion (as much for the author as anyone else), all Java code in the text is sorted so that all data fields come before any methods. Keep in mind when reading your own or others' code that this need not be the case.

Line 12 in Listing 4.2 defines the field apple, a label for an OvalSprite. In previous programs, we combined, on the same line as the local definition, the assignment of a newly created sprite to the name. Here we separate them so as to put all initialization of fields into the setup method.

The definition creates a name that can be used to label a sprite; no sprite has actually been created. That is delayed until line 19 is executed and **new** is called to create a OvalSprite.

The difference between a *type* or **class** and an *object* or *instance* of the class is the difference between the blueprints for a house and a house constructed from the blueprints.

If the blueprints are for a house in a subdivision, it might be the case that hundreds or thousands of specific houses are built from the exact same blueprint. Creation of the blueprint (like definition of the **class**) does not indicate that any houses (objects) of that type are built. Similarly, purchasing a lot (defining a variable as in lines 12 and 14) for a given kind of house does not build the house. Instead, having a lot (variable) and having a blueprint (class) means that we can contract to have a house built (call to **new**).

Line 18 defines a new *method* for NewtonsApple. A method is a *named piece of computation*; it can also be thought of as a new Java command. The first line of a method definition (where the method is defined) is called the method header. A method definition is a method header followed by a block of code defining the body of the method. The Java template is

```
<returnType> := <typeName> |
                void


<methodName> := <identifier>


<formalParameter> := <variableDeclaration>


<formalParameterList> := [<formalParameter> [, <formalParameter>]*]


<methodDeclaration> :=
  <accessLevel> <returnType> <methodName>(<formalParameterList>)


<methodDefinition> := <methodDeclaration>
                    <block>
```

```
<block> := {
            <statement>*
        }
```

- *<accessLevel>* : **public**

  This means that objects of types other than NewtonsApple (the type we are currently defining) can "call" the method. There is more on access levels in following chapters; for now, all methods should be **public**.

- *<returnType>* : **void**

  Methods can calculate and return values. This one returns nothing, so we use the special type, **void**, to indicate that no value of any kind is returned. This is enforced by the compiler.

- *<methodName>* : setup

  The name used to call this method. Naming in a computer program is important enough to fill most of the next chapter.

- *<formalParameterList>* : ()

  The parameter list here is empty. A *formal* parameter list is a list of *<variableDeclaration>*s.

  Compare that to the *actual* parameter list we saw in template in the last chapter that looks like a list of values to assign to variables: *<expression>*. It looks like these could go together in a local variable definition as in *<variableDeclaration>*= *<expression>*. This is no accident and we return to this point in Section 6.3 when discussing parameters in detail.

The body of a method, just like the body of a **class**, is contained inside curly braces (line 18's final { matches with the } on line 29). After all of that explanation, NewtonsAppleSprites draws two sprites on the screen as in Figure 4.3 on the next page, which shows what the game looks like when run.[5] Pressing **Start** has no effect because we have not provided a non-empty advance method.

An Experiment

How does advance work? How can we *animate* the apple sprite without using a transformer? Though we have set out to design the very simplest *game*, it does not result in the very simplest *program*. To get a feel for how FANG works, we write the simplest program that puts newton and the apple on the screen and has the apple fall on his head. Once. No scores, no catching, no random, just a red circle moving down the screen (and across a green square).

Building little experiment programs, to test out how things work, is a very good habit to get into. This program is a *prototype*, a proof of concept that is disposed of after use. Seeing how advance works in a stripped down program is important enough for the detour.

```
1   // package default
2
3   import fang2.core.Game;
4   import fang2.sprites.OvalSprite;
5   import fang2.sprites.RectangleSprite;
6
7   /** NewtonsApple pre-prototype */
8   public class NewtonsAppleAdvance
9     extends Game {
```

---

[5]The extra stripe of background to the right of the game space is caused by the name in the title bar being longer than will fit above the game space. This appears in screenshots in this chapter because of the NewtonsApple prefix on all of the program names.

Figure 4.3: `NewtonsAppleSprites`

```
10   // An OvalSprite field to name the apple
11   private OvalSprite apple;
12   // A RectangleSprite field to name newton
13   private RectangleSprite newton;
14
15   /**
16    * Update the game state: only game state here is where the apple is;
17    * let it fall each frame. Velocity is 0.10 screen/second.
18    */
19   @Override
20   public void advance(double secondsSinceLastCall) {
21     apple.translateY(0.10 * secondsSinceLastCall);
22   }
23
24   // First pass at defining the sprites for the game
25   @Override
26   public void setup() {
```

```
27      apple = new OvalSprite(0.10, 0.10);
28      apple.setColor(getColor("red"));
29      apple.setLocation(0.50, 0.00);
30
31      newton = new RectangleSprite(0.10, 0.10);
32      newton.setColor(getColor("green"));
33      newton.setLocation(0.50, 0.90);
34
35      addSprite(newton);
36      addSprite(apple);
37    }
38 }
```

Listing 4.3: `NewtonsAppleAdvance.java`

Listing 4.3 shows a program almost identical to `NewtonsAppleSprites` but for the insertion of lines 15–22 (and the changed line numbers after those lines). Methods in the source code for this book are sorted alphabetically after the fields (which are *mostly* sorted alphabetically; some related field definitions are kept together regardless of name). This makes it easy to find methods by name in the source code.[6]

Line 20 defines a method (What is the method header? What are the *parts* of the method header?), `advance`. Because `advance` overrides the version in `Game`, it is called each time through the game loop. `secondsSinceLastCall` is a number, somewhere close to 0.05 (one-twentieth).

Line 21 calls a method on `apple`. Because `apple` is a *field*, the `apple` referred to in `advance` is the same one referred to in `setup`. Each time through `advance`, the number of seconds since the last call is multiplied by the number of screens per second the apple should fall. For the experiment 1 screen, every 10 seconds or 0.1 screen/second was chosen. This is far too slow for a reasonable game but it gives us time to watch the sprite move.

The product of the time and the velocity gives us a distance, in screens. That value is passed in to the `translateY` method. All sprites have `translateY`, which takes a distance, in screens, and translates the location of the given sprite by that distance. `translateY` (and `translateX` and `translate` (which takes an x and a y value)) differ from `setLocation`: the `translate` family moves the sprite *relative* to its current location while `setLocation` moves the sprite to an *absolute* position on the screen.

Try running `NewtonsAppleAdvance`. See what happens. How can you further slow down the apple? How could you make the apple move faster? Why does the apple pass in front of Newton? How could you change that?

Because `NewtonsAppleAdvance` looks just like `NewtonsAppleSprites`, there is no screenshot (it has to be running to really make an impression). This is the end of working with `NewtonsAppleSprites`; back to making `NewtonsApple`.

Another Method

The `apple` should not always fall from the center of the screen. That would make the game too easy. Better would be to have the computer pick a random number on the range [0.0–1.0][7] (`Game` has a `randomDouble` method that does just that) and use that to set the x-coordinate of `apple`.

We could put the call to `randomDouble()` right in line 19 of `NewtonsAppleSprites`. That randomly positions the first apple. A random position is needed *whenever* a new apple is dropped onto the screen. The random number code, if put directly in the constructor, must be repeated at least once. It is much better practice to have a single copy of the code called from each of the places that needs it.

---

[6]It also makes it easier to picture where the different partial listings go in the original file. Partial listings are all printed with line numbers to simplify finding them in the electronic listings.

[7]Range notation in this book uses square brackets, [and], to indicate that the range is *inclusive* at that end, and parentheses, (and), to indicate that the range is *exclusive* at that end. The range [0.0–1.0) means the set of numbers d such that $0.0 \leq d < 1.0$.

The Do not Repeat Yourself Principle.   (DRY) Whenever possible, you should not repeat yourself when writing a computer program. As you learn to use iteration and delegation, when you do the same thing over and over, with little changes, it is always worthwhile to define a new method that takes the little changes as parameters.

Software engineering is the study of effectively writing high-quality code. The DRY principle is possibly the simplest rule of software engineering, yet it is one of the most effective when consistently applied.[8]

Why not repeat yourself? Because updating behavior requires updating every copy. Two copies of apple placement code means if you change how the apple is placed, you must remember to change every copy. Two days from now you will not remember how many copies you made, and missing one introduces inconsistencies into the program. Remember the DRY principle whenever you find yourself copying code; it may still be necessary to repeat yourself occasionally but reciting "DRY" over and over tends to make code better.

How would we define a helper method to *randomly* position the apple somewhere at the top of the screen to begin its fall? To begin writing a method, we need to know its header; the header of a method depends on its name, which, in turn, depends on *what* the method does.

The name and the purpose are intertwined. This is an example of bottom-up design because we need to be able to drop the apple at a different location each time the apple is dropped; the user has no meaningful choices if the apple always appears right above Newton.

The apple is randomly positioned along the top of the screen *each* time a new apple is dropped. We could call our new command `dropApple`. What is the method header of `dropApple`? It calls `setLocation` on a field, so it needs no parameters (it always does exactly the same thing). It does not calculate anything for us, so it has a **void** return type. For now all methods are **public** and we decided on the name already.

Listing 4.4 shows *just* the `dropApple` method with its header comment. The 'DropApple[9] version of the game is almost the same as 'Sprites except for the lines 15–20.

```
15   /**
16    * place the apple at random x-coord at top of screen.
17    */
18   public void dropApple() {
19     apple.setLocation(randomDouble(), 0.00);
20   }
```

Listing 4.4: `NewtonsAppleDropApple.java`: `dropApple` method

Notice that the method does not have a `@Override` annotation right before the method header. Why not? Because `Game` (and other higher FANG and Java classes) does *not* define a method with the same method header; in fact, no class directly or indirectly extended by `NewtonsApple` defines a method named `dropApple`. The `@Override` annotation belongs only before methods that override a definition in a higher class (*higher* in the **extends** hierarchy).

There is one other change in 'DropApple: line 27 no longer calls `apple.setLocation`. Instead it reads

```
27   dropApple();
```

It is necessary to call `dropApple` explicitly because FANG knows nothing about it and cannot call it automatically for us. So, *after* creating a new apple, but before `setup` finishes, we need to call `dropApple`; since it sets the apple's location, it seems reasonable to replace the call to `apple.setLocation` with the call to our new method.

---

[8]The current author first encountered the DRY principle in this form while reading Hunt and Thomas' *The Pragmatic Programmer*. [HT99]

[9]Read 'DropApple as `NewtonsAppleDropApple`; the suffix serves as a shorthand reference to the many versions of `NewtonsApple`.

Numbers in Java

What is a `double`? It is a type, like `Game` or `RectangleSprite`. It is a built-in (to Java) *numeric type*. The other built-in, numeric type we use is `int`.

Two questions spring to mind when we see the type names `double` and `int`: why are there two *different* types of numbers in Java and why are these the only type names we have seen that begin with lowercase letters?

In reverse order: the two types are *not* classes; in Java all standard class names (and all classes we write in this book) begin with a capital letter. `double` and `int` are different in that variables referring to these types *cannot be used to call a method with a dot*. There is more on the differences between classes and plain old data types in Section 5.3

There are two different number types in Java because computers deal with whole numbers, *integers*, and numbers with a fractional part, *floating-point numbers*[10] with different instructions. The numbers stored inside the computer, in the bits and bytes, are integers unless we use them to *encode* a floating-point number.

The details are well beyond the current discussion but a variable of type `int` can store a whole number between about -2 billion and +2 billion. When you type a number into a Java program and there is no decimal point in what you type, the number is treated as an `int` value by Java: `0`, `-102`, `1023`, all are examples of `int` *literals*, values literally typed into the program.

A floating-point number can hold numbers with a fractional part. A `double` can be typed in literally as in `0.10`, `0.50`, `0.00`. The trailing zeros do not change the values stored but they make the numbers stand out as being fractions between 0.0 and 1.0. Notice that `0` (an `int` literal) and `0.0` (a `double` literal) are *not* the same thing. The range for `double` is much larger than that for `int` but it cannot store every integer value in the range. More on the range in the next chapter.

The name `int` makes sense: it is the first three letters of *integer*, the type of number it holds. What does `double` mean? There is another floating-point type in Java, `float` (a name that makes sense!); the range of `float` is larger than that of `int`, but it keeps only about seven significant digits (total before and after the decimal place). Many floating-point calculations need more digits of *precision*, so the FORTRAN programming language introduced the idea of normal or *single-precision* floating point numbers and higher-precision, *double-precision* floating point numbers which keep about sixteen digits. The name `double` comes from *double-precision floating point* and is much easier to type and remember.

Keeping Score

The discussion of numeric types was prompted by the use of `randomDouble()` in the `dropApple` method. According to the documentation for `Game` (because there is no explicit object and dot in front of the method name, the method is called on the `NewtonsAppleDropApple` object on which `dropApple` was called), calling `randomDouble()` "Generates a shared random double on the range [0.0, 1.0)." "Shared" means the method works across networked games; not something we care about here. Since we need a random screen location, this is just the range we want to use, so it is what we pass in to `apple.setLocation` in `dropApple`.

Numeric types are also used to keep score. What is the score in `NewtonsApple`? The ratio between the number of apples caught and the number of apples dropped. This means we need to *count* apples dropped and apples caught. Which kind of number would we use for counting apples?

Disregarding applesauce, apples are discrete units, so we would use `int`, adding 1 to the number dropped whenever an apple is dropped and adding 1 to the number caught whenever an apple is caught.

Wait a minute. When is "whenever an apple is dropped"? It is exactly when `dropApple` is called. We can modify `dropApple` so that it does two things: positions the apple along the top edge of the screen *and* increments the number of apples that have been dropped.

We need a place to store the apples dropped count. Is it a *local variable* or a *field*? A local variable (inside `dropApple`) is not available to any other method, in particular, whatever method displays the score. This means that a local variable has too limited a scope. `applesDropped` is an `int` *field*.

---

[10]The decimal point in a floating-point number could be between any pair of digits; the decimal point in an integer is always to the right of its rightmost digit.

Adding the field to the class and updating `dropApple` results in Listing 4.5. The **import** lines and header comment are excluded in the interest of length but because there are changes in several different spots a complete listing of the **class** definition makes sense.

```java
public class NewtonsAppleJustSetup
  extends Game {
  // ----- visual representations of the apple and physicist -----
  /** on screen representation of the apple; a small red circle */
  private OvalSprite apple;

  /** on screen representation of Newton; a small green square */
  private RectangleSprite newton;

  // ----- keeping and displaying the score -----
  /** number of apples caught */
  private int applesCaught;

  /** number of apples dropped */
  private int applesDropped;

  /** on-screen current score; update contents when score changes */
  private StringSprite displayScore;

  /**
   * place the apple at random x-coord at top of screen.
   */
  public void dropApple() {
    apple.setLocation(randomDouble(), 0.00);
    applesDropped = applesDropped + 1;// another apple dropped
  }

  /**
   * The method called by FANG before the game starts. Include all
   * "one-time" instructions in setup.
   */
  @Override
  public void setup() {
    // initialize the score
    applesCaught = 0;
    applesDropped = 0;

    // The apple is small and red; its initial position is set randomly
    // in the dropApple routine (called here and when apple bottoms out)
    apple = new OvalSprite(0.10, 0.10);
    apple.setColor(getColor("red"));
    dropApple();

    // newton is small, green, at the middle bottom of the screen.
    newton = new RectangleSprite(0.10, 0.10);
    newton.setColor(getColor("green"));
```

```
62     newton.setLocation(0.50, 0.90);
63
64     displayScore = new StringSprite();
65     displayScore.setLineHeight(0.10);
66     displayScore.setColor(getColor("white"));
67     displayScore.topJustify();// move location to upper-left corner
68     displayScore.leftJustify();
69     displayScore.setLocation(0.00, 0.00);
70
71     displayScore.setText("Score: " + applesCaught + "/" +
72       applesDropped);
73
74     // must add all sprites we want drawn (or moved) to the game
75     addSprite(apple);
76     addSprite(newton);
77     addSprite(displayScore);
78   }
79 }
```

Listing 4.5: `NewtonsAppleJustSetup.java`: `dropApple` method

The field `applesDropped` is defined on line 30: **private** means only `NewtonsApple`'s methods can manipulate it. **int** is the integer type. Where does `applesDropped` get an initial value?

It is important to think about the difference between the order of *definition* and the order of *execution*. In the rules for the World War II wargame *Panzerblitz*, for example, normal combat is defined on page 5, minefield attacks on page 9, and the standard turn sequence on page 11. The turn sequence begins:

1. German player resolves any Minefield attacks against Russian units.

2. German player announces which of his units are attacking which Russian units, and what attack techniques are being used.

3. German player resolves all Normal combat . . .

4. . . . (Steps 4–8 omitted) [Pan70]

Though minefield attacks were defined on page 9, *after* the definition of normal combat, each turn begins with minefield attacks *before* resolving normal combat. The definition of the rules is in one order: movement, combat, obstacles (including minefields), and turn sequence. Execution begins with the turn sequence which refers to the others in the order they are "called."

In a FANG `Game`-extending class, `setup` is the first, automatically called method, so execution begins there. The first three lines of `setup`, lines 49–51, set the value of the **int** fields. So `applesDropped` is set to 0 (the number of apples already dropped) in line 51. The `apple` field is initialized (with a call to **new**) in line 55; `setup` finally calls `dropApple`.

This means "going backward" in the code. Execution of `setup` is suspended (but remembered) and execution begins at line 39 (the first line in the body of `dropApple`). The `apple` is randomly located at the top of the screen and the number of apples dropped is incremented.

```
40   applesDropped = applesDropped + 1;
```

What does this line mean? If we read = as "is assigned the value of," the line reads "applesDropped gets the value of applesDropped plus one." This makes sense if we consider the <expression> (that's what comes after the = here as well as in a definition) is evaluated *before* the assignment is made.

A variable refers to some thing, in this case an integer. Using the variable with the plus sign (on the right of the = or *assignment operator*) means "the value of" the variable. The expression calculates the "value of applesDropped plus one" and assigns that value to some variable. In this line the *some variable* is applesDropped, the same variable used in the expression.

The first time dropApple runs we know that applesDropped was *assigned* the value 0 (in line 51). The right-hand side (rhs) of the assignment operator is 0 + 1 or 1. This is stored in applesDropped. Each time line 40 is executed, the value of applesDropped goes up by one. Details on how Java stores different kinds of values is deferred until the next chapter.

Lines 64–72 in Listing 4.5 construct the score showing sprite setting its color, contents, and location. Lines 67–68 use methods unique to StringSprite which move the location *inside the sprite*. Sprite locations are at the center of the sprite but it is sometimes useful to have the location of a string at the left or right edge or along the top or bottom. Together the two lines move the location to the upper-left corner of the sprite.

This makes it easier to align strings and keep them in a given location even when their text value changes (and might change width). By putting the location in the upper-left corner and anchoring that in the upper-left corner of the game screen (look at the location in line 69), no matter how many digits the score grows to, the word "Score:" stays in the same place.

Review 4.3

(a) Why do programmers indent their code blocks?

(b) In which methods can **private** fields be used?

(c) Is OvalSprite a class or an object?

(d) Is SomethingYouHaveNeverHeardOf a class or an object?

(e) What does **void** mean?

(f) Name two numeric types (these are types capable of storing a number).

(g) PolygonSprite is one Sprite-extending type. Name three other Sprite-extending types (these are types capable of holding 2D graphic and geometric information).

(h) What does the StringSprite method topJustify do?

(i) What does the StringSprite method leftJustify do?

(j) Compile and run NewtonsAppleAdvance.

    (a) Change line 21 to read apple.translateY(0.10); how does the program change? Explain the difference.

    (b) Move line 21 to line 37, as the last line of the setup method (advance has nothing between the braces). What happens now? Explain the difference.

4.4 Selection

To complete our game, the advance method must do four things:

1. Move Newton to where the player's mouse is,

2. Move the apple down the screen,

3. Check if apple is caught,

4. Check if apple hit the ground.

The code for these is longer than any method we have yet written. The steps, as comments, serve as guideposts in the code:

```
38    public void advance(double secondsSinceLastCall) {
39      // (1) Move newton so his x-coordinate matches x-coordinate of mouse
44
45      // (2) Translate apple down screen; velocity * time = distance
47
48      // (3) Check if newton has "caught" the apple
55
56      // (4) Check if the apple has hit the ground (y-coordinate >= 1.0)
62    }
```

Listing 4.6: `NewtonsApple`: structure of `advance`

Notice the line numbers are not contiguous. The comments were pulled from the finished version of `advance`. The remainder of this section fills in the invisible lines in this listing.)

No Such Object

Before filling in the code in the above template, we take a slight detour. Consider a modified version of checkers where we want to reward the player who last captured an opposing checker. At the beginning of each player's turn, if he were the last to capture a checker, he gets a cookie. If we have a special square beside the board where we put the last captured checker, looking at it at the beginning of each turn, the moderator can determine whether or not the current player gets a cookie.

What "value" does the "last captured checker" have at the beginning of the game? In fairness, which player should be rewarded with cookies before either has captured a checker? We need a special value that indicates that there is no such component, no "last captured checker."

In Java, the special value meaning no such object is `null`. This is different than a method that returns `void`: `void` means that no value is ever returned; a method that returns an object can return `null` to indicate that there is no such object (right now; if you call it again the return value might change). Back from the detour.

To move `newton`, we need to get the player's mouse location. Extract the x-coordinate from the mouse location and set the x-coordinate of `newton` to the new value. This is trickier than it sounds: what if the player stared the game but has moved her mouse out of the game to answer an IM? There *is* no location for her mouse *inside the game*. FANG indicates this by returning `null` from `getMouse2D()` when the mouse has no location in the game.

```
39      // (1) Move newton so his x-coordinate matches x-coordinate of mouse
40      Location2D position = getMouse2D();
41      if (position != null) {
42        newton.setX(position.getX());
43      }
```

Listing 4.7: `NewtonsApple`: Moving Newton

If the player's mouse is in the game, move `newton`. In any other case, leave `newton` alone. Listing 4.7 shows the code.

The `!=` symbol reads as "is not equal to," so, if `position` is not `null`, set `newton`'s x-coordinate to the `position`'s x-coordinate. The `if` statement is how selection is written in Java.

The `if` Statement

Selection is choosing one rule over another. In checkers, **if** you jump over an opposing checker, **then** you get to remove the checker. Or, in chess, **if** the king is under threat and there is no way to get him out of threat, **then** the player whose king is under threat loses.

Each of these two examples has the rule follower either doing or not doing something. It is also possible to select from two (or even more) different paths: **if** the temperature is above sixty degrees Fahrenheit, **then** wear shorts or **else** wear long pants.

Where does this come into play in `NewtonsApple`? Three places: we must make sure the user's mouse location exists before we can use the dot notation with it; we need to be able to check if Newton caught the apple and adjust the score and drop a new apple if so; we need to check if Newton missed the apple and it hit the ground, and adjust the score and drop a new apple if so. We examine the `if` statement shown in the previous section, present the Java template for `if` statements, and explore Boolean expressions.

Lines 41–43 of `NewtonsApple` are the `if` statement that checks whether the player has a mouse position. FANG indicates that there is a valid mouse position by returning a non-`null` value; if the value returned from `getMouse2D()` is `null`, there is no valid mouse position in this frame.

"Frame" refers to one iteration through the game loop. The term comes from movie animation: one picture on the screen is one frame of film. Computer animators took the term and used it to talk about the refresh time for computerized scenes. From there it moved over to computer games with animation on the screen.

Never use a dot with a `null` value.   If `position` were `null`, the expression `position.getX()` would cause the program to crash (halt with an error). If there is ever a chance that an object variable might have `null` as a value, you must use an `if` statement to protect against using the dot with it.

If execution were simply sequential, having line 42 appear in advance would mean that it *must* execute every frame (a method executes from top to bottom when called *unless* the flow of control through the method is modified by selection or iteration statements). The `if` statement on line 41 evaluates a *Boolean expression*, an expression which is either **true** or **false**, and executes the body of the `if` statement if and only if the expression is **true** when evaluated. Whether the body is executed or not, when the `if` statement finishes, execution continues with the next executable line in the method.

The Java template for the `if` statement is

```
<thenStatement> := <statement>

<ifStatement> := if (<booleanExpression>)
                    <thenStatement>
```

The template for `<statement>` begins to fill out:

```
<statement> := <localVariableDefinition> |
               <expression>; |
               <ifStatement> |
               <block>
```

The `<thenStatement>` is any single statement; when you need to select more than one statement, put a block there with any number of statements in it. For consistency, in the book we *always* use curly braces around even single statements; you should be aware for reading other programmers' code that these are not necessary when there is a single statement.

Also notice that an expression, followed by a semicolon, is also a statement. The book sometimes talks about "assignment statements" by which the author means an assignment expression with a semicolon after it, making it a statement.

There is an alternate template for the `if` statement, the `if/else` version of the statement:

```
<elseStatement> := <statement>

<ifStatement> := if (<booleanExpression>)
                   <thenStatement>
                 [else
                   <elseStatement>]
```

The meaning of the **if/else** version is that Java evaluates the expression, and if it is **true**, the *<thenStatement>* is executed and the *<elseStatement>* is skipped over; if the Boolean expression is **false**, the *<thenStatement>* is skipped over and the *<elseStatement>* is executed. Exactly one of *<thenStatement>* or *<elseStatement>* is executed depending on the value of the Boolean expression.

Boolean Expressions

What is a Boolean expression? It is an expression with a truth value. One form of Boolean expression is a comparison of two values. Consider the following snippet of code:

```
int x = 13;
if (10 < x) {
  x = x - 1; // Line A
}
```

Does Line A get executed? Yes, because the < operator means "less than" and it applies to numbers just as you would think that it would: it returns **true** if the left-hand side is less than the right-hand side and **false** otherwise.

Java has six standard comparison operators: ==, !=, <, <=, >, and >=. These read "is equal to," "is not equal to," "is less than," "is less than or equal to," "is greater than," and "is greater than or equal to," respectively.

Two character operators must be typed with no space between the two characters. Less than or equal to is typed <=; the sequence <~= is interpreted as the operator less than followed by the assignment operator (and, since that sequence of operators makes no sense, the Java compiler complains).

Pay special attention to the "is equal to" operator, == and do not confuse it with the "is assigned the value of" or assignment operator, =. The first compares two expressions, returning a truth value; the second evaluates the expression on the right and assigns that value to the name on the left. x = 13 in the above snippet assigns 13 to the variable x whereas x == 13 would return **true** after the above assignment. Java flags the use of = in a Boolean expression as an error.

Another type of Boolean expression is a call to a method that returns a Boolean value. For example, the Game class has a method called isGameOver(). This method takes no parameters and returns **true** if the game is over and **false** otherwise. The main video game loop uses this Boolean method to determine whether to do the loop again or not. Actually, it uses the logical inverse of this method. To invert a Boolean expression, making **true false** and *vice versa*, place an ! in front of the expression (and read it as "not"). To have an **if** statement based on the game continuing, you could have

```
if (!isGameOver()) {
  someStringSprite.setText("Game Continues");
} else {
  someStringSprite.setText("Game is OVER");
}
```

Knowing these two ways of getting Boolean values, we know enough to finish expanding the four requirements of advance into actual code.

Review 4.4

(a) The statements of a method body are executed in sequential order unless specified otherwise. Suppose you sometimes want a statement to execute and other times do not want it to execute. How could you indicate that the order of statement execution should not be sequential and instead should execute the statement depending upon a condition?

(b) When evaluating a Boolean expression in Java, what are the two possible outcomes?

(c) What is the difference between `score = 2` and `score == 2`?

4.5 Finishing `NewtonsApple`

We have examined the code for moving Newton to the same x-coordinate as the player's mouse; we even decided that we didn't need to do anything if the mouse was not available to our game.

We saw how to move the apple; now we need to decide on its velocity. We want the game to be easy, so we use a fall rate of one screen every three seconds or 0.33 screen/second.[11] The amount that the `apple` falls in any given time period is still velocity × time.

```
45    // (2) Translate apple down screen; velocity * time = distance
46    apple.translateY(0.33 * secondsSinceLastCall);
```

Listing 4.8: `NewtonsApple`: Moving `apple`

Sprites can detect intersection with other sprites. This is done using a Boolean method called `intersects`, which takes as a parameter another sprite to test for intersection with. This method lets us check if Newton caught the apple. **If** the apple is caught, update the number of apples caught and drop a new apple.

```
48    // (3) Check if newton has "caught" the apple
49    if (apple.intersects(newton)) {
50      applesCaught = applesCaught + 1;// another apple caught
51      displayScore.setText("Score: " + applesCaught + "/" +
52        applesDropped);
53      dropApple();
54    }
```

Listing 4.9: `NewtonsApple`: Catching `apple`

We know the apple was missed if the apple's location reaches the ground, or when the y-coordinate of `apple` is greater than or equal to 1.0 (the bottom of the screen). Listing 4.10 shows the body of the `advance` method with the comments and the code filled in; this paragraph refers to lines 56–61.

```
38    public void advance(double secondsSinceLastCall) {
39      // (1) Move newton so his x-coordinate matches x-coordinate of mouse
40      Location2D position = getMouse2D();
41      if (position != null) {
42        newton.setX(position.getX());
43      }
44
45      // (2) Translate apple down screen; velocity * time = distance
46      apple.translateY(0.33 * secondsSinceLastCall);
```

---

[11]Constant velocity is *not* how things fall in the real world; it seems that this simplification might have kept Newton from discovering gravity!

```
47
48    // (3) Check if newton has "caught" the apple
49    if (apple.intersects(newton)) {
50      applesCaught = applesCaught + 1;// another apple caught
51      displayScore.setText("Score: " + applesCaught + "/" +
52        applesDropped);
53      dropApple();
54    }
55
56    // (4) Check if the apple has hit the ground (y-coordinate >= 1.0)
57    if (apple.getY() >= 1.0) {
58      displayScore.setText("Score: " + applesCaught + "/" +
59        applesDropped);
60      dropApple();
61    }
62  }
```

Listing 4.10: NewtonsApple: Missing apple

That completes advance by updating the state of the game: the two movable sprites are moved (one only if there is a viable new location) and the two scoring conditions are checked. The score is updated if necessary and a new apple is dropped again, if necessary.

A note on "dropping a new apple": That phrase is potentially misleading. This game does something that a lot of games (and other computer programs, for that matter) do: it reuses an already created resource when that resource is no longer in use by the user. There is really only one apple in the game. When it is caught or goes splat, that exact same apple is teleported to the top of the screen and magically becomes the *new* apple. The player does not care about this (the old apple is no longer of interest) and we are not required to call **new** all of the time.

Review 4.5

(a) What Sprite method is used to determine if two sprites overlap each other?

(b) Why is it okay to recycle the apple sprite? What would we have to do if we wanted to create a new apple sprite each time it was dropped? *Where* would you put the code to construct the new apple?

4.6   Summary

For a player's choices to be meaningful, a game must have different outcomes depending on the sequence of choices the player makes. Not every choice leads to a different ending but some sequence of choices must. This requires that the rules of the game include selection as well as sequence.

Computer Program Design

Design is problem solving. Designing a computer program is not quite solving the potential user's problem, but instead describing *how* to solve that problem to a computer. The user can run the program and solve as many instances of the given problem as he or she likes.

Game design, like program design, is an indirect approach to creating something: the game designer is designing an experience, the experience the user has while playing. Yet the designer can specify only the game the user plays. Games can be thought of as having four basic elements: aesthetics, story, mechanics, and technology.

Problem-Solving Techniques

Simple problem-solving techniques can be combined together using five different methods:

- *sequence:* do things in the order they are written.

- *selection:* choose, based on some criteria, which rules to follow.

- *iteration:* do some set of rules over and over again.

- *delegation:* collect some set of rules into a named subprogram.

- *abstraction:* encapsulate rules and components together into a new type.

Java Method Headers

In Java, a named subprogram is called a *method*. A method is defined with a *header* and a body, the body containing the set of rules run when the method is called.

The four parts of a method header are

- *access level:* so far methods are defined `public`;

- *return type:* the type returned by the method or `void` if there is no type to return;

- *name:* the name of the method;

- *parameter list:* in parentheses, the collection of type/name pairs representing.

Selection

In Java, selection is done with the `if` statement. The `if` statement takes a *Boolean* expression, an expression which is either `true` or `false`. If the expression is `true`, then the body of the `if` statement is executed. If the expression is `false`, then the body of the `if` statement is skipped; if there is an `else` clause, the body of the `else` is executed.

FANG Classes and Methods

4.7 Chapter Review Exercises

Review Exercise 4.1 What Java type has values `true` and `false`?

Review Exercise 4.2 Describe the *video game loop*.
- (a) What are the three parts of the video game loop?
- (b) What *methods* does FANG permit you to override to hook into the video game loop?

Review Exercise 4.3 What is a *Boolean expression*?

Review Exercise 4.4 What is a *block*?

Review Exercise 4.5 Start with `NewtonsApple.java`. Modify the program to drop your first name rather than a red `OvalSprite`. The gameplay remains unchanged.

Review Exercise 4.6 The `if` statement is Java's version of which of the problem-solving techniques?

Java Templates

```
<accessLevel> := public |
                 protected |
                 private

<fieldDeclaration> := <accessLevel> <variableDeclaration>;
```

```
<returnType> := <typeName> |
                void

<methodName> := <identifier>

<formalParameter> := <variableDeclaration>

<formalParameterList> := [<formalParameter> [, <formalParameter>]*]

<methodDeclaration> :=
  <accessLevel> <returnType> <methodName>(<formalParameterList>)

<methodDefinition> := <methodDeclaration>
                         <block>

<block> := {
             <statement>*
           }
```

```
<thenStatement> := <statement>

<elseStatement> := <statement>

<ifStatement> := if (<booleanExpression>)
                   <thenStatement>
                 [else
                   <elseStatement>]
```

```
 <statement> := <localVariableDefinition> |
                <expression>; |
                <ifStatement> |
                <block>
```

Review Exercise 4.7

(a) How many times can the setColor line in the following code be executed? Give all possible values.

```
public void setup() {
  double x = randomDouble();
  RectangleSprite rs = new RectangleSprite(1.0, 1.0);
  if (x < 0.5) {
    rs.setColor(getColor("dark violet"));
  }
  addSprite(rs);
}
```

(b) What are the possible colors of rs in the above listing?

(c) What is the scope of the variable rs?

Review Exercise 4.8 What does null mean in Java?

Review Exercise 4.9 What can you *not* legally do with a null reference in Java?

4.8 Programming Problems

Programming Problem 4.1 It is mentioned in the chapter that NewtonsApple uses an unrealistic model of gravity.

(a) The given game uses constant velocity. What is a more realistic model of gravity?

(b) To implement constant acceleration, you would need to replace the constant screen velocity (in advance) with a variable.

 i. Define a *field* in the class called velocity with the type **double**.

 ii. In dropApple, initialize the value of velocity to 0 (screen/second).

 iii. In advance, replace the use of the constant 0.33 with the field. (Question: What would the program do if you compiled and ran it now? If you're not sure, why not try it?)

 iv. Also in advance, increment velocity by 0.16.

Programming Problem 4.2 Given that the Game class has a randomColor() method that returns a Color (the type of object expected by Sprite.setColor method)

(a) *Where* would you change the code so that each time the apple was restarted at the top of the screen, it was set to a random color?

(b) Go ahead and add the required line to the right method.

Programming Problem 4.3 Start with NewtonsApple.java.

(a) Modify the program replacing newton with a heart or another shape using three different sprites. Make sure that the whole thing moves with the mouse.

(b) Make the apple "fall" from the right side of the screen to the left side of the screen.

(c) Make the heart move vertically on the left edge of the screen.

(d) Replace the OvalSprite with an ImageSprite of your favorite animal.
This changes the meaning of the game, does it not? From discovering gravity to finding loving homes for cute little animals. This idea of *skinning* or *rebranding* a game with just a change in the graphics (and here, a rotation of the gameplay through 90 degrees) is often used for Web-based "advergaming," games designed for advertising. Ian Bogost's *Persuasive Games* [Bog07] has more on this phenomenon along with some interesting insight into what happens to the game with a new skin.

Programming Problem 4.4   Start with NewtonsApple.java. Modify the program so that instead of limiting newton to moving horizontally, newton moves with the mouse all over the screen. This is, in many ways, easier than limiting the movement to a single dimension.

Programming Problem 4.5   Design a pursuit/evasion game similar to NewtonsApple. The "apple" should begin falling above the player's square. Then, when the player moves out of line with the falling object, it should correct its trajectory by moving 0.05 screen toward the player. If the player's x-coordinate is smaller than that of the apple, the apple should subtract 0.05 from its x-coordinate in this frame. If the player's x-coordinate is greater, then the apple should add 0.05 to its x-coordinate. The player starts with five lives, losing one each time the apple hits their character on screen.

This assignment purposely did not describe what "game" is being played. Can you provide a credible *backstory* about the game to put the gameplay into an interesting context? Would the backstory be helped if you changed the name of either the item falling or the player's representation? See Bogost's *Persuasive Games* [Bog07] for more thoughts on meaningful play.

Chapter

5

Components: Names, Types, Expressions

We have examined what a game *is*: a collection of components, each with some number of attributes, and a collection of rules determining how the components interact. The combination of the components and rules also provides the player with meaningful choices that impact the outcome of the game.

In Chapter 4 we wrote our first game, a Java program that made extensive use of the sequence and selection techniques of combining problem solutions. We also started to figure out how to design programs in a top-down manner. This chapter continues using the top-down design approach, creating a game with multiple cooperating classes; it also presents more information on defining fields and local variables.

5.1 Chance in Games

Have you ever considered how many games have an element of chance in them? If you spin a spinner, throw dice, flip a coin, or shuffle cards, that is chance. Often players get the "hand they were dealt" and must use their skill to overcome any random adversity they face.

Chance, also referred to as randomness, is found in FANG in the form of random numbers. The apple in NewtonsApple was positioned with a random x-coordinate each time it began its drop down the screen. The game would have been much less fun had the apple appeared in the same spot every time.

This chapter uses FANG random numbers to model dice and implement a dice game. Historically, dice games are wagering games [Kni00]. Rather than virtual money, our game is played for a pile of virtual matchsticks.

What Do Dice *Do*?

What do dice *do*? As a component in a game, what does a die provide *to* the game? A die provides a number (the face showing) and can be made to select another number randomly (by rolling). Not as common, but a die can be placed with a given number facing up, perhaps to indicate a score.

What does a die do when viewed from a lower level of abstraction: what *state* does the die have? Just as *game* state captures the current configuration of a game, the *state* of a part of the game (or an object in a Java program) captures the current configuration of that thing. A die "contains" its current face value: this is its state. Its state can be changed by rolling. This simple view of a die lets us model one and build a game using several of them.

119

EasyDice Rules

EasyDice is a game with two six-sided (cube) dice. The player makes a wager on his "winning" the current turn and then the turn begins. The *value* of a throw of the dice is the sum of the pips on the face of the two dice. Rolling a four and a two gives the value of six to the roll.

EasyDice turns consist of wagering and rolling. A player's turn begins by placing a wager. If the player wins he collects twice his wager (coming out ahead by the amount of the wager); if he loses the turn, he loses the wager. At the end of the turn a player is either ahead or behind by his wager amount.

The player's initial roll of the dice either wins the turn immediately or sets the value rolled as the *point* for this turn. An initial value of seven or eleven wins a turn of EasyDice on the first roll. Any other value is the point for the remainder of the turn.[1]

When a turn continues with a point, the player rolls repeatedly until a seven or the point is rolled. If the turn-ending roll was the point, the player wins and collects twice his wager. If the turn ending roll was seven, the player loses the turn and forfeits his wager.

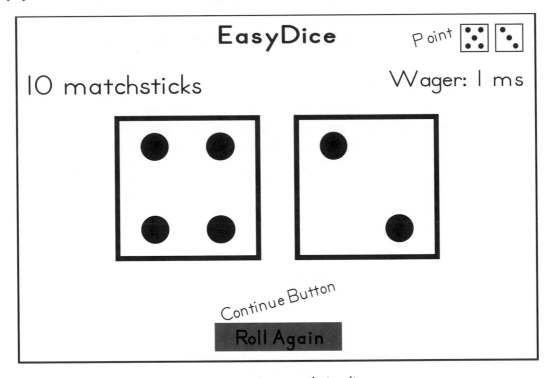

Figure 5.1: EasyDice game design diagram

In Figure 5.1 you can see a simple layout for the EasyDice: the current roll of the dice is in the middle, the point (from the first roll) is recorded on two dice in the upper-right corner of the screen, and the player continues to make rolls by pressing the "button" in the middle of the screen.

Look at the "button" that is really a rectangle and a string displayed one over the other on the screen.[2] To press the button, the player clicks within the box. The game waits for a button to be pressed by checking for a mouse click within the RectangleSprite representing the button. When the button is pressed, the state of the game is changed.

---

[1]This is the biggest simplification in EasyDice; in craps there are a number of values (two, thee, and twelve) which immediately end the turn with the player *losing* the turn. Additionally, there are a lot of different side bets possible in a real craps game.

[2]This description applies to buttons in most graphical user interfaces, too.

Easier Dice

How would you draw, using FANG sprites, the dice in Figure 5.1? A RectangleSprite of white with some number of black OvalSprite pips drawn in front of it. Given the location of one of the dice is (0.6, 0.5), where are the pips drawn? You need to know both the value on the die *and* the scale of the die. There are four dice in two different scales. The dice look dauntingly complex.

We leave dice with pips as an exercise at the end of the chapter (see Programming Problem 5.4). Instead we simplify them to show a large digit representing the face value. Figure 5.2 shows the same game state as the previous figure with the face of each die replaced with a digit representing its value.

Figure 5.2: EasyDice game design with text faces

The design of the game is done using a *public protocol*, a listing of the expected method headers. By writing our game to the protocol, converting from one type of die to the other should be painless.

Cooperating Classes: Our Own Sprites

FANG, like most software frameworks, is not an application but rather an application toolkit. It comes with low-level pieces that can be combined with some user-provided programming to make game components and games. Game components are *objects* in Java, so types of components are **class**es.

The EasyDice description implies three different types of components, three different **class**es: the game class, EasyDice, which has the rules for the whole game; the button class, EasyButton, which EasyDice can ask whether the user has clicked it or not; and the die class, OneDie.

It is tempting, given only one button and four dice, to forgo writing separate **class** files for them, and instead put the RectangleSprite and StringSprite objects on the screen in the game and manipulate them directly as NewtonsApple did.

This is wrong for two reasons: students need to see how to write their own classes — these classes are particularly simple to write — *and* putting the code directly in the game makes it almost impossible to use in a different game. What if we wanted to implement a FANG version of the game Pig from Chapter 11? We would have to position the one die on the screen by creating rectangle and oval sprites. The mixing of different levels of abstraction is not good practice.

Instead we define the *public protocol* for each of the two component classes, the list of public method headers each provides. As a proof of concept we write a demonstration program that rolls two dice over and over using just the public protocols of the die and button. We do not need to know how the dice or button classes are implemented to *use* them. Following sections use stepwise refinement to implement the classes so that the demonstration program runs.

Defining a Public Protocol

The public protocol of a class is the collection of all public methods (and fields) that it has. It catalogs all *services* that an object of that type provides as well as how to ask for the service. With a die we can think of the services as create, roll, set(n), and get. The services are to create a new die, roll the die to change its number randomly, set the number to n and get the current number on the die.

The public protocol is the *interface* between two different levels of abstraction. If we look down on OneDie from inside of EasyDice, there is no need to know *how* it works. In fact, knowing *how* it works is detrimental to staying focused on the game-level abstractions rather than the die-level abstractions. The game only needs to "know" what services are provided and how to request them.

To use OneDie in a FANG program, it needs to have, in addition to the "die" methods, methods for locating, rotating, scaling, etc.

Wait! If we *extend* a Sprite-derived **class**, we get the appearance methods for *free*. The public protocol of a class *inherits* the public protocol of the class it **extends** (and, transitively, all of the classes that class **extends** up to a class that does not extend any other class).

```
public class OneDie
    extends ...Sprite {
    // create a new die (initialize to 1?)
    public OneDie(...) ...
    // get the current state of the die
    public int getFace() ...
    // set the current state of the die
    public void setFace(int newFace) ...
    // randomly change the state of the die
    public void roll() ...
}
```

The constructor's parameter list is undetermined. The one-line comments try to make clear what each method does. These methods *are* the services provided by one die. A program *using* the die can "request" a service by calling the named method.

These four methods, all defined to be **public**, are the only visible methods in our OneDie class. Looking at the list, we have no idea how any of them work. But we don't care because we can *use* OneDie without knowing any more.

Before we can write a program that uses OneDie we need EasyButton's public protocol.

What Is a Button?

A button is a rectangle and some text; that is its *appearance*. What is a button's public protocol? A button can be constructed, it can change the text displayed on it, it can "say" whether or not it was pushed, and it can do whatever a sprite can do. The public protocol for EasyButton is

```
public class EasyButton
  extends ...Sprite {
  public EasyButton(...) ...
  public void setText(String message) ...
  public boolean isPressed() ...
```

When a button is on the screen, the game can call the isPressed method to see if the button was pressed during the current *frame* (the current iteration of the game loop). What is the *return type* of isPressed? **boolean** is the Java type for truth values, **true** and **false**. This means that isPressed is designed to be used whereever a Boolean expression is needed (as in an **if** statement). The public protocol suffices to *use* an EasyButton.

Designing with a Public Protocol: `RollDice`

We design a program using only the public protocols of OneDie and EasyButton to demonstrate that we can use them with just this information. The program RollDice displays two dice and a button. When the user presses the button, the game rolls both dice.

By our definition this is not really a game: the player *can* decide to press the button or not but the decision has no meaningful impact on the outcome of the game. It is a good demonstration of design using a class's public protocol.

```
1   // package default
2
3   import fang2.core.Game;
4
5   /**
6    * Demonstration game using OneDie and EasyButton classes: Roll two big
7    * dice every time the button saying "Roll Dice" is pressed.
8    */
9   public class RollDice
10    extends Game {
11    /** the button at the bottom of the screen */
12    private EasyButton button;
13
14    /** the left die */
15    private OneDie leftDie;
16
17    /** the right die */
18    private OneDie rightDie;
19
20    /**
21     * Advance the game one frame.
22     *
23     * @param  secondsSinceLastCall  time since last advance
24     */
25    @Override
26    public void advance(double secondsSinceLastCall) {
27      if (button.isPressed()) {
28        leftDie.roll();
29        rightDie.roll();
30      }
```

```
31      }
32
33      /**
34       * Set up the game for play. Initializes all of the sprites (either
35       * here or in other setup functions).
36       */
37      @Override
38      public void setup() {
39        button = new EasyButton();
40        button.setScale(0.5);
41        button.setLocation(0.5, 0.85);
42        button.setColor(getColor("yellow"));
43        button.setTextColor(getColor("navy"));
44        addSprite(button);
45
46        button.setText("Roll Dice");
47
48        leftDie = new OneDie();
49        leftDie.setScale(0.33);
50        leftDie.setLocation(5.0 / 18.0, 0.5);
51        addSprite(leftDie);
52
53        rightDie = new OneDie();
54        rightDie.setScale(0.33);
55        rightDie.setLocation(13.0 / 18.0, 0.5);
56        addSprite(rightDie);
57      }
58    }
```

Listing 5.1: RollDice demonstration program

Lines 11–17 define three *fields*, variables belonging to the whole game. This means that they are in scope (visible) in all methods in the class. Unlike FANG classes, these two classes have no **import** statements.

Java looks for named classes either in the classpath (as we saw in the examples in previous chapters) or, if there is no **import** statement, it looks in the current directory. As long as OneDie and EasyButton are defined in the same directory as RollDice, **import** statements are unnecessary. Java can do this because the class name, the .java file, and the compiled .class file all have the same name.

Lines 38–57 are setup; setup runs before advance but sorts after advance in sorted source code. The parameter lists for the OneDie and EasyButton classes are empty. The remainder of setup matches what we have done before: location, color, and scale setting and adding sprites to the game. Line 43 is new: what is the setTextColor method of EasyButton?

A button is composed of two different visual elements: the rectangle and the text. If programmers can customize colors of some constituent part, they want to customize *any* constituent part. EasyButton uses setColor to set the color of the rectangle and adds the setTextColor to permit setting the color of the text.

These two methods, neither provided in the way we want them by any Sprite-extending class, are not part of the public protocol above. This is typical: the first program using a public protocol demonstrates just what is *missing* from the class. It is good to find this out before investing in implementing an entire new class.

Lines 26–31, advance, checks if the button is pressed. Using an **if** inside, advance calls it over and over, every frame. For any frame where the button was clicked, each die is rolled. The short, easy-to-understand advance provides confidence that the public protocols designed above are right.[3] We were able to focus on the higher level of abstraction without worrying about the details of the objects we used.

Now, to a lower level of abstraction: it is time to implement EasyButton. The immediate problem is that we need to combine two sprites, the rectangle and the string, into a single sprite.

Review 5.1

(a) What is a *public protocol*

(b) Why is it possible to write a solution using a `class` only knowing its public protocol?

(c) Name three *different* services (i.e., ones not named for other classes) provided by each of the following classes:

   (a) StringSprite

   (b) Game

   (c) OvalSprite

   (d) OneDie

   (e) EasyButton

(d) Is there an argument to be made for naming setColor for EasyButton anything other than setColor? Could the use of setColor be confusing for programmers using the class?

(e) What is the **double** parameter to advance? What values would you expect it to have?

(f) Without changing any pips *location*, just making them visible or invisible, how few pips could you use to display all of the possible faces on a regular 6-sided die?

(g) Before you launch into writing a program, it is important to thoroughly understand the problem. This section describes the game EasyDice. Here are some questions to make sure you understand the rules.

   (a) What first roll would cause the player to lose immediately?

   (b) Assume the player wagers 3 match sticks and rolls the following numbers: 4, 8, 12.

      i. What number on the next roll would cause the player to win 6 match sticks (the originally wagered 3 and 3 more)?

      ii. What number on the next roll would cause the player to lose the originally wagered 3 match sticks?

(h) Only very simple programs are written in a single class. Most classes use other classes. For example, NetwonsApple used the OvalSprite class, which is part of the FANG Engine. Some classes such as NewtonsApple are meant to run on their own, and others like OvalSprite are *helper* classes. Helper classes are not meant to run on their own, but instead their purpose is to help other classes.

This section describes three classes: OneDie, EasyButton, and RollDice. Which ones are helper classes? Which class do you run? Hint: the one that you run extends Game.

(i) What would happen if you left out the advance method of RollDice?

5.2 One More Sprite: `CompositeSprite`

FANG permits the *composition* of multiple sprites together into a single sprite. If you have experience working with vector drawing programs[4] and have used the **Group Objects** command, you have some idea what this is like.

A CompositeSprite is a sprite that behaves as if it has its own screen. addSprite in a CompositeSprite adds the sprite to the composite. When the composite is scaled, moved, or rotated, all component sprites are automatically scaled, moved, or rotated according to their position in the composite.

---

[3]It is a truism in computer science (and the rest of the world) that there is more than one way to do anything. There are alternative designs for the public protocols of dice and buttons that would also be "right." We are confident that our design works well with FANG.

[4]*Inkscape, Adobe Illustrator*, etc.

A Screen within a Screen

A `CompositeSprite` is almost identical to the screen you see. Other sprites can be added to it. The center of the composite (the location of the composite) is (0.0, 0.0) *inside* the composite sprite. You set the location of objects in the composite relative to this point. You can then set the location of the whole composite relative to the game screen.

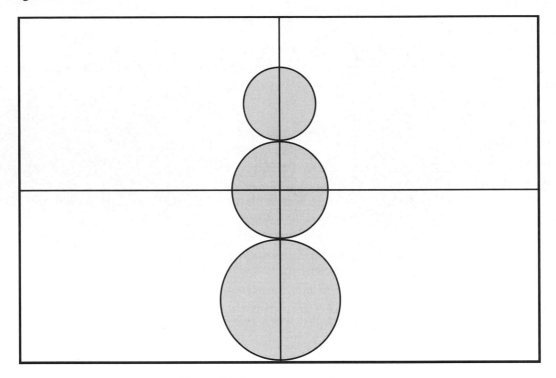

Figure 5.3: Snowman `CompositeSprite`

Figure 5.3 shows the design of a snowman `CompositeSprite`. The x-axis and the y-axis are shown in the drawing along with three `OvalSprites`. The important thing to note is that the positions of the three "snowballs" are along the y-axis, spaced out so that they are just touching.

```
1   // package default
2
3   import fang2.core.Game;
4   import fang2.sprites.CompositeSprite;
5   import fang2.sprites.OvalSprite;
6
7   // FANG Demonstration program: CompositeSprite
8   public class Snowman
9     extends Game {
10    private CompositeSprite redSnowman;
11
12    // spin the snowman about 4 times a minute; see how everything
13    // moves relative to (0.0, 0.0) ON the snowman; 24 degrees/second
14    @Override
```

```
15   public void advance(double secondsSinceLastCall) {
16     redSnowman.rotateDegrees(24.0 * secondsSinceLastCall);
17   }
18
19   // add three circles to snowman, add snowman to scene
20   @Override
21   public void setup() {
22     redSnowman = new CompositeSprite();
23
24     OvalSprite head = new OvalSprite(0.3, 0.3);
25     head.setColor(getColor("SCG Red"));
26     head.setLocation(0, -0.25);
27     redSnowman.addSprite(head);
28
29     OvalSprite middle = new OvalSprite(0.4, 0.4);
30     middle.setColor(getColor("SCG Red"));
31     middle.setLocation(0.0, 0.0);
32     redSnowman.addSprite(middle);
33
34     OvalSprite bottom = new OvalSprite(0.5, 0.5);
35     bottom.setColor(getColor("SCG Red"));
36     bottom.setLocation(0, 0.35);
37     redSnowman.addSprite(bottom);
38
39     // snowman scaled and placed off center on screen
40     redSnowman.setLocation(0.67, 0.67);
41     redSnowman.setScale(0.50);
42     addSprite(redSnowman);
43   }
44 }
```

Listing 5.2: Snowman demonstration program

The Snowman program is a demonstration program in the flavor of those presented in Chapter 3: light on comments, short, and complete. Notice that in setup addSprite is called four times: three times on redSnowman and once on the game (with redSnowman as the parameter). The locations of the three snowballs are inside the CompositeSprite.

To demonstrate that the three OvalSprites are treated as a single unit, the program rotates the snowman about four times a minute. The screenshot for this program is of a slightly modified version of the program, one which adds white lines as the x and y axes of the CompositeSprite. This is so you can easily spot the center of the snowman.

To show how the two different coordinate systems interact, Figure 5.5 shows the Snowman program before pressing **Start**. The CompositeSprite snowman was positioned at (0.67, 0.67) and scaled to 0.50. The axes in the drawing are at the snowman's origin. The white coordinates labeling the head and bottom of the snowman are the coordinates of the centers of the circles *inside the snowman's coordinate system*. Whenever a sprite is added to a CompositeSprite, the location is relative to the origin of the CompositeSprite.

The red coordinates are the coordinates *in the screen coordinate system* of the center of each of the snowballs. The call-out dimension shows the diameter of the middle snowball *in screen units*. Looking at the code, we see that line 29 constructs middle with a size of (0.4, 0.4). Because redSnowman was scaled to 0.50, the size of everything *inside* the composite sprite measured with units from *outside* the composite sprite are halved.

Figure 5.4: Running AxisSnowman

That explains the coordinate of the head in screen coordinates: 0.67 y on the screen is 0.00 y on the sprite. -0.35 y on the sprite is 0.67 + (-0.35 * 0.50) or distance times scale. The result is 0.495, the y-coordinate of the head in screen coordinates.

Think, for a second, what the *screen* y-coordinate of head is when the redSnowman has rotated 25 degrees. Now stop thinking about that and be happy to use CompositeSprite.

Button, Button, Defining a Button

As demonstrated above, it is possible to define a CompositeSprite on the fly, in the setup method of a Game extending class. This is useful if you have need of exactly one of some kind of grouped sprite and its only state is visual (e.g., location, scale, rotation).

When using multiple snowmen *or* if the snowman should keep additional information it is better to extend CompositeSprite. Demonstrating the snowman is the one time we build a CompositeSprite directly from a Game. It is better to extend CompositeSprite and build the composite sprite in the constructor of the new sprite.

Doing this for the snowman is left as an exercise for the reader. The next section begins implementation of the EasyButton class.

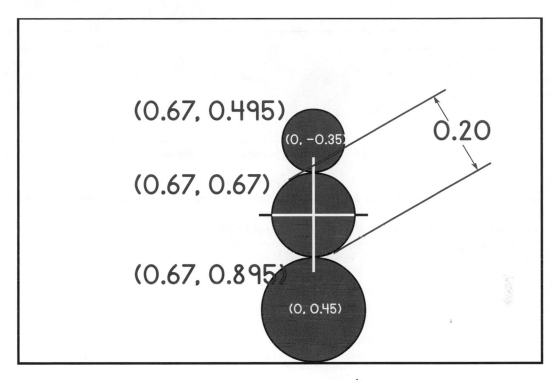

Figure 5.5: Snowman CompositeSprite coordinate systems

Writing a Constructor

A method header has four parts: access level, return type, name, and, in parentheses, the formal parameter list. The header is followed by a block containing the statements that are the body of the defined method. A *constructor* breaks this rule of four for method headers: it has no return type. Further, the name of a constructor is the same as the name of the class. The header of a constructor is

```
<className> := <identifier>


<formalParameter> := <typeName> <variableName>


<formalParameterList> := [<formalParameter> [, <formalParameter>]*]


<constructorDeclaration> :=
    <access-level> <class-name>(<formalParameterList>)


<constructorDefinition> := <constructorDeclaration>
                              <block>
```

(The first three templates are duplicated from previous chapters to make this template easier to read.)

That the constructor name must match the **class** name makes sense if you think about how **new** is used with the name of the class to be created. It looks like a method call, and now we know, that it *is* a method call, a call to the constructor method. The constructor's job is to initialize the fields within the object, to set everything up so that the class is ready for use. Listing 5.1, line 39 shows the initialization of button:

```
39    button = new EasyButton();
40    button.setScale(0.5);
41    button.setLocation(0.5, 0.85);
42    button.setColor(getColor("yellow"));
43    button.setTextColor(getColor("navy"));
44    addSprite(button);
```

Listing 5.3: RollDice demonstration program

After **new** is a call to the constructor. It names the type that is being constructed. The second requirement, that there is no return type, is strange until you realize that a constructor is initializing the type for which it is named.

Listing 5.4 shows the first portion of the EasyButton definition.

```
12  public class EasyButton
13    extends CompositeSprite {
14    /** the button at the bottom of the screen */
15    private final RectangleSprite button;
16
17    /** text displayed, centered, on the button */
18    private final StringSprite buttonMessage;
19
20    /**
21     * Construct new button. Horizontal, FANGBlue with same color text.
22     */
23    public EasyButton() {
24      button = new RectangleSprite(1.0, 0.5);
25      addSprite(button);
26      buttonMessage = new StringSprite();
27      addSprite(buttonMessage);
28    }
```

Listing 5.4: EasyButton: definition and constructor

This **class extends** CompositeSprite. It inherits the *public protocol* of a sprite plus the public protocol of a composite sprite (e.g., addSprite). The two fields, button and buttonMessage, refer to the RectangleSprite and the StringSprite after they are created. Fields referring to those sprites are necessary to implement the setColor, setTextColor, and setText methods.

Fields are **private** because they are *not* part of the public protocol of the class. They are not part of the public protocol because we want to control what other objects can do to the sprites *inside* the button. Rotating the whole button makes sense (it is a sprite); rotating the *text* and only the text inside the button does not make sense.

The constructor, lines 23–28, constructs two sprites, a rectangle and a text string. Both are positioned at (0.0, 0.0) *inside* the CompositeSprite and then they are both added using addSprite. Remember the layering order of sprites; the layering order inside a CompositeSprite is the same as it is in a regular screen, so the rectangle is added before the text.

On the screen, all sprites *in* the CompositeSprite are drawn between the sprite just below and the sprite just above the composite. This means that the button stacks, as a whole, on the screen as you probably expect.

Internally it makes sense to set the largest dimension of the CompositeSprite to 1.0 so that the locations run from (-0.5, 0.5). Doing this means that whatever value scaling is put on the CompositeSprite, in the longest dimension, that is the size the sprite has on the screen. So, the background of the button is 1.0 wide by 0.5 high. Set the width of an EasyButton to 0.33, and the width of the rectangle, on the screen, is 0.33.

What does addSprite with nothing in front of it mean? In setup of Snowman it was redSnowman.addSprite. What is the difference? In setup, calling addSprite alone adds the sprite to the current object, an instance of the Game-derived Snowman class. The sprite would be added to the screen, not the composite.

Similarly, just addSprite in EasyButton adds the sprite to the current object, an instance of the CompositeSprite-derived EasyButton class rather than to any screen. Line 44 of Listing 5.1 adds a new EasyButton to the game.

Modifying State and Overriding Methods

EasyButton *is* a CompositeSprite in the same way that a ham sandwich *is* a sandwich. Anything you can do with a generic sandwich you can do with the more specialized **ham** sandwich. Of course, there are things you can do with a ham sandwich, such as get the ham, which are not possible for arbitrary sandwiches.

While it is possible to setColor on any Sprite or Sprite-derived class, only EasyButton supports setTextColor. Jumping to the end of EasyButton.java, Listing 5.5 shows the set... methods for EasyButton.

```java
47  /**
48   * Set the color of the background rectangle
49   *
50   * @param  color  the color to set the rectangle to.
51   */
52  @Override
53  public void setColor(Color color) {
54    button.setColor(color);
55  }
56
57  /**
58   * Set text message; resize to fit in one line
59   *
60   * @param  message  the new message for the button to display
61   */
62  public void setText(String message) {
63    buttonMessage.setText(message);
64    // adjust size of text message to fit on the button
65    buttonMessage.setWidth(0.75);
66  }
67
68  /**
69   * Set the color of the text on the button.
70   *
71   * @param  color  the color to set the text to
72   */
73  public void setTextColor(Color color) {
74    buttonMessage.setColor(color);
75  }
```

Listing 5.5: EasyButton: set methods

Lines 62–66, the setText method, uses the identically named method of StringSprite. The String parameter (a type for holding sequences of characters) is passed directly to buttonMessage's setText method. The scale of the message is reset so that its width fits in the middle 75% of the displayed button.

A CompositeSprite is also a Sprite, so it has a setColor method. The version defined for Sprite does not set the color of any elements in a CompositeSprite. We must *override* setColor with a new version in EasyButton.

Lines 53–55 provides a version of setColor with the same header as the one defined in a parent class. The @Override on line 52 is called an *annotation*. An annotation can be thought of as a specialized type of comment, a comment that is processed by the compiler.

As a comment, line 52 tells the programmer that this is a specialized version of setColor, replacing the version provided above in CompositeSprite (or, if there is none at that level, the one in Sprite).

The compiler reads the annotation and, for @Override, it makes sure that there *is* a method higher up in the class hierarchy to be overridden. If there is no such method, the @Override annotation throws an error.[5]

The local setColor method sets the color of the rectangle to the Color parameter passed into it. This is similar to the setText method above as it forwards the work to the appropriate sprite within the composite. The Color type is a Java-defined type; importing java.awt.Color is necessary so that this method compiles.

Lines 73–75 are almost identical to setColor except that they set the color of the StringSprite within the composite. Notice that this method does *not* override another, identically named method. The parameter passed to setTextColor is forwarded to the setColor method of the buttonMessage field. These two color-setting methods show why we kept references to the two sprites in the composite.

Game.getCurrentGame()

The only remaining method in EasyButton's public protocol is isPressed. isPressed returns **true** if a mouse button was pressed during this frame and the mouse was inside the button when it was clicked; it returns **false** otherwise. How can we determine where the mouse is and whether or not it was clicked?

Looking back at NewtonsApple, we see that the getMouse2D method provides the Location2D object where the mouse was during a given frame. Since we did not define it and it is not called with a variable and a dot, the method must be defined in Game, and we get it for "free" when we extend Game.

Keep in mind that getMouse2D returns **null** when there is no valid mouse location. **null** is a special value meaning "no object."

```
35   public boolean isPressed() {
36     // The current game may have a mouse click or not.
37     Location2D mouseClick =
38       Game.getCurrentGame().getClick2D();
39     if (mouseClick != null) {
40       if (intersects(mouseClick)) {
41         return true;
42       }
43     }
44     return false;
45   }
```

Listing 5.6: EasyButton: isPressed

Section 3.3 explained how to use *JavaDoc* documentation to examine the classes and public methods provided by FANG and Java. The Game class supplies several mouse checking methods.

In addition to getMouse2D which returns the location where the mouse is every frame (if it is within the game window), there is also getClick2D which returns the location where the mouse was *clicked* during any frame *during which it was clicked*. Just like getMouse2D, clickMouse2D returns a Location2D. The important methods in Location2D are getX and getY which get the x-coordinate and y-coordinate of the location.

---

[5]There are other annotations available; they can be recognized by the @ symbol starting their name. They are beyond the scope of a beginning book.

If the player clicked any mouse button since the last call to advance, Game.getClick2D() returns the location of the mouse click in screen coordinates. If the player hasn't clicked any mouse button *or* the mouse is not in the window at all, this method returns . . . . Any guess as to what it returns if there is no location where a click took place?

It returns `null` to indicate that there is no mouse click available. isPressed starts by calling getClick2D and testing (using selection) whether the value is `null`.

There is a problem. getClick2D is not defined in the Sprite-derived classes but rather in Game. How can an EasyButton get a reference to the current game? If we could get the current game, we could use a dot and getClick2D to call the method.

The Game class provides a utility method called getCurrentGame, which takes no parameters and returns a reference to the currently running game. We can call getClick2D on that reference.

Lines 37–38 do just that, assigning the result to the local variable mouseClick. Sprites use Game.getCurrentGame() to access game services such as getting random numbers and getting user input.

isPressed must return a `boolean` value in order to compile. Lines 41 and 44, only one of which is executed on any call to isPressed, use the `return` statement to do this. The Java template for `return` is

```
<returnStatement> := return <expression>;
```

Here the expression after codereturn is evaluated and that value is returned as the result of the method. isPressed returns `true` if the mouse was clicked (mouseClick != null) *and*, if the mouse was pressed, the mouse click location intersects the button (the button was clicked *on*). In addition to being able to test for intersection between two sprites, we can test for intersection of a location with a sprite. intersects(mouseClick) in line 71 is a Boolean method returning `true` if the click is inside the CompositeSprite. The click and the sprite's boundaries are in *screen* coordinates (you must change the location to internal coordinates if you want to test intersection with subsprites; see CompositeSprite documentation for details).

When Java executes `return`, the expression is evaluated and the execution of the method returns control to the calling method (no other lines in the called (returning) method are executed). If line 41 executes, line 44 cannot execute until ifPressed is called again.

There is no need to use an `else` in this case. The routine is a couple of lines shorter but still clear. Only if *both* `if` statement conditions are `true` does the method return `true`. If either is false, the method executes line 44 and returns `false`.

void methods and return   If a method is of type `void`, return has the form

```
<returnStatement> := return <expression>; |
                     return;
```

This is because there is no expression of type `void`. All that happens when this `return` statement is run is that the method immediately returns control to the caller. No value is ever returned from a `void` method.

Review 5.2

(a) In *sprite coordinates* what are the x- and y-coordinates of a CompositeSprite?

(b) What is a *constructor*?

(c) How is a constructor's method header different from that of any other method?

(d) Which line(s) in Listing 5.4 calls the EasyButton constructor? How do you know it is calling a constructor?

(e) Which line(s) in Listing 5.1 defines the EasyButton constructor called in the previous question?

(f) What is wrong with the following statement?

```
OvalSprite ovalSprite1 = new OvalSprite("Loopy");
```

(Hint: You may need to consult the documentation for OvalSprite.)

5.3   Java Types

In a game, every component has a type. The type of the component determines what rules apply to that component. In chess, for example, a queen is one type of component, a king is another type of component. In addition to a type, components also have state. Game state is the complete configuration of the game; by analogy, the state of any component is its subset of the game state. A queen has color, a starting square, and a current square.

To move your queen, you need to be able to find her. The rules are defined for the type, the state is defined for an instance of the type (the black queen and the white queen follow the same rules but are not the same piece), and, in order to use a piece, you must be able to refer to it in some way. Playing chess in the dark, it might be impossible to find your queen after moving her once. You know she is out there but she is useless unless you can refer to her.

Note that it is possible to describe what a queen can do without actually having any actual, physical queen piece. All of this discussion applies, by analogy, to objects in Java programs.

In Java, every object has a *type*. A type defines a list of rules and state that each *instance* of the type (or *object* of the `class`) has. The public protocol determines what outsiders can ask objects of the class to do.

The state, typically `private`, is kept in `fields` and is available to the methods. The value in a field is specific to one instance of the type. In order to call methods on an object, we must be able to find it. A *reference* is a way of finding an object. A reference is a name that labels or refers to the object.

The type of an object determines *what* we can ask it to do; a reference to an object determines *how* we can ask it to do something.

A *variable*, which can be a local variable, a field, or a formal parameter, is defined with a type and a name. The definition sets aside a *memory box*, some space in memory to hold some value. What gets stored in the memory box depends on the type of the variable. Java has the context for interpreting the contents of the memory box because of the variable definition. To avoid awkward phrasing, the rest of this section uses *variable* generically for any identifier defined with a type.

The remainder of this section discusses what all variables have in common and then covers the two different types of types in Java, *classes* and *plain old data*.

Variables and Fields

Variables have types.   A variable is defined with a type name just before it. The type of a variable determines what kinds of values can be stored in it.

Variables must be initialized.   A variable has no particular value when defined. It receives a value through *assignment*. An *assignment statement* has the template:

```
<assignment-statement> := <variable-name> = <expression>;
```

The `<expression>` is evaluated for a value and that value is placed in the memory box associated with the `<variable-name>`. The previous value stored in the memory box is lost as soon as the new value is stored there. The types of the variable and the expression must be compatible; more on compatible types in Section 5.4.

The Java compiler is acutely aware of uninitialized local variables. Using one triggers a compiler error as in the following code:

```java
public boolean isPressed() {
  // The current game may have a mouse click or not.
  Location2D mouseClick;
  // vvvvv Compiler Error vvvvv
  if (mouseClick.getX())
  // ^^^^^ Compiler Error ^^^^^
}
```

Java determines that between the definition of the local variable `mouseClick` and `getX` call using `mouseClick`. (read as "mouseClick (dot)"), there is no way `mouseClick` was given a value. The Java compiler protects you from this kind of error. It cannot always do this: fields and parameters cannot be tracked like this.

Variables have scope.   In Java every variable is defined inside a block. Formal parameters are considered to be defined within the body of the method they are part of. The range of the program where the variable is visible, the variable's *scope*, is determined by the block within which it is defined. Local variables are in scope from the line where they are defined until the end of the enclosing scope.

Formal parameters are in scope for the entire body of the method where they are defined. Fields are in scope for the *entire* class block in which they are defined. This includes *before* the line where they are defined.

It is possible to write your classes with all fields defined at the very end. The argument in favor of writing classes that way is that you can put all of the public protocol methods at the top of the `.java` file, and users of the class can stop reading before they look at the fields. Code for this text is meant to be studied, so the implementation details are important. The authors come from a time when languages had a strict define before using rule and they're just more comfortable with what they know.

The next two sections look at the two types of types in Java.

Classes

A *class* is a type defined in a `.java` file using the **class** keyword. By convention, class names begin with a capital letter so that they are easy to recognize. An *instance* of a class or an *object* of the class type is *constructed* using the **new** operator and the name of a constructor for the class.

Class variables are *references*.   A variable of a class type (remember the capital letter at the beginning) refers to the actual object rather than containing the actual object. What does this mean?

- To get a reference to a new object in memory requires a call to **new**.

- A class variable may refer to no object at all: **null**.

- A class variable may refer to, at most, one object in memory at a time.

- What object a variable refers to can be changed through assignment.

- More than one label can refer to the same underlying object in memory.

- A reference can be used, with the dot operator, to call a method on the object referred to (or, if it has public fields, to manipulate the fields). A **null** reference should never be used this way.

Imagine a Java object is a car. The **class** definition is the blueprint for building the car and calling **new** orders a new car. As with **new** in Java, if we wanted to refer to the car returned, we would need some label. One convenient label would be a license plate; you could assign the car to a given license plate and then refer to it through the license plate from then on. Note that, while against the law, our analogy permits an arbitrary number of license plates per vehicle.

In Section 3.1 we saw that the computer's RAM can be considered a long sequence of memory locations, each with its own address. Further, in that section and those surrounding it, we saw that the meaning of contents of memory depend on the type of value encoded into that memory location. This is important here because defining a variable associates the variable with a specific memory location *and* determines the type of value encoded into a memory location.

The boxes in memory can contain only one value at a time. Whenever a value is assigned into a memory location, whatever was in the location previously is destroyed. When a memory location holds a reference to an object, assigning a different reference to the variable (storing the reference in the memory location associated with the variable's name) *destroys* the previous reference but it does nothing to the object referred to.

With the license plate analogy, a license plate refers to, at most, one car at a time, and changing the car which the license plate labels removes any connection between the license plate and its previously associated car.

Assignment of an object to an object variable causes the assigned variable to refer to the assigned object. The variable is a *memory box*, a space in memory that can hold a reference to an object somewhere else in memory.

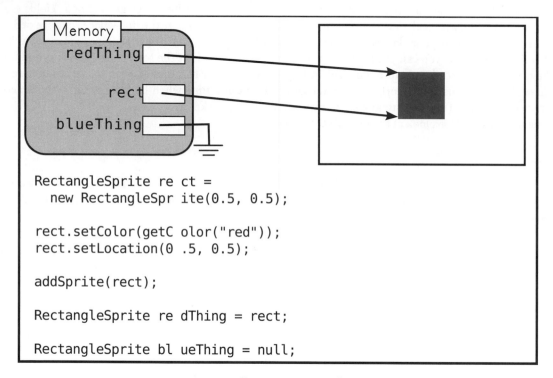

```
RectangleSprite re ct =
  new RectangleSpr ite(0.5, 0.5);

rect.setColor(getC olor("red"));
rect.setLocation(0 .5, 0.5);

addSprite(rect);

RectangleSprite re dThing = rect;

RectangleSprite bl ueThing = null;
```

Figure 5.6: Illustrating Java references

Figure 5.6 illustrates how object variables work. The area labeled "Memory"[6] has boxes that can hold values. The boxes are not drawn next to each other because that is not something we need to know. We just need three boxes, one labeled for each `RectangleSprite`.

Both `rect` and `redThing` refer to the same rectangle, the one in the center of the screen. `blueThing` refers to no object at all or `null`. The `null` reference is pictured as the electrical *ground* symbol, indicating that there is nothing referred to.

Given the situation in the figure, what would change if the following line were executed?

```
redThing.setLocation(0.25, 0.25);
```

The rectangle would be moved from the center of the screen to the upper-left corner of the screen. Note that either of the references to the rectangle could have been used to move it.

What is the value of x after the following code snippet executes?

---

[6]The handwriting font is used for the label to remind us that this is something like how it really works, but this is a high-level, human view of memory. The model is good enough to use until a computer organization or architecture course is taken.

```
rect.setLocation(0.60, 0.90);
double x = redThing.getX();
```

The first line moves the rectangle again, down and to the right, and the second queries the x-coordinate of the rectangle. Since redThing refers to the rectangle that was moved (with setLocation) to the point (0.60, 0.90), x is assigned the value of 0.60.

Plain Old Data

Not everything in Java is an object;[7] some types are so simple that Java provides facilities to manipulate them directly without putting them into an object. These simple types, *plain old data*, are not instantiated, have no null value, do not share underlying values, and cannot be used to call methods.

Plain old data (POD) types are type names that begin with lowercase letters: **int, double, boolean**.[8] A POD variable *always* has a value. You cannot always figure out what value it has from reading the source code but it always has a value.

plain old data variables hold values. Class variables are labels and assignment does not copy the object; it just makes a new reference to the same object. POD values are copied on assignment because they do not refer to anything: they *are* the thing.

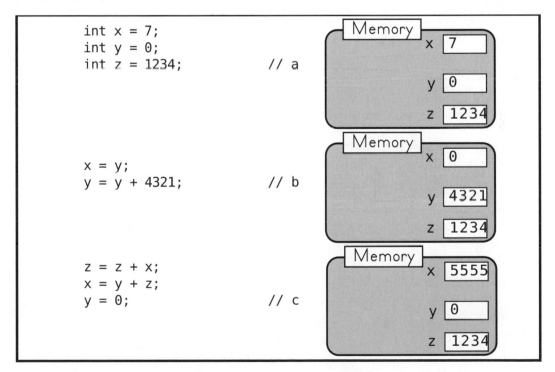

Figure 5.7: Illustrating POD variables

---

[7]This is not true of all object-oriented languages. In Squeak, for example, everything is an object from the number 9 to the character 'Q' to the mathematical constant *Pi*. Java is a hybrid language with both objects and primitive types. Primitive data types improve both the speed and the size of computer programs.

[8]And a handful of others including **char** for printable characters.

Figure 5.7 illustrates how POD variables work: when they are assigned a value, the value itself is stored in the "memory box" to which the variable refers. The interpretation of the memory box depends on the type as always. In the **(a)** diagram of memory, all three variables, x, y, and z, have been given values.

In the code for **(b)**, x is assigned y. This means that the value stored in the memory box of y is copied and replaces the value in x. The value in the box y is then added to 4321 yielding 4321. That value is then put into y, replacing the value that was there.

This is different than what we saw with rect and redObject in the previous section: when the referenced value was manipulated through either value, because they shared an underlying object somewhere in memory, both variables "saw" the change.

Here, as soon as y's value of 0 is copied into x, there is no longer any association between y and x. No matter what happens to *either* of them, the other cannot reflect the change.

Finally, after the last three lines are executed, the values shown in part **(c)** end up in the variables.

The biggest thing to remember (and the Java compiler reminds you) is that you cannot call methods using POD variables. The dot operator, called the *dereferencing* operator, takes a reference on the left and an accessible field or method on the right and makes the call (or gets the field). Since POD variables are not references and there are no methods or fields defined for them, the dot operator does not work with POD variables.

Review 5.3

(a) What is *scope*?

(b) How can you determine whether a variable names a local variable or a field?

(c) How can you determine whether an identifier names a class or an object?

(d) If the value stored in a variable is shared among multiple methods, say setup and advance, should the variable be defined local or as a field?

5.4 Calculating with the Computer

An *expression* is a piece of code that returns a value. Examples we have seen include
`new RectangleSprite(0.10, 0.10)`,
`applesCaught + 1`, and
`apple.getY() > 1.0`. Like variables, expressions have types. The type of an expression determines what you can do with it. If the type of the expression is a class type, it is a reference to an object and can be used to call a method. If the expression is a POD type, then it can be used to assign to (or pass into) a compatible variable (or parameter).

The Java template for an expression is

```
<op> := + | - | * | / | \% |
        == | != | < | <= | >= | > |
        \&\& | '||' |
        =


<post-op> := ++ | --


<pre-op> := ++ | -- |
            + | - |
            !


<methodCall> := [<object>.]<methodName>(<actualParameterList>)
```

```
<expression> := <literal> |
                new <typeName>(<actualParameterList>) |
                <methodCall> |
                <expression> <op> <expression> |
                <expression> <post-op> |
                <pre-op> <expression> |
                (<expression>)
                <methodCall>
```

Literals   Literal values are values literally typed into the text of the program. Examples include 1.0, **true**, 12, "Hello, World!", and **null**. All literal values *except* for strings and **null** have POD types. 1.0 is **double**, **true** is **boolean**, and 12 is of type **int**.

The value "Hello, World!" is of type String, the only class type value that can appear literally in a program. **null** is a literal meaning "no such object" and can be assigned to any class type variable.

Variables   A variable is an expression. When it appears in an expression, the value stored in the variable is used in the expression. When a variable appears alone on the right-hand side of an assignment, the value stored is copied to the variable on the right-hand side.

A variable has its defined type in an expression.

new   As we have said before, the **new** operator followed by a call to a constructor (the name of the class and the actual parameter list) creates space for an instance of the class and calls the constructor to initialize the space.

The expression has the type of the object constructed and returns a reference to that object.

Unary and Binary Operations   Java has unary and binary operators. Different operators have different types and expect different types of subexpressions. Note that in the template the template operator | is also part of a Java operator, '||'. The primes around the vertical bar indicate that the value inside the primes is the <op>.

Arithmetic Operators   The first line of operators is arithmetic operators. Java supports the standard four calculator operators plus one more.[9]

The four include + for addition, - for subtraction, * for multiplication, and / for division. Prefixing - changes the sign of the following expression and prefixing +, while legal, has no effect. The following example expressions are followed by their type and value in a comment:

```
1 + 4              // (a) int,     5
12 - 100           // (b) int,    -88
1.3 + 7            // (c) double,  8.3
1.0 + 4.0          // (d) double,  5.0
3 * 5              // (e) int,     15
3 + 2 * 3          // (f) int,     9
5.0 / 2.0          // (g) double,  2.5
5 / 2              // (h) int,     2
```

[9]As well as several designed for operating at the bit level. Not all operators supported by Java are in this list.

If both operands (the subexpressions on either side of the operator) are `int`, then the result is `int`. If either operand is `double`, then the type of the expression is `double`. Notice (c) were the `int` is *widened* into a `double` and then added to the `double`[10] (h) sometimes surprises students. Because both subexpressions are `int`, the division is done as `int` division: 2 goes into 5 2 times with some remainder.

Example (f) above is 9, *not* 15 because of the *precedence* of operators, the rules that govern the order of application of operations in a complex expression. As was the case in math class, multiplication and division operators have higher precedence than addition operators. 3 + 2 * 3 is evaluated as if it were 3 + (2 * 3), *not* (3 + 2) * 3. The programmer can use parentheses (as in the explanation) to change the order of operators; subexpressions in parentheses are evaluated before applying the operator that the parentheses are an operand for.

Could we get the remainder in that last expression? The `%` operator is the *modulus* operator. Given two `int` subexpressions, it returns the *remainder* when dividing the first number by the second: 5 % 2 is 1 and 19 % 7 evaluates to 5.

Prefix operators: + and - can appear *before* an arithmetic expression, too. + means the sign of the expression remains unchanged, and - means that the sign of the expression is inverted.

Increment and decrement operators: ++ and - - are operators that have *side-effects* on the variable to which they are applied. Each comes in a prefix (written before the variable) and a postfix (written after the variable) version.

The side-effect on the variable is the same whether the operator is pre- or postfixed: `<integerVariableName>++` adds 1 to the named variable as does `++<integerVariablename>`. Similarly, `<integerVariableName>--` and `--<integerVariablename>` each subtract 1 from the value stored in the variable.

The difference between pre- and postfix versions is in the value they return. The prefix version of the operator *preincrements* (or *predecrements*) the variable, returning the value *after* the change. The postfix version of each operator *postincrements* (or postdecrements) the variable, returning the value the variable had *before* the operator was applied (before the value is changed).

```
int a = 0;
int b = a;    // just copy a: a = 0, b = 0
int c = ++a; // preincrement: a = a + 1, then c = a: a = 1, c = 1
int d = a++; // postincrement: d = a, then a = a + 1: a = 2, d = 1
--b;          // no assignment so b = b - 1 = -1 (pre/post does not matter)
b--;          // b = b - 1 = -2 (was -1 after previous statement)

int e = ++a + b++ + --c + d--;
// a = 3    3 : pre
// b = -2      -3 : post
// c = 0            0 : pre
// d = 0                 1 : post
// e =     3 + -3 +   0 + 1 = 1
```

The comments explain how the values change. This book prefers the preincrement or predecrement form and always calls them for the side-effect. Mixing ++ or - - in more complex arithmetic expressions is never worth the confusion. Avoid mixing them with assignment or any other complex expression.

Comparison Operators   The next row contains the six comparison operators. They work for POD types and return a `boolean` value depending on the comparison. The first two, "is equal to" and "is not equal to", that is, == and !=, *can* be used to compare class types. They compare the two references: if two class variables a and

---

[10]Numeric types with bigger ranges are considered "wider" than types with smaller ranges. It is always safe to widen a numeric value; it is not always safe to narrow one, so Java never does it automatically.

b refer to exactly the same object then a == b is **true**; if they refer to two different objects which are supposed to have the same value (say, two different String objects each containing the character sequence "Nicholas"), because they are different objects, a == b is **false**.

Boolean Operators   Boolean expressions such as those returned by comparison operators can be combined: && means "and" and || means "or"; the prefix operator ! means "not." There is more on combining Boolean expressions as we make more use of them for selection and iteration.

Assignment   Assignment is an operator and assignment is an expression. That means it returns a value. The value it returns is the value assigned to the variable. This permits code that chains assignment operators together to set several variables to a given value all on one line. Do not do that! There is no example of that type of expression.

Parenthesized Expression   Parentheses can be used to change precedence, as mentioned above in arithmetic expressions.

Calling a Method   The last entry in the *<expression>* template is a call to a method. It includes calling a method on the current object as in

```
addSprite(apple);
```

It also includes calling a method on any expression that evaluates to a reference to an object (any number of expression dot parts can come before the actual call):

```
apple.setColor(getColor("blue"));

Game.getCurrentGame().randomDouble(-1.0, 1.0);
```

This is a crash course in what an expression is; the text continues to use the different types and operators and explains them again as we go.

Review 5.4

(a)   What is the result of each of the following expressions? Include the type and the value.

(a) `111 / 10`

(b) `111 % 10`

(c) `2 + 5 + 6 * 7`

(d) `1.0 / 100`

(e) `1 / 100`

(f) `9 * (2 + 99 / 11)`

(g) `1 + 2.5`

(h) `3.8 / 2`

(i) `100 -100.0`

(j) `5 / 2`

(b)   What are the values of any variables with changed values after each of the following statements? You may assume they are executed in the order they are labeled.

```
int a = 10;
int b = 100;
int c = 1000;

double x = 9.0;
double y = 100.0;
double z = 176.5;
```

(a) `++a;`

(b) `b++;`

(c) `c = a++ * ++b;`

(d) `x = y / a;`

(e) `z = 1 / 3;`

(f) `z = 1.0 * (++a / 13);`

(g) `z = z / 3;`

(h) `x = x * x + a;`

(i) `y = y + y * a`

(j) `z = z * 6.0;`

5.5 Naming Things in Java

What is in a name? Would an object by any other name not compute as fast?[11]

Identifiers are used to name methods, classes, fields, local variables, labels, parameters, and more. Naming conventions on what kinds of names to choose for different things in Java have developed to assist programmers reading code to determine the kind of thing named. This section is derived from the Java standard naming conventions.[12]

Components: Named with Nouns

Variables, the names we are most concerned with in this chapter, should be in mixed upper and lower camel-case beginning with a lowercase character; as with methods, the lowercase initial letter is to indicate that the variable is contained *within* a `class` (or within a block within a class) rather than being a class itself. Variable names should consist of a descriptive noun or noun phrase. Variable names can be defined directly in the scope of a `class` (an *instance* variable or a *field* of the class), in the *parameter list* of a method, or inside a method's body.

The amount of description required in a name is inversely proportional to the size of the scope of the variable. An instance variable holding the number of keystrokes entered by the user might be named `keys`, `keysNumb`, or `totalNumberOfKeystrokes`. The last name in the list reads as a phrase describing what the value in the number *means*.

The second choice seems reasonable until you go back to work on your code after a long weekend. It is hard to remember whether you used "Numb" or "Number" and was it "numbKeys" or the other way around? There are a lot of different things that could be named "keys": the actual values typed in by the user, some collection of objects found in the game world and used to open doors, and even a count of the number of keys pressed. It makes sense, at the `class` level, to make sure you give a full description of the variable.

If the variable were defined inside a method named `getKeyboardStatistics`, then a shorter name would make sense: `keyCount`, `count`, or even, perhaps, `keys`. These are acceptable because the name is used within a limited context where other meanings of "key" are unlikely to confuse readers of the code.

Constants: Unchanging Values

The one exception to naming variables in camel-case is for a special kind of variable: the *named constant*. A named constant can be recognized because it is defined with two special keywords, `static final`. These variables should be named with all uppercase letters and with underscores, "_", used to separate the words. Named constants are named with nouns or noun phrases and are defined at the class level. Examples might include

```
static final double ROAD_X = 0.10;
static final double SITTER_X = 0.20;
static final double HOUSE_X = 0.90;
```

---

[11] Apologies to the Bard.

[12] http://java.sun.com/docs/codeconv/html/CodeConventions.doc8.html

These named constants represent the x-coordinates of the road, sitter, and house, respectively. When they appear in a setLocation parameter list, it should be obvious whether or not they are being used correctly.

Consistency in code makes your code easier for a programmer to read. Any programmer, including you, can tell at a glance whether a name names a component, a rule, or an attribute.

Rules: Named with Verbs

Methods, the rules defined inside a **class**, should be in mixed upper and lower camel-case, starting with a lowercase letter. The camel-case makes the name easier to read. Consider setColor: the capitalized letters make it obvious that this name consists of three words. Compare that with a couple of variations: setcolor and SETFILLCOLOR. The variants are more difficult to read, especially after some practice reading camel-case code. The lowercase initial letter indicates that this name is contained within a **class**, not, itself, a class name.

Methods should be named with descriptive verbs or verb phrases. Two naming conventions are that Boolean methods, methods that return a truth value, typically begin with is (think isPressed from EasyButton), and fields are accessed through *getters* and *setters*, methods named get<*FieldName*> and set<*FieldName*>. Note that the first character of the field name is capitalized to put the method name in camel-case.

Classes: Named with Adjective-noun Phrases

Component-type names, the names of **class** or *type names* (as well as **interface** names), should be in mixed uppercase and lowercase letters, with each word inside the name capitalized.[13] We have seen examples in the names of our sample programs, NewtonsApple, FANG-defined types, RectangleSprite, OvalSprite, and standard Java types, String. Note that as String is a single word; there is no internal capitalization.

When selecting a name for a **class**, use a descriptive noun (a person, place, or thing) or noun phrase. This is because a type represents a type of object and objects are *things*. Translating traditional physical games into Java, we might find types such as ChessPiece, SixSidedDie, PlayingCard, DeckOfCards. Be consistent in number when naming things (singular or plural nouns); this text uses plural nouns for collections of objects and singular nouns in all other case. This means that DeckOfCards should contain a collection of PlayingCard objects.

Review 5.5

(a) Define *expression*.

(b) What is a *literal* value?

    (a) Given an example of an **int** literal.

    (b) Give an example of a String literal.

    (c) Give an example of a **boolean** literal.

    (d) Give an example of an OvalSprite literal. (This *is* possible.)

(c) What is an *operator*? Name four Java operators, at least one not an arithmetic operator. Describe what the operators do; include the type of subexpression(s) they require and the type of the resulting expression.

(d) What does the expression 12 + 11 * 4 + 7 evaluate to?

    (a) What is the type of the result?

    (b) How would you change the expression so that it evaluated the rightmost sum before the multiplication?

---

[13]Mixed case with internal words capitalized is also known as *camel-case* because the resulting names seem to have humps in them: CamelCaseIdentifier, DrumSet, WhisperingWind.

(e) What is the % operator? What types of subexpressions does it require? What is the type of the result? How is % related to /?

(f) How can you tell if / represents *integer division* or *floating-point division*?

(g) Given x is an **int** that has been initialized and oval refers to an OvalSprite,

   (a) how would you set oval to the color "cornflower blue"?

   (b) how would you set oval to "cornflower blue" if x is a positive number?

   (c) how would you set oval to "cornflower blue" if x is a positive number less than 100?

(h)

   (a) What logical operator means "and"?

   (b) What logical operator means "or"?

   (c) What logical operator means "not"?

5.6   Finishing EasyDice

Defining a Die

Just as we implemented the EasyButton public protocol above, here we implement the OneDie public protocol. By extending StringSprite, OneDie inherits all of StringSprite's public protocol: location, color, scale, rotation, and even text.

   The extension is so that OneDie can add the state necessary to model one die. The state of a die is the value showing on the face of the die. An **int** variable or field is necessary; which makes more sense? The state of the die (and of most objects) is needed in *all* methods: it should be one or more fields.

```
 1 | // package default
 2 |
 3 | import fang2.core.Game;
 4 | import fang2.sprites.StringSprite;
 5 |
 6 | /**
 7 |  * This class, extending StringSprite, represents one six-sided die.
 8 |  * That is, a cube used for generating random numbers. The faces are
 9 |  * marked from 1 to 6.
10 |  */
11 | public class OneDie
12 |   extends StringSprite {
13 |   /** the value of the die; range is 1-6 */
14 |   private int face;
15 |
16 |   /**
17 |    * Initialize a OneDieStringSprite object with default values
18 |    */
19 |   public OneDie() {
20 |     setFace(1);
21 |   }
22 |
23 |   /**
24 |    * Get the current value of face.
25 |    *
```

```
26    * @return  [1..6], the current value of the die
27    */
28   public int getFace() {
29     return face;
30   }
31
32   /**
33    * Roll this die: get currentGame(), use randomInt and setFace.
34    */
35   public void roll() {
36     setFace(Game.getCurrentGame().randomInt(1, 6));
37   }
38
39   /**
40    * Set value of face to newFace and update displayed value if newFace
41    * is legal; otherwise leave face unchanged.
42    *
43    * @param  newFace  the new value for face
44    */
45   public void setFace(int newFace) {
46     if ((1 <= newFace) && (newFace <= 6)) {
47       face = newFace;
48       setText(Integer.toString(face));
49     }
50   }
51 }
```

Listing 5.7: OneDie class

The constructor, lines 19–21, is simple: just set the face to 1. Using setFace to do the work here is an application of the DRY principle.

We *could* assign a value to face and call setText in the constructor. That would duplicate the code that is now in setFace. What if we wanted to change how the die displays its state, say, with the French word for the face value (make it a language learning game)? We would have to update both setFace and the constructor. By having one method that does all of the setting and displaying of the state, we have only one spot to have to update.

Line 36 uses getCurrentGame() to access the currently running game. The Game provides randomInt; line 36 gets a random integer on the range [1–6], passing it to setFace. Again, calling setFace assures that all housekeeping for setting a face value is performed.

Because face is **private**, we must provide a way for classes using OneDie attributes[14] to access the "value" of the die. We add a *getter*; a method that provides read access to the value of a private attribute is referred to as a getter (it "gets" the value) and is typically named get + attribute name. Lines 28–30 return the current value of face.

A getter (1) is **public** since it gives access to something not otherwise available; (2) returns the same type as the type of the attribute being "getted"; (3) typically does nothing more than return the value.

The one other thing we might want to do is set what face is up. This is particularly true for the two "point dice" in the upper-right corner of the design. They are not rolled but rather are set to a given value so that the user can remember her point. As with a getter, a **private** attribute can have a *setter*. A setter takes a single

---

[14]Notice that while we design OneDie, we think of it as an object maintaining its state in fields; when designing classes that *use* our OneDie, our class, itself, is a type for fields of that class.

parameter of the same type as the attribute and updates the value of the attribute. A setter, like `setFace` on lines 45–50, can protect the private field from being set to illegal values (such as values outside [1–6] for a die). Line 46 protects the rest of the setting code from setting an illegal value.

Line 48 sets the *text* value of this sprite, updating the displayed value. The code `Integer.toString(face)` converts an integer to a `String`, and a `String` is exactly the type needed to call `setText` on a `StringSprite`.

Given this definition, you might be asking yourself why we bother to define `face` to be private. We needed 14 lines to define the getter and setter and, together, they pretty much provide the same access to the field as would have been provided by defining the attribute to be **public**. Some trade off: fourteen extra lines or one fewer character.

Wait just a second, though. In the definition comment for `face`, it says the value should be limited to values 1 through 6. If `face` were **public**, then it would be possible to write the following code:

```
OneDie die;
...
die.face = 8;
```

Of course, it is possible, with the current definition, to have the same effect (to violate the stated constraint on the type, that its `face` value be limited to integer values from 1 to 6) by writing

```
OneDie die;
...
die.setFace(8);
```

But `setFace` updates the value of `face` only if it is valid. The logical "and" applied to the two comparisons evaluates to **true** only when both subexpressions evaluate to **true**. The left subexpression is **true** only if `newFace` is greater than or equal to 1; the right subexpression is **true** only if `newFace` is less than or equal to 6. The two together are only **true** for the six values we consider in range.

Notice two things: (1) It was necessary to write two separate comparisons (the value being compared had to be typed twice); this is different than the way you might write it in mathematics but it is how it must be done in Java. (2) The way the two comparison expressions are written is done to indicate that the value of `newFace` is being constrained between 1 and 6; it is possible to write either comparison with `newFace` on either side of an appropriate comparison operator but this ordering was chosen to improve readability of the code.

Having defined `EasyButton` and `OneDie`, we design `RollDice` using just their public protocols compiles and runs. Each time the button is pressed, the dice roll; remember that sometimes they randomly roll the same value. Also, make sure you press **Start** because the `EasyButton` works only if the game loop is running.

Now on to writing `EasyDice`. Note that from this point forward, we do not need to talk about `EasyButton` or `OneDie` except in terms of their public protocols. This greatly simplifies our programming problem.

State of the Game

Consider the game described at the beginning of the chapter. Even given the two classes we have defined, the game is complex. What must we keep track of? The description describes a pile of matchsticks, a wager of a matchstick, a "point," and four dice on the screen. Looking at what "point" means, we also need to be able to differentiate between a first roll and all subsequent rolls.

```
15    /** bank balance; game ends when this goes to 0 after a bet */
16    private int bank;// value
17    private StringSprite bankDisplay;// display
18
19    /** player's current bet */
20    private int bet;// value
```

```
21    private StringSprite betDisplay;// display
22
23    /** the button */
24    private EasyButton button;
25
26    /** the left die */
27    private OneDie dieLeft;
28
29    /** the right die */
30    private OneDie dieRight;
31
32    /** the value the player is trying to match */
33    private int point;
34
35    /** the left point die */
36    private OneDie pointDieLeft;
37
38    /** the right point die */
39    private OneDie pointDieRight;
40
41    /** is there an active bet? */
42    private boolean rolling;
```

Listing 5.8: EasyDice fields

All of this game state requires a lot of fields. Lines 16–17 define the bank (the pile of matchsticks) and lines 20–21 define the wager. There are two variables for each because we track the number of matchsticks as an int and have a pretty display sprite with the description and value showing on the screen. It is always a good idea to label values you show to the user so that she knows what they mean.

The button, the four dice, and the point are self-explanatory. The dice are named "left" and "right" to indicate which die of each pair they are, and the dice in the upper-right corner showing the current point have "point" in their name. Naming fields consistently greatly improves the readability of your code.

The last field, rolling, is used to determine if we are rolling subsequent rolls in a turn of easy dice (and trying to match the point before getting seven) or waiting to place a bet and make our first roll. There is more on rolling when we define advance.

With the fields defined, what must setup do? Rather than try to list everything in detail, let's look at it from a high level:

```
setup button
setup bank
setup bet
setup dice
```

The pseudocode is a top-level view in the process of stepwise refinement. In fact, it is, with each statement in the algorithm replaced with a call to a method.

```java
66   public void setup() {
67     setBackground(getColor("green"));
68     rolling = false;
69     buttonSetup();
70     bankSetup();
71     betSetup();
72     diceSetup();
73   }
```

Listing 5.9: EasyDice setup

The first two lines were snuck in to set the color of the game field and set the initial state to *not* rolling. The four *<something>*Setup() methods are straight forward; in the interest of brevity they are not listed in the chapter because each just constructs and adds the sprites for each part of the game display.

advance is really two methods. There is work to do if we are waiting for the first roll and *different* work to do if we are rolling for a point. That sounds like an application of selection *and* stepwise refinement:

```java
51   public void advance(double dT) {
52     if (!isGameOver()) {
53       if (!rolling) {
54         advanceWaiting(dT);
55       } else {
56         advanceRolling(dT);
57       }
58     }
59   }
```

Listing 5.10: EasyDice advance

The real work for either case is pushed off until we define the given method. Each method, advanceWaiting and advanceRolling, sits and spins its wheels until the button is pressed. The body of each is a big **if** (button.isPressed()) statement. If the button is pressed, the dice are rolled and the state of the game is updated accordingly.

```java
100   private void advanceWaiting(double secondsSinceLastCall) {
101     if (button.isPressed()) {
102       // place and show wager
103       bet = 1;
104       bank = bank - bet;
105       betDisplay.setText("Bet: " + bet);
106       bankDisplay.setText("Bank: " + bank);
107
108       int roll = rollTheDice();
109
110       // check for a win on the first roll
111       if ((roll == 7) || (roll == 11)) {
112         win();
113       } else {
114         // copy roll dice up to the point
115         pointDieLeft.setFace(dieLeft.getFace());
116         pointDieRight.setFace(dieRight.getFace());
```

```
117
118         // set new point, set rolling flag, and change button text
119         point = roll;
120         rolling = true;
121         button.setText("Roll to match point");
122       }
123     }
124   }
```

In advanceWaiting, when the button is pressed, a wager is made. The dice are rolled. If the roll is a winning number for a first roll, call the win method. Otherwise update the point dice to display the same faces as the game dice (lines 115–116), point to be the sum of the dice (line 119), set rolling to true since we are now rolling for a point, and, finally, change the button text to indicate that we're rolling for point.

```
81   private void advanceRolling(double dT) {
82     if (button.isPressed()) {
83       int roll - rollTheDice();
84       // game wins, loses, or keeps going. Nothing to do to keep going
85       if (roll == 7) {// lose
86         lose();
87       } else if (roll == point) {// win
88         win();
89       }
90     }
91   }
```

In advanceRolling, when the button is pressed, we roll the dice. If the roll equals 7, the player loses. Else, if the roll equals the point, the player wins. In any other case, rolling continues. Note that win and lose are defined to update the wager and the bank, and to set rolling false.

The finishRolling, lose, rollTheDice, and win methods are private methods which sort to the end of the .java file. They are private because they are implementation details; no class outside of EasyDice needs to know they exist.

```
200   private void finishRolling() {
201     bet = 0;
202     bankDisplay.setText("Bank: " + bank);
203     betDisplay.setText("Bet: " + bet);
204
205     rolling = false;
206     button.setText("Bet 1 matchstick");
207   }
208
209   /**
210    * Player lost wager; bank remains unchanged, finish rolling.
211    */
212   private void lose() {
213     if (bank == 0) {
214       // if out of matches, game is over
```

```
215      setGameOver(true);
216    }
217    finishRolling();
218  }
219
220  /**
221   * Roll the game dice. Return the sum of the pair of dice.
222   *
223   * @return   the sum of the newly rolled dice
224   */
225  private int rollTheDice() {
226    dieRight.roll();
227    dieLeft.roll();
228    return dieLeft.getFace() + dieRight.getFace();
229  }
230
231  /**
232   * Player won wager; return twice wager to bank finish rolling.
233   */
234  private void win() {
235    bank = bank + (2 * bet);
236    finishRolling();
237  }
```

Listing 5.13: `EasyDice` end of the class

`win` and `lose` both fix up the bank value and call `finishRolling`. As the programmer wrote `win` and `lose`, they ended up having a lot of code in common. Not wanting to repeat the code, the common work was factored out. The `win` method adds winnings to the bank; the `lose` method does not need to do any bank manipulation because the wager was taken out of the bank when it was made. That does mean if the bank is 0 after losing, the player is out of matches and the game ends.

`finishRolling` updates the display messages on the screen, resets `rolling` to **false**, and updates the text on the button.

`rollTheDice` is modeled on `RollDice.advance`. Each die rolls and then the sum of the two dice is returned.

Review 5.6

(a) Why is it better to have `face` defined as a **private** field with a getter and a setter rather than as a **public** field?

(b) Listing 5.10 on page 148 shows the `EasyDice` advance method. What *helper methods* are called from it? If you look only at this listing, can you determine what the *parameter lists* of the helper methods are?

(c) Why is `finishRolling` a separate method? Would you have made it its own method? Explain your answer.

5.7 Summary

Chance and EasyDice

Chance or a random element is part of many games using spinners, dice, and cards. In FANG the `Game` class provides several methods for getting random numbers: `randomInt` and `randomDouble`, each with several signatures,[15] return random integers and random double values, respectively. The different signatures permit you to specify the range.

When classes are defined in the same directory, the Java compiler can find the required files through the name of the class when it is used in another class; there is no need for **import**.

`OneDie` **extends** `StringSprite` for two reasons: to *inherit* the public protocol of `StringSprite` and to add *state* to the resulting object. The *class* defines the field `face` to represent the state; each *object* has its own copy of `face` so that different dice can have different values.

Designing with Public Protocols

A *public protocol* is the collection of all public methods and fields in a **class**. The methods are *services* that objects of the given type can perform. The method header indicates how to call for the service, what actual parameters you must pass in, and what value, if any, you can expect back.

With a **class**'s public protocol, it is possible to design a program that *uses* the **class**. The public protocols of classes in the Java standard libraries are documented in the provided *JavaDoc* Web pages. FANG provides its own *JavaDoc* Web pages.

Types

Java types divide into two large kinds: *class types* and *plain old data (POD) types*. Table 5.7 summarizes the similarities and difference of the two kinds of types.

	Class Types	POD Types
Naming	Use initial UppercaseLetter with "camel case"	all lowercase
User-definable	Yes	No
Use as operand	No; exceptions: `String` and the POD "wrapper" classes (i.e., `Integer`, `Double`, `Boolean`).	Yes, for operators defined for their type
Literal values	Only `null` and "string"	Yes
Variables hold	A *reference* to an object	A *value*
Assignment	Copies one *reference* over the other *reference*. Underlying object is *shared*. Previous value in memory box is overwritten.	Copies one *value* over the other *value*. After assignment, nothing shared. Previous value in memory box is overwritten.
Initial value	Must call **new** to construct an object	The memory box always has *some* value. Cannot use with **new**
Use to call methods?	Yes	No
Multiple references	An object can have any number of references.	A given memory box has only one name (variable). No shared object (no object at all)
"No Such" value	Yes: `null`	No

Table 5.1: Comparing `Object`-derived and plain old types.

Variables have *scope*, the section of the program source where they are visible. A variable's scope is the block in which the variable definition appears. Variables are defined with a *type* that determines what kinds of expressions can be assigned to them.

---

[15]The *signature* of a method is the name of the method and the number and types of the parameters in the parameter list. It is a subset of the *method header* (it does not include the return type or access level).

Expressions

An expression is a piece of code that returns a value. Simple expressions are literal values, variables, new expressions, and method calls. Expressions are built up of simpler subexpressions by combining the subexpressions with *operators*. All expressions have types.

Literal values, such as 3.1415 or "One Two Three," are evaluated by the compiler and compiled directly into a program. Variables, fields and local variables alike, are names for values that are filled in (using assignment) at run-time. The new operator allocates memory and calls a *constructor* to initialize the space into an object. Method calls, where a method is named and parameters (if any) are provided, can return values.

Operators have *precedence*, which determines the order in which they are applied. 4 + 3 * 2 is 10 (4 + (3 * 2)) rather than 14 ((4 + 3) * 2). Parentheses can be used to specify order of application and to make it clearer even when they are not required.

All expressions have types. The extends relationship between two types means that the child class *is-a* or is an example of its parent class. A every running shoe is a shoe, after all.

5.8　Chapter Review Exercises

Review Exercise 5.1 What does *override* mean?

  (a) What *annotation* is used to indicated that one method overrides another?

  (b) Where is the annotation typed?

  (c) What does the compiler do if a non-overriding method has the annotation?

Review Exercise 5.2 What are the four parts of the method header? How do you indicate that a method returns a value to the calling method?

  (a) What goes in the method body to actually return the value?

Review Exercise 5.3 The state of a class is defined by the fields defined within the class and the fields of the extended class. What class does EasyButton extend? What fields does EasyButton define? Name one method EasyButton inherits from the class it extends.

Review Exercise 5.4 The types in the standard Java class libraries are classes within packages that start with java or javax. Visit the Java documentation and list three classes in the java.lang package.

Review Exercise 5.5 The types in the FANG class libraries are classes within packages that start with fang2. Visit the FANG documentation and list three classes in the fang2.sprites package.

Review Exercise 5.6 What are the six comparison operators for comparing numeric expressions? What does each one mean? Where, in each operator, can you insert whitespace without changing the meaning?

Review Exercise 5.7

  (a) In what package(s) is (are) OvalSprite defined in FANG?

  (b) How many classes named OvalSprite are in the FANG libraries?

  (c) How many different ovals can you have in one game?

  (d) Explain any difference between the two numbers.

Review Exercise 5.8 Explain why face is a *field* in the OneDie class.

Java Templates

```
<className> := <identifier>


<formalParameter> := <typeName> <variableName>


<formalParameterList> := [<formalParameter> [, <formalParameter>]*]


<constructorDeclaration> :=
    <access-level> <class-name>(<formalParameterList>)


<constructorDefinition> := <constructorDeclaration>
                            <block>
```

```
<returnStatement> := return <expression>; |
                    return;
```

```
<op> := + | - | * | / | \% |
        == | != | < | <= | >= | > |
        \&\& | '||' |
        =


<post-op> := ++ | --


<pre-op> := ++ | -- |
           + | - |
           !


<methodCall> := [<object>.]<methodName>(<actualParameterList>)


<expression> := <literal> |
                new <typeName>(<actualParameterList>) |
                <methodCall> |
                <expression> <op> <expression> |
                <expression> <post-op> |
                <pre-op> <expression> |
                (<expression>)
                <methodCall>
```

Review Exercise 5.9 OneDie has a getter and a setter for the face field. Looking at the class listing, Listing 5.7, answer the following questions.

    (a) What is the name of the *getter*?

    (b) What is the name of the *setter*?

    (c) face is an **int**. What are the return types of the getter and the setter? Why?

    (d) face is an **int**. What are the parameter lists of the getter and setter? Why?

Review Exercise 5.10 Given the following setup method

```
public void setup() {
  addSprite(new OvalSprite(0.10, 0.40));
  // now move it to the center of the screen
}
```

    (a) why is it difficult to "now move it" at the comment line?

    (b) Rewrite the method and move the oval to the center of the screen.

Review Exercise 5.11 After the following setup method runs, how many ovals are on the screen? (If you are not sure, try writing a simple FANG game to figure it out.) Explain your answer.
Where is (are) the oval(s) on the screen?

```
public void setup() {
   OvalSprite oval = new OvalSprite(0.1, 0.1);
   oval.setLocation(0.25, 0.25);

   oval=new OvalSprite(0.1, 0.1);
   oval.setLocation(0.75, 0.75);

   addSprite(oval);
   addSprite(oval);
}
```

Review Exercise 5.12 After the following setup method runs, how many ovals are on the screen? (If you are not sure, try writing a simple FANG game to figure it out.) Explain your answer.
Where is (are) the oval(s) on the screen?

```
public void setup() {
   OvalSprite oval1 = new OvalSprite(0.1, 0.1);
   oval1.setLocation(0.25, 0.25);

   OvalSprite oval2=oval1;
   oval2.setLocation(0.75, 0.75);

   addSprite(oval1);
   addSprite(oval2);
}
```

Review Exercise 5.13 After the following setup method runs, what does the StringSprite display on the screen? (If you are not sure, try writing a simple FANG game to figure it out.) Explain your answer.

```
public void setup() {
   int x = 5;
   StringSprite textSprite = new StringSprite("x is "+x);
   textSprite.setLocation(0.5, 0.5);
   textSprite.setWidth(0.9);
}
```

Review Exercise 5.14 After the following setup method runs, what does the StringSprite display on the screen? (If you are not sure, try writing a simple FANG game to figure it out.) Explain your answer.

```
public void setup() {
    int x = 5;
    int y = x;
    StringSprite textSprite = new StringSprite("x is "+x+" y is "+y);
    textSprite.setLocation(0.5, 0.5);
    textSprite.setWidth(0.9);
}
```

Review Exercise 5.15 After the following setup method runs, what does the StringSprite display on the screen? (If you are not sure, try writing a simple FANG game to figure it out.) Explain your answer.

```
public void setup() {
    int x = 5;
    int y = x;
    ++y;
    StringSprite textSprite = new StringSprite("x is " + x + " y is " + y);
    textSprite.setLocation(0.5, 0.5);
    textSprite.setWidth(0.9);
}
```

Review Exercise 5.16 What color is the RectangleSprite displayed on the screen filled with?

```
    RectangleSprite lemon = new RectangleSprite(0.2, 0.2);
    lemon.setColor(getColor("yellow"));


    RectangleSprite lime = lemon;
    lime.setColor(getColor("green"));


    addSprite(lemon);
```

Review Exercise 5.17 State which of the following collection of possible identifiers are *not* legal in Java and why they are not legal:

(a) oneFish

(b) ReD

(c) findSmallest

(d) Bilbo Baggins

(e) NDX

(f) ingredient

(g) 2fish

(h) Go!

(i) FarFetched

(j) 123BrockportLn

(k) mouseEvent

(l) FryingPan

(m) SIZE_OF_SQUARE

(n) Alan_Turing

(o) flash cards

(p) student-grade-point-average

(q) LionTigerLeopardPumaCougarCount

(r) Orca#

(s) alpha_Bravo

(t) BrockportLn123

Review Exercise 5.18 Classify each of the following identifiers as either a type (`class`) name, a method, a variable, or a constant.

(a) `DirtyDozen`

(b) `color`

(c) `createCheckerKing`

(d) `YEAR_LINCOLN_WAS_BORN`

(e) `myGameProgram`

(f) `GolfClub`

(g) `findSmallest`

(h) `LENGTH_OF_SHIP`

(i) `nameOfCountry`

(j) `getCaptainsName`

(k) `MAXIMUM_NUMBER_OF_PIRATES`

(l) `PlayingCard`

(m) `currentPokerHand`

(n) `getHighCard`

(o) `ChessPiece`

(p) `getRasberryCount`

(q) `firstMove`

(r) `castleToKingside`

(s) `numberOfRasberries`

(t) `SmallInteger`

Review Exercise 5.19 What is the scope of the variable `blueLine` in the following listing?

```
class Something
  extends Game {
  public void gamma() {
    (a)
  }

  public int delta(int a) {
    (b)
  }

  LineSprite blueLine;

  public void setup() {
    (c)
  }
}
```

Review Exercise 5.20 What is the text in the label after this code is executed?

```
StringSprite results = new  StringSprite();
addSprite(results);

int x, y, z;
String cubit = "atom mixed replication";

x = 10;
y = 100;
z = y;

y = 2 * y;

x = z * x;

results.setText(cubit.substring(1,7) + " (" + x + ", " + y + ", " + z + ")");
```

Review Exercise 5.21 The following program defined in BadGame.java does not compile. Why not?

```
1  import fang2.core.Game;
2  import fang2.sprites.OvalSprite;
3  public class BadGame
4    extends Game {
5    public void setup() {
6        OvalSprite oval=new OvalSprite(0.1, 0.1);
7        addSprite(oval);
8    }
9
10   public void advance(double secondsSinceLastCall) {
11       OvalSprite oval;
12       oval.setLocation(getMouse2D()); // compiler error here
13   }
14 }
```

(a) How would you fix that problem?

(b) There is another, logical error in the program. Assume the programmer meant for oval to track the player's mouse. What is wrong with the body of advance?

5.9 Programming Problems

Programming Problem 5.1 Take the Snowman.java program as a base and design a CompositeSprite-extending class, SnowmanSprite. This can be done in two steps.

(a) Make a SnowmanSprite.java file and build a constructor for the class. The constructor should instantiate three OvalSprites of appropriate sizes and position them so that the center of the snowman is the center of the middle ball *and* the overall height of the snowman is 1.0 screens (width is determined by the width of the bottom ball).

You can test this sprite by building a simple Game that adds ten sprites with random locations and random rotations. You might want to try setting random colors for each as well.

(b) Modify SnowmanSprite by overloading the setColor method. Although CompositeSprite *has* a setColor method, the method does not set the color value of sprites within the composite.

Programming Problem 5.2 *Pig* is a simple dice game for children. Two players begin with a score of 0, adding some number to their scores from rolling a single die on their turn. The first to 100 wins the game.

On his turn a player rolls one die at a time and keeps a running total of the rolls. At any time the player may end his turn and add the total for all rolls that turn to his total. A player's turn is also over when he rolls a 1 or a "pig"; when a player rolls a pig, the turn ends and the player receives 0 points for the turn.

Design a two-player (alternating on the same machine) game of Pig. You should display both scores, whose turn it is, the turn score, and two buttons (one for ending the turn, one for rolling again). The game logic becomes a bit more difficult in tracking two different buttons.

Chapter 11 presents a console version of *Pig*.

Programming Problem 5.3 Start with EasyDice.java. Modify the program for two players alternating play on the same machine.

(a) Which variables represent the state that must be duplicated for each player? Which do not?

(b) How does the program track which player's turn it is? What state changes to mark the change of turn? How is the change of turn signaled to the players? You may assume that the players are able to pass the mouse from one to the other when the turn changes.

(c) When is the game actually over? What message could you show?

Programming Problem 5.4   Modify EasyDice to use dice with pips. This takes several steps.

(a) A new class, OneDiePips, must be defined. It must use the OneDie public protocol. Make a copy of OneDie.java and

    i. Modify the copy so that it compiles.

    ii. Modify EasyDice so that it uses OneDiePips.

    iii. Run the modified EasyDice; can you see any difference from the original version at this point?

(b) A die which is a rectangle with ovals on it does not extend StringSprite. What class should it extend? Change it so that it extends that class.

(c) The CompositeSprite version of OneDiePips has more state than just the face. It needs a background rectangle and seven pips (as shown in Figure 5.8). Only 1 to 6 of the pips are visible at any given time. Add the necessary fields. Give the pips reasonable names so that you know which one is which from the name.

    i. What size should the background rectangle be? It is a square and it should scale well (so scale 0.33 makes the background 0.33 screens across): what inside size should it have?

    ii. What are the coordinates of the center of each of the pips if the background rectangle is centered at (0.0, 0.0) (in sprite coordinates)?

    iii. Initialize the eight new fields in setup and modify OneDiePips so that it compiles. You want to remove the setText call from setFace but leave the rest of that method in place. When you run this version, the dice should show up with seven pips (no matter what the value of the face field is). That is to be expected.

(d) The Sprite class has two methods, hide and show, which turn on and off the visibility of a sprite. Use them in setFace to turn on and off the appropriate pips so that the die shows the value of the face field. Hint: It is probably easiest to turn off *all* pips and then just turn on the ones you want. That way there is only one multi-way **if-else if** statement.

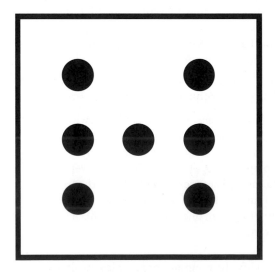

Figure 5.8: Seven Pips

Rules: Methods, Parameters, and Design

We have seen how to use top-down design to go from a description of public protocols to a computer program. This chapter continues that while going deeper into the *delegation* problem-solving technique through the use of *methods*. We also create an animating countdown timer using *iteration* through FANG's built-in iteration of the advance method.

6.1 A Simple Arcade Game: SoloPong

One of the earliest, commercially successful computer games was Atari's *Pong* coin-operated video game. This chapter designs a FANG version of *Pong*, a handball simulation called *SoloPong*. The ball starts at a random location on the left half of the screen with a random, nonzero velocity. The player's paddle, limited to moving up and down near the right edge of the screen, must keep the ball from reaching the right edge of the screen. The score goes up each time the player successfully hits the ball. Before the ball is released, a three-second countdown is displayed so that the player can prepare.

The *SoloPong* design diagram is Figure 6.1 on the next page. The advance method is responsible for everything that happens (no transformers are used). To manage the complexity of advance, the ball, paddle, and countdown timer define their own advance methods, and SoloPong.advance *ticks* them every frame.

All three screen-visible objects, the ball, paddle, and timer, are sprites with their own state (whenever you hear "*something* with state" you should be thinking: "create a class that **extends** *something*.").

Physics of Bouncing

How is a *ball* different from an OvalSprite? Think back to what made an apple different from an OvalSprite. The fact that we moved it during advance. The apple had *velocity*, a speed and a direction that it was moving.

Where was the apple's velocity stored? The distance that the apple moved was calculated in NewtonsApple.advance and apple.translateY was called from there. The speed of the apple was the coefficient of the change in time in advance and the direction was along the positive y-axis (straight down). The velocity was hard-coded into NewtonsApple.

A ball *is-a*[1] OvalSprite that has a velocity. Because it tracks its own velocity, the ball can be told to "advance itself" just by passing the elapsed time to it. With variable velocity, the ball can bounce off walls by updating

---

[1]The term *is-a* is a term of art used in computer science when discussing the **extends** relationship. With OvalSprite it would flow much better to say *is-an*, but that term is not typically used.

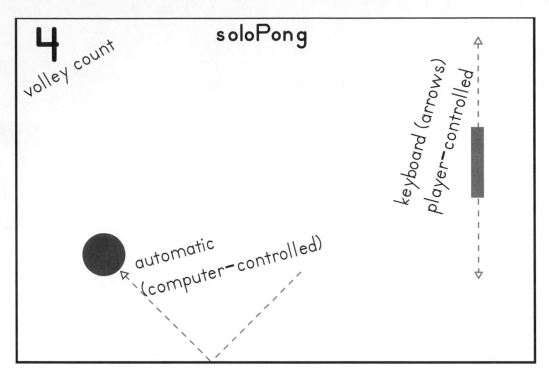

Figure 6.1: *SoloPong* game design diagram

the velocity when it detects a collision with a wall; similarly, it can bounce off other sprites when a collision is detected. If *each* ball object tracks its own independent velocity, each can have its own velocity. Multiple balls are almost as easy to add as a single ball.

How can velocity be tracked? The velocity in NewtonsApple was in a fixed direction, so it was just a speed, a single **double** literal. To permit movement in any direction in a two-dimensional game, velocity must have two dimensions. The two dimensions could be a heading and a speed (these are *polar coordinates* centered at the ball) or as components, an x-speed and a y-speed (*Cartesian coordinates*).

Either method permits arbitrary velocity (both direction and *magnitude*; the magnitude is the speed along the direction of travel). If we look at the design diagram, all interaction is with *axis-aligned surfaces* (lines that are either vertical or horizontal; lines running in the same direction as one of the axes). The physics of bouncing is easier to understand when modeled with the velocity in Cartesian coordinates.

The movement rules, more complex than those in previous games, simulate physics to create a believable simulation of the real world.[2] Because we are modeling physics, the two new fields in the PongBall class are deltaX and deltaY. In physics, Δ, the Greek letter delta, is used to mean change, so Δ_x and Δ_y are the change in position in the x-coordinate and y-coordinate.

How does a billiard ball bounce off a cushion? Figure 6.2 shows a ball moving from right to left, striking the bottom edge of the figure, a cushion off which the ball bounces. To the right of the point of impact the velocity of the ball is represented with the two components deltaX and deltaY. Each "time step" (frame), the location of the ball moves deltaX in the x-dimension and deltaY in the y-dimension. Using FANG's advance method to drive the simulation means the velocity should be expressed in screens/second; then a time unit is a second, and multiplying by the seconds elapsed between calls to advance scales the velocity appropriately.

---

[2]For a sufficiently loose interpretation of *believable*.

Our simulation assumes perfectly *elastic* collisions: neither the ball nor the cushion changes shape, no energy is lost in heating them up, no friction causes the ball to spin along the cushion, etc. A *model* of reality, by definition, simplifies reality. The important thing in using a model in a computer program is making sure that it is as simple as possible but that it captures all of the important features of reality. Elastic collisions are close enough to reality for SoloPong purposes.

What happens to the velocity of the ball when it hits the cushion? When we look at the drawing, it seems that the velocity after the impact is the same as that before *except* deltaY has changed sign.

When a ball hits a surface, the component of the velocity perpendicular to the surface struck reverses direction. The new velocity has the same size or *magnitude*; just the direction has changed. If the ball strikes a horizontal surface, the y-component of the velocity (perpendicular to the surface struck) changes sign. The x-component (parallel to the surface struck) is unchanged.

Reacting to a collision with *any* surface takes the same form; the portion of the velocity perpendicular, or *normal*, to the surface struck is reversed in direction. The two hard parts of arbitrary collision reaction are determining *where* two objects struck one another and *what* the normal of the surface at the point of collision is.

A first approximation of an arbitrarily shaped sprite is to use its *bounding box* or the smallest axis-aligned rectangle that contains all of the sprite. Using a bounding box means that we reflect only off horizontal or vertical surfaces. Figure 6.3 on the following page shows how a bounding box would fit around a grey rectangle sprite. The two balls bouncing off it show how a ball would bounce if it hit one edge of the bounding box or if it hit two edges at the same time. To the left, the four regions are marked with slanted lines to show where the ball struck a vertical or a horizontal edge. In the corners, the moving ball bounces off the corner or off both a horizontal and a vertical surface, as shown by the cross hatching in the diagram.

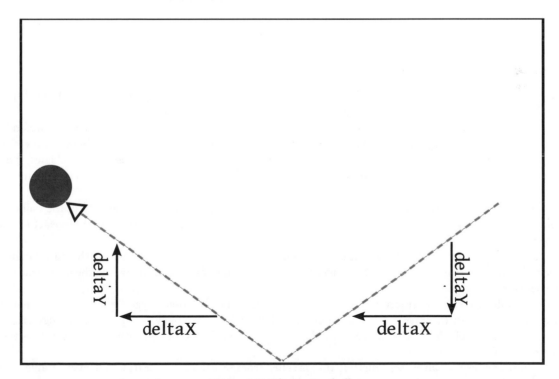

Figure 6.2: A bouncing ball

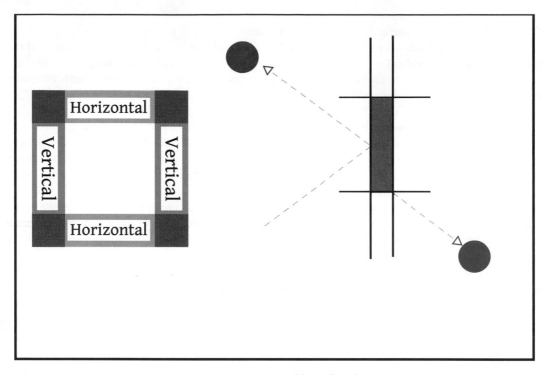

Figure 6.3: Bouncing and bounding boxes

Objects with Their Own Advance

What sort of objects are the ball, countdown timer, and paddle that are part of SoloPong? What type of sprite should each extend and what extra information does each need?

What state must the ball have? We want to know where the ball is (its current x-coordinate and y-coordinate): that is already part of Sprite. There is a type, fang2.core.Sprite. Each *<some>*Sprite class **extends** Sprite. That means the publicly declared methods in Sprite are available to all *<some>*Sprite classes; it also means that when we write a class that **extends** a *<some>*Sprite class, it is part of our new sprite's public protocol, too.

In addition to knowing where the ball is right now, the ball sprite tracks the velocity of the ball as an x-component and a y-component. The ball should look like, well, a ball. That implies that PongBall **extends** OvalSprite.

The countdown timer is like OneDie: it is a StringSprite extended to track a number (in this case a number of seconds). In each frame it updates the timer, changing the color of the text, and fading the displayed value into the background.

The paddle tracks its position and a velocity. The difference between a paddle and a ball is that the ball *always* moves. In its advance the paddle checks whether any arrow keys are pressed. If they are, the paddle applies its velocity in the appropriate direction. Since it looks like a rectangle, PongPaddle **extends** RectangleSprite.

Do these sprites *need* an advance method that is called from SoloPong.advance (this call, every frame, is the "tick" described above; some game engines even name their advance method "tick")?

NewtonsApple moved all sprites directly in advance. EasyDice used two different "advance" methods, one for each of the states the game could be in. It, too, animated the sprites from those advance methods.

History of *Pong*

What was the first video game? One oft-cited contender is 1972's *Pong* from Atari. *Pong* was the first commercial blockbuster in video games but it was 25 years late to the party to be the first video game.

In 1947 Goldsmith and Mann created a radar screen simulator using *analog* circuits to track a missile flight on a cathode ray tube (CRT); a CRT is the big picture tube in older television sets and computer monitors. They called their invention a "cathode ray amusement device" on the patent application they were granted in 1948. With a name like that it is hard to see how it failed to capture the public imagination.

Communications engineer and originator of *information theory* Claude Shannon published a chess playing program in *Philosophical Magazine* before anyone, himself included, had ever programmed an actual computer to play chess [Sha50].

Pong is not even the first video game to play ball. In 1958 William Higginbotham, a nuclear

Figure 6.4: Pong on a Home TV

physicist at Brookhaven National Laboratory, wanted to have something interesting in his lab for the annual visitors' day. The veteran of the Manhattan project wrote that he thought "it might liven up the place to have a game that people could play, and which would convey the message that our scientific endeavors have relevance for society." [Bro09]. He was right, and people stood in line to play the game, connected to a tiny oscilloscope. It showed a side view of a tennis court and the ball arced across the screen, pulled down by "gravity" as players used dials and a single button to control their "racket."

Allan Alcorn, an electrical engineer, built the first Atari *Pong* prototype for Atari, which had a pinball machine route covering various locations in the Stanford University area. The prototype was installed in a local bar and seemed moderately successful. Unfortunately, after a few days, the prototype machine began to malfunction. Alcorn was dispatched to fix it and found that the problem was that the payment system was choked with quarters: the game was *too* successful.

Nolan Bushnell, Atari's founder, wrote an article about games and the computer business 25 years later. He discussed the greatest lesson the Pong team learned from that first product: "One: People will not and hate to read instructions. Two: If people cannot get up the learning curve in 15 seconds they will not spend the second quarter. Three: If you must give instructions make them short, direct, and in as large a font as possible. With the game Pong over 20 years ago the instructions we used were very simple—there are those that think they could be a metaphor for life. The guidelines for use were:

> Insert Quarter.
> Ball Will Serve Automatically.
> Avoid Missing Ball for High Score." [Bus96]

Bushnell's article is interesting because he lists a number of general computer innovations that got their start in computer games. Included in the list are joystick and dial input, collaborative computing, and even sprites. The current author is in fair company in claiming that "All of computer science can be found inside of games."

What responsibilities would `SoloPong.advance` have if it had to do everything?

```
advance(deltaT) // deltaT - delta of time
  if (waiting to start play)
    if (spacebar pressed)
      start countdown timer
  if (countdownTimer is counting down)
    decrement timeRemaining
    if (timeRemaining <= 0.0)
      countdownTimer NOT counting down
    else
      animate based on time remaining
  else
    move ball according to ball velocity
    move paddle according to keyboard
    if (ball hit wall)
      if (wall is bounce wall)
        update ball velocity
      if (wall is score wall)
        update score
        move ball to start position
        wait to start play
    if (ball hit paddle)
      update ball velocity
```

Three different game states (the top level **if-else if**) each with multiple responsibilities. Computer scientists tame complexity by decomposing complex problems into simpler problems and composing the solutions to the simpler problems into a solution of the more complex problem.

Give each sprite its own `advance` method. `SoloPong` just keeps track of which sprites need to be advanced (the real work being left to the sprites).

```
advance(deltaT)
  if (waiting to start)
    if (spacebar pressed)
      countdownTimer.startTimer(3)
      beginCountdown
  else if (counting down)
    countdownTimer.advance(deltaT)
    if (countdownTimer.isExpired())
      beginPlay
  else if (playing)
    ball.advance(deltaT)
    paddle.advance(deltaT)

    if (ball.isOutOfBounds())
      beginWaiting
```

The parameter of `SoloPong.advance` is `deltaT`? Δ_t is the change in the variable t or time. We use `deltaT` for the moment (it shortens to `dT` in future chapters). The important thing to take away from this is that when overriding a method, the *type* of each of the parameters must be the same and they must be in the same order, but the local *name* of the parameter does not matter to Java.

Review 6.1

(a) The velocity in the `Ball` class is separated into the horizontal component and the vertical component, or x-velocity and y-velocity for short. In the FANG coordinates:

  (a) Does a positive x-velocity mean the ball is moving left or right?

  (b) Does a positive y-velocity mean the ball is moving up or down?

  (c) What would be the sign (positive or negative) of the x- and y-velocities if the ball was moving up and to the right?

(b) What happens to the x-velocity when the ball collides with a horizontal wall? With a vertical wall?

(c) What happens to the y-velocity when the ball collides with a horizontal wall? With a vertical wall?

(d) If the *names* of formal parameters don't matter to Java when overloading a method, what *does* matter?

(e) The formula D = R * T describes the relationship between distance, rate (velocity), and time.

  (a) If the ball is moving horizontally at a rate of 0.5 screen per second (moving right) for a duration of 0.04 second, what distance does the ball travel to the right (in the unit screens)?

  (b) If the ball is moving horizontally at -0.66 screen per second (moving left) for a duration of 0.04 second, what distance does the ball travel?

6.2 Top-down Design

Top-down design is decomposing a complex problem into a collection of less complex problems along with a solution to the complex problem composed of solutions to the simpler problems. This is how we designed the `OneDie` and `EasyButton` classes. We went from a public protocol down to running implementations. This section again applies the process, teasing out the different levels of abstraction used.

Pretend that It Works

The first step of stepwise refinement is a game of "let's pretend." When working at a higher level, decompose the high-level solution into a composition of solutions of lower-level, simpler problems. Define the information necessary to solve the simpler problems and figure out how the high-level solution can provide that information to the lower-level solutions. This means examining the parameters necessary for the higher-level solution and determining how they are passed on to the lower-level solutions.

So, how would we write the actual `advance` method for `SoloPong` using the "pretend it works" approach? Assume that we have working ball, paddle, and countdown timer implementations and that appropriately named fields are declared in `SoloPong` (e.g., `countdown` is a `CountdownTimer`).

```
39  public void advance(double deltaT) {
40    if (isWaitingToCountdown()) {
41      if (getKeyPressed() == ' ') {
42        beginCountingDown();
43      }
44    } else if (isCountingDown()) {
45      countdown.advance(deltaT);
46      if (!isCountingDown()) {
47        beginPlaying();
48      }
49    } else if (isPlaying()) {
50      paddle.advance(deltaT);
51      ball.advance(deltaT, paddle);
```

```
52
53        if (ball.isOutOfBounds()) {
54            beginWaitingToCountdown();
55        }
56    }
57 }
```

Listing 6.1: PongBall: advance

(advance sorts near the beginning of SoloPong.java.) SoloPong has three game states: waiting to countdown, counting down, or playing. Rather than trying to specify how to test what state we are in, push the details off by pretending we can write three Boolean methods: isWaitingToCountdown, isCountingDown, and isPlaying.

Putting off the decision on how to determine the current state means we do not know how to *change* the state of the game. How does the game move to the playing state when the countdown finishes? Put off the decision by defining beginPlaying, beginWaitingToCountdown, and beginCountingDown. Each puts the game into the given state.

Having assumed that the detailed methods work (pushing the details down to the next level of abstraction), we write the complete game control, combining those lower-level solutions into the game of SoloPong.

Refining Solutions: Multiple Levels of Abstraction

We *used* the CountdownTimer class (line 45, countdown.advance(deltaT);). The public protocol of CountdownTimer needs to provide the advance method with an appropriate method header. We pushed off all other detailed decisions about CountdownTimer to a lower level of abstraction. It is time to descend to that level.

Determining Necessary Methods

A digital kitchen timer, the kind used to make sure oatmeal cookies don't burn, serves as an analogy for our countdown timer class. What can you do with a kitchen timer?

The timer permits you to set the countdown value, start the countdown, see the remaining time, and check if the time has expired. These capabilities sound like methods in the CountdownTimer class:

```
class CountdownTimer {
  public void setTimer...
  public void startCountdown...
  public double getRemainingTime...
  public boolean isCountdownExpired...
}
```

Anything missing from the public protocol? How do we *get* a kitchen timer? At home we go to the junk drawer and pull the timer out; Java needs to be able to create one. We need a **public** constructor. The kitchen timer has a built-in clock circuit that automatically counts time; we need some way to "tick" the timer. That is what the call to countdown.advance in Listing 6.1 is all about. The new protocol:

```
class CountdownTimer {
  public CoundownTimer...
  public void setTimer...
  public void startCountdown...
  public double getRemainingTime...
  public boolean isCountdownExpired...
  public void advance(double deltaT) { ... }
}
```

Method Headers

What do the rest of the method headers look like? To set the time, we need the time to set. The other four methods need no parameters (though it might be a valid design to have a constructor that took the initial countdown time; we separate the construction and setting). Also, if we intend to have the timer appear on the screen, displaying the countdown, we should extend a sprite class capable of displaying a string. CountdownTimer's public protocol looks like this:

```
class CountdownTimer
  extends StringSprite {
  public CoundownTimer() { ... }
  public void setTimer(double remainingTime) { ... }
  public void startCountdown() { ... }
  public double getRemainingTime() { ... }
  public boolean isCountdownExpired() { ... }
  public void advance(double deltaT) { ... }
}
```

A design rule of thumb is to give all fields and methods as *restrictive* an access level as possible. If it can be **private**, make it **private**. Separating implementation details from the public protocol is *encapsulation*: the implementation details are encapsulated inside the class, protected from meddling from outside code by restrictive access levels.

Review 6.2

(a) Top-down design expresses a problem solution in terms of "solved" simpler problems. The simpler problems are then solved using an application of top-down design at a lower level of abstraction.

- (a) In Java, how are the "simpler problem" solutions expressed when writing the solution to the higher-level problem?
- (b) What three simpler classes are used to solve the "problem" of writing SoloPong?

(b) What is the public protocol of CountdownTimer? Can you think of any other methods that *should* be there that are not?

6.3   Delegation: Methods

A *method* is a named subprogram. It is *named* so that it can be *called* from other methods. It can take *parameters* that can change its behavior from call to call. Some methods calculate and return *values*; value-producing methods can be used as expressions.

The definition of a method does not execute any code. It just gives a name to the body of the method, code that *can* be executed by calling it. Think of it as a recipe: by writing a recipe in a cookbook, the author has *defined* how to make delicious oatmeal cookies; the definition, however, produces no cookies. When some cook *executes* the recipe (method) with the appropriate ingredients (parameters), they produce warm, wonderful cookies.

Defining New Rules: Declaring Methods

A method must be defined inside a class definition. The first line of a method definition is known as the *method header*. The header has four parts: the access level, the return type, the name of the method, and the parameter list.

The term "method header" is not a universal term. It is much more common to talk about a *method signature*. A method's signature is its name and the *types* of its parameters (it is not uncommon to say "formal parameter list" instead of the list of types, but the *names* of the formal parameters are not part of the signature). Java uses the method signature to identify overridden methods (explained in Section 6.3).

The access level has four possible values: `public`, `protected`, `private`, and empty. The (final) Java template for access level is

```
<access-level> := public |
                  <empty> |
                  protected |
                  private
```

(*<empty>* means literally nothing or an "empty string.")

From most restrictive to least restrictive, the meaning of each access level is

`private` Only the class containing the field or method declaration can access it.

`<empty>` The declaring class *and* any class declared in the same *package* (folder) can access the field or method. This behaves as `private` for all classes *except* classes in the same folder as the defining class; for classes in the same folder, the empty access level behaves as `public`.

`protected` The declaring class *and* any class that `extends` that class (either directly or indirectly) can access the field or method. This behaves as `private` for all classes *except* classes extending the defining class; for child classes, `protected` behaves as `public`.

`public` Any class that has a reference to the declaring type can access the field or method.[3]

The return type is just a type, as when declaring fields and variables, or the keyword `void`. Calling a `void` method is not an expression; it is a statement because a `void` method cannot return a value (which is the definition of what an expression does).

The name of the method is any valid Java identifier (starts with letter or underscore, continues with letters, underscores, and digits). Naming conventions, or how to select *good* method names, was discussed in the previous chapter.

Finally, the *formal* parameter list is a list of zero or more type and name pairs (the meaning is investigated in Section 6.3 below). Parameters communicate values from the caller to the called method.

Calling a Method

Delegation has two parts: definition and invocation. Definition describes what happens when the method *is* called; calling the method suspends the calling method and transfers control to the defined subprogram.

Execution begins at the beginning of the body of the method and executes each statement in sequence until running off the end of the method or executing a `return` statement. Selection permits selecting one execution path while skipping others.

Consider living on a college campus. Over time you internalize where you are living. You can find your way home from the bookstore, the dining hall, and even your computer science lab. That internalized knowledge of *how* to get back to the room, the directions you know, is a definition of a "go home" method in your head. Having it defined in your head does not do anything. Something happens only when you tell yourself: "Now, go home from here."

When you call your method, your internal directions evaluate the parameter, "here," and you are off. It is possible that going home was part of some larger sequence of instructions ("change clothes for volleyball," for

---

[3] A `public` *field* can be seen and modified from any class, not just the defining class. The present authors consider `public` fields terrible design.

example). The key is that "go home" does not know anything about that. In fact, the larger set of instructions is suspended until you complete "go home" (which is a good thing if the next step in changing for the game is "remove pants").

Analogously, when setup calls someSprite.setColor(blue), the parameters are evaluated and the instructions in setup are suspended. setup stops making progress while setColor executes.

The rule follower which was performing the instructions in setup sets a bookmark so that it can return to the exact spot setColor was called. setColor does not know it was called from setup or advance or any other method. It does whatever it does with the given actual parameters. When setColor returns (which includes running off the end of the method), control returns to the bookmark in setup.

The definition of a method constructs a new, named rule. Calling the method suspends the method containing the call, marking the *return address* (the bookmark) to which control returns, and it executes the definition from the beginning. For any given rules follower, exactly *one* method is the currently active method.

Parameters: Customizing Rules

Returning to the cooking analogy for a moment, consider a step in the cookie recipe that says Cream together the butter and the sugar. What does that mean? Fortunately, in a fairly complete cookbook such as *The Joy of Cooking*, there is a section on techniques, and the novice cook can look up the definition: Cream together: Mix the ingredients together until they are light and creamy.

What are the ingredients? The author of the definition of Cream together does not know what recipe(s) use the technique, so cannot know the ingredients to be mixed together.

In the cookie recipe, the call is for creaming together the butter and the sugar: that is, the value for which the ingredients serves as a placeholder. When we apply the technique at this point in the cookie recipe, those are the actual ingredients used in the mixing.

Consider a liver dumpling recipe. It might contain the instruction Cream together the egg, liver paste, and breadcrumbs. What are the ingredients this time? It is the list provided when the technique was called.

The analogy is good but goes only so far: in Java, the placeholders are *formal parameters*, declared between the parentheses in the header of the method declaration; there must be one parameter in the formal parameter list for each parameter in the actual parameter list in the call, and the types must match.[4]

It seems limiting to have to specify the types of formal parameters when defining a method. It permits *overloading* a method name, having multiple methods with the same name.

For example, we have used multiple versions of getColor from Game, including ones with the following headers:

```
public Color getColor(String colorName)
public Color getColor(String colorName, int opacity)
public Color getColor(Color currentColor, int opacity)
```

Java differentiates them by their *signature*: the name of the method (which they all share) and the types of the parameters. The three method signatures are

```
getColor(String)
getColor(String, int)
getColor(Color, int)
```

The parameter list in the method header is the *formal* parameter list; it declares local variables that have scope of the body of the method. The ingredients in the technique's *definition*, the formal parameter, is what gets mixed when cream is called.

---

[4]This is the greatest shortcoming of the analogy; in the cookbook, the ingredients applies to any number of items specified in the call. Java method signatures typically require the exact number and type of items to be specified.

The *actual* parameter list is the list of expressions that provide values to the parameters. The term, the butter and the sugar, in the recipe *calling* for creaming is the value actually assigned to the formal parameter on this call.

When assigning a variable with an = operator, the expression on the right-hand side of the assignment is evaluated and the result is copied into the variable named on the left-hand side. In parameter passing, the expression is the actual parameter which is evaluated and the result is copied into the formal parameter. Control is transferred to the called method just *after* all parameters are assigned.

Just as with assignment, the expression (in the actual parameter list) is evaluated and the result is copied into the memory location associated with the formal parameter. Control is transferred to bounceOffOfSprite *after* the value is assigned to the formal parameter.

If there are more than one formal parameter, the actual parameter list must have as many expressions as the formal list has type/name pairs. Values are assigned by position: the left-most actual parameter evaluates and is assigned to the left-most formal parameter's memory location; the second to the left actual parameter expression is evaluated and assigned to the second to the left formal parameter's memory location; and so on.

Passed by Value

Java parameters are passed by value . The actual parameter expression is evaluated and the *value* is copied into the formal parameter's memory location.

The assignment metaphor holds. After the value is copied, the formal and actual parameters are no longer associated. Consider passing a POD parameter:

```java
// package default

import fang.core.Game;
import fang.sprites.StringSprite;

class PODParameters
  extends Game {
  public void fiveTimes(double x) {
    x = x + x + x + x + x;
  }

  public void setup() {
    int k = 9.0;
    fiveTimes(k);

    StringSprite s = new StringSprite(Double.toString(k));
    s.setWidth(0.80);
    s.setLocation(0.5, 0.5);
    addSprite(s);
  }
}
```

Listing 6.2: PODParameters.java

What does s display on the screen? The constructor call in line 16 creates a StringSprite containing the value of k. What is the value of k at that line.

It is set to 9.0 in line 13. The method fiveTimes is called. The actual parameter expression k is evaluated and the result (9.0) is copied into the formal parameter, x, in fiveTimes.

Inside fiveTimes, the value of x changes. Nothing happens to k. This is visualized in Figure 6.5. The red labels and lines in memory are there for humans reading the diagram.

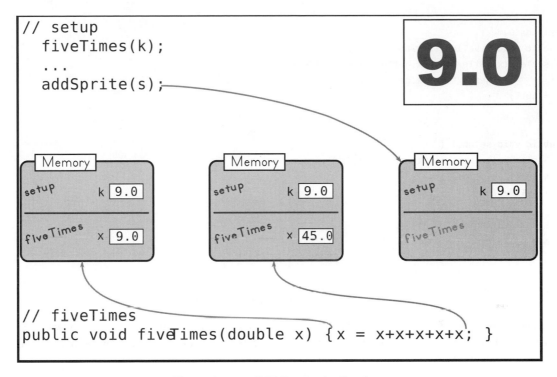

Figure 6.5: POD: POD Parameter Passing

The three views of memory are marked with arrows indicating where, in the execution sequence, they apply. When control passes to fiveTimes, the state of memory is that shown on the left. The expression x + x + x + x + x is evaluated to 45.0 and assigned to x; the middle snapshot of memory shows conditions just after 45.0 is assigned, overwriting the previous value. Finally, when the called method ends, control returns to the caller, setup at the top of the diagram. Everything set aside for fiveTimes is released back to the system. The right-most snapshot shows this.

Execution runs off the end of the body of fiveTimes, so control returns to the bookmark in the calling method. Execution of setup continues from where it was suspended. Line 16 executes, evaluating Double.toString(k) by evaluating the parameter k (value: 9.0) and passing that value to the toString method. toString converts the **double** that it was passed into a string of characters with its value and returns that string: "9.0". The StringSprite constructor is passed that string and the scale value 0.80 and constructs a StringSprite with the given text.

The program PODParameters displays a great big "9.0" in the middle of the screen.

What about object parameters? If we changed the types of x and k to StringSprite, could a change to x change k? The answer is "No, but . . . ."

Object variables are *references* to objects. The following code, a modification of Listing 6.2, passes a StringSprite in to the method fiveTimes. What value does the StringSprite k display?

```
1  // package default
2
3  import fang.core.Game;
4  import fang.sprites.StringSprite;
5
6  class ObjectParameters
```

```
 7  extends Game {
 8  public void fiveTimes(StringSprite x) {
 9  x.setText(x.getText() + x.getText() + x.getText() +
10           x.getText() + x.getText());
11  x = null;
12  }
13
14  public void setup() {
15    StringSprite k = new StringSprite("q");
16    k.setWidth(0.16);
17    fiveTimes(k);
18
19    k.setLocation(0.5, 0.5);
20    addSprite(k);
21  }
22 }
```

Listing 6.3: `ObjectParameters.java`

Line 15 constructs a `StringSprite` somewhere in *Object Memory*. Figure 6.6 illustrates this by showing a section of memory labeled "objects." Java sets aside memory in this area (which is always there in a running Java program, even when it is not drawn) for all **new** objects.

The `StringSprite` in *Object Memory* holds all of the fields of a `StringSprite`. For simplicity the illustration shows just the text value (written in double quotes to indicate that it is a string of characters) and the x and y values of the location of the sprite. These fields are shown for illustration; know that all the fields of an object are stored in the memory set aside by the call to **new**.

Line 15 assigns the result of the **new** operator to k. Line 16 calls `fiveTimes` with k as the actual parameter. The expression k evaluates to a reference to a `StringSprite` and the value of that expression is copied into the formal parameter x. Control transfers to `fiveTimes`.

The left-most memory in the figure shows memory just after `fiveTimes` begins execution. Though k and x are separate variables in memory, they both refer to the same underlying object. Again, parameter passing by value is just like assignment from the actual parameter(s) to the formal parameter(s).

When x.`setText` is called with five concatenated copies of the text already in the `StringSprite`, the sprite *in Object Memory* is changed. This is seen in the middle memory snapshot. The value of x is changed by assignment in line 11 and that, too, is shown in the middle memory diagram. Notice that neither action in the called method changed the value of k, the variable used as the actual parameter.

Finally, `fiveTimes` returns control to `setup` and the execution resumes right after the call to the method (where the compiler kept a "bookmark" before transferring control to the called method). The right-most memory snapshot shows the situation after line 18: the location, the two other fields shown in the `StringSprite` object, was updated from (0.0, 0.0) to (0.5, 0.5). The string displayed, in the upper-right corner, is "qqqqq."

Methods as Functions: Returning Values

Method calls can be expressions. When the return type of a method is anything but **void**, the expression returns some value. **void** is not a type but rather a word meaning "nothing."

Listing 6.4 shows `getRemainingTime` and `isExpired` from `CountdownTimer`. `CountdownTimer` has a **double** field called `remainingTime` which holds the seconds remaining in the countdown.

`getRemainingTime` is what we have called a *getter*, a **public** method permitting outside classes to see some internal state of our class. This is safe because the public protocol determines how much state is exposed. Besides, there is no requirement that the method return a field; the timer could store the expiration time in Greenwich Mean Time and *calculate* the remaining time on each call to `getRemainingTime`. The getter just gives

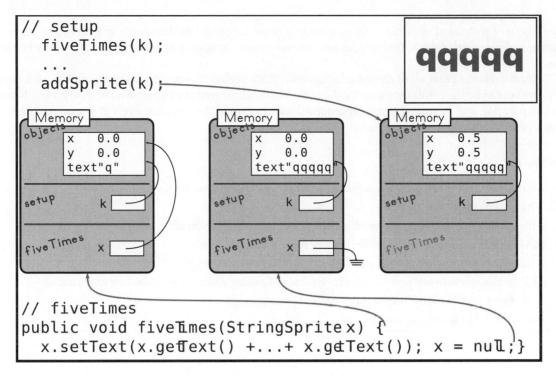

Figure 6.6: Java Object Parameters

clients of this class a way to query an instance's state. A client of a class is one that *uses* the class: SoloPong is a client of CountdownTimer and would use the getters to query the state of a timer.

```
64    public double getRemainingTime() {
65      return remainingTime;
66    }
73    public boolean isExpired() {
74      return remainingTime <= 0.0;
75    }
```

Listing 6.4: CountdownTimer: functions

The **return** statement on line 65 evaluates the expression following it and returns that value as the result of calling the method.

If there were 10.34 seconds remaining to countdown and somewhere in SoloPong.advance the following (hypothetical) line were executed,

```
double t = countdown.getRemainingTime();
```

a memory box for a **double** is set aside, labeled with the identifier t, the method is called (no parameters to pass), and 10.34 is returned. The value 10.34 is stored in t.

isExpired returns a **boolean** value. Java naming conventions suggest that **boolean** methods be named is<*Something*> where <*Something*> describes what it means when the method returns **true**.

The expression on line 74 is a *Boolean expression*: it compares two **double** values using the <= operator. It returns **true** when the timer is expired (when there is 0.0 or fewer seconds remaining) and **false** otherwise.

The <= is used instead of == because there is no way to be sure that the ticks come at intervals to make the counter end up *exactly* on 0.0. This way, as soon as remainingTime touches or crosses zero, the method returns true.

Delegation is the creation of named subprograms. It is a perfect fit with stepwise refinement: each named subprogram can be the solution to a particular subproblem uncovered at a higher level of abstraction. Naming the computation and providing it with appropriate parameters protects higher levels of abstraction from the details of solving the given subproblem.

Review 6.3

(a) What is the difference between *defining* a method and *calling* a method?

(b) What is a method *signature*?

(c) Which fields of an object are stored in the "object memory" region after a call to new?

(d) How does a *constructor* header differ from a regular method header?

(e) What is the difference between a public method and a private method?

(f) Why is calling a void method not an expression, but calling a non-void method an expression?

(g) Must every method have one or more parameters?

(h) Consider the following Game code:

```
public void setup()
{
   OvalSprite oval=new OvalSprite(0.1, 0.1);
   modify(oval);
   addSprite(oval);
}

private void modify(OvalSprite oval)
{
   oval.setLocation(0.5, 0.5);
}
```

Where on the screen is the oval displayed? (If you are not sure, try writing a simple FANG game to figure it out.) Explain your answer.

(i) Consider the following Game code:

```
public void setup()
{
   OvalSprite oval=new OvalSprite(0.1, 0.1);
   modify(oval);
   addSprite(oval);
}

private void modify(OvalSprite oval)
{
   oval=new OvalSprite(0.1, 0.1);
   oval.setLocation(0.5, 0.5);
}
```

Where on the screen is the oval displayed? (If you are not sure, try writing a simple FANG game to figure it out.) Explain your answer.

6.4 Expressions Redux

An expression is a piece of code that returns a value. What is the type and the value of the expression in the line marked (a)?

```
int p = 1001;

"p = " + p // (a)
```

The expression is an application of the + operator. As we saw earlier, the type of an addition expression depends on the types of the subexpressions being added. If they are both **int** . . . no, the first expression is *not* an **int**. If one is **double** and the other is **double** or **int** . . . no, that is not the case either.

What is the *type* of "p = "? It is a sequence of characters enclosed in double quotes. It is a String[5] literal. It is a class-type literal.

What does an expression of the type String + int *mean*? Java uses + for *concatenation* of String values. When left-hand subexpression is a String, no matter what type the right-hand subexpression has, Java converts it into a String and appends it to the end of the left-hand side String, returning a new String containing all of the characters in a row.

The left-hand side is "p = " and the right-hand side is the **int** p. When a variable appears in an expression, it returns its value; p stores 1001. Java converts the **int** into a String.[6], getting "1001"

The string "1001" and the **int** 1001 are not the same thing. In Java it is possible to multiply an **int** by another **int**; it is not possible to multiply a String by anything.

After conversion, the two strings are concatenated and the result of the whole expression is the string "p = 1000". In the given code snippet, the String is created as the expression is evaluated. Since nothing is done with the expression, it is thrown away.

When concatenating a String with any plain old data type, Java uses the *<Type>*.toString(*<type>*) method where *<Type>* is the name of the wrapper for the POD type (Integer for **int**, Double for **double**, Boolean for **boolean**, etc.). To explicitly convert p to its String equivalent, we could call Integer.toString(p) before the concatenation:

```
int p = 1001;

"p = " + Ineger.toString(p) // (a) - just the same!
```

java.lang.String is a class type. Objects of type String can be used to call methods.

The *Other* Literal Value: String

Modern computer languages have a type to hold variable length sequences of characters. In Java the standard type is java.lang.Sting. All types defined in the java.lang library are automatically imported into every program.

String is a class type and can be used to declare variables. String is also unique among class types in Java: there are String literals and String operators.

A String literal is a sequence of characters enclosed in double quotes ("). Examples include "simplecomputer", "*.*", and "101". Inside double quotes, whitespace (spaces and tabs) is significant; a String literal *cannot* span multiple lines in Java.

Java (taking after its predecessor languages C/C++) permits *escaped character sequences* to express characters that are difficult or impossible to type into a String (or **char**) literal. An escaped character is a two-character sequence that is replaced with a single special character. The first character of the sequence, the *escape character*, is a slash, \. The following table shows the most common escape character sequences:

---

[5]String, java.lang.String *is* a standard Java class.
[6]With an implicit call to Integer.toString method.

Escape Sequence	Meaning
\n	New line — an end-of-line marker
\r	Carriage return — another end-of-line marker
\t	Tab
\"	A quote character (that does not mark the end of the string)
\	A slash (or else it escapes the next character)

As shown above, String is the only class for which the + operator works. It is the concatenation operator, "gluing" strings together when they are "added." If the left-hand subexpression is not already of type String, Java automatically converts it to a String before concatenation. String values, though stored in the *Object Memory*, are *immutable* or unchangeable. That is why fiveTimes took a StringSprite rather than a String. Java's authors took great pains for String to behave almost like it is a primitive type.

Listing 6.5, StringValues, demonstrates how to declare String variables, how to concatenate them, and how to assign values to the variables. It also demonstrates some of the String methods.

```java
16  public void setup() {
17     final double STRING_HEIGHT = 0.04;// a named constant. Used to step
18                                  // strings down screen
19     double yPosition = STRING_HEIGHT;// represents the y position of
20                                  // the next string sprite
21     String userFirstName = "Claes";
22     String userLastName = "Bos-Ladd";
23     // concatenation
24     String userFullName = userFirstName + " " + userLastName;
25
26     // Constructor takes a string and then the scale.
27     StringSprite msg1 = new StringSprite("userFirstName = " +
28         userFirstName);
29     msg1.setLineHeight(STRING_HEIGHT);
30     msg1.setLocation(0.5, yPosition);
31     yPosition = yPosition + STRING_HEIGHT;
32     addSprite(msg1);
33
34     StringSprite msg2 = new StringSprite("userLastName = " +
35         userLastName);
36     msg2.setLineHeight(STRING_HEIGHT);
37     msg2.setLocation(0.5, yPosition);
38     yPosition = yPosition + STRING_HEIGHT;
39     addSprite(msg2);
40
41     StringSprite msg3 = new StringSprite("userFullName = " +
42         userFullName);
43     msg3.setLineHeight(STRING_HEIGHT);
44     msg3.setLocation(0.5, yPosition);
45     yPosition = yPosition + STRING_HEIGHT;
46     addSprite(msg3);
47
48     StringSprite msg4 = new StringSprite(
49         "userFullName.toLowerCase() = " + userFullName.toLowerCase());
50     msg4.setLineHeight(STRING_HEIGHT);
```

```
51    msg4.setLocation(0.5, yPosition);
52    yPosition = yPosition + STRING_HEIGHT;
53    addSprite(msg4);
54
55    StringSprite msg5 = new StringSprite(
56        "userFullName.toUpperCase() = " + userFullName.toUpperCase());
57    msg5.setLineHeight(STRING_HEIGHT);
58    msg5.setLocation(0.5, yPosition);
59    yPosition = yPosition + STRING_HEIGHT;
60    addSprite(msg5);
61
62    StringSprite msg6 = new StringSprite(
63        "userFullName.substring(6, 9) = " +
64        userFullName.substring(6, 9));
65    msg6.setLineHeight(STRING_HEIGHT);
66    // "Claes Bos-Ladd" [6-9) = "Bos"
67    //  00000000001111
68    //  01234567890123
69    msg6.setLocation(0.5, yPosition);
70    yPosition = yPosition + STRING_HEIGHT;
71    addSprite(msg6);
72  }
```

Listing 6.5: `StringValues` setup

The various `StringSprite` values are constructed with the results of various `String` expressions. The expressions begin with text identifying what string feature is being demonstrated; the result of calling the identified method is concatenated on the identifier. The second parameter to `StringSprite` is the scale of the resulting sprite.

`String` includes methods to convert the case of the characters in the string: `toUpperCase` and `toLowerCase` each return a copy of the `String` on which they are called with the case of all letters converted as you would expect. `substring` returns a copy of some part of the string: `substring(<start>)` copies from the `<start>` position to the end of the string; `substring(<start>, <end>)` copies the characters from `<start>` up to but *not including* `<end>`. The start and end values are the indexes of the letters. The *first* letter in a `String` has an index of 0.

The comments in lines 66–68 in Listing 6.5 show the value of `userFullName` and give the character index below each character (read the numbers downward in column). Index 06 is B, so the characters on the range $[6-9)$[7] yield the substring "Bos". Figure 6.7 shows the results of running `StringValues`.

Object Expressions

Object expressions are expressions returning an object type. An object-typed variable or a call to **new** is an object expression.

```
new RectangleSprite(1.0, 0.5)
```

This call to **new** calls the constructor for the type `RectangleSprite`. It returns a reference to the newly constructed object somewhere in object memory. To date we have always assigned the result of this call to a variable. This is necessary only if we want to be able to call the result by name, that is, use a label for it. It is legal to use the above expression anywhere a `RectangleSprite` is permitted:

---

[7]The range notation: "[" means the range includes the lower bound and ")" means it does *not* include the upper bound.

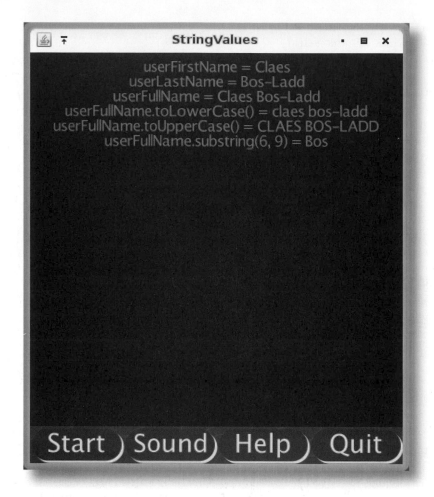

Figure 6.7: Running the compiled StringValues program

```
addSprite(new RectangleSprite(1.0, 0.5));
```

This would add the new sprite to the game (or CompositeSprite). Without a label for the sprite we cannot change its color or scale or rotation or, well, anything.

Using Object Methods

A more complex object expression is the result of calling a method which returns an object type. Consider lines 48–49 in StringValues, duplicated here:

```
48    StringSprite msg4 = new StringSprite(
49        "userFullName.toLowerCase() = " + userFullName.toLowerCase());
```

Listing 6.6: StringValues: 48–49

The subexpression userFullName.toLowerCase() calls the toLowerCase method (defined in the String class) on the String referenced by userFullName. A duplicate string is returned with all upper-case letters converted to their lower-case equivalents and all other characters unchanged.

Chaining Method Calls

The "dot notation" calls methods using a reference to an object. A variable (or field or parameter) of a class type is a reference to an object (or, possibly, **null** to indicate it refers to no object at all). The return value of **new** and the return value of an object-returning method are also *references to objects*. They can be used on the left-hand side of the dot to call methods on the object.

```
62    StringSprite msg6 = new StringSprite(
63        "userFullName.substring(6, 9) = " +
64        userFullName.substring(6, 9));
```

Listing 6.7: `StringValues`: 62–64

How could `msg6` be changed so that the last three characters were `"BOS"` instead of `"Bos"`? A call to `toUpperCase` on the string holding `"Bos"` would do the trick. There is no *variable* holding the string. Change the lines to read:

```
62        StringSprite msg6 = new StringSprite(
63            "userFullName.substring(6, 9) = " +
64            userFullName.substring(6, 9).toUpperCase());
```

Listing 6.8: `StringValues`: 62–64 (modified)

Modified line 64 *chains* the call to `toUpperCase` onto the results of the call to `substring`. Calls can also be chained onto the results of **new**.

Review 6.4

(a) Is `String` a class type or a plain old data type? (Hint: Think about naming conventions.)

(b) What does *immutable* mean?

(c) What `String` method do you use to get a copy of some sequence of characters in the string? What parameters (if any) does the method take?

(d) What *operator* is used to *concatenate* two `Strings` together into a single string?

(e) What does the literal character `'\n'` mean?

(f) The `String` method `charAt(int n)` returns the character at position n in the string. What parameter would you pass in to get the *first* character in the string? The *second* character? The *seventh* character?

6.5 Finishing Up SoloPong

What is the public protocol for `PongBall`? The game needs to be able to construct a ball, tick the ball, set the velocity, and check if the ball has gone out of bounds. A ball is an `OvalSprite` with velocity. The constructor needs enough information to construct a `OvalSprite` plus to set the velocity of the ball. The constructor takes four parameters: `width`, `height`, `deltaX`, and `deltaY`.

The ball must bounce off the walls and the paddle but all bouncing methods are **private**, called from `advance` when the ball is ticked.

```
class PongBall
  extends OvalSprite {
  public PongBall(double width, double height,
                  double deltaX, double deltaY)...
  public void advance(double deltaT, Sprite paddle)...
```

```
    public boolean isOutOfBounds()...
    public void setVelocity(double deltaX, double deltaY)...
}
```

The signatures of the methods are what one would expect except for advance. Previously, advance just took a time. Here it takes time and some Sprite. Why?

The key is the answer to the question: what object or objects have references to the paddle? The paddle, a sprite of some sort, is constructed in SoloPong. The *game* constructs the ball, too. The game "knows" about both the ball and the paddle; the ball has no direct reference to the paddle. It needs a reference to the paddle to determine if it has struck the paddle. The game can provide the necessary information when it calls PongBall.advance.

```
19    private double deltaX;
20    private double deltaY;
21
22    /**
23     * Create a new PongBall. Specify the size and the initial velocity of
24     * the ball.
25     *
26     * @param  width   width of the ball in screens
27     * @param  height  height of the ball in screens
28     * @param  deltaX  initial horizontal velocity in screens per second
29     * @param  deltaY  initial vertical velocity in screens per second
30     */
31    public PongBall(double width, double height,
32                    double deltaX, double deltaY) {
33      super(width, height);
34      // A scope hole: two detltaX are in scope (line 9, line 25)
35      // Deepest nested block in scope wins: line 25
36      // this.deltaX refers to the field (line 9)
37      this.deltaX = deltaX;// set FIELD to the parameter value
38      this.deltaY = deltaY;// set FIELD to the parameter value
39    }
```

Listing 6.9: PongBall: Constructor

Listing 6.9 shows the fields and constructors of PongBall. The fields are deltaX and deltaY. Lines 31–32 are the header of the constructor (the line is wrapped to print clearly). It takes four **double** parameters.

Line 33 calls a method named **super** with two **double** parameters. What is **super** and where is it defined? The keyword **super**, as the first statement in a constructor, calls the constructor of the *superclass* of the current class. The superclass is the class that the current class *directly* **extends**.

Line 33 calls the OvalSprite constructor that takes two **double** parameters. If we look at the documentation, that constructor takes the width and the height of the oval to construct. The width and height parameters are exactly those values in this constructor.

This is the first time we have had to do this because Java has a concept of a *default constructor*. The default constructor is the constructor (if there is one) with no parameters. *If* the superclass has a default constructor *and* that is the constructor our class needs, there is no need to include an explicit call to **super()** (the call with no parameters): Java makes the call implicitly before giving control to our constructor.

EasyButton extended CompositeSprite and used the default CompositeSprite constructor. It need no explicit call to **super** since an implicit **super()** was generated by Java.

Scope Holes

Lines 37 and 38 are strange: the same variable name appears in the line twice, once with `this.` in front of it, once without. What does the comment, mentioning a *scope hole*, mean?

Scope, as we have seen, is where a variable or method name is usable. A field, such as `deltaX`, is *in scope* throughout the class definition body (both before and after the line declaring the field). `deltaX` is in scope at the beginning of line 37.

There is a problem: the constructor has a parameter called `deltaX`. A parameter is in scope for the body of the method for which it is declared. Between the end of line 32 and the end of line 39 there are *two* different variables named `deltaX` in scope.

Java's rule for resolving this sort of conflict is simple: whatever definition is closest to the current line in terms of curly braces wins. Count the depth of each definition, adding one to depth for each opening curly brace that is still open when the variable is defined (consider parameters to be in the method body). Do the same for a given line using the variable name. Whichever definition is closest to the same level as the reference is the one chosen.

```
class PongBall ... {
  private double deltaX; // depth 1
  private double deltaY; // depth 1

  ...

  public PongBall(double width, // depth 2
                  double height, // depth 2
                  double deltaX, // depth 2
                  double detlaY) { // depth 2
    ... deltaX ... // which deltaX? depth == 2
  }
  // which deltaX? only one in scope!
}
```

The unqualified name, `deltaX`, within the constructor, refers to the parameter. This creates a scope hole, a place where the field `deltaX` "should" be in scope but where it is masked by another use of the same name.

The constructor must assign the value of the parameter `deltaX` to the field `deltaX`. In Java, inside of any method, there is a reference to the object on which the method was called. The reference is `this`. In the constructor, `this.deltaX` is the field (no matter what names the parameters have) and `deltaX` is the parameter. Lines 37 and 38 both use `this` to overcome the scope hole.

An entire subsection on scope holes: why not just use different names for the parameters and the fields? Until now we have and it would be perfectly legitimate to do so here.

The scope hole was created to illustrate Java's rule for resolving multiple declarations of the same name at different scope levels. It is also standard Java programming practice to name constructor parameters for the fields they initialize. It is important for a learning Java programmer to be comfortable with the idiom and using `this.` to refer to the nonlocal declaration. Programs are written for the compiler *and* other programmers. It is important to be able to read and write standard idioms in your preferred programming language.

Another use of `this`

```
47  public PongBall(double width, double height) {
48    this(width, height, 0.0, 0.0);
49  }
```

Listing 6.10: `PongBall`: The Other Constructor

Listing 6.10 shows a *second* constructor for `PongBall`. This raises a lot of questions: Why have two constructors? How does the compiler decide which one to call? What is **this** doing on line 48; it looks like it should be **super**.

The second constructor permits the user to construct a `PongBall` without bothering to specify the initial velocity. It is convenient if the method constructing the ball cannot know the velocity (as is the case in `SoloPong.setup`).

The compiler can tell the difference between multiple methods with the same name, *overloaded* methods, by comparing the actual parameter list with all of the signatures for methods with the given name. When the number and types match, the compiler knows which one to call. Because expressions (the actual parameters) have types, the compiler can figure out the match when compiling the program.

The signatures of different methods (or constructors) with the same name must be different. Since they cannot differ in the method name, they must differ in the number or types of the parameters in the parameter list. The signature does not include the return type or access level, so neither of those impact the choice.

Just as a constructor can call a superclass constructor by specifying a call to **super** as the first statement in the constructor, a constructor can call a different constructor of the *same* class by calling **this** as the first statement in the constructor. This is a good application of the DRY principle: the four parameter constructor does all the real work; it is the *canonical* or standard constructor. All other constructors call that constructor, providing appropriate default values for missing parameters.

What default velocity should we use? The arbitrary answer is 0.0 screen/second in both dimensions. That is where the two 0.0s on line 48 come from.

Bouncing

Listing 6.11 shows bouncing off the edges for the ball. The various hit<*Some*>Edge methods check the minimum or maximum extent of the ball against the given edge of the screen.

Lines 230–232 show `hitBottomEdge` as an example. If the bottom edge is hit, the ball bounces off a horizontal edge (lines 135–137). The clear<*Direction*> methods make sure that the ball is not sticking past the edge.

Remember how in the `CountdownTimer` we could not be sure the remaining time would count down to *exactly* 0.0? The same problem applies to the ball hitting the edge of the screen. Notice that the test in `hitBottomEdge` is not for equality but for equal or larger. This is because the ball could move *past* the bottom edge (or any other edge).

```
115    private void bounceOffEdges() {
116      if (hitTopEdge()) {
117        bounceOffHorizontalEdge();
118        clearTop(0.0);
119      } else if (hitBottomEdge()) {
120        bounceOffHorizontalEdge();
121        clearBottom(1.0);
122      }
123      if (hitLeftEdge()) {
124        bounceOffVerticalEdge();
125        clearLeft(0.0);
126      }
127      /* else if (hitRightEdge()) {
128       * clearRight(1.0);} */
129    }
135    private void bounceOffHorizontalEdge() {
136      deltaY = -deltaY;
137    }
```

```
186   private void clearBottom(double y) {
187     if (y < getMaxY()) {
188       translateY(y - getMaxY());
189     }
190   }
230   private boolean hitBottomEdge() {
231     return (getMaxY() >= 1.0);
232   }
```

Listing 6.11: PongBall: bounceOffEdges

The problem is that our "reaction" to hitting an edge is to reverse the velocity in a given dimension. What if, for some reason, the ball does not move up onto the screen in the next frame? It is still hitting the bottom edge and the ball reverses vertical direction again. It wiggles up and down, trapped in the wall. If you have ever moved through a "solid" object in a game world, you have seen a manifestation of this sort of error.

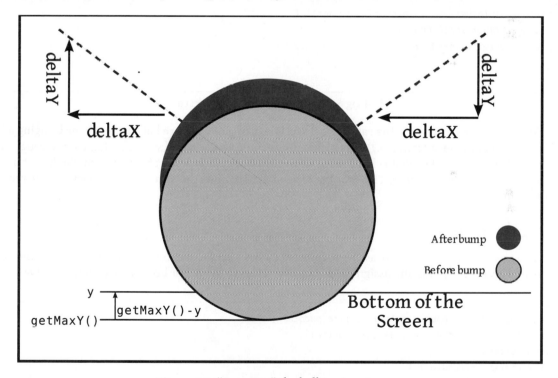

Figure 6.8: "Bumping" the ball in clearBottom

The fix is to "bump" the ball back onto the screen before the next frame begins. clearBottom makes sure the bottom of the ball is *above* the given value by translating the ball up a little bit if necessary. The situation and the result of calling clearBottom is illustrated in Figure 6.8.

Bouncing off another sprite is just about the same. The biggest difference is that in order to intersect with, for example, the top of the paddle, the ball must be above the paddle and the paddle must cross the bottom edge of the ball. Figure 6.3 indicates why this is. The methods for determining above and intersects the edge are range checks on the minimum and maximum bounds in the x- and y-directions.

```
153   private void bounceOffSprite(Sprite other) {
154     if (leftOfIt(other) && intersectsRight(other)) {
155       bounceOffVerticalEdge();
156       clearRight(other.getMinX());
157     }
158     if (rightOfIt(other) && intersectsLeft(other)) {
159       bounceOffVerticalEdge();
160       clearLeft(other.getMaxX());
161     }
162
163     if (aboveIt(other) && intersectsBottom(other)) {
164       bounceOffHorizontalEdge();
165       clearBottom(other.getMinY());
166     }
167     if (belowIt(other) && intersectsTop(other)) {
168       bounceOffHorizontalEdge();
169       clearTop(other.getMaxY());
170     }
171   }
```

Listing 6.12: `PongBall`: `bounceOffSprite`

It would have been easy to write the range checks in-line in `bounceOffSprite` but that would be bringing a lot of unnecessary detail into Listing 6.12. As recommended in *Code Complete* [McC04], a tome on writing good code, named methods make what is happening clearer. Also note that some of the same methods that made `bounceOfEdges` work are used here. This is a sign of good design, when the same building blocks can be reused in a different way.

Refining the Design

`setVelocity` uses `deltaX` and `deltaY` as the parameter names. Just as the constructor does, it uses the **this** reference to access the fields and assign the parameter values to them. For brevity we do not list `setVelocity` here.

```
61   public void advance(double deltaT, Sprite paddle) {
62     translate(deltaX * deltaT, deltaY * deltaT);
63     bounceOffEdges();
64     if (intersects(paddle)) {
65       bounceOffSprite(paddle);
66       incrementScore();
67     }
68   }
```

Listing 6.13: `PongBall`: `advance`

Listing 6.13 shows what happens to the ball in every frame. By pushing details down to another level, the code is quite clear: move the ball according to its velocity, bounce it off the edges, and, if it has hit the paddle, bounce it off the paddle and increment the score.

Once more, because this `advance` method does *not* override a method in a parent class of `PongBall`, there are no constraints on its signature. That is why it is fine to take `paddle` as a parameter.

By passing in the paddle, the ball can handle all of its own bouncing *and* increment the score when hitting the paddle. Why is the type of the parameter `Sprite`? Aren't we defining a class, `PongPaddle`?

Yes, we are defining `PongPaddle`. `Sprite` as the parameter type makes a point about Java and extending classes: whenever a variable (field, parameter, local variable) expects a value of a particular class, *any* class that **extends** that class, directly or indirectly, is acceptable.

`advance` expects a `Sprite` for the second parameter. A `Sprite`, a `RectangleSprite`, a `PongPaddle`, even a `StringSprite` is acceptable.

The limitation when using superclass parameters is that the method is limited to the methods defined in the superclass. So, even if we pass in a `PongPaddle` that defined a `advance` method, `PongBall.advance` could not call `paddle.advance` because the compiler could not be sure that the value of `paddle` even *had* an `advance` method (since `Sprite` does *not*). The bouncing does not require any special knowledge of the type of the `Sprite`, so that is the type for `paddle`.

Reading the Keyboard

`PongPaddle` looks like `PongBall`: it extends a sprite, it has a velocity, it has its own `advance` method, and it has a `bounceOffEdges` method. The thing that makes it different is that in the `advance` method, the velocity is only used if an arrow key has been pressed.

Think about that for a moment: the ball simulates continuous motion, an "active component." In every frame the ball moves according to its velocity:

```
translateX(deltaX * deltaT);
translateY(deltaY * deltaT);
```

The same basic formula works for the paddle except it moves only when the player tells it to. If the player presses the left arrow key, velocity is applied to the left; if she press the right arrow key, velocity is applied to the right. Using `deltaX` as the horizontal velocity, the translation is by `deltaX * detlatT` times plus or minus 1. The plus is for moving right, the minus for moving left (x-coordinates get bigger to the right, smaller to the left).

As we have seen, reading the keyboard uses the `getKeyPressed()` and `[up,down,left,right]Pressed()` methods of the `Game` class. We now need that information in a different class, a non-`Game`-derived class. That means we need to get access to the current `Game` inside `PongPaddle`'s `advance`. The `Game` class has a special method, a **static** method, called `getCurrentGame`, which returns a reference to the current `Game`.

static Fields and Methods

What is a **static** method? The short answer is a method that has no **this**. The longer answer is that a **static** method is one that belongs not to an *instance* of a class but rather to the *class* itself.

The difference has two immediate consequences: we can call a **static** method without having called **new** to create an object or instance, and inside a **static** method we cannot access *any* fields or methods that are not also **static**. Static methods are called by prefixing the method name with the name of the class rather than a reference to an instance:

```
Game.getCurrentGame()
```

The second consequence means that **static** is contagious: any method or field used from a **static** method is infected and becomes **static**. Fields, too, can be **static** (we saw **static final** fields in Section 5.5). More discussion of **static** methods, including a modified Java method template, comes later when we write our own **static** methods.

For right now, we use the `getCurrentGame` method to get a reference to the current game whenever we need it. So, we can now write the `advance` method for the `PongPaddle` class:

```
47  public void advance(double deltaT) {
48    if (Game.getCurrentGame().upPressed()) {
49      translateY(-deltaY * deltaT);
50    }
51    if (Game.getCurrentGame().downPressed()) {
52      translateY(deltaY * deltaT);
53    }
54    if (Game.getCurrentGame().leftPressed()) {
55      translateX(-deltaX * deltaT);
56    }
57    if (Game.getCurrentGame().rightPressed()) {
58      translateX(deltaX * deltaT);
59    }
60    bounceOffEdges();
61  }
```

Listing 6.14: PongPaddle: advance method

The value returned from Game.getCurrentGame() is a reference to a Game. A dot can be applied, chaining a call to another method, one belonging to an instance of a Game. Game.getCurrentGame().upPressed() is **true** when the user has pressed the up arrow key (see Game documentation). The four **if** statements move the paddle according to the key(s) pressed by the player and the velocity set for the PongPaddle.

The game design calls for constraining the paddle to vertical movement. What velocity values would have this effect? A zero x-component means that the paddle cannot move horizontally. A non-zero y-component means the paddle does move vertically. A positive y-component makes the direction of movement match the arrow key being pressed (try a negative velocity for a crazy, mixed-up game).

Why does the PongPaddle have an x-component to its velocity? Two reasons: sometimes it is easier to solve a more general problem than it is to solve a very specific problem, and it almost always a good idea to reuse code you already understand. The ball velocity code is code we have examined and it moves the ball in two dimensions. That code, modified to check on what keys were pressed, works to move the paddle. We could even modify the game to have the paddle move horizontally at very little cost.

What does it mean for the paddle to "bounce" off of the edge? When the paddle moves a little bit off the edge, we want to move it back immediately. The paddle never moves past the edge so, when we detect that it has, we back it up:

```
71  public void bounceOffEdges() {
72    if (getMinY() < 0.0) {
73      translateY(0.0 - getMinY());
74    }
75    if (getMaxY() > 1.0) {
76      translateY(1.0 - getMaxY());
77    }
78    if (getMinX() < 0.0) {
79      translateX(0.0 - getMinX());
80    }
81    if (getMaxX() > 1.0) {
82      translateX(1.0 - getMaxX());
83    }
84  }
```

Listing 6.15: PongPaddle: bounceOffEdges method

The distance the paddle is moved is just enough to put the errant edge back on the screen; this is just like the ball's clear<*Direction*> methods. The translation is done only if the paddle edge is past the edge of the screen.

Laziness as a Virtue

There is a successful programming language, Perl, which is known for three things among computer programmers: some of the craziest combinations of punctuation as valid variable names (for example, $_ and $@ are both regularly used system variables), having more than one way to do *anything*, and for having been developed out of laziness. The inventor of Perl, Larry Wall, praises laziness as a virtue because if you're too lazy to get right to work, you'll think about what you need to do. Perl grew out of a report that Wall had to type up every week with data he had to go across campus to read off another computer. He automated the process and added parameters so that he could change the report format. The result is the "Practical Extraction and Report Language" or Perl.

Laziness also means to look for general solutions that use parameters to specify them. Take, for example, the PongPaddle advance method. How hard would it be to modify the game to bounce a ball up in the sky while the paddle moved across the bottom of the screen? The paddle is already ready (just set the shape and the velocities). The ball would need a little work.

Of course, some part of the code is specific to the problem at hand. We end this chapter looking at the six state-handling methods we pretended into existence at the beginning of the chapter.

```
17    /** The ball */
18    private PongBall ball;
19
20    /** Countdown timer */
21    private CountdownTimer countdown;
22
23    /** The paddle */
24    private PongPaddle paddle;
25
26    /** Press space to start message */
27    private StringSprite pressSpace;
28
29    /** The display of the score */
30    private StringSprite volleysSprite;
```

Listing 6.16: SoloPong: Fields

Listing 6.16 shows the fields at the beginning of SoloPong, the Game-extending class. All but volleySprite and pressSpace were discussed earlier in the chapter.

SoloPong inherited a getScore and a setScore method, methods that can keep score in a **private** field in Game. In PongBall.advance, the call to incrementScore uses getScore to get the current score and setScore to add one to it.

```
65    @Override
66    public void setScore(int score) {
67      super.setScore(score);
68      volleysSprite.setText(Integer.toString(getScore()));
69    }
```

Listing 6.17: SoloPong: setScore

volleySprite displays the current score. To make sure volleySprite is properly updated, SoloPong overrides setScore:

This use of **super** calls the named method defined at or above our superclass. Recall (from Section 4.1) that Java starts at the bottom of the **extends** hierarchy of the constructed type (the one named after **new**) looking for the lowest definition of an overridden method. The call to **super**.setScore starts the search at our superclass (Game) rather than at the most extended class (SoloPong, the current class). The call means Game does whatever it does to keep the score. Line 68 then uses getScore to get the game's score, convert it to a String, and set the sprite's text.

pressSpace is a StringSprite that says "Press Space to begin." It is only visible when the game is waiting to count down.

```
146    /**
147     * Are we in the counting down state?
148     *
149     * @return  true if we are, false otherwise
150     */
151    private boolean isCountingDown() {
152      return countdown.isVisible();
153    }
154
155    /**
156     * Are we in the moving ball state?
157     *
158     * @return  true if we are, false otherwise
159     */
160    private boolean isPlaying() {
161      return ball.isVisible();
162    }
163
164    /**
165     * Are we in the waiting to countdown state?
166     *
167     * @return  true if we are, false otherwise
168     */
169    private boolean isWaitingToCountdown() {
170      return pressSpace.isVisible();
171    }
```

Listing 6.18: SoloPong: Check State

Only one of the three sprites, ball, pressSpace, and countdownTimer, is visible at any given time. ball is visible while playing. pressSpace is visible while waiting to countdown. countdownTimer is visible while counting down. The Sprite methods show and hide change whether or not a sprite is visible. Because only one is visible at a time, the state-testing routines in Listing 6.18 are all one liners.

```
114    /**
115     * Whatever state we were in, move us to the counting down state
116     */
117    private void beginCountingDown() {
118      ball.hide();
119      countdown.show();
```

```
120     pressSpace.hide();
121     countdown.setTimer(COUNTDOWN_SECONDS);
122     countdown.startTimer();
123   }
124
125   /**
126    * Whatever state we were in, move us to the moving ball state.
127    */
128   private void beginPlaying() {
129     ball.show();
130     countdown.hide();
131     pressSpace.hide();
132     startBall(ball);
133     setScore(0);// no volleys yet
134   }
135
136   /**
137    * Whatever state we were in, move us to the waiting to countdown
138    * state.
139    */
140   private void beginWaitingToCountdown() {
141     ball.hide();
142     countdown.hide();
143     pressSpace.show();
144   }
```

Listing 6.19: `SoloPong`: Set State

The first three lines of the `begin<StateName>` methods are the same: each sets the visibility of the three patron sprites to match the state beginning. After that `beginWaitingToCountdown` is done, `beginCountingDown` sets the countdown time and starts the timer, and `beginPlaying` sets the score to 0 and calls `startBall` to start `ball`.

The use of a method, `startBall`, and a parameter, the `ball`, is done with an eye toward having more than one ball in play. It also takes advantage of the fact that `ball` is a reference to a `PongBall` object, so that the location of that object can be set in the method.

```
179   private void startBall(PongBall theBall) {
180     double xVelocity = randomDouble(0.2, 0.4);
181     double yVelocity = randomDouble(0.2, 0.5);
182
183     if (randomInt(2) == 1) {
184       xVelocity = -xVelocity;
185     }
186     if (randomInt(2) == 1) {
187       yVelocity = -yVelocity;
188     }
189
190     theBall.setVelocity(xVelocity, yVelocity);
191     double xLocation = randomDouble(0.2, 0.4);
192     double yLocation = randomDouble(0.3, 0.7);
193     theBall.setLocation(xLocation, yLocation);
```

```
    }
```

Listing 6.20: SoloPong: startBall

The ball's velocity is randomly selected from a moderate range of possible values. Notice that 0.0 is *not* in the range of possible velocity values. Think about why not. To avoid having 0.0 in the range, a positive number is chosen and then, to mix up the starting movement, the sign is flipped half of the time. The ball is randomly placed in an imaginary box on the left-hand side of the screen.

Review 6.5

(a) In Listing 6.9 on page 180, what does `super` on line 33 mean? What method does it call?

(b) In Listing 6.10, what does `this` on line 48 mean? What method does it call?

(c) In Listing 6.9 on page 180, line 37 reads `this.deltaX = deltaX`; Which variable names the field and which names the local parameter?

(d) What is a *scope hole*? What does `this.deltaX` have to do with the scope hole in the `PongBall` constructor?

(e) What does a constructor *do*? When is a constructor called? How does Java determine which overloaded constructor to call?

(f) The code in Listing 6.14 is written so that `PongPaddle` can move in any direction. How is it constrained to moving only in the y-dimension? (Hint: Examine values of variables used to calculate the translation distances.)

(g) All of the sprites in `SoloPong` are added during `setup`, yet not all of them are visible when the game starts. How is this done?

(h) One measure of complexity in a program is the length of methods. What is the longest method in `SoloPong` or any sprite classes written in this chapter?

6.6   Summary

Delegation

Delegation is the creation of new named rules. In Java this is done by defining methods. The four parts of the header remain the access level, the return type, the name of the method, and the parameter list.

The *access level* can be `private`, `protected`, `public`, or nothing. `private` means that access to the method (or field) is limited to just the class in which it appears. `protected` means the same as `private` except for classes extending the current class; child classes of the current class can access `protected` fields and methods. `public` means that any class that has a reference to the current class can call the method (or access the field). Having no access level means that the method or field is accessible to the *package*; for the moment, package can be considered the folder containing the source code file.

There are two different parameter lists: the *formal parameter list* is the one in the header, a list of types and names; the *actual parameter list* appears when the method is called and is a list of expressions. The formal parameters behave like local variables which are initialized with the values of the actual parameter list.

In Java parameters are passed by *value*. This means the expression's result is copied into the formal parameter; changes made to the formal parameter inside the method do not modify the actual parameter.

An apparent contradiction is references to objects; the reference is copied into the formal parameter but both the formal and actual parameter refer to the same value.

Delegation is how top-down design can be applied. By assuming that the next lower level of solutions exist, a method can be written. Then, the simpler problems represented by the design of the submethods are approached by defining the methods.

Scope

The *scope* of a variable is where the name is visible. Fields are in scope from the opening curly brace of the `class` to the closing curly brace. Formal parameters are in scope throughout the block defining the body of the method. All other variable declarations are in scope from the line where they are declared until the end of the block in which they are declared.

6.7 Chapter Review Exercises

Review Exercise 6.1 What is the purpose of adding parameters to methods?

Review Exercise 6.2 What is the difference between *actual* and *formal* parameters?

Review Exercise 6.3 Methods can be *overridden* and methods can be *overloaded.* What is the difference between the two?

Review Exercise 6.4 What is a method *signature*? How is it different from a method header?

Review Exercise 6.5 How are two overloaded methods with the same name differentiated by Java? What part of the signature must be different?

Review Exercise 6.6 How are the two parameter lists matched up? How are actual parameter values assigned to formal parameters?

Review Exercise 6.7 Would it make sense to have a constructor for `PongBall` that takes only an initial velocity? Why or why not? If it makes sense, can you write it?

Review Exercise 6.8 Assume you write a `makeAllTheSprites` method that takes no parameters.

(a) How would you call `makeAllTheSprites` from `setup`?

(b) Describe what happens to the running version of `setup` when `makeAllTheSprites` is called.

Review Exercise 6.9 Describe the *public protocol* of a class.

Review Exercise 6.10   What is the type of `x` at each of the lettered lines?

```
public void someMethod(double x) {
  // (a)
  if (x > 100.0) {
    String x = "Hello, World!";
    {
      int x = 10;
      // (b)
    }
    // (c)
  } else {
    // (d)
  }
  // (e)
}
```

Review Exercise 6.11 Using the code in the previous exercise, describe where there is a *scope hole* for `x`.

Review Exercise 6.12 Given this declaration statement:
```
String name = "FANG";
```
what are the values of the following expressions:

(a) `name.toLowerCase()`

(b) `name.substring(2)`

(c) `name.substring(2, 4) + name.substring(0, 2)`

(d) `name.replace('F', 'B')`

Review Exercise 6.13 Consider `Game.getCurrentGame()`.

(a) What is the *type* returned by this method?

(b) What does it mean that `Game.` is the name of a *class* rather than a reference to an instance?

(c) Can you write the header for `getCurrentGame`?

Review Exercise 6.14 What is the value of `k` at the lettered lines?

```java
public void alpha(int k) {
  // (a)
  k = k + 100;
  // (b)
}

public int beta(int k) {
  // (c)
  return k * 2;
}

public void setup() {
  int k = 13;
  // (d)
  alpha(k);
  // (e)
  int j = beta(k);
  // (f)
  k = j;
  // (g)
}
```

Review Exercise 6.15 Use the following definition of `SomeClass` to answer the question below.

```java
class SomeClass extends Object {
  public int doA() {...}
  private int doB() {...}
  public double doC() {...}
  private double doD() {...}
}
```

Which of the following statements are legal inside the `OtherClass.user` method (definition below)? Explain why each statement is or is not legal.

```java
class OtherClass extends Object {
  public void user() {
    SomeClass sc = new SomeClass();
    // questions are here
  }
}
```

(a) `int a = sc.doA();`

(b) `int b = sc.doB();`

(c) `double c = sc.doC();`

(d) `double d = sc.doD();`

(e) `int e = sc.doC();`

(f) `int f = sc.doD();`

(g) `double g = sc.doA();`

(h) `double h = sc.doB();`

Review Exercise 6.16 What color is the rectangle on the screen after this code executes?

```
public void aleph(RectangleSprite rect) {
  rect.setColor(getColor("blue"));
}

public RectanlgeSprite beth(RectangleSprite rect) {
  rect.setColor(getColor("black"));
  return rect;
}

public void setup() {
  RectangleSprite rs = new RectangleSprite(0.5, 0.5);
  rs.setLocation(0.5, 0.5);
  addSprite(rs);
  // what color if we stop here?

  aleph(rs);
  // and if we stop here?
  rs = beth(rs);
}
```

Review Exercise 6.17 What method does Game provide to examine the player's mouse position? What method dose Game provide to examine the player's keyboard?

6.8   Programming Problems

Programming Problem 6.1   Write a computer program that creates a tenth of a screen red square that bounces around the screen. When the player clicks the mouse on the moving square, the color should change to cyan and then, when it is clicked again, it turns back to red. Also keep track of the number of times the user successfully clicks on the square (don't bother keeping track of misses).

This problem should be implemented *incrementally*. Three levels of refinement might be:

(a) Make a program with a red bouncing square. You need a reference to the bouncing square that is visible to multiple routines; what should you be thinking about *where* to declare the label for the bouncing ball. (*Hint: Look at PongGame for some guidance on creating a bouncing object.*)

Why?   Animating a bouncing `RectangleSprite` seems to have the simplest subset of the functionality required by this program. So this seems to be the smallest program that does *something* along the path to a program that fulfills the requirements described above.

(b) Add a score. This would require a numeric component that is visible from multiple methods (`preCodeHook`, some display building method, and the mouse listener (see below)). Also, add a label on the screen so that the player can see his square

(c) Modify your bouncing program so that the bouncing square has a `MouseListener` listener for pressing/releasing the mouse. When the player clicks, if they are on the bouncing square, increment the score and randomly reposition the square with a random velocity (so that the player cannot score multiple times with quick clicking).

Playtesting.   Though this game is very, very simple, it offers an interesting chance to do some playtesting to balance difficulty and enjoyment of the game. First, think about what you could do to make the game easier.

The two ideas that come to mind are to make the target bigger or to make it move more slowly (or some combination of both). For the purposes of this exercise we leave the size fixed and manipulate the speed.

Where is the *velocity* of the moving square set? Change the speed to one-half of its current value and play the game. It is easier; is it more fun? It probably will be if you found the previous speed too difficult. Try doubling the velocity from the original value. Is the resulting game more fun? Or is it frustratingly difficult?

Now that you know the fun/challenge ratio for three different settings, you can work out the setting that makes the game most enjoyable for you. Note that in the *real world*, playtesting involves a lot more testers and an average of the results typically sets the difficulty level of the final game. Think a little bit about how you could accommodate gamers of different abilities and keep an eye on the **Playtesting** sections in other Programming Problems.

Programming Problem 6.2   Going back to `OneDie.java`, can you add an animation to the dice? When the dice are `rolled`, they should start randomly changing the visible face once every quarter of a second and should "roll" for two seconds (both values should be fields and should have get/set methods).

`EasyDice` has to be modified so that it asks the dice if they are still rolling. If they are, ignore user input. This implies the following changes to the public protocol for `OneDie`:

```
public void setFaceTime(double secondsPerFace) ...
public double getFaceTime() ...
public void setRollTime(double secondsToRoll) ...
public double getRollTime() ...
public boolean isRolling() ...
```

Make sure you provide good comments for the methods (and the fields that you add).

Programming Problem 6.3   Start with `SoloPong.java`.

(a) What changes would be necessary to handle two balls at the same time? How would you be able to start the balls so that their arrival at the paddle is somewhat staggered?

(b) Modify the game so that two balls are started whenever one ball is started. Also, change only the state of the game to waiting to start play when *both* balls go out of play.

(c) Modify the game so that the second ball comes into play whenever the volley count (with one ball) goes to 10. After I get 10 volleys, a new ball appears so that I can get volleys twice as fast.

Playtesting. Look at the two two-ball variations spelled out here. Try each a few times. Which seems to make for more interesting gameplay? Why do you think that is? Would it make the game more interesting to have the two balls move at different velocities?

Programming Problem 6.4 Start with `SoloPong.java`. Modify `PongBall` so that after each volley it speeds up by 5%. Does this variation make the game more fun?

Programming Problem 6.5 Add a target object to the game. Create a class which when struck by the `PongBall` disappears. Disappearance is handled either by moving the object off the screen or calling `Sprite.removeFromCanvas()`.[8]

Notice that if you have one object that can disappear when struck, you can have an arbitrary number of them and you could build a *Breakout* clone.

---

[8]The `removeFromCanvas` method does *not* remove the sprite from the canvas; instead, it schedules the removal of the sprite after the current frame finishes. This makes sure that the updating of game state never references a sprite that has already been removed. Generally there is no visible difference but it is worth knowing.

7

Components Meet Rules: Classes

By extending Game and various sprites, previous games have applied the abstraction technique. This chapter reviews how Java classes are defined in detail. It also exploits the "N" in FANG by presenting the first *networked* game. It also introduces Java's *standard output stream*, a way to print messages to a console window. The output is not as pretty or flexible as that provided by StringSprite but setup is easy and it can be used in non-FANG programs.

7.1 Playing Together

From the start FANG was designed with an emphasis on networked games, games with multiple players playing at different computers, perhaps in the same room and perhaps halfway across the globe. Getting input from multiple players is almost identical to getting input from a single player. FANG games can run inside Java-enabled Web browsers *and* they can run on the desktop; you can easily distribute the game to multiple players on computers of different capabilities.

Network Programming with FANG

To keep the focus on the networking aspects of our game, we implement a classic childhood game: *Tic-Tac-Toe*.

TicTacToe is a game of position. The board is a 3×3 grid of squares. Two players alternate turns, each placing his or her symbol, an X or an O, in one of the squares. Play continues until one player has created a line of three of his or her symbols horizontally, vertically, or diagonally on the board or there are no more spaces on which to move.

If a player succeeds in getting three in the row, he or she wins. If the game ends without three in a row, the game is a tie or, in *Tic-Tac-Toe* terms, a "Cat's Game."

A multiplayer version of the game demonstrates the networking capabilities of FANG. Each player runs a separate copy of TicTacToe; the separate copies use FANG communication to alternate turns. The game determines when the game ends in one or the other player winning or a cat's game.

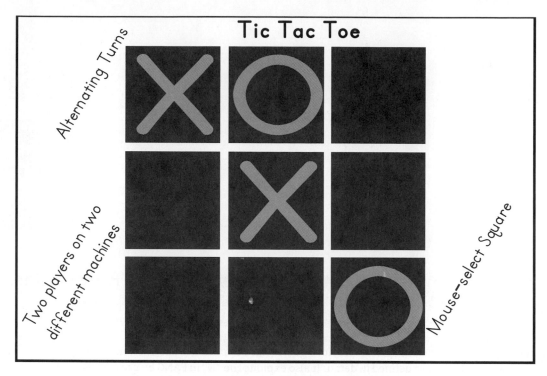

Figure 7.1: `TicTacToe` game design diagram

Sharing State: Where's the Game?

When multiple players share a computer game without sharing a computer, how do the programs communicate? *What* do the various copies of the game communicate? If there are multiple copies of the game, where does the *game* really reside?

A *process* is a running program .[1] Communication between processes is known as *interprocess communication* (IPC). IPC is handled by the *operating system*; different systems support different kinds of IPC.

The *Internet protocols* are a widely supported collection of communications protocols that work on many different hardware and operating system platforms. One reason they are so widely supported is that they are built using multiple *layers of abstraction* where each lower layer advertises a public protocol and each higher layer is implemented using only the next lower layer's public protocol.

The Internet protocols provide a reliable mechanism for transferring messages from one process to another on the same or different computers, assuming the computers are attached to a network medium or the Internet. The Internet is a network of networks implementing machine addressing, message routing, and the actual delivery of messages from machine to machine.

Passing messages relies on the Internet protocols; what should our game processes say to one another when running the game? The answer depends on *where* the game lives.

Multiple process, cooperating to play a game, could store the game state in one of three places:

1. In one process

2. Part of the state in each process

---

[1]As opposed to the bytecode or machine code sitting in a file which is called a `program`. In this text we are this precise only when it is absolutely necessary.

3. A copy of all of the state in each process

If all of the state lived in one process, that process would be the *server* process and all other processes are called *clients*. Input is collected at each client and routed to the server; the server decides how the game state changes and communicates what to display back to each client.

Client and server should be familiar from use of the Web: a Web *server* keeps a collect of Web pages, a Web browser (client) requests pages from the server, and the server decides what pages the client gets.

If the game processes are *peers*, each the same as any other and each keeping only a *part* of the state, each process shares changes to its local state with all other peers. A peer-to-peer communications pattern is seen in many instant messaging programs and file-sharing systems such as Bittorrent.

Both of these configurations assure a consistent view of the world because any portion of the game state (any given field or instance of a class, for example) is kept by exactly one process. The server has *all* game state and each peer has the only copy of the part of the game state for which it is responsible.

A single copy of game state is an application of DRY and the consistency is a good thing. The downside is that the single keeper of some game state introduces a single point of failure: if the server dies, there is no game. Also, to get information about part of the game, a message must travel from the interested process to the keeper of the state and back again before the process can use it.

In a peer-to-peer configuration where every process maintains the entire state of the game, there is no need to send messages to get information: all game state is maintained locally. In order to make sure that all versions of the one game remain consistent, the game could share the input stream from each peer with every other peer.

It is required that all peers play all input from *all* processes back in exactly the same order. This last model, where all games simply process the same sequence of input to remain in synch has an obvious vulnerability: if for some reason my game did something different with the input, my view of the game would not match yours. If I rewrote my game to give me hidden knowledge (say, seeing your cards in a card game), then I would be cheating.

FANG uses this third method because the input stream to FANG games is typically fairly small, so sharing one or more such streams across the network is not too bandwidth intensive.[2]

Every single-player game you have written already uses this model. To handle multiplayer games well, all FANG games create a server that can fully order multiple input streams and then sends all input to that server. In a single-player game, the server just beams the same stream back to the game; in a multiplayer game, multiple input messages are ordered by their arrival time at the server, and the merged stream is shared across all processes.

Every process running `TicTacToe` has the complete tic-tac-toe game inside of it: all `GameTile` showing Xs and Os, the turn indicator, all of it. The game resides at every process; the processes use a server to order the input stream and every game processes the merged input stream so as to remain in a state consistent with all others.

Distributing the Game Loop

How is distributing the input handled in the video game loop?

Reviewing: Display; Get Input; Update State

The game loop has three parts:

- Display the current game state,

- Get user input,

---

[2]Bandwidth is the number of bits per second a given communication stream requires. For any given connection to the Internet, more low-bandwidth applications can run across it at the same time than high-bandwidth applications.

• Update game state according to current state and user input.

Each copy of TicTacToe runs the game loop in a separate process. The local game handles input two different ways: when the user presses a key or moves the mouse, that information is *forwarded to the game server*; when input is received from the game server, it is available to update the game state. How can FANG games differentiate between input from different players?

Sharing Information

GameTile is like EasyButton (review Section 5.1 if you need to): an isPressed method checked from TicTacToe.advance to check if the player has clicked on a given tile.

Rather than using the getClick2D() method of the current game (an empty parameter list), GameTile uses the getClick2D(playerID) where playerID is an **int** identifying each different player in a multiplayer game. The first player is player 0, the next player to join is player 1, and so on. In a single-player game the only player has playerID equal to 0. In TicTacToe the two players are player 0 and player 1.

```
79   public boolean isPressed(int playerID) {
80     // The current game may have a mouse click or not.
81     Location2D mouseClick = Game.getCurrentGame().getClick2D(playerID);
82     if (mouseClick != null) {
83       if (intersects(mouseClick)) {
84         return true;
85       }
86     }
87     return false;
88   }
```

Listing 7.1: GameTile isPressed

isPressed looks almost identical to isPressed in EasyButton: it gets the current game, fetches the mouse click location, and checks if the mouse location intersects this sprite. The differences are the parameter, **int** playerID on line 80, and the use of the parameter when calling getClick2D in line 126. This means that our game cares about which player clicked the button.

Alternating turns means isPressed is called with the current player's ID. On X's turn, the game cares only about clicks by player 0; on O's turn, the game cares only about clicks by player 1.

Player numbers are assigned when a multiplayer game is started. That is covered later in the chapter. The next section looks at the *abstraction* problem-solving technique in Java.

Review 7.1

(a) Does FANG support building multiplayer games?

(b) Where does the game state reside in a multiplayer FANG game?

(c) How does FANG keep multiple copies of game state consistent?

(d) The Game.getMouse2D is overloaded. Called with no parameters it returns information for the first player. How can you call getMouse2D to get location information for a different player? How do you think you would get a mouse click from a player other than the first?

7.2 Abstraction: Defining New Types

Java classes permit the construction of *abstract data types*. An abstract data type (ADT) consists of three parts: a public protocol, a private implementation, and a strict limitation of interaction with the type to the public protocol. This section discusses the definition of an ADT and how the `class` mechanism in Java makes it easy for programmers to define their own data types.

What is a Type?

What is a type? Is it the same as a `class`? No: a `class` is a type and is the way Java programmers define their own types, but POD types are also types (but not classes). We look at what an abstract data type is.

Abstract Data Type

An *abstract data type* is a type with three parts:

1. A *public protocol*. Also called the *interface*. The collection of services the program may request from instances of the type. This is the collection of public methods, fields,[3] and exported internal types.[4]

2. A *private implementation*. Also known as a "layout in memory." For classes this means the private fields, methods, and internal types. For non-classes the idea of a layout in memory makes more sense; the bits inside the POD type have an interpretation defined by the language designers and that is the implementation.

3. Interaction is limited to the public protocol. No code using the type is permitted to access the private implementation directly; all access to the value of the type is through the interface.

Java's `double` type is an abstract type. The public protocol includes declaring `double` variables, the standard arithmetic operators (+, -, *, and /) that work with `double`, and the *cast* operator, the prefix (`double`) that forces Java to treat a given expression as having the type `double`: `double` x = (`double`) 1 / 4; evaluates as 1.0 / 4 returning 0.25.

What is the private implementation. We don't know. In fact, we don't *want* to know. If we learn the internal representation of a floating point number and we decide to manipulate the representation directly (ignoring point 3 above), we must take responsibility for any constraints that the representation has. Otherwise our manipulation might set a `double` in memory to a value that cannot be used to encode a `double`.

Imagine designing a `RationalNumber` class. A rational number is a number that can be expressed as an integer fraction: $\frac{p}{q}$ for integers p and q. What would make a good implementation?

Two `int` fields, p and q, make sense. Using this implementation, what constraints, if any, are there on what values of p and q represent *legal* rational numbers?

Division by zero does not yield a rational number; the denominator of a rational number should never be permitted to be 0. Yet, if the fields p and q are `public`, other programmers can bypass our methods and directly manipulate the implementation (the equivalent of our directly changing the bits inside of a `double` in a memory box).

If we "know," by examining the public protocol and limiting access *to* the public protocol, that q cannot be 0, we can freely divide by q whenever we want to without causing a divide by zero exception.

Alternatively we could count on programmers checking the value of q. Every time q is to be used for division, the code must check whether or not it is 0. This works so long as the class convention is well documented and *every single programmer* working on the class adheres to the convention.

---

[3]This book eschews `public` fields except for fields representing constants: `public static final` fields cannot be changed after they are first assigned, so they can safely be made public.

[4]Java permits `class` declarations *inside* of `class` declarations; this book does not explore nested classes.

One missed check leaves a serious bug lurking in the code. An *intermittent* bug, one that appears only some of the time. Such a bug is difficult to find because the programmer must first determine when it happens. By repeating the *reproduction steps* to trigger the bug, the programmer can *begin* to determine the cause and the fix for the bug.

It makes sense to centralize the zero check in the `setQ` method and limit access to `q` to the constructor and that method. Avoid repeating yourself, avoid *forgetting to* repeat yourself, and protect the code from intermittent bugs. The same argument applies to data fields in all abstract data types.

Our Own Types

We have looked at public protocols, the way of specifying the top-level interaction of a new type. The public protocol determines where we begin stepwise refinement for the class.

The point of *abstraction* is dividing a problem into a group of cooperating types. Each type is responsible for one particular aspect of the problem. The types are combined to create a working program. `TicTacToe` extends `Game`; the display of the game uses `GameTile` which extends `CompositeSprite`. The game also uses string sprites to display information on the screen.

Structure of `class` Files

The Java template for a `<classDeclaration>` (extended) is

```
<classDeclaration> := <accessLevel> class <className>
                      extends <parentClassName>


<classBody> := {

            <definition>*
          }


<definition> := <fieldDeclaration> |
              <methodDefinition> |
              <classDefinition>
```

A class consists of a series of field, method, and (we now know) nested class definitions. That is the *syntax*, what is required by Java. The order of the definitions inside the class is not important to Java: all definitions are in scope for the block in which they are defined.

Programmers who have to orient themselves in unfamiliar code appreciate a more structured approach. The code for this book has been sorted to consistently use the following ordering:

```
public class <className>
  extends <parentClassName> {
 // static field definitions
 // static method definitions

 // field definitions
 // constructor definitions
 // method definitions
}
```

Inside each group the elements are grouped by access level: **public**, **private**, **protected**, default. In practice this means **public** followed by **private**.[5]

---

[5] *Simple Games* does not find much use for the **protected** access level.

What is a *static* definition? Static fields and methods are fields and methods defined for the *class* and not for individual *objects* of the class. There is a single copy of the field (or method) for all instances of our class no matter how many instances there are.

Looking at GameTile, we see two **static**, **final** fields:

```
20    /** the constant (final), class-wide (static) Color for the tile */
21    public static final Color DEFAULT_COLOR =
22      Game.getColor("dark violet");
23
24    /** the constant (final), class-wide (static) Color for the text */
25    public static final Color DEFAULT_CONTENT_COLOR =
26      Game.getColor("lavender");
```

Listing 7.2: GameTile named constants

The first *modifier* before the field type, name, and value is **public**. The entire section on abstract data types spells out that **public** and fields do not mix. What makes these fields special? The *second* modifier.

The keyword **final** declares that a field (or variable) cannot be changed after it is set. Lines 21–22 define and initialize the field DEFAULT_COLOR. The field is *constant* from that point on as the compiler does not permit using the field name on the left-hand side of an assignment statement.

The **final** keyword documents a field or variable as having a constant value. It is, in a way, a comment the compiler can enforce. One use for a **final** field is as a named constant. When a literal value is used in a lot of different places, it makes sense to document *what* it means by replacing it with a well-named constant. It keeps you from repeating yourself unnecessarily.

There is another benefit to constants. How would you change the color used by the foreground or background of a GameTile? With the named constants it should be clear. If there were a large number of setColor calls with colors specified by literal strings, which ones should you change? You would not want to globally replace "dark violet" because some places it might remain the right color. Named constants differentiate on how a given value is being used, improving documentation and maintainability.

```
31    /** Current content of this tile */
32    private String content;
```

Listing 7.3: GameTile content

What is the difference between a **static** field and a non-**static** field? Line 32 declares an *instance* field (non-**static** field) called content. Each GameTile has its own content. Otherwise, setting the content of the center tile to "X" would fill all of the tile with "X". The memory diagrams showing *Object Memory* show instance fields stored in each and every object constructed.

What about **static** or *class* fields? There is only one copy of DEFAULT_COLOR for *all nine* GameTile. There is only one memory box used to store it for the *class*. The difference between the DEFAULT_COLOR of a GameTile and the color of a tile should be clear: all tile share the default starting color but any given tile could have its color changed without affecting any other tile.

This field is safely **public** because it is **final**; no one can change it. It is **public** so the game TicTacToe using GameTile can access the default color if it is interested in using the color for something else.

How could TicTacToe access the **static** field? Instance fields/methods appear after a reference to an instance of the type and a dot (or, in a method *inside* a class, without anything, thereby implying **this**. in front of them). A **static** or *class* field/method uses the name of the class followed by a dot: GameTile.DEFAULT_COLOR.

Lines 22 and 26 show examples of using a **static** method: the Game class defines several getColor methods as **static** methods. Since the value of the **final**, **static** is set before the program really starts running, we cannot access getCurrentGame. Fortunately, Game, the class, is available.

Constructing Instances of Our Type

The *constructor* for our class must initialize all *instance* fields, the "regular" fields we have been using all along. The constructor header is special in two ways: it has no return type and it has the class name as its name. The return type makes no sense because the constructor is initializing an object of the type it constructs.

When you call `new`, Java looks at the type being constructed. It sets aside enough memory in *Object Memory* to hold all of the fields of an instance of that type. The more fields you have, the more space an object of that type takes in memory.

The constructor matching the actual parameter list is called with `this`, referring to the newly allocated memory. The memory is somewhere in the RAM being used by the Java virtual machine. The constructor initializes all of the instance fields (which either explicitly or implicitly are prefixed with `this.`, located inside the memory Java just allocated).

```
28    /** The background of the tile */
29    private final RectangleSprite background;
30
31    /** Current content of this tile */
32    private String content;
33
34    /** the visible content of the tile */
35    private final StringSprite displayContent;
36
37    /**
38     * Construct a new GameTile: content = ""
39     */
40    public GameTile() {
41      background = new RectangleSprite(1.0, 1.0);
42      background.setColor(DEFAULT_COLOR);
43      addSprite(background);
44      content = "";
45      displayContent = new StringSprite();
46      displayContent.setLocation(0.00, 0.075);
47      displayContent.setColor(DEFAULT_CONTENT_COLOR);
48      addSprite(displayContent);
49    }
```

Listing 7.4: `GameTile` constructor

The three fields of `GameTile` are shown in lines 28–35 in Listing 7.4. They match those in `EasyButton`: a background square, a string sprite to show the content, and a string containing the content. Two fields, `background` and `displayContent`, are marked as `final`.

After each is assigned a value in the constructor, neither can be assigned another value. Again, `final` is a promise to the compiler (and programmers reading the code) that the value does not change after the first assignment.

In the interest of simplicity we have not used `final` before this point for our fields. It is considered good design practice to use `final` whenever possible. It simplifies reasoning about when things might change.

```
96    public void setColor(Color color) {
97      background.setColor(color);
98    }
```

Listing 7.5: `GameTile` `setColor`

Key thing to notice about **final**: while background is a **final** field and the *object* it references cannot be changed, the non-**final** fields *of* the object referred to by background can be changed.

The setColor method calls background.setColor; the contents of the memory box background do not change though the contents of the object (in *Object Memory*) do change.

The content field is not **final** because we provide a setContent method that changes the content, and String objects are immutable, so they behave like POD. In order to change what the string contains means constructing a brand-new string with the new contents.

```
107    public void setContent(String content) {
108      if (content.length() > 1) {
109        content = content.substring(0, 1);
110      }
111      this.content = content;
112      setText(content);
113    }
```

Listing 7.6: GameTile setContent

Notice that we use the ability to *validate* the value being set in setContent (something we could not do if content were **public**). We make sure that if the value has more than one character, we chop it down to its first character. The content is displayed very large in the tile and more than one character would overwrite another tile.

Documenting Our Types

A type is documented by the combination of header comments, typically written in *JavaDoc* style, and any necessary in-line comments. On large projects, there may well be external documentation, design documents, requirements documents, and component tests. At a minimum you should include a header comment for every class, every field, and every method defined in the class.

The *JavaDoc* program, by default, extracts header comments for **public** and **protected** elements, generating a linked collection of HTML pages which can be viewed with a Web browser. The use of the javadoc tool is beyond the scope of this book but the formatting used for class, field, and method comments is compatible with it.

Document Intent

Over and over you have been admonished to document your intent. This means that your comments, header, and otherwise should speak to someone who already knows Java as well as you do. Explain why the class/method/field exists as well as why someone would want to use it.

Documentation is another level of abstraction that a competent programmer keeps in mind: dividing solutions into multiple cooperating classes and using stepwise refinement to develop methods are language ways of taming complexity with levels of abstraction. The comments on a class, method, or field give you a slightly higher level to explain the function of your class in a natural language. The documented intent serves as a table of contents for the bit of code it comments on, helping the reader find his way around your code.

Review 7.2

(a) What are the three parts of defining an *abstract data type*?

(b) Can you define an abstract data type in Java? If so, how are the three parts of the definition realized in Java?

(c) If you create five instances of a given class:

(a) How many copies of each of the class's `static` fields are created?

(b) How many copies of each of the class's instance fields are created?

(d) What does the keyword `final` mean when applied to field?

(e) How does documentation help with top-down design?

7.3 Finishing the Game

Listing 7.7 shows `TicTacToe`'s `advance` method. As long as the game is not over, check whether the current player has moved. If not, `advance` is done.

How can a `TicTacToe` game end? The current player makes her move and wins the game (only the current player can possibly win the game if it was not a winning game before she moved). Alternatively, the current player makes her move into the last remaining empty tile and the game ends in a draw.

If the current player has moved, check if the game ended with a win or a draw. If the game has not ended, it is the other player's turn.

```
47   public void advance(double dT) {
48     if (!isGameOver()) {
49       if (hasCurrentPlayerMoved()) {
50         if (isWinner()) {
51           handleWin();
52         } else if (isCatsGame()) {
53           handleCatsGame();
54         } else {
55           nextTurn();
56         }
57       }
58     }
59   }
```

Listing 7.7: `TicTacToe` advance

The names of the methods in `advance` serve as documentation. It makes much more sense to read the current listing rather than

```
47   public void advance(double dT) {
48     if (!isGameOver()) {
49       if (methodA()) {
50         if (methodB()) {
51           methodC();
52         } else if (methodD()) {
53           methodE();
54         } else {
55           methodF();
56         }
57       }
58     }
59   }
```

Listing 7.8: `TicTacToe` *obfuscated* advance

While the current author claims that there is no such thing as completely self-documenting code,[6] this code is fairly simple to follow because of the names chosen.

Top-down design of a Game-extending program begins in advance. This means the method is at a high level of abstraction. The high level is evident in the lack of parameters; the details on which the methods work is put off to another, lower level of detail.

The Tic Tac Toe Board

A TicTacToe board hass nine tiles, three rows of three. How should it be represented? The board is nine GameTile variables. Each tile knows how to determine if a given player has clicked it. hasCurrentPlayerMoved checks each tile to see if it is unoccupied (GameTile.isOccupied hides the details of how a square knows whether or not it is occupied) and the current player has clicked on it. If so, the player has moved.

Naming fields becomes annoying when there are nine variables that are pretty much the same except for where they are in the grid.

```
21   /** Nine game tiles. Named t<row><col>. */
22   private GameTile t00, t01, t02;
23   private GameTile t10, t11, t12;
24   private GameTile t20, t21, t22;
66   public void setup() {
67     setBackground(getColor("green"));
68     currentPlayerID = 0;
69     currentPlayerSymbol = "X";
70     turnsTaken = 0;
71     t00 = makeGameTile(0.17, 0.17);
72     t01 = makeGameTile(0.50, 0.17);
73     t02 = makeGameTile(0.83, 0.17);
74     t10 = makeGameTile(0.17, 0.50);
75     t11 = makeGameTile(0.50, 0.50);
76     t12 = makeGameTile(0.83, 0.50);
77     t20 = makeGameTile(0.17, 0.83);
78     t21 = makeGameTile(0.50, 0.83);
79     t22 = makeGameTile(0.83, 0.83);
80     setTitle(currentPlayerSymbol + "'s Turn: TicTacToe");
81   }
```

Listing 7.9: TicTacToe setup

The nine GameTile are named according to their location in the board, each row numbered from [0–2] and each column numbered from [0–2]. Computer scientists almost always count from 0. Lines 22–24 show that when fields or local variables (but *not* formal parameters) are declared, the type name can be followed by a comma-separated list of field or variable names. The Java template is

```
<fieldDeclaration> :=
  <accessLevel> <typeName> <variableName1> [, <variableNamei>]* ;


<localVariableDefinition> :=
  <typeName> <variableName1> [, <variableNamei>]* ;
```

[6]Advocates for self-documenting code claim that with properly chosen field and method names, it is possible to write computer code that needs no comments to be understood. The earlier argument that comments serve as a table of contents or outline to the code to which they apply seems to say that a good level of comments always makes code easier to follow. This does not excuse *poor* naming conventions, it just says that good naming and good commenting compliment one another to make code readable.

This permits the definition of an arbitrary number of fields (or local variables) of the same type in a single statement. The book uses one per line unless there is a reason not to. These tile are defined three per line on three lines because their layout documents where each is on the board.

Initializing nine tiles and not repeating ourselves takes a `makeGameTile` method. `GameTile` are all the same except for their location in the game; `makeGameTile` takes the center of the game tile as its parameters. `makeGameTile` returns a reference to the tile constructed; the call can be assigned to one of the nine tile fields (lines 71–79). The other fields in the game state are the current player's id, the current player's symbol, and a turn counter. All three are initialized before the game tile in `setup`.

Starting a Multiplayer FANG Game

How does FANG know a game is multiplayer? Given that a game *is* multiplayer, how do multiple players connect to the server? And who starts the server anyway?

```
33   public TicTacToe() {
34     // Call the default constructor for Game
35     super();
36     // set the number of players required for a game
37     setNumberOfPlayers(2);
38   }
```

Listing 7.10: <code>TicTacToe</code> constructor

This is the first `Game`-derived class for which we have defined a *constructor*. Typically we have been able to use the standard settings for everything in a `Game` *or* we have modified the value inside `setup`. Unfortunately, by the time `setup` is run, the number of players in the game has already been determined. The number of players must be set earlier.

FANG always uses the *default* constructor when building a `Game`-derived class. Line 35 is included to remind us that any constructor must call some constructor of the parent class. Here we are calling the default constructor of `Game`. This is the same constructor that would be called if line 35 were omitted or commented out; the line makes what happens explicit. After the constructor returns, the `numberOfPlayers` (a `Game` field) is set to 2.

When you run the program, FANG sees the number of players before calling `setup`. If it is a multiplayer game, you enter the multiplayer *lobby* as in Figure fig:ComponentsMeetRules:screenshotTicTacToe-lobby.

The lobby has three text fields and a button. From the bottom up, the **Connect & Start Game** button connects to the server described by the next field up, the **Name of game server**. The author's primary machine is named "BigRedOne," which is why this field contains that name automatically. When running an applet, the game server is assumed to be the Web host that served the applet; when running an application, the server is assumed to be the `localhost`.

Number of players indicates the number of players expected to play the game. While it can be changed from the lobby, `TicTacToe` cannot handle a different number of players. Finally, **Name of this game** is a name you can provide for the session you are running. This permits multiple sessions of the same game to use the same server and still be differentiated.

Our game session is named "t-cubed". If there are already sessions of this game running and waiting for players on the server, the drop-down box contains the name of the sessions already running. After typing in "t-cubed" and pressing the **Connect & Start Game** button, the first player sees a waiting screen as in Figure 7.3.

When a second player starts a copy of the program, he sees the same lobby. He can direct the program to any machine he wishes by typing the IP address or domain name into the **Name of game server** field. The screenshot shows the "BigRedOne" name for the game server.

The list of sessions running the current game on the current server contains one entry, "t-cubed." If that name is picked and the second player presses the button, two players connect to the same session of a game requiring two players and the game begins.

Figure 7.2: Lobby for `TicTacToe`

After the lobby is the beginning of the game. Figure 7.4 shows a game familiar from all previous FANG games. Either player may press **Start** and the game begins. The player who chose the name for the session in the game lobby is player 0; the second player to join the session is player 1 and so on if there are additional players. Each game can also determine the ID of the local player, the player interacting with the current FANG window. In this game, that is not important, but in some games, such as a card game where only the local player's hand should be visible, it is.

Player Turns

```
191  private boolean hasCurrentPlayerMoved() {
192    return
193      isPlayersMove(t00) || isPlayersMove(t01) || isPlayersMove(t02) ||
194      isPlayersMove(t10) || isPlayersMove(t11) || isPlayersMove(t12) ||
195      isPlayersMove(t20) || isPlayersMove(t21) || isPlayersMove(t22);
196  }
```

Figure 7.3: Waiting for a second `TicTacToe` player

```
206   private boolean isPlayersMove(GameTile gt) {
207     if (!gt.isOccupied() && gt.isPressed(currentPlayerID)) {
208       gt.setContent(currentPlayerSymbol);
209       ++turnsTaken;
210       return true;
211     } else {
212       return false;
213     }
214   }
```

Listing 7.11: `TicTacToe` moving

Figure 7.5 shows the view of two processes, each running `TicTacToe`, at the beginning of player 1's first turn. Player 0 had moved when `hasCurrentPlayerMoved` returns **true**. It makes nine calls to `isPlayersMove`, checking each tile in turn to see if it is where the current player has moved. Listing 7.11 shows the two methods.

`hasCurrentPlayerMoved` is an example of a very long (though not complicated) Boolean expression. A logical *or*, `||`, also called a *conjunction*, is **true** if either or both of the operands it joins are **true**. A long conjunction such as this is **true** if any of its subexpressions are **true**.

Figure 7.4: Joining "t-cubed" `TicTacToe` session

isPlayersMove takes a `GameTile` parameter, and it determines if the player *can* move there (it must currently be empty) and whether the player *did* move there (was the tile clicked by the current player). If he can and did, put his symbol in the tile and add one to the move count.

```
225    private boolean isWinner() {
226      return
227        row1(currentPlayerSymbol) ||
228        row2(currentPlayerSymbol) ||
229        row3(currentPlayerSymbol) ||
230        col1(currentPlayerSymbol) ||
231        col2(currentPlayerSymbol) ||
232        col3(currentPlayerSymbol) ||
233        diag1(currentPlayerSymbol) ||
234        diag2(currentPlayerSymbol);
235    }
```

Listing 7.12: `TicTacToe` isWinner

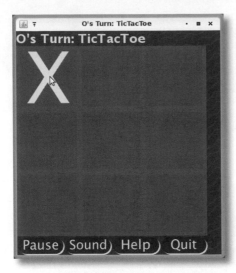

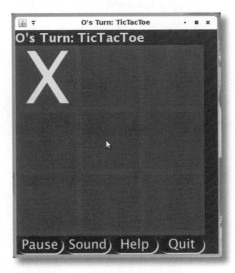

Figure 7.5: `TicTacToe` on O's first turn

The `isWinner` method is another long conjunction. This time, however, it calls eight *different* methods. There are eight methods because there are eight different ways to win: three rows, three columns, and two different diagonals. Detail of one method suffices as the other seven are almost identical; it would be nice to have some way to avoid repeating ourselves here (Programming Problem 8.4 kicks things off in getting rid of repeating, something to look forward to for interested readers).

```
280    private boolean row1(String p) {
281      return t00.getContent().equals(p) && t01.getContent().equals(p) &&
282        t02.getContent().equals(p);
283    }
```

Listing 7.13: `TicTacToe` `row1`

`row1` (and all the other individual win checkers) takes a player symbol, a `String`, as its sole parameter. That is possible because only the player who just moved could have won. So we don't have to call `isWinner` with both symbols. It would not be that much harder to call it twice (or once for each player). Knowing what player we are checking simplifies the individual win checking methods.

Comparing objects.   Note the use of the `equals` method to compare the contents of a `GameTile` with the player's symbol. This method is defined in the base class of *all* Java classes, `Object` and is overridden in objects that need a special way to compare themselves for equality. The `equals` method takes an `Object` as its parameter and compares the given object to **this**. For a `String`, `equals` returns **true** if the two strings have exactly the same number of characters and both strings match in each character position.

What about ==? That is what we used to compare **int** and **double** values. Why not use it for Object and its child classes? Java *permits* the comparison of Object-derived classes with double equals; comparing them with == has a different meaning than what we normally mean.

If we create two new String objects, each with the same contents:

```
String one = new String("Hello, World!");
String two = new String("Hello, World!");
boolean doubleEquals = (one == two);
boolean equalsMethod = (one.equals(two));
```

What are the values of doubleEquals and equalsMethod? the first Boolean expression, using == returns **true** if and only if the two references refer to the same object in *Object Memory*; it returns false otherwise. The equals method, on the other hand, does whatever String defines to be the comparison operation for objects of its type (this is an example of encapsulation in a type; the meaning of "equality" is left to the implementer of the class).

The two Boolean expressions return **false** and **true**, respectively. This is the circumstance on the left-hand side of Figure 7.6.

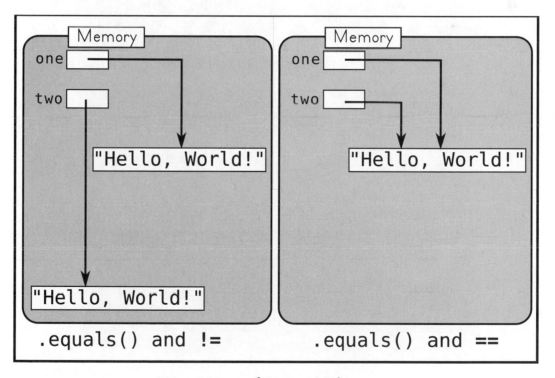

Figure 7.6: Java references, == and equals()

On the right-hand side of the figure is the result of the following code snippet:

```
String one = new String("Hello, World!");
String two = one;
boolean doubleEquals = (one == two);
boolean equalsMethod = (one.equals(two));
```

The only difference is that the value assigned to two is *not* a newly created string with the sequence of characters "Hello, World!," but rather a reference to the already created string containing those characters. Since the sequence of characters in one and two (or rather, the actual strings to which they refer) is the same, this code sets equalsMethod to **true**; since the values *inside* the references are the same, doubleEquals is also set to **true**. Now back to our regularly scheduled program.

The isCatsGame method is simple: it checks if the number of moves is nine. If nine moves have been made, there are no empty squares. If there is no winner (already checked), the game ends in a tie.

The handle . . . methods are also simple: they determine a message to display and call endGame with the text of the message to display.

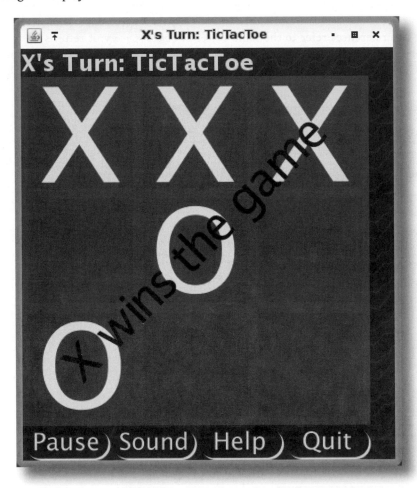

Figure 7.7: X wins TicTacToe

```
245    *
246    * @return  a newly created {@link GameTile} positioned at the given
247    *          location
248    */
249   private GameTile makeGameTile(double x, double y) {
250     GameTile result = new GameTile();
```

```
251     result.setScale(0.3);
252     result.setLocation(x, y);
253     addSprite(result);
254     return result;
```

Listing 7.14: TicTacToe endGame

The endGame method builds a StringSprite with the message (who won or that it is a tie) and puts it on the screen as you can see in the image above. It also calls setGameOver, a method in Game. That means advance does no more work (look at line 48; isGameOver returns **true** after it is set).

Both games in the session see the exact same sequence of input. When either player moves or clicks his or her mouse, the information goes to both versions of the game. The only clicks that make a difference, though, are those by the current player on empty squares (isPlayersMove makes sure the square is empty and isPressed in GameTile takes a player number to make sure that only that player's clicks count). Even though two "different" versions of the game are running, the input stream is shared so that the two games unfold identically. The games you have built in previous chapters can also be extended for multiple players.

Review 7.3

(a) Describe how the advance method in Listing 7.7 illustrates top-down design.

(b) Listing 7.9 initializes many tiles. What variable refers to the middle tile of the board? What variable refers to the upper-right tile? The lower-left?

(c)

   (a) What principle motivated the development of makeGameTile?

   (b) Explain, in your own words, why makeGameTile was written.

   (c) Approximately how long would setup be without makeGameTile?

   (d) What are the parameters to makeGameSquare?

(d) Can one server host three different games of TicTacToe? How would a player know which game she was joining? Where in the game lobby would you determine what game to join?

7.4 Summary

Network Communications

A running program or *process* can communicate with other running processes across the network. FANG, through Java, supports multiplayer games where multiple players run the same game in multiple processes.

Network communications can be from *client* processes to *server* processes where the servers provide some special service to the clients. The client/server application architecture usually runs many clients connecting to one server. Alternatively, a swarm of *peers*, duplicates of the same program, can connect and, as a group, provide a service to their members.

FANG uses a client/server architecture. The server portion runs, and all clients send their input to the server. The server sorts all of the input into a particular order and sends it to all of the clients. Clients run the game only with the input they get back from the server. This lets each program run the program from the beginning and, since they see the exact same sequence of input, the programs remain synchronized.

Abstraction

Abstraction is the encapsulation of rules and data together in a new type, an *abstract data type*. An abstract data type has three parts:

1. A *public protocol* or *interface*. The collection of public methods.

2. A *private implementation*. Also known as a "layout in memory." For classes this means the private fields and methods and internal types.

3. Interaction is limited to the public interface.

Abstraction permits a part of the solution to be wrapped up inside a `class` so that users can focus solely on the public protocol to use it, and the implementer is safely insulated from where the type is being used.

FANG Classes and Methods

Java Templates

```
<classDeclaration> := <accessLevel> class <className>
                        extends <parentClassName>


<classBody> := {

            <definition>*
          }

<definition> := <fieldDeclaration> |
            <methodDefinition> |
            <classDefinition>
```

7.5   Chapter Review Exercises

Review Exercise 7.1 If there were three players in a networked game, how would you check to see if the first payer had typed 'y'?

Review Exercise 7.2 What are the advantages of sharing just the input stream in a FANG game? What risks are there?

Review Exercise 7.3 If I told you I was running `TicTacToe` on my computer, `nonesuch.potsdam.edu`, and I had started session `t-cubed`, describe the steps you would take to connect to my session.

Review Exercise 7.4 Where do you specify the number of players necessary to start a multiplayer game?

Review Exercise 7.5 What is a `static final` field for? What advantages are there to using named constants?

Review Exercise 7.6 Why do you think using `final` whenever possible is a good idea? Or, if you want to argue the contrary, why is it *not* a good idea? Support your position with consideration of how easy/difficult your code is to understand, how long your code is, and how much effort the code is to change.

Review Exercise 7.7 Why do we use setter methods rather than making fields `public`?

Review Exercise 7.8 If `String` (`java.lang.String`) is *immutable*, what can you tell me about *all* of its fields.

Review Exercise 7.9 When using a `static` method in `RectangleSprite`, what comes before the dot?

Review Exercise 7.10 What does the annotation `@Override` before a method mean? What checks does the compiler perform for you when it is there? What does it tell the programmer?

Review Exercise 7.11 How would you let *either* player in TicTacToe pick the next square to move to? (Note: This makes for a mildly interesting "click as fast as you can" sort of game; it is *not* a good game.)

Review Exercise 7.12

What is the advantage of making as many methods **private** as possible? Are or are not these methods part of the public protocol of the class? If not, what *are* they a part of?

7.6 Programming Problems

Programming Problem 7.1 Start with TicTacToe.java. Modify the program to play a 4×4 game (with four in a row required to win).

(a) Does it seem likely that GameTile requires changing?

(b) Where would you declare new GameTile fields?

(c) Make sure to modify makeGameTile so it sets the right sizes. Modify setup to construct all 16 tiles.

(d) How many ways are there to win in the new game? Write the required helper functions and rewrite isWinner accordingly.

(e) Is there anything else that must be changed?

Programming Problem 7.2 Start with TicTacToe.java. How would you modify the program so that it can be played in a single FANG instance with the players passing the mouse back and forth? What is the *minimum* changing you can do?

Programming Problem 7.3 Start with SoloPong.java. Modify SoloPong so that it plays a two-player version of the game. Add a second paddle. The paddle constructor should take a player number as a parameter so that each paddle responds to just one player.

Playtesting. Play the game some and consider adjusting how the ball starts: for example, a random but more central location with the direction determined by the last player to miss the ball. The game needs a new score so each player's score can be kept individually.

Programming Problem 7.4 One shortcoming of TicTacToe is that it plays a single game and must be restarted to play a new game. Can you modify the game so that it advances to a new game when the current game is over? Or, better, that it pauses for 10 seconds so players can see the results and then starts the game over.

Switch which player is X and which is O. What changes when player 1 is X and player 0 is O?

Programming Problem 7.5 Look at Problem 5.3. Modify the two-player version of EasyDice to make it a networked, multiplayer game. If you have a one-machine solution, the real multiplayer solution should be very simple (though EasyButton must be modified to make it like GameTile).

Programming Problem 7.6 Look at Problem 5.2 for a description of the game of *Pig*. Using OneDie and, perhaps, EasyDice, you can build a multiplayer game of Pig. Start with making it two player; after the next chapter you should be able to extend it to an arbitrary number of players.

Collections: ArrayList and Iteration

When writing TicTacToe, much of the length of the program was taken up with methods to test for winning combinations. If we examine related methods, say, row*<n>*, it is interesting how similar they are to one another.

```
280    private boolean row1(String p) {
281      return t00.getContent().equals(p) && t01.getContent().equals(p) &&
282        t02.getContent().equals(p);
283    }
292    private boolean row2(String p) {
293      return t10.getContent().equals(p) && t11.getContent().equals(p) &&
294        t12.getContent().equals(p);
295    }
304    private boolean row3(String p) {
305      return t20.getContent().equals(p) && t21.getContent().equals(p) &&
306        t22.getContent().equals(p);
307    }
```

Listing 8.1: TicTacToe the row winning methods

Note that all three use the same form, a logical or between three calls to the equals method. equals is the standard way of checking whether or not two objects are equal. What is interesting is the similarity of the names of the variables at the beginning of each chained call to equals.

Notice that the three methods are actually identical except for the names of the variables: row1 uses field names beginning t0; row2 uses field names beginning t1; row3 uses field names beginning t2. Given our desire to avoid repeating ourselves, this seems wasteful. Further, imagine the changes necessary to extend the game to play 4×4 tic-tac-toe. More methods with more similar variables in each method.

There has to be a way to get Java to do the work, to have it calculate which variable we want to address at run-time, saving the programmer work and headache at compile time.

This chapter is about *collections*, objects that contain other objects. A collection has some method of indexing to recover individual objects in the collection. We start with collections indexed by small integers so that we can *loop* across all entries in the collection, executing the same code on each entry.

8.1   Flu Pandemic Simulator

This is a book about games. Why is there a section titled "Flu Pandemic Simulator"? The topic is certainly too dark for a book on simple computer games and it is surely too complex for a beginning programming book.

Actually, neither of the statements in the preceding sentence is true. A pandemic simulator may well be dark but the idea of simulating the real world, using numbers taken from real pandemics, can give users of the program some feeling for how dangerous such a situation could be. It provides that insight *before* anyone dies. Also, by adding some game elements, with the player directing limited protective resources, players can understand why proactive preventive measures are a good idea. It also gives the author a good chance to introduce the ideas of serious games.

A pandemic simulator is also not too difficult to program. The world, in such a simulation, consists of people in a village. The villagers are modeled as simply as possible: each maintains its own health and its own visual representation. Age, gender, hair color, name, all might be interesting features of a real person but the point of a computer model is to simplify as much as possible. All we are interested in is the progression of a single illness; a "person" is narrowed down to his or her health and the number of days he or she has been in that state of health.

For example, the simplest model would be HEALTHY and SICK as the states of health. Healthy people do not become sick spontaneously (they must be exposed to someone sick) and sick people become well after three days in bed. This description approximates the common cold. The only model parameters missing are the mortality rate (percentage of people killed by the disease), the infection rate (percentage of people exposed to the illness who become ill), and some way of modeling exposures (who might see the sick person and become sick themselves).

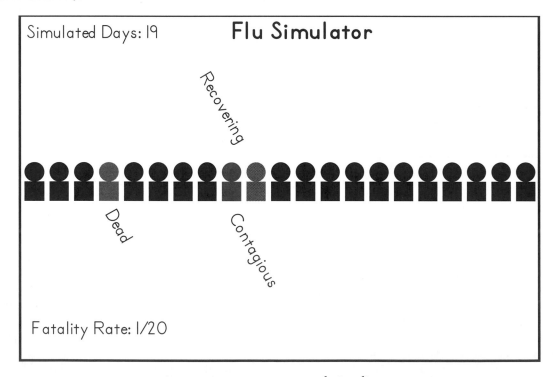

Figure 8.1: FluSimulator game design diagram

The *FluSimulator* represents the village as a row of people in the middle of the screen. Each sprite's color reflects the health of the person being modeled. The design also introduces a more complex model of disease:

infected individuals are sick but not contagious for some amount of incubation time; for some amount of time, they are contagious; and for another amount of time, they are sick but recovering. Both healthy and dead individuals do not change their state spontaneously. This means there are five states of health (and five colors in the final game): DEAD, HEALTHY, SICK, CONTAGIOUS, and RECOVERING.

Introduction to Discrete Time Simulation

Once we conceptualize a simplification of a person as his or her state of health, how does the pandemic unfold over time? The missing dimension of our simulation is time. Like movement, in the real world, time unfolds continuously, an analog value. In the computer, time is modeled as moving forward in discrete steps, digitally. Time in the pandemic simulation jumps forward one day at a time with a day's worth of changes applied at the same time.

Why choose a day? Because that seems like a reasonable level when we look at a disease that lasts about a week. Modeling traumatic blood loss would require a much shorter, say, one-minute, time step, and modeling continental drift would require much longer, say, a million-year, time step. Discrete time steps, tuned to the simulation being written, greatly simplify the math over a continuous time model.

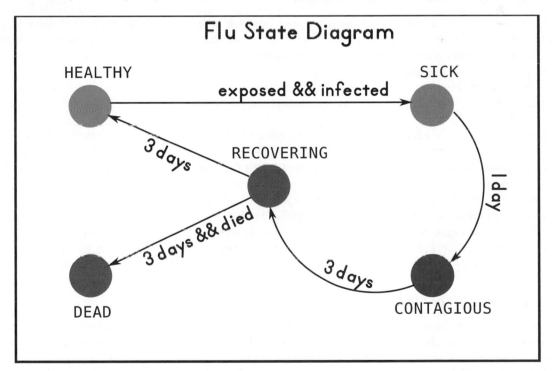

Figure 8.2: Flu Health State Diagram

A *state diagram* as seen in Figure 8.2 describes an object's states and how the states change.

Circles represent states, each labeled with the name of the health state. Arrows indicate permitted *transitions*, how a person's health can move from one state to another. The transitions are labeled with the conditions necessary for the change to be made. A HEALTHY person becomes sick if he or she is *exposed* to the illness and becomes *infected*. There is *no* way for a HEALTHY person to die (go directly to the DEAD state). Transitions marked with times are crossed automatically after the person has spent the requisite time in the state at the tail of the arrow.

Notice that there are *no* transitions out of DEAD: dead is dead and there is no coming back. There are also two transitions out of RECOVERING, one marked "3 days && died", the other just marked "3 days". After three days pass, a check is made to see if the person was killed by the disease (based on the *mortality rate* of the disease). If they died, dead is dead. If they survived, then they are healthy. Random numbers are used to determine whether an exposed individual becomes infected, if a recovering individual dies, and who is exposed to contagious individuals.

The disease model is somewhat unrealistic (e.g., people seldom die right before they should have recovered, the disease progresses at the same rate in everyone, the infection and mortality rates are the same for everyone) but it is simple to program.

At the end of each day a person checks his current health state and the number of days he has been in the current state. With that information, he can determine whether or not he should transition to a new health state. If the person is leaving RECOVERING this is also the point where the simulation decides if he lives or dies.

It says that "a person checks . . . ." What that really means is that Person provides a nextDay method that advances the person's disease (if any).

Defining Neighbors and Chance of Infection

How is a person exposed? Once a person is exposed, how is it determined if she is infected? Look back at Figure 8.1; notice that the villagers are all in a row. For our model, that represents the main street through the village. Proximity along the line relates to proximity in the village. We use a simple social model, one where people, sick or well, can visit their "neighbors."

Neighbors are those villagers within some fixed distance to the left and the same fixed distance to the right of the person. With a three-person neighborhood, the CONTAGIOUS person's neighborhood is represented by the pink rectangle.

In our social model, each person interacts with a fixed number of neighbors per day (any number of which may, in fact, be the same neighbor or even herself). If the person happens to be CONTAGIOUS when interacting with a neighbor, the neighbor is *exposed* to the disease (the first condition of the transition from HEALTHY to SICK). When a person is exposed, the *virulence* or contagiousness of the disease is consulted and if the exposed person was HEALTHY and a random number says she was infected, she becomes SICK.

The implementation of the social model is simplified further: only CONTAGIOUS villagers check which neighbors they visit and might expose. There is no check to see if neighbors *of* the CONTAGIOUS come over to visit the CONTAGIOUS person on any given day. The infection rates are lower than they would be in the model described above. Programming Project 8.3 discusses extending the program with a symmetric social model.

Putting a Game in the Simulation

FluSimulator is a *simulation* rather than a game. We have components (villagers) and we have rules (both a disease model and a social model); so what is missing? The "player" has no decisions to make and cannot influence the outcome of the simulation. The player is not *playing*, he is just watching.

There are several ways to extend this into a game: let the player move people around on the screen to change the social model and exposure; give the player a limited number of vaccines which make people immune; give the player a limited amount of medicine which increases recovery or lowers mortality or infection rates. These extensions are left as programming exercises because of the large amount of new material to get the simulation running.

This chapter introduces *console* programming, printing output to the console window. Console output is used to introduce the syntax and meaning of Java collections. The simulation's core class, Person, is designed, a list of Persons is built, and the collection techniques are used to step the simulation clock forward, determine when the simulation is over, and determine the overall mortality rate of the disease.

Review 8.1

(a) In a state diagram, which parts are the *states*? Which are the *transitions*? What do the *state labels* mean? What do the *transition labels* mean? Which way do the arrows point?

(b) How long is a person SICK before becoming CONTAGIOUS?

(c) Counting the person themselves, how many Persons are there in a neighborhood?

(d) How should either end of the village be handled? What is the left-most villager's neighborhood?

(e) What other attributes, beyond sickness and days sick, might be worth modeling? What sorts of people have higher or lower infection, mortality, or exposure rates? Keep your answers in mind when reading the Programming Problems.

8.2   Console I/O: The System Object

Java has a System object. The full name of the System type is java.lang.System; types defined in the java.lang *package*[1] need not be **imported**: Java automatically **imports** them into every program.

The *JavaDoc* for System shows its whole public protocol is **public static** methods and three **public static** fields. Yes, this book admonishes you to never create **public** fields, yet Sun uses them in the System class. The authors stand by their admonition: do not define nonconstant **public** fields.

The **public** field, System.out, is the standard output stream where console output is printed.

Standard Output: System.out

Using *JavaDoc*, System.out is of type PrintStream. In the documentation, that type name is a link to the documentation for the type. Clicking on it, one can read the public protocol for a PrintStream.

PrintStream names two methods of interest: print and println. Each of these methods appears with about ten different signatures. Each signature has a single parameter and each is of a different type so that Java can differentiate the overloaded method name. Each method's documentation is similar: "Prints an *integer*" where *integer* is replaced by the type of the formal parameter.

PrintStream.print prints the value of the expression passed to it, leaving the "print point" just after the last character printed, and PrintStream.println, does the same but advances the print point to the beginning of the next line right *after* printing the value of its parameter. The no parameter version, PrintStream.println(), advances the print point to the next line.

```
1   // package default
2
3   import fang2.core.Game;
4
5   /**
6    * This "game" has no sprites. In setup it just prints "Hello, World!"
7    * to the standard output console. This is a demonstration of how
8    * System.out can be used.
9    */
10  public class HelloWorld
11      extends Game {
12      /**
13       * Print out one line. That is all the setup required
```

---

[1]The fully qualified names of classes are some collection of *packages*, separated by dots, and, at the end, the class name. If no package names are specified, it means that the class is in the current directory; classes defined in the same directory do not need to be **imported** at all.

```
14    */
15    @Override
16    public void setup() {
17      System.out.println("Hello, World!");
18    }
19  }
```

Listing 8.2: `HelloWorld` Demonstrate `System.out`

Listing 8.2 is a lot like `EmptyGame.java`: it creates an empty game window. The interesting difference is what happens in the window where the program was run.[2]

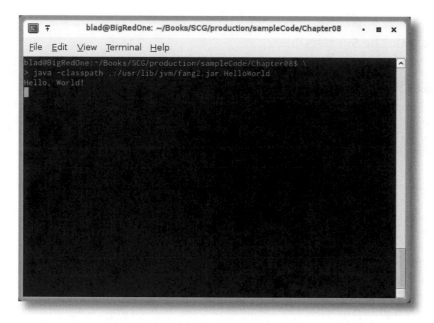

Figure 8.3: Console output of `HelloWorld`

Figure 8.3 shows the command line window where the program was run after being compiled.[3]

Poor-man's Debugger

What good does console output do us? It can be used to give the user feedback that does not fit well into the game display. Because `print` and `println` can print many different types, it is easy to add lines that print out the current values of a variable at several points. Consider the output of `PrintASprite.java`.

```
1  // package default
2
3  import fang2.core.*;
4  import fang2.sprites.RectangleSprite;
```

---

[2]If you are programming in a browser using JavaWIDE or another online IDE, you need to open your Java Console to see console output. Exactly how to do that is browser specific.

[3]The `classpath` in the screenshot is that on the author's main machine; run the program with the correct `classpath` for your environment.

```
5
6   /**
7    * Demonstrate how a Sprite class object prints out using
8    * System.out.println.
9    */
10  public class PrintASprite
11    extends Game {
12    /** The value to print out. */
13    private Sprite someField;
14
15    /**
16     * Creates a rectangle sprite for the field; print field value several
17     * times to show toString method
18     */
19    @Override
20    public void setup() {
21      System.out.println("someField = " + someField);
22      someField = new RectangleSprite(0.25, 0.25);
23      System.out.println("someField = " + someField);
24      someField.setLocation(0.5, 0.5);
25      addSprite(someField);
26      System.out.println("someField:" + someField.getX() + ", " +
27        someField.getY() + " - " + someField.getWidth() + ", " +
28        someField.getHeight());
29    }
30  }
```

Listing 8.3: `PrintASprite` Demonstrate `System.out`

The game, declared a `Sprite` field, initializes it and adds it to the game. Intertwined in those actions, `setup` calls `println` to print information about `someField`. The book has insisted that you cannot use fields before initializing them. The first line of the output shows why:

```
~/Chapter08% java -classpath .:/usr/lib/jvm/fang2.jar PrintASprite
someField = null
someField = fang.sprites.RectangleSprite[x = 0.0, y = 0.0],
[w = 0.25, h = 0.25] color = FANG Blue
someField:0.5, 0.5 - 0.25, 0.25
```

The value of the uninitialized field is **null**; **null** is the reference value that means the reference refers to *nothing*. You cannot apply the dot operator (.) to the **null** pointer without causing a run-time error.

How is the expression `"someField = "`+ `someField` evaluated? The + operator is the `String` concatenation operator. We have seen that Java coerces POD types "added" to a `String` into a `String` value. An **int**, for example, is changed into a `String` by passing it to `Integer.toString`.

How is `someField` turned into a `String`? The Java base class `Object` defines a **public** `toString` method. *Any* object can be "turned into" a `String` by calling `toString`.

When Java needs a `String` and has, instead, a reference to an `Object`, it checks if the reference is **null**. If it is, the `String` is `"null"`. If the reference is non-**null** the `String` is the result of calling `toString` on the reference.

The `Object` definition returns a string containing some information about the location in *Object Memory* to which the reference refers. Any **class** has the option of overriding the inherited `toString` method.

When an overridden method is called on a reference, the program calls the deepest defined version of the method for the *constructed object type*. We need a better term for the constructed type.

Static and Dynamic Information   Some attributes or properties of a variable (or a program) can be figured out by the compiler at *compile-time*; compiler-knowable attributes are called *static* attributes. Some attributes of a variable cannot be known until *run-time*; attributes unknowable until execution are called *dynamic* attributes.

Static[4] attributes, because they are determined early, cannot change during execution. Static attributes include the value of literals (e.g., `"Wolverines!"`, `true`, `null`), the *signature* of a method, and the *defined type* of a variable. The defined type or, more simply, the *static type* of a variable is determined by the type used in the definition. The static type of `someField` is `Sprite`:

```
13    private Sprite someField;
```

Dynamic attributes include all values that *can* change either from one run to another or within any one run. Dynamic attributes include user input (which key was struck first), the *value* of a variable, and the *constructed type* of a variable. The constructed type or, more simply, the *dynamic type* of a variable is determined by the type passed to `new` when the object to which it refers was constructed. The dynamic type of `someField` is `RectangleSprite`:

```
22    someField = new RectangleSprite(0.25, 0.25);
```

When a method is called, Java searches for a method matching the required signature (a static attribute), starting at the dynamic type of the object on which the method is called and working its way up the `extends` hierarchy toward `Object`. `someField`'s dynamic type is `RectangleSprite`. The *JavaDoc* for `RectangleSprite` shows the `extends` hierarchy for the class:

```
java.lang.Object
+--extended by fang.core.Sprite
   +--extended by fang.sprites.RectangleSprite
```

`someField.toString()` calls the first method in the following list which is actually defined:

```
RectangleSprite.toString()
        Sprite.toString()
        Object.toString()
```

This is a more precise description of how Java selects which definition of an overridden method to call than was presented in Section 4.1

There is no definition of `toString` in `RectangleSprite`: the *JavaDoc* for `RectangleSprite` does not list `toString` in the *Method Summary*. `Sprite` *does* override `toString` with the following code:

```
/**
 * Return a string representation of the {@code Sprite}. The type,
 * location, size, and color of the {@code Sprite}.
 */
\@Override
public String toString() {
  return getClass().getName() +
    "[x = " + getX() + ", y = " + getY() +"], " +
    "[w = " + getWidth() + ", h = " + getHeight() + "] color = " +
    Palette.getColorName(getColor());
}
```

---

[4]This use of static should not be confused with the Java keyword `static`. The two are related: constructing an instance is dynamic; not needing an instance to call a `static` method is less dynamic. The concept of static attributes applies more broadly than the Java `static` keyword.

This code, reformatted to match, to an extent, the second and third lines of the output above, returns a string specialized for Sprite. It includes the name of the class of the Sprite followed by the location, the scale, and the color. These fields are fields all Sprite have in common. getClass is defined in Object and returns the dynamic class of an object; getName returns the name associated with a class.

Line 26 and following in Listing 8.3 prints out some of the same information in slightly different format. The name of the variable (entered as a literal string) is followed by the x, y, width, and height values. The last line of the output shows how the location and size of someField has changed by the end of setup.

There is a program (included in most modern integrated development environments (IDE)) called a *debugger*. A debugger lets you pause a program at an given line and examine the value of variables, look at field values inside of objects, and even stop the program when the value of a given variable changes.

Instruction on the use of a debugger is beyond the scope of this book but the use of System.out.print and System.out.println is a way of doing much the same thing. At various points in the program you can print out the location of a sprite to track how it moves. This can be helpful even with access to a debugger because a trace produced by a series of print statements can be saved in a file and analyzed with other tools.

Review 8.2

(a) Where does System.out.print print its output? How would you view it in your environment?

(b) What is the difference between print and println? Are there the same number of overloaded definitions for each method? (Hint: Look at the documentation.)

(c) Describe how Java determines which definition of an overridden method to call.

(d) Define what a *static* attribute is. Name two.

(e) Define what a *dynamic* attribute is. Name two.

(f) What is the meaning of the Java keyword **static**?

8.3 Iteration

Write a program that prints the numbers 0 through 9 on the console as part of setup. We hope that the following occurred to you:

```java
public void setup() {
  System.out.print(" " + 0);
  System.out.print(" " + 1);
  System.out.print(" " + 2);
  System.out.print(" " + 3);
  System.out.print(" " + 4);
  System.out.print(" " + 5);
  System.out.print(" " + 6);
  System.out.print(" " + 7);
  System.out.print(" " + 8);
  System.out.print(" " + 9);
  System.out.println(); // start new line
}
```

Two things to note: each of the first ten lines differs from the others by only a single character (violates at least the spirit of DRY) and the code would be hard to extend to 100 or 1000 numbers.

We must use Java *iteration* to do the same thing (or almost the same thing) over and over again. The following code does the trick:

```
14   public void setup() {
15     for (int i = 0; i != 10; ++i) {
16       System.out.print(" " + i);
17     }
18     System.out.println();
19   }
```

Listing 8.4: Iteration iteration

The *semantics* or the meaning of this language construct is based on the three parts of the **for** statement inside the parentheses. The three parts, separated by the semicolons, are described in the Java template for the **for** statement:

```
<forStatement> ::= for (<init>; <continuation>; <nextStep>)
                        <statement>


<statement> := <localVariableDefinition> |
               <expression>; |
               <forStatement> |
               <ifStatement> |
               <block>
```

The *<body>* of the **for** loop is the collection of statements that are *iterated* or done many times. The *<init>* or *initialization* part of the **for** statement is executed *once* before any other parts of the statement are evaluated or executed.

In the counting loop above, the *<init>* is **int** i = 0; this declares a local variable and sets the value of the variable to zero. Note that it is not *necessary* to declare a *loop-control variable* in the *<init>* though it is often convenient. The value of the loop-control variable determines how many times a count-controlled loop executes.

Question: What is the *scope* of i? The scope is the whole **for** statement. The variable i is visible inside all three parts of the **for** statement *and* throughout the <body>.

After initialization, execution of the **for** loop continues by evaluating *<continuation>*. *<continuation>* is a Boolean expression. When *<continuation>* evaluates to **true**, the *<body>* is executed once; when it is **false**, execution continues *after* the body of the **for** statement. This is similar to an **if** statement in that the *<thenStatement>* is executed or skipped depending on the value of a Boolean expression.

In our sample loop above, when i is not *exactly* equal to 10, the body of the loop is executed. As you can see, right after initialization, i != 10 is **true**, so the body is executed.

Each time the statement finishes executing *<body>*, execution of the **for** loop continues with the execution of *<nextStep>* and reevaluating *<continuation>*.

If *<continuation>* is **true**, the body of the loop and *<nextStep>* are executed and the continuation condition is rechecked. The body of the loop and the next step are executed so long as the continuation is **true.**

In the sample loop, *<nextStep>* is ++i. The ++ operator increments the variable to which it is applied. The next step operation is to increment i. The body of the loop prints out a space and i. The loop prints [0–10][5] on the console.

One way to view the execution is to "unroll" the loop, writing down all of the parts as if they were to be executed sequentially. The check of *<continuation>* becomes an **if** statement, and if it is **false** (or its compliment is **true**), then the pseudo-statement EXIT runs and execution continues with the labeled statement at the end of the listing.

The comments trace what is happening as each part of the **for** loop executes:

---

[5]Or [0–9]; the asymmetric range notation matches the way the **for** loop range is expressed inside the *<init>* and *<nextStep>* parts of the statement.

```
int i = 0;                   // init: i = 0
if (!(i != 10)) EXIT;        // continuation
System.out.print(" " + i);   // body: " 0"
++i;                         // nextStep: i = 1
if (!(i != 10)) EXIT;        // continuation
System.out.print(" " + i);   // body: " 1"
++i;                         // nextStep: i = 2
if (!(i != 10)) EXIT;        // continuation
System.out.print(" " + i);   // body: " 2"
++i;                         // nextStep: i = 3
if (!(i != 10)) EXIT;        // continuation
System.out.print(" " + i);   // body: " 3"
++i;                         // nextStep: i = 4
if (!(i != 10)) EXIT;        // continuation
System.out.print(" " + i);   // body: " 4"
++i;                         // nextStep: i = 5
if (!(i != 10)) EXIT;        // continuation
System.out.print(" " + i);   // body: " 5"
++i;                         // nextStep: i = 6
if (!(i != 10)) EXIT;        // continuation
System.out.print(" " + i);   // body: " 6"
++i;                         // nextStep: i = 7
if (!(i != 10)) EXIT;        // continuation
System.out.print(" " + i);   // body: " 7"
++i;                         // nextStep: i = 8
if (!(i != 10)) EXIT;        // continuation
System.out.print(" " + i);   // body: " 8"
++i;                         // nextStep: i = 9
if (!(i != 10)) EXIT;        // continuation
System.out.print(" " + i);   // body: " 9"
++i;                         // nextStep: i = 10
if (!(i != 10)) EXIT;        // continuation
EXIT:
System.out.println();        // After loop
```

<init> is executed exactly *once*. <continuation> is evaluated one more time than the body of the loop (it must evaluate to **false** once). nextStep is executed once after each execution of the body of the loop.

This is, in many ways, similar to setup and advance: setup is run once *before* the main video game loop is entered. After the game is entered, the body of the main video game loop includes a call to advance.

Practice Loops

This section explores iteration by describing numeric sequences and **for** loops for printing them out. Commonalities between the loops are reviewed at the end of the section.

More Numbers

How would you change the example loop given above to print the numbers 0 through 99? We want 100 different numbers.

```
for (int i = 0; i != 100; ++i) {
  System.out.print(" " + i);
}
System.out.println(); // start new line
```

Clearly the change was just in the <continuation>: the 10 became 100. This is right but not aesthetically pleasing: there are too many numbers on one line. What if we want to print 7 numbers per line (with no more than 7 on the last line since 7 does not divide 100 evenly)? We need to check, inside the loop, whether we need to insert a new line. The program starts a new line whenever i is a multiple of 7: a line before 0, 7, 14, 21, ... This means there is a new line started before the first number is printed; we examine how to avoid that after the loop works.

Remember that the <body> of the loop is a collection of statements; it can contain calls to methods, **if** statements, or even more **for** loops.

```
for (int i = 0; i != 100; ++i) {
  if (i % 7 == 0) { // remainder of 0
    System.out.println(); // start new line
  }
  System.out.print(" " + i);
}
System.out.println(); // start new line
```

Here we test if i is a multiple of 7 by using the *modulus* operator, %. The modulus operator takes two **int** expressions and divides the first by the second, returning the *remainder* in the division. The definition of a number being a multiple of another number is that it have a remainder of 0 when divided by the number. The Boolean expression in the **if** statement is **true** exactly when i is a multiple of 7.

To get rid of the first newline, it suffices to test if i is *not* zero as well as the multiple of 7 test:

```
12   public void setup() {
13     for (int i = 0; i != 100; ++i) {
14       if (((i % 7) == 0) && (i != 0)) {
15         System.out.println();
16       }
17       System.out.print(" " + i);
18     }
19     System.out.println();
20   }
```

Listing 8.5: MoreNumbers iteration

The output of this loop is

```
~/Chapter08% java -classpath .:/usr/lib/jvm/fang2.jar MoreNumbers
0 1 2 3 4 5 6
7 8 9 10 11 12 13
14 15 16 17 18 19 20
21 22 23 24 25 26 27
28 29 30 31 32 33 34
35 36 37 38 39 40 41
42 43 44 45 46 47 48
49 50 51 52 53 54 55
56 57 58 59 60 61 62
63 64 65 66 67 68 69
70 71 72 73 74 75 76
77 78 79 80 81 82 83
84 85 86 87 88 89 90
91 92 93 94 95 96 97
98 99
```

The columns do not line up (single digit numbers print in a single space whereas double digit numbers use two) but there are seven elements per line.

What could a **for** loop do other than print a table on System.out? Listing 8.6 uses iteration to add randomly colored and located RectangleSprites.

```
13  public void setup() {
14    for (int i = 0; i != 10; ++i) {
15      RectangleSprite curr = new RectangleSprite(0.1, 0.1);
16      curr.setLocation(randomDouble(), randomDouble());
17      curr.setColor(randomColor());
18      addSprite(curr);
19    }
20  }
```

Listing 8.6: IterateSquares iteration

Figure 8.4 shows an example run of this program. This example uses iteration but not console output; these two techniques are independent of one another.

Not Starting at 0

How would you print (on the console) the numbers from 10 up to 99? The easiest way is to change *<init>*: rather than set i to 0, set it to 10.

```
12  public void setup() {
13    for (int i = 10; i != 100; ++i) {
14      if (((i % 7) == 0) && (i != 0)) {
15        System.out.println();
16      }
17      System.out.print(" " + i);
18    }
19    System.out.println();
20  }
```

Listing 8.7: NotFromOne iteration

Figure 8.4: A Sample Run of IterateSquares

The output of this program is

```
~/Chapter08% java -classpath .:/usr/lib/jvm/fang2.jar NotFromOne
10 11 12 13
14 15 16 17 18 19 20
21 22 23 24 25 26 27
28 29 30 31 32 33 34
35 36 37 38 39 40 41
42 43 44 45 46 47 48
49 50 51 52 53 54 55
56 57 58 59 60 61 62
63 64 65 66 67 68 69
70 71 72 73 74 75 76
77 78 79 80 81 82 83
84 85 86 87 88 89 90
91 92 93 94 95 96 97
98 99
```

Again, this is correct (the numbers printed are [10–99]) but it is not aesthetically pleasing. It would look better to have 7 elements on the first line and every line after except, possibly, for the last (how many numbers are printed? Is that number a multiple of 7? If not, how many elements are on the last line?).

The trick here is that the value i in this example serves two purposes: it contains the value to print next *and* it counts how many items have been printed. That second function must be done some other way now. How can we determine how many elements have been printed so far? Having that number, we could check if *it* is a multiple of 7 and start a new line.

The first time through the loop 0 elements have been printed. The second time 1 element and each additional time, one more than the iteration before. A new int variable, numberPrintedSoFar, can be introduced, initialized to 0, and incremented every time a number is printed. The two purposes of i are now separated: i contains the value to be printed, and numberPrintedSoFar counts how many items have been printed.

```
12  public void setup() {
13    int numberPrintedSoFar = 0;
14    for (int i = 10; i != 100; ++i) {
15      if (((numberPrintedSoFar % 7) == 0) &&
16          (numberPrintedSoFar != 0)) {
17        System.out.println();
18      }
19      System.out.print(" " + i);
20      ++numberPrintedSoFar;
21    }
22    System.out.println();
23  }
```

Listing 8.8: NotFromOneFixed iteration

Listing 8.8 shows the setup from the fixed version counting from a number other than one. The fixed output is

```
~/Chapter08% java -classpath .:/usr/lib/jvm/fang2.jar NotFromOneFixed
 10 11 12 13 14 15 16
 17 18 19 20 21 22 23
 24 25 26 27 28 29 30
 31 32 33 34 35 36 37
 38 39 40 41 42 43 44
 45 46 47 48 49 50 51
 52 53 54 55 56 57 58
 59 60 61 62 63 64 65
 66 67 68 69 70 71 72
 73 74 75 76 77 78 79
 80 81 82 83 84 85 86
 87 88 89 90 91 92 93
 94 95 96 97 98 99
```

Not Counting by 1s

How can we iterate across the first ten *non-negative multiples of 7*? There are multiple different answers: MoreNumbers could be modified so that i is printed only when it is a multiple of 7 (the if statement is already there); the loop could be modified so that i takes on only multiples of 7; the loop could *count* the number of multiples printed and the value to be printed could be calculated separately.

The first and last approaches are left as exercise (see Chapter Review 1 and 2). The second approach seems promising: 0 is the first multiple of 7 to be printed; the beginning of the sequence is 0, 7, 14, 21, ... Each is 7 more than the one before. *<nextStep>* is modified to i = i + 7:

```
12   public void setup() {
13     for (int i = 0; i != 70; i = i + 7) {
14       System.out.print(" " + i);
15     }
16     System.out.println();
17   }
```

Listing 8.9: CountBySeven iteration

Listing 8.9 shows that *<nextStep>* can be any statement for advancing to the next iteration. *<continuation>* is also changed because the first ten multiples of seven are those less than 70. The output of the program is

```
~/Chapter08% java -classpath .:/usr/lib/jvm/fang2.jar CountBySeven
0 7 14 21 28 35 42 49 56 63
```

Never Execute the Body

Finally, what if continuation is **false** from the beginning? Consider

```
12   public void setup() {
13     for (int i = 0; i < 0; ++i) {
14       System.out.print(" " + i);
15     }
16     System.out.println();
17   }
```

Listing 8.10: NeverExecuteBody iteration

What is the output of this snippet of code? The variable is initially 0 which is *not* less than 0. The *<continuation>* is **false** from the start and the *<body>* (and *<nextStep>*) is never executed. The only output is a newline, printed by line 16.

About Iteration

In Java, **for** is one of the main ways of implementing iteration. Most of our examples used != in the *<continuation>*; this is idiomatic in the language *if* you know the exact value the loop control variable takes at the end of the iteration. When we count by 1, this is pretty simple. The instance of counting by 7 was harder since we had to figure what value the variable would take (it had to be a multiple of 7).

Some programmers consistently use < (instead of !=) to indicate to the reader that the loop is counting *up*. Then, when counting down (using --i in place of ++i for *<nextStep>*), they use >. This can help document your intention for the values of the loop-control variable.

It is also idiomatic to start counting with 0. Computer scientists start counting with 0 because when there is a collection of objects (as described in the next section), they are indexed by integers starting with 0. The reason is that a collection can be stored as the computer address of the whole collection and a given element is found by adding the index times the size of each object.

There are multiple ways to write even a count-controlled loop. Listing 8.9 counts to 70 by 7s; it could, instead, have counted to 10 by 1s and multiplied the index by 7 when passing it to println. Writing that version is left as an exercise for the reader.

Review 8.3

(a) What are the three parts in parentheses of a `for` loop?

(b) How could you determine if the value in the `int` variable `counter` were a multiple of 13?

(c) How many stars does the following code snippet print on the console? (Hint: If you have trouble figuring it out, type it into `setup` of an empty game and see what happens.)

```
for (int i = 0; i != 17; ++i) {
  System.out.print("*");
}
System.out.println();
```

Explain how you arrived at your answer.

(d) How many stars does the following code snippet print on the console? (Hint: If you have trouble figuring it out, type it into `setup` of an empty game and see what happens.)

```
for (int i = 0; i != 17; ++i) {
  System.out.print("**");
}
System.out.println();
```

Explain how you arrived at your answer.

(e) How does the program start a new line on the console?

(f) Can the body of a `for` loop add sprites to a game?

8.4   Collections: One and Many

Can we combine what we just learned about iteration with the code from `TicTacToe`? Can we avoid repeating ourselves in three (or eight) different routines for checking for a winning row of symbols?

The answer is no: the names we give variables such as `t11` exist only at *compile-time*. They are *static attributes* that are used by the compiler and then thrown away (the running program uses only the memory addresses of the memory boxes used by each variable). There is no way to iterate over those names at run time. Fortunately most programming languages support *collections* or *containers*, objects that can contain multiple other values.

Java has a standard collection library in the `java.util` package as well as one built-in collection type. The *array*, the built-in collection, is constructed by specifying exactly the number of entries the collection can contain, and that number cannot vary over the life of the array. The fixed size is a limitation we want to avoid, so *Simple Games* uses arrays only where necessary.

`java.util.ArrayList` is constructed without the need to specify the number of entries and can grow to accommodate an arbitrary number of entries. This flexibility is not free: where an array can be a collection of *any* Java type, `ArrayList`s are limited to contain only *object* types.

The trade-off is a good one, and the book uses the `ArrayList` collection as much as possible.

Declaring an `ArrayList`

The import required to use `java.util.ArrayList` is

```
import java.util.ArrayList;
```

The `ArrayList` type is special: it is a *generic* type. This means that when declaring a variable or field of the `ArrayList` type, you must also specify the *type* of the elements the collection contains.

Listing 8.11 declares an `ArrayList` field on line 16. The elements in the list[6] are `Integer`, the object type that wraps the POD **int** type. `Integer` can be an element of `ArrayList` and automatically behaves like an **int** when it needs to.

```
1  // package default
2
3  import fang2.core.Game;
4
5  import java.util.ArrayList;
6
7  /**
8   * Demonstrate how an ArrayList prints using System.out.println.
9   */
10 public class PrintAnArrayList
11   extends Game {
12   /**
13    * ArrayList of Integer (we will put in some numbers and do things
14    * with them)
15    */
16   private ArrayList<Integer> theTable;
17
18   /**
19    * Create the ArrayList; print out some information about it
20    */
21   @Override
22   public void setup() {
23     System.out.println("theTable = " + theTable);
24     theTable = new ArrayList<Integer>();
25     System.out.println("theTable = " + theTable);
26     System.out.println("theTable.size() = " + theTable.size());
27   }
28 }
```

Listing 8.11: `PrintAnArrayList` on `System.out`

The console output of `PrintAnArrayList` is

```
~/Chapter08% java -classpath .:/usr/lib/jvm/fang2.jar PrintAnArrayList
theTable = null
theTable = []
theTable.size() = 0
```

`PrintAnArrayList`, like `PrintASprite`, demonstrates that the field `theTable` is initially **null** (printed in line 23). The collection is instantiated on line 24; notice that the constructor called by **new** operator includes the name of the element type just like the declaration of the field. Line 25 prints out the value of the `ArrayList`. The second line of output shows the value of `theTable` is "[]". Why?

The `toString` method of `ArrayList` is inherited from **class** `java.util.AbstractCollection`; the exact location of the method is not as important as our ability to find the documentation for the method that is called (it helps us debug). According to the documentation:

---

[6]To avoid confusion with the built-in *array* type in Java, when `ArrayList` is mentioned in the text, it is referred to as a *list*. This matches Java nomenclature because the `ArrayList` type **implements** (like extends) the `List` **interface** (like **class**).

```
toString

public String toString()

Returns a string representation of this collection. The string
representation consists of a list of the collection's elements in the
order they are returned by its iterator, enclosed in square brackets
(''[]''). Adjacent elements are separated by the characters '', '' (a
comma and a space). Elements are converted to strings as by
String.valueOf(Object).

Overrides:
    toString in class Object
Returns:
    a string representation of this collection
```

The two square brackets on the second line of output indicate that the ArrayList is not null but it is empty. This is confirmed by the last line of console output where the size of the ArrayList is 0.

Filling a Collection

An ArrayList is a line of elements. Each element has a place in the line and that place is its *index*. The index of the first element in an ArrayList is 0 (computer scientists love counting from 0). The valid indexes in an ArrayList run from 0 to size() -1.

Elements are added to the end of an ArrayList with the add method. It takes an element type as its parameter and adds the value to the end of the list.

Listing 8.12 extends the printing of theTable to include adding four elements to the list.

```
20  public void setup() {
21    System.out.println("theTable = " + theTable);
22    theTable = new ArrayList<Integer>();
23    System.out.println("<> theTable = " + theTable);
24    System.out.println("<before> theTable.size() = " + theTable.size());
25    theTable.add(63);
26    System.out.println("<63> theTable = " + theTable);
27    theTable.add(56);
28    System.out.println("<56> theTable = " + theTable);
29    theTable.add(49);
30    System.out.println("<49> theTable = " + theTable);
31    theTable.add(42);
32    System.out.println("<42> theTable = " + theTable);
33    System.out.println("<after> theTable.size() = " + theTable.size());
34  }
```

Listing 8.12: PrintAnArrayList2 onSystem.out

In the output, just below, lines are prefixed with the element just added to the ArrayList. After each call to add, the whole list is printed out.

```
~/Chapter08% java -classpath .:/usr/lib/jvm/fang2.jar PrintAnArrayList2
theTable = null
<> theTable = []
<before> theTable.size() = 0
<63> theTable = [63]
<56> theTable = [63, 56]
<49> theTable = [63, 56, 49]
<42> theTable = [63, 56, 49, 42]
<after> theTable.size() = 4
```

After adding four elements, the four elements are in the ArrayList *in the order they were added.* This is similar to addSprite: with plain add, the newest item is "on top" in the sense that it is last in the ArrayList.

We want to modify the content of the list. We want the first ten non-negative multiples of seven in the list in ascending order. 0 first, 7 second, and so on until 63 is last. How could we modify Listing 8.12 to do this?

We could easily cut and past the four lines in that program and modify each of them. The authors hope you are reciting "DRY" under your breath and wondering how to use iteration. If the first ten multiples of seven failed to make you say that, what if we wanted the first thousand?

```
12   public void setup() {
13     for (int i = 0; i != 70; i = i + 7) {
14       System.out.print(" " + i);
15     }
16     System.out.println();
17   }
18 }
```

Listing 8.13: CountBySeven iteration (again)

Listing 8.13 is a repeat of CountBySeven. The body of the loop is just a call to System.out.print; we need to call add and then, to see what is happening, print out theTable. Listing 8.14 lists the modified setup.

```
22   public void setup() {
23     System.out.println("theTable = " + theTable);
24     theTable = new ArrayList<Integer>();
25     System.out.println("<> theTable = " + theTable);
26     System.out.println("<before> theTable.size() = " + theTable.size());
27     for (int i = 0; i != 70; i = i + 7) {
28       theTable.add(i);
29       System.out.println("<" + i + "> theTable = " + theTable);
30     }
31     System.out.println("<after> theTable.size() = " + theTable.size());
32   }
```

Listing 8.14: PrintAnArrayList3 iteration

As in PrintAnArrayList2, each time the table is printed out, the line is prefixed with the last entry added. add, when called with one parameter, tacks the new entry onto the end of the list.

The output of `PrintAnArrayList3` is

```
~/Chapter08% java -classpath .:/usr/lib/jvm/fang2.jar PrintAnArrayList3
theTable = null
<> theTable = []
<before> theTable.size() = 0
<0> theTable = [0]
<7> theTable = [0, 7]
<14> theTable = [0, 7, 14]
<21> theTable = [0, 7, 14, 21]
<28> theTable = [0, 7, 14, 21, 28]
<35> theTable = [0, 7, 14, 21, 28, 35]
<42> theTable = [0, 7, 14, 21, 28, 35, 42]
<49> theTable = [0, 7, 14, 21, 28, 35, 42, 49]
<56> theTable = [0, 7, 14, 21, 28, 35, 42, 49, 56]
<63> theTable = [0, 7, 14, 21, 28, 35, 42, 49, 56, 63]
<after> theTable.size() = 10
```

There is a *two*-parameter version of `add` that takes an index and an element. The element is added to the list *at the given index*. This means the index of any elements already in the list at or after the given index is moved up one slot to make room for the new entry.

So far we know:

- An `ArrayList` is a generic object type.

- *Generic* means that the type name requires another type name between angle brackets to be complete *and* that type must be an object type: for example, `ArrayList<Integer>`.

- Somewhere above `ArrayList` the `toString` method is overridden to print out the contents of the list.

- The `add` method adds elements at the end of the list or at a given location (one- or two-parameter versions).

Iteration: Traversing a Collection

After inserting elements into a collection, how can we access them again? The previous section showed how to convert the entire contents of the list into a `String`; we want to be able to access the individual elements put into the collection. This lets us treat the one collection as a collection of *variables*.

How would you declare an `ArrayList` that could hold `GameTile` elements? How would you put nine `GameTile` into the `ArrayList`? This section focuses on how you would access each element so that you could check for a winner in a game of `TicTacToe` (see Programming Problem 8.4 for more guidance on using an `ArrayList` in `TicTacToe`).

The method to get an element, given its index, is `get`. The return type of `get` is whatever element type was used when declaring the `ArrayList`. This is what a generic type does for us: it sets the parameter type for `add` to be the element type and the return type of `get` to the same type. `get` returns a reference to the element in the `ArrayList` at the given index.

Manipulating Each Element

We can use the `size` method along with our standard loop construct to print out all of the elements in an `ArrayList`

```
17   public void setup() {
18     theTable = new ArrayList<Integer>();
19
20     for (int i = 0; i != 70; i = i + 7) {
21       theTable.add(i);
22     }
23
24     System.out.println("<after>");
25     for (int j = 0; j != theTable.size(); ++j) {
26       System.out.print(" " + theTable.get(j));
27     }
28     System.out.println();
29   }
```

Listing 8.15: `PrintAnArrayList4` iteration

The direct printing of the `ArrayList` is removed. Instead we use the loop in lines 25–27 to call `get`, once for each element in the `ArrayList`. `j` crosses the range [0–10). The first element in `theTable` has the index 0; the last has the index `theTable.size() -1`.

The console output of this program is

```
~/Chapter08% java -classpath .:/usr/lib/jvm/fang2.jar PrintAnArrayList4
<after>
 0 7 14 21 28 35 42 49 56 63
```

Notice that the elements are in the same order we inserted them (and that we saw them when `toString` was used to print them). We can call any method in the public protocol of the element type.

Updating Elements

Let us revisit `IterateSquares.java`. The new version, `BoxParade.java` has an `ArrayList` of `RectangleSprites` containing all of the sprites constructed and added to the game. `advance` loops across the list of squares, moving each one on each frame. The result is an animated parade of squares up the screen.

```
1  // package default
2
3  import java.util.ArrayList;
4
5  import fang2.core.Game;
6  import fang2.sprites.RectangleSprite;
7
8  /**
9   * Randomly place some number of rectangle sprites. Then move them
10  * upward at a fixed rate, looping them around off the top of the screen
11  * to the bottom.
12  */
13 public class BoxParade
14   extends Game {
15   /** The collection of RectangleSprites */
16   ArrayList<RectangleSprite> boxes;
17
```

```
18    /**
19     * 10 randomly colored and placed rectangles on the screen
20     */
21    @Override
22    public void setup() {
23      // Make sure you initialize the collection!
24      boxes = new ArrayList<RectangleSprite>();
25
26      for (int i = 0; i != 10; ++i) {
27        RectangleSprite curr = new RectangleSprite(0.1, 0.1);
28        curr.setLocation(randomDouble(), randomDouble());
29        curr.setColor(randomColor());
30        addSprite(curr);
31        boxes.add(curr);
32      }
33    }
34
35    /**
36     * Move all the rectangles upward at a fixed speed.
37     */
38    @Override
39    public void advance(double dT) {
40      for (int i = 0; i != boxes.size(); ++i) {
41        boxes.get(i).translateY(-0.5 * dT);// move up
42        if (boxes.get(i).getY() < 0.0) {// loop around at top
43          boxes.get(i).setY(1.0);
44        }
45      }
46    }
47 }
```

Listing 8.16: BoxParade iteration in setup and advance

Line 24 calls **new** to construct the new collection. This is an important step (the program crashes without it) and an easy one to forget. Line 31 (which is where the program crashes without the **new** in line 24) was not needed in IterateSquares. It adds a reference to the new square to boxes.

The body of the **for** loop in advance, lines 40–44, moves one RectangleSprite up the screen at the rate of 1 screen every two seconds. The loop changes which sprite is being moved, iterating over all elements in boxes so that all 10 sprites move.

The **if** statement just wraps a square around from the top of the screen to the bottom of the screen (like a WrapTransformer) so that the parade can continue.

An important point here (and a lot of other places in the remainder of the book): whenever you find yourself thinking, "I want to do *blah* to every element in a collection," you should think of a loop. Here, *blah* is "move upward." In the previous example, PrintAnArrayList4, *blah* was "print a space followed by the element."

Finding an Element

What else could we do with an ArrayList? We could search for a specific element. It might be that we want to know whether a certain value is in the list or we might want to find the minimum or maximum value. Check each element in the ArrayList against the value being searched for (or the best result found so far). The *blah* for every element is "compare to the searched for value" or "compare to the best result so far."

To put this in action we modify BoxParade so that the element that is closest to the top of the screen is colored red. This requires us to be able to find the index of the box with the smallest y-coordinate. An outline of advance becomes

- If there is a new highest box:

    - Restore color of old highest box
    - Copy color of new highest box
    - Color new highest box red

- Move all boxes up the screen

    - If a box goes off the top, wrap it around

Deferring the details of finding the highest box to indexOfHighestBox, advance is shown in Listing 8.17.

```
70    int currHighest = indexOfHighestBox();
71
72    if (currHighest != highest) {
73      boxes.get(highest).setColor(highestColor);
74      highest = currHighest;
75      highestColor = boxes.get(highest).getColor();
76      boxes.get(highest).setColor(getColor("SCG Red"));
77    }
```

Listing 8.17: BoxParadeWithRed advance

indexOfHighestBox returns the index (integer used with get) of the box with the lowest y-coordinate. If that index is different than it was before (as stored in the field highest), we need to reset the color of the *old* highest box, change the highest field, save the current color of the highest box (so we can restore it later), and change the color of the highest box to red. Though it is not listed in the book, setup initializes highest and highestColor so that they have appropriate values the first time through advance.

How does indexOfHighestBox work? It returns an index, an **int**. The body of the method begins by "guessing" that box 0 is the highest box. It does this by initializing indexOfHighestSoFar to 0. When the method ends, indexOfHighestSoFar is the value returned by the method.

```
51    public int indexOfHighestBox() {
52      int indexOfHighestSoFar = 0;
53
54      for (int nextIndexToCheck = 0; nextIndexToCheck != boxes.size();
55          ++nextIndexToCheck) {
56        if (boxes.get(nextIndexToCheck).getY() <
57            boxes.get(indexOfHighestSoFar).getY()) {
58          indexOfHighestSoFar = nextIndexToCheck;
59        }
60      }
61
62      return indexOfHighestSoFar;
63    }
```

Listing 8.18: BoxParadeWithRed.java iteration

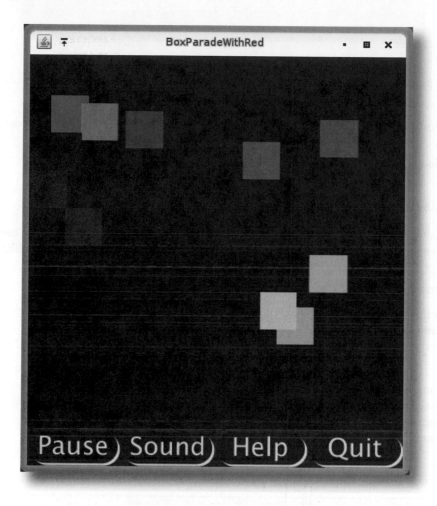

Figure 8.5: BoxParadeWithRed snapshot

After the guess is initialized, it is necessary to check each box in boxes to see if the box is higher than the guess; the guess remains the highest square seen so far. Listing 8.18 shows the method. The **for** loop compares the y-coordinate of the current highest to each box in turn. When one is found that is higher, indexOfHighestSoFar is changed to the current index. When the loop finishes, indexOfHighestSoFar contains the index of the highest box in the whole list.

Figure 8.5 shows a snapshot of BoxParadeWithRed. The red box is closer to the top of the screen than any other at the moment. As soon as it wraps to the bottom, however, for a couple of frames, at least, the box that overlaps wins and is colored red.

Review 8.4

(a) What does *generic* mean?

(b) How would you declare an ArrayList to contain elements of the following types:

    (a) Double

    (b) OvalSprite

    (c) `CompositeSprite`

    (d) `Person`

(c) How would fill an `ArrayList<Integer>` with the first ten multiples of 19?

(d) What does `ArrayList.size` return? What does the value mean?

(e) On what does the return type of `get` depend? For each of the lists in Section Review 2 above, what is the return type of `get`?

(f) "I want to do *blah* to every element in a collection." What should you be thinking?

8.5   `ArrayList` Is an Object

What can we do with a `ArrayList`? `ArrayList` is a standard class type provided by Java; we can look at the *JavaDoc* documentation for the class and get a list of all of the methods declared within its public protocol.

The Public Protocol

Much of this section is copied from the *JavaDoc* page for `ArrayList` in the Java 1.6[7] release.

Constructor Summary

```
ArrayList<E>()
```

constructs an empty list of element type `E` with an initial capacity of ten. The initial capacity is the number of times you can call one of the `add` methods before the class has to move things around in memory to accommodate more elements. An `ArrayList` can contain an arbitrary number of elements.

Method Summary

```
boolean add(E e)
void add(int index, E element)
```

The first version appends the specified element to the end of this list. The second inserts the specified element at the specified position in this list. Either one results in an `ArrayList` with one more element in the list.

```
void clear()
```

This method removes all of the elements from this list. No matter how many elements were in the list *before* the call, there are 0 elements after the call (`size()` returns 0).

```
boolean contains(Object o)
int indexOf(Object o)
```

The `contains` method returns **true** if this list contains the specified element. It uses `equals()` method to find a match. `indexOf` returns the index of the first (lowest-numbered) occurrence of the specified element in this list, or -1 if this list does not contain the element; `indexOf` also uses `equals` to determine whether or not an element matches the given value. These would not have worked for our `indexOfHighestBox` because they use only `equals` which does not find a minimum or maximum value of a field.

```
E get(int index)
```

Returns the element at the specified position in this list.

---

[7]Only methods that work in 1.5 as well as 1.6 are listed (the `isEmpty` predicate is omitted) to support the use of older Java installations.

```
E set(int index, E element)
```

Replaces the element at the specified position in this list with the specified element. This method returns the value previously at this location.

```
E remove(int index)
boolean remove(Object o)
```

The first removes the element at the specified position in this list, returning the value that used to be there (and moving all of the elements with higher indices down one location). The second version removes the first occurrence of the specified element from this list, if it is present. It returns `true` if a matching element was found and removed; `false` if no match could be found. It uses `equals` as defined in the element type to find a match.

These are the basic methods for use with all `ArrayLists`. Summarizing what we know one more time:

- An `ArrayList` is a generic object; the type is named with as `ArrayList<ElementType>` where the `ElementType` is an object type.

- The constructor for an `ArrayList` requires the same generic type specification as a variable declaration.

- An `ArrayList` is an object. This means interaction uses the dot notation we use with other objects.

- `add` adds elements to the list, `get` gets individual elements in the list by index, and `size` returns the current number of elements in the `ArrayList`.

- The indexes of an `ArrayList` start at 0. Valid indexes of `ArrayList` A (with any element type) are on the range [0–A.size()). As noted previously, 0 is inclusive, A.size() is not.

- Whenever you think, "I need to *blah* every element in the list," you should immediately think, "I need to use a loop."

Review 8.5

(a) How would you remove all of the elements from an `ArrayList` with one statement?

(b) What does `remove(int)` do? What happens to `size()` after a call to `remove`? What happens to the index of the last element (assuming `remove` does not leave the list empty)?

(c) What is the constructor call for an `ArrayList` of `PolygonSprites`?

8.6 Finishing the Flu Simulation

We finally know enough to create our simulation. Given a `Person` class to represent villagers, we can represent the village as an `ArrayList<Person>`. Setup requires adding enough people to the village and selecting some number of them to be the initial victims of the disease.

The simulation runs until all villagers are either dead or healthy. Each day of the simulation, individuals advance their disease (if any) to the following day; each contagious person is exposed to some number of his or her neighbors chosen at random.

The state of the `Person` is similar to the state we saw in `SoloPong`; `Person` defines useful *predicate* methods for checking the state.

A predicate is a method that returns `true` or `false`; a predicate is also known as a Boolean method. `Person` also provides transition methods, methods for putting a `Person` into a given state. This makes it easy to translate the state diagram in Figure 8.2 into Java code.

The Person Class Public Protocol

If we look at the above description of Person, the class's public protocol begins to take shape.

```
public class Person
  extends CompositeSprite {
  Person();

  public boolean isContagious();
  public void makeContagious();
  public boolean isDead();
  public void makeDead();
  public boolean isHealthy();
  public void makeHealthy();
  public boolean isRecovering();
  public void makeRecovering();
  public boolean isSick();
  public void makeSick();

  public void finishRecovery();
  public void expose();
  public void nextDay();

  public void setColor(Color color);
}
```

The middle 10 methods are related to the five different states that the person can be in. The predicate returns **true** when the person is in the named state and **false** otherwise. At this point, treating Person as an abstract data type, we neither know nor care how that class encodes its current health state. That is an implementation detail left for a lower level of abstraction.

The setColor method overrides the method for CompositeSprite and colors all of the parts of the person with the same color. The state of the person is expressed in the color he displays in the village (we can watch who is sick or contagious, etc.).

The three methods above setColor are important for the simulation. The first, finishRecovery, is called to determine whether or not the person got well after the recovery period. In the state diagram, when the person finishes recovering, he might die or might become healthy; this method makes the appropriate transition.

The expose method exposes this person to the disease. There is a fixed chance of catching the disease when exposed, so a healthy person has a chance of becoming sick when he is exposed.

Finally, nextDay advances the person one day into the future. If he is sick, the illness runs one more day into its course; if he is dead or healthy, nothing happens. nextDay operates on *this* person; an individual Person has no idea about finding its neighbors; that is the simulation's job.

Implementation

The implementation of Person begins with the definition of a large number of named constants. Recall that named constants are **static final** fields that are assigned once. They can be used in the code to make the meaning clearer. They also serve as a single place to make changes.

The constants can be divided into three groups. The first group is the states of the Person's health.

Health is kept as an **int** field, and each of these values is used to indicate that the person is in a given state. The method isSick can just check if the health field is equal to SICK.

```
28    private static final int DEAD = -1;
29    private static final int HEALTHY = 0;
30    private static final int SICK = 1;
31    private static final int CONTAGIOUS = 2;
32    private static final int RECOVERING = 3;
```

Listing 8.19: Person health constants

The second set of constants is the chances of infection and death with the disease along with the number of days the person spends in each stage of the illness. The infection and mortality rates are very high but they match the high-end estimates of the flu pandemic of 1918; one reason for clearly marking these values is that the simulation outcome changes a great deal when they change.

```
18    /** Number of days spent in each of the states of health */
19    public static final int DAYS_SICK = 1;
20    public static final int DAYS_CONTAGIOUS = 3;
21    public static final int DAYS_RECOVERING = 3;
22
23    /** Chance of infection and death */
24    public static final double INFECTION_CHANCE = 0.50;
25    public static final double MORTALITY_RATE = 0.20;
```

Listing 8.20: Person sickDays constants

Finally, the last group of constants is colors. These colors are the colors the person is displayed with when he is in each of the different states of health. The particular choices here were for shades of green except when the person is dead (grey) or contagious (golden). That makes it easy to follow the spread of the disease.

```
34    /** Color constants for each of the states of health */
35    private static final Color COLOR_DEAD = Game.getColor("dark gray");
36    private static final Color COLOR_HEALTHY = Game.getColor("green");
37    private static final Color COLOR_SICK = Game.getColor("green yellow");
38    private static final Color COLOR_CONTAGIOUS =
39        Game.getColor("goldenrod");
40    private static final Color COLOR_RECOVERING =
41        Game.getColor("yellow green");
```

Listing 8.21: Person color constants

Fields

The fields of a Person are the health, the count of days they have been at a given level of sickness, and the body parts displayed for the person.

```
43    /** visible body parts; colored to indicate health state */
44    private final RectangleSprite body;
45    private final OvalSprite head;
46
47    /** current state of health; drawn from states above */
48    private int health;
49
```

```
50    /** days a person has been sick (or greater) */
51    private int sickDay;
```

Listing 8.22: Person fields

Initializing a Person requires initializing the sprites that make up the body and initializing health and sickDays. A newly-created person is assumed to be healthy; we use makeHealthy to avoid having to worry about any extra stuff we need to do to make the new person healthy.

```
57    public Person() {
58      body = new RectangleSprite(0.5, 0.5);
59      body.setLocation(0.0, 0.25);
60      head = new OvalSprite(0.5, 0.5);
61      head.setLocation(0.0, -0.25);
62      addSprite(head);
63      addSprite(body);
64      makeHealthy();
65    }
```

Listing 8.23: Person constructor

State Management

The ten middle methods, the state management methods, are all similar. isHealthy and makeHealthy stand for all ten routines.

```
113    public boolean isHealthy() {
114      return health == HEALTHY;
115    }
158    public void makeHealthy() {
159      sickDay = 0;
160      health = HEALTHY;
161      setColor(COLOR_HEALTHY);
162    }
```

Listing 8.24: Person <is|make>Healthy

isHealthy checks for equality between health and the HEALTHY constant. Both the field and the constant are plain old data, so == suffices; because == returns a Boolean value, the predicate returns the result of the comparison.

makeHealthy is no more involved: the number of days at a given level of illness is set to 0, health is set to the right constant, and the color is set to reflect the new health level.

The other eight methods are just the same with the names of the constants suitably changed.

Random Chance

The two methods finishRecovery and expose use random numbers to decide what happens to this person's health. When a person reaches the end of his recovery period, finishRecovery uses the mortality chance to determine if he dies; if he lives, he recovers and is healthy again.

```
71  public void expose() {
72    if (isHealthy() &&
73        (Game.getCurrentGame().randomDouble() < INFECTION_CHANCE)) {
74      makeSick();
75    }
76  }
82  public void finishRecovery() {
83    if (Game.getCurrentGame().randomDouble() < MORTALITY_RATE) {
84      makeDead();
85    } else {
86      makeHealthy();
87    }
88  }
```

Listing 8.25: `Person` random chance methods

Similarly, expose checks if this person is healthy and if he is, it uses the chance of infection to determine if he becomes sick. Notice that the chance of mortality and infection are numbers between 0 and 1; the lower the number, the less chance that the event occurs. Here a random number between [0.0–1.0) is generated with randomDouble(), and that value is tested against the chance. If the random number is less than the chance, the chance event happens; otherwise the chance event does not happen.

Day by Day

Finally, the nextDay method moves the villager's illness forward one day. That means if he is healthy or dead, there is nothing to do. If he is sick, sickDay is incremented and the number of days he has been at this sickness level is checked against the appropriate DAYS constant. If enough time has elapsed, the method to move to the next state is called. Notices that finishRecovery is called at the end of the RECOVERING state because we don't know whether to make the person healthy or dead.

```
186  public void nextDay() {
187    if (!isHealthy() && !isDead()) {
188      ++sickDay;
189
190      if (isSick() && (sickDay >= DAYS_SICK)) {
191        makeContagious();
192      } else if (isContagious() && (sickDay >= DAYS_CONTAGIOUS)) {
193        makeRecovering();
194      } else if (isRecovering() && (sickDay >= DAYS_RECOVERING)) {
195        finishRecovery();
196      }
197    }
198  }
```

Listing 8.26: `Person` nextDay

Updating the Village

Now that Person is implemented, how does a discrete-time simulation work? We need to set up the village: create an ArrayList of Person, populate it with healthy people, and infect a few of them. The simulation updates the village once per "day"; this means using a timer to determine when the number of seconds per day have elapsed. These two top-level methods are the public protocol of the simulation game.

Setting up the Village

The listing below shows the fields and the setup method of FluSimulator. village holds all of the villagers. The number of villagers is determined by a constant, NUMBER_OF_VILLAGERS; as in Person, named constants are used to make the meaning of the value clear (and permit changing them in a single place).

```
12  /** Number of neighbors exposed to a contagious villager per day */
13  public static final int EXPOSED_PER_DAY = 3;
14
15  /** Maximum neighbor visiting distance */
16  public static final int NEIGHBOR_DISTANCE = 3;
17
18  /** Patients zero are initially ill patients. */
19  public static final int NUMBER_OF_PATIENTS_ZERO = 2;
20
21  /** The number of individuals in the village */
22  public static final int NUMBER_OF_VILLAGERS = 20;
23
24  /** Clock seconds per simulated day */
25  public static final double SECONDS_PER_DAY = 1.0;
```

Listing 8.27: FluSimulator constants

The constants define the size of the village, the number of visitors per day, the size of the neighborhood, the seconds per day of the simulation, and the number of initially sick villagers.

Listing 8.28 shows the fields and setup. The number of villagers determines the number of times **new** Person is called. The number of villagers is also used to determine the scale of each villager's sprite so that they all fit in a single line across the screen.

```
27  /** Number of days elapsed since the beginning of the simulation. */
28  private int dayCount;
29
30  /** String sprite assigned to display the day count. */
31  private StringSprite dayCountDisplay;
32
33  /** The collection of Person representing the village. */
34  private ArrayList<Person> village;
56  public void setup() {
57    // how big is each villager (so they all fit in one line)
58    double scale = 1.0 / NUMBER_OF_VILLAGERS;
59
60    // set aside space for the collection (no Persons yet)
61    village = new ArrayList<Person>();
62
63    for (int i = 0; i < NUMBER_OF_VILLAGERS; ++i) {
64      // construct one person
65      Person nextVillager = new Person();
66      nextVillager.setScale(scale);
67      nextVillager.setLocation((i * scale) + (scale / 2), 0.5);
68      addSprite(nextVillager);
69
70      // add one person to village
```

```
71      village.add(nextVillager);
72    }
73
74    dayCount = 1;
75    dayCountDisplay = new StringSprite();
76    dayCountDisplay.setScale(0.1);
77    dayCountDisplay.leftJustify();
78    dayCountDisplay.setLocation(0.2, 0.1);
79    dayCountDisplay.setText("Day #" + Integer.toString(dayCount));
80    addSprite(dayCountDisplay);
81
82    infectPatientsZero();
83
84    scheduleRelative(this, SECONDS_PER_DAY);
85  }
```

Listing 8.28: `FluSimulator` setup

Why is the expression for `scale` **1.0** / NUMBER_OF_VILLAGERS? Remember that the division operator, /, when applied between **int** values, returns the integer quotient. **1** / NUMBER_OF_VILLAGERS, where the number of villagers is greater than 1, always returns the **int** value of 0. By making the first literal in the expression a **double** (by including the decimal point in the literal), the whole expression is forced to be a **double**, and the number of villagers is changed into a **double** with the same value (so that 20 is *coerced* into the **double** 20.0) and the right value is calculated.

Line 67 uses the loop control variable to calculate the x-coordinate of the location of each villager. The first villager is centered so that its left edge touches the left edge of the screen; its x-coordinate is half of its width or `scale` / 2. Each following villager is one "villager width" to the right of the previous one; since i starts at 0 and goes up by 1 each time through the loop, i * `scale` is the total width of the villagers to the left of villager i. This is the same technique used to solve Chapter Review 2.

With 20 villagers (number determined by the constant NUMBER_OF_VILLAGERS), the game looks like this:

Making an Alarm

The last line of `setup` is something new. It is a call to a method, `scheduleRelative`. The `scheduleRelative` is a way of scheduling an event to take place some time in the future. FANG schedules the event either at a fixed time after the beginning of the game (using `scheduleAbsolute`) or at some amount of time after the moment the action is scheduled (using `scheduleRelative`). The two parameters to either `schedule` method are an `Alarm` and a number of seconds. Neither timer runs before the game is started or when the game is paused.

What is an `Alarm`? An `Alarm` is an *interface* defined in FANG.

An **interface** is like a **class** in that it is defined inside a file with the same name as the **interface**, and all of the methods are declared inside the **interface** body block. An **interface** is different from a **class** in that any class can **implement** any number of interfaces, and an interface provides no "already working" methods or fields. The **interface** just defines a public protocol that a class can choose to implement with methods having the required signatures. Any class implementing the interface can be assigned to a variable of the *interface's* type (which can be used to call any method in the **interface**).

```
<interfaceName> := <identifier>

<parentInterfaceName> := <identifier>
```

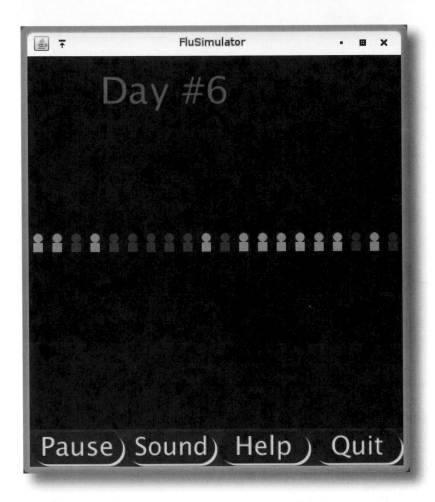

Figure 8.6: The FluSimulator

```
<interfaceDeclaration> :=
    <accessLevel> interface <interfaceName>
      [extends <parentInterfaceName> [, <parentInterfaceName>]*]


<interfaceBody> := {
                    [<methodDeclaration>;] *
                  }


<interfaceDefinition> := <interfaceDeclaration>
                           <interfaceBody>



<interfaceFile> := [<packageID>]
                <imports>
                <interfaceDefinition>
```

For the moment, all we need to do is note that the Alarm interface declares a single method, **public void** act(). When the scheduled time comes, FANG calls the act method automatically.

We could, of course, keep track of elapsed time on our own, counting down some period of time using the dT parameter passed to advance. That is how the CountdownTimer class in Section 6.2 works.

This time we implement an interface, let FANG do the timing for us, and call our act method when the timer expires. act advances the simulation one day and checks whether the simulation continues. If the simulation continues, it schedules another simulation update.

```
40  public void act() {
41    spreadInfection();
42    advanceSimulatedTime();
43    // schedule the next update unless the simulation is quiescent
44    if (simulationContinues()) {// schedule a new call in the future
45      scheduleRelative(this, SECONDS_PER_DAY);
46    } else {
47      endgameStatistics();
48    }
49  }
```

Listing 8.29: FluSimulator act

act is a good example of the "pretend it works" approach to top-down design. The problem that it solves is what to do to advance the simulation's time clock one day into the future. There are two things to do each day: spread the infection and advance time for the villagers. Having advanced time, we can check if the simulation is quiescent: if no health values can change just through the passage of time, the simulation is over.[8]

Leaving spreading the infection for a couple of paragraphs, what do we do to advance time one day for every villager. We want to "advance time one day for every villager in the ArrayList village." What should you be thinking?

```
91   private void advanceSimulatedTime() {
92     for (int currentVillagerNdx = 0;
93          currentVillagerNdx != village.size(); ++currentVillagerNdx) {
94       Person villager = village.get(currentVillagerNdx);
95
96       villager.nextDay();
97     }
98     // increment the day count and display it
99     ++dayCount;
100    dayCountDisplay.setText("Day #" + Integer.toString(dayCount));
101  }
```

Listing 8.30: FluSimulator advanceSimulatedTime

Advancing simulated time means traversing the entire ArrayList, calling a method to advance time on every element. The **for** loop in advanceSimulatedTime is formatted across multiple lines. It is customary to break the contents of the parentheses of a **for** loop at the semicolons so that the *<init>*, *<continuation>*, and *<nextStep>* are not broken across lines. The body of the loop here just copies a reference to the next villager into the villager variable. This works because the entries in village are references, and the assignment just makes two variables, one inside the ArrayList and one declared on line 94; both refer to the same Person. Using

---

[8]All villagers are healthy or dead. No one can become sick, contagious, or recovering ever again.

Using the villager reference, nextDay is called for the Person. As we saw in the last section, nextDay advances any existing illness by one day, changing the person's state (and color) if necessary.

The last two lines in advanceSimulatedTime update the time display at the top of the screen (see Figure 8.6 to see the day number message).

Spreading the Illness

To spread the illness, we need to find all contagious villagers and have them exposed to their neighbors. The number of neighbors they should be exposed to and how to pick neighbors to expose are left for another pass through the top-down design cycle. That said, the spreadInfection method is straightforward:

```
228    private void spreadInfection() {
229      for (int currentVillagerNdx = 0;
230        currentVillagerNdx != village.size(); ++currentVillagerNdx) {
231      Person villager = village.get(currentVillagerNdx);
232      if (villager.isContagious()) {
233        handleContagiousVillager(currentVillagerNdx);
234      }
235     }
236    }
```

Listing 8.31: FluSimulator spreadInfection

We must check each and every villager. If he or she is contagious, we handle a contagious villager. Handling a contagious villager means picking some number of neighbors and exposing them:

```
161    private void handleContagiousVillager(int contagiousVillagerNdx) {
162      for (int numberOfExposed = 0; numberOfExposed != EXPOSED_PER_DAY;
163         ++numberOfExposed) {
164      int exposedVillagerNdx = selectNeighbor(contagiousVillagerNdx);
165
166      if (isValidNdx(exposedVillagerNdx)) {
167        village.get(exposedVillagerNdx).expose();
168      }
169     }
170    }
```

Listing 8.32: FluSimulator handleContagiousVillager

The loop here, rather than going over all of the villagers, runs just EXPOSED_PER_DAY times (convince yourself that this is true by looking at the code). The constant EXPOSED_PER_DAY is set to 3; this loop picks three neighbors of each contagious villager and, if the neighbor is actually a valid index into the village, it exposes the neighbor, giving her a chance of becoming sick.

Remember, the model of the illness (the chance of getting sick, what happens when an already sick person is exposed, etc.) is all in the Person, and the model of how villagers interact (who is exposed to whom, how to find neighbors, number of villagers, etc.) is in the FluSimulator. This is an example of using different levels of abstraction to overcome complexity. It is also a good example of some bottom-up design in that the Person was written before the game and it has all the right methods already defined.

Selecting a neighbor is done by taking the index of a villager and adding a random number to it. The random number is on the range [-3,3] (where 3 is the value of the NEIGHBOR_DISTANCE constant).

```
196   /**
197    * Select a neighbor of the villager at currNdx. Returned value will
198    * be within NEIGHBOR_DISTANCE of currNdx.
199    *
200    * @param    currentVillagerNdx   the index of the villager for whom we
201    *                                must select a neighbor
202    *
203    * @return   an "index" of a neighbor; index in quotes as it might be
204    *           outside the legal range for village
205    */
206   private int selectNeighbor(int currentVillagerNdx) {
207     int neighborNdx;
208     neighborNdx = currentVillagerNdx +
209       randomInt(-NEIGHBOR_DISTANCE, NEIGHBOR_DISTANCE);
210
211     return neighborNdx;
212   }
```

Listing 8.33: FluSimulator selectNeighbor

This listing includes the method header comment to show you that it mentions that this method can return "index" values that are out of range. It is important that you document your intent and any limitations of your methods. If you include this in the header comment, users of this method know that they are responsible for range checking. You can easily picture what the isValidNdx does (called from line 166 inside handleContagiousVillager). If a non-valid villager is picked, it is assumed no villager was exposed that time around.

Finishing the Simulation

The simulation is over when health states cannot change any more. When is that? If all of the villagers were healthy, none could spontaneously get sick. Similarly, if all the villagers were dead, none would suddenly get better. The other three health states have out arcs that depend only on the number of days in the health state. If any villager is neither dead nor healthy, the simulation must continue.

```
108   private boolean anySick() {
109     boolean sawSick = false;
110
111     for (int currentVillagerNdx = 0;
112          currentVillagerNdx != village.size(); ++currentVillagerNdx) {
113       Person villager = village.get(currentVillagerNdx);
114       sawSick = sawSick || villager.isSick() ||
115         villager.isContagious() || villager.isRecovering();
116     }
117
118     return sawSick;
119   }
220   private boolean simulationContinues() {
221     return anySick();
222   }
```

Listing 8.34: FluSimulator simulationContinues

simulationContinues is just a new name for the anySick method. Why? Because the name simulationContinues explains what the method is being asked about, the Boolean value it returns. anySick, in turn, explains what it does, returning **true** if there are any sick villagers and **false** if there are not. There might well be other uses for the anySick method, other than checking if the simulationContinues. The separation of the two methods makes reuse of anySick simpler.

How can we determine if any villager is sick? We need to check each villager, and if he is sick or contagious or recovering, set a flag to **true**. If we start with the flag set to **false** and test every villager, the final value of the flag is **true** if and only if there is at least one non-dead, non-healthy villager.

This could be done with an **if** statement inside a loop (we have to check every villager). Instead, here, lines 111–112 use a Boolean expression to reset the value of the flag, sawSick, each time through the loop. The new value of sawSick is **true** if any one of the four Boolean subexpressions is **true**. Once sawSick is **true**, it remains **true** until the end of the method. sawSick *becomes* **true** on the first villager who is neither dead nor healthy. This loop checks whether *any* element in the ArrayList meets some criteria.

When the simulation ends, there is a report on how many villagers died. A new StringSprite is created with the information in it and it is added to the game. The interesting part is how we figure out how many villagers are dead. Given anySick above, consider how you would approach writing countOfTheDead.

```
127   private int countOfTheDead() {
128     int numberOfDead = 0;
129
130     for (int currentVillagerNdx = 0;
131         currentVillagerNdx != village.size(); ++currentVillagerNdx) {
132       Person villager = village.get(currentVillagerNdx);
133
134       if (villager.isDead()) {
135         ++numberOfDead;
136       }
137     }
138
139     return numberOfDead;
140   }
```

Listing 8.35: FluSimulator countOfTheDead

We go through every villager and if he is dead, add one to a counter. Initialize the counter to 0 before we start and after we have checked every villager we have the total number of the dead. Lines 134–136 check if the current villager is dead and increment the counter. The loop control and local variable villager are done just as they are in the other loops in this section.

The only method we have not mentioned yet is infectPatientsZero. This is called from setup and provides the initial infection. The code is almost identical to handleContagiousVillager except that the villagers are picked at random across the whole village and, rather than being exposed, each is directly made sick. That way there is always at least one infected person at the beginning of the simulation. The number of initial patients is determined by the value of the NUMBER_OF_PATIENTS_ZERO constant at the top of the simulation.

Review 8.6

(a) How can you use a **for** loop to find if *any* element in the village is dead?

(b) Which class, FluSimulator or Person, has the disease state diagram in it?

(c) Which class determines how big a neighborhood is? What code would you change to pick a neighbor from anywhere in the village?

(d) What is an `interface`?

(e) What is an `Alarm`? What method does `FluSimulator` have in order to `implement Alarm`?

(f) When is `FluSimulator.act` called?

8.7   Summary

Discrete Time Simulation

`FluSimulator` is a *discrete time simulation*: time in the simulation jumps from one point of interest to the next. For this simulation the time interval is fixed at one simulated day.

The village is modeled as a *collection* of `Person` objects. The `Person` object models the disease, which is represented by a *state diagram*. In a state diagram, states are represented by circles, transitions are depicted by arrows, and the labels on arrows indicate when the transition is permitted.

Dynamic and Static Attributes

Static attributes of a program, a class, or a variable are attributes that could be known at *compile-time*. Because they are known early, static attributes cannot change during the execution of a program. Static attributes include the declared type of a variable, the signature of a method, and the names of fields, methods, and classes.

Dynamic attributes of a program, a class, or a variable are attributes that cannot be known until *run-time*. Any value that can change from run to run or during a single run of a program must be dynamic. Dynamic attributes include the constructed type referred to by an object variable, a nonconstant variable's value, and user input.

Java uses the dynamic type of a variable (the constructed type of the referred to object) to determine which overridden method to call. It calls the lowest override of the method in the hierarchy starting at the dynamic type. Inside a method, `super.<methodName>` can be used to start the search at the current class's parent rather than at the bottom dynamic type (lets an overriding method call the method it overrides).

Iteration

Iteration, doing something over and over, is one way of building complex rules out of simpler rules. This chapter presents the Java `for` loop.

A `for` loop has four parts: an initialization, a continuation expression, an advance to next step statement, and a body. The loop does the initialization and immediately tests the continuation expression. If the expression is `true`, the body and then the next step statement are executed. The expression is reevaluated after each execution of the next step. When it evaluates to `false`, execution continues *after* the end of the loop.

A *count-controlled loop* is a loop that is performed a known number of times. All `for` loops in this chapter were count-controlled.

`ArrayList`

Java supports *collections*, classes that can contain a number of objects of some element type.

Arrays (no examples given) are a built-in collection type. They can hold any type as elements. `java.util.ArrayList` is a standard collection type which can hold any *object* type.

- An `ArrayList` is a generic object; the type is named with an `ArrayList<ElementType>` where the `ElementType` is an object type.

- The constructor for an `ArrayList` requires the same generic type specification as a variable declaration.

- An `ArrayList` is an object. This means interaction uses the dot notation we use with other objects.

- `add` adds elements to the list, `get` gets individual elements in the list by index, and `size` returns the current number of elements in the `ArrayList`.

- The indexes of an `ArrayList` start at 0. Valid indexes of `ArrayList` A (with any element type) are on the range [0–A.size()). As noted previously, 0 is inclusive; A.size() is not.

- Whenever you think, "I need to *blah* every element in the list," you should immediately think, "I need to use a loop."

Interface

An **interface** is like a Java class except that it *cannot* have any implementation details. It is a *public protocol*. An **interface** is declared in a .java file like a class. Another class can implement the **interface** by providing an implementation for every method defined in the interface. Note: an interface-defined method cannot have a body block in the **interface**. It ends with a semicolon.

Java Templates

```
<forStatement> ::= for (<init>; <continuation>; <nextStep>)
                     <statement>

<statement> := <localVariableDefinition> |
               <expression>; |
               <forStatement> |
               <ifStatement> |
               <block>
```

```
<interfaceName> := <identifier>

<parentInterfaceName> := <identifier>

<interfaceDeclaration> :=
    <accessLevel> interface <interfaceName>
      [extends <parentInterfaceName> [, <parentInterfaceName>]*]

<interfaceBody> := {
                     [<methodDeclaration>;] *
                   }

<interfaceDefinition> := <interfaceDeclaration>
                            <interfaceBody>


<interfaceFile> := [<packageID>]
                   <imports>
                   <interfaceDefinition>
```

8.8   Chapter Review Exercises

Review Exercise 8.1   Starting with MoreNumbers, Listing 8.5, modify only the *body* of the loop so that it prints only the non-negative multiples of 7 less than 100.

Review Exercise 8.2   Starting with Iteration, Listing 8.4, modify only the *body* so that it prints the first ten non-negative multiples of 7 rather than the first ten non-negative integers.

Review Exercise 8.3   How many stars does each of the following code snippets print on the console?

(a)

```
for (int j = 0; j != 13; ++j) {
  System.out.println("*");
}
```

(b)

```
for (int j = 0; j != 13; ++j) {
  if ((j % 2) == 0) {
    System.out.println("*");
  }
}
```

(c)

```
for (int j = 0; j != 13; ++j) {
  System.out.println("***");
}
```

(d)

```
for (int j = 0; j != 13; ++j) {
  System.out.print("*");
  System.out.print("*");
  System.out.println("*");
}
```

(e)

```
for (int j = 0; j != 13; ++j) {
  if ((j % 3) == 0) {
    System.out.println("**");
  } else {
    System.out.println("*");
  }
}
```

Review Exercise 8.4   Write a loop that prints your name on the console 100 times. Each copy should start on a new line.

Review Exercise 8.5   How can you have multiple expressions, printed on different source lines, appear on one line on the console?

Review Exercise 8.6   How would you declare an ArrayList of GameTile?

Review Exercise 8.7   What is the output of the following snippet of code?

```
for (int q = 20; q != 100; q = q + 10) {
  System.out.println("and q = " + q);
}
```

Review Exercise 8.8 How would you remove all entries from theTable?

```
private ArrayList<Integer> theTable;
// ... theTable = new ...
// ... theTable.add (a number of times)


// your code goes here
```

Review Exercise 8.9 How would you print out the number of elements in an ArrayList?

Review Exercise 8.10 Can you declare an ArrayList of **double** to hold the y-coordinates of a collection of Sprite? How would you do it (if you can).

Review Exercise 8.11 Write a **for** loop that fills a ArrayList<Sprite> with 19 randomly colored OvalSprite.

8.9 Programming Problems

Programming Problem 8.1 Take FluSimulator as a starting point. Modify the program so that it displays the model parameters on the screen while the simulation is running. Model parameters determine the model of illness that is being simulated: EXPOSED_PER_DAY, NEIGHBOR_DISTANCE, and NUMBER_OF_PATIENTS_ZERO; INFECTION_CHANCE, MORTALITY_RATE, DAYS_SICK, and DAYS_RECOVERING. Some parameters are in different classes.

Programming Problem 8.2 Starting with FluSimulator, modify the program so that the final statistics include the number of villagers who have *never* been sick.

Think about what object(s) could possibly track this information. FluSimulator and Person are the two candidates.

How would FluSimulator keep track of whether or not villager number 13 had been sick? This is not easy. How would villager 13 keep track of whether or not she had become sick?

Having chosen where the state resides, modify the program:

(a) Add the state to Person. What *type* is the new state? What value should it be initialized to in the constructor? When does the state change? Does it make sense to have a *getter* to expose the state to users of the class? Does it make sense to have a *setter* that permits users of the class to change the state?

(b) Modify the statistics gathering code so that it goes through the ArrayList and *counts* the number of entries which have never been sick. Counting matching entries is a count-controlled loop with a count variable declared outside the loop.

What value is the count variable initialized to before the loop? When (in the loop) is the count variable incremented?

Programming Problem 8.3 Modify FluSimulator to have a *symmetric* social model. On any given day, *every* HEALTHY villager must also (in addition to CONTAGIOUS villagers) determine which of the neighbors she interacts with. If the villager is HEALTHY and she interacts with a neighbor who is CONTAGIOUS, she is exposed.

Run both programs, unmodified FluSimulator and the symmetric version. What is the difference in infection rates? How does the difference change in relation to the INFECTION_CHANCE?

Programming Problem 8.4 Start with TicTacToe from Chapter 7. Replace the nine variables, t00 through t22, with a single ArrayList of GameTile.

(a) Modify the constructor to use two *nested* count-controlled loops to construct the nine tiles. The outer loop should loop across row numbers and the inner across column numbers. Inside the inner loop, call `makeGameTile` with a location calculated by the two loop indexes.
(Hint: a private `locationFromIndex(int ndx)` method makes the code clear. You can read the values to return on lines 69–77 in `TicTacToe.java`.

(b) Write a helper routine with the header

```
private int index(int row, int col)
```

The method returns the index (in the `ArrayList`) of the element at the given (`row`, `col`) position. The method can be used to generate the index of any tile given its row and column.

(c) Modify `row<n>()` and `col<n>()` methods to use count-controlled loops. `diag<n>()` is more difficult but `index` from the previous question makes it possible.

(d) Combine the three `row<n>()` methods into a single `row` method that checks all three rows in one **for** loop.

(e) Combine the three `col<n>()` methods into a single `col` method that checks all three rows in one **for** loop.

(f) *Optional* If you rewrote the `diag<n>()` methods, combine the two `diag<n>()` methods into a single `diag` method that checks both diagonals in one **for** loop.

(g) Compare the number of lines the new program has with those the original `TicTacToe` had. How does the clarity of the code compare?

Programming Problem 8.5 Modify `BoxParade` so that it is a parade of circles.

Programming Problem 8.6 Modify `BoxParade` so that it is a parade of `Person`. There is no need to advance the time for the people in the parade.

Programming Problem 8.7 Modify `FluSimulator` so that once a person has been sick, she is more difficult to infect. This requires a new state, `HEALTHY_WITH_ANTIBODIES`. When a `Person` recovers, she goes to the new state rather than back to `HEALTHY`. The new state is the same as `HEALTHY` except the infection rate is halved.

(a) Draw the new state diagram.

(b) Add the new state, constants, and methods to `Person`.

(c) Is there any need to modify `FluSimulator` itself?

Programming Problem 8.8 Modify `FluSimulator` so that the player starts with one dose of vaccine. This requires a new state for `Person`: `IMMUNE`.

(a) When the player clicks on a `Person`, if there are available doses of vaccine and the person is not immune, make her immune and reduce the number of vaccines by one. What class handles vaccines? How can you determine if the player clicked on a `Person`?

(b) Give the player a new dose of vaccine every three days. The number of days and the number of initial doses are both good playtesting variables. Having too many doses makes the game too easy.

Programming Problem 8.9 Modify `FluSimulator` so that while the village is still represented as a single main street (one `ArrayList`), the persons on the screen are laid out on five rows. (or one row if there are less than 25 of them). The first row should have the first fifth of the people, the second the second fifth and so on.

This is a good extension to combine with Programming Problem 8.8.

9

Multidimensional Data Structures

In the last chapter we looked at the use of the `ArrayList` type as a collection of objects. The `ArrayList` is limited in that it must hold object types; this is not a big problem because Java provides object "versions" of the built-in plain old data types — `Integer`, `Double`, and `Boolean` — to match the built-ins we have worked with. It also supports automatically using the value of the object versions as the plain old data types when necessary.

Java automatically *unboxes* a `Boolean` appearing in an **if** statement, converting it to a **boolean** when that is needed. Alternatively, when we called `add` on an `ArrayList<Integer>` with a literal **int** value, Java automatically *boxed* the value, putting the **int** value into an `Integer` passed in to `add`.

The big win with `ArrayList` over built-in arrays is that `ArrayList`s are *dynamically* sized; they can grow as necessary to hold whatever number of elements are needed.

This chapter continues working with `ArrayList`s: this time it is `ArrayList` with `ArrayList` elements. Two-dimensional data structures where a content element is found by getting the *row* in which it resides and then getting the entry at a given *column*.

9.1 Rescue Mission

Consider a job as a lifeguard. A large number of nonswimmers have fallen into the river and are being swept to their doom. Your job is to throw a rescue ring to each, saving the swimmers before they fall off a waterfall. *RescueMission* is just such a game. As shown in Figure 9.1, the swimmers are laid out in a grid. They move back and forth across the screen. Each time a swimmer touches the edge of the screen, the group moves closer to the bottom of the screen. At the bottom of the screen, the rescuer stands, launching a rescue ring into the group in an attempt to save the swimmers. The game is over when a swimmer reaches the bottom of the screen. The game advances to the next level when the last swimmer in the block is rescued: each level is a faster version of the level before.

Above the grid of swimmers is a lane for an occasional "fast swimmer," something like a swimmer but moving across the screen more quickly than the swimmers and only going across the screen once. Fast swimmers appear at random times, are worth about twice the greatest value of any of the other swimmers, and serve to tempt the player to go for the brass ring.

When the ring is launched, it flies straight up the screen where it was launched. The ring continues until it rescues a swimmer (fast or otherwise) or goes off the top of the screen. Only one ring can be launched at a

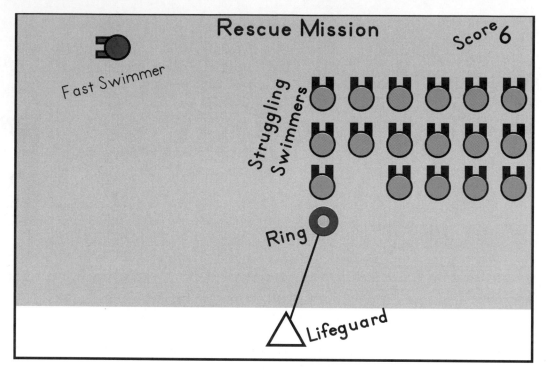

Figure 9.1: RescueMission game design diagram

time. This gives the player a resource management problem to solve: the farther away the target is from the rescuer, the longer the player must wait to throw the ring again.

This game is interesting for several reasons: given four rows of six swimmers each, there are almost thirty sprites on the screen at the same time, many more than we have previously handled; all of the sprites (except for the score) move; the swimmers (and the fast swimmer at the top of the screen) are *animated* in that they change appearance while moving across the screen.

Having so many different sprites moving according to so many different rules (swimmers move left to right until someone hits the wall; the rescue ring moves up from where it was launched; the rescuer moves left to right, controlled by the user's keyboard; the fast swimmer moves from side to side occasionally; the rope is a decoration connecting the rescuer to the rescue ring), it is essential that we divide to conquer. Each sprite class has its own advance method, encoding its own movement rules.

Consider how to call advance for each of thirty sprites. If you look back at Chapter 7 and TicTacToe, you see that there was a lot of repeating of code to handle just nine sprites on the screen. One argument in favor of using ArrayList collections is that they are composed of multiple elements and we can process each element in them within a loop. Using iteration keeps us from having to repeat ourselves.

Iteration permits the use of thirty swimmers. Rather than having to devise an algorithm to convert from a one-dimensional collection (a single ArrayList) to a two-dimensional layout (the Swimmer sprites on the screen), we introduce a two-dimensional data structure, an ArrayList of ArrayLists of sprites.

Before we get there, though, we look at the public protocols of the sprites in the game and see what we can learn about having lots and lots of moving sprites, each based on the CompositeSprite.

Review 9.1

(a) Assume you have the following `ArrayList` declaration:

```
    ArrayList<Sprite> swimmer;
```

What is the type of an individual element of `swimmer`?

    (a) How would you access the first element of `swimmer`?

(b) Assume you have the following ArrayList declaration:

```
    ArrayList<ArrayList<Sprite>> swimmer;
```

What is the type of an individual element of `swimmer`?

    (a) How would you access the first element of `swimmer`?

    (b) How would you access the first `Sprite` of `swimmer`?

9.2   Inheritance

Looking at the design in Figure 9.1, we see that there appear to be four different classes of sprite: `Rescuer`, `RescueRing`, `Swimmer`, and `FastSwimmer`. Game implementation begins by examining the public protocol of each of these sprites.

Rescuer

Let's start simple: what does the `Rescuer` need in its protocol? Note that we want to be able to have the rescuer move at some speed (a speed we can easily change so that we can tweak our game) according to keyboard input. Does that sound familiar? It should, since Chapter 6's `PongPaddle` class did almost exactly that. The movement velocity was held in the paddle class, which included getter and setter methods for the velocity as well as a routine to bounce the paddle off the edges of the screen. Using `PongPaddle` as a pattern, `Rescuer`'s public protocol looks like this:

```
class Rescuer
  extends CompositeSprite {
  public Rescuer(double deltaX, double deltaY)...
  public void setVelocity(double deltaX, double deltaY)...
  public void setDeltaX(double deltaX)...
  public void setDeltaY(double deltaY)...
  public void advance(double dT)...
  public void bounceOffEdges()...
  public double getDeltaX()...
  public double getDeltaY()...
}
```

Note that there are two ways to set the velocity, either in one dimension at a time or both at the same time. In this program the y-coordinate of the velocity is always zero but, as discussed with `PongPaddle`, the more general problem is sometimes easier to solve (and before this section is over, this should be abundantly clear).

The rescuer "bounces" off the edge of the screen in the same way that the `PongPaddle` bounced off the edge: the user cannot move the sprite past the edge of the screen.

Swimmer

Each individual Swimmer moves at a given speed, first one way and then the other way, across the screen. Again, reaching back to SoloPong, this is a lot like the ball, moving in a straight line until it bounces off the edge of the screen. The public protocol of Swimmer looks like this:

```
class Swimmer
  extends CompositeSprite {
  public static void bumpTheWall()...
  public static void clearBumpTheWall()...
  public static void hasBumpedTheWall()...

  public Swimmer(int score, double deltaX, double deltaY)...
  public void setVelocity(double deltaX, double deltaY)...
  public void setDeltaX(double deltaX)...
  public void setDeltaY(double deltaY)...
  public void advance(double dT)...
  public void bounceOffEdges()...
  public double getDeltaX()...
  public double getDeltaY()...

  public void setScore(int score)...
  public int getScore()...
}
```

The *individual* swimmer protocol is similar to that found in Rescuer; by individual we mean non-**static**. The **static** methods are there so that *all* of the Swimmer objects reverse direction when *any* swimmer touches the edge of the screen.

The score value of a Swimmer is how many points the swimmer is worth when rescued. It is variable so that each row of swimmers can have a higher value than the one below it. The exact score is determined in the game when the swimmers are constructed.

RescueRing

The RescueRing is either waiting to be thrown or has been thrown. If it is waiting to be thrown, it should simply move along with the Rescuer; if it has been thrown, then it moves according to its current velocity until it rescues a given Swimmer or it hits the edge of the screen. The public protocol is

```
class RescueRing
  extends CompositeSprite {
  public RescueRing(double deltaX, double deltaY)...
  public void setVelocity(double deltaX, double deltaY)...
  public void setDeltaX(double deltaX)...
  public void setDeltaY(double deltaY)...
  public void advance(double dT)...
  public void bounceOffEdges()...
  public double getDeltaX()...
  public double getDeltaY()...
}
```

FastSwimmer

The FastSwimmer is a Swimmer extended with two states: waiting and swimming. While waiting the FastSwimmer randomly determines when it should launch into swimming. While swimming it just moves according to its current velocity. The public *protocol* of FastSwimmer is the same as that of Swimmer. In fact, any FastSwimmer *is a* Swimmer, so the one class **extends** the other:

```
class FastSwimmer
  extends Swimmer {
}
```

FastSwimmer overrides all of the non-**static** member functions of Swimmer because they perform slightly differently (in particular, FastSwimmer has no impact on bouncing the rest of the swimmers off walls and fast swimmers don't really bounce off the edge: fast swimmers go to the waiting state when they hit an edge).

The following screenshot shows the grid of swimmers as well as the fast swimmer zipping across the top of the screen.

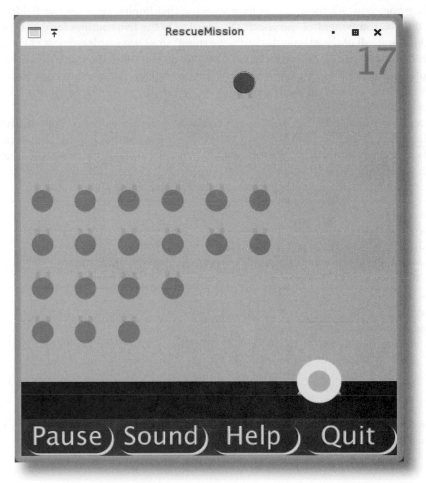

Figure 9.2: A Screenshot of RescueMission with a FastSwimmer

Is-a

The emphasis in the sentence above, that FastSwimmer *is a* Swimmer, indicates a special relationship between the two classes: every FastSwimmer is first a Swimmer and then something more. This relationship is so common in object-oriented programming that computer scientists have turned it into a single word: *is-a*. When one class extends another, any child class object *is-a* parent class object.

What this means is that anywhere where a parent class object is expected, you can replace it with a child class object. Consider a landscaping plan. If there is to be a tree at the northeast corner of the yard, it is possible to plant an apple tree there. This is because an apple tree *is-a* tree. There are things you can do with an apple tree that you cannot do with any arbitrary tree: sit under it and discover gravity, pick an apple; there is nothing you can do with an arbitrary tree that you cannot do with an *apple* tree: plant it, prune it, water it, etc.

Extracting Common Functionality

Looking back over the three public protocols for Rescuer, RescueRing, and Swimmer, we see that the three of them have much in common. All three classes have velocity; that implies each has two fields for holding the x-component and the y-component of the velocity in addition to the five routines for getting and setting the velocity. More than that, all of the classes do the "same thing" in advance, at least most of the time: translate the current position of the sprite by the velocity (in screens/second) times the frame delay time (in seconds). The DRY principle dictates that we should avoid repeating ourselves. We want to have some way to factor the two fields and their associated methods along with advance and bounceOffEdges out of all three classes and define them once rather than three different times.

How do classes share implementation? How can two classes use the same method? We have been using this capability since the beginning of the book: any class that extends another inherits the parent class's public protocol. So, to have a single copy of the fields and common definition of most of the methods, all three classes must extend a class with those methods in the public protocol. If we call the missing link in this hierarchy SpriteWithVelocity, we split the three classes into four with the following pubic protocols:

```
class SpriteWithVelocity
  extends CompositeSprite {
  public SpriteWithVelocity(double deltaX, double deltaY)...
  public void setVelocity(double deltaX, double deltaY)...
  public void setDeltaX(double deltaX)...
  public void setDeltaY(double deltaY)...
  public void advance(double dT)...
  public void bounceOffEdges()...
  public double getDeltaX()...
  public double getDeltaY()...
}

class Rescuer
  extends SpriteWithVelocity {
  public Rescuer(double deltaX, double deltaY)...
}

class RescueRing
  extends SpriteWithVelocity {
  public RescueRing(double deltaX, double deltaY)...
}
```

```
class Swimmer
  extends SpriteWithVelocity {
  public static void bumpTheWall()...
  public static void clearBumpTheWall()...
  public static void hasBumpedTheWall()...

  public Swimmer(int score, double deltaX, double deltaY)...
  public void setScore(int score)...
  public int getScore()...
}
```

The number of classes is one higher than it was before, but each of the subclasses of SpriteWithVelocity is simpler. All of the classes override advance and bounceOffEdges, but each class is simpler because of the *abstraction* of the velocity out of several classes. With comments, SpriteWithVelocity.java is just under 200 lines of code; this code would have to appear in each of the three classes that now inherit it.

This is primarily an example of sharing implementation and features through inheritance. While each Swimmer is-a SpriteWithVelocity (and the same for Rescuer and RescueRing), we are not using that fact. FANG *does* use an is-a relationship in the heart of the video game loop.

Displaying Sprites

As a reminder, the main video game loop in FANG is

```
setup
while (not game over)
  displayGameState
  getUserInput
  advance
```

The part we are interested in is displayGameState. How does FANG display all of the different sprites on the screen? Inside FANG is a class called AnimationCanvas, which has a field called sprites of type ArrayList<Sprite>.[1] Each time through the video game loop, AnimationCanvas's paintSprites method is called. It is called with an object of type Graphics2D; a Graphics2D represents the current window on the video screen where the program is running. The paintSprites method looks something like this:

```
class AnimationCanvas ... {
  ...
  ArrayList<Sprite> sprites;
  ...
  private void paintSprites(Graphics2D brush) {
    for (int i = 0; i != sprites.size(); ++i) {
      sprites.get(i).paintInternal(brush);
    }
  }
  ...
}
```

---

[1]The *actual* type of sprites is more complicated than ArrayList; it is much more similar to an ArrayList<ArrayList<Sprite>> where each ArrayList<Sprite> is the collection of sprites entered with the same z-ordering or layering number. What we present as a single loop is actually a nested pair of loops, one selecting the layer and the inner one selecting each Sprite on the layer (and even this is a simplification).

What is special about this? It is an example of code using the is-a relationship. The elements of sprites are of type Sprite as far as this code knows. You know that what you called addSprite with was a RectangleSprite or a Swimmer or a StringSprite. The Sprite class provides a method called paintInternal; each specialized type of Sprite provides a version of paintInternal that knows how to put a rectangle or an oval or an image or even an entire composite collection of other sprites onto the screen. That way the specialized actions of each of the special types of Sprite take place even though all AnimationCanvas needs to know is that all Sprite objects know how to paintInternal.

In the landscaping example, imagine each tree knows how to makeBlooms. To have the whole garden bloom, it is enough to cycle through all of the trees and call makeBlooms for each tree. The apple trees make apple blossoms, cherry trees make cherry blossoms, and pine trees might not actually have flowers in the more traditional sense, so they might do nothing.

The is-a relationship is the power we leverage in using abstraction to tame complexity. By separating the details of how each paintInternal method works from the details of figuring out when paintInternal is called for each Sprite, we limit the details we must remember at any given moment.

The ability to call a superclass method based on the *static* type of the reference and have the lowest overridden method in the *dynamic* type hierarchy is called *polymorphism*. Polymorphism lets FANG keep a single collection of Sprite but still be able to support classes that change the behavior of Sprite methods.

Overriding superclass methods in the subclasses permits calls to those methods to behave polymorphically. A Sprite reference that refers to an EasyButton can call setColor because *every* Sprite has a setColor method. But instead of doing what Sprite.setColor does, EasyButton.setColor is called, and it sets the color of the background of the button (see Listing 5.5 on page 131).

The next section looks at how we can have collections that hold collections, and the section after that discusses animated sprites. After that we return to the RescueMission game and look at how to use SpriteWithVelocity to share several useful methods among multiple classes.

Review 9.2

(a)   This section discusses two versions of the public interface to the Rescuer class: one that extends CompositeSprite and another one that extends SpriteWithVelocity. What is the benefit of extending SpriteWithVelocity as opposed to directly extending CompositeSprite?

(b) What does *polymorphism* mean?

(c) What is gained by including the SpriteWithVelocity class within the hierarchy of classes?

(d) What **class**'s version of translateX is called at the marked line? Explain your answer.

```
public class SuperDuperSprite extends Sprite {
  ...
  @Override
  public void translateX(double dX) { ... }
  ...
}
...
public class MyGame extends Game {
  public void advance(double dT) {
    Sprite mySprite = new SuperDuperSprite();
    mySprite.translateX(100); // what version?
  }
}
```

(e) In Java, how is the *is-a* relationship expressed?

(f) What does it mean to say that a `RectangleSprite` is-a `Sprite`?

(g) Which of the following are true and which false:

    (a) `RectangleSprite` is-a `OvalSprite`.

    (b) `CompositeSprite` is-a `Sprite`.

    (c) `Swimmer` is-a `CompositeSprite`.

    (d) *If* `Fire` is-a `CompositeSprite` then `Fire` is-a `Sprite`.

9.3 Multidimensional Collections

Before we work on declaring `ArrayLists` of `ArrayLists` (that is where this is going), let's take a quick look at two *nested loops*. Iteration such as "Remove the smallest numbered card from this deck of numbered cards, placing it on the table in front of you," can, itself, be iterated as in "Remove one smallest card (as described previously) once for each card in the deck." The algorithm described is something like (this is *not* actual Java):

```
for(i = 0; i != #of cards; ++i) {
  for (j = 0; j != #of cards still in deck; ++j) {
    if this one is smallest see so far, grab it
  }
  Lay the card you grabbed on the table
}
```

What is the result of following the above instructions? The cards are placed on the table in *ascending order*. The deck of numbered cards is sorted when this algorithm finishes. We use sorting later. For the moment just note that the idea of iterating iteration is not as foreign to you as it might seem.

Nested Loops

Remember that the body of a **for** loop can be *any* Java code that is valid in a method body.[2] This means that it is legal to have a loop inside another loop.

Consider the following code. How many asterisks are printed?

```
for (int i = 0; i != 5; ++i) {
  for (int j = 0; j != 3; ++j) {
    System.out.println("*");
  }
}
```

Looking at the second **for** line and the *<init>*, *<continuation>*, and *<nextStep>* parts, we can see that j takes on all of the values from [0–3) or 0, 1, and 2. When the loop control variable begins at 0, the next step increments the loop control variable, and the comparison uses != (or <) some number, n, the body of the loop is run n times. This is the *idiomatic* way to write a count-controlled loop, a loop that runs a certain number of times. This is the way a Java programmer writes such a loop; it makes it easy to read and to reason about the loop.

How many times is the body of the outer loop executed? Reading the **for** line, we see that it, too, is an idiomatic count-controlled loop. That means it runs five times.

---

[2]Java does not support nested method or type declarations. You cannot define a method *inside* the body of another method nor can you define a **class** *inside* the body of a method. The same is true of code inside a **for** loop; the **for** loop must, itself, be inside some method.

The inner loop body draws a asterisk each time it is executed. Each time the inner loop is executed (in total), it draws three asterisks. Since the inner loop *is* the body of the outer loop, it is executed five times. Five times (once for each loop iteration) there are three asterisks drawn; this means there are fifteen asterisks drawn, one per line (each is drawn using println which starts a new line).

Two Loops, Two Dimensions

The above code prints out a single, vertical line of asterisks; how would you change it to print out all of its asterisks on a single line and only after printing all of them start a new line? That would mean changing the println to print (so it does not start a new line) and then adding System.out.println() after the end of the loops. All fifteen asterisks in a single line:

```
for (int i = 0; i != 5; ++i) {
  for (int j = 0; j != 3; ++j) {
    System.out.print("*");
  }
}
System.out.println();
```

What code would print out five lines of three asterisks each? In this case we want to use print in the inner loop (to keep the asterisks on a single line) and then, whenever the outer loop is about to end, start a new line with the System.out.println().

```
for (int i = 0; i != 5; ++i) {
  for (int j = 0; j != 3; ++j) {
    System.out.print("*");
  }
  System.out.println();
}
```

If you use the fact that we know, because the loop is written idiomatically, the number of times the outer loop executes is five, that means, because println is inside the loop (and not inside of any other loop), this code prints five lines. Since each line also has whatever is printed by the inner loop, each line has three asterisks.

Multiplication Table

How would you write a game that displayed a multiplication table on the screen? This is different than printing asterisks because we want to position things on the screen. It is similar, though, because we need to process something with two dimensions. We start by displaying a simple multiplication table. We then look at how to put references to displayed elements into a two-dimensional data structure and how to traverse a two-dimensional data structure.

```
8   public class MultiplicationTable
9     extends Game {
10    /** The number of columns of numbers in the table */
11    public static final int COLUMNS = 10;
12
13    /** The number of rows of numbers in the table */
14    public static final int ROWS = 6;
15
16    /** StringSprite + space between them */
```

```
17  public static final double SPACING = 1.0 /
18    (1 + Math.max(ROWS, COLUMNS));
19
20  /** Scale of StringSprites (for leaving space) */
21  public static final double ACTUAL_SCALE = SPACING - 0.02;
22
23  /** Color for entries labeling the table */
24  public static final Color LABEL_COLOR = getColor("misty rose");
25
26  /** Offset from edge to labels (on top or left) */
27  public static final double LABEL_OFFSET = SPACING / 2.0;
28
29  /** Color for entries in the table */
30  public static final Color TABLE_COLOR = getColor("yellow green");
31
32  /** Offset to first row or column (top/left) */
33  public static final double TABLE_OFFSET = LABEL_OFFSET + SPACING;
```

Listing 9.1: `MultiplicationTable.java` constants

`MultiplicationTable` begins with a collection of constant values. The number of rows and columns, the size of each `StringSprite` and the size in which each sprite is positioned (the scale of the sprite is smaller so there is space between entries), the offset of the first entries in the tables, and the first entries of the label rows and columns are calculated based on the spacing of the entries. Finally, the colors of the table entries and the labels are specified. Notice that all of the constants are **static**, meaning that there is only one copy, no matter how many `MultiplicationTable` objects are instantiated, and **final**, meaning that they can be assigned to only once. By assigning to the **static final** values at the same time they are declared makes it easier for others to come along later and change the constant values; if we make consistent use of ROWS, we need change only that constant to change the number of rows of in the table.

```
39  public void setup() {
40    labelRows();
41    labelColumns();
42    fillProductTable();
43  }
```

Listing 9.2: `MultiplicationTable.java` setup

The listing above is another example of the power of top-down design. `setup` calls just three routines, `labelRows` and `labelColumns` to place the row and column labels on the screen and `fillProductTable`, which places all of the products.

```
76  private void labelRows() {
77    double yOffset = TABLE_OFFSET;
78    double xOffset = LABEL_OFFSET;
79    for (int row = 0; row != ROWS; ++row) {
80      makeOneEntry(xOffset, yOffset, row, LABEL_COLOR);
81      yOffset += SPACING;
82    }
83  }
```

Listing 9.3: `MultiplicationTable.java` labelRows

labelRows serves to explain both label methods. There is a count-controlled **for** loop that runs ROWS times for numbers in the range [0–ROWS). It creates a StringSprite each time through the loop and it changes the yOffset by the spacing value each time through the loop. Each StringSprite is placed directly below the one before it on the screen (the xOffset does not change). The text inside each StringSprite is the value of the loop control variable.

How do we know the value of the text? Look at the body of makeOneEntry:

```
98    private StringSprite makeOneEntry(double x, double y, int value,
99        Color color) {
100       StringSprite tableEntry = new StringSprite();
101       tableEntry.setScale(ACTUAL_SCALE);
102       tableEntry.setLocation(x, y);
103       tableEntry.setColor(color);
104       tableEntry.rightJustify();
105       tableEntry.setText(Integer.toString(value));
106       addSprite(tableEntry);
107       return tableEntry;
108    }
```

Listing 9.4: MultiplicationTable.java makeOneEntry

Setting the color, scale, and location are typical for creating any sprite. The rightJustify method sets the position of a StringSprite to the right edge of the string. This means the unit digits align vertically. What is the text set to in line 105? The value parameter is of type **int**; this is *not* an object type. There is no way to call value.toString (you cannot apply the dot operator to non-object types). The object type, Integer, provides a **static** method, toString, which takes a single **int** as its parameter and it converts the value to a string.

Declaring a Two-Dimensional ArrayList

Now that we have some feeling for how to use nested loops to work with two dimensions of data, we now look at how to declare a two-dimensional data *structure*, an ArrayList of ArrayLists. This section focuses on creating a two-dimensional list of Swimmers; for the moment we only use the objects' Sprite protocol functions, though we declare the array list to hold Swimmer objects.

```
21    public static final int ROWS = 4;
22    public static final int COLUMNS = 6;
64    /** 2-dimensional container of Swimmer's */
65    private ArrayList<ArrayList<Swimmer>> swimmers;
```

Listing 9.5: RescueMission: Declaring swimmers

Listing 9.5 shows the declaration of swimmers inside the RescueMission class (RescueMission extends Game). The two **static final int**s are the number of rows and columns of swimmers. Having named constants and using them consistently means that changing these numbers in lines 21 or 22 changes the number of swimmers throughout the program.

Just as before, the declaration of an ArrayList type consists of the word ArrayList followed by the element type in angle brackets. Unlike in the last chapter, here the elements of swimmers are not sprites but rather are *lists of sprites*. After it is properly initialized, swimmers.get(0) returns the first ArrayList<Swimmer> in the field.

An ArrayList can have any object type as its element type, and ArrayList<...> is an object type, so it is legal to have elements which are, themselves, ArrayLists. Inside the angle brackets must be a complete object-type name; ArrayList is a *generic type*, so to be a complete type we must provide the element type of the collection. We want the inner collections to contain Swimmer objects. This is just what the declaration on line 65 does.[3]

Having declared a field which holds lists of lists, how do we initialize it? Obviously at some point we need to call **new** and set the value of the field to the result. What constructor is called? The question then is what do we pass to add to add new elements to the list of lists.

```
347  private void setupSwimmers() {
348    final double swimmerOffset = objectScale / 2.0;
349    final double lowestRowY = swimmerOffset + (ROWS * objectScale);
350    swimmers = new ArrayList<ArrayList<Swimmer>>();
351    for (int row = 0; row != ROWS; ++row) {
352      ArrayList<Swimmer> currentRow = new ArrayList<Swimmer>();
353      double rowY = lowestRowY - (row * objectScale);
354      int rowScore = row + 1;// higher row = higher score
355      for (int column = 0; column != COLUMNS; ++column) {
356        Swimmer current = new Swimmer(rowScore, swimmerDX, swimmerDY);
357        current.setScale(objectScale);
358        current.setLocation(swimmerOffset + (column * objectScale),
359          rowY);
360        addSprite(current);
361        currentRow.add(current);
362      }
363      swimmers.add(currentRow);
364    }
365  }
```

Listing 9.6: RescueMission: setupSwimmers

The setupSwimmers method from RescueMission sets up the list of lists and the elements in it. Line 350 calls **new** to construct swimmers; the constructor is of type ArrayList<ArrayList<Swimmer>>. Ignoring lines 353–362 for a minute, we can see that line 352 constructs a new ArrayList<Swimmer> and line 363 adds that new list to swimmers.

How many times are lines 352 and 363 executed? The loop control variable, row, is initialized to 0 and is incremented each time through the loop, and the loop is exited when row is ROWS. That means the loop runs across the integer range [0–ROWS). The number of rows added is ROWS (set to 4 as we saw above in line 21).

What happens when we stop ignoring lines 353–362? Line 353 calculates the y-component of all sprites on the current row. The first row is the lowest row on the screen, the second the next one up, and so on. Line 349 calculated the y-component of the lowest row (the *highest* y value because of the inverted y-axis). Each row we subtract row number times height of a row from that value. Similarly, the score for rescuing swimmers in the lowest row is 1, the second row up is 2, and so on for each row. The score for all swimmers in a row is calculated in line 354.

The loop in lines 355–362 is executed with column across the integer range [0–COLUMNS), or COLUMN times (set to 6 in line 22 above). Inside the loop we create one Swimmer sprite. That sprite is scaled, located, added to the game (so it is in the list used in AnimationCanvas), and added to the current row's ArrayList. Six Swimmers are added to each row and four rows are added to swimmers: there are 24 Swimmer sprites added to the game.

We could have added any number of sprites to the game with addSprite. This code is powerful because we retain the ability to access each individual Swimmer sprite because we have the collection of collections of Swimmers.

---

[3]In this book we do not include spaces within the angle brackets. The type of swimmers is ArrayList<ArrayList<Swimmer>>. It should be noted that spaces are permitted within and around the angle brackets and some sources recommend using ArrayList< ArrayList< Swimmer > > as the spacing for this type name. The alternate spacing is required in some programming languages, and students should be aware that it is legal in Java.

Traversing a Two-Dimensional `ArrayList`

How can we use `get` to get each `Swimmer`? In the last chapter we saw that to do *anything* with every element in an `ArrayList` means to use a count-controlled loop, iterating across all of the elements and using the `get` method to retrieve each entry.

That suggests the following model of code for calling `advance` on each and every `Swimmer` in `swimmers`:

```
for (int row = 0; row != ROWS; ++row) {
  ArrayList<Swimmer> currentRow = swimmers.get(row);
  for (int column = 0; column != COLUMNS; ++column) {
    Swimmer curr = currentRow.get(column);
    // do something with curr here
  }
}
```

This is *exactly* what is done in the `moveEverything` method of `RescueMission` except that, instead of having a variable holding a reference to the current row, we just use `swimmers.get(row)` whenever we need the current row.

```
227   private void moveEverything(double dT) {
228     fastSwimmer.advance(dT);
229     rescuer.advance(dT);
230     ring.advance(dT);
231     for (int row = 0; row != ROWS; ++row) {
232       for (int column = 0; column != COLUMNS; ++column) {
233         Swimmer curr = swimmers.get(row).get(column);
234         if (curr != null) {
235           curr.advance(dT);
236         }
237       }
238     }
239   }
```

Listing 9.7: `RescueMission`: `moveEverything`

In `moveEverything`, the fast swimmer, rescuer, and rescue ring are moved first (lines 228–230); we return to these objects a little later, but just consider that advance moves each one according to its movement rules outlined above. The two nested loops look just like the ones shown in the previous snippet except for line 219, which uses two chained calls to `get`. The key thing to note is that `get` returns an element of the `ArrayList` no matter what type the elements have. Line 233 is parsed as follows:

```
Swimmer curr = swimmers.get(row).get(column);
             = (swimmers.get(row)).get(column);
```

The result of `swimmers.get(row)` is an `ArrayList<Swimmer>` (just like in the earlier snippet), and applying `get` to that array list yields a `Swimmer` just like the previous snippet.

What about the `if` statement inside the loop? In the previous section we saw that we added the results of calling **new** `Swimmer` 24 times; how can any element be `null`?

At the beginning of the level no entry *can* be `null`. The question is, what happens when a swimmer is rescued? The game is played by launching the rescue ring, and if the rescue ring intersects a swimmer, that swimmer is rescued and the score for that swimmer is added to the player's score. How is the rescue of the `Swimmer` in the 2D `ArrayList` indicated?

There are two possible answers: We could use the hide method defined in Sprite to turn the swimmer invisible or we could actually remove the swimmer from the array list by putting a null reference in its place. The if statement should make it clear which design decision was made in this program. We briefly examine the path not taken and then look at the implications of null references in our grid.

Using hide. When a Sprite is hidden, it remains on the screen and it returns true if there is an intersection test with any other sprite, where the visual representation of the hidden sprite *would have* intersected with the other, had it been visible. Hidden (invisible) sprites still intersect with other sprites. They also have locations and bounds, so it is possible for them to intersect with the edges of the screen.

A hidden sprite is still "there" and an additional check is required with each intersection test to have our game pretend that they are not. The advantage to using null is that the Java Virtual Machine yells if we dereference (use the dot operator on) a null reference, whereas it does not yell if we forget to check whether a given sprite is hidden. While errors, especially run-time errors, are annoying, in this case they make finding missing reference checks easier to find. In the other case we might just see odd bouncing behavior but be hard pressed to narrow down where to look for it.

There is a set method for ArrayList objects that takes an index (just like get) and a new value to put in the ArrayList at that location. Rescuing the Swimmer at the position (row, column) in the grid is done by rescueSwimmer:

```
297  private void rescueSwimmer(int row, int column) {
298      Swimmer curr = swimmers.get(row).get(column);
299      setScore(getScore() + curr.getScore());
300      removeSprite(curr);
301      swimmers.get(row).set(column, null);
302      ring.startReady();
303  }
```

Listing 9.8: RescueMission: rescueSwimmer

The FANG removeSprite method is analogous to addSprite but it removes the reference sprite from the list used inside of AnimationCanvas. We then update the location where the sprite was to contain null. Notice that we do not remove rows, just individual Swimmers.

Looking at the description of the game, we see that a level ends when the player rescues all of the swimmers in the grid and the game ends when a swimmer reaches the bottom of the water. Detecting each of these conditions requires *traversing*[4] across the swimmers collection. Each does something a little bit different with each element.

Counting the Remaining Swimmers

A level is finished when the last swimmer, from swimmers, is rescued. This means the FastSwimmer does not count for ending the level. How can we determine how many swimmers remain? We can count how many non-null references remain in swimmers. Again, doing *anything* with every element in an ArrayList means we should be thinking about a count-controlled loop. For a two-dimensional collection, we should be thinking about two *nested*, count-controlled loops.

```
248  private int remainingSwimmerCount() {
249      int numberOfSwimmers = 0;
250      for (int row = 0; row != ROWS; ++row) {
251          for (int column = 0; column != COLUMNS; ++column) {
```

___
[4]"to travel or pass across, over, or through" [AHD00]

```
252        Swimmer curr = swimmers.get(row).get(column);
253        if (curr != null) {
254            ++numberOfSwimmers;
255        }
256      }
257    }
258    return numberOfSwimmers;
259  }
```

Listing 9.9: RescueMission: remainingSwimmerCount

The remainingSwimmerCount method starts by initializing the count to 0. In a pair of nested loops, the outer looping over rows and the inner looping over the columns, curr is set to refer to each Swimmer in the structure, one after the other. The if statement (which should look very familiar) tests if curr is not null. As long as the reference isn't null, the swimmer counts. The body of the if statement increments the return value. When the loops finish, the count is returned.

Examining this method now is an example of bottom-up design: we know we need this ability to test for the end of a level. Now we have a command that gives us the swimmer count. We look at how to launch a new level later in this chapter.

Finding the Lowest Swimmer

The *game* ends when the lowest row of swimmers on the screen reaches the bottom of the water — when the lowest y-coordinate of one of the lowest Swimmer sprites is greater than or equal to the bottom of the water. If we could get a reference to one of the lowest sprites in the swimmers collection, the Boolean expression testing for the game being over is straight forward:

```
((getLowestSwimmer() != null) &&
 (getLowestSwimmer().getMaxY() >= water.getMaxY()))
```

Now, how does getLowestSwimmer work? It should return a reference to any Swimmer in the lowest row on the screen. Looking back at setupSwimmers, we find that row 0 is the lowest row. Unfortunately, it is possible that the player rescued *all* of the swimmers in the bottom row (they are all set to null, as discussed above; we have not seen the rescue code yet, but we know it should null out the rescued swimmers).

What we need to do is go through the list of lists and check for the first non-null value. Again, we should be thinking of a nested pair of count-controlled loops.

```
204  private Swimmer getLowestSwimmer() {
205    Swimmer lowest = null;
206    for (int row = 0; ((lowest == null) && (row != ROWS)); ++row) {
207      for (int column = 0; ((lowest == null) && (column != COLUMNS));
208          ++column) {
209        Swimmer curr = swimmers.get(row).get(column);
210        if (curr != null) {
211          lowest = curr;
212        }
213      }
214    }
215    return lowest;
216  }
```

Listing 9.10: RescueMission: getLowestSwimmer

This pair of loops should look familiar: the loop control variable is initialized to 0 and incremented until it reaches the end of that dimension's size. The Boolean expression in the middle of the **for** loop is extended, though: these loops also end as soon as a non-**null** swimmer is found. So, assuming that all of the swimmers remain, when both row and column are 0, the **if** statement on line 210 evaluates to **true**, so the variable lowest is set to curr (or swimmers.get(0).get(0)). This is not **null**, so the (lowest == **null**) expression is **false** and each loop ends early (remember: **false** *and* anything is **false**).

Bottom-up Design

Using remainingSwimmerCount and getLowestSwimmer as building blocks lets us write two Boolean methods, checkIsGameOver and checkIsLevelOver. In advance we can call these methods in **if** statements. Notice that these two methods are quite simple; the reason for writing them as methods is to make the selection statements "self-documenting."[5]

```
183    private boolean checkIsGameOver() {
184      return ((getLowestSwimmer() != null) &&
185        (getLowestSwimmer().getMaxY() >= water.getMaxY()));
186    }
191    private boolean checkIsLevelOver() {
192      return (remainingSwimmerCount() == 0);
193    }
```

Listing 9.11: RescueMission: checkIs...

Checking for the game being over is easy: checkIsGameOver evaluates the Boolean expression given earlier, returning **true** if there is a surviving swimmer *and* that swimmer has reached the bottom of the water.

The Boolean expression should have you scratching your head. We know that **false** and anything (**true** or **false**) is **false** but if (getLowestSwimmer() != **null**) is **false**, then getLowestSwimmer() must have returned **null**. That means the expression after the && throws a *null-pointer exception*. getLowestSwimmer().getMaxY() cannot be evaluated without causing the program to crash.

Java uses the fact that **false** and anything is **false** to avoid this problem. Using something called *short-circuit Boolean evaluation*, Java evaluates a complex Boolean expression only until it knows the result. Expressions at the same level are evaluated from left to right. If the expressions are joined by && (such an overall expression is called a *conjunction*); as soon as Java evaluates one expression as **false**, it can stop evaluating the expression because the result is known.

Similarly, with Boolean expressions joined by the || operator (called a *disjunction*), as soon as Java evaluates one expression to **true**, it can stop evaluating as the overall expression's value must also be **true**. Many modern languages use short-circuit Boolean evaluation to permit tests to make sure expressions are safe to evaluate (what we do in lines 184–185) and to speed up programs (if the answer is known, why do any more processing to evaluate the expression?).

checkIsLevelOver just counts the number of swimmers remaining and compares that number to 0; if there are 0 swimmers, all have been rescued and the current level is over. We return to having multiple levels after a slight diversion into animation and how we can animate our Swimmer class.

Review 9.3

(a) Give the code to declare a one-dimensional ArrayList of Sprites called swimmer.

(b) Give the code to declare a two-dimensional ArrayList of Sprites called swimmer.

---

[5]The scare quotes are here because some programmers argue that properly written code is always self-documenting, whereas others claim that such a term is an oxymoron. As discussed in earlier chapters, the current authors believe in a balance between comments that document the programmer's *intent* and the use of good names and an appropriate level of abstraction in support of readable code.

(c) Assuming you have a two-dimensional `ArrayList` of `Sprites` called `swimmer`, how would you access the third `Sprite` in the second `ArrayList` of `Sprite`.

(d) What is the output of the following code:

```
int count=0;
for(int i=0; i<3; ++i)
  for(int j=0; j<5; ++j)
    ++count;
System.out.println(count);
```

(e) What is the difference between the `ArrayList` methods `set` and `add`?

(f) Is it possible to put a `null` value into an `ArrayList`?

(g) Suppose you have a `Sprite` x that may or may not be `null`. In the event that the sprite is below the bottom of the screen (past 1.0 in the y direction) and it is not `null`, you want to move it to the center of the screen. Here is the code you use to do this:

```
if(x.getY()>1.0 && x!=null)
  x.setLocation(0.5, 0.5);
```

Unfortunately this causes a `NullPointerException`. Your professor instead suggests you change the code to be:

```
if(x!=null && x.getY()>1.0)
  x.setLocation(0.5, 0.5);
```

This code works and does not throw a `NullPointerException`. Why?

9.4 Animation

Animation, "the act, process, or result of imparting life, interest, spirit, motion, or activity" [AHD00], is nothing new. From the falling apple in `NewtonsApple` to the color-changing villagers in the `FluSimulator`, all of the games we have written since Chapter 2 have added interest through motion and activity. This section reviews what we have done before and talks about how to animate `Swimmer` sprites in `RescueMission`.

Smooth Move: Animating Sprites

At its core, animation, be it computer animation or traditional painted celluloid animation, is really a loop. If you look at film and a film projector, you find that the film is a long stream of pictures, each printed on the celluloid at a fixed distance from the previous and following pictures. The projector aligns the film so that one of the pictures is projected through the optics. When the projector is running, a given picture is held for a short, fixed amount of time. For a much shorter amount of time, a shutter blocks the projection of the light through the film and, at the same time, the film is moved to the next frame.

That sequence, show frame–update frame, sounds familiar. It is, in fact, the first and last steps of the video game loop:

- Display the current ~~game~~ *film* state,

- ~~Get user input,~~

- Update ~~game~~ *film* state according to current state ~~and user input~~.

This means that we can, already, see how we should include animation inside our objects: advance in our various sprite classes enforces movement rules according to the game and also animates the appearance of the sprite at some rate.

Making Use of advance on the Objects

Looking at moveEverything in Listing 9.7, we see that advance is called for every Swimmer in the grid to make it move. If each swimmer should wave his or her arms back and forth in an effort to get the player's attention, that is where we should put the code to animate the sprite.

Let's look at Swimmer.advance:

```
13  public class Swimmer
14    extends SpriteWithVelocity {
101    public void advance(double dT) {
102      super.advance(dT);
103      decrementTimer(dT);
104      if (runIntoLeftWall() || runIntoRightWall()) {
105        bumpTheWall();
106      }
107    }
```

Listing 9.12: Swimmer: advance

Lines 13–14 are included in the listing to remind us that a Swimmer is-a SpriteWithVelocity. In advance on line 102, the call to super.advance(dT) is a call to the advance method provided by that class. Whenever possible we use the commonly defined implementations of methods from SpriteWithVelocity to justify our extracting the code. SpriteWithVelocity.advance(**double**) has just one line in the body:

```
9   public class SpriteWithVelocity
10    extends CompositeSprite {
42    public void advance(double dT) {
43      translate(dT * deltaX, dT * deltaY);
44    }
```

Listing 9.13: SpriteWithVelocity: advance

If a sprite has velocity, it is advanced by moving it according to how long it has been from the last frame and how fast it should be moving.

Lines 104–106 in Listing 9.12 handle bumping into the wall. The bumpTheWall method is **static**. What does **static** mean again? There is no **this**. The method and the field it manipulates are shared by *all* Swimmers. If *any* Swimmer touches the wall, then *all* Swimmers see the change in the shared field. More on this in a minute.

Line 103 handles animation timer. Each Swimmer has a timer. When the timer runs out, then the *state* of the Swimmer is updated. This should sound a lot like how FluSimulator ran except that each sprite has its own timer rather than using a FANG timer class.

```
31   /** Which animation frame is currently showing? */
32   private int frame;
44   /** animation timer; expires with call to timerExpried */
45   protected double timer;
164  protected void decrementTimer(double dT) {
165    timer -= dT;
166    if (timer <= 0) {
167      timerExpired();
168      startTimer();
169    }
170  }
```

```
177    protected double getTimerCountdownTime() {
178      return SECONDS_PER_FRAME;
179    }
206    protected void setTimer(double timer) {
207      this.timer = timer;
208    }
213    protected void startTimer() {
214      setTimer(getTimerCountdownTime());
215    }
221    protected void timerExpired() {
222      setFrame((frame + 1) % FRAME_COUNT);
223    }
```

Listing 9.14: Swimmer: All about timers

The timer field is **private**; the methods for manipulating the value are all **protected** because it is assumed that classes extending Swimmer treat those as *extension points*, spots where the child class can modify its behavior relative to the parent class.

The key concept is that the method getTimerCountdownTime is used to get the amount of time the timer takes before expiring; it is called from startTimer whenever the timer needs to be restarted. Note that getTimerCountdownTime in Swimmer just returns a constant value; it is possible to use any amount of calculation or state information to determine the timing (we see this in FastSwimmer where the timer determines how long the swimmer waits off screen *or*, if the timer is on the screen, how long each animation frame is).

When the timer is decremented (the call to decrementTimer is inside advance for Swimmer and should be in that method for all subclasses of Swimmer), a check is made to see if the timer has crossed 0.0 (has expired). If the timer expires, calls are made to timerExpired and startTimer to restart the timer. Since the state may have changed, the call to getTimerCountdownTime may return something different.

In Swimmer, in line 222, timerExpired calls setFrame. What is the value of the parameter expression passed to setFrame? frame and FRAME_COUNT are both **int** fields, one **static** (Which one? Notice how even capitalization conventions, consistently applied, improve readability of expression). So, frame + 1 is an integer one greater than frame.

What is the % operator again? It is the *modulus* or remainder operator. If FRAME_COUNT is set to 4, the result of modulus is an integer on the range [0–4]. frame is cyclic, taking on the values 0, 1, 2, 3, 0, 1, . . . and so on. This frame number is how we know how to change the appearance of the Swimmer sprite.

```
188    protected void setFrame(int frameNumber) {
189      frame = frameNumber % FRAME_COUNT;
190      if (frame == 0) {
191        rotate(20);
192      } else if (frame == 1) {
193        rotate(20);
194      } else if (frame == 2) {
195        rotate(-20);
196      } else if (frame == 3) {
197        rotate(-20);
198      }
199    }
```

Listing 9.15: Swimmer: setFrame

The code for setFrame shows that the swimmer is rotated relative to its current facing. Assuming frame 0 is the nominal position, when advancing to frame 1, the swimmer rotates 20 degrees clockwise. With frame

2, the swimmer returns to the nominal position (rotates 20 degrees counterclockwise). Advancing to frame 3, the swimmer rotates 20 degrees counterclockwise from the nominal position. When the frame goes to 0 again, the sprite returns to the nominal position.

This is a very simple state machine where the frame number records the current state and setFrame updates the frame number and the appearance of the sprite. Note that this cyclic state is maintained "automatically" by calling decrementTimer in advance.

Using timer's Extension Points

How can we use the timer in FastSwimmer? There is one requirement put on us to use it: FastSwimmer.advance must call decrementTimer, either directly or by delegating some or all of its work to Swimmer.advance through a call to **super**.advance.

We cannot call Swimmer.advance. The **static** method bumpTheWall is called when a swimmer, using Swimmer's advance method hits a wall. The FastSwimmer hitting the wall should not cause the grid of swimmers to change direction and move closer to the bottom of the screen. To avoid this, FastSwimmer.advance does all of its work locally:

```
40  public void advance(double dT) {
41    decrementTimer(dT);
42    if (isSwimming()) {
43      translate(dT * getDeltaX(), dT * getDeltaY());
44    }
45  }
```

Listing 9.16: FastSwimmer: advance

It calls decrementTimer and then, if the fast swimmer is on the screen and swimming, it translates the location according to the current velocity. This is a case of repeating ourselves: why can't we reuse the advance method declared in SpriteWithVelocity? Wasn't avoiding just this sort of code in *all* of the sprites in this game the point of factoring out the super class?

Short answer: Yes. The point was to reuse implementation. Unfortunately there is no Java notation for talking about the definition of a method in the class above the class above the current class. That statement tells us what **super**, used with a dot, actually does: the expression following the dot is evaluated as if it had been written in the body of the class above the current one. Typically that means that it calls a method defined in the class the current class extends. But if the closest definition of a named method is farther up the hierarchy, **super** refers to that definition. It always refers to the lowest definition that happens *above* the current class.

Because we don't want Swimmer.advance and there is no way from FastSwimmer to specify SpriteWithVelocity.advance, we were reduced to copying the method body into our advance.[6] We are lucky in this case that there is a single line to copy; if the processing were more complex, it would make sense to move the actual movement code out to its own protected method so that it could be called from SpriteWithVelocity.advance and any other advance where it was needed.

Review 9.4

(a) The advance method is called in the Game class and on Sprites at about 25 times per second when the processor and video cards can keep up. When running at 25 frames per second, in seconds how quickly must each frame be computed and displayed? This is the reason that the advance method must always finish its work quickly in order to maintain smooth motion in your game.

---

[6]Some programming languages, such as C++, support picking and choosing which ancestor class's implementation to call; that power comes at the cost of having to know more of the class hierarchy.

(b) When extending a class, is it possible to call methods of that class that are `public`? `private`? `protected`?

(c) Digital animations are created by displaying frames at such a rapid rate that it looks like the objects in the animation are moving. Do some Internet research to determine the typical frame rate of:

(a) High definition television

(b) Modern movies

(c) A video game console of your choice
Cite your sources when reporting this information.

(d) Sometimes a class is extended to provide new functionality by adding entirely new methods, and other times a class is extended to customize the existing functionality by overriding the implementation of existing methods.

(a) List the new functionality provided in the `Swimmer` class by listing the methods written in `Swimmer` that are not within `SpriteWithVelocity`.

(b) List the methods in the `Swimmer` class that override existing methods within the `SpriteWithVelocity`.

9.5   Finishing Rescue Mission

This section finishes `RescueMission` by finishing a discussion of the code of `FastSwimmer`, and then we look at how multiple levels are supported in FANG.

Launching a `FastSwimmer`

There is one `FastSwimmer` in the game; sometimes it is swimming across the screen and sometimes it is waiting. This is an object with two states. When constructed, a `FastSwimmer` is waiting; it changes from swimming to waiting when it reaches the edge of the screen and `bounceOffEdges` is executed.

```
167  protected void timerExpired() {
168    if (isSwimming()) {
169      super.timerExpired();
170    } else {
171      launch();
172    }
173  }
```

Listing 9.17: FastSwimmer: `timerExpired`

The `timerExpired` method (as mentioned above) launches the fast swimmer. When it begins waiting, the `FastSwimmer` sets a random waiting time on the range [0–MAX_TIME_OFF_SCREEN) seconds. When the timer expires, since the state is waiting (`isWaiting` returns **true**), `isExpired` calls `launch`. If the fast swimmer is already swimming, the timer is used to animate the swimmer by calling **super**.`timerExpired` and reusing the animation code written for `Swimmer`.

```
115  private void launch() {
116    startSwimming();
117    if (Game.getCurrentGame().randomDouble() < 0.5) {
118      launchLeftToRight();
119    } else {
120      launchRightToLeft();
121    }
122  }
```

```
129  private void launchLeftToRight() {
130    setLocation(0.0, 0.1);
131    setRotation(90);
132    setVelocity(speedX, speedY);
133  }
140  private void launchRightToLeft() {
141    setLocation(1.0, 0.1);
142    setRotation(-90);
143    setVelocity(-speedX, speedY);
144  }
```

Listing 9.18: FastSwimmer: launch...

When a fast swimmer launches, the state is changed to swimming (startSwimming is called). This changes the state, makes the sprite visible, and sets the frame number to 0. launch "flips a coin" or rather gets a random number from the Game. If the number is less than half, the fast swimmer moves left to right; otherwise it moves right to left. The two methods for actually positioning the swimmer and setting the velocity do what you would expect.

Naming methods well is an important skill. It would be possible to save 10–25 lines by moving the bodies of launchLeftToRight() and launchRightToLeft() directly into launch. Each call would be replaced by three lines of code. It would greatly decrease the readability of launch, and additional comments would be necessary to explain the code.

The current structure separates the decision about what direction the swimmer should move from how it is set to move in a given direction. The separation of functionality into small, independent units makes life easier for the programmer. Each method should do one thing and should have a name that reflects the one thing that it does. If you're having trouble coming up with a good name for a function, think carefully about whether it really does only one thing.

In the current structure it would be easy to have newly created FastSwimmers always start moving left to right. It would also be easy to change the chances that the swimmer goes in either direction without having to worry whether any code for launching needed to change.

The Rescuer and the Ring

How are swimmers rescued and how does the Rescuer move across the bottom of the screen. The movement of the rescuer is limited like that of the paddle in SoloPong in Chapter 6. Rescuer reuses the advance method of SpriteWithVelocity.

```
44  public void advance(double dT) {
45    Game curr = Game.getCurrentGame();
46    if (curr.keyPressed()) {
47      char key = curr.getKeyPressed();
48      if ((key == KeyEvent.VK_LEFT) || (key == KeyEvent.VK_KP_LEFT)) {
49        setVelocity(-Math.abs(getDeltaX()), getDeltaY());
50        super.advance(dT);
51      } else if ((key == KeyEvent.VK_RIGHT) ||
52          (key == KeyEvent.VK_KP_RIGHT)) {
53        setVelocity(Math.abs(getDeltaX()), getDeltaY());
54        super.advance(dT);
55      } else if (key == KeyEvent.VK_SPACE) {
56        ring.startFlying();
57      }
```

```
58        }
59      }
```

Listing 9.19: `Rescuer: advance`

The resetting of the x-component of the velocity (lines 49 and 53) use the `Math` class, a class that has only **static** methods. `abs` is the absolute value or the magnitude of the number without regard to sign. It is always a nonnegative number. Since we don't know whether the rescuer was last moving from left to right or reverse that, we convert the x-component to a positive value (it must be non-zero for the rescuer to move) and then invert it if the swimmer is moving to the left.

If the user presses the space bar, the rescue ring is launched. The rescue ring, like the `FastSwimmer`, is a sprite with two states: ready and flying. When the ring is ready, it is "attached" to the rescuer, matching location with the rescuer each frame.

```
100     public void advance(double dT) {
101       if (isFlying()) {
102         super.advance(dT);
103         rescueRope.setStart(rescuer.getLocation());
104         rescueRope.setEnd(getLocation());
105       } else {
106         setLocation(rescuer.getLocation());
107       }
108     }
```

Listing 9.20: `RescueRing: advance`

If the ring is ready, it is not flying. Line 106 executes, moving the rescue ring to the location occupied by the rescuer. The first branch of the **if** statement uses the super definition of `advance` to move the ring.

A line is drawn between the rescuer and the rescue ring (or rather, the line sprite `rescueRope` has its end points set to be the location of the rescuer and the location of the rescue ring). The rope is purely aesthetic; no other sprites interact with it.

Changing the state of a `RescueRing` takes place in `startFlying` and `startReady`: `startFlying` is called in `Rescuer.advance` (when space bar is pressed); `startReady` is called from the constructor, `bounceOffEdges`, and `isRescuing`. The rescue ring keeps flying until it rescues a swimmer (regular or fast) or it hits an edge of the screen. With this feature the game values accuracy very highly.

Rhythm in Games

How the `RescueRing` behaves is a central design decision for this game. How many rings can the rescuer throw at one time? What is the "recharge time" between rings? The decision for `RescueMission` was that there is only one ring, and once it is thrown, it travels in a straight line until it rescues a swimmer or moves off the top of the screen.

This decision means that pressing the space bar calls `startFlying` but that method does nothing unless the ring is currently ready; if the ring is already flying, `startFlying` does nothing. This means that there is only one ring in flight. The ring is returned to the ready state when it rescues a swimmer or goes off the screen, so the limitation in `startFlying` enforces just the design described above.

This design decision forces the players to trade off their long-range accuracy (say for hitting the fast swimmer) and the need to throw the rescue ring rapidly. This particular mechanic was lifted from the retro game on which `RescueMission` was modeled, *Space Invaders.* In Taito's arcade *Space Invaders,*[7] there was an additional rain of missiles from the grid of invaders and a series of destructible forts between the invaders and the player.

---

[7]*Space Invaders*, released in 1978, remains trademarked by Taito.

There was no good story reason for the swimmers to want to harm the rescuer (and the game is already almost 1400 lines long), so that was left out.

```
114  public void bounceOffEdges() {
115    if (isFlying() && runIntoAnyWall()) {
116      startReady();
117    }
118  }
195  public void startFlying() {
196    if (isReady()) {
197      readyForLaunch = false;
198      rescueRope.show();
199      rescueRope.setStart(rescuer.getLocation());
200      rescueRope.setEnd(getLocation());
201    }
202  }
207  public void startReady() {
208    if (isFlying()) {
209      readyForLaunch = true;
210      rescueRope.hide();
211      setLocation(rescuer.getLocation());
212    }
213  }
```

Listing 9.21: RescueRing: States and Bouncing

Internally, RescueRing uses a **boolean** field, readyForLaunch, to keep track of its state. When the field is **true**, the ring is in the ready state; when the field is **false**, the ring is in the flying state. Lines 197 and 209 take care of setting the field according to the state the ring is changing to.

When the ring is flying, the rescue rope should be visible; when it is ready, the rope should not be visible. Finally, each state-setting method adjusts the location of either the ring or the rope, depending on what the new state is.

Bouncing off the edges is running into a wall. When that happens, the flying ring goes from flying to ready (line 116 above).

```
160  public boolean isRescuing(Sprite victim) {
161    return isFlying() && (victim != null) && intersects(victim);
162  }
```

Listing 9.22: RescueRing: isRescuing

How does a ring rescue a swimmer? The action needed to rescue the swimmer is actually beyond the scope of RescueRing; it is something that the *game* is in charge of. The ring does have a **boolean** method, isRescuing, which takes a swimmer as a parameter and returns **true** if the swimmer and the ring are intersecting.

Note that this method uses short-circuit Boolean evaluation to make sure that intersects is not called with null. The null check is necessary because of how we decided to handle rescued swimmers: they are set to null when rescued. By putting the check here, we can write a simple iteration to handle checking each and every swimmer to see if it has been rescued.

The iteration is in RescueMission.rescueIfPossible. The nested loops in Listing 9.23 look similar to those used in moveEverything; the only difference is that rather than checking against null, the if statement checks if the ring is rescuing the given swimmer. Remember that there is a null test inside of isRescuing, so this is safe. If the check returns **true**, the method calls rescueSwimmer.

```
273    private void rescueIfPossible() {
274      if (ring.isFlying()) {
275        for (int row = 0; row != ROWS; ++row) {
276          for (int column = 0; column != COLUMNS; ++column) {
277            Swimmer curr = swimmers.get(row).get(column);
278            if (ring.isRescuing(curr)) {
279              rescueSwimmer(row, column);
280            }
281          }
282        }
283      }
284      if (fastSwimmer.isSwimming() && ring.isRescuing(fastSwimmer)) {
285        rescueFastSwimmer();
286      }
287    }
```

Listing 9.23: RescueMission: rescueIfPossible

After the loop, the fast swimmer is checked to see if it is being rescued. It is necessary to check isSwimming on the fast swimmer because it cannot be rescued if it isn't visible. It might be possible to intersect with it even when it is off the screen (the reason we remove Swimmer sprites from the list of lists to rescue them).

```
264    private void rescueFastSwimmer() {
265      setScore(getScore() + fastSwimmer.getScore());
266      fastSwimmer.startWaiting();
267      ring.startReady();
268    }
297    private void rescueSwimmer(int row, int column) {
298      Swimmer curr = swimmers.get(row).get(column);
299      setScore(getScore() + curr.getScore());
300      removeSprite(curr);
301      swimmers.get(row).set(column, null);
302      ring.startReady();
303    }
```

Listing 9.24: RescueMission: rescue...

To rescue the fast swimmer we add the fast swimmer's score to the game score and reset the state of the fast swimmer (to waiting) and the rescue ring (to ready). To rescue a regular swimmer we do just the same thing but regular swimmers don't have a waiting state. Instead we set the location where the sprite is in the grid to null, see line 301, and remove the sprite from the FANG data structure so that it is no longer painted as part of each frame; see line 300.

Levels in FANG

The concept of Game in FANG is a little more complicated that this text has let on. Internally FANG keeps a list of Game-derived class objects. The first item in the list is the current game (and is what is returned by the call Game.getCurrentGame). When the current game really finishes, FANG automatically calls the next game in the list. If there is no next game, then FANG terminates the program.

Each game in the list can be considered a level. When a level is over (when all swimmers in the grid are rescued), we can create a new RescueMission, add it to the list of games FANG maintains, and then really end the current game. That is exactly what happens in advance:

```
104   public void advance(double dT) {
105     moveEverything(dT);
106     bounceEverything();
107     rescueIfPossible();
108     if (checkIsLevelOver()) {
109       addGame(new RescueMission(level + 1, getScore(),
110           swimmerDX * LEVEL_SPEEDUP, swimmerDY * LEVEL_SPEEDUP));
111       finishGame();
112     } else if (checkIsGameOver()) {
113       addGame(new EndOfGame(getScore()));
114       finishGame();
115     }
116   }
```

Listing 9.25: `RescueMission: advance`

Everything is moved, then everything is bounced off the edges of the screen, and every swimmer is checked for a rescue. If the level is over (there are no remaining swimmers in the grid), a new game is added by calling `addGame` with a newly constructed game. The new game is constructed with a level number, the current score, and slightly higher speeds for the swimmers.

If those four parameters are necessary for constructing a `RescueMission`, how does FANG know what values to use for the first level? The short answer is that it doesn't. FANG requires every `Game`-derived class to have a default constructor; the default constructor is the no-parameter constructor. When creating the first level, FANG calls the default constructor.

```
75   public RescueMission() {
76     this(1, 0, SWIMMER_DX, SWIMMER_DY);
77   }
88   public RescueMission(int level, int initialScore, double swimmerDX,
89     double swimmerDY) {
90     this.scoreSprite = null;
91     this.level = level;
92     this.swimmerDX = swimmerDX;
93     this.swimmerDY = swimmerDY;
94     this.initialScore = initialScore;
95   }
```

Listing 9.26: `RescueMission: Constructors`

Applying the DRY principle, we just forward the default constructor to the four-parameter constructor providing initial values: level 1, score 0, and the named constants for swimmer velocity.

The only odd thing remaining in `advance` is line 113 (in Listing 9.25). What is `EndOfGame`? It is used with `new`, so it must be a class. Is it part of FANG? Looking at the documentation we see that the answer is no. It is a fairly simple "game," one which takes a score as a parameter to its constructor and displays a `StringSprite` on the screen. It is like the drawings and examples in Chapter 2: it has a `setup` method but no `advance`.

This use of a level to mark the end of the game is similar to how many video games actually work. They have modes of operation such as attract mode (show pretty video or pictures to get players interested), setup (setting up the game), the lobby (waiting to play multiplayer games), the game itself, loading screens, and high-score or end-of-game levels. Note that it would be fairly simple to add a small `advance` to `EndOfGame` that would start a new game of `RescueMission` when the player pressed the space bar.

```
1    // package default
2
3    import fang2.core.Game;
4    import fang2.sprites.StringSprite;
5
6    /**
7     * The "game" is really just a level of the main game. It is
8     * constructed to display a message on how well the player did (it is
9     * initialized with the player's score) and then the setup creates a
10    * centered end-of-game message.
11    */
12   public class EndOfGame
13     extends Game {
14     /** the score provided to the constructor */
15     private final int initialScore;
16
17     /**
18      * Construct a new EndOfGame level. Requires the score to display for
19      * the player.
20      *
21      * @param  initialScore  the player's score
22      */
23     public EndOfGame(int initialScore) {
24       this.initialScore = initialScore;
25     }
26
27     /**
28      * Setup the display information on the screen.
29      */
30     @Override
31     public void setup() {
32       setScore(initialScore);
33       StringSprite announcement = new StringSprite();
34       announcement.setText("GAME OVER\nFinal Score: " + getScore());
35       announcement.setScale(1.0);
36       announcement.setLocation(0.5, 0.5);
37       addSprite(announcement);
38     }
39   }
```

Listing 9.27: EndOfGame: Whole Class

Review 9.5

(a)   Often it is simpler to create and add most or all of the sprites your game will need, and then make them visible or invisible as necessary. What are the Sprite methods for making a Sprite visible or invisible?

(b)   The Sprite class has an intersects(Sprite) method. Does this intersects method take into account whether the sprite is visible or invisible, on or off the screen? Consult the FANG Engine API to read the documentation on the intersects method.

9.6   Summary

Nested Loops

The body of a `for` loop can contain any valid Java code. This means that it can, by definition, include another `for` loop. A collection of loops, one inside another, is called *nested loops*. To determine how many times the body of the inner-most loop executes, it is necessary to determine how many times the body of each loop executed and then *multiply* the values together. This is simple for count-controlled loops that run a fixed number of times; it is more difficult if termination conditions of the loops are more complex.

When working with a two-dimensional structure like a multiplication table, it is useful for you to think of using two nested loops (one loop for rows, an inner loop for columns).

Collections of Collections

While nested loops permit generating two-, three-, and higher-dimensional things, keeping the data for such a structure typically requires a list of lists (of lists of lists of . . .). That is, where a loop per dimension permits discussing a multidimensional creation such as a multiplication table, a collection per dimension permits keeping the structure around.

An `ArrayList` of `ArrayLists` of some object gives a two-dimensional data structure that can hold a "table" or grid of the element objects. To fill such a structure requires two nested loops (one for rows and one for columns) and $rows \times columns + rows + 1$ calls to `new`: one for each element in the table or $rows \times columns$ calls for those, one for each row or $rows$ calls for those, and one call for the whole list of lists.

Traversal of a data structure means passing over all of the elements in the structure. For a list of lists, this implies a pair of nested loops. In this chapter we saw how to count elements of a list of lists with a given attribute (not being `null` in our case) and how to find the first element with a given attribute (again, not being `null`, though the `if` statement could be modified fairly simply).

Because `ArrayLists` can hold only references, all plain old data types have object equivalents: `Integer` for `int`, `Double` for `double`, and `Boolean` for `boolean`.

Inheritance

An oak *is-a* tree just as a cherry tree *is-a* tree. This relationship means that any time a generic **tree** is required, either an **oak** or **cherry tree** would be acceptable as a **tree**.

In Java, an object of any class that `extends` another (either directly or through a chain of intermediate classes) is-a(n) object of the ancestor class as well. A `CompositeSprite` is-a `Sprite`, a `RescueMission` is-a `Game`, and a `Rescuer` is-a `SpriteWithVelocity`, is-a `CompositeSprite`, is-a `Sprite`, and is-a(n) `Object`.

Animation

Animation, the changing of the appearance of a `Sprite`, is similar to regular movement of a sprite on the screen. The only difference is if the frequency of the updates should be different than calls to `advance`. This chapter demonstrated how to use a timer and how to include `protected` *extension points*, methods that can be overridden in subclasses to extend or modify the behavior of the timer in specific subclasses.

Combining overridden methods and the is-a relationship yields the important object-oriented programming principle of *polymorphism*. Polymorphism is having many forms; the superclass provides a method that can be used in the general case (the timer expires), and the subclasses provide specialized implementations of the extension point routines that are called through the superclass reference.

Levels in FANG

The Game class in FANG has an addGame method that adds a Game-derived class to the list of games to be run by the current game. When a running game calls finishGame, the currently running game is taken off the front of the list of games, and if there is any game remaining in the list, the first is started as the next game or next level.

The chapter makes use of this by constructing increasingly more difficult levels of the same game when all of the swimmers are rescued. It also uses this fact to create a special end-of-game level which displays a message for the players showing their scores. This is where a level could be built to read/save high scores or the game could be started over.

9.7   Chapter Review Exercises

Review Exercise 9.1 It is possible to put one loop inside another loop. What is this structure called?

Review Exercise 9.2 If you have an ArrayList of ArrayLists, how many loops are necessary to iterate over all of the individual elements.

Review Exercise 9.3 If you have **class** A **extends class** B, which is the super class (also called base class) and which is the subclass (the more specialized class or the one with additional functionality)?

Review Exercise 9.4 Between **public**, **private**, and **protected**, which access level is used to indicate an extension point for a class (a method that can be overridden when extending the class but not called by an outside class)?

Review Exercise 9.5 Give a high level overview of how you can make a multilevel game out of several existing single-level games.

Review Exercise 9.6 Simulating two moving objects bouncing off of each other is more challenging than you might initially think. Part of bouncing is determining if two objects intersect.

In this problem, we are simply going to simulate one-dimensional intersections. A simulation such as this could determine when two trains are passing each other on parallel tracks. Suppose you have two line segments, one from a to b and the other from c to d where a is not necessarily less than b and c not necessarily less than d. Figure 9.3 shows three different train positions, only one of which has the trains intersecting.

Complete the following method to determine if the two segments intersect. Write a small program to test the method. Be sure to create enough test cases to show that your code works for *all* possible inputs (not just those in the figure).

```
/**
 * Determines whether or not two segments overlap;
 * segment endpoints are not ordered.
 * @param a an endpoint of the first segment
 * @param b the other endpoint of the first segment
 * @param c an endpoint of the second segment
 * @param d the other endpoint of the second segment
 *
 * @ return true if the segments overlap, false otherwise
 */
public boolean doOverlap(int a, int b, int c, int d){
  <your code here>
}
```

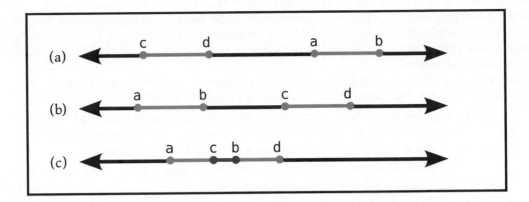

Figure 9.3: Intersecting Trains

Review Exercise 9.7 Air traffic controllers perform a job where mistakes can cost hundreds of lives. Training on a simulator would be a far less risky way to get some experience before controlling real air traffic. As part of a simulation development team, it is your job to determine if the elevation of any planes are too close. Complete the following method to evaluate if any planes are near collision.

```
/**
 * Determine if one plane is too near any other planes.  The plane is
 * too near if its altitude is within 500 meters of any other plane
 * in the vicinity.
 * @param planeAltitude the altitude of one plane (m)
 * @param allOthersAltitude the altitude of all nearby planes (m)
 *
 * @return true if planeAltitude is within 500 meters of any other
 * plane's altitude otherwise false (all planes more than 500 meters
 * from planeAlititude)
 */
public boolean otherPlanesTooClose(int planeAltitude,
                        ArrayList<Integer> allOtherAltitudes){
    <your code here>
}
```

(a) Fill in otherPlanesTooClose method.

(b) How many comparisons between altitudes are necessary when there are 10 other planes and none are within 500 meters?

(c) How many different cases should you test? One, obviously, is when there is one other and it is within 500m. Another is when there is one plane and it is *not* within 500m. Describe as many different kinds of cases as you can (no need to list every possible length of allOtherAltitudes, but only testing list of length 1 is inadequate).

(d) Write a test program that generates your test cases and calls otherPlanesTooClose. Make sure your test program prints out all failed tests including the parameters, the expected result, and the actual result.

Review Exercise 9.8 How could you use two-dimensional lists to implement a *Battleship* board?

Each player begins with a 10×10 grid of squares and a fleet of five ships of varying lengths (lengths appear after each ship's name): aircraft carrier (5), battleship (4), cruiser (3), submarine (3), and destroyer (2). To set up the game, each player places his or her fleet in their grid, each ship placed horizontally or vertically across the given number of squares.

Players then take turns selecting squares in his or her opponent's grid, shooting at any ship occupying the square. The goal is to sink the enemy's fleet before a player's own fleet is sunk.

(a) Each player sees two boards: one with his or her ships on it and one with his or her shots on it. What are the elements in each of the `ArrayList`s? In each case there are four values for each square: occupied by a section of a ship, occupied by a *sunken* section of a ship, shot at, or empty.

(b) How would each board be displayed for each player? Player 0 should see ships and sunken ships on his board and sunken ships and shots on his opponent's board. If the player does not "see" something, it means that the board shows that square as clear.

9.8 Programming Problems

Programming Problem 9.1

Caterpillar Games   The following games start with a simple game in `Caterpillar.java`. The program has a caterpillar with ten segments follow the mouse.

As written, the game has no rules; it is just a software toy.

Part I

Making it into a game:

The `Caterpillar` can be much like a `Snake` in the popular cellphone game of that name. A piece of food appears randomly on the screen (the food is some sprite of your choosing). The player's goal is to guide the caterpillar to the food without ever intersecting with itself. Each time a food sprite is "eaten," the caterpillar grows a new tail segment. The steps to do this include:

(a) Store the segments of the caterpillar in an ArrayList called segments.

(b) Add food to the game but don't yet provide any interaction with the caterpillar.

(c) Make it so that when the head of the caterpillar touches the food, the caterpillar adds a segment at the end. Place this code in a method called checkFood and call this method from advance. Use the code in setup for an example. Make sure the newly added segment has an AttractorTransformer that chases the old last segment and that you set the min distance (similar to the way it is done in setup).

(d) Make a method called doesOverlap that checks to see if the head of the caterpillar (first in the ArrayList) intersects any of the other segments. This method should return a boolean. Make it so that the caterpillar follows the mouse only so long as the result of doesOverlap is false.

(e) Add a score. Make the score the number of elements in the segments ArrayList.

(f) Provide a timer that counts down. Allow the player to continue controlling the caterpillar only while there is still time left.

Part II

Other interesting extensions:

(a) Increase the time when the caterpillar eats food.

(b) The basic game prevents only the head of the caterpillar from intersecting with the other segments. Modify the game so that no two segments more than three segments apart in the ArrayList can overlap (segments next to each other and even two away normally overlap as the caterpillar moves). This mod requires nested **for** loops, or a **for** loop and a helper method with a loop in it.

(c) Devise a two-player version of the game. One way to do this is to provide two caterpillars, and the head of either caterpillar cannot move when it is intersecting the other caterpillar.

Remember that each caterpillar is tracking a *different* mouse.

Programming Problem 9.2

Herding Cats   This game is about getting a bunch of cats all in the same place. There is one human that the cats all run from. Also, some cats run from each other. Once all of the cats are herded, another one pops out of nowhere and the herded cats scatter. The goal it so see how many cats you can herd. Here's how to write the game:

(a) Make a game with a single sprite field called human. The human should take up about one-twentieth of the screen. The location of this sprite should be controlled by the mouse. The sprite could be a simplified version of Person from Chapter 8 (no need to get sick).

(b) Add an instance field called cats, which is an ArrayList<Sprite>. Define a method called addCat. addCat takes no parameters, creating and returning a cat sprite (your choice on appearance) which is about one-tenth of the screen (it's a huge cat). The method places the cat at a random location on the screen, adds it to the game, and adds it to cats.

Have setup create the human and call addCat thee times. The human should move and the cats should ignore the human (some say the simulation of reality can stop here).

(c) Each cat needs aRepelTransformer that moves the cats away from the human at a speed of 0.4 screen/second. They also need a StayOnScreenTransformer to keep them on the screen; they can be herded into corners.

(d) Add the following catsHerded method that returns **true** when all of the cats are within one-fifth the screen of each other:

```
public boolean catsHerded() {
  for (int i = 0; i < cats.size(); ++i) {
    for (int j = i + 1; j < cats.size(); ++j) {
      Location2D first = cats.get(i).getLocation();
      Location2D second = cats.get(j).getLocation();
      if (first.distance(second) > 0.2) {
        return false;
      }
    }
  }
  return true;
}
```

In advance, check if all of the cats are herded. When they are herded, randomly place another cat on the screen (using addCat).

(e) Modify addCat so that every cat in the ArrayList is set to a random location. This makes the cats scatter when a new cat is added.

   i. What does addCat now do? Can you state it clearly in one sentence? Methods are a little bit like paragraphs in writing: each should have a "thesis statement," the one thing that it does. Does the new addCat have such a statement?

   ii. Would it be better to write a new method, scatterCats, that randomly places all cats on the screen? In advance, when cats are herded, call scatterCats and addCats. Both of the resulting methods have only a single purpose and so are easier to compose to do new things.

(f) The game is still too easy. To make it more challenging, when a new cat is added, it should run away from one or more of the existing cats. Use the RepelTransformer to make the cat run away from half of the existing cats. The cats should run away from each other at about half the speed the cats run away from the human.

(g) Add a sprite that shows how many cats you are currently herding. This is the score in the game.

(h) Modify the difficulty level by making the cats run away faster or slower.

Programming Problem 9.3 Modify RescueMission so that the FastSwimmer comes in two different flavors, fast and really fast. The differences between the two are the speed with which they cross the screen (really fast swimmers are twice as fast as the current fast swimmers) and the points they are worth: fast swimmer should be worth what it is worth now and a very fast swimmer should be worth double that.

This does not involve a new Sprite. Instead, some fraction of the time, when the fast swimmer is launching, it sets itself as a very fast swimmer. The rest of the time it is just a fast swimmer. You need to track the base score and base speed and then set the values to double those values if the swimmer is to be very fast.

If you want, you can change the color of the swimmer when it is very fast.

Programming Problem 9.4 This is a larger project that is more research than programming oriented.

In order to verify that the flu epidemic simulator works, a researcher decides to use actual test subjects. As part of his study, he gives out free pizza to students, but the students do not know that he injected some slices with live flu virus. He plans to count the number of absences in his school to see if it matches the results of his simulation.

Consult the Association of *Computing Machinery (ACM) Code of Ethics* and cite the guidelines violated by listing the number of the guideline along with a summary of the guideline and how it was violated. Describe a more ethical way for the researcher to validate his model. Make sure *your* suggestion does not violate any of the guidelines in the *ACM Code of Ethics*.

Programming Problem 9.5 Start with TicTacToe from Chapter 7. Replace the nine variables, t00 through t22, with an ArrayList of ArrayList of GameTile.

(a) How is the board initialized? The constructor should use two *nested* count-controlled loops to construct the nine tiles and place them in the two-dimensional board. How many times must the ArrayList constructor be called (perhaps with different element types)?

(b) Modify row<n>(), col<n>(), and diag<n>() methods to use count-controlled loops

(c) Combine the three row<n>() methods into a single row method that checks all three rows in one **for** loop.

(d) Combine the three col<n>() methods into a single col method that checks all three rows in one **for** loop.

(e) Combine the two diag<n>() methods into a single diag method that checks both diagonals in one **for** loop.

(f) Compare the number of lines the new program has with those the original TicTacToe had. How does the clarity of the code compare?

10

Scanner and String: Character Input

So far all of our games were *self-contained*. They are self-contained in the sense that they don't rely on any files other than their Java source code and then, after being compiled, the compiled `.class` files. The resulting games are simple: distributing the game depends only on passing along the `.class` file.[1]

The flip side of being self-contained is that the game *must* be recompiled to change any values it works with. This is not how most programs work. You do not need to recompile **Microsoft Word**® each time you want to edit a different document. You don't have to recompile the `javac` executable each time you want to compile a different program. This is because these programs interact with the *file system* on the computer where they run. The only instance where we have interacted with the file system is when loading an `ImageSprite`.

The games also lack a memory: when run, a game has no way to tell if this is the first, the one hundredth, or the one millionth time it has run. There is no concept of an enduring high score or restoring from a saved game.

Random numbers change the play from run to run (remember `NewtonsApple`: the starting location of the `apple` changes randomly each time it is dropped but the two sprites on the screen are fixed at compile time), but each run is completely independent of every other run.

This chapter introduces the Java `Scanner` class. A `Scanner` can be connected to a Web resource or a file on the local hard drive, permitting the game to change behavior based on the contents of the resource without needing to be recompiled. Think about games with multiple different levels: the same game is being played but the exact layout of the game changes. Programs in this chapter only read resource files; writing files is deferred until Chapter 12.

10.1 Designing Hangman

Imagine a two-player game where one player, the chooser, selects a word and exposes the number of letters to the other player, the guesser. The guesser guesses letters, one at a time, and the game is over when the guessing player guesses all of the letters in the word or when he misses six times. This game could be played with paper and a series of tick marks; when the sixth tick is written, the guesser loses and the chooser exposes the rest of the word.

---

[1]Along with any required `.jar` Java archive such as `fang2.jar`.

This is an example of a simple word game with simple rules: pick a word, guess letters, count misses, mark matches, guess word, or miss too many letters. It lacks a good story, though. The description is too dry.

Enter *Hangman*: instead of tick marks, the chooser draws a gallows at the beginning of the game and on each missed letter draws a new body part hanging from the gallows; when the last body part is drawn, the guesser is "dead." This is an example where a story (perhaps a bit morbid) can add interest to an otherwise dry game design.

This particular word game has been around for almost a century and a half: "The origins of Hangman are obscure, but it seems to have arisen in Victorian times." [Aug03] It comes from a time when hanging was an almost common occurrence.

Our Hangman game pits the human player, as the guesser, against the computer playing as chooser. The design diagram shows that the screen has four sprites on it: the score, the gallows, the word being guessed, and the alphabet selector.

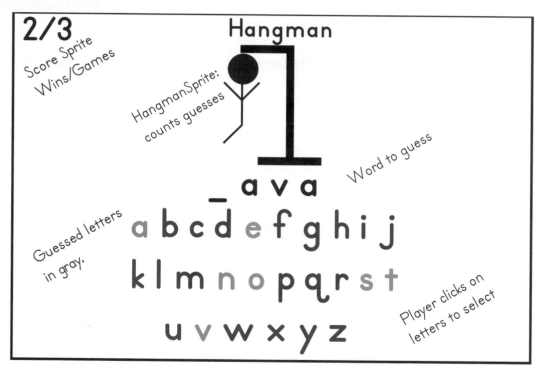

Figure 10.1: Hangman game design diagram

Looking at the diagram, we see that there seem to be a lot more than four sprites on the screen: the alphabet is 26 characters and the hangman/gallows has at least six parts. Top-down design means that we use *abstraction* to conquer the complexity in this program. We design the interfaces of the four classes we use in the game and implement the game using those interfaces. All of the new concepts in this chapter are in the game and not in the sprite classes.

Public Protocols

ScoreSprite

The ScoreSprite in the upper-left corner of the game implements a scoring model just like that found in NewtonsApple back in Chapter 6. It is just wrapped up in a class that knows how to initialize, how to record a win, and how to record a loss. That means the public interface for the class is:

```
public class ScoreSprite
  extends StringSprite {
  public ScoreSprite()...
  public ScoreSprite(int wins, int games)...
  public void lose()...
  public void win()...
}
```

The sprite is added to the game, properly positioned. Whenever the game is won or lost, win or lose is called and the ScoreSprite fixes up its score[2] and updates the displayed value. The overloaded constructors provide flexibility: the sprite can be initialized to any arbitrary value. The number of wins cannot be greater than the number of games played.

HangmanSprite

The HangmanSprite is a composite of the gallows and the victim. Note that the hangman takes the place of the tick marks, so it is really a second score indicator. It shows the score for the current game while the ScoreSprite shows the scores across multiple games.

Thinking about it as a score indicator gives us the insight to build the public interface:

```
public class HangmanSprite
  extends CompositeSprite {
  public HangmanSprite()...
  public void clear()...
  public void incrementState()...
  public void setColor(Color color)...
  public boolean stillKicking()...
}
```

The local setColor method sets the color of the victim's body to the new color. clear clears the state so that no body parts are on display (sets the score to 0). incrementState adds one to the state and displays a new body part. stillKicking returns true until the victim is finished being hung. They are finished when all of the body parts are visible.

GuessableWord

The word to be guessed is displayed in the middle of the screen. It is a StringSprite with additional state. It tracks the word to be guessed and the progress of the guess (it shows "_" characters where unguessed letters are and the letters where they have been guessed). The public interface is

```
public class GuessableWord
  extends StringSprite {
  public GuessableSprite(String word)...
  public void expose()...
  public boolean guess(char letter)...
  public boolean isGuessed()...
}
```

---

[2]Going back and fitting the ScoreSprite into NewtonsApple is left as an exercise for the interested reader.

A `GuessableWord` is initialized with the word to be guessed. As part of the implementation, it prepares the displayed version of the word. So long as `isGuessed()` is **false** (`!isGuessed()` is **true**), the game continues. Each time the user picks a letter, the letter is passed to `guess`: if the letter is in the word, it is exposed and `guess` returns **true**; if the letter is not in the word, then the displayed word is unchanged and `guess` returns **false**.

AlphabetSelector

The user must be able to pick letters to guess. This could be done with the keyboard, with the mouse, or with both. For simplicity, we focus on just using the mouse (extending the sprite to handle keyboard input is presented as an exercise).

An additional problem in `Hangman` is that the guesser would like to keep track of letters already guessed; if the letter is *in* the word, it is easy to remember, but if it is not in the word, it is not clear how `AlphabetSelector` remembers that it has been guessed. The `AlphabetSelector` contains `LetterSprites`, sprites which have a ready and a used state; they are shown in two different colors and only ready letters are selectable by the player. The appearance provides feedback to the user that they shouldn't reselect letters and the sprite state keeps them from making the mistake.

```
class AlphabetSelector
  extends CompositeSprite {
  public AlphabetSelector()...
  public char selectedChar()...
  public void unselectAll()...
}

class LetterSprite
  extends StringSprite {
  public LetterSprite(char letter)...
  public char getLetter()...
  public Color getReadyColor()...
  public Color getUsedColor()...
  public boolean isReady()...
  public boolean isUsed()...
  public void setReadyColor(Color readyColor)...
  public void setUsedColor(Color usedColor)...
  public void startReady()...
  public void startUsed()...
}
```

The public interface of `LetterSprite` is included to make the operation of `AlphabetSelector` clearer. When an `AlphabetSelector` is built, it contains 26 `LetterSprites`, all initialized to the ready state. `selectedChar` returns either a letter (if one was selected) or the *null character*, the **char** with a value of zero, otherwise. If a letter was selected, the corresponding `LetterSprite` is changed from the ready to the used state.

Once a `LetterSprite` is in the used state, it cannot be selected again. To permit restarting with the whole alphabet selectable again, the `unselectAll` method is provided.

Hangman: The Game

Given these classes, since they do most of the work, designing `Hangman` is straightforward. This chapter does take guidance from the design of `NewtonsApple` in Chapter 4: we build two different versions of the program. In the text, both are referred to as `Hangman`. The listing captions make clear whether the line numbers refer to the version in HangmanWithStub, the first version, or Hangman. The methods in 'WithStub are all found in Hangman, some with more capability and many at slightly different line numbers.

The setup routine is broken into four subroutines, one for each of the sprites discussed above. They are created, scaled, located, and colored according to the design diagram shown above. We skip covering the game's setup method in detail because it is so similar to code we have already covered.

```
38  public void advance(double dT) {
39    if (isGameOver()) {
40      if (getKeyPressed() == ' ') {
41        setGameOver(false);
42        startOver();
43      }
44    } else {
45      char ch = alphabet.selectedChar();
46      if (ch != '\0') {
47        if (gamePhrase.guess(ch)) {
48          if (gamePhrase.isGuessed()) {
49            scoreSprite.win();
50            doneWithGame("Congratulations");
51          }
52        } else {
53          hangman.incrementState();
54          if (hangman.isDead()) {
55            gamePhrase.expose();
56            gamePhrase.setColor(getColor("red"));
57            scoreSprite.lose();
58            doneWithGame("You lose!");
59          }
60        }
61      }
62    }
63  }
```

Listing 10.1: HangmanWithStub: advance

Hangman uses a single level (and level type), unlike Chapter 9's RescueMission. Instead Hangman has two different states: game over and game not over.

Style note.   The if statement here is written with *positive logic* or without using not, !, at the beginning of the Boolean expression. Software engineering studies have shown that positive logic is easier for human programmers to understand and maintain. [McC04]

If the game is already over, the game is waiting for the user to press the space bar to restart the game. The game ended with a call to doneWithGame (see Listing 10.2). A message indicates how the game ended and instructions to press the <Spacebar> to continue. The game loops, doing nothing, until the user presses the <Spacebar>. The Game startOver method restarts the current Game: the sprites and alarms are all canceled, setup is called once, and then the game enters the main loop. It is almost the same as adding the current game to the list of games and then calling finishGame.

While the game is running, the **else** clause, lines 45–60, executes. Line 45 gets the selected letter from the alphabetSelector. If the player has not yet picked a letter (how they pick a letter has yet to be determined), the selector returns '\0', the null character.

If the player *has* just selected a letter, the letter guessed is passed in to the `GuessableWord` object. `guess` returns **true** if the letter was found in the hidden word, **false** if not.

If the `guess` letter was in the word, the player might have just won the game. If the guess was not in the word, tell the hangman and check if the player died. If the game ended, either well or poorly, display an end of game message, update the score, and set the game over. If the player loses, expose the word so that he knows what word was missed.

```
84  private void doneWithGame(String endOfGameMessage) {
85    StringSprite restartMessage = new StringSprite(endOfGameMessage +
86        "\nPress <space> to play again.");
87    restartMessage.setScale(0.9);
88    restartMessage.setLocation(0.5, 0.75);
89    addSprite(restartMessage);
90    alphabet.hide();
91    setGameOver(true);
92  }
```

Listing 10.2: `HangmanWithStub`: `doneWithGame`

The `doneWithGame` method creates a new `StringSprite` containing two lines: the given message and a game restart line. The sprite is positioned in the bottom half of the screen, the `AlphabetSelector` is hidden, and the game is set to over.

These two methods are the only two needed for playing the game. The rules for picking a letter, for guessing a letter in a hidden word, and for keeping track of scores are abstracted away from the game program itself; all it has to do is coordinate communication between the pieces that know how to play the game.

Stub Methods

We examine one of the setup methods because it leads us to a way of applying top-down design, the idea of *stub methods*. A stub method is a temporary implementation of a method, a simple implementation that permits compiling and testing of higher-level methods. A stub method is an implementation of the design admonition, "Pretend that it works."

```
132  private void setupGamePhrase() {
133    String pickedPhrase = pickPhrase();
134    if (pickedPhrase == null) {
135      System.err.println("Unable to find a phrase with which to play!");
136      System.exit(1); // error exit code
137    }
138    gamePhrase = new GuessableWord(pickedPhrase);
139    gamePhrase.bottomJustify();
140    gamePhrase.setWidth(0.7);
141    gamePhrase.setLocation(0.5, 0.6);
142    addSprite(gamePhrase);
143  }
150  private String pickPhrase() {
151    // TODO: Replace with real load/select code.
152    return "cats and dogs";
153  }
```

Listing 10.3: `HangmanWithStub`: `setupGamePhrase` and `pickPhrase`

At line 133, setupGamePhrase calls pickPhrase. Lines 150–153 represent a stub implementation of pickPhrase. The method just returns a fixed phrase. Every time the game is played, the chooser chooses the exact same phrase.

This does not make for a good Hangman game but it does make for a *playable* and (more importantly) *testable* Hangman game. With the stub implementation for pickPhrase in place, we can compile HangmanWithStub and all of the supporting classes without knowing anything about opening files for input.

We debug the mechanics of the game separately from the problems of locating a file full of possible phrases, reading that file into memory, and picking a word from that list. As always, separating problems into different levels either by delegation (as we have done here) or abstraction (as partitioning Hangman into the four specialized sprite classes) helps us overcome complexity.

We detour now to discuss how java runs a compiled .class file from the command line, how we can specify parameters to a program when it is run, and how FANG has started the program for you automatically behind the scenes.

Review 10.1

(a) What is a *stub* method? Why would you write one?

(b) What is a null character? How is a null character literal typed?

(c) What are the states of a LetterSprite? What do they mean?

(d) What are the states of the Hangman (or HangmanWithStub) game? How are the states differentiated in advance?

(e) Why should programmers prefer positive logic when writing Boolean expressions? What *is* positive logic?

10.2   Starting Programs

Remember the introduction of *operating systems* in Section 2.3? An operating system is a program that can start and stop *other* computer programs. One of the biggest differences between operating systems is the rules the operating system uses when beginning the execution of a program. An executable program that runs directly on a given CPU requires more than just the right CPU: it also requires the right operating system so that it is properly loaded into memory and the correct *entry point* is chosen to begin execution.

An example of this difference lies in the executable formats for *Microsoft Windows*, *Linux*, and *Apple OSX*. All three operating systems run on computers with an Intel or compatible CPU; all three operating systems use sequences of instructions drawn from the exact same instruction set as do programs which any of the operating systems can start.

Without special adaptation, however, programs compiled on OSX cannot be started directly on a Windows computer, nor can Windows executables be started directly by Linux, and so on. The instructions in the program depend on the CPU but how the program starts depends on the CPU and the operating system.

This is of interest to us because we are programming using the Java programming language. Rather than compiling to machine code run directly on any given CPU (or loaded by any given operating system), the javac compiler compiles to .class files containing *bytecodes* to be interpreted by the java virtual machine program.

The java interpreter is like an operating system in that it has a defined convention for how it starts a program. When you run a given .class file, java calls a specific **static** method, the method with the following header:

```
public static void main(String[] args)
```

We address the meaning of the two square brackets later in this section. When java is run with the command line:

```
~/Chapter10% java -classpath .:/usr/lib/jvm/fang2.jar Hangman
```

304 SCANNER AND STRING: CHARACTER INPUT

the Java interpreter sets up all appropriate library connections, loads the Hangman class, and then calls Hangman.main with the previous header.

The complete *lifecycle* of an application is

- Load the named .class file

- Call main in loaded class

- Terminate program when main returns

"Wait," you are thinking, "Nowhere in this book have we written a main method. Looking at Hangman.java (and HangmanWithStub.java), we see that there is no such method." FANG uses the standard Java inheritance model to provide a version of main for you. In GameLoop.class, there is a **static** main method with the right header.

When Java runs an *application*, it calls main as defined by the class named on the command line calling the interpreter. In FANG the default implementation of main is both the simplest and the most complex method in the library. It is simple in *what* it does: it determines the class that was specified on the command line for Java, makes sure the class extends GameLoop, calls the default constructor for that class, and then calls runAsApplication. It is complicated in that figuring out what class was specified when the program was run and then calling the constructor for a type that is unknown at compile time requires some deep knowledge of Java.

This simplified definition ignores some convoluted details. We continue to ignore them. The remaining question is what does runAsApplication do?

Applets vs. Applications

One powerful feature of FANG is its ability to run exactly the same code as either an application (with a call to java from the command line) or as an *applet* inside of a Java-enabled Web browser.

What is an applet and how is it different from an application? An applet is a class that extends java.applet.Applet, a Java library class. The lifecycle of an applet is

- Load named .**class** file

- Construct (with default constructor) an object of the given class

- Call init on the new object

- While browser is running:

  - Call start when page containing applet is entered
  - Call stop when page containing applet is exited

- Call destroy on the applet object

Because the applet runs inside the context of a Web browser,[3] it is not started with a call to main because the Java virtual machine has already started and is running the browser's version of main.

What does that mean for a FANG game? A FANG game must run as either an applet or an application and it must *not* require recompiling to change from one to the other. If FANG provides its own main and that main acts like an applet browser, implementing the applet lifecycle outlined above, all started from a call to main, then a FANG program can run like an applet no matter how it is started.

---

[3]or another applet browser such as appletviewer in the JDK.

Notice that this is another separation of function, the splitting of a problem into component parts that are solved independently. Rather than worry about "How to start and run a program as an applet or an application," FANG solves the problems of "How to run a program as an applet" and "How to provide a `main` which starts an applet running inside of an application."[4]

Both applets and applications can be customized by providing parameters to specify how the program should run. These parameters are just like parameters passed to any method except that they are all `String`. The next section discusses how to interpret the arguments passed into `main` and how FANG saves those parameters for you so that you can have access to them without having to override `main` yourself. The section after next describes how to pass in and use parameters in applets. This information is important because, by the end of the book, we want to be able to write our own programs without the FANG library.

In addition to customizing the way applications run, applets also can receive parameters but not via the command line. Because applets are typically run within a Web browser, their parameters are passed in via HTML. Between the start and end applet tags, parameter tags can be supplied. For example, you could pass in the parameters `one` and `two` in the following way:

```
<applet ...>
   <param name"="one value"="alpha></param>
   <param name"="two value"="bravo></param>
</applet>
```

Accessing the parameters is done in the same way in the `setup` method, as shown in Listing 10.6.

Many modern IDEs provide a way to run programs as either an applet or an application without explicitly specifying the console or HTML parameters. Consult the documentation of your own IDE to determine how to set these when you run your program.

`public static void main(String[] args)`

Because of the way Java handles inheritance, any class that `extends GameLoop` can provide its own `main` method with the above header; such a method overrides the method defined in `GameLoop`. If you want FANG to run as usual, your `main` method must end with the following method call:

```
InitializeApplication.fangMain(args);
```

You must **import** `fang.util.InitializeApplication` to call this method. `fangMain` is the wrapper around all of the complexity mentioned above so we do not drill down any deeper here.

What can you do in `main`? And what is the meaning of `String[] args`? In reverse order: `String[] args` is an *array* of `String` objects, and `main` can do anything that is built into Java.

An array is like an `ArrayList` in that it is a Java collection, a single object containing other objects. An array is unlike an `ArrayList` in its syntax and public interface. To illustrate this and where we are going with writing non-FANG programs, the next section develops a console-only program that prints all of its command line parameters to the console. It does *not* use any part of FANG.

Writing `main`

`PrintAllArguments` in Listing 10.4 treats `args`, the array of arguments, just like any other collection.

---

[4]One of the authors (Ladd) originally wrote a different toolkit with an inherited `main` method in summer 2006 as part of an early version of this book. The current implementation of `main` and its support code is based on code written for the ACM's Java Task Force's Java toolkit [RBC+06].

```
1  // package default
2
3  /**
4   * A program showing how to use a for-loop to iterate across the
5   * arguments passed in to the program when it is run.
6   */
7  public class PrintAllArguments {
8    /**
9     * The main program: java PrintAllArguments starts by calling this
10    * public static method. The method just uses a for-loop and
11    * System.out.println to print each argument on a line by itself.
12    *
13    * @param  args  The command-line arguments
14    */
15   public static void main(String[] args) {
16     System.out.println("PrintAllArguments:");
17     for (int i = 0; i != args.length; ++i) {
18       System.out.println("  args[" + i + "] = \"" + args[i] + "\"");
19     }
20   }
21 }
```

Listing 10.4: `PrintAllArguments`

The following table gathers the differences between an `ArrayList` and an array starting with those shown in this code and including a couple of other cases.

Array	ArrayList	Description
array.length	list.size()	The array exposes a *field* whereas the list exposes a method.
array[i]	list.get(i)	The array uses square brackets to indicate individual items.
array[i] = "x"	list.set(i, "x");	The square brackets generate the element location so that it can be used to get and set the given element.
array = new String[n]	list = new ArrayList<String>()	The array constructor is called when square brackets containing the number of elements is appended to the element type. The default constructor is called for each of the n element locations as part of construction; while entries can be reset, the number of elements in an array cannot be changed after construction. The list is initially empty; add and remove, expand and contract the list as necessary to fit the current number of elements.

What does `PrintAllArguments` do? Given different command lines, what is the output?

```
~/Chapter10% java PrintAllArguments
PrintAllArguments:

~/Chapter10% java PrintAllArguments alpha bravo charlie
PrintAllArguments:
  args[0] = "alpha"
  args[1] = "bravo"
  args[2] = "charlie"

~/Chapter10% java PrintAllArguments "alpha bravo charlie"
PrintAllArguments:
  args[0] = "alpha bravo charlie"
```

In the first instance, there are no command line arguments after the name of the class file for Java to load. Line 16 prints the name of the program. The `length` of args is 0, so the **for** loop is never executed.

The second instance has three words appearing after the name of the program, `alpha`, `bravo`, and `charlie`. The words are separated from the name of the class and from each other by some number of spaces. With three different words, `args.length` is 3, so the loop executes three times and the three `String` values are printed.

The last example shows how the command line interpreter, provided by the operating system (`bash` on Linux in this case), groups multiple words together. The command line arguments after the name of the class are similar to those in the second case, but enclosed in double quotes. This causes the command line interpreter to treat the string enclosed in the quotes as a single argument. `args.length` is 1, and `args[0]` (remember, `[0]` is equivalent to `.get(0)` for an `ArrayList`), the only `String` in the argument array, is printed.

Arguments in FANG Programs

The FANG library processes command line arguments by breaking them into two types: *named* and *unnamed* arguments. An argument of the form `name=value` (where the whole thing is one word according to the command processor) is a named argument. FANG collects all named arguments with the same name and puts the values into an `ArrayList` of `String`, one entry for each time the same name appears. The `ArrayList` is available from the `getNamedArgs(String name)`, a **static** method in `InitializeApplication`.[5]

All other arguments, those without an equal sign, are grouped together as unnamed attributes. They are put into an `ArrayList` which you can access with a call to `getUnnamedArgs()`. `PrintAllArgumentsFANG` demonstrates how unnamed arguments work.

```
1  // package default
2
3  import java.util.ArrayList;
4
5  import fang2.core.Game;
6  import fang2.util.InitializeApplication;
7
8  /**
9   * Uses FANG methods to get the arguments passed into the program.
10  */
11 public class PrintAllArgumentsFANG
```

---

[5]Due to Java applet limitations, there is no way, in a FANG program running as an applet, to get a list of the names of all named parameters. The code in this section works as described when run as an application. You must *know* the names of named parameters in order to get them from inside a running applet.

```
12    extends Game {
13    /**
14     * List all the command-line arguments on standard output.
15     */
16    @Override
17    public void setup() {
18      ArrayList<String> args = InitializeApplication.getUnnamedArgs();
19      System.out.println("PrintAllArgumentsFANG:");
20      for (int i = 0; i != args.size(); ++i) {
21        System.out.println("  args[" + i + "] = \"" + args.get(i) + "\"");
22      }
23    }
24  }
```

Listing 10.5: `PrintAllArgumentsFANG`

```
~/Chapter10% java -classpath .:/usr/lib/jvm/fang2.jar \
              PrintAllArgumentsFANG
PrintAllArgumentsFANG:

~/Chapter10% java -classpath .:/usr/lib/jvm/fang2.jar \
              PrintAllArgumentsFANG alpha bravo charlie
PrintAllArgumentsFANG:
  args[0] = "alpha"
  args[1] = "bravo"
  args[2] = "charlie"

~/Chapter10% java -classpath .:/usr/lib/jvm/fang2.jar \
              PrintAllArgumentsFANG "alpha bravo charlie"
PrintAllArgumentsFANG:
  args[0] = "alpha bravo charlie"
```

(The \ characters are continuation characters; the lines continue onto the next line. They can be typed on a single line in most command line interpreters. They are necessary so that the lines fit on the printed page.)

The discussion for the three different executions of the program match those given above for `PrintAllArguments`. The real difference between the two programs is that FANG does the work of reading the array and puts it all in an `ArrayList` for you.

```
1  // package default
2
3  import java.util.ArrayList;
4
5  import fang2.core.Game;
6  import fang2.util.InitializeApplication;
7
8  /**
9   * Uses FANG methods to get the arguments passed into the program.
10   */
11  public class NamedArgumentsFANG
12    extends Game {
13    /**
```

```
14     * List all the command-line arguments on standard output.
15     */
16    @Override
17    public void setup() {
18      System.out.println("NamedArgumentsFANG:");
19      ArrayList<String> names = InitializeApplication.getArgumentNames();
20      for (int i = 0; i != names.size(); ++i) {
21        ArrayList<String> args = InitializeApplication.getNamedArgs(
22            names.get(i));
23        for (int argumentNdx = 0; argumentNdx != args.size();
24            ++argumentNdx) {
25          System.out.println("  args[\"" + names.get(i) + "\"][" +
26              argumentNdx + "] = \"" + args.get(argumentNdx) + "\"");
27        }
28      }
29    }
30  }
```

Listing 10.6: NamedArgumentsFANG

Named arguments are similar but are grouped by name. The getArgumentNames method returns a list of all names used for arguments; this list can be empty. If you look at the code in NamedArgumentsFANG, notice that it is a pair of nested loops because the collection of named arguments is a list of lists (a two-dimensional data structure).

```
~/Chapter10% java -classpath .:/usr/lib/jvm/fang2.jar \
              NamedArgumentsFANG one=alpha two=bravo
NamedArgumentsFANG:
  args["two"][0] = "bravo"
  args["one"][0] = "alpha"
```

The order of the strings in the list returned by getArgumentNames is, for all intents and purposes, random. This is because of the internal structure used to store the lists of arguments. Note that getArgumentNames does not work in an applet. Sorting collections is covered in Chapter 11.

Review 10.2

(a) How can you determine the size of an *array*? How do you get the element with index 4?

(b) What are the command line arguments passed to PrintAllArguments in each of the following:
   (a) PrintAllArguments babylon five
   (b) PrintAllArguments two fifty one ninety seven
   (c) PrintAllArguments two "fifty one""ninety seven"

(c) What are the named command line arguments passed to PrintAllArgumentsFANG in each of the following:
   (a) PrintAllArgumentsFANG first=babylon second=five
   (b) PrintAllArgumentsFANG w=a x=b y=c
   (c) PrintAllArgumentsFANG "all=a b c"

(d) Is it possible to get a listing of the names of all named parameters in an *applet*?

10.3   Different Iteration

So far *iteration* has been synonymous with the `for` loop in Java. This is because we have limited ourselves to
count-controlled loops. To review, a count-controlled loop is a loop where, at the time the loop begins, the
computer knows the number of times the loop runs. We use a `for` loop to implement count-controlled loops
because the three parts of the `for` loop, the `<init>`, `<continuation>`, and `<nextStep>`, capture the operation of a
count-controlled loop very well.

The variable used to count must be initialized, it must be tested against some ending value, and it must
be incremented each time through the loop. These three steps match the three parts of the `for` loop almost
exactly.

In `RescueMission` in Chapter 9, the `getLowestSwimmer` method modified our standard count-controlled loop:

```
204  private Swimmer getLowestSwimmer() {
205    Swimmer lowest = null;
206    for (int row = 0; ((lowest == null) && (row != ROWS)); ++row) {
207      for (int column = 0; ((lowest == null) && (column != COLUMNS));
208          ++column) {
209        Swimmer curr = swimmers.get(row).get(column);
210        if (curr != null) {
211          lowest = curr;
212        }
213      }
214    }
215    return lowest;
216  }
```

Listing 10.7: `RescueMission`: `getLowestSwimmer`

In lines 206 and 207, the Boolean expression for `<continuation>` extends the standard count-control test of
having reached some bound with a test for `lowest` being `null`. The loop runs for some number of iterations or
until the body of the loop sets `lowest` to a non-`null` value. A loop that runs over and over until some condition
is met is known as a *sentinel-controlled* loop.

A sentinel is a guardian or, in our case, a marker. It marks the end of some phase of processing. Imagine
writing a method to generate a random multiple of 3 between 0 and some given positive value, `bound`.[6]

If we ignore the need to have a multiple of 3, the method is fairly simple to write:

```
public int randomMultipleOfThree(int bound) {
  int multipleOfThree = Game.getCurrentGame().randomInt(bound);
  return multipleOfThree;
}
```

This is just a wrapper around a call to `randomInt` in the current game. This method could be defined in
a game or a sprite, any class that imports `fang.core.Game`. The value returned may or may not be an actual
multiple of 3. How can we make sure it is?

The `randomInt` method returns a number on the range `[0-bound)`. What are the odds that that number is a
multiple of 3? If all numbers are equally likely, then one in three should be a multiple of 3. So one-third of the
time the above method should work. Is that good enough? No, we want it to work every time.

So, if we call `randomInt` three times, if each choice has a one in three chance of being a multiple of 3, we
have a one in one chance of getting a multiple of 3, right? **Wrong.** With random numbers there is a chance

[6]There are alternative approaches to this problem that do not use iteration at all. Exploring them is left as an exercise for the
interested reader.

that any number of them in a row is not a multiple of 3. The chance gets smaller and smaller the more times we select a random number, but the number of times we must select *cannot be known* when the method begins. This cannot be a count-controlled loop.

We use a new construct, the `while` loop. First we show an example loop inside `randomMultipleOfThree` and then we present the template.

```
public int randomMultipleOfThree(int bound) {
  int multipleOfThree = Game.getCurrentGame().randomInt(bound);
  while (!((multipleOfThree \% 3) == 0)) {
    multipleOfThree = Game.getCurrentGame().randomInt(bound);
  }
  return multipleOfThree;
}
```

A `while` loop takes a single Boolean expression after the word `while`. When the `while` line is executed, the expression is evaluated. If it evaluates to `true`, then the body of the loop is executed; at the end of the body of the loop, execution returns to the `while` line, reevaluating the Boolean expression. When the Boolean expression evaluates to `false`, execution skips over the body of the loop and continues execution with the following statement:

```
<whileStatement> ::= while (<continuation>)
                        <statement>

<statement> := <localVariableDefinition> |
               <expression>; |
               <forStatement> |
               <whileStatement> |
               <ifStatement> |
               <block>
```

The `while` statement looks a lot like an `if` statement and some students confuse the two. It is important to keep in mind that a `while` statement *cannot* have an `else` clause. Also, the body of an `if` statement is executed zero or once (depending on the Boolean expression); the body of a `while` statement is executed zero or *more* times with an unbounded value for *more*.

So, looking back at `randomMultipleOfThree`, if the first number chosen is a multiple of 3, then `multipleOfThree % 3` is 0. The Boolean expression `((multipleOfThree % 3) == 0)` is `true`, so the logical inverse (or not) of that is `false`. The key is we wrote an expression that is `true` at the sentinel value and then applied a logical not to it. The loop runs while the sentinel check does *not* evaluate to `true`.

De Morgan's Laws

Note that the Boolean expression in our multiple of 3 method can be simplified: if we push the logical not, `!`, into the expression it modifies, we can rewrite the expression according to the following:

```
(!((multipleOfThree \% 3) == 0)) = ((multipleOfThree \% 3) != 0)
```

This removes a level of parentheses. It also reverses the logic from

```
while (!P) {
  ...
}
```

to

```
while (Q) {
    ...
}
```

where P and Q are Boolean expressions and !P = Q or !P and Q have the same truth values for all possible values of variables they reference. This helps us use positive logic which, as mentioned earlier, has been shown to be easier for programmers to understand.

August De Morgan (1806–1871) was a logician who was influenced by George Boole's work and formally stated a couple of simple rules, rules for simplifying expressions with logical not in them. The following two lines use == to show that the two expressions are logically equivalent.

```
!(P && Q) == !P || !Q
!(P || Q) == !P && !Q
```

So, how can we use this? Consider a **while** loop to pick a random number which is either a multiple of 10 or a multiple of 11 or both. The Boolean expression can be built up:

```
((n \% 10) == 0) // multiple of 10
((n \% 11) == 0) // multiple of 11
((n \% 10) == 0) || ((n \% 11) == 0) // either 10 or 11
(!((n \% 10) == 0) || ((n \% 11) == 0)) // not 10/11
```

This expression makes sense in that it was developed by expressing the sentinel condition, the condition where the loop should stop, and then that expression was logically inverted. This is the way a sentinel-controlled loop is typically built up.

The expression is not the simplest form to read for following programmers. It would make sense to push the ! into the expression. That is done by applying the second of De Morgan's Laws:

```
(!((n \% 10) == 0) || ((n \% 11) == 0))
!((n \% 10) == 0) && !((n \% 11) == 0)
((n \% 10) != 0) && ((n \% 11) != 0)
```

The expression is first rewritten as an and of the inverse of the two subexpressions. The not is pushed into the subexpressions (it would work if they were && or || expressions as well). We do not spend a lot of time working on simplifying logical expressions though this is a skill a programmer should develop.

Review 10.3

(a) Write a loop that generates a random integer between 1 and 100 and exits only when the random number is even.

(b) Write a **while** loop that finds the first power of two larger than 10000.

(c) Write a **while** loop that finds the largest power of two smaller than the **int** variable magicNumber.

(d) What is a sentinel? What does it have to do with **while** loops?

(e) Using De Morgan's Laws, simplify the following Java Boolean expressions:

    (a) `!((x < y) && (a != b))`

    (b) `!((getScore() > 10) || isGameOver())`

    (c) `!((a == b) || ((x < 10) && (y < 10))`

    (d) `!((x != null) && ((x.isBig()) || (x.isMean())))`

    (e) `!((z > 1.3) || (b <= 1.9) )`

    (f) `!(isVisible() && (w < 0))`

    (g) `!(command.equals("far") || command.equals("near"))`

    (h) `!((x < 100) && ((x % 3) != 0))`

10.4 String Manipulation

In Section 3.1, we saw that internally digital computers work only with discrete integers. This design influenced the tasks early computers were put to: space and atomic physics including the first atomic bomb, ballistics tables for artillery, and payroll and tax calculations.

The deepest insight presented in that section was that arbitrary *types* of values can be encoded for storage and manipulation in a digital computer. Computers are a *universal medium* in that any other medium can be encoded into a digital representation. This insight was first used when business computing became standard and continues as audio, video, and even immersive 3D environments are digitized and distributed using networks of digital computers.

This section looks at String and the char elements that make them up. char is a POD type representing a character. We look at more String methods and how String objects compare for ordering.

The char Data Type

Back in Chapter 2, the comparison was made between printable characters and *bytes* in the computer. A byte, eight binary digits or bits, can hold 256 different values. If you consider just the characters in a textbook (ignoring for the moment color or font values), how many different characters are you likely to see?

If the language of the text is English, the alphabet accounts for 52 letters (upper and lower case), common punctuation probably account for another 18 characters, and the digits account for another 10. That gives about 80 characters. Why encode characters in 256 values when 128 will do — or, if we were less liberal with punctuation and mixed case, perhaps even as few as 64 different values?

There are two answers to the question of why not: memory is free, and powers of two powers of two are powerful. Modern technology makes RAM memory and other memory devices very inexpensive. Saving 12.5% in memory costs more in convenience than it saves in memory. The other reason is that a byte is 8 bits and 8 is a power of 2. Thus, $256 = 2\char94 8 = (2^2)^3$. This has benefits in building and programming binary circuitry at the heart of a modern computer.

Given that we have more encodings than characters in English, we can extend the characters encoded to include those used in most Western European languages by adding accents, umlauts, and some special characters. The characters are encoded using the ASCII character coding sequence.[7]

The "Western European" limitation in the previous paragraph is indicative of where computers were developed and deployed. Other alphabets such as Cyrillic, Greek, Tamil, Thai, Arabic, Hebrew, and the like are used in many modern programs by using a two-byte character encoding scheme (known as Unicode). Operating with Unicode characters is an important part of internationalizing computer programs but, with that said, we are not going to discuss Unicode characters any further in this text. Unicode embeds the ASCII encoding to simplify working with Western European encoded legacy data.

How are characters encoded? Given a character, let's say 'A', what value is stored in a byte to represent it? The short answer: who cares?

We don't care what value 'A' has[8] because that is an implementation detail. In fact, there are only three important pieces of information to remember about the ASCII encoding sequence:

1. The capital letters are contiguous. 'A' has an encoding one smaller than that of 'B' which is one smaller than that of 'C', and so on.

2. The lowercase letters are also contiguous. 'a' is one smaller than 'b' which is one smaller than 'c', and so on.

3. The digit characters are contiguous. '0' is one smaller than '1', '0' is two smaller than '2', and nine smaller than '9'.

---

[7] American Standard Code for Information Interchange.

[8] Though all of the current authors do waste some portion of their brains remembering how 'A', 'a', and '0' are encoded.

Remembering that a character is stored in a single byte (ignoring Unicode) and that there are three contiguous ranges in the encoding, ['A'-'Z'], ['a'-'z'], and ['0'-'9'] are the only implementation details we need to remember.

Character

The Character type is like Integer, Double, and Boolean, an object type that lets us create ArrayLists and provides many utility functions. Among the methods provided by Character are a series of static character classification routines. Some of these are summarized in the table below:

Method Name	Description
isDigit(**char** ch)	**true** if ch is a digit; otherwise **false**.
isLetter(**char** ch)	**true** if ch is a letter; otherwise **false**.
isLowerCase(**char** ch)	**true** if ch is a lowercase letter; otherwise **false**.
isUpperCase(**char** ch)	**true** if ch is an uppercase letter; otherwise **false**.
isSpaceChar(**char** ch)	**true** if ch is the space character; otherwise **false**.
isWhitespace(**char** ch)	**true** if ch is considered whitespace by Java; otherwise **false**.
char toLowerCase(**char** ch)	returns lowercase equivalent to ch if it is a letter; otherwise returns ch unchanged.
char toUpperCase(**char** ch)	returns uppercase equivalent to ch if it is a letter; otherwise returns ch unchanged.

Table 10.1: Character Classification and Translation Routines

The value returned by Game.getKeyPressed() is a **char**, so these methods can be applied to the values entered by the user. Imagine we wanted to call setGameOver with **true** if the user pressed either an uppercase or lowercase 'q' (for 'q'uit). The following **if** statement makes that easy:

```
if (Character.toLowerCase(getKeyPressed()) == 'q') {
  setGameOver(true);
}
```

By forcing the case to be lower, we effectively ignore case. Notice that we use == to compare **char** values. It is also possible to use less than and greater than comparisons for individual characters. For example, we could write myIsUpperCase(**char** ch) as follows:

```
boolean myIsUpperCase(char ch) {
  return (('A' <= ch) && (ch <= 'Z')) ;
}
```

The Boolean expression is **true** when the value in ch (the encoding for the letter) is greater than or equal to the encoding of 'A' and when the value in ch is less than or equal to the encoding of 'Z'. Using the first rule of ASCII, that the uppercase letters are contiguous, any capital letter must be encoded between those values, and only those 26 values encode uppercase English letters. This version of isUpperCase only handles English letters, not extended Western European letters (e.g., 'ö' and 'Ê') nor Unicode characters; the Character version does handle those characters.

String: The Public Interface

A Java String is an *immutable* sequence of **char** values. Immutable simply means unchangeable; once a String has been constructed, it is not possible to change individual characters. Consider:

```
String one = "cat";
String two = "fish";


one = one + two;
```

How many `String` objects are created by this code? Is it even legal (if a `String` is immutable, how does the last line work?)? This code is legal because both `one` and `two` are *references* to `String` objects. The last assignment just changes *what* `String` one refers to without changing the `String` containing `"cat"`. The first line constructs a literal `String` (all doubly quoted strings in Java code are converted to constructor calls by the compiler automatically). The next line constructs a second literal string. The last line calls the + operator for `String`. + takes two `String` operands and returns a new `String` containing the characters of the first operand followed by the characters in the second operand. `one` ends up referring to the third `String` constructed by this code, a `String` containing the characters `"catfish"`.

`ArgumentCharacters` is a FANG program printing the characters in its argument, one character per line.

```
1  // package default
2
3  import java.util.ArrayList;
4
5  import fang2.core.Game;
6  import fang2.util.InitializeApplication;
7
8  /**
9   * Read unnamed arguments, print out the first argument one character
10  * per line. Demonstrates how a String is a collection of char.
11  */
12 public class ArgumentCharacters
13   extends Game {
14   /**
15    * If there are any unnamed command-line parameters, then get the
16    * first one and print out the characters, one per line. If there are
17    * no parameters, print out a message to that effect.
18    */
19   @Override
20   public void setup() {
21     System.out.println(getClass().getName());
22     ArrayList<String> args = InitializeApplication.getUnnamedArgs();
23     if (args.isEmpty()) {
24       System.out.println("  No unnamed argument provided");
25     } else {
26       String firstArgument = args.get(0);
27       for (int i = 0; i != firstArgument.length(); ++i) {
28         System.out.println("  str.charAt(" + i + ") = '" +
29           firstArgument.charAt(i) + "'");
30       }
31     }
32   }
33 }
```

Listing 10.8: `ArgumentCharacters`

A String is sequence of characters. This means we can write a loop to iterate over the characters in a string.

This program has a new feature at line 21: rather than our typing in the name of the program's class (as we have done up until this point), the program takes advantage of Java's runtime class identification. Java knows the *dynamic* class of an object and keeps a reference to a Class object for that class; getting the class of the current object is as easy as calling getClass. The Class class is not always easy to follow but the getName method does just what you would think it would: it gets the name of the class, the *actual* class of the object on which getClass was called.

The first line of output, the name of the program, is generated by printing the String returned from getClass().getName() in line 21.

Using the FANG method for getting command line arguments, it checks to make sure there is at least one command line argument. If there are none, an error message is printed and setup finishes. Otherwise, the first command line argument is fetched and referred to with firstArgument. Each character in firstArgument is then retrieved using the charAt method with an index. Each character is printed on its own line using System.out.println. Sample output is given below.

```
~/Chapter10% java -classpath .:/usr/lib/jvm/fang2.jar \
            ArgumentCharacters
ArgumentCharacters
  No unnamed argument provided
```

```
~/Chapter10% java -classpath .:/usr/lib/jvm/fang2.jar \
            ArgumentCharacters alpha bravo charlie
ArgumentCharacters
  str.charAt(0) = 'a'
  str.charAt(1) = 'l'
  str.charAt(2) = 'p'
  str.charAt(3) = 'h'
  str.charAt(4) = 'a'
```

Notice that only the first unnamed argument is processed by the program.

```
~/Chapter10% java -classpath .:/usr/lib/jvm/fang2.jar \
            ArgumentCharacters "alpha bravo charlie"
ArgumentCharacters
  str.charAt(0) = 'a'
  str.charAt(1) = 'l'
  str.charAt(2) = 'p'
  str.charAt(3) = 'h'
  str.charAt(4) = 'a'
  str.charAt(5) = ' '
  str.charAt(6) = 'b'
  str.charAt(7) = 'r'
  str.charAt(8) = 'a'
  str.charAt(9) = 'v'
  str.charAt(10) = 'o'
  str.charAt(11) = ' '
  str.charAt(12) = 'c'
  str.charAt(13) = 'h'
  str.charAt(14) = 'a'
  str.charAt(15) = 'r'
  str.charAt(16) = 'l'
  str.charAt(17) = 'i'
  str.charAt(18) = 'e'
```

What else can you do with a `String`? In Listing 6.5 on page 176, `StringValueDemonstration.java`, we saw the `toUpperCase()`, `toLowerCase()`, and `substring(start, end)` methods. The first two methods return a copy of the `String` on which they are called, one containing the `Character.toUpperCase(ch)` result for every character in the original string (or `Character.toLowerCase(ch)`, as appropriate).

`substring(start, end)` takes two **int** values and returns a new `String` containing the character sequence starting at the given `start` location (note in previous output shows `String` like `ArrayList` and arrays are indexed from 0) up to but not including the `end` position.

There is an overloaded definition of `substring(start)`; it returns a new `String` containing the character sequence starting at the `start` location and continuing to the end of the `String`. (Quick review: an *overloaded* method is one where there are more than one with the same name, only differentiated by their headers. In this case, one version has two integer parameters, the other only one.)

The `indexOf` method takes a `String` parameter and returns the index of the left-most occurrence of the parameter in the `String` on which `indexOf` was called or -1 if there is no match. There is an overloaded version that takes an character and returns the index of the left-most occurrence or -1. Each has another overloaded variation that takes a second parameter, an index where the search should start. It returns the left-most occurrence *at or after* the given index. `indexOf` is used in `GuessableWord` to count the number of underscores remaining in the word to guess.

```
92    public int unguessedLetterCount() {
93      /** how many matches have been found */
94      int underscoreCount = 0;
95
96      /** where is the most recent underscore found */
97      int justMatchedIndex = showWord.indexOf('_', 0);
98      while (!(justMatchedIndex == -1)) { // negative logic is bad!
99        ++underscoreCount;
100       justMatchedIndex = showWord.indexOf('_', justMatchedIndex + 1);
101     }
102     return underscoreCount;
103   }
```

Listing 10.9: `GuessableWord`: `unguessedLetterCount`

On line 97, `justMatchedIndex` is initialized to the index of the left-most underscore in the field `showWord`; `showWord` was initialized to contain an underscore and a space for each letter to be guessed (double-spaces the word to make it easier to count the number of characters for the player).

To count the number of letters as yet unguessed, this method loops through the shown word, matching `'_'` characters *after the most recent match*. Each time a match is found, a counter is incremented. When no more matches are to be found, the current count is the total number of underscores.

Line 98 is a sentinel-controlled loop. For teaching purposes, to make it clear that it is a sentinel-controlled loop, the condition on the **while** loop is left in a negative logical form. The sentinel is a location of -1 because -1 is never a valid index into a `String`.

When designing a sentinel-controlled loop and choosing a sentinel, a good rule of thumb is to use a value that *cannot* appear as a legitimate value. If the sentinel *could* be a legal value, how can your program tell the difference between a legitimate and a sentinel occurrence? Once you define the context necessary to differentiate between the two values, you have defined your actual sentinel value, the contextualized occurrence of the value which is never a legitimate value.

`String` is special in Java in that it is the only object type for which you can directly write literal values. One reason that it is immutable is so that it behaves as much as possible like a plain old data type. The biggest departure in behavior between POD and `String` is in comparing values.

String.compareTo(String)

Consider writing a method that takes two `int` parameters and returns the larger of the two values. Consider how you would write this method, `myMax`, for a moment before you read on.

The method should return `int` as well as take two `int` parameters. Since the parameters are arbitrary values (they are not heights or coordinates or anything), a and b make sense as names. The body of the method should be an `if` statement comparing the two numbers and returning the larger value:

```java
int myMax(int a, int b) {
  if (a > b) {
    return a;
  } else {
    return b;
  }
}
```

Convince yourself that this works by walking through the code with a few different values. In particular, what happens when the two integers are equal?

Looking at the code, we see a Boolean expression using the > comparison operator. If we want to overload `myMax` so that it works with `char` or `double`, the plain old data types, the body of the overloaded methods would look identical; only the header line changes.

Since `String` is supposed to behave like a POD, it is tempting to try comparing two `String` using > (or >= or even ==). Java does not compile the following code:

```java
String myMax(String a, String b) {
  if (a > b) {
    return a;
  } else {
    return b;
  }
}
```

The compiler gives the following error message (this output was edited to put the error message in the middle of the code):

```java
String myMax(String a, String b) {
  if (a > b) {
      ^
      StringCompare.java:5: operator > cannot be
      applied to java.lang.String,java.lang.String
    return a;
  } else {
    return b;
  }
}
```

The comparison would *compile* with == or != in the middle, but it would not mean what you probably think that it would mean (more on that below).

Java defines a special `interface` called `Comparable`, and all `Comparable` objects (`String` is one) provide a `compareTo` method. The method takes a `String` as its parameter and compares the string on which `compareTo` is called to the parameter, returning a negative number, 0, or a positive number, depending on the order of the two strings: if the called-on string is before parameter, return a negative number; if the called-on string and parameter are equal, return 0; and if the called-on string comes after the parameter, return a positive number. The following rewrite of myMax works for String:

```
String myMax(String a, String b) {
  if (a.compareTo(b) > 0) { // a after b
    return a;
  } else {
    return b;
  }
}
```

There is also an equals method, defined in Object, that returns **true** if two String objects contain the same sequence of characters, and **false** otherwise. The following expressions are all **true**:

```
"stop".equals("s"+"top")
("abc" + "def").equals("abcdef")
"catfish".substring(3).equals("fish")
```

It is important to note that the following expression returns **false** on the author's machine:

```
"catfish".substring(3) == "fish"
```

This is because ==, when applied to object or *reference* types, compares the references, not the referents. So, since "fish" is a String constructed by a call to **new** before the program starts running, and the result of the call to substring is a newly created String copying the letters 'f', 'i', 's', and 'h' out of a different statically constructed literal String, they are not the exact same object, so the == comparison returns **false**.

While == and != *can* be used to compare objects, the general rule is that they should *not* be used to compare objects. All objects have an equals method, and most types implement a meaningful comparison when they override the version provided by Object.

What Order?

What order is used when comparing String with compareTo? The myMax method neatly sidestepped needing to know. In Java, Strings are compared in *lexicographic order*, which means that they are compared in dictionary order. If two strings contain only lowercase or only uppercase letters, then they are sorted into alphabetic order according to the left-most character that differs between them. "cab" comes before "cat" and "capacitor" because 'b' comes before 't' or 'p'. If one string is a prefix of the other (the letters in one of the strings runs out before a differing character is found), then the shorter word comes first. "cab" also comes before "cabal" and "cable", too.

The "only lowercase or only uppercase" stipulation above was to make the examples easy to include. What actually happens is the two strings are compared, character by character, from left to right. As soon as a position differs, the two Strings compare in the order of the differing characters. For ASCII characters, whichever of the characters has a smaller ASCII code comes first. Because uppercase letters are contiguous and lowercase letters are contiguous, this works out to being alphabetic order as long as we don't compare uppercase to lowercase letters.[9]

The Java String class also provides the compareToIgnoreCase method, which ignores differences between uppercase and lowercase letters. The call "someTHING".compareToIgnoreCase("SoMeThInG") returns 0 (the two strings are equal).

---

[9]For those interested, all uppercase letters sort earlier than any lowercase letter. Digits sort before any uppercase letter.

It is worthwhile to look at the documentation for the `java.lang.String` class because it is a very central class, one used for a lot of useful things. We now look at how we can read a text file on a computer into a `String` or a list of `String`; once we can do that, having `Hangman` pick a different word is as easy as reading a list of words and picking one at random.

Review 10.4

(a) What does the `charAt` method of the `String` class do?

(b) What does immutable mean?

(c) How many `String` objects are created in the following segment of code? Remember that `Strings` are immutable.

```
String x = "Hello";
x = x + x;
```

(d) The Java API has an extensive set of `String` methods. List at least five methods in the `String` class that have a `String` return type. Becoming familiar with the basic Java class methods such as those in the `String` class will help you become a more efficient programmer.

(e) What does the `String`'s `compareTo` method do? What are the possible return values?

(f) Why should you use the `equals` method when comparing strings instead of the equals operator (`==`)?

(g) Consult the Java API and describe in your own words what all of the `substring` methods in the `String` class do (you should be able to find more than one). Give examples of how these work. You may either create your own examples or give ones from the Java API documentation.

10.5   Reading Files

Section 3.1 introduced random access memory (RAM), the memory inside the computer, and disk drives, non-volatile memory stored outside the RAM memory. Because the disk drive's storage capacity is much larger than that of the RAM and the user stores different things on the drive, things they want to be able to find again, to send to others, and to reopen in various computer programs, the disk drive has a *file system*, a method to add user specified names to locations on the disk drive.

This section covers how to interact with the file system, opening a specific file for input and reading the values from a file into a running Java program.

Opening a File for Input

There are two steps in reading input from a text file: connecting a Java data structure to a specific file on the disk (or on the network) and reading and disassembling the contents of the file. We introduce three classes in this section: `java.io.File` and `java.net.URL` to provide an internal representation for a file system object on the disk or the network, and `java.util.Scanner` for scanning through the contents of the file, extracting each word or each line.

Along the way we see a new Java construct, the **try** . . . **catch** block. This is a construct that is a lot like an **if/else** statement except that the first block, the **try** part, is always run and the **catch** part is executed *only* if there is an exception while running the **try** block. An exception is an error or some other unexpected condition.

Applets, Applications, and Security

In addition to the differences between applications and applets discussed in Section 10.2, there are also differences in what each can and cannot do based upon security restrictions. Imagine if visiting the wrong Web page could accidentally expose the entire contents of your home computer including all of your stored passwords and other private information to the owners of the Web site. Browsing the Web would certainly be a dangerous activity! The developers of Java wanted to make the Web more interactive through the use of applets, but not more dangerous — it was important to restrict the access levels of untrusted applets.

While there are many details about what applets can and cannot do according to various security policies, there are two essential restrictions placed on applets.

Applets cannot read from or write to the local file system. If applets were allowed to read arbitrary files on your own personal computer, then they might access sensitive information you would prefer to keep private, such as financial information and e-mails sent and received. If applets were allowed to write to the local file system, they could erase existing files or install viruses without your knowledge. The implications of this security with respect to applets is that you cannot read files in the same way using the File class — instead the applet must use the URL class to read files from the Web server (not your personal computer).

In general, it is not possible to write files directly to the Web server.[10]

Applets can make network connections only to the server from which they are downloaded. Applets running on your computer must be restricted from damaging remote computers. They should also be restricted from accessing possibly sensitive information you have stored on other computers using your local browser's credentials.

An example of the type of damage that can be done by making unauthorized network connections is the distributed denial of service attack that brought down Twitter on the morning of August 6, 2009 (see http://www.nytimes.com/2009/08/08/technology/Internet/08twitter.html?_r=1 for more information). This attack used a botnet, a large collection of compromised computers. The botnet exhausted Twitter's resources by all tweeting at once. The implication of this security restriction is that you can read files from the server where the applet is hosted and you can connect to this same server for other purposes such as distributing the communications between players of a networked multiplayer game.

If you plan on making sophisticated applets, you will want to become more familiar with many more of the security policies placed upon applets. One final detail that is important to note about programming applets is that if you are using an IDE to write your program, be aware that many IDEs run applets in an unrestricted environment (i.e., they can do everything an application can do), but when these same applets are actually posted to a Web site, they will run in a more restricted environment. Practically, what this means is that the applet that runs perfectly in your IDE may not run at all when posted to the Web. In this way, it is always important to thoroughly test your applets once deployed to make sure they function as expected.

Specifying a Filename

Think, for a minute, about your hard drive (or, if you prefer, your USB thumb drive or a networked drive to which your computer is connected). It is composed of a large number of *sectors*, units which are addressed by numbers (the exact nature of the numbering scheme is unimportant).

The computer operating system permits allocation of the sectors for use in *files* and *folders*; a folder can also be called a *directory*. Modern graphical user interfaces use a *desktop metaphor* where files are stored together in folders which can, themselves, be arranged in other folders in a hierarchical storage system. You might keep your Java programs together in a CS101 folder which is inside a SchoolWork folder.

---

[10] It is possible to send information to the Web server via a POST message, much in the way that forms and files are uploaded in music, video, and photo sites. These sites are set up in a way to make sure the uploaded files are safe to upload onto the server and do not contain malicious material such as unauthorized scripts or viruses.

When specifying a file name on the command line, you use slashes between folder and file names. From the point of view of the SchoolWork folder, the NewtonsApple source file would have the name CS101/NewtonsApple.java.[11] The concatenation of folders and finally a file name is called a *file path* or *path name*.

A path name can begin with a slash as in /home/blad/SchoolWork, in which case the hierarchy is anchored at the *root* of the file system.[12] A path name starting with a slash is an *absolute path name*; no matter where you are inside the file system, an absolute path name always refers to exactly the same file on the system.

If a path name does *not* begin with a slash, the name is a *relative path name*; the hierarchy starts at the *current directory* and searches downward from there. The first example here specified that the path CS101/NewtonsApple.java applies if you start in the SchoolWork folder.

We specify file names using relative path names. When you run a Java program, the current folder is the folder where you run it. If I run ExistsFile.java with the following command line:

```
~/Chapter10% java -classpath .:/usr/lib/jvm/fang2.jar ExistsFile pets.txt
```

and the command line parameters are treated as file names, the file specified is ~/Chapter10/pets.txt.

What is ExistsFile? It is a program that demonstrates how to **import** the File class in Java, how to call the constructor, and how to query a File object to see if it refers to a file that exists on the system. The code is as follows:

```java
 1  // package default
 2
 3  import java.io.File;
 4
 5  /**
 6   * A program that reads its command-line arguments, treating each as
 7   * the name of a file. Create an ExistsFile object with the name of the
 8   * file. Then check if the file exists.
 9   */
10  public class ExistsFile {
11    /** Java reference attached to file on file system */
12    File file;
13
14    /**
15     * Create a new ExistsFile with the file pointed to the named file.
16     *
17     * @param  fname  the name of the file to connect to; the named file
18     *                 need not exist (it will be checked in exists()).
19     */
20    public ExistsFile(String fname) {
21      file = new File(fname);
22    }
23
24    /**
25     * The arguments are assumed to be the names of files. Each is opened
26     * and echoed to the screen.
27     *
```

---

[11]Microsoft Windows derivatives have a file system ported from Unix with some changes. The most noticeable difference is the use of \ instead of / between levels in the file name hierarchy. This book consistently uses /; feel free to translate it as you read.

[12]On Microsoft systems this is also done with a letter followed by a colon as in C:. This is known as a disk name. Microsoft operating systems have multiple file system roots.

```
28  * @param  args  command-line arguments; should name files to be
29  *                checked for existence
30  */
31  public static void main(String[] args) {
32    for (int argNdx = 0; argNdx != args.length; ++argNdx) {
33      ExistsFile nextFile = new ExistsFile(args[argNdx]);
34      nextFile.exists();
35    }
36  }
37
38  /**
39   * Check if the file exists, printing an appropriate message.
40   */
41  public void exists() {
42    if (file.exists()) {
43      System.out.println("\"" + file.getName() + "\" is a file.");
44    } else {
45      System.out.println("\"" + file.getName() + "\" is NOT a file.");
46    }
47  }
48 }
```

Listing 10.10: `ExistsFile`

The `main` method is modeled on the one used to cycle across command line parameters. For each command line parameter, an `ExistsFile` object is constructed. On line 21 that constructor calls the `File` constructor. The most common version of the `File` constructor takes a `String` containing a path name. The constructed `File` object then refers to that location in the file system.

In the program, line 42 calls the `exists` method on the newly created `ExistsFile` object. All that method does (see lines 31–36) is call the `exists` method of the `File` object. That Boolean method returns **true** if the file exists and **false** if it does not.

The output of the previously shown command line is

```
~/Chapter10% java -classpath .:/usr/lib/jvm/fang2.jar ExistsFile pets.txt
"pets.txt" is a file.
```

This assumes that there is a file with the given name in the current folder.

try . . . catch and Exceptions

The file `EchoFile.java` is almost identical to `ExistsFile.java`. The difference is that the `exists` method is replaced by an `echo` method:

```
46  public void echo() {
47    if (file.exists() && file.canRead()) {
48      try {
49        Scanner echoScanner = new Scanner(file);
50        String line;
51        while (echoScanner.hasNextLine()) {
52          line = echoScanner.nextLine();
53          System.out.println(line);
54        }
```

```
55        echoScanner.close();
56      } catch (FileNotFoundException e) {
57        System.out.println("PANIC: This should never happen!");
58        e.printStackTrace();
59      }
60    } else {
61      System.out.println("Unable to open \"" + file.getName() +
62        "\" for input");
63    }
64  }
```

Listing 10.11: EchoFile: echo

If the file exists (as in ExistsFile, file is a field that was initialized in the constructor) and the file is readable, then we go into the body of the if statement. If either of the conditions is not met, then we print an error message and return from the method.

We look at lines 49–55 at two levels of abstraction. First, we look at how a file is opened and read line by line. Assuming all goes well, lines 49–55 run and the contents of the file are copied onto the screen. Line 49 creates a Scanner associated with file. A Scanner is an internal Java representation of a text file. The Scanner keeps track of a *current position* inside the file it is reading. As values are read from the Scanner, the current position moves through the input file; a Scanner can read the next word or line *and* can be queried to see if there is anything more to read at the current position.

The while loop on lines 51–54 is a sentinel-controlled loop that runs until there are no more lines of input to be read. Each time through the body of the loop, line is set to the contents of the next line in the file the Scanner is scanning and then line is printed to standard output.

This loop is a special sentinel-controlled loop, an *end-of-file-controlled (eof-controlled) loop*. The hasNext and hasNextLine methods return true so long as the current position in the file is not at the end of the file. The loop ends when the input file is exhausted.

Assuming pets.txt contains the names of one author's family pets, the output of running this program would be

```
~/Chapter10% java -classpath .:/usr/lib/jvm/fang2.jar EchoFile pets.txt
Explorer
Frodo
Grace Murray Hopper
```

What could go wrong?   When associating a Scanner with a file in the file system, many things could go wrong: the file might not exist (because some folder in the path name does not exist or the file itself does not exist); the file might be protected so that only authorized users can read it (imagine a password file); even if the file exists and is readable, something could change while the program is running which changes things (a different program could delete or replace the file); if the file is on removable media, the entire device containing the file could be ripped out (think pulling a USB thumbdrive or disconnecting an MP3 player).

One way to deal with this would be to provide a Scanner predicate, allIsWell. After each call to next, the programmer is expected to call allIsWell to check if there was an error or not. Such an if statement at line 53 would more than double the size of this loop. Remember, too, that similar checks would be necessary after the constructor and the call to close.

There would be a lot of if statements. So many, in fact, that a lot of programmers would skip putting them in; most of the time, if the file exists, reading the whole thing finishes with no problems. So if we just check on the constructor, then we are "safe." Of course, we aren't really safe; we just get away with ignoring errors most of the time. When errors happen, our program crashes with ugly error messages.

Many older programming languages use a system similar to the one described, and error checks were routinely ignored. To avoid this *and* keep the code uncluttered with the error checks, Java uses *exceptions*. An exception is a software signal that Java can **throw** to indicate an *exceptional condition*. Most exceptional conditions are errors.

An `Exception` (a Java type) is an object that a method can construct and **throw**. When thrown, the exception requires the running program to terminate the current method call and the method that called that and the method that called that and so on until it reaches a **try** . . . **catch** block. If there is no such block and Java gets up to `main`, the program terminates because of the exception. The author assumes that every student reading has seen the dread

```
Exception in thread "main" java.lang.NullPointerException
```

message. This is the Java Virtual Machine catching the exception.

The programmer can wrap a method that might throw an exception in a **try** block followed by some number of **catch** phrases. Lines 52–58 in `echo` are an example of code within a **try** block. If any problem occurs, an exception is thrown and the **catch** block runs with the parameter set to the exception thrown.

If the file named does not exist, the `Scanner` constructor throws an exception, one specifying that the file does not exist. We specifically catch that kind of exception on line 59, and the block on lines 59–62 executes with `c` set to the exception thrown.

The `printStackTrace` method of exceptions prints out where the error occurred (by giving what Java methods were executing when it occurred). Robustly dealing with exceptions is very sophisticated; this book catches them and, in general, ends the current task or, if nothing more can be done, ends the program.

The Java template for a **try** . . . **catch**...**finally** statement is

```
<exceptionalStatements> := <statement>*


<tryCatchFinallyStatement> :=
    try {
        <exceptionalStatements>
    } catch (<exceptionType1> <identifier1>) {
        <statement>*
    } [ catch (<exceptionTypei> <identifieri>) {
        <statement>*
    } ]*
    [ finally {
        <statement>*
    } ]

<statement> := <localVariableDefinition> |
               <expression>; |
               <forStatement> |
               <ifStatement> |
               <tryCatchFinallyStatement> |
               <block>
```

This says that the keyword **try** comes before a block. In the block, go the statements that might cause an exception. After the block, go one or more **catch** clauses. After the keyword **catch** comes a type/identifier pair, creating what is effectively a formal parameter for the **catch** clause. The identifier is in scope for the block of the catch clause. Optionally, a **finally** clause comes at the end.

If an exception happens while the code in the **try** block is being processed, then the execution of that code stops and control passes to the first matching **catch** clause. A **catch** clause matches if the exception thrown can be assigned to the formal parameter of the **catch** clause (if the type of the exception thrown is a subclass of the type of exception caught). No matter whether the `try` block completed *or* a `catch` clause completed, the `finally` block is executed before the statement ends.

Reading a File into a Collection

How can you read the contents of a text file into a collection? We write two variations on this theme: one that reads the file word by word and one that reads the file line by line. Each program get the name of exactly one file to read from the command line. It then reads the file using an appropriate eof-controlled loop, adding elements to a list of `String`. Finally we print out all of the entries in the list so that we can see how the file was read. The next section uses the list of lines read as the list of phrases for playing `Hangman`.

Reading a Text File by *Word*

The `main` method is a lot like that in the echo and exists programs. The biggest differences are that the program expects exactly one file name command line argument. We check the size of the argument array and do the work only if there is a single argument. If the number of arguments is wrong, print an error message and let `main` finish.

```
34   public static void main(String[] args) {
35     if (args.length == 1) {
36       String fname = args[0];
37       TextFileByWord byWord = new TextFileByWord();
38       byWord.listLoadFromFile(fname);
39       System.out.println("----- listPrint -----");
40       byWord.listPrint();
41       System.out.println("----- listPrint -----");
42       System.out.println("There were " + byWord.listSize() +
43         " words in " + fname);
44     } else {
45       System.out.println(
46         "Usage: provide exactly one (1) file name on command-line.");
47       System.out.println("Program Terminating");
48     }
49   }
```

Listing 10.12: `TextFileByWord`: `main`

The other difference is that the `TextFileByWord` object has a larger public protocol: the default constructor, the `listLoadFromFile` method (which now takes the file name), a `listPrint` method, and a `listSize` method. This is an attempt to make sure each method has a single, well-defined purpose. While the printing could have been included directly in the `loadListFromFile` method, it would have made using the same code in a program that did not print out the contents impossible (or require a new and different load method). Single-purpose methods mean we can combine them as we see fit in the order we choose to call them.

`listSize` and `listPrint` are fairly obvious, being based on code we saw when we started working with single-dimensional `ArrayLists`:

`strings` is initialized with an empty `ArrayList<String>` in the constructor (not shown). When a file is successfully read, as in Listing 10.14, `strings` refers to the newly read list. This means that `listSize` can safely call `strings.size` (`strings` is not `null`) and `listPrint` can safely call `strings.size` and `strings.get`.

```
17   ArrayList<String> strings;
82   public void listPrint() {
83     for (int i = 0; i != strings.size(); ++i) {
84       System.out.println(strings.get(i));
85     }
86   }
93   public int listSize() {
94     return strings.size();
95   }
```

Listing 10.13: TextFileByWord: the collection

It would have been possible to include the marker lines, lines 39 and 41 in main, directly in listPrint. Why would this be a bad idea?

This code is based on that seen in echoFile earlier in this chapter.

```
57   public void listLoadFromFile(String fname) {
58     File file = new File(fname);
59     if (file.exists() && file.canRead()) {
60       try {
61         ArrayList<String> localStrings = new ArrayList<String>();
62         Scanner scanner = new Scanner(file);
63         String word;
64         while (scanner.hasNext()) {
65           word = scanner.next();
66           localStrings.add(word);
67         }
68         strings = localStrings;
69         scanner.close();
70       } catch (FileNotFoundException e) {
71         System.out.println("PANIC: This should never happen!");
72         e.printStackTrace();
73       }
74     } else {
75       System.out.println("Unable to open \"" + fname + "\" for input");
76     }
77   }
```

Listing 10.14: TextFileByWord: listLoadFromFile

listLoadFromFile, based on EchoFile.echo in Listing 10.11 on page 323, associates a Scanner with the named file (if the file exists and can be read). The **try** . . . **catch** construct protects against a FileNotFoundException. Assuming the loop finishes (without an error), the scanner is closed as all files should be closed and, because there was no error, the newly read list is assigned to strings.

To read *word by word*, the Scanner methods hasNext and next are used to check for and read the next *token*. By default, Scanner breaks its input up on whitespace; each value returned by next is a string of non-whitespace characters. The output of this program, when run on pets.txt, is

```
~/Chapter10% java -classpath .:/usr/lib/jvm/fang2.jar \
            TextFileByWord pets.txt
----- listPrint -----
Explorer
Frodo
Grace
Murray
Hopper
----- listPrint -----
There were 5 words in pets.txt
```

Why five when there are only three pets? Because words are separated by whitespace, the last pet name, "Grace Murray Hopper," is parsed as three separate tokens. If we look back at the echoed content of the file, there are five separate words, one on each of the first two lines and three on the third line; the output is what we should expect.

What if we used a different file, say numbers.txt?

```
~/Chapter10% java -classpath .:/usr/lib/jvm/fang2.jar \
            EchoFile numbers.txt
100 101
3.1415
1000000

eins 2 THREE IV
```

Key things to note about the contents of the file: there is a mix of "numbers" and "words." But Scanner uses whitespace to mark out words. There are only words, some of which have digits as characters. How many words are there in numbers.txt?

```
~/Chapter10% java -classpath .:/usr/lib/jvm/fang2.jar \
            TextFileByWord numbers.txt
----- listPrint -----
100
101
3.1415
1000000
eins
2
THREE
IV
----- listPrint -----
There were 8 words in numbers.txt
```

It is worth noting that Scanner does have nextInt and nextDouble, both capable of reading text representation of a number and converting it to an **int** or **double** with the appropriate value; we use them in the following chapters.

Reading a Text File by *Line*

To read a file line by line with a Scanner is almost the same as reading it word by word. The next and hasNext methods are replaced with calls to the nextLine and hasNextLine methods. TextFileByLine.java is the same as TextFileByWord.java except for the contents of the listLoadFromFile method:

```
57  public void listLoadFromFile(String fname) {
58    File file = new File(fname);
59    if (file.exists() && file.canRead()) {
60      try {
61        ArrayList<String> localStrings = new ArrayList<String>();
62        Scanner scanner = new Scanner(file);
63        String line;
64        while (scanner.hasNextLine()) {
65          line = scanner.nextLine();
66          localStrings.add(line);
67        }
68        strings = localStrings;
69        scanner.close();
70      } catch (FileNotFoundException e) {
71        System.out.println("PANIC: This should never happen!");
72        e.printStackTrace();
73      }
74    } else {
75      System.out.println("Unable to open \"" + fname + "\" for input");
76    }
77  }
```

Listing 10.15: TextFileByLine: listLoadFromFile

Running this program generates the following output:

```
~/Chapter10% java -classpath .:/usr/lib/jvm/fang2.jar \
            TextFileByWord pets.txt
----- listPrint -----
Explorer
Frodo
Grace Murray Hopper
----- listPrint -----
There were 3 lines in pets.txt

~/Chapter10% java -classpath .:/usr/lib/jvm/fang2.jar \
            TextFileByWord numbers.txt
----- listPrint -----
100 101
3.1415
1000000

eins 2 THREE IV
----- listPrint -----
There were 5 lines in numbers.txt
```

"Grace Murray Hopper" is treated as a single line (the line was read *including* the embedded whitespace) and the fourth line in numbers.txt, a blank line, is read and treated as a line. Calling nextLine reads from the current file position to the end of the current line. The end of a line is marked by a special sequence of characters.

Among the characters in the ASCII sequence are non-printing *control* characters. One is the null character, '\0'. Two others are the *carriage return* character, '\r', and the *new line* character, '\n'. Different operating systems use different combinations of carriage return and new line characters to mark the end of the line.[13] The Scanner uses the native version of end-of-line marker for the system on which it is running.

The combination of `try . . . catch` and the eof-controlled `while` loop using a Scanner is a very important Java idiom. Many program assignments in the remainder of this book call for reading a file of a given format. It is worth practicing with this construct until it becomes comfortable.

Using URL Input in Applets

All of the above examples used the class File for connecting the Java program to a file on the local disk. Applets are restricted from reading files directly, but they can read files using the URL class instead of the File class.

Most of the programs in this section followed a similar pattern: get a file name, construct a File, use the File to construct a Scanner, use the Scanner to read the information. Using a URL object in an applet is similar: get a file name, construct a URL, use the URL.getInputStream() method and construct a Scanner, use the Scanner to read the information.

```
File file = new File(fname);
if(file.exists() && file.canRead()) {
    Scanner scanner
      = new Scanner(file);
    ... read contents
}
```

```
URL url = MyClass.class.getResource(fname);
if(url != null) {
    Scanner scanner
      = new Scanner(url.openStream());
    ... read contents
}
```

Similar to using the File class, the path of the file must be specified. In this example, the current path is the path to the MyClass class file, and the name fname is interpreted relative to this path. For example, if MyClass is located on the server at http://www.fangengine.org/example/MyClass.class, and fname is "ch10/contents.txt", the snippet looks for the file http://www.fangengine.org/example/ch10/contents.txt, the base URL of MyClass, http://www.fangengine.org/example/ plus fname. In the event that the supplied URL does not exist at that location, then the result from calling getResource returns **null**. Checking that url != **null** is similar to checking for file.exists() && file.canRead() for a file.

The code comparing opening a Scanner with File and with URL is pure Java and generalizes to all applications and applets. FANG provides a convenient way to get the URL in the Game class via the getGameResource method. This method returns a game resource as a URL relative to package of a particular game. For example, if your game were in the package ch10, then you could put all of the files and resources in their own folder called ch10/resources. To get the URL pointing to a particular resource, you could make a call such as getGameResource("resources/words.txt").

Review 10.5

(a) What is a File? What is a URL? What do they have in common in this section?

    (a) How is a Scanner constructed using a File? Include the protective **if** statement to make sure all is well with the file.

    (b) How is a Scanner constructed using a URL? Include the protective **if** statement to make sure all is well with the URL.

---

[13]Unix (and Linux) uses \r, MacOS uses \n, and Microsoft operating systems use \r\n.

(b) What is the *sentinel* condition when reading a `Scanner` by word?

(c) Write the loop to read a `Scanner` line by line and print the values to standard output.

10.6   Finishing Hangman

Now it is time to finish the `Hangman` program. First, the program reads a named file for potential words and selects one from the list at random. The program removes each word as it is used to avoid repeats. We then look at the `AlphabetSelector` object, in particular the code that checks for mouse clicks on sprites that are inside a `CompositeSprite`.

Replacing the Stub

We now know how to get the command line arguments provided to our FANG program, how to treat such an argument as the name of a file, and how to open that file for input, reading the contents into a collection.

Before we look at the code, how are we going to store the "words" in the data file? Are we playing `Hangman` with single words or do we permit multi-word phrases? Looking at the popularity of game shows based on the same premise as `Hangman`, we see that permitting either words or phrases makes sense.

If we permit embedded spaces in a phrase, how does the program know where a phrase begins or ends? One phrase per line is easy to parse and easy to explain to possible creators of phrase files.

If we cannot read the file for input, or there is no named file, then we end the program. This is because we have no way to select a word for the player to guess.

Listing 10.16 shows the replacement `pickPhrase` method. The line numbers changed because of the additional methods (e.g., `listLoadFromFile`, `getFname`) and fields.

```
32    /** the list of possible phrases to choose for the player to guess */
33    ArrayList<String> phrases = null;
243   private String pickPhrase() {
244     if ((phrases == null) || phrases.isEmpty()) {
245       listLoadFromFile(getFname());
246     }
247     if (phrases == null) {
248       return "cats and dogs";//
249     }
250     int phraseNdx = randomInt(0, phrases.size());
251     return phrases.remove(phraseNdx);
252   }
```

Listing 10.16: `Hangman`: `pickPhrase`

If the list of strings, `phrases`, is **null** or empty, this method calls `listLoadFromFile` that is almost identical to that in `TextFileByLine`. If, after trying to load `phrases` it remains **null**, return the stub phrase. This makes sure that if there is a problem the game can go on.

When `phrases` is not empty (by loading, if necessary), a random phrase index is selected, that phrase is removed from the list, and the removed phrase is returned as the result of `pickPhrase`. This code takes advantage of the fact that `ArrayList.remove` returns the element that was removed.

The `getFilename` method checks for a program argument named `"words"` first; if there is one, that is assumed to be the name of the file or resource for finding the word list. If there is none, then the method gets the unnamed arguments and returns the first one. If, for some reason, no word file name is available, the method returns `"phrases.txt"`.

```
113    private String getFname() {
114      // try to use the named parameter from the applet/application
115      String name = getParameter("words");
116
117      if (name != null) {
118        return name;
119      }
120      // try to use the unnamed parameter from the application
121      ArrayList<String> args = InitializeApplication.getUnnamedArgs();
122      if (args.size() > 0) {
123        return args.get(0);
124      } else {
125        // give up - we don't have a file name
126        return "phrases.txt";
127      }
128    }
```

Listing 10.17: Hangman: getFilename

If it is passed a null file name or there is some other problem reading the word file, listLoadFromFile prints a message to standard output and returns, leaving phrases set to null (and we get the stub phrase).

If all goes well, listLoadFromFile converts all phrases to lowercase because AlphabetSelector has no shift key. That leads us to the only remaining tricky code: AlphabetSelector.

Tracking Used Letters

In RescueMission, we used nested count-controlled loops to check each swimmer for intersection with the rescue ring. Almost the same code could have been used to determine whether the user had clicked the mouse inside of any swimmers. That code is the conceptual basis of the selectedChar method in AlphabetSelector.

```
114    private LetterSprite selectedChar(Location2D insideClick) {
115      LetterSprite selected = null;
116      if (insideClick != null) {
117        for (int row = 0; row != letters.size(); ++row) {
118          ArrayList<LetterSprite> currRow = letters.get(row);
119          for (int column = 0; column != currRow.size(); ++column) {
120            LetterSprite curr = currRow.get(column);
121            if (curr.intersects(insideClick) && curr.isReady()) {
122              selected = curr;
123            }
124          }
125        }
126      }
127      return selected;
128    }
```

Listing 10.18: AlphabetSelector: selectedChar

The private selectedChar takes a mouse click as a parameter, returning a reference to the *ready* LetterSprite with which the click intersects and null if there is no such sprite. Remember that LetterSprite

Figure 10.2: Hangman with the AlphabetSelector

has the ready and the used state. The code uses nested **for** loops to check each letter in the list of lists inside the object.

Figure 10.2 shows the poor fellow about to be rescued from the gallows. Notice how the letters change state depending on whether or not they have been clicked. The j LetterSprite is about to be returned from selectedChar.

selectedChar is overloaded. The signature of the one in Listing 10.18 takes a Location2D, the FANG class representing two-dimensional points (such as where a mouse has been clicked).

Listing 10.19 shows the no-parameter version. This method is **public**. Remember that overloaded methods are differentiated only on their signatures, so that neither access level nor return type plays any part in that.

```
38  public char selectedChar() {
39    char letter = '\0';
40    Location2D outsideClick = Game.getCurrentGame().getClick2D();
41    if (outsideClick != null) {
42      Location2D insideClick = getFrameLocation(outsideClick);
43      LetterSprite letterSprite = selectedChar(insideClick);
```

```
44      if (letterSprite != null) {
45         letterSprite.startUsed();
46         letter = letterSprite.getLetter();
47      }
48   }
49   return letter;
50 }
```

Listing 10.19: `AlphabetSelector: selectedChar`

Line 40 calls `getClick2D` on the current game to get the player's mouse click. If the value is non-`null`, then it is translated from the game's coordinates to the `CompositeSprite`'s coordinates.

A `CompositeSprite` has sprites inside it and they each have a location, which is in *sprite coordinates*. The mouse click (if there is one) is in *screen coordinates*. To check for intersection, the mouse click and the sprite must both be in the same coordinate space.

Line 40 uses `CompositeSprite.getFrameLocation` to translate the click. The method takes a `Location2D` relative to the origin in the game with (0.0, 0.0) in the upper-left corner and transforms it into the coordinate system of the sprite where (0.0, 0.0) is located at the center of the sprite.

The transformation also takes into account rotation and scaling. This is why the parameter passed to `selectedChar(Location2D)` is called `insideClick`, to communicate to other programmers that the location must be in sprite coordinates.

If the value returned from `selectedChar(Location2D)` is non-`null`, then the `LetterSprite` is set to the used state and the letter represented on the letter sprite is returned as the value of `selectedChar()`.

Review 10.6

(a) How are overloaded methods differentiated by Java?

(b) Under what conditions does the `pickPhrase` in the final `Hangman` return the stub phrase?

(c) What method translates a *screen location* into a `CompositeSprite` *sprite location*? Look up in the documentation the name of the method to go the other way.

(d) The default file name, `"phrases.txt,"` appears on line 126 of `Hangman.java`, and the default phrase, `"cats and dogs,"` appears, directly in the code, on line 248. Does this strike you as good software engineering practice? What would be a better approach?

10.7 Summary

Starting Programs

All Java application programs begin by calling the `main` method belonging to the class named on the `java` command line. The header of `main` is

```
public static void main(String[] args)
```

`args` is an *array* of `String`.

An *applet* begins with a call to `init`.

To run as an application, FANG uses a "pretend" `main`, **void** `InitializeApplication.fangMain(String[] args)`. This method is the last method called from `main` (the real one) in a FANG application. It starts the FANG game as if it were an applet running inside a Web browser.

Never call `InitializeApplication.fangMain` unless you are writing a `main` for a FANG program.

Arrays

Arrays are containers. As in `ArrayList`, it is possible to access individual elements. None of the syntax is the same:

Array	ArrayList	Description
`array.length`	`list.size()`	The array exposes a *field* whereas the list exposes a method.
`array[i]`	`list.get(i)`	The array uses square brackets to indicate individual items.
`array[i] = "x"`	`list.set(i, "x");`	The square brackets generate the element location so that it can be used to `get` and `set` the given element.
`array - new String[n]`	`list = new ArrayList<String>()`	The array constructor is called when square brackets containing the number of elements is appended to the element type. The default constructor is called for each of the `n` element locations as part of construction; while entries can be reset, the number of elements in an array cannot be changed after construction. The list is initially empty; `add` and `remove`, expand and contract the list as necessary to fit the current number of elements.

`while`

The `for` loop is not the only loop construct Java provides. The `while` loop is a loop that takes a Boolean expression, executes the body of the loop, and reevaluates the expression. The body of the loop is executed so long as the expression is `true`.

The `while` loop is used for loops where the number of times the loop runs is not known when the loop begins. If the count is known, a *count-controlled loop* using `for` makes sense.

A `while` loop can be *sentinel-controlled*: it runs until some sentinel or "guard" condition happens indicating that the loop should stop.

Exceptions

Java run-time errors are signaled using *exceptions*, types derived from `Exception`. Code can *catch* exceptions and attempt to recover from them (if that is possible) or give the user some meaningful error message. If an exception is *thrown* and not caught, the program crashes.

The construct for catching exception is the `try . . . catch` statement. The code, which can throw an exception, is put in the `try` block, and `catch` clauses are supplied for all types of exceptions that are to be caught. If an exception is thrown, the first matching `catch` is invoked. A `try . . . catch` statement can have a `finally` clause: no matter how the statement finished, the `finally` clause is executed on the way out.

Reading Files

A `File` object represents a file in the file system. It is constructed with the *path* to the file. A file path can be relative or absolute. When a file is constructed, it provides methods to test if the program can use the file: `exists` for if the file exists, `canRead` for if the file can be read, and `canWrite` for if the file can be written.

A `URL` object represents a *Uniform Resource Locator*, a reference to a resource somewhere on the Web. In FANG, a `URL` is typically created by calling `Game.getGameResource` with the name of a game resource file.

Either a `File` or an `InputStream` (`URL.openStream()`) can be used to construct a `Scanner`.

A `Scanner` is an input reading class designed to take an input text file apart into *tokens*. A `Scanner` can easily read a file *word-by-word* or *line-by-line*:

```
Scanner scanner;
// initialize scanner here
while (scanner.hasNext()) {
  String word = scanner.next();
  // do what you want with each word
}
scanner.close()
```

```
Scanner scanner;
// initialize scanner here
while (scanner.hasNextLine()) {
  String line = scanner.nextLine();
  // do what you want with each line
}
scanner.close()
```

10.8   Chapter Review Exercises

Review Exercise 10.1 Write a **for** loop that concatenates all of the arguments passed in to `main` and prints them on the console. This should *not* be a FANG program.

Review Exercise 10.2 Given the following **for** loop:

```
int x;
String separator = "";
for (x = 0; x < 100; x = x + 19) {
  System.out.print(separator + x);
  separator = ", ";
}
```

(a) What is the output generated by this loop?

(b) Write an equivalent **while** loop.

Review Exercise 10.3 What parameters are passed to a `File` constructor? What do they mean?

Review Exercise 10.4 What parameters are passed to `Game.getGameResource`? What do they mean?

Review Exercise 10.5 How do you construct a `Scanner` from a `File`?

Review Exercise 10.6 How do you construct a `Scanner` from a `URL`?

Java Templates

```
<whileStatement> ::= while (<continuation>)
                        <statement>
```

```
<exceptionalStatements> := <statement>*

<tryCatchFinallyStatement> :=
    try {
        <exceptionalStatements>
    } catch (<exceptionType1> <identifier1>) {
        <statement>*
    } [ catch (<exceptionTypei> <identifieri>) {
        <statement>*
    } ]*
    [ finally {
        <statement>*
    } ]

<statement> := <localVariableDefinition> |
              <expression>; |
              <forStatement> |
              <whileStatement> |
              <ifStatement> |
              <tryCatchFinallyStatement> |
              <block>
```

Review Exercise 10.7 The following setup method is for putting words all over the screen based upon input from a text file. Ideally, the text file loaded exists, but in case it does not, an appropriate error message should be displayed. Modify the following code to provide a meaningful and visible error message in the event the file to be loaded does not exist. Do not use System.out in your modified code.

```java
@Override
public void setup() {
  try {
    File file = new File("wordCloud.txt");
    Scanner scanner = new Scanner(file);
    for (String word = scanner.next(); word.charAt(0) != 'q';
        word = scanner.next()) {
      StringSprite text = new StringSprite(word);
      text.setSize(scanner.nextDouble());
      text.setLocation(scanner.nextDouble(), scanner.nextDouble());

      addSprite(text);
    }
  } catch (FileNotFoundException e) {
  }
}
```

Review Exercise 10.8 Rewrite the following `for` loops as `while` loops

(a)

```
File file = new File("wordCloud.txt");
Scanner scanner = new Scanner(file);
for (String word = scanner.next(); word.charAt(0) != 'q';
    word = scanner.next()) {
  StringSprite text = new StringSprite(word);
  text.setSize(scanner.nextDouble());
  text.setLocation(scanner.nextDouble(), scanner.nextDouble());
  addSprite(text);
}
```

(b)

```
ArrayList<Sprite> bubbles = new ArrayList<Sprite>();
for (int i = 0; i < 10; ++i) {
  Oval oval = new Oval(0.1, 0.1);
  bubbles.add(oval);
}
```

(c)

```
// assume this code comes after previous part
for (int i = 0; i < bubbles.size(); ++i) {
  bubbles.get(i).setLocation((i + 0.5) / 10, (i + 0.5) / 10);
}
```

10.9   Programming Problems

Programming Problem 10.1   Add an introductory mode to one of the games you have written or modified:

(a) Make a new game with an appealing look. Somewhere in the game screen add the message "Press <Spacebar> to Start."

(b) In `advance` of the new game, place the following code:

```
if(getKeyPressed() == ' '){
  Game next = new <YourGameName>();
  addGame(next);
  finishGame();
}
```

Place the new game in the same directory as the old game and run the new game. FANG begins by displaying your new game with the message in it. When the user presses the <Spacebar>, the new game finishes, launching the previous game.

The new level is often referred to as the "attract mode" for the original game. It is a level designed to attract people with quarters to the arcade game version of the game. Most console games have an attract mode as well.

It is typical to design the attract mode to show off how the game is played. You could use a modified version of the game itself, one that plays by itself. The only input it checks for could be the space to advance to the real game.

(c) The next step is to modify the game so that when the game ends it calls addGame with a new attract level and then calls finishGame. The original game is unloaded and a new attract level begins, giving the player the chance to start a new game by pressing space.

Programming Problem 10.2 Make an arcade with three of the games you have written or modified in previous chapters. This is similar to Programming Problem 10.1.

(a) Make a starting game called Arcade. This should show the names of each game as a StringSprite. Provide instruction that the player should click on the name of the game she wants to play.

(b) In Arcade.advance check if any of the StringSprites in the game menu were clicked. When a game entry is clicked, the following lines launch the appropriate game:

```
Game next=new <MenuGameName>();
addGame(next);
finishGame();
```

There is a different type of game constructed for each different game name the player can pick.

It is possible to include the most distinctive sprites from one or another of the three games in the arcade to decorate the menu. It is also possible to combine the arcade menu with the attract mode described in Programming Problem 10.1.

(c) Modify the three games so that when the game ends (or the user presses a "get me out of here" key), the game returns to the Arcade game.

The following code snippet, from an advance method, checks for the Esc key (upper-left hand corner of most keyboards).

```
if(getKeyPressed()==KeyEvent.VK_ESCAPE){
  Game next=new Arcade();
  addGame(next);
  finishGame();
}
```

Programming Problem 10.3

Trivia! In this problem, you will write a basic trivia game. The game will work by loading a trivia file and asking 10 randomized multiple choice questions. This game can be extended in an almost endless variety of ways.

The format of a trivia file Each trivia file contains some number of *questions*. Each question is four lines long with a prompt followed by the correct answer on the next line and two distractors (wrong answers), each on separate lines following the correct answer. Here is an example of what a trivia file could look like:

```
Who are the authors of Simple Games?
Ladd and Jenkins
Tom and Jerry
Rocky and Bowinkle
When was the textbook published?
After 2009
In the dark ages
At the dawn of time
```

(a) Write a class called `QuestionSprite` that extends `CompositeSprite`. This class should have a `StringSprite` called `question` and an `ArrayList` of `StringSprites` called `answers`. It should arrange the questions and answers on the screen without overlapping or extending beyond the screen. You may want to consult the FANG API documentation about the methods `set/getWidth` and `set/getHeight`. For now, the answers should be listed on the screen in the order they are given in the constructor. Here is the public interface of `QuestionSprite`:

```
/**
 * makes a question and any number of given answers.
 * The first answer in the ArrayList is always the right answer
 * and it is followed by distractors.
 *
 * @param question the prompt for the correct answer
 * @param answers the list of candidate answer with the correct
 * answer as the first answer
 */
public QuestionSprite(String question, ArrayList<String> answers)


/**
 * determines if an answer has been clicked
 *
 * @return true if an answer was clicked this frame, false otherwise
 */
public boolean answerClicked()


/**
 * determines if the correct answer has been clicked.  This method
 * should be used in conjunction with answerClicked to determine
 * when the right or wrong answer has been clicked.
 *
 * @return true if the correct answer was clicked this frame, false
 * if no answer has been clicked or the wrong answer has been clicked
 */
public boolean answerClicked()
```

(b) Write and test a class called `TriviaGame` that extends `Game`. During this step, just make and add a `QuestionSprite`. Make sure to test `QuestionSprite` with long and short questions and answers to make sure the formatting is correct.

(c) In `QuestionSprite`, randomize the order of the answers. Here's one strategy for doing this:
    i. Make an `ArrayList` of `Doubles` called `vertical`.
    ii. Iterate over all of the answers and add the y-location to the `vertical`.
    iii. Call the method `Collections.shuffle` on the `vertical`. This randomizes the order of the elements in the `ArrayList`.
    iv. Iterate over the `vertical` and call `setY` on each corresponding element of `answers`.

(d) Test your changes in `TriviaGame`.

(e) Modify `TriviaGame` to read a `Trivia.txt` file that has one question with three answers. Use this question and these answers to make the `QuestionSprite`.

(f) Add an `ArrayList` of `QuestionSprites` called `questions` to the fields of `TriviaGame`. Read from the file `Trivia.txt` to fill the `ArrayList` with `QuestionSprites`. Add only the first `QuestionSprite` to the screen on this step.

(g) After filling `questions` from the file, call `Collections.shuffle` to randomize the order of the questions. Now the first question should appear randomly selected from all questions in `Trivia.txt`.

(h) Add in a score. Every time the player clicks on the wrong answer, a point is deducted. When the player clicks on the right answer, a point is added, the first element of the questions `ArrayList` is removed (both from the `ArrayList` and the screen), and the new first element of questions is displayed.

(i) Make a design decision about how long the game continues. This could be a given number of seconds, number of clicks, or a number of questions. Implement your design decision.

(j) Enhance the look of the game. This could include using pictures for each question, including some simple text animation when the answer selected is right or wrong, or any number of other ideas. Use your creativity.

C
h
a
p
t
e
r

11

Console I/O: Games without FANG

We know half of what we need to know about standard console input and output. To date we have used System.out to print values to standard output. This chapter addresses the missing half by introducing how we read information from standard input. With both standard input and standard output, we can write a game that does not use FANG at all.

11.1 Another Dice Game: Pig

In this chapter we implement a computer-mediated version of the folk dice game *Pig*. *Pig* is a *jeopardy dice game*, a term coined by Reiner Knizia in *Dice Games Properly Explained* [Kni00]. In a jeopardy dice game, players' decisions are between protecting current gains or risking current gains in search of greater gains.

In *Pig*, players take turns rolling a single 6-sided die. If they roll a 1 (a "pig") they lose their turn and add nothing to their score; any other roll is added to their *turn total*. After any roll adding to their turn total the rolling player may choose to *hold*, ending their turn and adding the turn total to their *score*. The winner is the first player with a score greater than or equal to 100.

A console game is limited to text input and text output: no mouse, no sprites, no FANG. The design of Pig is shown in Figure 11.1 on the next page.

The design shows two columns on the screen; the actual program uses only System.out without any screen control (no way to reposition the output point to a given row/column) so that the output is really in one column scrolling off the top as more is printed below.

Notice that the design differentiates between things typed by the players and things printed on the screen by the program. Further, notice that whenever the program expects input from the user, it provides a *prompt*. As with any game we have designed, it is important to keep the player informed as to what is expected of him or her (and when).

There are two phases of the game in the design. Initially the game asks for the players' names. When all of the players are represented, some player types "done" and the initialization of the game is finished. After that the game is played by taking turns.

Looking at the design, one can see the video game loop in action:

- Show the current player his roll,

- Prompt the user for what he wants to do,

- Update the state of the game by either rolling again or holding the total for the turn.

Which player has control alternates by turn. When a player holds or rolls a pig, the state of the game is updated and the next player's turn begins. Notice that each time around all of the players, the game also displays the current standings (in the order in which players take their turns). When a player holds and puts his score over 100, the game is over and the standings are printed one last time, this time *sorted* in descending order by score.

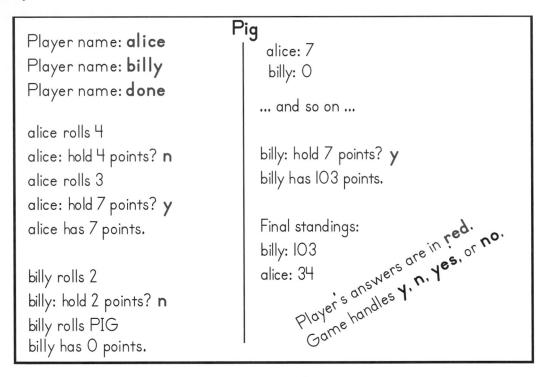

Figure 11.1: Design of *Pig* Game

The remainder of this section focuses on the design of the classes of `Pig`. The chapter then introduces pure console I/O and the idea of sorting a collection.

Pig and Its Classes

As we have seen before, a non-FANG program requires a **public static void** main method. In FANG the default version of this method constructs an object of the right class (the class that is specified on the command line) and calls a particular method on it (`runAsApplication`, though we use the more friendly name, `play`). Basing our class on that, we have, as a first pass for a design, something like this:

```
public class Pig {
  public static void main(String args[])...
  private Pig()...
  private void play()...
}
```

Information Hiding

Why is the Pig constructor **private**? Because it *can* be. Another principle of software engineering is the Need to Know principle: limit the scope and visibility of all fields and methods as much as possible. If a method *can* be **private**, make it **private**. Always prefer the most restrictive visibility possible.

The Pig constructor can be **private** because it is called only in Pig.main (the main method declared inside the Pig class). The only call to the constructor is in a method declared in the same class. A **private** constructor is possible.

Limited visibility is desirable for two reasons, both related to design and, more importantly, redesign of the class. Changing the header of a **private** method or the type of a **private** field can impact only the single Java file in which the change is made. No other file need be edited or even recompiled. Isolating change like this makes changes much less complex.

Similarly, any special requirements of our class, say, that the list of players never be **null** or some such, is documented in the Java file implementing the class *and* **private** fields, and methods can be modified only by changing the source code containing them. This means the programmer should be working at the level of abstraction represented by the class when working on the **private** parts. All non-**static** methods of Pig are declared to be **private** for this reason.

What does play do? Looking at the design, we see that there are three phases of the game: getting the players' names, playing the game, and finishing the game. The first and last phases are not game loops. Getting the players' names could be wrapped up in a method of its own as could announcing the winner of the game (that is what happens when the game ends). Playing the game is, itself, a video game loop. The extended design is

```
public class Pig {
  public static void main(String args[])...
  private Pig()...

  // ----- main game phases -----
  private void getPlayersNames()...
  private void play()...
  private void announceWinner(Player winner)...

  // ----- video game loop -----
  private void showState(Player curr)...
  private void handleUserTurn(Player curr)...
  private boolean continueGame(Player curr)...

  // ----- player list handling -----
  private Player getPlayer(int n)...
  private int indexOf(Player p)...
}
```

Five methods take a `Player` object reference as a parameter and a sixth returns a `Player` object reference. What is a `Player`? We design the class below. For the moment a `Player` holds all of the information necessary to identify players and know how they are doing in the game.

The three video game loop methods take the current player so that they can tell whose turn it is. `showState` shows the player's current score and, if this is the first player, shows the standings of all players. It is possible to show the standings before each player's turn but it seems to make more sense to show them once per round.

The `handleUserTurn` method has a player take a turn. Consider that taking a turn involves showing the player the state of her turn, letting her decide if she wishes to continue, and then updating the state of her turn. This "get user input" portion of the video game loop of `Pig` invokes another video game loop.

The `continueGame` method updates game state and returns **true** if the game should continue and **false** if the game is over. `Pig` ends when one player wins the game. Only one player's score can change during any given turn (the current player), so only one player needs to be checked. In games where any player's state might change during any turn it would be necessary to traverse the list of players, checking each one to see if there was a winner.

The `getPlayer` and `indexOf` methods are for working with the list of `Player` objects. `getPlayer` takes an index into the list of `Players` and returns the `Player` object associated with that location. The `indexOf` method is the inverse function, taking a `Player` in the list of `Players` and returning the index where that `Player` is. The name `indexOf` is a Java standard name for methods that convert from an element to its index (we have seen `String.indexOf` for finding the index of a `String` or **char** in a `String`, for example).

Now, what is a `Player`? Imagine that you were keeping track of an ongoing game of `Pig` with pencil and paper. What information would you keep track of? You need to know whose turn it is (that is the turn number passed to the various methods in `Pig`), and the name and the score for each person playing.

When you find the need to group information together into a unit, that is when you should think of creating a class. It would be possible to design `Pig` without having a `Player` class but keeping the score and the name together in a single object makes life much simpler. What does the interface for the `Player` class look like?

```
public class Player {
  public Player(String name)...
  public String getName()...
  public int getScore()...
  public void takeTurn()...
  public String toString()...
}
```

When announcing the winning player, `Pig` needs access to the name and the score of the winning player. That is why the two `get*` methods are provided. `takeTurn` is the method that gets input from the user. As the name suggests, it actually does much more: it rolls the die, tracking the player's turn score, and, when the player chooses to hold, updates the player's score. It also handles the player rolling a pig, ending his turn without changing his score. As noted earlier, it is another, smaller video game loop.

The `toString` method is a method declared in `Object`, the class that *all* Java classes extend. If a class lists no parent class, then it implicitly **extends** `Object`. The `toString` method returns a `String` representation of the object on which it is called. This permits `print`/`println` methods to print out any object. When a reference to an object is passed to `print` (as in `System.out.print`), the object's `toString` method is called and the result is printed to standard output.

This is an example of *polymorphism*, having many forms. The method has the header **public void** `print(Object obj)` and internally it calls `obj.toString()`. Java calls the lowest overriding implementation of a method, so if `obj` is *really* a `Player`, then the overridden `toString` is called.

Formal, Actual, Static, Dynamic

In the *header* and definition of `public void` `print(Object obj)`, the parameter `obj` is a *formal* parameter. It is said to have a *static* type of `Object`;[1] a static attribute is any attribute of the program that could be known at *compile time*.

When `print` is called, as in `System.out.println(somePlayer)`, the parameter `somePlayer` is an *actual* parameter. In the scope where the call is made, `somePlayer` has a static type that can be determined from the declaration: `Player somePlayer;` The static type is `Player`. Because `somePlayer` is passed into the parameter `obj`, both of these references share *dynamic* type; the dynamic attribute is any attribute that can be known only at *runtime*.

The dynamic type of a reference can be determined only from the call to **new** that returned the reference. The type that was constructed *is* the dynamic type of the object.

```
Player somePlayer;
...
somePlayer = new Player("ralph");
...
System.out.print(somePlayer);
...
```

In the above code we see that the *dynamic* type of `somePlayer` is the same as the *static* type of `somePlayer`. It is not always this easy to determine the dynamic type of a variable or parameter. Consider the code for `print`:

```
public void print(Object obj) {
...
String someString = obj.toString();
...
}
```

What is the *dynamic* type of `obj`? It depends on what actual parameter is matched with the formal parameter `obj`. In the previous listing, `print` is called with `somePlayer`. In that case the dynamic type of `obj` is `Player` and the static type of `obj` is still `Object`.

Why do we care? Because overriding methods permits polymorphic behavior, behavior where the same code (that inside of `print`) behaves differently depending on the *dynamic* type of the objects on which it operates due to overriding of methods (`toString` in this example).

Review 11.1

(a) What does *polymorphic* mean? How does it apply to object-oriented programming?

(b) Define the terms *formal*, *actual*, *static*, and *dynamic*.

(c) How is a method called *polymorphically*?

(d) What is information hiding? How does it produce easier-to-maintain code? What is the rule of thumb about access levels?

---

[1]The term *static attribute* is not directly related to Java's **static** keyword.

11.2 Pure Console I/O

Section 10.2 described how Java programs begin execution: the interpreter begins and looks for the `public static void` main method provided by the class named on the command line. Section 8.2 describes how to use `System.out` to print information on the screen. The following program uses printing to standard output in the main method to implement the quintessential "Hello, World!" program.[2] This program is similar to `HelloWorld.java` in Listing 8.2 but this version does not use FANG, so it must provide its own main method.

```
1   // package default
2
3   /**
4    * Greeting program. Standard output for a non-FANG console I/O program
5    */
6   public class Hello {
7     /**
8      * The main program. Just prints out a greeting on standard output.
9      *
10     * @param  args  command-line arguments; ignored by this program
11     */
12    public static void main(String[] args) {
13      System.out.println("Hello, World!");
14    }
15  }
```

Listing 11.1: `Hello`: Print Generic Greeting

Notice that the method comment for main explicitly states that the parameter, args, is ignored by the method. It is, in almost all cases, bad form to have unused parameters. According to a 1986 study discussed in the software engineering book *Code Complete*([CCA86] cited in [McC04]), methods with unused parameters in the parameter list are twice as likely to contain errors as those without unused parameters. Correlation is not causality, but unused parameters can imply a poorly designed public protocol that could imply a poorly executed implementation.

main is the primary exception to the admonition against having unused method parameters: the main method header must *exactly* match that in the Java language definition in order for the Java interpreter to be able to start the program.

The next program shows two new things: `System.in` is an object much like `System.out` but for standard input (the keyboard) rather than output, and `Scanner` has a constructor that takes an `InputStream`. As we first saw in Chapter 10, a `Scanner` can take apart the text in an input file. In this case the values typed on the keyboard are treated as the values found in the file.

```
1   // package default
2
3   import java.util.Scanner;
4
5   /**
6    * Greeting program. Standard output for a non-FANG console I/O program;
7    * user provides her name at a prompt.
```

---

[2]The "Hello, World!" program is a short text program presented in almost every introduction to a computer programming language. It derives from a sample in Kernighan and Richie's 1974 book *The C Programming Language* [KR78]. The original actually printed "hello, world" without capitals or the exclamation point. The C programming language was developed to implement the original Unix operating system (which, through many twists and turns, begat the Mac OSX and Linux operating systems).

```
 8   */
 9   public class YourNameHere {
10     /**
11      * The main program. Prompt user for her name and print a greeting
12      * for her.
13      *
14      * @param  args  command-line arguments; ignored by this program
15      */
16     public static void main(String[] args) {
17       Scanner keyboard = new Scanner(System.in);
18       System.out.print("What is your name? ");
19       String userName = keyboard.next();
20       System.out.println("Hello, " + userName + "!");
21     }
22   }
```

Listing 11.2: YourNameHere: Personalized Greeting

Line 18 prints a prompt for the user. It is good form to make sure the user knows what to do next (this is important in text programs just as it is with games). Line 19 uses Scanner.next to read from the input associated with the Scanner called keyboard. Since System.in is, by default, associated with the keyboard, the program halts, waiting for the Scanner to finish reading the input. Line 20 prints out a greeting customized for the named user. An example run of the program could look like this:

```
~/Chapter11% java YourNameHere
What is your name? Dr. Marcus Welby
Hello, Dr.!
```

There is something wrong. The program paused until the user pressed the <Enter> key but it read only one word. Why is that?

Looking back at line 19, we see that the next method is used. By default, next parses the input stream into *tokens* where a token is defined as a sequence of non-whitespace characters separated by whitespace characters.

When you call next, the Scanner goes down to the input stream to which it is attached (more on how this corresponds to disk files below) and asks for some number of characters. It reads characters, skipping over all whitespace (actual space characters, tabs, and end-of-line characters; anything for which Character.isWhitespace returns true). Once it sees a non-whitespace character, it keeps reading characters until a whitespace character is found (and the whitespace character is *unread* so that the file read pointer rereads the character the next time the file is read).

One thing to note about using Scanner with the keyboard: on most operating systems the standard configuration has characters delivered to Java for reading *line by line*. Even though the user typed the four characters "Dr. " as the first four characters of the line of input, Java cannot see them until <Enter> is pressed at the end of the line.

There is no universal way to change console input from line-based to character-based mode from Java. Explaining operating system- and shell-specific methods is beyond the scope of this text, so we assume that console input is in line mode for the remainder of the book.

How can we change YourNameHere so that it reads Dr. Welby's whole name? To read a whole line with a Scanner from a text file we use nextLine. That works with a Scanner wrapped around standard input just as it does when reading a file. With line 19 changed (and the program renamed to YourWholeNameHere.java, available in this chapter's sample code) to use nextLine, the earlier console session would look like this:

```
~/Chapter11% java YourWholeNameHere
What is your name? Dr. Marcus Welby
Hello, Dr. Marcus Welby!
```

InputStream Files and Collections

What is an InputStream and how is it different than a File? As we discussed in Chapter 10, a File object is an internal representation of a file in the local file system (typically on a hard drive or some USB storage device). A File refers to a given location in the namespace of the file (the complete path name including hierarchical folder names); there may or may not be an actual file with that name. The File object can be queried to see if the file exists and what rights the program has to the file.

The File object does not refer, in any way, to the *content* of the file. It is possible to instantiate a Scanner with the File object so that the content of the named file is accessible. Under the hood, how does Java represent the content of a file?

The problem facing operating system writers is that information can come from multiple different devices: the hard drive, USB devices, DVD drives, the keyboard, and so forth. One of the operating system's primary functions is to simplify a program's interaction with the actual hardware.

Computer scientists want to banish the details of any given device to the operating system so that they can interact with *any* device without caring about the type of the device. Again, *abstraction* is a powerful tool with which to confront complexity.

The original Unix operating system from the early 1970s treated all devices and files as character sequences. This meant that any program that could process a character sequence could process content coming from the keyboard, the network, a disk, or even some string stored in memory. Standard input and standard output (and the standard error channel) are, internally, just files or just character sequences.

The C programming language, developed for the Unix operating system, is a direct ancestor of modern Java, and the internal view of file contents as sequences of characters is a result of that heritage.

When a Scanner is constructed with a File, the Scanner constructor builds a InputStream associated with the file. A *stream* in this case is just a sequence of characters. InputStream supports read and close, two of the major operations we want to perform on input text files. The read method returns the next character[3] and close disassociates the stream from the content to which it is attached. The InputStream child class FileInputStream can be constructed with a File and gets its stream of characters from the given disk file.

Internally, the InputStream or one of its descendants keeps track of the file read pointer and signals when the end of file is reached (it is possible to indicate the end of file on standard input; the exact key combination to press is operating system dependent).

Beyond String Input

Consider writing a console program that takes two integers and adds them together. The program would not be hard to write: use a Scanner attached to the keyboard (standard input) to read something from the user. If we used next or nextLine we would get back a String. Though there are ways to convert String values to numeric values, we want, if possible, to directly get integers from the user.

Scanner, as we have seen, has nextInt. We can just call that method twice to add a pair of numbers and print the sum:

```
1 // package default
2
3 import java.util.Scanner;
4
```

---

[3]The actual return type is an int rather than a byte. The reason for this discrepancy is not relevant to the current discussion.

```
5   /**
6    * Prompt user for two integers. Print the sum of the two integers.
7    * Program then halts.
8    */
9   public class AddTwoNumbers {
10    /**
11     * The main program. Prompt user for two integers and add them
12     * together. DOES NOT WORK AS EXPECTED!
13     *
14     * @param  args  command-line arguments; ignored by this program
15     */
16    public static void main(String[] args) {
17      System.out.println("AddTwoNumbers:");
18      Scanner keyboard = new Scanner(System.in);
19
20      System.out.print("Number: ");
21      int first = keyboard.nextInt();
22
23      System.out.print("Number: ");
24      int second = keyboard.nextInt();
25
26      System.out.println("Sum of " + first + " + " + second + " = " +
27        first + second);
28    }
29  }
```

Listing 11.3: AddTwoNumbers

When the code is run, the output is

```
~/Chapter11% java AddTwoNumbers
AddTwoNumbers:
Number: 100
Number: 121
Sum of 100 + 121 = 100121
```

What is wrong with the code? The sum of two 3-digit numbers should never be a 6-digit number. Looking at the code, we see that printing the program identifier and the prompts should have no effect on the final sum. The nextInt calls also look right. In fact, when we look at the output for a moment, "100121" = "100" + "121." In line 27, the + operator is being treated not as integer addition but as String concatenation.

Whenever the compiler can determine that the element to the left of a + is a String, then the plus sign means concatenation. The + at the end of line 26 is a concatenation operator; first is converted to a String and tacked onto the end of the String to print. That means the + on line 27 is also interpreted as a concatenation operator.

We need to convince Java to do integer addition of first + second *before* applying the concatenation operator and building the output string. When we want to change the order of evaluation in an expression, we use parentheses. Wrapping parentheses around (first + second) on line 27 yields the following:

```
~/Chapter11% java AddTwoNumbersRight
AddTwoNumbersRight:
Number: 100
Number: 121
Sum of 100 + 121 = 221
```

Again, `AddTwoNumbersRight.java` is included in the chapter's sample code. It differs from the previous listing only in the parentheses in line 27.

Sentinel-controlled Loops and User Input

The final program we examine in this section combines a sentinel-controlled loop with reading input from the user. When we look at our previous programs, it seems that whenever we read information from standard input, we first must print out a prompt on standard output. Rather than having to remember both steps every time we require input, it would make sense to factor the two steps out into a single method that we could call whenever we wanted to read the next line from the user.

The method, `getLine`, defined in lines 22–26, does exactly what we want: given a prompt, it shows the prompt to the user (and even appends a space on the end) and then returns the next line of text typed by the user.

```java
1   // package default
2
3   import java.util.Scanner;
4
5   public class SentinelControlledLoop {
6     /**
7      * static means there is only one; keyboard can be used in multiple
8      * methods
9      */
10    private static Scanner keyboard = new Scanner(System.in);
11
12    /**
13     * Get a line from the user. Prints the prompt on the console followed
14     * by a space. Then waits for user to enter a line and returns the
15     * full line of text to the calling method.
16     *
17     * @param   prompt  the prompt to print for the user.
18     *
19     * @return  the line entered by the user (everything up to but not
20     *          including the <return> key)
21     */
22    public static String getLine(String prompt) {
23      System.out.print(prompt);
24      System.out.print(" ");
25      return keyboard.nextLine();
26    }
27
28    /**
29     * Main program. Uses getLine to prompt user and read lines in a
30     * sentinel controlled loop. User enters the sentinel value "done"
31     * when they want to quit. All other lines are converted to upper-case
32     * and echoed back.
33     *
34     * @param  args  command-line arguments - ignored by this program
35     */
36    public static void main(String[] args) {
```

```
37    String line = "";
38    while (!line.equalsIgnoreCase("done")) {
39      line = getLine("Line to capitalize ('done' to finish):");
40      if (!line.equalsIgnoreCase("done")) {
41        System.out.println(line.toUpperCase());
42      }
43    }
44  }
45 }
```

Listing 11.4: SentinelControlledLoop

Why is keyboard not defined inside of getLine? And what does line 10 actually mean? The keyboard Scanner is opened on standard input and, it is hoped, it can be used to read all user input it is necessary to read. Since we expect to call getLine over and over, it does not make sense to construct a new Scanner to read the next line and then the next line and so on. It makes much more sense to read everything from one Scanner that is shared by all read routines.

Since getLine is called from main and main is **static**, getLine *must* be **static**. As mentioned in Chapter 6, the **static** qualifier is infectious: methods *and* fields accessed directly from **static** methods must be **static**.

The "and fields" part is new. It explains why keyboard must be declared **static**. Why does line 9 have an assignment directly in the line where the field is declared? Because Java permits all fields (just like local variables) to be initialized when they are declared. This book does not use the define and initialize syntax on regular fields because it can be very confusing to understand *when* the initialization takes place.[4] A **static** field must be initialized this way if the initialization is to take place before any other code in the class.

That means the call to **new** in line 9 takes place *before* main is called by Java. We use the in-line initialization syntax for all **static** fields and *only* for **static** fields.

After all of that, main is somewhat anticlimactic. The field line is initialized to the empty string and so long as it is not the word "done", the loop reads a line from the user (using getLine); if the line is not "done", then the line is echoed in upper case.

What happened to the DRY principle? Looking at lines 38 and 40, we see that the same test is done twice in very rapid succession. Why? The problem is known in computer science as the "loop and a half" problem. The problem is where, in the loop, to read a value into line. If we read the value in first thing, as we do here, then there is a problem with the last time through the loop. After having read "done," we should *not* execute the body of the loop. There must be an **if** statement and it must have the same Boolean expression as the **while** statement.

Alternatively we could move the reading of the value from the keyboard from the beginning to the end of the loop. That would mean that the last line would be read and then the loop would cycle back to the top, the Boolean expression would return **false**, and the body of the loop would not execute. The following code shows the idea:

```
36  public static void main(String[] args) {
37    String line = getLine("Line to capitalize ('done' to finish):");
38    while (!line.equalsIgnoreCase("done")) {
39      System.out.println(line.toUpperCase());
40      line = getLine("Line to capitalize ('done' to finish):");
41    }
42  }
```

Listing 11.5: SentinelControlledLoop2

---

[4]Non-**static** fields have values assigned just before the constructor begins execution. It is not *that* hard to explain when, but it is much clearer to have all initialization of fields explicitly written in the constructor so that the programmer can see the order of execution and know all starting values.

We have moved the problem from the last line of input to the *first* line of input. The first time through the body of the loop, what value should `line` have? In line 36, what do we initialize it to? The only real answer is to duplicate the code from line 39 in line 36 as well. So we can choose to have to handle an extra half of a loop at the beginning or the end of the input.

Review 11.2

(a) Explain the difference between `Scanner.next` and `Scanner.nextLine`.

(b) How is a sentinel-controlled loop used to let a user terminate an input loop?

(c) Write a `while` loop that prompts the user for names of stocks, one per line, until they enter "finished."

(d) Modify the `while` loop in the previous question to keep the longest line entered by the user and print it out when the loop ends. Where does the variable for holding the longest have to be declared?

(e) Write a `while` loop that prompts the user for integer test scores. The user should enter a negative number when done.

11.3   Sorting a Collection

Pull all the hearts out of a standard deck of cards and shuffle them. How would you sort them? We want to describe the process in sufficient detail that we could convert it into a computer program. A detailed description of a method of calculation is known as an *algorithm*. An algorithm is a *finite* sequence of explicit, detailed instructions that proceed from an *initial state* through a *finite* series of intermediary states to a *final state*. An algorithm must be finite so that we can write it down in a finite amount of time, and the algorithm must terminate in a finite amount of time as well (hence the finite series of states requirement).

Algorithms can be expressed at various levels of abstraction. We have used a mix of a high-level description in English combined with a more formal description of most of our algorithms in Java.

The initial state for our algorithm is any arbitrary shuffled ordering of the 13 hearts. The final state is the same set of 13 cards in descending order, ace high. Consider, for a moment, how you would sort the deck. Consider how you would *describe* how to sort the deck to an eager child. You can neither see nor touch the cards but you can tell the child what to do with them. And your rules must work for any valid initial state.

Here is a possible description at a fairly high level in English:

```
pick up the deck
while your hand is not empty
  find the largest card in your hand
  swap largest card with the top card in your hand
  place top card on pile on table
```

Assuming the first step in the loop works, the algorithm works (each card added to the pile is the largest remaining, so that the pile is built from biggest to smallest) *and* the algorithm must eventually halt (there are fewer cards in the hand each time through the loop; the hand must eventually be empty).

The only problem is the first step in the algorithm: it is too complicated. We need to describe, in explicit detail, how to find the largest card in the hand.

We now express this algorithm in terms of looking at a card, comparing its value to that of one other card, keeping track of a location in the hand, and swapping a pair of cards. These are pretty much fundamental steps in handling a deck of cards.

```
pick up the deck
while your hand is not empty
  // ----- find the largest card in your hand
  assume top card is largest
  for each card below the top
    if the current card is larger than the largest so far
      largest so far is now current card
  largest so far is largest card
  // -----
  swap largest card with the top card in your hand
  place top card on pile on table
```

This algorithm is not limited to working with cards in a deck. Given an `ArrayList` of objects, we can get any value by index, keep track of a location by keeping its index, and, using `get` and `set`, swap values in the `ArrayList`. The only thing challenging is knowing how to order two objects. We look at how to do that by comparing `Integer` objects using greater than, comparing other objects just by comparing one of their fields, and how to use `compareTo` with `String`.

Sorting Integer Objects

```java
1  // package default
2
3  import java.util.ArrayList;
4  import java.util.Arrays;
5
6  /**
7   * Initialize a literal ArrayList, print it, then sort it and print it
8   * again. The three method sort matches the example algorithm in SCG
9   * chapter 10.
10  */
11 public class SortIntegers {
12   /**
13    * Initialize a list of {@link Integer} values and sort them using an
14    * insertion sort (find largest remaining, put it in the right spot).
15    *
16    * @param  args  command-line arguments ignored by this program
17    */
18   public static void main(String[] args) {
19     System.out.println("SortIntegers:");
20     ArrayList<Integer> theInts = new ArrayList<Integer>(Arrays.asList(9,
21         4, 2, 8, 3, 17, 10, 15));
22
23     System.out.println("Before:");
24     System.out.println(theInts);
25
26     sort(theInts);
27
28     System.out.println("After:");
29     System.out.println(theInts);
30   }
```

```
31
32    /**
33     * Find the index of the largest value inside of aList at or after the
34     * given starting index
35     *
36     * @param   aList       reference to the list in which the index of
37     *                      the largest element is to be found
38     * @param   startIndex  start searching at this index in the list
39     *
40     * @return  a number >= to startIndex, an index into aList; if
41     *          startIndex is out of range, will return startIndex;
42     *          otherwise will always return a valid index
43     */
44    private static int largestIndex(ArrayList<Integer> aList,
45      int startIndex) {
46      int largestNdx = startIndex;
47      for (int contenderNdx = startIndex + 1;
48          contenderNdx != aList.size(); ++contenderNdx) {
49        if (aList.get(contenderNdx) > aList.get(largestNdx)) {
50          largestNdx = contenderNdx;
51        }
52      }
53      return largestNdx;
54    }
55
56    /**
57     * Sort aList in descending order. Uses {@link
58     * #largestIndex(ArrayList, int)} and {@link #swap(ArrayList, int,
59     * int)} to do much of the work.
60     *
61     * @param  aList  the list to sort
62     */
63    private static void sort(ArrayList<Integer> aList) {
64      for (int firstUnsortedIndex = 0; firstUnsortedIndex != aList.size();
65          ++firstUnsortedIndex) {
66        int largestIndex = largestIndex(aList, firstUnsortedIndex);
67        swap(aList, firstUnsortedIndex, largestIndex);
68      }
69    }
70
71    /**
72     * Swap elements aList[a] and aList[b] (using array notation). Works
73     * for all valid index value for a and b (even if they are equal).
74     * Does not do anything crafty when they are equal.
75     *
76     * @param  aList  list in which elements should be changed
77     * @param  a      an index into aList
78     * @param  b      an index into aList
79     */
80    private static void swap(ArrayList<Integer> aList, int a, int b) {
```

```
81      Integer temp = aList.get(a);
82      aList.set(a, aList.get(b));
83      aList.set(b, temp);
84    }
85  }
```

Listing 11.6: SortIntegers

In SortIntegers, lines 20–21 initialize the variable theInts with a *literal list*. A literal value is one typed into the source code. The java.utils.Arrays package contains **static** methods for working with arrays. The one used here takes an arbitrary number of arguments and returns a List containing the right element type. The ArrayList constructor can take a list and copy all of the elements into the newly created ArrayList.

Line 24 and line 29 print out the contents of theInts. Because ArrayList overrides toString in a sensible way (it calls toString on all of the elements in the list, wrapping them in square brackets and separating them with commas), we can just pass the object to println. The output of this program is

```
~/Chapter11% java SortIntegers
SortIntegers:
Before:
[9, 4, 2, 8, 3, 17, 10, 15]
After:
[17, 15, 10, 9, 8, 4, 3, 2]
```

The sort method, lines 63–69, follows the algorithm given above except that rather than placing numbers on the table, all numbers are kept inside the array. The front part of the array is sorted (from largest to smallest) and the back part of the array remains to be sorted. Each time through the loop in sort, one more element from the unsorted part is moved to its right position, and the sorted part of the array is extended by one. Before the loop runs at all, 0 elements are known to be in sorted order; after performing the loop n times (where n is the number of elements in the array), each iteration adding one element to the sorted region, all n elements are in sorted order.

The sort method uses firstUnsortedIndex to keep track of the index (in the list) of the first element in the unsorted region. At the beginning of the method, firstUnsortedIndex is set to 0 (all elements are unsorted). The body of the loop finds the index of the largest element in the unsorted region by calling largestIndex. The second parameter to largestIndex tells the method where to start looking for the largest element; by starting at firstUnsortedIndex, it finds the largest element in the unsorted region. Knowing the index of the largest element in the unsorted region, we just swap that value with the first value in the unsorted region; the largest element is now in the right place and we can move firstUnsortedIndex forward by one.

Figure 11.2 shows the sorting of this particular list visually. The left column shows the situation just before the call to swap at line 67 in the sort method. The pink region of the list is unsorted, the triangle atop the list is the index of the first unsorted value, and the red triangle below the list is the index of the largest element in the unsorted region.

Looking from the first list to the second list, you can see that the element indexed by the red triangle was swapped with that indexed by the white triangle *in the first list diagram*. The values 17 and 9 were swapped. That put 17 in its sorted place in the list; the first location is sorted, the rest of the list remaining unsorted.

The right column shows what happens inside largestIndex the first time through the loop. The white triangle is the startIndex parameter. The red triangle represents the largestNdx variable; on line 46 it is initialized to be the startIndex. The loop control variable, contenderNdx, represented in the drawing by the red question mark, cycles through all of the values from one more than the startIndex through the last valid entry. Each time through the loop, the value of the element indexed by contenderNdx and the value of the element indexed by largestNdx are compared.

If the contender is larger than the largest, largest must be updated. You can see that the red triangle (largestNdx) moves when 17 is compared with 9. Finally, after contenderNdx is past the end of the list, we know

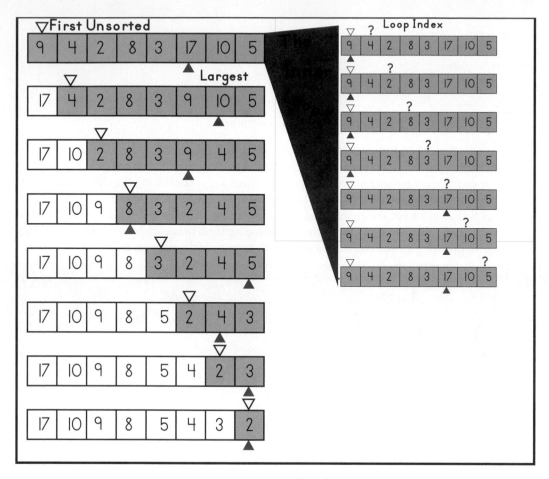

Figure 11.2: Sorting a list of Integer

that largestNdx really is the index of the largest value at or to the right of startIndex, so it is the value returned by the method (line 53).[5]

Note that in line 49 we use > between two Integer objects. Earlier it was mentioned that direct comparison between objects was not supported (and even equality tests test only for exact reference identity). Why does this compile and run? Since version Java version 1.5, Integer and the other object wrappers for plain old data types automatically convert themselves to plain old data types with the right values when Java requires plain old data types. This is called *autounboxing* where the Integer object is considered a *box* around the int. Java also supports *autoboxing*, the conversion of a POD type to its corresponding box type when necessary.

Sorting Player Objects

How could we sort a collection full of Player objects if the Player interface were (duplicated from Section 11.1)

---

[5]The drawings and approach were inspired by Chapter 11, "Sorting," of John Bentley's *Programming Pearls, 2E.* [Ben00]. The book is a collection of columns originally written for the Association of Computing Machinery's *Communications* magazine. They are insightful, readable software engineering case studies that most computer science students can understand.

```
public class Player {
  public Player(String name)...
  public String getName()...
  public int getScore()...
  public void takeTurn()...
  public String toString()...
}
```

It depends on *how* we want to sort Players. If we sort in descending order, what makes one Player larger than another? At the end of a game of Pig we want to sort the objects by their score. This means that in largestIndex we compare the result of getScore() called on the two elements in the list rather than directly comparing the objects. The following code is from Pig; the names of the methods were prefixed with sp_ and slightly shortened so that they would group together in the source code file and print more clearly. The following three methods are the last three definitions in the Pig class (the comments have been elided in this listing).

```
253   private int sp_LargestIndex(ArrayList<Player> standings,
254     int startIndex) {
255     int largestNdx = startIndex;
256     for (int contenderNdx = startIndex + 1;
257       contenderNdx != standings.size(); ++contenderNdx) {
258       if (standings.get(contenderNdx).getScore() >
259         standings.get(largestNdx).getScore()) {
260       largestNdx = contenderNdx;
261       }
262     }
263     return largestNdx;
264   }
273   private void sp_Sort(ArrayList<Player> standings) {
274     for (int firstUnsortedIndex = 0;
275       firstUnsortedIndex != standings.size(); ++firstUnsortedIndex) {
276       int largestUnsortedIndex = sp_LargestIndex(standings,
277         firstUnsortedIndex);
278       sp_Swap(standings, firstUnsortedIndex, largestUnsortedIndex);
279     }
280   }
291   private void sp_Swap(ArrayList<Player> standings, int a, int b) {
292     Player temp = standings.get(a);
293     standings.set(a, standings.get(b));
294     standings.set(b, temp);
295   }
```

Listing 11.7: Pig: sort

Except for the change in the types and calling aList standings, sp_Sort and sp_Swap correspond exactly to sort and swap in SortIntegers.java. The important thing to take away from the swap method is that swapping two values (in a collection or not) requires a *temporary* variable to hold one of the values, because as soon as a new value is assigned to a variable, the old value is gone. The type of the temporary variable must match the type of the two values being swapped.

Even sp_LargestIndex is very similar to largestIndex in the integer program. Lines 258–259, where the comparison between two scores is made, is different than line 49 (in part because it is longer and therefore prints on two lines). In one case, the two values returned by get are compared directly; in the other, the values returned by get are used to get a particular field on which the list is to be sorted.

Sorting String Objects

SortStrings.java is almost identical to SortIntegers.java. We look at the main method where the list to be sorted is declared and the largestIndex method where the actual comparison takes place.

```
18  public static void main(String[] args) {
19    System.out.println("SortSrrings:");
20    ArrayList<String> someAnimals = new ArrayList<String>(Arrays.asList(
21        "dog", "cat", "hamster", "catfish", "pig", "aardvark",
22        "zebra"));
23
24    System.out.println("Before:");
25    System.out.println(someAnimals);
26
27    sort(someAnimals);
28
29    System.out.println("After:");
30    System.out.println(someAnimals);
31  }
45  private static int largestIndex(ArrayList<String> aList,
46    int startIndex) {
47    int largestNdx = startIndex;
48    for (int contenderNdx = startIndex + 1;
49        contenderNdx != aList.size(); ++contenderNdx) {
50      if (aList.get(contenderNdx).compareTo(aList.get(largestNdx)) >
51          0) {
52        largestNdx = contenderNdx;
53      }
54    }
55    return largestNdx;
56  }
```

Listing 11.8: SortStrings: main and largestIndex

The type of the list, someAnimals, is an ArrayList of String. That means that the swap method (not shown) has a temporary variable of type String. It also means that the > comparison we used in SortIntegers is not available; autounboxing works only for classes that wrap POD types, and a String does not have a corresponding POD type.

Looking back to Section 10.4, we see that the compareTo method is how objects (other than POD wrappers) should be compared. a.compareTo(b) returns a negative integer if String a comes before b in an ascending dictionary sort order, 0 if they are equal String values, and a positive integer if a comes after b. We are sorting in *descending* or reverse order, so we want the largest or last in dictionary order. So, if the contender compared to the largest is positive, the contender comes after the largest or, in other words, is larger than the largest. That is what line 50 does. A run of SortStrings looks like this:

```
~/Chapter11% java SortIntegers
SortSrrings:
Before:
[dog, cat, hamster, catfish, pig, aardvark, zebra]
After:
[zebra, pig, hamster, dog, catfish, cat, aardvark]
```

Review 11.3

(a) What does swap(ArrayList<Integer> aList, **int** a, **int** b) do? What do the parameters mean?

(b) What does String.compareTo return in the following cases:

    (a) "goliath".compareTo("david")

    (b) "pepper".compareTo("salt")

    (c) "spam".compareTo("spam")

    (d) "source".compareTo("unreal")

    (e) "java".compareTo("cplusplus")

    (f) "picard".compareTo("kirk")

(c) Would it be better to have largestElement, which returns the largest element in the given range, rather than largestIndex? Why or why not?

11.4   Finishing Pig

Looking back at the design of Pig in Figure 11.1 on page 344, we see that the program appears to ask the user for two different *kinds* of input: complete lines for the players' names and yes/no answers the rest of the time. Consider for a moment: what should the game do if the user is prompted for a yes/no answer and he answers "catfish"?

There are a couple of ways to handle this: define every answer other than the string "yes" to *mean* "no" as a default answer; make "yes" the default answer; try to deal with whatever is typed in each location where the answer is used to make a decision; build a method that prompts the player over and over until he gives an acceptable answer.

The last choice in the list has at least two advantages over the others: it uses levels of abstraction to hide complexities that are only part of getting the player to answer yes/no from any code using the answer and it centralizes all of the code to handle "wrong" answers in a single place (we do not repeat ourselves).

Static Input Methods

Pig has two **static** input methods; both rely on the declaration and initialization of the **static** keyboard field.

```
40   public static boolean answersYes(String prompt) {
41      String userAnswer = "";
42      // sentinel: userAnswer is a valid answer
43      while (!userAnswer.equalsIgnoreCase("y") &&
44          !userAnswer.equalsIgnoreCase("n") &&
45          !userAnswer.equalsIgnoreCase("yes") &&
46          !userAnswer.equalsIgnoreCase("no")) {
47        userAnswer = getLine(prompt);
48      }
```

```
49    // userAnswer: "y", "yes", "n", or "no"; first letter differentiates
50    return userAnswer.substring(0, 1).equalsIgnoreCase("y");
51  }
61  public static String getLine(String prompt) {
62    System.out.print(prompt);
63    System.out.print(" ");
64    return keyboard.nextLine();
65  }
```

Listing 11.9: `Pig`: Input Routines

These methods are defined right before `main` in the body of the class. `getLine` is just as it was defined earlier in the chapter.

The `answersYes` method is a Boolean method that returns **true** if the user answers yes to the prompted question. The body of the method is a sentinel-controlled loop. It ignores all input lines until a sentinel value is entered. The final line is processed after the loop terminates so we avoid the loop-and-a-half problem.

The sentinel condition in `answersYes` is when `userAnswer` is equal to "yes" or "no" or "y" or "n" without regard to case. It is possible to write all of the possible upper/lowercase mixes for "yes" and "no" ($2^3 = 8$ and $2^2 = 4$ possibilities, respectively; generating them is left as an exercise for the interested reader) but Java provides a simpler solution. In addition to `equals`, the `String` class provides a `equalsIgnoreCase` method. It does what its name suggests: it compares two strings permitting upper and lower case versions of the same letter to evaluate as the same.

To express the sentinel condition, we need to call `equalsIgnoreCase` four times, combining the results in a disjunction with the logical or operator, ||. The sentinel condition is **true** when

```
userAnswer.equalsIgnoreCase("y") ||
userAnswer.equalsIgnoreCase("yes") ||
userAnswer.equalsIgnoreCase("n") ||
userAnswer.equalsIgnoreCase("no")
```

evaluates to **true**.

To use the Boolean expression of the sentinel condition in the **while** loop, we need its logical inverse. We need **while** (!<*sentinel*>) {...}. Or

```
!(userAnswer.equalsIgnoreCase("y") ||
  userAnswer.equalsIgnoreCase("yes") ||
  userAnswer.equalsIgnoreCase("n") ||
  userAnswer.equalsIgnoreCase("no"))
```

The expression makes sense: it is the inverse of the sentinel condition. What if having ! in front of such a long Boolean expression makes you uncomfortable? Would it be possible to use De Morgan's laws to distribute the ! into the expression? Yes. Remember that the rules say || goes to && and each subexpression is inverted:

```
!userAnswer.equalsIgnoreCase("y") &&
!userAnswer.equalsIgnoreCase("yes") &&
!userAnswer.equalsIgnoreCase("n") &&
!userAnswer.equalsIgnoreCase("no")
```

This is exactly the expression in the **while** loop's Boolean expression on lines 43–46. Breaking it up on the operators (and keeping the parts on each line at the same level) makes it easier for a programmer to follow. It also keeps the lines short enough to print in the book.

The body of the loop prompts the user for a line of input and reads a line from keyboard. Rather than repeat that code from the body of getLine, the loop just calls getLine.

Line 50 is reached only if the sentinel condition is **true** (the inverse of the sentinel is **false**). That means userAnswer is one of the four values. The user answers yes if it is equal to "y" or "yes". We could test for either of these with an || in a Boolean expression. It is also possible to note that the first character of each of the affirmative answers is "y", extract the first character, and test if it *is* "y". There is an argument to be made that this code is too clever (especially if it needs a comment to say what is happening) but it is clear enough that it stayed in the game.

The Main Method

The main method is the first method executed by the java interpreter.

```
74  public static void main(String[] args) {
75    Pig game = new Pig();
76    game.getPlayersNames();
77    if (game.isPlayable()) {
78      game.play();
79    } else {
80      System.err.println("Not enough players to make game playable.");
81    }
82  }
```

Listing 11.10: Pig: main

As described earlier, this method borrows from FANG in that it constructs a new object of the type Pig and then calls specific methods to have that object play the game. The getPlayersNames() method fills the collection of Player objects (it is implemented in the next section). isPlayable is a Boolean method that checks to make sure there are enough players to play the game; at present it checks for at least two, but it could be changed to check for at least one if the game should support solitaire play. Finally, if there are enough players, the play method is called; play is the game loop for Pig and is detailed in the second following section.

The Player Collection

The game must keep track of a collection of Player objects. The field holding them is a list called standings. The previous section on sorting objects by a field value revealed this collection. The following listing collects together the declaration and methods (other than sorting) that manipulate standings:

```
21   private final ArrayList<Player> standings;
28   private Pig() {
29     standings = new ArrayList<Player>();
30   }
119  private Player getPlayer(int n) {
120    return standings.get(n);
121  }
130  private void getPlayersNames() {
131    String playerName = "";
132    while (!playerName.equalsIgnoreCase("done")) {
133      playerName = getLine("Next player's Name ('done' to exit):");
134      if (!playerName.equalsIgnoreCase("done")) {
135        standings.add(new Player(playerName));
```

```
136        }
137      }
138    }
158    private int indexOf(Player p) {
159      int ndx = -1;
160      for (int i = 0; i != standings.size(); ++i) {
161        if (standings.get(i) == p) {
162          ndx = i;
163        }
164      }
165      return ndx;
166    }
173    private boolean isPlayable() {
174      boolean hasPlayerList = standings != null;
175      boolean hasEnoughPlayers = hasPlayerList && (standings.size() > 1);
176      return hasPlayerList && hasEnoughPlayers;
177    }
```

Listing 11.11: Pig: The Players

The field is declared to be an ArrayList<Player>. The methods are in the source file (and in the listing) in alphabetical order except that the constructor comes first.

All the constructor does is initialize the field. Looking back at main, we see that the next method called after the constructor is getPlayersNames. The method prompts the user for each player's name and adds that name to the collection until the user enters the sentinel value; this is exactly the loop-and-a-half problem. This one solves it with the repeated Boolean expression (while it could be changed to use the other method). For each name that is typed in, a new Player is created and added to standings. The newly minted Player has a score of 0 (we present the Player class in detail below).

isPlayable demonstrates a useful technique for making Boolean expressions easier to read: use named subexpressions to clarify what is going on. Make an effort to separate the rules for determining, for example, if the game is playable, from how the various rule conditions are determined.

Here the game is playable if there is a player list and there are enough players. Line 176 says this explicitly. The rule is clear and you don't need to look at lines 175 and 174 (to see how we determine if the list exists or the number is big enough) unless you need to drill down to a less abstract, more detailed level.

getPlayer is a convenience method. It would be possible to write standings.get(i) everywhere getPlayer is called, but by wrapping it in a method, it would be possible to use a different collection if we wanted to. The indexOf method is the *inverse* of getPlayer: getPlayer takes a small integer and converts it into a Player; indexOf takes a Player and converts it back into a small integer. Notice that indexOf handles looking up a Player, which is *not* in standings. Handling that situation appropriately (returning an invalid index makes sense and matches what Java does in its collection libraries) argues that this must be a method so that the code is written only once.

indexOf is necessary so that we can tell when it is the first player's turn (so we can print the standings). That is part of showing the state of the game and is therefore properly part of the game loop.

Java Random Numbers

All previous games have relied on fang2.core.Game to provide random numbers. There were two reasons for this: Game is a central class in *any* FANG program, and under the hood, FANG coordinates random number generation across multiplayer games so that every instance of the game sees the same sequence of numbers. More on how that last bit is accomplished below.

Remember the FANG multiplayer architecture runs a complete copy of the game for each player and the input to each game is interleaved into the exact same sequence of input for every instance. If the game were a multiplayer version of EasyDice, each game would call the local method Game.randomInt when the player whose turn it is pressed the button. It is important that all instances of the game generate the same die roll; otherwise it would be possible for the player to win in one instance and lose in another. FANG provides a wrapper around the Java random number facility that automates the coordination of the sequences in all shared instances.

Java provides a class called Random, which is a *pseudo-random number generator*. This means that the numbers generated by Random may *look* random (even at a deep mathematical level) but they are *not*. The numbers are generated in a fixed but very, very, very large cycle. If your program uses more than $2^{48} = 281474976710656$ random numbers in any given run, the sequence may begin to repeat. It is likely that anyone around to see the beginning of the sequence, however, has moved on to a better place.[6]

Computers are *deterministic*: given a starting state and a sequence of input, a computer always ends in the same state. We count on this when we enter finances into a spreadsheet or use a calculator application. It is not conducive to producing truly random numbers. The random sequence produced by Java's Random class is good enough.

Where in the sequence a Random starts generating values is determined by a *seed* value. It is possible to construct two Random objects with the same seed: "If two instances of Random are created with the same seed, and the same sequence of method calls is made for each, they will generate and return identical sequences of numbers." (Java 1.6 *JavaDoc* for java.util.Random) This is how FANG manages multiplayer random numbers. All random numbers in an instance of a FANG game come from one Random object *and* all Random objects in a multiplayer game start with the same seed.

To use Random directly, first construct one and then use the nextInt and/or nextDouble methods to generate random numbers. The Random constructor comes in two flavors: when called with an **int**,[7] the integer value is used to seed the pseudo-random number generator. This means that if you call the same sequence of routines on the random number generator, you get the same sequence of random numbers. This is good for testing.

When called with no parameters the Random constructor takes some portion of the JVM's current time clock as a seed value. Because the portion it uses includes the highest frequency bits of the clock, no two runs of a program are likely to get the same seed (though it is possible).

To use the Random instance, there are two flavors of nextInt and one of nextDouble defined (there are other methods for other types but they are beyond the scope of this chapter):

Type	Method	Range
int	nextInt(**int** n)	[0–n)
int	nextInt()	[Integer.MIN_VALUE–Integer.MAX_VALUE]
double	nextDouble()	[0.0–1.0)

The range for the no-parameter version of nextInt is the range of all possible **int** values, from -2^{31} through $2^{31} - 1$. These values are stored as named constants in Integer and the names were used in the table.

In Pig, Player has a **static** field, random, shared by all Player objects. The rollOneDie method uses random.nextInt(6) to get a random number on the range [0–5]. Since one die actually rolls on the range [1–6], the method adds one to the random number and returns the result.

As a rule of thumb, to generate a random integer on the range low to high, the following expression works:

```
random.nextInt(high - low + 1) + low
```

The number of different values is high -low + 1 (for a number on the range 1 through 6 there are 6 - 1 + 1 = 6 different values). The random number is on the range [0-n) where n is the number of different values. Adding low shifts the value up to the right range (for the six-sided die, random.nextInt(6 -1 + 1) + 1 or random.nextInt(6) + 1).

---

[6] At 10,000 random numbers per second, the cycle takes almost seven centuries to complete.

[7] The actual type is **long**, a "long integer." Because a **long** is *wider* than an **int**, an **int** can be used to set the parameter.

The Game Loop

The game loop itself is in the `play` method, a method that determines which `Player` is taking her turn and calls appropriate methods to show the state, get user input, and update the state of the game.

```java
106  private boolean continueGame(Player curr) {
107    boolean currHasWon = curr.getScore() >= GAME_SCORE;
108    return !currHasWon;
109  }
145  private void handlePlayerTurn(Player curr) {
146    curr.takeTurn();
147  }
200  private void play() {
201    int turn = 0;
202    Player curr = null;
203    boolean playing = true;
204    while (playing) {
205      curr = getPlayer(turn);
206      showState(curr);
207      handlePlayerTurn(curr);
208      playing = continueGame(curr);
209      turn = nextTurn(turn);
210    }
211    announceWinner(curr);
212  }
230  private void showState(Player curr) {
231    boolean isFirstPlayersTurn = (indexOf(curr) == 0);
232    if (isFirstPlayersTurn) {
233      System.out.println();// improve readability of output
234      System.out.println("Standings:");
235      showStandings();
236    }
237    System.out.println();// improve readability of output
238    System.out.println(curr);
239  }
```

Listing 11.12: `Pig`: Game Loop

`play` and the three main game loop methods are shown together in Listing 11.12. Again, the methods are in alphabetical order, so `play` is near the middle. Each time through the loop, `curr` is set to the current `Player` by calling `getPlayer` with the turn number. That `Player` is then passed to each of the three methods to show, get input for, and update the state of the game. `showState` prints out the current player (the last two lines of the method). If it is the first player's turn, it also prints out the complete standings. This is where the `indexOf` method is called; notice again the use of a name for the **boolean** expression. The reason for the expression `indexOf(curr) == 0` is documented right on line 231 and the reason for the **if** statement is documented right in the next line.

The `handlePlayerTurn` method forwards the real work of getting input from the user to the `Player.takeTurn` method.

The `takeTurn` method looks like a game loop itself. The loop is slightly skewed in that updating the state happens at the beginning; if you rewrite it so that it is at the end, you'll find this loop has a loop-and-a-half quality to it.

```
56   public void takeTurn() {
57     int turnTotal = 0;
58     boolean rolledPig = false;
59     boolean heldPoints = false;
60     while (!rolledPig && !heldPoints) {
61       // ----- update state of turn -----
62       int roll = rollOneDie();
63       rolledPig = (roll == 1);
64       // ----- show state of turn -----
65       if (rolledPig) {
66         System.out.println(name + ": Rolled PIG!");
67       } else {
68         System.out.println(name + ": Rolled " + roll);
69       }
70       // ----- get user input for turn -----
71       if (!rolledPig) {
72         turnTotal += roll;
73         heldPoints = Pig.answersYes(name + " with " + turnTotal +
74             " points this turn, would you like to hold your points?");
75       }
76     }
77
78     // Could have gotten here for two different reasons; only update
79     // score if player held the points.
80     if (heldPoints) {
81       incrementScore(turnTotal);
82     }
83
84     System.out.println(name + " ends turn with " + score + " points.");
85   }
```

Listing 11.13: Player: takeTurn

In the loop we roll one die and check if the player rolled a pig. The state of the turn is printed and, if the roll was not a pig, she is asked if she wants to hold with the current turn total. Note that lines 73–74 are a call to Pig.answersYes. That **public static** method isolates interaction with standard input, which is why it has **public** visibility.

The loop finishes when the sentinel condition is reached: rolledPig || heldPoints. The inverse of the sentinel condition is the Boolean expression in the **while** loop.

The sentinel combines two different reasons for exiting the loop. Line 80 makes sure the score is updated only if the player held her points. Finally, upon leaving the method, it prints a short message letting the player know how her turn went.

```
94   public String toString() {
95     return name + ": " + score;
96   }
```

Listing 11.14: Player: toString

When Pig needs to print information about a Player, it passes the object to println. As discussed above, println calls the object's toString method. Player overrides toString to return the name and the score of the player.

After calling `handlePlayerTurn` in `play`, Pig calls `continueGame` with the current player. How does a game of *Pig* end? When someone wins by having a score higher than the required score. When do players' scores change? Only at the end of their own turns; it is not possible for a player to change the score of any other player. We continue to play so long as the current player has not won the game. Lines 107–108 determine if the current player has won and return the inverse of that for continuing the game.

The only two things that Pig does that we have not looked at in detail are to print the whole standings table and to announce the winner. Printing the standings table is just looping over the contents of `standings`, passing each entry to `println` (using the `toString` override again). After the game loop ends (because someone won), the winner is announced.

```
90   private void announceWinner(Player winner) {
91      sp_Sort(standings);
92      System.out.println("Final Standings:");
93      showStandings();
94      System.out.println(winner.getName() + " wins with " +
95         winner.getScore() + " points.");
96   }
```

Listing 11.15: Pig: `announceWinner`

To announce the winner, `standings` is sorted in descending order by `score` (`sp_Sort` was examined in the previous section). The standings table is printed and a line identifying the winner is printed. The final line is redundant but it is important for winners to feel recognized; it improves the feel of the game for most players.

Review 11.4

(a) Why does `Player.takeTurn` look so much like a game loop?

(b) Are there any turn-based games where a player other than the player taking his or her turn could win the game? Is the "optimization" of just checking the current player's total painfully obvious?

(c) Do the named Boolean variables and methods make the logic easier to follow? Can you think of problems you have completed for earlier chapters where you could have used this approach?

11.5   Summary

Pure Console I/O

When running an application, `System.out` is attached to the standard output, `System.err` is attached to the standard error stream, and `System.in` is attached to the standard input stream.

`System.in` can be used to construct a `Scanner`. Such a scanner can then be used to read input typed by the user.

Console input can be in line or character mode. This book assumes it is in line mode, so no input can be read until the user presses the <Enter> key.

In addition to `next` and `nextLine`, `Scanner` provides `nextInt` and `nextDouble`. Each skips over whitespace and reads the next "word" (like `next`) and tries to interpret the word as either an **int** or a **double**. Each uses the `Integer.parseString` or `Double.parseString` method to do the conversion.

To share one `Scanner` attached to the keyboard, this chapter (and subsequent console-focused programs) define a **static** field for the `Scanner`, wrap it around the keyboard when the field is initialized, and then use that field for all keyboard reading. This avoids the cost of creating and destroying a new `Scanner` for every read of user input. It also permits consuming only part of a given line with the rest remaining for another read.

A sentinel-controlled loop can be used to make sure that the user provides input from some particular set. It is possible to wrap a sentinel-controlled loop in a method so that the method does not return a value until the player enters something the method understands.

"Literal" Lists

An `ArrayList` can be constructed and initialized with a collection of entries. One way to get a list of values is to use `java.util.Arrays`. `Arrays.asList` takes an arbitrary number of parameters (all of the same type) and returns a list with the given values. This can be used, with Java's autoboxing (wrapping POD values as objects automatically), to create lists of `Integer` from a sequence of literal **int** values.

Sorting

A collection, either an `ArrayList` or an array, can be sorted. This chapter presented the *insertion sort*. To sort in descending order (largest first), the following is the algorithm:

```
for every position in the collection from 0 to size-1
  find largest element at or after position
  swap largest element into position
```

To sort in descending order, replace `largest` with `smallest`.

Java Random Numbers

FANG random number methods are not available in non-FANG programs. Instead you use Java's standard `java.util.Random` class. It can be constructed with or without a *seed number*. Constructed with no parameter, it takes some part of the current time as its seed and generates a different sequence during each run. Constructed with a fixed integer seed, the sequence returned is the same from run to run. The `Ransom` methods introduced in this chapter were

Type	Method	Range
int	`nextInt(int n)`	[0–n)
int	`nextInt()`	[`Integer.MIN_VALUE–Integer.MAX_VALUE`]
double	`nextDouble()`	[0.0–1.0)

11.6   Chapter Review Exercises

Review Exercise 11.1 How can you wrap a `Scanner` around the user's keyboard (or standard input)?

Review Exercise 11.2 What impact does the console being in "line mode" have on reading input from the user's keyboard?

Review Exercise 11.3 How do you construct a `Random` object?

Review Exercise 11.4 How would you get a random integer on the range [1–100] from a `Random` variable, random?

Review Exercise 11.5 Given an `ArrayList` of `Integer` called `theTable`, write a method to find the index of the smallest value in the list.

Review Exercise 11.6 Given an `ArrayList` of `Integer` called `theTable`, write a method to find the index of the smallest value in the list *except for the first element*.

Review Exercise 11.7 Describe how the *insertion sort* works.

Review Exercise 11.8 Why must there be a temporary value in `swap`? What, if anything, is wrong with this rewrite:

```
private static void swap(ArrayList<Integer> aList, int a, int b) {
  aList.set(a, aList.get(b));
  aList.set(b, aList.get(a));
}
```

11.7   Programming Problems

Programming Problem 11.1   Build a "pretend" game. The game starts by placing some number of ovals. This simulates starting a game with a number of obstacles placed on the screen.

   (a) Write Obstacles01, which randomly selects a size on the range [0.25–0.50) and randomly places 10 ovals of the given size on the screen. All 10 ovals should be the same color.

   (b) A configuration file permits the obstacles to be placed at specific locations every time the game is played. Further, a nonprogrammer could write his own configuration file without needing to know any Java.
       The configuration file is a text file with the following format:

       <size>
       <x0> <y0>
       <x1> <y1>
       ...
       <xn> <yn>

       <size> is the size (in screens) of each of the ovals. The *<xi><yi>* pairs are the location of the center of each of the ovals. The number of ovals placed is determined by the number of lines in the configuration file.
       The following sample data file places two ovals on the screen as shown in Figure 11.3: each is a quarter of the screen across, one placed at (0.3, 0.4) and the other at (0.7, 0.8).

       0.25
       0.3 0.4
       0.7 0.8

       Write Obstacles02, modifying Obstacles01, that reads such a file in setup. This iteration should have the name of the file hard-coded into the compiled program.

   (c) Modify Obstacles02 into Obstacles03 and let the player specify the name of the obstacle file at *run-time*. At this point the "game" is really using a configuration file.

Programming Problem 11.2   Read the description of the file format in Programming Problem 11.1. You need to write a console program to determine whether or not a given file is in the right format.
   Your program begins by prompting the user for a file name to check. It then checks the syntax of the file (this means the formatting and *not* the meaning). The file is in the correct format if it contains an odd number of numbers.
   After evaluating the file, the program should print out a message including the name of the file and whether or not it is properly formatted.
   If you think about the design: What does the "main" method in the object do (e.g., play in Pig)? It should handle validating *one* file, already knowing its name. That moves the "get name of file" out to main and permits any number of files to be processed just by putting a loop in main.

Programming Problem 11.3   In games that involve randomness, sometimes it is hard to evaluate if your strategy is good or if you were just lucky this time. One way around this is to try out the strategies with a predictable sequence of random numbers.

Figure 11.3: ObstacleReader reading sample file

For Pig, when you construct your random number generator, pass it a parameter of 0. random is a **private static** field of Player, initialized on Player.java:14.

Now every time you play, the dice roll the same sequence. You can use that to develop a good strategy and always test the strategy. Once you have a good strategy against a zero seed, try passing in a different seed value. This changes the constant sequence (though the sequence is the same as long as the new seed is passed into the constructor). Does your strategy still work?

After tweaking the strategy, try going back to zero seeding and see if it still works.

Programming Problem 11.4 How could we resume a game of Pig after being interrupted? If Pig could save the state of the game in a file, then we could modify the program to read such a file. File writing is presented in Chapter 12. This exercise just reads an already-generated state file.

```
<playerCount>
<name0> <score0>
<name1> <score1>
...
<nameN> <scoreN>
<currentPlayerName> <currentTurnRoll>
```

Here are the contents of an example file with two players, Sonic and Luigi:

```
2
Sonic 23
Luigi 14
Luigi  2
```

Modify `Pig` so that you can enter in the name of a text file that can be read to resume a game already in progress. If the user enters an empty file name, set up the game as it is set up now. If the user enters a non-empty file name, parse the file, create the players, set the scores, and set the turn for the named player.

Programming Problem 11.3 looks at how to save a game of `Pig`.

Programming Problem 11.5   Write a console-based game of `EasyDice` from Chapter 5.

Programming Problem 11.6   The game of `Memory` is a card game where all of the cards are placed face down in a random order.

On each turn the player turns up two cards of her choosing. If the two cards are matched, then they are won and remain face up. If the two cards are different, they are placed face down again. The game continues turning up pairs until all pairs have been found.

Write this game using `StringSprites` to represent the card values. Place a `RectangleSprite` over each `StringSprite`. When the user clicks on a RectangleSprite, hide it to reveal the text underneath. If two rectangles reveal `.equal` text values, leave the `RectangleSprites` hidden; otherwise show them again. The game ends when the player finds the last pair. The score is the number of tries it takes to finish. Low scores are better than high.

The strings for matching come from a configuration file. One word per line, the program should produce two `StringSprites` containing the text of each word.

The program should read the entire file and place the `StringSprites` in a list. Shuffle the list.

Determine the size of the grid for laying out cards by finding the largest integer whose square is less than the number of cards. Scale all of the string sprites to an appropriate fraction of the screen.

Using nested count-controlled loops, lay the cards down, placing a clickable `RectangleSprite` over each word.

Programming Problem 11.7   Look at Programming Problem 11.6. Modify `Memory` so that it is a two-player networked game. One consequence of the way FANG shared game state across the network is that a copy of the data file is required at *each* player's computer.

Can you actually make the game multiplayer for an arbitrary number of players? Where could you keep the scores for an arbitrary number of players?

Programming Problem 11.8   Write a program to graphically show the frequency of letters in a file. This sort of program can help in breaking cipher systems or solving CryptoQuips in the newspaper.

Use an `ArrayList` to store the frequency of the letters. The list is indexed by each letter's offset into the alphabet: index 0 is for 'a', 1 for 'b', 2 for 'c', and so on.

Conversion from a character to its corresponding index (and back again) can be done with the following methods:

```
/**
 * Get the index for a letter. Return -1 if it is not a letter
 *
 * @param   letter  character containing a letter (maybe)
 *
 * @return  -1 if it is not a letter; index on [0-26) of letter in
 *          alphabet otherwise
 */
```

```java
public int getIndex(char letter) {
  if (Character.isLetter(letter)) {
    char lower = Character.toLowerCase(letter);
    return lower - 'a';
  }
  return -1;
}


/**
 * Get the lowercase letter associated with the
 *
 * @param   index   index in [0-26)
 *
 * @return  the lowercase letter in the range or space if number is
 *          out of range
 */
public char getLetter(int index) {
  if ((0 <= index) && (index < 26)) {
    return (char) ('a' + index);
  }
  return ' ';
}
```

(a) Design a Game that prompts the user for the name of a text file. Read the file word by word (skipping whitespace). With each character in each word call getIndex and print out the index of the letter.

(b) Modify the program so that it initializes an ArrayList of counters. There should be 26 counters, one for each letter.

For each letter, if getIndex returns a negative number, do nothing. If it returns a value on the range [0–26), increment the corresponding counter.

When the program finishes reading the file, print the table of letters and frequencies out to standard output. The next step is to build a visual representation of this data.

(c) After reading the file, construct appropriate sprites to present the relative frequency of the different letters. A *histogram* or bar chart is traditional: each table entry is translated into a RectangleSprite with a width of one-twenty-sixth of the screen wide and a height proportional to the number of times the given letter appears. For this to work, you must find the largest entry in the list. All other heights of the rectangles are scaled by the frequency of the letter divided by the largest entry.

Alternatively, FANG sprites make creating a pie chart possible. Here you need to determine the total number of letters to scale the various arcs.

Finally, a "new media" style presentation could be generated using letters where the height of each letter is proportional to the letter frequency. This permits a more "random" layout of the letters in various spots (and transparencies) on the screen. Be careful about scaling; it is easy to lie with statistics when using two-dimensional objects to represent relationships in one-dimensional data.

C
h
a
p
t
e
r

12

More Streams: Separating Programs and Data

In previous chapters we have seen how to write console programs where we can treat standard input and standard output as input and output files. We have also seen how to read information from a file so that a single game can change its behavior without being recompiled. This chapter adds the finishing touches to input and output with text files: we see how to open output files on the disk and save information to the file, information that can be read by the same or another program.

This chapter uses the same console-based input approach found in the previous chapter so that the programs written in this chapter do not use FANG. The game in this chapter is Twenty Questions; we build a computer opponent that gets smarter and smarter the more it plays.

12.1   Outsmarting the Player: Twenty Questions

The game of *Twenty Questions* is an old game, dating back to antiquity, according to Mansfield Walsworth who researched the game back in 1882 (the date is not a typographical error) [Wal82]. It is also at the heart of the 20Q Website, http://www.20q.net, a computerized opponent that can guess, in 20 questions, what you are thinking of. The information gathered by the online game was packaged into the successful 20Q line of portable game systems from Radica Games (Mattel) [Rad].

In the two-player version of the game, one player chooses an object from an agreed upon domain. The other player is then permitted to ask 20 yes-or-no questions in an attempt to guess the chosen object. For example, assume Anne and Billy are playing in the animal domain. Billy has selected a dolphin. A possible game sequence could be

> Anne: "Does it have four legs?"
> Billy: "No."
> Anne: "Does it have wings?"
> Billy: "No."
> Anne: "Is it a reptile?"
> Billy: "No."
> Anne: "Is it a fish?"
> Billy: "No."
> Anne: "Is it an amphibian?"

Billy: "No."
Anne: "Is it a mammal?"
Billy: "Yes."
Anne: "Does it swim?"
Billy: "Yes."
Anne: "Is it a whale?"
Billy: "No."
Anne: "Is it a dolphin?"
Billy: "Yes."

In nine questions Anne zeros in on the answer. Somewhat surprisingly, with 20 questions, if each question divides the remaining elements of the domain in half, the questioner can differentiate between $2^{20} = 1048576$ different objects. It is literally possible to find one in a million.

How can we convert Twenty Questions into a computer game? Two possibilities jump out: make a two-player game where the computer just provides a communications medium, and have the computer play one of the two roles in the game. A two-player version of Twenty Questions would have the "game" acting more like an instant messaging program than an actual game; none of the rules of Twenty Questions would really end up inside the program.

What would the program need to do to play each of the roles? If we look back at Hangman, reading a data file containing a collection of animals (or other domain objects) and selecting one at random is easy. Breaking arbitrary yes-or-no questions down, interpreting them, and then answering them correctly is far beyond the scope of our current programming skills.

Alternatively, the file contains a collection of yes-or-no questions and guesses of domain objects (animals) related to each sequence of "Yes" or "No" answers provided by the user. The structure of the file is more complex than the data file we used in Hangman. Rather than being a single line containing a single phrase, each item stored in the file is a *record* with multiple field values stored across multiple lines. The exact format of the data file depends on the structure of the question and answer classes; there is one line per *field* in the class. We now digress in the process of designing the question and answer classes to examine an interesting variation on how to read a book.

Choose Your Own Adventure

The *Choose Your Own Adventure* series was a collection of "interactive" children's books from the 1970s and 1980s. The format of the book was that the reader began on page 1 and read the page. The page would describe the current situation and, at the bottom of the page, would provide suggested resolutions to some problem. Each resolution directed the reader to a different page in the book, so that the book was read nonlinearly (selection rather than sequence controlled the order of the pages). The series was popular — with more than 120 titles and many different imitators.

Readers of this book, 40 years after the fact, should not be particularly excited by these books. Many of them have been translated onto the World Wide Web where *hypertext links* take the place of page numbers. Each of the resolutions is linked to the Web page where the outcome is described and another choice presented to the user.

Figure 12.1 is a picture of several pages from a choose your own adventure-style story. Notice that each white page presents the user with a decision to make. In this snippet, each decision has only two outcomes; there is no requirement that that be true.

The pink pages have no selections on them. They represent endings of the story. Each page has a page number on the bottom; it is assumed that there are other pages in the book, but none of the other pages can be reached by starting from page 1 and going only to the pages named as part of decision pages. The page numbers are widely distributed (as they were in the original series) so that it is not easy to "look ahead" by

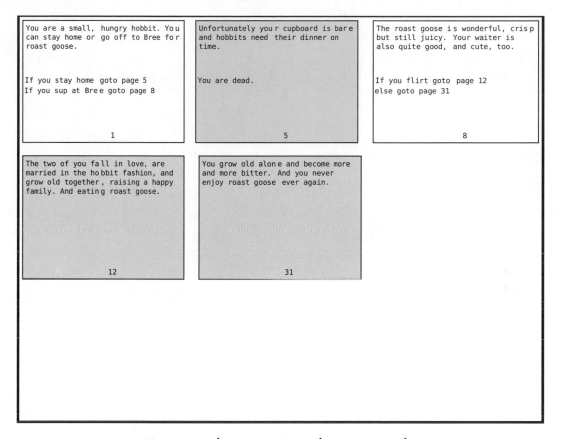

Figure 12.1: Choose Your Own Adventure example

turning one or two pages ahead to see if the outcome of some branch of the adventure is good or bad for the reader.

The story in the figure, such as it is, has three possible outcomes: you die of starvation, you grow old and bitter alone, or you meet the love of your life and have a happy ending. Seeing all of the pages for all of the paths through the book makes it obvious that this book is not "interactive" in the sense that it reacts to the reader by changing due to previous actions. It is equally clear, however, that the *story*, from the point of view of a reader an any given page, *is* interactive. If the reader is making meaningful choices, then this is a form of a game by our working definition.

Why are we interested in a 50-year-old literary device[1] widely used in children's books?

We are looking for a structure where we can store questions and answers in an easy to read manner (so we can load it from a file). The structure must also encode the relationship between the questions and the answers. Once the player tells us that his animal has four legs, the game should no longer guess that the animal is a dog.

The choose-your-own-adventure book provides us with such a structure: each page is either a decision point for the user (a question) or an ending (an answer). The structure of the book is linear (the pages are printed in a fixed order in the book or stored in a fixed order in an input file), so it is easy to read. The structure of the story is encoded in the page numbers (indexes into an `ArrayList`) associated with each choice on a decision page.

---

[1]Raymond Queneau, a French novelist/poet, pioneered the form with his 1959 *Story As You Like It*, and Julio Cortázar, an Argentine au-

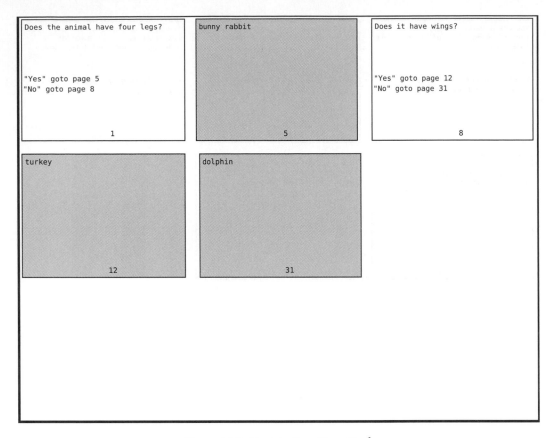

Figure 12.2: Twenty Questions Book

Figure 12.2 is identical to the previous figure except that the text in each page has been changed. Instead of telling a story about a hobbit, the book now plays a game of Twenty Questions (or is it Two Questions?). Notice that on the white pages, let's now refer to them as Question pages, the two choices are now universally labeled "Yes" and "No." Each label is then followed by a "goto page #" just as before. The pink pages, let's refer to them as Answer pages, now each hold just the name of a domain object. When processing an Answer page, we read the text to be "Is it a(n) . . ." where ". . ." is the name of a domain object.

To demonstrate playing the game, we pick an animal, begin at page 1, answer the questions, and turn to the indicated pages. First we pick one of the animals the book knows, a turkey.

The game progresses as follows: On page 1, "Does the animal have four legs?"; our answer is "No", so we turn to page 8. On page 8, "Does it have wings?"; our answer is "Yes" so we turn to page 12. On page 12, "Is it a(n) turkey?"; our answer is "Yes", so the game was won by the book.

Suppose we had selected a penguin instead of a turkey. The first two questions would go exactly as they did before. It is only on page 12, when we are asked if we had chosen a turkey, would our answer change from "Yes" to "No" and the book would be stumped.

If the book is immutable, and its contents cannot be changed (as most printed books in the real world are), we could win every time we played with the book by picking penguin. We won once and now know we will win every time. In fact, this book is very limited and knows only three animals; all other animals stump it.

thor, used it in his 1964 *Hopscotch*. Both of these experimental novels had great influence on the development of hypertext and interactive fiction. See Chapter cha:TextAdventure for more.

If the book is, instead, mutable, and we can add new pages and modify existing pages, then the book can be extended, made smarter. What if when we stumped it we were asked for two things: what we had chosen and a question to tell the difference between the new and the wrong animal.

On page 12, "Is it a turkey?"; our answer is "No", so the book is stumped. "What is your object?"; "penguin." "What yes/no question would differentiate between 'turkey' and 'penguin'?"; "Does it eat fish?" "Which answer means 'penguin'?"; "Yes."

Now we add two pages to the end of the book. Assuming the book had 100 pages in it before, the new pages are numbered 101 and 102. One is a question, "Does it eat fish?" and the other is an answer, "penguin." The "Yes" direction from the new question goes to the new answer (remember that we asked) and "No" goes to the wrong answer (page 12, remember). Finally, the question on page 8 cannot guess "turkey" when the answer is "Yes"; instead it must ask the new question.

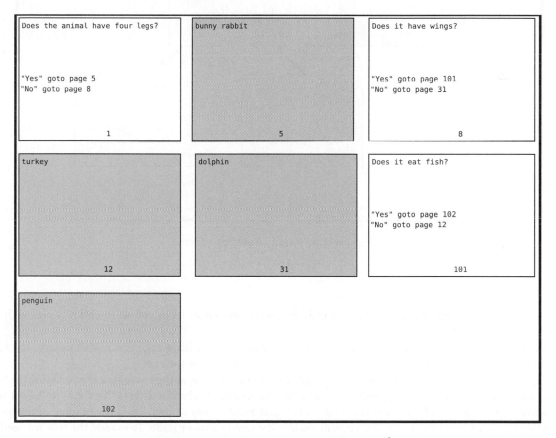

Figure 12.3: Smarter Twenty Questions Book

The smarter book now knows four animals. In Figure 12.3, the updated information is written in red: the text on the new pages, the page numbers on the new pages, and the fixed-up page number on the question before the wrong answer.

Another way to look at the data in the pages of our Twenty Questions books is by moving the pages around and drawing connections between the pages as in Figure 12.4 on the next page.

This drawing shows what computer scientists call a *tree*. A tree is a collection of nodes where one node is designated the *root* of the tree. All nodes but the root have exactly one node referring to them: the node referred to is the child of the referrer; the referrer is the parent of the referred to node. Page 1 is a parent of page 8. A consequence of having only one parent and a single root is that it is possible to traverse the tree

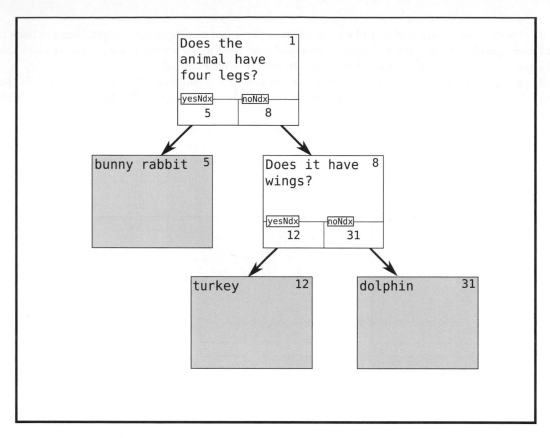

Figure 12.4: Twenty Questions Tree

from the root to any other node in the tree only following references from parent to child. Nodes with no children are *leaf* nodes.[2]

Looking at Figure 12.4, you can see that computer scientists have little experience with nature: the root of the tree is at the top of the figure and the leaves are all drawn below the root.

Playing Twenty Questions with the book is really a matter of starting at the root of the tree, reading the text on the current page, and then, depending on whether the answer to the question is "Yes" or "No", continue down the tree to the yes-child or the no-child. This is just another way of visualizing the reading of the book.

When the book loses the game, the current node is the wrong answer node. To extend the tree we need to build a small tree consisting of the new question, the wrong answer leaf, and the new answer leaf, and then replace the reference to the wrong answer from the question that was its parent with a reference to the new question.

It is useful to notice that we can still get from the root to all of the nodes in the tree: since we could get to the last question in the game and we didn't change its parent, we can still get there. Further, the last question now refers to the new question, so we can get to the new question. The new question refers to both the wrong and the new answer. It is still possible to follow a path of yes and no references to get from the root of the tree to any node. The wrong answer page, in particular, has the same page number and is still reachable. The path from the root to the wrong answer goes through one more question than it did before.

---

[2]Except for the direction of the arrows, a *Twenty Questions Tree* should remind you of a class hierarchy diagram. Computer scientists still talk about `Object` being the root of the Java class hierarchy and any class with no child classes as a leaf class.

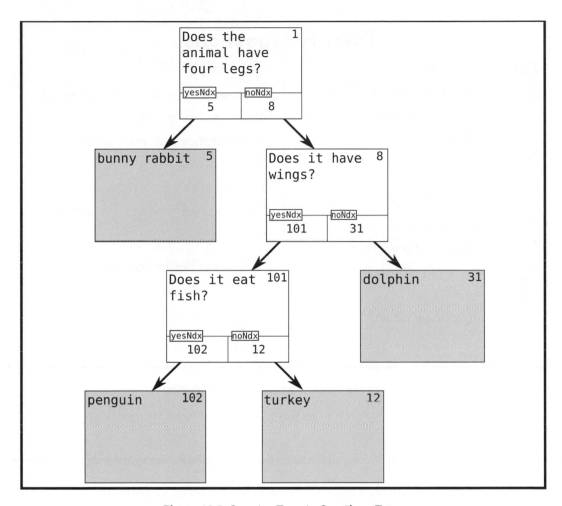

Figure 12.5: Smarter Twenty Questions Tree

Designing Our Classes

If we look at the description of a choose your own adventure story, there appear to be three classes of objects: the book, the question pages, and the answer pages. An AdventureBook is a collection of pages. Any given page can be either a question or an answer. How can we have a collection of different kinds of objects? If the objects in the collection extend the same class, the collection can have the superclass as the *static* type of its elements, whereas the *dynamic* type of each element can be any of the specific subclasses.

An AdventureBook object is a collection of AdventurePages where an AdventurePage is either a Question or an Answer. The AdventureBook is separate from the game so there is one more class, the main class, TwentyQuestions.

What does the game look like while we are playing it? Figure 12.6 shows an example. Just like in Pig in the previous chapter, the program should accept yes-or-no answers without regard to case and permitting single letter abbreviation.

It is also necessary to be able to prompt the user for an arbitrary string of input so that he can supply the name of the domain object he was thinking of and the new question text. This means that TwentyQuestions has three **public static** methods, just like Pig. The main method constructs a TwentyQuestions object and calls three methods on it: load to load the information from the question file, play to actually play the game as long

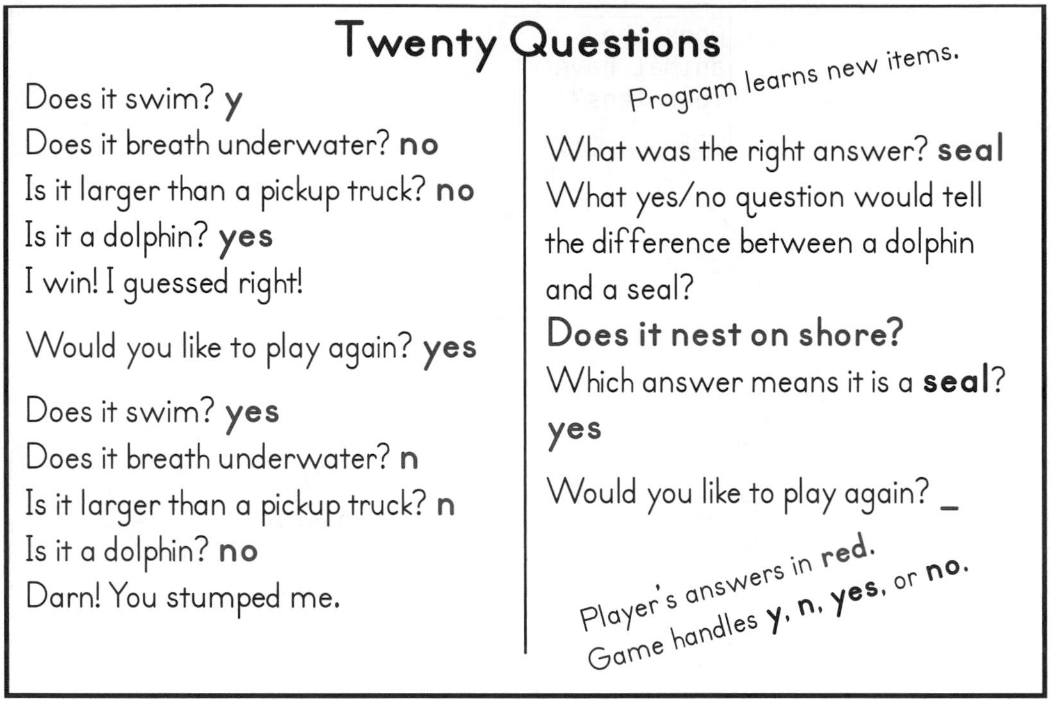

Twenty Questions

Does it swim? **y**
Does it breath underwater? **no**
Is it larger than a pickup truck? **no**
Is it a dolphin? **yes**
I win! I guessed right!

Would you like to play again? **yes**

Does it swim? **yes**
Does it breath underwater? **n**
Is it larger than a pickup truck? **n**
Is it a dolphin? **no**
Darn! You stumped me.

Program learns new items.

What was the right answer? **seal**
What yes/no question would tell
the difference between a dolphin
and a seal?
Does it nest on shore?
Which answer means it is a **seal**?
yes

Would you like to play again? _

Player's answers in red.
Game handles **y, n, yes,** *or* **no.**

Figure 12.6: `TwentyQuestions` Program Design

as the player wants to, and, optionally, `save` which saves the information known by the program back into the question file.

The call to `save` is necessary so that any new domain objects added by the player are "remembered" by the game the next time it is played. Remember the discussion of *RAM* and *disk drives* in Section 3.1. The RAM is the *working memory* of the computer. It is where the Java program, local variables, and objects constructed with `new` reside. It is volatile, meaning its contents last only as long as the computer is running. It is actually worse than that in a sense: the contents of the RAM memory belonging to a Java program last only as long as the program is running.

The information about telling the difference between a turkey and a penguin must be *saved* onto the hard drive. The content of the file on the hard drive is nonvolatile. It remains the same until the file is deleted or overwritten. In particular, if the saved information in the file is of the right format (one we have not yet discussed), then the `load` method can be used to reload the smarter Twenty Questions information the next time the game is played. In turn, this means that the more people play the game, the more elements are added to the collection of domain objects and the better the game becomes.

The main class's public protocol looks something like this:

```
public class TwentyQuestions {
  public static boolean answersYes(String prompt)...
  public static String getLine(String prompt)...
  public static void main(String[] args)...

  private TwentyQuestions()...
  private void load(String fname)...
  private void play()...
```

```
private void save(String fname)...
```

The constructor and the playing methods are **private**, just like those in Pig, because they can be. They are called from the main method *in the same class definition*. They can be **private**.

```java
66  public static void main(String[] args) {
67    String fname = null;
68    if (args.length == 1) {
69      fname = args[0];
70    } else {
71      System.out.println("Usage: java TwentyQuestions <fname>");
72      System.out.println("  where <fname> is the data file name");
73      System.out.println();
74      System.out.println(
75        "Alternatively, what file would you like to load?");
76      Scanner scanner = new Scanner(System.in);
77      fname = scanner.nextLine();
78    }
79
80    TwentyQuestions game = new TwentyQuestions();
81    if (game.load(fname)) {
82      game.play();
83      if (TwentyQuestions.answersYes("Save guessing data?")) {
84        game.save(fname);
85      }
86    }
87  }
```

Listing 12.1: TwentyQuestions main

Given the TwentyQuestions protocol, the main method almost writes itself. The main things it does is get a file name from the user, construct a new TwentyQuestions object, and then use the load method to load the data file for the game. The play method plays the game with the user. Finally, if the user wants to save the changed game data, the save method is called.

The AdventureBook needs to support the same load, play, and save sort of methods. The AdventurePage class uses indexes into the book to keep track of the parent and any child nodes (in the tree), so the AdventureBook has to behave like an ArrayList and support getting an entry by index, finding the index given a page, adding a new entry, and being able to determine the size of the book overall. These requirements lead to a public protocol of the form:

```java
public class AdventureBook {
  public static AdventureBook readBookFromFile(String fname)...
  public static void writeBookToFile(String fname, AdventureBook book)...

  public void add(AdventurePage page)...
  public AdventurePage get(int pageNumber)...
  public int indexOf(AdventurePage page)...
  public void play()...
  public int size()...
```

Because an AdventureBook is treated like a collection, we need to support some of the standard collection methods such as size and get as well. We want to be able to find the page number of a given page inside the book.

Loading is done through a **static** method that loads a whole book from a named file, returning a reference to the new book. A load method like this must be **static** because it must be callable *before* any AdventureBook object has been constructed.

A **static** load method like this is sometimes known as a *factory*, a method that wraps up calls to **new** so that the implementation details of the constructor don't need to be known by *clients* of the class. A client is any class using objects of a given class. TwentyQuestions is a client of AdventureBook. If we consider the parameter list for constructing an AdventureBook to be an implementation detail, wrapping the call to **new** inside a factory hides the detail from TwentyQuestions and the programmer writing it.

The save method is also **static** to remain parallel with the loading method. It is very good practice to make sure that the parameters to methods that go together conceptually are at the same level of abstraction; it would be possible to write writeBookToFile to take an open file rather than a file name. That would make it hard for programmers using the class to remember which takes a file name and which takes an open file. This way the related methods are "the same" in their protocol.

The two node types found in the book, Question and Answer, have a lot in common. Looking at the picture of the tree, we see that both contain text, both have a parent, and both have a page number. It is also possible to play both kinds of pages. This gives us a feeling for the public protocol for AdventurePage:

```
public abstract class AdventurePage {
  public static AdventurePage readPageFromFile(AdventuerBook book,
                                        Scanner scanner)...
  public static void writePageToFile(AdventurePage page,
                               PrintWriter out)...
  public int getNdx()...
  public String getText()...
  public abstract boolean play()...
```

The readPageFromFile is another example of a factory, a method that constructs either an Answer or a Question, depending on what type of page is specified in the input file (the formatting described below). This factory takes the place of a *polymorphic constructor*. Remember that a polymorphic method is a method that is overridden in subclasses. The code calls the method on an object of some *static* type but the version of the method that executes depends on the *dynamic* type of the object referred to.

Since the dynamic type of an object depends on the constructor that is called, an actual polymorphic constructor makes no sense in Java. This factory method is the next best thing. The input file connected to the Scanner encodes the desired dynamic type in some way, and readPageFromFile reads the encoding and uses an **if** statement to call **new** Answer(. . .) or **new** Question(. . .). The factory returns a reference to the superclass AdventurePage but inside the method it calls the constructor of one of the subclasses of that class. More on why this is a good idea later when we discuss the file format.

What does **abstract** mean? It appears twice, once modifying the class AdventurePage and once modifying the method play. An **abstract** class is a class that contains one or more **abstract** methods. An **abstract** method is a method that provides only a header; an **abstract** method has no method body. As a consequence of having "empty" methods, Java does not permit programmers to call constructors of **abstract** classes directly. An **abstract** class can be instantiated only by some subclass which extends it *and* overrides all **abstract** methods.

Another way to think of a **abstract** method is as one that provides only the protocol. The header of the method provides the return type, name, and parameter list that must be overridden, so it describes one aspect of the class's protocol. Since no implementation is provided, all non-**abstract** subclasses must provide an implementation. AdventurePage references can be used to call play but it is always the play method defined in a subclass.

A `Question` is a page that has two additional indexes, one to turn to if the answer to the question on the page is "Yes" and another to turn to if the answer is "No." Turning to the next page after asking the question is embedded in the `play` method. The only other operation that needs access to the index values is `userProvidesNewAnswer`, the method that extends the tree with a new question and a new answer. The extension method is part of the protocol because it is called from `play` in an `Answer` node (that is where the game finds out that it has guessed wrong). The protocol for `Question` is

```
public class Question
  extends AdventurePage {
  public Question(...)... // don't know header yet
  public boolean play()...
  public String toString()...
  public void userProvidesNewAnswer(Answer wrongAnswer)...
}
```

An `Answer` is even simpler. It has to implement `play`, constructor(s), and `toString`. The `toString` method is in both `Question` and `Answer` so that we can print out the content of a tree and see if it is put together the way we think it is. Remember that `toString` is provided by `Object` and that it is used by `System.out.println` to convert object instances for printing. The whole `Answer` protocol is

```
public class Answer
  extends AdventurePage {
  public Answer(...)... // don't know header yet
  public boolean play()...
  public String toString()...
}
```

Before we delve further into **abstract** classes and how to encode domain knowledge for a *smart* computer program, we take time to extend our knowledge of file I/O to include file output. That way we can write text files as well as read them.

Review 12.1

(a) How does one page in a Choose Your Own Adventure book refer to other pages? How is that related to how `Question` objects refer to other `AdventurePages`?

(b) What does **abstract** mean when applied to a class declaration?

(c) What does **abstract** mean when applied to a method declaration?

(d) What is a *tree*? Where is the tree's root? What is a *leaf*?

(e) How many different objects could be differentiated if the game were limited to 15 questions? Is there anything in the structure of our game that actually limits it to 20 questions?

12.2   Reading and Writing Files

In the last two chapters we have seen how to open files for input using the `File` class and then read them with the `Scanner`. In the last section we saw how to use `Scanner` to read standard input; we were able to leverage what we know about reading from data files to read from standard input.

Since Chapter 8 we have, on and off, used `System.out`, a `PrintWriter` object, to write text on the console. In this section we leverage what we have seen about writing to standard output to help us write output files.

System.out and Output Files

Looking at the System documentation, we see that the **public** field out[3] is a PrintWriter. If we follow the documentation link over to PrintWriter, it is nice to see that it has a constructor that takes a File. It looks like we can construct a PrintWriter in almost the same way we construct a Scanner and then use the writer the same way we use System.out. Output does not appear in the window with the command line but is saved in a file stored in the file system.

Two important caveats.   When a PrintWriter is constructed with the name of an existing file and you, the user who ran Java, have permission to overwrite the file's contents, any existing contents are lost. In most graphical user interfaces, when saving over an existing file, programs ask if you are sure you want to overwrite the existing file contents. You can write a program that does that, but PrintWriter is of low enough level that when you open the file (call the object constructor), the file is reset to have a length of 0 characters waiting for you to write new contents. You must also *always* close your output files. There are file systems that can lose the contents of a file if the program terminates with any output file unclosed. Very few *modern* file systems do this but it is important to make it a habit to close all files (but especially output files).

For practice writing a file, let's modify AddTwoNumbersRight.java so that instead of writing the sum to standard output, the program instead writes it to a file. We prompt the user for the name of a file in which to save the results, prompt the user for two numbers to add, and then add them, storing the results in the output file.

```java
19  public static void main(String[] args) {
20    System.out.println("FileTwoNumbersRight:");
21    Scanner keyboard = new Scanner(System.in);
22
23    System.out.print("Results file name: ");
24    String fname = keyboard.nextLine();
25    File outFile = new File(fname);
26    try {
27      PrintWriter out = new PrintWriter(outFile);
28
29      System.out.print("Number: ");
30      int first = keyboard.nextInt();
31
32      System.out.print("Number: ");
33      int second = keyboard.nextInt();
34
35      // Print results in the file
36      out.println("Sum of " + first + " + " + second + " = " +
37        (first + second));
38      out.close();
39    } catch (FileNotFoundException e) {
40      e.printStackTrace();
41      System.err.println(
42        "Program cannot make useful progress: terminating.");
43      System.exit(1);
44    }
45  }
```

Listing 12.2: FileTwoNumbersRight

---

[3]Just a reminder: Good object-oriented design abhors *public* access for fields.

Most of `main` is familiar. Even the `try` ... `catch` block is familiar; we have just not used it for `PrintWriter` objects before. Just like when creating a `Scanner`, it is possible that the file represented by the `File` object cannot be found. Typically `PrintWriter`, because it is opening the file for output, creates a file. But it is possible that the user does not have permission to create the named file for some reason. If that happens, then an exception is raised by the `PrintWriter` constructor. This program moved all of the useful code inside the `try` block because a failure to open the output file moots any values calculated by the program. The exception is handled by reporting it and terminating the program.

Let's run the program:

```
~/Chapter12% java FileTwoNumbersRight
FileTwoNumbersRight:
Results file name: sum.txt
Number: 100
Number: 121

~/Chapter12% java EchoFile sum.txt
Sum of 100 + 121 = 221
```

Notice that there was no output from the program after the second number was entered. The program simply terminated. When `EchoFile` (see Listing 10.11) was run (at the next command line prompt), it echoed the contents of the newly created output file. Java does not add any extension to a file name. The full name, `sum.txt`, was provided to the `File` constructor.

When a `PrintWriter` is constructed with the name of an existing file, the contents of the file are truncated (the size is set to 0), and then anything printed to the output file is appended to the file pointer which is then moved to the end of the input.

So, if we run the program a second time with the same file name but different input, the following console session results:

```
~/Chapter12% java EchoFile sum.txt
Sum of 100 + 121 = 221

~/Chapter12% java FileTwoNumbersRight
FileTwoNumbersRight:
Results file name: sum.txt
Number: 87
Number: -5

~/Chapter12% java EchoFile sum.txt
Sum of 87 + -5 = 82
```

The first run of `EchoFile` shows that the contents of `sum.txt` are just what they were at the end of the last session. We then run the sum program and look at the new contents. One reason for choosing the numbers that we did are because the results line is *shorter* (in characters) than the previous results line. If any characters were left from the previous file contents, we should see them at the end of the line after "= 82".

Review 12.2

(a) Assume you create a `File` referring to an existing file on the system. You then use the `File` to construct a `PrintWriter`. You write some lines to the `PrintWriter` and close the file. When were the original contents of the file lost?

(b) Could you print a `Sprite` into a file? How would you do it? Would it include enough information to restore the `Sprite` at some later time?

12.3   Data-driven Programs

Consider a commercial game program for a moment. What makes Epic Game's *Unreal Tournament* series of first-person shooters so popular? There are many arguments to be made in favor of gameplay decisions made by the designers along with the powerful graphics engine underlying the game. The author would argue that there is an additional factor: user-created content.

Unreal Tournament and many other popular games come with *level editors* that permit motivated players to build their own game levels. These user-designed levels can then be shared with other owners of the game. These user-generated *game mods* (short for "modifications") give creative players a new level (pun intended) of interaction with the game and give other players a way to extend their interaction with the game in new environments. Popular mods can even go on to become their own games.[4]

What is a level editor? It is a program that permits users to place virtual game objects inside virtual game spaces and to attach actions, or some sort of code, to them. The details of writing a mod or using a level editor is beyond the scope of this book since we are focused on writing games in Java, not the various modification languages of commercial game engines. What is important to us is what happens when you press the "Save" button in the level editor.

What gets saved and how does whatever gets saved become a new map, character, or game? The following discussion assumes the saved information is a new map but the general features are independent of the exact type of mod written. The level editor saves a *data file* that describes the new map. The format of the data file depends on the game engine being used; both the level editor and the game itself were written with a particular format in mind.

When the game is run, among the various command line parameters it supports is a map file name. If you include a command line parameter of the form `--map-file-name=MyNewMap`,[5] the game starts not in its standard first level but instead in the world described in the new map file.

The important thing to notice is that the *program*, the game itself, is not changed. The modder does not need access to the source code of the game, nor does he need to compile source code into executable code. The format saved by the level editor is the same format used by the game's own levels.

Separating the code (the compiled game) from the data (the level files), the game has increased flexibility. During development the game designers can make changes without needing to compile the whole program; this is a major time savings since compiling a moderately complicated game on a single computer can take upwards of two hours. Since changes are inexpensive (in terms of time), game designers can try many different things to find the ones that work. The separation also makes it possible to sell downloadable content to extend the life of the game and provide additional revenue to the game company. And, as discussed above, separating code and data permits the user community to mod the game and even develop new games atop the existing game.

Human-readable Data Files

In the previous chapter we wrote Hangman to use an external word list file. That was a separation of data and code. It would be possible to have multiple word files, perhaps by natural language. You could then play Hangman in German or English, Dutch or French. There could also be different files for different skill levels. If the player were asked for her school grade level, then the game could open one of a dozen different word lists and play a game tailored for the player's level.

One thing to note about the Hangman data file is its format: each line represents one entry, one phrase (or word) that the game uses to challenge the player. Knowing this is how the file is laid out, anyone could produce a data file for Hangman. This is a major advantage to using a plain text file of some format.

---

[4]*Quake* spawned *Team Fortress*, *Half-life* was modded into *Counter Strike*, and *Unreal Tournament* spawned *ChaosUT* and *Tactical Ops*; these examples barely scratch the surface, focusing only on mods that became separately distributed games and only on first-person shooter games. The range of maps, new characters, weapons, gameplay modes, and the like is much, much larger.

[5]This syntax is fictional but similar to that found in several commercial games.

The next section looks at how objects more complex than a `String` can be encoded and stored in a human-readable and, more importantly, human-editable format. Knowing how the game data files are formatted, we can write `TwentyQuestions` files to guess animals (as we develop in the chapter), famous politicians, Roman trading centers, or anything else we wish.

Review 12.3

(a) Name three advantages of having a data-driven program.

(b) Why are human-readable data files important?

(c) What is a *game mod*? How would you explain it to your grandmother?

12.4 Encoding Objects to Read or Write Them

The power of separating programs from data comes from the ability to use the exact same program to play multiple different games. The ability to play more than one game is dependent on being able to build a data structure that supports at a minimum sequence and selection. Once the data structure is developed as the heart of the game, it is necessary to encode it so that different structures can be saved into data files and a data file can be specified when the executable is run.

Pages and Books

In Section 12.1 we looked at how a choose-your-own-adventure story could be stored in a book. As an analogy, a book is a good fit with an `ArrayList`: the elements (pages) are stored in sequence, each is associated with a small integer (page number), and, by containing a small integer, one page can refer to another page. Equally important, the reference from one page to another page does *not* require the referred to page to exist when the reference is made; the page need exist only when following the reference.

This makes loading/saving a linear representation of a book simpler than it could be. If every page *referred to* by a page must have been loaded before the referring page can be loaded, it would be necessary to sort the pages of the book so that leaves were in the file before any internal node that referenced them. The root of the tree would have to be the very last page read from the book file.

So, an `AdventureBook` is a linear container of `AdventurePage` objects. If we look back at the design of the protocols of the `AdventurePage`, `Question`, and `Answer`, what fields to they each have for implementation? That is, how can the protocol be implemented. We need to determine the data contained in the objects before we can determine how to store any of these objects into a text file (for reading or writing).

Let's start by agreeing to label each page in the text file with the type of the page. If we have a single question with two answers on the following pages, the text file would look something like this:

```
Question
...
Answer
...
Answer
...
```

Listing 12.3: Skeleton of an `AdventureBook` file

The ellipses stand for whatever information, in whatever format, is required for defining a `Question` or an `Answer`. Looking back at Figures 12.2–12.5, we see that every page has a page number, text, and a reference to its parent page, and that every page belongs to some particular book.

How can these common features be represented in the text file? A text file contains the pages of a particular book: the book the pages are in is indicated by the file they are in. The book file must contain every page in the book: the pages are numbered, implicitly, from the beginning of the file. Figure 12.7 shows the skeleton tree matching the skeleton data file in Listing 12.3

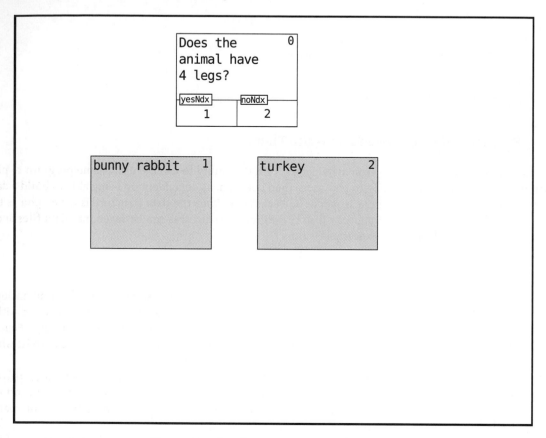

Figure 12.7: Reading a Twenty Questions Tree

The tree shows the page number assigned to each of the pages when they were read in from the file: since they are stored in a Java collection it is convenient to use 0-based numbering. The layout of the page indicates the parent/child relationship between the pages, but we have not yet specified the formatting for all of the fields.

In `Hangman` we used one line per item. Here we have committed to multiple lines. An `Answer` needs text and the page number of its parent. That sounds like two additional lines. A `Question` has the same information, text and the parent page number, as well as the page numbers for its yes and no following pages. Given a line per page number, the data file for a very simple game tree would look like this:

```
Question
Does the animal have four legs?
-1
1
2
Answer
bunny rabbit
```

```
0
Answer
turkey
0
```

This is the file representation of the tree in Figure 12.8.

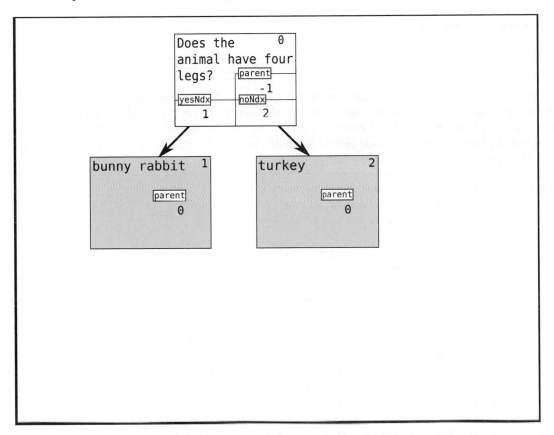

Figure 12.8: Finishing Reading a Twenty Questions Tree

AdventurePage

The common information is stored in `AdventurePage` and the specialized information for `Question` is stored in that subclass. We look at the *constructors* for the three page classes. The one thing to note is that an `Answer` or a `Question` constructor is called right *after* the label is read. So the read marker is at the beginning of the text line. We see how to arrange that when we discuss the factory method's implementation.

```
50    /** the book to which this page belongs */
51    private final AdventureBook book;
52
53    /** the index of the parent node */
54    private int parentNdx;
55
```

```
56    /** this node's text value */
57    private final String text;
68    protected AdventurePage(AdventureBook book, String text,
69      int parentNdx) {
70      this.book = book;
71      book.add(this);
72      this.text = text;
73      setParentNdx(parentNdx);
74    }
```

Listing 12.4: `AdventurePage` constructor

The `AdventurePage` constructor copies the three parameters into the class's fields. The only *interesting* bit is where the page is added to the book. This makes sure that every new page is actually in the book it references as its containing book. Notice that there is no field for the page number of this page. That is because we can always use the book's `indexOf` method to find our index in the collection (which is the page number of the page). This is another application of the DRY principle.

```
20    public Answer(AdventureBook book, Scanner scanner) {
21      this(book, scanner.nextLine(), scanner.nextInt());
22      scanner.skip(".*\n");// skip to the end of the line
23    }
34    public Answer(AdventureBook book, String text, int parentNdx) {
35      super(book, text, parentNdx);
36    }
```

Listing 12.5: `Answer` constructor

`Answer` has two constructors and no fields (beyond those inherited from `AdventurePage`). The second constructor passes its parameters to the `AdventurePage` constructor. The first constructor is called with a `AdventureBook` and a `Scanner` with the read pointer at the beginning of the text line. Line 21 reads the next line from the input as the text and then reads an integer (on the next line) as the index of the parent page. These values are passed directly into the other constructor.

There is a problem at the end of line 21: `nextInteger` leaves the read pointer at the character following the integer's characters. The read pointer is at the end of the line with the integer rather than at the beginning of the next line. This is a problem because if a call were made to `nextLine`, it would read from the read pointer to the end of the line with the integer.

We want to skip over everything up to and including an end-of-line character. The `Scanner` class has a `skip` method that takes a `String` describing the pattern to skip over. In the pattern, "." means any character, "*" means 0 or more of what comes before (just like in our Java template grammar), and the slash n is the end of line marker. Line 22 skips over anything up to and including an end of line marker. Just what we want.

```
15    /** reference to the no tree */
16    private int noNdx;
17
18    /** reference to the yes tree */
19    private int yesNdx;
32    public Question(AdventureBook book, Scanner scanner) {
33      this(book, scanner.nextLine(), scanner.nextInt(), scanner.nextInt(),
34        scanner.nextInt());
35      scanner.skip(".*\n");// skip to the end of the line
36    }
```

```
56    public Question(AdventureBook book, String text, int parentNdx,
57      int yesNdx, int noNdx) {
58      super(book, text, parentNdx);
59      setYesNdx(yesNdx);
60      setNoNdx(noNdx);
61    }
```

Listing 12.6: `Question` constructor

The `Question` constructors look a lot like the `Answer` constructors: the one passed an `AdventureBook` and a `Scanner` reads all of the values from the input file and passes them to the other constructor; the other constructor takes five parameters, passing three up to `AdventurePage` and setting the two local fields to the appropriate values. The two local fields are `yesNdx` and `noNdx`, the page numbers that follow this question if the answer is "Yes" or "No."

The Factory

So, where do the `Answer` and `Question` lines in the data file come in? The factory method (the *polymorphic constructor*) can construct either an `Answer` or a `Question` from the contents at the read pointer of the `Scanner` passed into the method. The decision of which type of page to construct is made by reading the next line.

```
27    public static AdventurePage readPageFromFile(AdventureBook book,
28      Scanner scanner) {
29      String questionOrAnswer = scanner.nextLine();
30      if (questionOrAnswer.equals("Question")) {
31        return new Question(book, scanner);
32      } else {
33        return new Answer(book, scanner);
34      }
35    }
```

Listing 12.7: `AdventurePage readPageFromFile`

The `readPageFromFile` method is **static** so that it can be called before any pages are actually constructed. It is passed an `AdventureBook`, to which the next page read is added, and a `Scanner`. The `Scanner` provides the next line from the file. Since we assume the input stream is positioned at the beginning of a page record (either three or five lines long, beginning with the name of the class), the method reads the next line and compares it to `"Question"`: if it is equal, a `Question` constructor is called; otherwise an `Answer` constructor is called. Remember that the `AdventurePage` constructor (called from the subclass constructor) adds the page to the book. This makes sure that the read page is given an index (its own page number) as well as having a reference from the book.

If there were a third type of page we would have to write a new `AdventurePage` subclass and update the factory so that it could handle the new kind of page. Reading data from a text file is often discussed using database terms: each page in the text file is a *record* composed of a type identifier and some number of *fields*.

AdventureBook

The factory can, given an open input text file, read the next page record. The constructors for the pages, as we saw above, leave the input read marker just past the end of the last line of the record. How can such a method be used to read a file?

`AdventurePage.readPageFromFile` is similar in function to `nextLine` in `Scanner`: `nextLine` reads from where the input marker is, constructing a `String` until it reaches the end of the current line; the input marker is left just past the end of line marker and the newly constructed object is returned. A sentinel-controlled loop that looks much like our other file reading loops should be used to read in all of the pages for a book.

```
32    public static AdventureBook readBookFromFile(String fname) {
33      File file = new File(fname);
34      AdventureBook book = null;
35      try {
36        Scanner scanner = new Scanner(file);
37        book = new AdventureBook(scanner);
38        scanner.close();
39      } catch (FileNotFoundException e) {
40        book = null;// return an error value
41      }
42      return book;
43    }
79    private AdventureBook(Scanner scanner) {
80      pages = new ArrayList<AdventurePage>();
81
82      while (scanner.hasNextLine()) {
83        AdventurePage.readPageFromFile(this, scanner);
84      }
85    }
```

Listing 12.8: AdventureBook readBookFromFile

The **static** readBookFromFile method takes a file name and opens the file for input, if possible. If it is possible, then a new AdventureBook is constructed using the Scanner attached to the input stream; if there is a problem, **null** is returned.

The important lines in the constructor are 82–84: it is an eof-controlled loop. If there is another line in the file, then there is another page. The loop reads until there are no more lines; each call to the page factory consumes one page record from the input file, leaving the read marker just past the last line of the record. When the last record is read, the last line of the record is also the last line of the file so that there are no more lines available. The loop ends and the book is full of pages.

Writing Out Data

After playing TwentyQuestions, a player might have updated the data in the AdventureBook. How is an AdventureBook written out to a data file? It is done with a **static** method, writeBookToFile. This method is **static** to parallel the read method (it would make equal sense to make the save method non-**static**).

```
56    public static void writeBookToFile(String fname,
57      AdventureBook bookToSave) {
58      File file = new File(fname);
59      try {
60        PrintWriter out = new PrintWriter(file);
61        bookToSave.save(out);
62        out.close();
63      } catch (FileNotFoundException e) {
64        System.err.println("Problem opening " + fname + " for output.");
65        System.err.println("Decision tree contents unsaved.");
66      }
```

```
 67      }
151      private void save(PrintWriter out) {
152        for (int i = 0; i != pages.size(); ++i) {
153          AdventurePage.writePageToFile(pages.get(i), out);
154        }
155      }
```

Listing 12.9: `AdventureBook writeBookToFile`

When `writeBookToFile` is called, it is passed a file name and a `AdventureBook`. The method attempts to open the named file for output. If all goes well, the file content is truncated, and then `AdventureBook.save` is called. `save` uses a count-controlled loop to traverse the `pages` list, calling `writePageToFile` with each page in `pages` in turn along with the open output file. When `save` finishes, `writeBookToFile` closes the output file and returns.

If there was a problem opening the named file, a message is printed and the method returns. Notice that it returns *without* having saved anything. It prints an error message giving that information to the user.

Lines 64–65 use `println` but not with `System.out`. The `System` class has three file handles, one for standard input, `in`, one for standard output, `out`, and one for standard error (or, in better English, "the standard error channel"), `err`. Everything we have seen about using the `PrintWriter System.out` applies to using the `PrintWriter System.err`.

When running from the command line, `out` and `err` are typically both attached to the screen for output. In some operating systems it is possible to split the output so that each goes to a different place.[6] It is good programming practice to split "regular" output from error messages so that we make sure to print output to `out` and error messages to `err`.

The `AdventurePage` class's `writePageToFile` method is also **static** to parallel the read method. It takes two parameters: the `PrintWriter` where the record should be saved (written) and the page to write. The `save` method of the page does the real work.

```
 45      public static void writePageToFile(AdventurePage page,
 46        PrintWriter out) {
 47        page.save(out);
 48      }
153      protected void save(PrintWriter out) {
154        out.println(getClass().getName());
155        out.println(getText());
156        out.println(getParentNdx());
157      }
```

Listing 12.10: `AdventurePage writePageToFile`

It is common for overriding methods in subclasses to literally extend the function of the method defined in the superclass. `Question.save` does whatever `AdventurePage.save` does *and then* does whatever special stuff it does to handle `Question` objects.

`AdventurePage.save` must be called by all overriding definitions *before* they write anything to the output text file. This is why it is **protected** (subclasses must be able to call it). An `AdventurePage` is written by writing the name of the class of the page (`getClass`, defined in `Object`, is *polymorphic*: it returns the dynamic class of the object) on a line, then the text on the next line, and the parent page index on the next line. Any subclass that must save more information, say, `Question`, writes additional information following the base information. `Answer` has no additional information; there is no need to override the method in `Answer`.

---

[6]The details on doing this are operating system and command line processor specific and are beyond the scope of this book.

```
248   protected void save(PrintWriter out) {
249     super.save(out);
250     out.println(getYesNdx());
251     out.println(getNoNdx());
252   }
```

Listing 12.11: `Question` save

`Question.save` overrides `AdventurePage.save`; in line 249 it calls the superclass definition of the `save` method. After the three lines written by `AdventurePage.save`, `Question` adds the yes and no page indexes, each on its own line. This matches the input format expected by the input factory described earlier.

Review 12.4

(a) How are the types of different objects encoded in the data files for our program?

(b) What is a *factory*? How are the `Question` and `Answer` objects created by a factory? What is the static return type of the factory method?

(c) What does **protected** mean? Why is `AdventurePage.save` declared to be **protected**? How do subclass `save` methods use it?

(d) In `Question.save`, how do you call `AdventurePage.save`?

12.5   Finishing the Game

The I/O of the game uses the same methods developed in the last chapter, and the structure of the main game, as described above, is also very similar: a new `TwentyQuestions` object is constructed and its three methods, `load`, `play`, and `save`, are called in that order.

The `load` and `save` methods use the `AdventureBook` methods `readBookFromFile` and `writeBookToFile`, the methods described in the last section. All that is left to examine is the `play` method and the corresponding `play` methods in the book and page objects. As we look at `play` we also come up against the `userProvidesNewAnswer` method, the method by which the game gets smarter. These two pieces, `play` and learning, are addressed in separate subsections below.

Recursion: Circular Invocation

Looking at Figure 12.9 on the facing page, how would you use the diagram to play a game of `TwentyQuestions`? One easy way is to take a coin and mark the page you are on. When you move the coin onto a page, you ask the question. When the player answers, you just move the coin to a new page and *do the same thing again*.

One key thing to notice about the decision tree view of the book: *each* `Question` is the root of a decision tree. That means if we know what to do at the root of the whole tree, we know what to do for each and every question.

We examine the code from the top down, from `TwentyQuestions` down to the individual pages. Notice the separation of concerns as we go down: at `TwentyQuestions`'s level we ask if the user wants to play again (and again and . . .); at the `AdventureBook` level we play one game starting at the root; at the `Question` or `Answer` level the focus is on displaying the state for the user, getting user input, and updating the state of the game.[7]

---

[7]We hope that last set of three things sounds familiar.

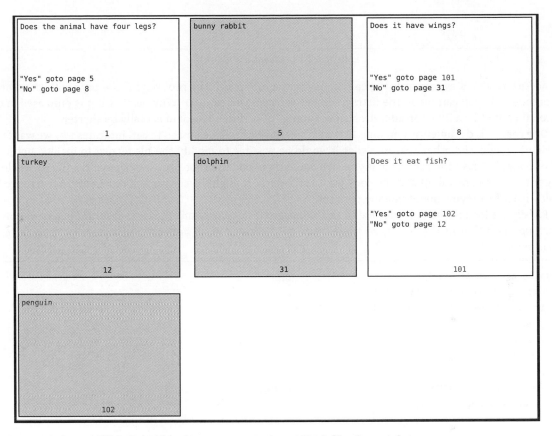

Figure 12.9: Smarter Twenty Questions Book (duplicate of Figure 12.3

```
105   private void play() {
106     boolean playing = true;
107     while (playing) {
108       book.play();
109       playing = TwentyQuestions.answersYes(
110           "Would you like to play again?");
111     }
112   }
```

Listing 12.12: TwentyQuestions play

The play method in TwentyQuestions has the book play one game and then asks the user if he wants to play again. This is a sentinel-controlled loop with an ending condition when the user says no more. It is also an example of reusing code we already wrote: since we have answersYes, we call it to ask if the user wants to play again, just as we call it to ask the various questions in the game.

```
19    /** the index of the root page in the book */
20    private static final int rootNdx = 0;
130   public boolean play() {
131     return get(rootNdx).play();
```

```
132   }
```

Listing 12.13: AdventureBook play

AdventureBook.play forwards the call to play in the root page. The root page is the page with the rootNdx as its index. As you can see in the listing, rootNdx is a constant set to 0. Why name it if it is only used in one place? It cannot be a DRY consideration since typing "0" on line 131 would actually be shorter.

One reason is documentation. Line 131, with rootNdx as the value passed to get, indicates *why* we want that particular page. The other reason is that it would be possible to modify the file format to include not just a list of pages but also the root page index. We could then load the root page index from the file (it would no longer be a constant value) and the code would still work. It might be convenient to be able to rearrange the book without worrying about moving the root.

Finally we look at the play method in the two page classes. Remember, play is **abstract** in AdventurePage; it has *no* definition in that class, so there must be overrides in all concrete (non-**abstract**) subclasses of AdventurePage.

```
69   public boolean play() {
70     int nextPageNdx = NO_SUCH_PAGE;
71     if (TwentyQuestions.answersYes(getText())) {
72       nextPageNdx = getYesNdx();
73     } else {
74       nextPageNdx = getNoNdx();
75     }
76     AdventurePage nextPage = getBook().get(nextPageNdx);
77     return nextPage.play();
78   }
```

Listing 12.14: Question play

In Question we see the complete game loop for TwentyQuestions: the call to answersYes displays the question in the text (shows the state) and waits for an answer from the user (gets user input). Based on the input (was it "Yes" or "No?"), a next page is selected and play is called on that page (state is updated *and* the loop starts over).

Two related things to notice: there is no explicit loop construct here; instead play calls play to start the loop over again. Each iteration of the loop is one call to play, and the method calls itself if another iteration is needed.

A method that calls itself (same name, same header, same class of object) is a *recursive* method. Recursion is an alternative way to implement iteration. For some data structures, in particular, trees and other linked-together structures (graphs), recursion can be conceptually simpler than writing a loop. Here we recur to play at the next question after the current question (think about moving the coin and asking the question). When the user reaches an Answer, the play method on Answer does not recur, so it returns **true** or **false**; so the Question.play that called it returns that value to the Question.play that called it, which returns that value to the Question.play that called it which . . . . You get the idea.

```
48   public boolean play() {
49     String guess = "Is it a(n) " + getText() + "?";
50     if (TwentyQuestions.answersYes(guess)) {
51       System.out.println("I am so smart! I win!!!");
52       return true;
53     } else {
54       System.out.println("Darn, you stumped me.");
55       getParent().userProvidesNewAnswer(this);
```

```
56        return false;
57    }
58  }
```

Listing 12.15: `Answer play`

`Answer.play` builds a question out of the item to be guessed and asks it of the player (again, show state, get input from user). If the player answers "Yes", we can just return **true** because we (the game) won.

If the player answers "No", then we don't know enough domain objects. The player has one we don't know. So, let's get the parent of the wrong answer (it is a `Question`) and have it fix up the contents of the tree. We then return **false** because we lost the game.

A Learning System

Section 12.1 described how to fix up the decision tree/book when it failed to guess a domain object. That description is reflected in the `userProvidesNewAnswer` method. The method is longer than any other we have seen and it has more internal comments than we have seen since `NewtonsApple`. It is not difficult but it is long.

```
109  public void userProvidesNewAnswer(Answer wrongAnswer) {
110      // Get the name of the correct object
111      String correctAnswerText = TwentyQuestions.getLine(
112          "What were you thinking of?");
113
114      // And a question to differentiate right from wrong
115      String differentiatingQuestionText = TwentyQuestions.getLine(
116          "What question could differentiate between a \"" +
117          wrongAnswer.getText() + "\" and a \"" + correctAnswerText +
118          "\"?");
119
120      // And whether "yes" means the new object or not
121      boolean newAnswerIsYes = TwentyQuestions.answersYes(
122          "Which answer means \"" + correctAnswerText +
123          "\" is the right answer?");
124
125      // Make a new answer and a new question. Attach the two answers,
126      // right and wrong, to the yes/no or no/yes positions of the new
127      // question (according to what the player told us)
128      Answer correctAnswer = new Answer(getBook(), correctAnswerText,
129          NO_SUCH_PAGE);
130
131      Answer newYes = null;
132      Answer newNo = null;
133      if (newAnswerIsYes) {
134        newYes = correctAnswer;
135        newNo = wrongAnswer;
136      } else {
137        newYes = wrongAnswer;
138        newNo = correctAnswer;
139      }
140
141      Question differentiatingQuestion = new Question(getBook(),
```

```
142        differentiatingQuestionText, getNdx(), newYes.getNdx(),
143        newNo.getNdx());
144
145    // Fix up the last question so instead of guessing wrongAnswer, we
146    // ask differentiatingQuestion. Need to know whether the wrongAnswer
147    // came from the yes or the no branch of the last question
148    if (isYesChild(wrongAnswer.getNdx())) {
149      setYesNdx(differentiatingQuestion.getNdx());
150    } else {
151      setNoNdx(differentiatingQuestion.getNdx());
152    }
153  }
```

Listing 12.16: Question userProvidesNewAnswer

The method asks the player for the name of her new domain object, a question to differentiate between the new and the wrong objects, and how to answer the question to mean the new object.

It then builds a new Answer object without a parent (the parent is fixed up when the new question is constructed). The answers, new and wrong, are matched with yes and no answers so that the differentiating question can be constructed. Lines 141–143 make the new question, adding it to the book, and fixing up the parent fields of the two Answer objects referenced. setYesNdx is listed here; setNoNdx is parallel.

```
231  private void setYesNdx(int yesNdx) {
232    this.yesNdx = yesNdx;
233    if ((yesNdx != NO_SUCH_PAGE) && (yesNdx < getBook().size())) {
234      getBook().get(yesNdx).setParentNdx(getNdx());
235    }
236  }
```

Listing 12.17: Question setYesNdx

When the yesNdx in the differentiatingQuestion is set, the parentNdx of the page (since both Answer objects are already in the book, they already have valid indexes) referenced is set to the current page.

Finally, the current Question must be updated. Why? Because this Question refers to the wrong answer (we called the method on the wrong answer's parent, remember?). It must refer, instead, to the differentiatingQuestion. Only difficulty: do we fix up the yesNdx or the noNdx? Depends on whether the wrong answer's index is in the yesNdx or not. isYesChild returns **true** if the given index is the yesNdx (again, a named method to explain *why* we compare the two indexes).

We look at one more method, AdventurePage.getParent. The method is fairly simple in concept: go to the book, get the object with the parent's index, and return that object. The problem? The pages in the book are AdventurePages and all parents must be Questions. This method could just return an AdventurePage object, leaving the problem of how to convert an AdventurePage to a Question to the calling method.

That is a bad design: changing the static type of a reference involves error checking and putting that off to the point of *call* of getParent is the wrong kind of lazy. It makes more sense to make the change in one place, especially since we know that in a properly constructed decision tree any parent *must*, of necessity, be a Question page. We can avoid error checking since we know what type of AdventurePage it must be.

```
124  protected Question getParent() {
125    if (getParentNdx() != NO_SUCH_PAGE) {
126      return (Question) getBook().get(getParentNdx());
127    } else {
128      return null;
```

```
129        }
130      }
```

Listing 12.18: AdventurePage getParent

Line 126 uses `get` on the book; that returns a `AdventurePage`. The `(Question)` in front of the expression is a *cast operator*. We saw type casting briefly in Chapter 7. The form of a cast operator is the name of a class inside a pair of parentheses. If the expression following is-a `Question`, then the whole expression is a reference to that `Question`. If, perchance, the expression is *not* actually a `Question`, then the cast fails and the result is **null**.

Most object-oriented programs should not need casts. In fact, this program needs casts because we use numeric references into the `pages` list rather than Java references to hook questions to answers.[8] This one cast is unfortunate but it does not completely invalidate the class structure of the program.

There are a handful of helper methods that were not described in detail in the chapter. This is because simple getter and setter methods should be easy to understand. The choice of **private** or some other access should also be understandable: choose **private** unless, for some reason, you cannot.

Review 12.5

(a) What is type casting? How is it used in `AdventurePage.getParent`? Why is it used in that method?

(b) How can an `Answer` tell whether it is a yes or a no answer to its parent?

(c) What is recursion? Why does it come up in this section?

12.6   Summary

Choose Your Own Adventure Books

A *Choose Your Own Adventure* book is an example of a printed *hypertext*: each page has a question and the next page to be read is determined by the answer selected by the reader. Pages are linked through the use of page numbers.

Choose Your Own Adventure books were used to construct a *tree* for playing `TwentyQuestions`. A tree labeling the major parts is shown in Figure 12.10 on the next page.

The *root* is a *node* with no *parent*. A tree has exactly one root. *Links* join nodes; in this picture, each link points from the *parent* to the *child*; when drawing a Java inheritance tree we point the arrows in the other direction.

A tree is *traversed* or crossed by starting at the root (which means the root can be found in some way) and choosing to follow the link to the *left subtree* or the *right subtree*; these are also known as the *yes subtree* and the *no subtree* in the chapter.

Links in our tree were stored as index values into the `ArrayList` of nodes (`AdventurePages`). The root is the node at index 0.

Saving and Restoring Trees

So long as the `ArrayList` is saved and restored in the exact same order, the references to other nodes by their indices remains valid across multiple runs.

---

[8]That leads to recursive data structures where a `Question` contains a reference to another `Question` and requires recursive methods for reading and writing the structures to text files. For the cost of one cast, the read and write routines are *much* easier to understand.

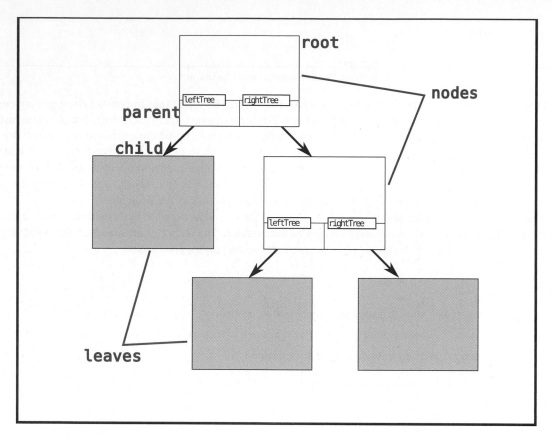

Figure 12.10: Computer science tree terms

Adding Nodes

New nodes are added to the tree by

- calling `add` to put the new node into the `ArrayList`,

- getting a reference to the node that should be the new node's parent by calling `get` with the appropriate index,

- updating the yes or no subtree value in the parent with the index of the new node,

- updating the parent value in the new node with the index of the parent.

No other nodes in the tree need to change.

Structured File Contents

When a file that can contain objects of multiple types is read, the type of each object must be encoded in the file. The type of object to create from any given *record* in the data file cannot be known until run-time. This dynamic value requires a *polymorphic constructor*, a constructor that initializes different types depending on parameters passed to the constructor.

Java does *not* have polymorphic constructors. Instead, the *factory pattern* is applied. A factory method is a `static` method that returns a superclass of all of the types that it can construct. The factory uses its parameters to determine what dynamic type is required and calls the correct constructor (through a standard static call to `new`). The new object is then initialized (by the object constructor) and a reference is returned by the factory.

```
public static AdventurePage readPageFromFile(AdventureBook book,
                                             Scanner scanner)
```

In this chapter, `AdventurePage` is a superclass of `Question` and `Answer`, so the factory, `readPageFromFile`, returns `AdventurePage`. For convenience the factory is also located in the `AdventurePage.java`. The required type is determined by reading `scanner` for a `String` encoding of the desired type.

Writing Files

The `PrintWriter` class is the type of `System.out`. A `PrintWriter` can be constructed with a `File`. This opens the file for *output* and *erases all previous content in the file.*

The `PrintWriter` has `print` and `println`, so writing to it is just like writing to `System.out`, the standard output. It is important to *close* any `PrintWriter` opened on a file to make sure the file system does not lose any output when the program terminates.

12.7   Chapter Review Exercises

Review Exercise 12.1 If you had the following is-a hierarchy:

```
HousholdObject
    Furniture
        Chair
        Sofa
        Ottoman
    Electronics
        Computer
        Stereo
            IPod
            Component
```

(a) Consider a *factory* method that can read a file encoding instances of any of these types. What is the return type of the factory method? Why?

(b) Suggest a way to encode the type of the next record in the input file. How would your factory match the encoding to an internal value?

(c) Now, suggest a different way to encode the type of the next record in the input file. Do *not* read the same type of value to determine the needed type. It is important to keep in mind that there are multiple possible encodings.

(d) What if you were reading a file that had only `Computer` and `IPod` objects in it? What return type *could* the factory method have in that case?

Review Exercise 12.2 What is *polymorphism*? How does it relate to *dynamic* and *static* attributes of programs and variables?

Review Exercise 12.3 Describe how a `Question` is written out in a file.

Review Exercise 12.4 The following `Question` stored in an `AdventureBook`'s pages collection at index 8. Answer the following questions about the contents of `pages` or explain why you cannot determine the answer.

```
parentNdx: 11
text: "Is it bigger than a breadbox?"
yesNdx: 5
noNdx: 9
```

(a) The smallest possible value for pages.size().

(b) The parentNdx of the AdventurePage at index 5.

(c) The yesNdx of the AdventurePage at index 11.

(d) The dynamic type of the AdventurePage at index 8.

(e) The dynamic type of the AdventurePage at index 9.

(f) The dynamic type of the AdventurePage at index 11.

Review Exercise 12.5 How many nodes in an AdventureBook should have parentNdx == AdventurePage.NO_SUCH_PAGE? Describe all such nodes.

Review Exercise 12.6 How many nodes in an AdventureBook should have noNdx == AdventurePage.NO_SUCH_PAGE? Describe all such nodes.

Review Exercise 12.7 You hire me to type in your animal data file because it is so much work. You agree to pay me a nickel per entry so after reading the whole file you have the program print out the number of AdventurePages read from the file. The number comes back as 112. You refuse to pay because the file is corrupt. How did you know?

Review Exercise 12.8 What would happen if a Question had the same value in its noNdx as it had in its parentNdx? What if noNdx and yesNdx were the same?

Where would you put tests to make sure these conditions never happened? Imagine making as few changes as possible.

Review Exercise 12.9 What is the most Answer nodes there can be in a AdventureBook with 7 pages? 15 pages?

Review Exercise 12.10 One easy way to play with the Scanner class is to construct Scanners to scan a String. For example, consider the following code snippet:

```
Scanner scanner = new Scanner("Hello Scanner");
String first = scanner.next();
String second = scanner.next();
System.out.println(first);
System.out.println(second);
```

The output is

```
Hello
Scanner
```

scanner reads, as its source, the string "Hello Scanner". What is the output of each of the following code snippets?

(a)
```
Scanner scanner = new Scanner("invader space");
String bet = scanner.next();
String aleph = scanner.next();

System.out.println(aleph);
System.out.println(bet + "s");
```

(b)
```
        Scanner scanner = new Scanner("one two three four");
        String a = scanner.next();
        scanner.next();
        String b = scanner.next();
        System.out.println("a and b are " + a + " " + b);
```

(c)
```
        Scanner scanner = new Scanner("The question is do you feel luck.");
        while (scanner.hasNext()) {
          String word = scanner.next();
          System.out.println(word);
        }
```

(d)
```
        Scanner scanner = new Scanner("One fish, two fish, read fish, view fish");
        while (scanner.hasNext()) {
          String s1 = scanner.next();
          String s2 = scanner.next();
          System.out.println(s1 + " " + s2);
        }
```

(e)
```
        Scanner scanner = new Scanner("Combine 2 5");
        String operation = scanner.next();
        int first = scanner.nextInt();
        int second = scanner.nextInt();
        int result = first + second;
        System.out.println("The result of " + operation + " is " + result);
```

(f)
```
        Scanner scanner = new Scanner("go left");
        String action = scanner.next();
        String direction = scanner.next();
        if (action.equals("go")) {
          if (direction.equals("left")) {
            System.out.println("You encounter a goblin.");
          } else if (direction.equals("right")) {
            System.out.println("You collect 100 gold coins.");
          } else {
            System.out.println("Where do you want to go?");
          }
        } else {
          System.out.println("What was it you wanted to do?");
        }
```

Review Exercise 12.11 Convert the following file into the AdventureBook tree it represents.

```
Question
Is it a super hero?
```

```
-1
1
2
Question
Does he/she spin webs?
0
5
6
Question
Is he/she a German spy?
0
3
4
Answer
Baroness Paula Von Gunther
2
Answer
Green Goblin
2
Answer
Wonder Woman
1
Answer
Spiderman
1
```

Review Exercise 12.12 Convert the following file into the AdventureBook tree it represents.

```
Question
Is it an even number?
-1
1
4
Answer
two
0
Answer
fifteen
4
Answer
three
4
Question
Is it prime?
0
3
2
```

Review Exercise 12.13 Convert the following file into the AdventureBook tree it represents.

```
Question
Does it eat plants?
-1
5
6
Answer
Diplodocus
X
Answer
Allosaurus
X
Answer
Triceratops
X
Answer
Velociraptor
X
Question
Does it have three horns?
0
3
1
Is it about the size of a human?
0
4
2
```

Review Exercise 12.14 Convert Figure 12.11 to a corresponding file representation.

Review Exercise 12.15 Convert Figure 12.12 to a corresponding file representation.

Review Exercise 12.16 Convert Figure 12.13 to a corresponding file representation.

Review Exercise 12.17 Put the following segment of code into main in a console application. Run the program and write down the output.

```
3    Random random=new Random(0);
4    for(int i = 0; i < 5; ++i){
5      System.out.println(random.nextInt(100));
6    }
```

Run the program again and write down the output. Was it the same?

Now get rid of the parameter passed to the Random constructor.

Run the program twice more, writing down the results each time. Do these two runs produce the same output? Are they the same as either of the first two runs?

The parameter passed to the Random constructor is called the *seed* value. Java does not produce truly random numbers; instead it produces numbers in a fixed sequence (of more than four billion different values). There is no obvious relationship between any two entries in the sequence.

Where it starts in that sequence depends on the seed value. Providing a seed value has the sequence start at the same spot each time. Providing no seed causes Java to use some part of the current clock time of the computer as the seed; the time used includes thousandths of a second, so it is unlikely that the same seed is used on multiple runs of the program.

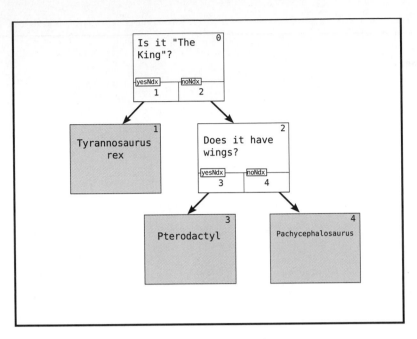

Figure 12.11: Dinosaur Questions Tree

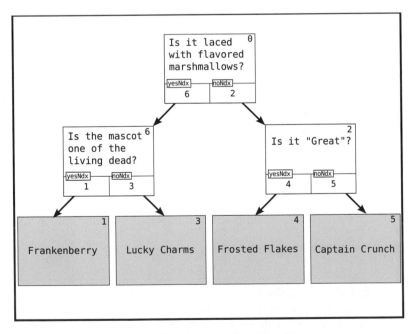

Figure 12.12: Dinosaur Questions Tree

The seed is provided to get a fixed sequence. This is important when testing games: with a fixed random sequence it would be possible to test `EasyDice` or `Pig` since we would know what the results *should* be.

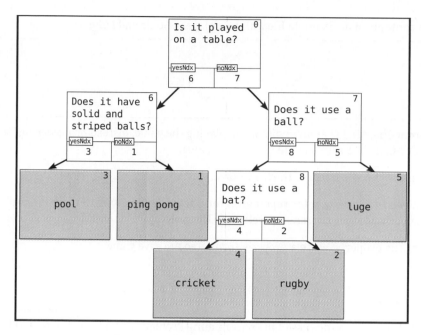

Figure 12.13: Dinosaur Questions Tree

12.8 Programming Problems

Programming Problem 12.1 Write a Twenty Questions editor. The program should be able to read and write Twenty Questions files. It should also be able to list the contents of the array list and permit the user to move pages around inside the AdventureBook, fixing up all references to the moved page.

The editor should also permit the user to easily reconnect entries. You will want to come up with a simple notation to permit the user to change the yesNdx of the Question in location 3 to refer to location 9. The program should include error checking to make sure no Question refers to nonexistent spaces and that index 0 always refers to a Question.

Programming Problem 12.2 Modify TwentyQuestions so that it does not create a tree that is more than 20 questions deep. It should lose on the twentieth and then ask the player if she wants to play again. This would actually limit the game to 20 questions.

It is possible to restructure the tree so that the questions highest in the tree do the best job of dividing the remaining field of contenders in half. The techniques for doing so are beyond the scope of this book but keep the idea in your head when you read Section 14.6, which also talks about dismissing half of the remaining contenders when searching for something.

Programming Problem 12.3 Programming Problem 11.4 looked at reading a saved game of Pig. A Pig game consists of some number of players, each with a score (between 0 and 100). The players take turns rolling so, the game state includes the players, their scores, and the player whose turn it is. The data file format for the game is

```
<playerCount>
<name0> <score0>
<name1> <score1>
...
<nameN> <scoreN>
<currentPlayerName> <currentTurnRoll>
```

Here are the contents of an example file with two players, Sonic and Luigi:

```
2
Sonic 23
Luigi 14
Luigi  2
```

Modify Pig from Chapter 11. At any point while playing the game, instead of answering "yes" or "no", the player can answer "save." To save the file the program must

- Prompt the user for the name of the file to save.

- Open the given file for output (or report an error if that is impossible). If there is a problem, permit the player to specify another file name or return to the game.

- If the file opens properly, write a properly formatted Pig save game.

- Close the file.

- Terminate the game.

When starting the game, as discussed in Programming Problem 11.4, the player should be able to specify the name of a save file rather than typing in player names to start a new game. The program should read the save file and begin the game where it left off.

Chapter

13

Lists of Lists and Collision Detection

We have spent some time working with non-FANG games, looking at running our own game loops and manipulating files. In this chapter we go back and write a more complex FANG program. The game takes advantage of the animation capabilities of FANG and explores different ways of modeling the internal structure of the game world at the same time. Since this program is longer than previous programs, this program takes advantage of a Java structuring mechanism, **package**s, to permit us, as programmers, to focus on one portion of the program at a time. BlockDrop also uses the factory pattern, multidimensional ArrayLists, and file input/output.

13.1 Designing BlockDrop

Just about everyone reading this book has, sometime in the last quarter century, played the game of *Tetris*. The game defined the "casual games" genre and has been ported, legally and illegally, to almost every game-capable platform ever developed. In this chapter we develop our own port[1] in FANG. In respect of the *Tetris* trademarks, our program is called *BlockDrop*.

The design of this game begins with a screenshot of the finished game in action; while this might seem backwards, you can just as easily imagine that the screenshot is of any *Tetris* clone and we are examining the elements and gameplay in an attempt to duplicate the game. If you plan on duplicating a game for anything other than learning and personal gratification, make sure you understand trademark law in your jurisdiction.

The key things to note in Figure 13.1 are the playing board in the middle of the screen where the different shaped tetraminoes (groups of four blocks) fall from the top. The pieces are steered and rotated as they fall with various keys. When a piece can no longer fall, the block freezes on the screen. Whenever a row is filled from one side to the other with blocks from one or more pieces, that row is removed and the player's score is increased by 1. The game ends when the top row is not empty (some portion of a frozen piece is in the top row).

The score, shown in the upper left corner of the screen, tracks the number of rows the player has eliminated. The box on the right of the screen is the "next piece box" showing the next piece to fall.

The tetraminoes are shown in Figure 13.2 along with their common letter designations.

Think about your favorite arcade or console game. What does the game do when no one is playing it? It shows a gameplay video or it plays itself in a level of the game or it shows the high scores. This is known as an

---

[1]In computing, to *port* is to rebuild a software system to run on a different computing platform; the resulting rewritten software is referred to as a *port*. *Tetris* has been widely *ported* to different operating systems and computers since it was first developed.

Figure 13.1: *BlockDrop* screenshot

attract screen, something that attracts the player to the game so that he or she presses the appropriate start button.

The attract screen for BlockDrop is a scrolling display of the ten highest scores earned in the game, challenging players to try their luck at getting on the leader board. In order to keep the high scores from one session of the game to the next, we keep a high score file. The HighScoreLevel and BlockDrop alternate; as one ends, it creates and starts the other.

With more than ten new classes (the two Game-extending classes discussed above and at least nine Sprite-extending classes), this is the longest game with the most files we have yet examined. How can we tame the complexity? The next section discusses software engineering, the computer science discipline focused on effectively writing correct, efficient code.

Review 13.1

(a) What is an *attract* screen?

(b) How does FANG handle attract screens? Does that seem like a reasonable way to do it?

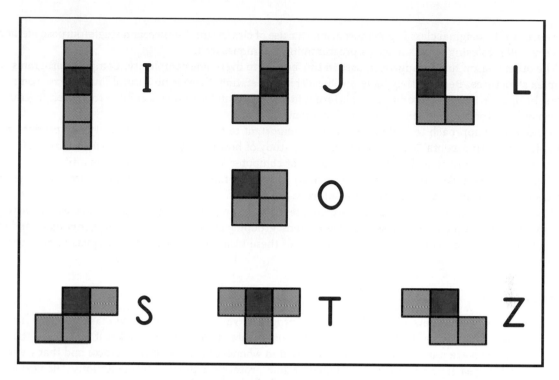

Figure 13.2: *BlockDrop* Tetraminoes

13.2 Software Engineering: Managing Complexity

One recurring theme of this book is *compartmentalization*: write short, single-purpose methods; design classes and interactions using only the public protocol; hide all fields and as many methods as possible by making them `private`. Two different impulses come together to drive this theme: to use object-oriented programming techniques well and to control complexity.

Object-oriented programming developed out of the study of *abstract data types* [ADTs]. The development of languages with programmer-defined *classes*, *inheritance*, *polymorphism*, and *encapsulation* created the object-oriented programming paradigm.

As we saw in Section 7.2, an abstract data type has three features: a *public* protocol, a *private* implementation, and interaction limited to the protocol. The last feature means that *clients* of the abstract data type cannot make use of any aspects of the private implementation. The separation of protocol from implementation means that the implementation can be changed without having to change client classes.

Notice that encapsulation, the ability to hide data and other details inside a class, done in Java with `private` members and methods, comes directly from the last feature of ADTs.[2] Java access modifiers in general are used to separate the public protocol from the private implementation. `protected` elements kind of cross the border between implementation and protocol: subclasses of a class with protected elements have interaction with the *implementation* of the base class. This is sometimes necessary for efficiency but it is, strictly speaking, a sharing of the implementation between the super- and subclasses.

Inheritance is the ability to extend an existing class, providing only that state and those behaviors that the new class needs. The ability to override existing behavior and have the overriding definitions used through

---

[2]ADTs predate object-oriented programming; we talk about how ADT concepts drove the development of object-oriented programming.

references to the original class is polymorphism. Our use of classes, inheritance, and single-purpose methods fits very well into using object-oriented programming techniques well.

The other reason for the approach used in this book is to overcome complexity. Computer programs are complex structures. Because they have no physical manifestation, there is no natural limit on *how* complex. A steel bridge can be only so complicated before it literally falls under its own weight; a computer program is limited only by the memory space within the computer.

A disciplined approach to building software is important to overcome the complexity and produce correct software in an acceptable amount of time. The study of how to do this is *software engineering*. Software engineering, generally considered a subdiscipline of computer science, is focused on quantifying software development costs, risks, and quality. Then, armed with quantitative analysis of existing projects, different approaches can be applied in an attempt to improve the metrics.

Among the practices studied in software engineering are program design patterns such as our factory, the separation of protocols and class implementations, grouping classes together into larger *modules*, and the reuse of existing code. This section presents each of these ideas and discuss how it applies to our current project.

Java interfaces

Every time we needed a new kind of "thing" in a program, we have created a new `class` in a new file. In defining a `class` we provide the public protocol and the private implementation. What if we relaxed the two requirements: that we must provide an implementation whenever we define an protocol and that we must start a new file for each new `class`. This section examines protocols without implementations. The next looks at packing more than one class into a single file.

Consider building a generic sorting class. The class should take an `ArrayList` of sortable objects, objects that implement the `compareTo` method, and, using `compareTo` and something like the sorting code we saw previously, it could *polymorphically* compare whatever actual objects were in the list, sorting the list.

We need a "superclass" that collects together all objects defining `compareTo`. All we need to do then is make sure any new "sortable object" just `extends` the "superclass." You can guess from the liberal use of scare quotes that there is a problem in declaring such a "superclass." There is.

Java has *single inheritance*: a given `class` can extend one other class. Every class, except for `java.lang.Object`, *must* extend exactly one other class. This means that the inheritance graph[3] is a *tree*, similar to the decision tree we saw in Chapter 12. While each node can have an arbitrary number of children, no node can have more than one parent. Only `Object`, at the root of the tree, can have no parent.

Sun wants to support sortable objects; any class extending the (imaginary) `SortableObject` class can be compared, one to another. So, imagine that we want to make a `SortableSprite` class. `SortableSprite` **extends** `Sprite` and can extend only one class (because of single inheritance).

Since `SortableSprite` must extend both `Sprite` and `SortableObject` and the inheritance graph must be a tree, either `Sprite` extends `SortableObject` *or* `SortableObject` extends `Sprite`. There is no other way that `SortableSprite` can have a single superclass *and* extend both of the other classes.

If `Sprite` extends `SortableObject`, then *all* `Sprite`-derived classes are already sortable, even if it makes no sense to discuss order between two `PolygonSprite` objects (let alone a `LineSprite` and an `OvalSprite`). So, `Sprite` does not extend `SortableObject`; only some of the subclasses of `Sprite` can meaningfully implement sorting.

But if `SortableObject` **extends** `Sprite`, Sun must ship our `Sprite` class in their standard libraries or they must extend a class from our third-party framework.[4] This means Sun has to include FANG with every Java installation, which makes no sense. Instead `Sprite` must extend sortable.

---

[3]A mathematical *graph* is a set of *nodes* that are joined into ordered pairs by a set of *edges*. The *inheritance graph* has classes as nodes and there is an edge between a class and its direct superclass.

[4]In a contract for Java (or other software), the provider, Sun Microsystems, is the *first party*. The end-user of the software, you, the programmer of the language, is the *second party*. FANG, provided to enhance Java but created by neither Sun nor you, is a *third party* product.

This is a paradox.

One possible fix would be *multiple inheritance*. Multiple inheritance permits one class to extend more than one other class. This greatly complicates the inheritance graph, in particular, when two parent classes of any class share, somewhere in their history, a common ancestor. Both Sprite and SortableObject extend Object. All of the Object fields appear in SortableSprite *twice*, once from each parent, and there is no easy way to differentiate them.[5]

Java's solution is the use of **interface**s to define just a *public protocol*. An **interface** is a *totally abstract* class. Where an **abstract** class can have methods, declared **abstract**, that have no implementation, an **interface** has only methods that have no implementation. An **interface** is declared just like a **class**: it is declared to be **public** so that it is visible to other classes, it is declared in a file with the same name as the **interface**, and the definition of the **interface** goes in a block after the name of the interface.

When writing a **class** that *implements* the methods named in the **interface**, the keyword **implements** goes between the name of the implementing class and the beginning of the class definition block. A class **extends** exactly *one* class, so only one class name appears after **extends**; any class **implements** an arbitrary number of interfaces so that the code contains a comma-separated list of all implemented interface names.

fang2.core.GameWindow, for example, implements two different interfaces. By implementing any required methods (those listed in the **interface** body), a GameWindow is-a WindowStateListener or an ActionListener.

```
public abstract class GameWindow
          extends JApplet
          implements ActionListener,
          WindowStateListener {
```

The above code, taken from GameWindow.java, shows how the GameWindow class **extends** something called a JApplet.[6] Looking at the **import** statements and Java documentation (Swing is a standard, first-party library for Java), we see that both of these interfaces are defined in the javax.swing package. We stop here with GameWindow and change our view to a class for BlockDrop, HighScore.

By implementing an interface, the object can be passed into methods that declare one of their formal parameters to have an interface type. We saw this with scheduleRelative in Chapter 8. The signature of the method is scheduleRelative(Alarm alarm, **double** seconds). The game, FluSimulator **implements** Alarm. That means it must define a **public void** act() method (the one method header in the Alarm interface).

We take a slight diversion from **interface** to motivate the idea of nested classes; the code for HighScore then **implements** an interface, giving us an example of how to do that.

Nested Classes

Between games of BlockDrop we display the high scores so far achieved. That means that there is an end-of-game level, HighScoreLevel. The main game, BlockDrop, needs to be able to communicate the name and score for a new high-scoring player but otherwise it knows nothing about high scores.

None of the visible elements discussed above in the game design know anything about high scores either. The HighScoreLevel must be able to keep a list of some number (say 10) high scores which group a name and a score, save the list to a file, load the list from a file, and sort the list. Note that the methods to do these things are *implementation details*. So, it turns out, is the existence of a class to group a name with a score. The HighScore class, the element type in the list of high scores, is an implementation detail of the HighScoreLevel. All of the fields and methods that are implementation details are encapsulated, hidden, **private** inside the class. HighScore should be, too.

---

[5]The details of the "dread diamond" are beyond the scope of this book because Java does not provide multiple inheritance.

[6]A JApplet extends Applet, and that is why FANG games can be run as applets inside of properly configured browsers. When they run as applications, FANG arranges to start the applet by calling runAsApplication (might be better to call that method startSuperSimpleAppletBrowser).

```
<classDeclaration> := <accessLevel> class <className>
                         [extends <parentClassName>]
                         [implements <interfaceName> [,<interfaceName>]*]


<classBody> := {

                   <definition>*

               }


<definition> := <fieldDeclaration> |
                <methodDefinition> |
                <classDefinition>
```

The extended Java template for **class** shows that a class definition can have, at most, one **extends** clause (with the value **extends** Object assumed if the clause is omitted) and an optional single **implements** clause with a comma-separated list of interfaces implemented by the class.

Java also supports *nested classes*, the inclusion of a **class** within the body of another class. A nested class can be given any Java access modifier, so it is possible to declare nested classes to be **public** to include them in the public protocol of the class or **private** to use them solely in the implementation.[7] The following listing shows the skeleton of the declaration of HighScoreLevel.HighScore. The **class** lines, the beginning of the definition block, and the closing curly braces of the definition block have been included.

```
21  public class HighScoreLevel
22    extends Game {
284   private class HighScore
285     implements Comparable<HighScore> {
394   }
395 }
```

Listing 13.1: HighScoreLevel.HighScore

Notice that the full name of the nested **class** is HighScoreLevel.HighScore. This is similar to the naming of **static** methods and fields. We tend to use the short name, HighScore, when no confusion results.[8]

The other thing to notice in this listing is that HighScore **implements** an **interface**. Looking at the documentation and the code provided by Java, we see that the definition of the interface is

```
public interface Comparable<T> {
    public int compareTo(T o);
}
```

The first thing to do is ignore T for the moment. If we just let T be some type, then we see that this looks like a **class** but with the word **interface** in place of **class**. It has a method in it, compareTo. Just like when a concrete class, one on which **new** can be called, **extends** an **abstract** class, any class that **implements** Comparable must have a method with the given header. An interface defines one or more headers for methods that implementing classes must define.

The <T> is an example of Java *generics*. We have been using Java generics with ArrayList for several chapters now. The definition of the **interface** simply says that the interface is generic, taking the name of a type between angle brackets. It also says that the parameter type of compareTo must be the same type as that in the generic angle brackets. Defining generic classes is beyond the scope of this book, so we now return to implementing Comparable<HighScore> (because HighScore values can be compared to other HighScore values).

---

[7]Or **protected**, again so that they are mostly private but available to subclasses.

[8]The compiler permits the use of the short name in the *scope* of the nested class. The nested class's scope extends throughout the enclosing class definition.

In order for `HighScoreLevel.HighScore` to implement the `Comparable` **interface**, it must override the required method with one having the right header *and* a method definition.

```
337    public int compareTo(HighScore rhs) {
338      if (rhs.name.length() == 0) {
339        return 1;
340      }
341      if (name.length() == 0) {
342        return -1;
343      }
344      if (score == rhs.score) {
345        return name.compareTo(rhs.name);
346      }
347      return score - rhs.score;
348    }
```

Listing 13.2: `HighScoreLevel.HighScore compareTo`

Tracing the code in `compareTo` we see that empty names always come after non-empty names. If neither `name` field is empty, then the `score` values are compared. If the `score` values are the same, then the `HighScore` objects compare in order by their `name` values (which means if they have the same `score` and `name`, they compare as equal, which is what we would expect). If the scores are different, they sort in order by the `score`.

Remember that `compareTo` guarantees only that the *sign* of the return value reflects whether **this** or `rhs` sorts first (negative means **this** is first; positive means `rhs` first). We do not have to use an **if** here: we just subtract the `rhs.score` from the **this**.`score`; if `rhs` is bigger, then the result is negative (**this** < `rhs`) and if **this** is bigger, the result is positive (**this** > `rhs`).

Note that the signature of a method does not include the *names* of the formal parameters in the parameter list. While the **interface** calls the parameter o, when overriding the method, any valid Java variable name can be used. `rhs`, standing for "right-hand side," was used to bring to mind the comparison operators shown in parentheses in the previous paragraph. **this** is on the left-hand side and the parameter is on the right-hand side. Headers match up on the number and type order of parameters. Notice that the `@Override` annotation is used here because we are overriding the *empty* definition of the **interface**.

One other thing to note: just as any class that directly or indirectly **extends** a superclass *is-a* superclass object, any class that directly or indirectly **implements** an interface *is-a* object of the interface type. `HighScore` is-a `Comparable<HighScore>`. We can use methods that depend solely on the methods described in an **interface** and we can even write our own methods that do. The next section shows how we can use Java-defined sorting methods to sort a collection of `Comparable` objects; an `ArrayList<HighScore>` is a collection of `Comparable` objects.[9]

Don't Reinvent the Wheel

Let's take a quick look at how `HighScoreLevel` holds the high scores:

```
39    /** the list of HighScore objects */
40    private final ArrayList<HighScore> highScores;
```

Listing 13.3: `HighScoreLevel highScores`

---

[9]`Comparable<T>` and `Comparable` are basically the same thing; the book uses `Comparable` when talking about the interface in general (any possible instance of T) and `Comparable<HighScore>` (or similar) when the type would make a difference. The sort routines are generic, handling any type that can be compared to itself.

The `ArrayList` containing the scores is a field called `highScores`. When a `HighScoreLevel` object is constructed, the high scores are all loaded from a file; when a new high score is recorded, the high scores are saved back to the file from which they were loaded.

```
214   private ArrayList<HighScore> loadHighScores(String fname) {
215     ArrayList<HighScore> hs = new ArrayList<HighScore>();
216     File highScoreFile = new File(fname);
217     try {
218       Scanner highScoreInput = new Scanner(highScoreFile);
219       while (highScoreInput.hasNextInt()) {
220         hs.add(new HighScore(highScoreInput));
221       }
222       highScoreInput.close();
223     } catch (FileNotFoundException e) {
224       // It is okay if there is no such file; we will just ignore this
225     }
226     return hs;
227   }
```

Listing 13.4: `HighScoreLevel` Loading and Saving

These two methods should look familiar: `loadHighScores` uses an eof-controlled loop to read `HighScore` records (format actually defined inside of `HighScore` so it is not of interest to us right now), and `saveHighScores` uses a count-controlled loop to go through the list of high scores, writing them out to the output file (again, the format of the writing is determined by the `toString` method of `HighScore` so that inside that class it is necessary to make sure the formats match; out here in the level, we just let `HighScore` do the work).

We look back at the level constructor that calls `loadHighScores`:

```
75    public HighScoreLevel(int currentScore, String fname) {
76      this.fname = fname;
77      this.currentScore = currentScore;
78      highScores = loadHighScores(fname);
79      while (highScores.size() < MAX_HIGHSCORE_COUNT) {
80        highScores.add(new HighScore(0, ""));
81      }
82      Collections.sort(highScores, Collections.reverseOrder());
83    }
```

Listing 13.5: `HighScoreLevel` Constructor

The level is constructed with a current score, the score the player made in the last game of `BlockDrop`, and the name of the high score file. `loadHighScores` is used in line 78 to load the high scores from the file. If there are fewer high scores than expected, then `highScores` is filled with unnamed 0 scores. This means that the list is never empty, so we don't have to check for that.

Finally, line 82 is executed. The `Collections` class, in the `java.util` package, is a class with a number of **static** methods that provide useful algorithms for working with collections. One such algorithm is sorting. `Collections.sort` comes in two flavors. The first takes just a `List` of `Comparable` objects. Note that `List` is an **interface** and an `ArrayList` is-a `List`. When provided with just a `List`, the sort is done in ascending order according to `compareTo`; the list has to be of `Comparable` so that they all have `compareTo`.

The second overload of `Collections.sort` takes a `List` of `Comparable` as before and a `Comparator`. We're not going to go into what a `Comparator` is except to say that it modifies the results of calling `compareTo`. In the case of the `Collections.reverseOrder()` `Comparator`, it just reverses the sign of the result, thereby reversing the sorting order. The list of high scores is sorted, but from highest down to lowest.

```
179   private void insertScore(int score, String name) {
180     highScores.set(highScores.size() - 1, new HighScore(score, name));
181     Collections.sort(highScores, Collections.reverseOrder());
182     saveHighScores();
183     if (showScores != null) {
184       removeSprite(showScores);
185     }
186     showScores = makeShowScoresSprite();
187     addSprite(showScores);
188   }
```

Listing 13.6: `HighScoreLevel insertScore`

The other place we need to sort the list is when we add a new high score. In Listing 13.6, you can see that the last score in the list is set to a new `HighScore` object with the new score and name. `highScore` is then sorted (in reverse order), the high scores are saved, and the screen is fixed up with a new `showScores` sprite. We examine when this code is called in the last section of this chapter where we describe how the `BlockDrop` and `HighScoreLevel` games communicate.

Java packages

When do we break a method down into several smaller methods? One answer is when we are doing stepwise refinement and working our way down from the main problem. We define a solution in terms of simpler problems that we pretend are working, putting off defining the additional methods until we think about the next lower layer of abstraction.

There is one other time: when we find a method growing too long or taking care of too much. Think back to Chapter 5 and the `EasyDice` program (see Listings 5.10–5.12). The game had two states: rolling the dice or waiting for the user to place a bet. Each one did something different when `advance` was called. When the author first wrote the program, he put all of the processing for both states directly in the `advance` method. The method was over 40 lines long, handled checking what state the game was in, and then, in both the `if` and `else` branches, checked if the button was pressed, and then it . . . Needless to say, breaking the method into three pieces, `advance` to determine game state, `advanceWaiting` to handle advancing one frame in the waiting state, and `advanceRolling` to handle advancing one frame in the rolling state, greatly improved the readability of the code. It limited the amount of context necessary to read any one of the three methods.

A similar problem occurs when writing a program with many classes. `BlockDrop` has fifteen different classes. When looking at a listing of all of the class names, we see that it can be overwhelming. The context a programmer must comb through to find one desired class is too much. Java supports limiting the context by grouping classes together into **packages**. With good package naming, it can be simpler to find a given class and, by keeping related classes together, it can be easier to reuse code in other projects.

The `BlockDrop` project has fifteen different class files. More than half of them are `Piece` and its subclasses. It would be nice if those files could be segregated off by themselves. There are then `HighScoreLevel` and `BlockDrop`: they are separate levels and should probably be separated in some way (they don't belong in the same context). In fact, the files in this project can be divided into four different groups:

```
core                        + classes for main game level
  BlockDrop.java            - main Game
  Board.java                - where the pieces fall
  NextPieceBox.java         - generates and shows new pieces
  ScoreSprite.java          - show the current score
highscore                   + classes for high score level
```

```
  HighScoreLevel.java          - Game handling high scores
  ScrollingMessageBox.java     - looping, scrolling string table
pieces                         + piece classes
  I_Piece.java
  J_Piece.java
  L_Piece.java
  O_Piece.java
  Piece.java                   - superclass of all pieces
  S_Piece.java
  T_Piece.java
  Z_Piece.java
util                           + general utility classes (core & piece)
  Position.java                - a position on the Board: row, column
```

Our source files are stored in a directory named for the current chapter, Chapter13. Splitting the files into the four named packages requires four steps:

- Move the source files to package subdirectories.

- Add a **package** line to each file.

- Add **import** for all classes not in the same **package**.

- Change the command line for compiling and running the program.

A *package subdirectory* is just a subdirectory with the same name as the **package** it contains. Forcing the file system (subdirectory) name to match the Java (package) name simplifies Java's task when searching for a file to fulfill an **import** statement. This is analogous to matching .java file names and their public class names.

Using our operating system we create the four subdirectories and move the source files down into them. The exact commands to create the directories depend on the operating system. We look at the output of listing the contents of the Chapter13 directory and its subdirectories. ls * lists the directories and their contents:

```
~/Chapter13% ls *
core:
BlockDrop.java  Board.java  NextPieceBox.java  ScoreSprite.java

highscore:
HighScoreLevel.java  ScrollingMessageBox.java

pieces:
I_Piece.java  L_Piece.java  Piece.java    T_Piece.java
J_Piece.java  O_Piece.java  S_Piece.java  Z_Piece.java

util:
Position.java
```

The **package** line is the key word **package** followed by the name of the package (the directory name) and a semicolon. The **package** line must be the first (non-comment) line in the file. It must be before any **import** or **class** or **interface** lines. The first line of HighScoreLevel.java is

```
1  package highscore;
```

Listing 13.7: HighScoreLevel **package**

The Java template for adding a **package** line to a Java source file is

```
<packageID> := <identifier>
<packageID> := package <packageName>;

<classFile> := [<packageID>]
               <imports>
               <classDefinition>
```

When the HighScoreLevel is showing, the player is expected to press the space bar to start the game (or, alternatively, to start at a higher level, press a digit for the starting level). When the key is pressed, the HighScoreLevel creates a new BlockDrop game with the appropriate level and then finishes

```
157   private void advanceScrollingScores(double dT) {
158     showScores.advance(dT);
159     if (keyPressed()) {
160       char key = getKeyPressed();
161       if ((key == ' ') || (('1' <= key) && (key <= '9'))) {
162         int level = 1;
163         if (('2' <= key) && (key <= '9')) {
164           level = key - '0';
165         }
166         addGame(new BlockDrop(level));
167         finishGame();
168       }
169     }
170   }
```

Listing 13.8: HighScoreLevel advanceScrollingScores

There is a problem for Java now. BlockDrop.java is not in the current directory when HighScoreLevel.java is compiled. You never had to think about **import** for any classes you wrote because they were always in the same directory as every other class you wrote (at least for any one project). Java just looked for the matching .java file in the current directory and all was well. Now, with multiple packages, you must explicitly tell Java where to find any classes not in the same package as the current class.

Given that the BlockDrop class is in the core package, HighScoreLevel needs the following included (so that line 166 can compile):

```
10   import core.BlockDrop;
```

Listing 13.9: HighScoreLevel **import** BlockDrop

(One other thing to note in advanceScrollingScores: we take advantage of the fact that the digit character codes are contiguous. In line 164 we convert from the code of a digit, say, '4', to the number 4 by subtracting the code for '0' from the value of key.

If we pretend that the digits begin at code 150, then, because they are contiguous, '0' = 150, '1' = 151, '2' = 152, etc. '4' = 154. '4' - '0' = 154 - 150 = 4. This calculation does not depend on the particular value for the code of '0'; in fact, 150 is *not* the code of '0' in the ASCII sequence.[10] What value it has is not important. The contiguous nature of digits (and lowercase letters, and uppercase letters) is the important thing to remember.)

We run javac and java in the *chapter root* directory. That used to be the same directory where the source code was; now the source code is below the root directory. We need to tell javac and java how to find the files.

---

[10]The author did that on purpose, to show that the encoded value of '0' does not matter to this argument.

```
~/Chapter13% javac -classpath .:/usr/lib/jvm/fang2.jar core/BlockDrop.java
```

Notice here that the name of the *file* to compile is the name of the *directory* followed by a slash (some operating systems use a different character) and then the full name of the file. The compiler is run in the directory above any package directory.

```
~/Chapter13% java -classpath .:/usr/lib/jvm/fang2.jar core.BlockDrop
```

Notice in the `java` execution line that the name of the *class* to run is the name of the *package* followed by a dot followed by the name of the class. We never noticed before that `javac` works with file names and `java` works with class names (except for leaving off the `.java` extension).

Moving files to packages lowers the cognitive overhead in keeping track of context when we are looking at them. Grouping files in well-named packages *documents* what they have in common and guides the reader of the code to find what she needs. Using packages requires moving the files, adding **package** and **import** lines, and changing the way you compile and run the program. The payoff, in ease of programming, is well worth a little bit of effort.

This section introduced some basic concepts of software engineering: Java **interface**s, nested classes, the use of built-in algorithms (`Collections` is your friend), and using **package**s to group your classes and make reading your code simpler. All of these were presented in terms of making code easier to understand, one of the driving forces in writing code for this book. When you go on to study software engineering in more depth, you find that many of them have even deeper benefits to your code and to the programmers who write and use it.

Review 13.2

(a) How is a nested class definition different than having a class in a package? Answer in both syntax and meaning terms.

(b) Given the name `LinkedList.Node`, is the **class** `Node` in a package or is it a nested class?

(c) What is the access level when nothing is specified? Would it make sense to call it *package level* access? Why or why not?

(d) What classes are defined in the `pieces` package?

(e) What is an **interface** and how is it different from a **class**?

13.3   When It's Safe to Move: Collision Detection

How is *Tetris*, or rather `BlockDrop`, played? How does a piece travel down the screen? In the original game, a piece appears, approximately centered, in the top row of the screen. At discrete time intervals it moves down the screen one block height (where each tetramino is composed of four blocks) at a time until it comes time to move and it cannot move down. The blocks then freeze on the screen in their current position.

We create each `Piece` as a FANG `CompositeSprite`. That way we can put the blocks into the `Piece` simply by setting their positions in the internal coordinate system.

Moving a `Piece` a discrete amount is actually quite simple. Rather than calling `translate` every frame with the product of the velocity and the frame time, we use a countdown timer to wait for some number of seconds and then translate the `Piece` by a full block size. This does mean that the block size (the apparent size of the blocks in the `Board`'s coordinate system) needs to be known but that can be calculated when scaling the `Piece`. Actually, if all of the `Piece` classes were the same size, then it would be easy to calculate. We expand this *same size* idea below.

The idea of a countdown timer was used in Chapter 6 (see Listings 6.4 and 6.1). We set a timer to the interval between moves, and decrement the timer value by `dT` each time through `advance`; when it crosses, 0 the timer has expired.

```
74  public void advance(double dT) {
75    int oldScore = score.getScore();
76
77    moveClock -= dT;
78    if (moveClock <= 0.0) {
79      updateBoard();
80      moveClock += moveDelay;
81    }
82
83    checkKeyPressed();
84
85    int newScore = score.getScore();
86    updateLevel(oldScore, newScore);
87  }
```

Listing 13.10: `BlockDrop advance`

We move the `Piece` and reset the timer and do it all over again, as shown in Listing 13.10. Each time `moveClock` expires, `updateBoard` is called (which moves the block down) and the timer is reset. The use of `+=` is to keep the time between movements as regular as possible; if one movement runs a little over, the next movement comes a little bit earlier.

```
178  private void updateBoard() {
179    if (!board.moveDownIfPossible()) {
180      if (board.isGameOver()) {
181        endThisGame();
182        return;
183      }
184      board.add(nextPiece.getPiece());
185      nextPiece.nextPiece();
186    }
187  }
```

Listing 13.11: `BlockDrop updateBoard`

The `updateBoard` method uses the `moveDown` method defined in `Board` to determine whether the current piece moved down or it was frozen. If it was frozen, then the game might be over. If not, move the `Piece` from the `NextPieceBox` (called `nextPiece`) and have it generate a new random `Piece`.

How can `moveDown` determine whether or not it is safe to move the current piece down one row? And what, exactly, *is* a row and a column? What are the implementation details of `Piece` and `Board` and how do they work together?

A Square Grid

Any *Tetris* clone has to deal with making sure that pieces are moved or rotated only when doing so does not move the piece (or some of its blocks) into an illegal position. An illegal configuration would have two blocks superimposed on the board or one or more blocks off of the board. This is an instance of *collision detection*: would moving the piece to the proposed new position collide with any of the frozen blocks on the board (or the edge)?

The collision detection needs to be done *before* moving the piece (or, alternatively, the piece has to be able to "back up" to where it was before the move) so that the piece never ends up in an illegal position. This means that our standard FANG `intersects` reaction after collision does not work.

How is a Piece stored? To make scaling pieces simple (all blocks in all pieces must have the same visual dimension *and* must be the same size as frozen blocks), all Piece objects should be square. Javier López, in his online *Tetris*-cloning tutorial [Ló08], simplifies things still further by placing all tetraminoes inside a 5×5 grid.

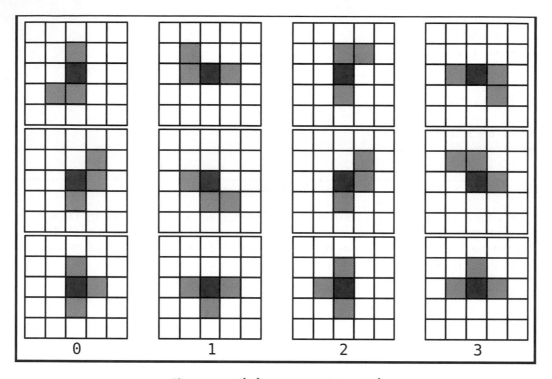

Figure 13.3: *BlockDrop* Tetraminoes Grid

Figure 13.3 shows three different pieces as they appear inside the grid in each of their four rotations. Using a 5×5 grid makes sure that all rotations of every piece fit completely within the grid; this is one of López's most effective simplifying contributions. The numbers along the bottom of the figure are the facing value (facing is a field of the Piece class). Rather than being able to rotate freely, the Piece is constrained to be in one of four facings. We number them [0–3] so that we can use modular arithmetic to cycle around the different facings.

The darker square marks the *pivot* square. It is the center of the grid. The piece rotates around that square. It is also the center of the CompositeSprite, the point around which it rotates. This makes showing the Piece in different orientations very easy.

There are *two* different representations for the same thing: the blocks that make up a Piece are represented by actual RectangleSprite objects with given positions inside the coordinate system of the sprite and also inside a 5×5 grid of references to RectangleSprites. Any given location in the grid is null if that position is empty in the piece and refers to one of the blocks making up the Piece otherwise.

This same dual view is used in the Board class. The Board is a CompositeSprite but it also maintains a grid of blocks where null means the position is free and non-null means that the position is occupied by the given RectangleSprite. The number of rows and columns in the Board grid is set when the constructor is called.

```
49   /** board grid; each location is either null or filled with a block */
50   private final ArrayList<ArrayList<RectangleSprite>> blocks;
86   public Board(ScoreSprite score, int rows, int columns) {
```

```
87      this.score = score;
88      this.rows = rows;
89      this.columns = columns;
90
91      blockSize = 1.0 / rows;
92
93      // Show one square width on each of 3 sides
94      edges = new RectangleSprite((columns + 2) * blockSize,
95          (rows + 1) * blockSize);
96      edges.setLocation(0.0, blockSize / 2);
97      setEdgeColor(DEFAULT_EDGE_COLOR);
98      addSprite(edges);
99
100     background = new RectangleSprite(blockSize * columns, 1.0);
101     setColor(DEFAULT_BACKGROUND_COLOR);
102     addSprite(background);
103
104     ulcX = -blockSize / 2 * (columns - 1);
105     ulcY = -0.5 + (blockSize / 2);
106
107     blocks = initBlocks();
108   }
```

Listing 13.12: Board Constructor

Both Board and Pieces have ArrayLists named blocks (or blocksByFacing; explanation below). These are the grids stored as lists of rows, each row being a list of RectangleSprites. The initBlocks method creates a two-dimensional list of lists of blocks, initializing all values to null. In the Board, this method is called once and the grid is then used to play the game. When a Piece is constructed, it is called four times, once for each facing the piece can have.

```
29    /**
30     * 4 facings * 5 rows * 5 columns: each facing has a 5 x 5 two dimensional
31     * description of the piece in that facing. Blocks are either null
32     * (empty) or non-null (full), referring to a {@link RectangleSprite}
33     * that goes in that {@link Position}.
34     */
35    private final ArrayList<ArrayList<ArrayList<RectangleSprite>>> blocksByFacing;
69    protected Piece(int facing, Color color) {
70      this.rows = 5;
71      this.columns = 5;
72      setColor(color);
73      position = new Position(0, 0);
74      this.facing = facing % 4;// make sure its safe
75      setRotationDegrees(90 * this.facing);
76      blocksByFacing =
77        new ArrayList<ArrayList<ArrayList<RectangleSprite>>>();
78      // for each facing, insert an empty blocks grid
79      for (int f = 0; f != 4; ++f) {
80        blocksByFacing.add(initBlocks());
81      }
```

```
82    }
```

Listing 13.13: Piece Constructor

The blocksByFacing field is, conceptually, four copies of the blocks field in the board. Just as Figure 13.3 shows four different facings for each of the pieces in it, so, too, does each Piece have a list of block grids, one for each facing. Rather than create each RectangleSprite in each of the facings, the four block grids share the same four blocks. We defer talking about that until after discussing collision detection. For now, just accept that the drawings in the figure represent the facing 0–3 block grids. Empty squares are null and filled squares are references to RectangleSprites. There are 25 references and four are to actual sprites.

How can we keep track of a Piece on the Board as it falls? It is enough to know the *board* position of some reference square in *piece*. Because we use position a lot, it makes a useful class. A Position has a row and a column field, both int and both with a getter and a setter. This lets us track the Position of a Piece by having a field, position:

```
44    /** Current position of this {@link Piece} (in unit-squares) */
45    private final Position position;
```

Listing 13.14: Piece Position

Along with the position, we also keep track of the current facing. Each facing is a quarter of a turn off the previous facing. This means that there are at most four different facings since four quarter revolutions is one full revolution, returning the spinning object back to its original orientation. We track facing as an int modulus 4.

The different facings have blocks in different locations. When a Piece is constructed, each different type of piece fills in a list of lists of Positions: it is a list with four lists in it, one for each *block* in the piece; each list has four Positions in it, one for each facing:

```
47    /**
48     * 4 blocks in a tetramino so there are 4 different lists in this. 4
49     * facings so 4 different positions for each block. These are the only
50     * non-empty locations in the cells for each facing. Note that the
51     * every block appears, by reference, in each facing of cells.
52     * Protected so that subclasses can set the value after calling the
53     * {@link Piece} constructor.
54     */
55    protected ArrayList<ArrayList<Position>> blockPositionByFacing;
```

Listing 13.15: Piece blockPositionByFacing

The blocks in a piece can be numbered, 0–3 (there are four blocks in every tetramino). Each block has a position inside the grid for each facing. Figure 13.4 repeats the figure of the blocks within a grid but this time each block in facing 0 is given a number.

The numbers are assigned, in facing 0, from the top row to the bottom row and, in any given row, from the left to the right. As the piece is rotated in each facing, each number follows the block to which it was assigned. In the J piece in the top row, block 0 begins in position row 1, column 2 or (1, 2). When the piece is rotated one quarter turn clockwise, the block moves to position (2, 3) in facing 1. Subsequently it moves to (3, 2) and (2, 1) in the next two facings.

The list of Position objects with values (1, 2), (2, 3), (3, 2), (2, 1) is the value of entry 0[11] of blockPositionByFacing in J_Piece.

---

[11]Tracking block 0.

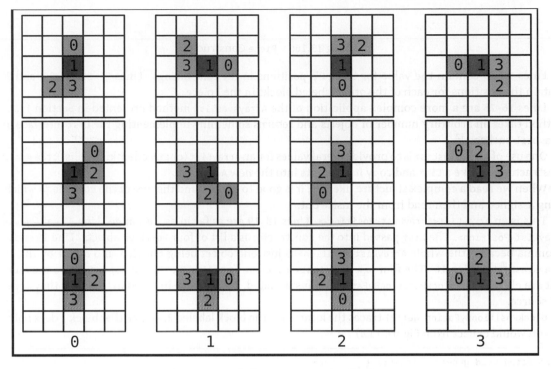

Figure 13.4: *BlockDrop* Tetramino Blocks

```
13   public J_Piece(int facing, Color color) {
14     super(facing, color);
15     blockPositionByFacing = new ArrayList<ArrayList<Position>>(Arrays
16         .asList(
17           new ArrayList<Position>(
18             Arrays.asList(new Position(1, 2), new Position(2, 3),
19               new Position(3, 2), new Position(2, 1))),
20           new ArrayList<Position>(
21             Arrays.asList(new Position(2, 2), new Position(2, 2),
22               new Position(2, 2), new Position(2, 2))),
23           new ArrayList<Position>(
24             Arrays.asList(new Position(3, 2), new Position(2, 1),
25               new Position(1, 2), new Position(2, 3))),
26           new ArrayList<Position>(
27             Arrays.asList(new Position(3, 1), new Position(1, 1),
28               new Position(1, 3), new Position(3, 3)))));
29
30     initialOffsetByFacing = new ArrayList<Position>(Arrays.asList(
31         new Position(-1, -1), new Position(-1, -1),
32         new Position(-1, -2), new Position(-2, -1)));
33
34     generateBlocks();
35   }
```

Listing 13.16: `J_Piece` Constructor

Lines 18–19 contain the value for block 0's positions in the four facings. Lines 21–22, 24–25, and 27–28 contain the positions for each of the other labeled blocks in the J piece.

Lines 16–28 are a more complex application of the `Arrays.asList` method presented in Section 11.3. The method takes an arbitrary number of objects and returns something implementing the `List` interface in the `java.util` package.[12]

One use of `Arrays.asList` is to provide literal values for an `ArrayList` (or any other kind of list); the `ArrayList` constructor can take a `List` and copy its contents into the new `ArrayList`.

When we read a complex structure like this, it is good to understand the *type* of the variable to which it is being assigned and then read from the inside out.

This is an `ArrayList<ArrayList<Position>>`. Lines 18–19 are as far in as we can go. Line 17 calls **new** on an `ArrayList<Position>`. The `List` passed into the constructor is a list of four `Position` objects. Line 19 ends with a comma because the whole `ArrayList<Position>` is just one object being bundled into a `List` by the call to `Arrays.asList` on line 16. The four **new** `ArrayList<Position>` lines (17, 20, 23, and 26) are where the four lists that are elements in `blockPositionByFacing` are instantiated, and they are inserted in the order they appear in the source.

`blockPositionByFacing.get(2)` traces the location of the block labeled 2. Notice that block 1 does not move (as you would expect from Figure 13.4).

```
342    protected void generateBlocks() {
343      for (int blockNdx = 0;
344           blockNdx != blockPositionByFacing.size();
345           ++blockNdx) {
346        ArrayList<Position> blockPositions
347            = blockPositionByFacing.get(blockNdx);
348
349        // Position block # blockNdx in its 0 facing; rotate sprite
350        // for other views
351        int row = blockPositions.get(0).getRow();
352        int column = blockPositions.get(0).getColumn();
353
354        // block at position (2, 2) is centered at location (0.0, 0.0)
355        double y = (row - 2) * squareEdgeSize;
356        double x = (column - 2) * squareEdgeSize;
357
358        // create the block
359        RectangleSprite block
360          = new RectangleSprite(squareEdgeSize, squareEdgeSize);
361        block.setLocation(x, y);
362
363        // color pivot darker; pivot is center square
364        if ((row == getRowSize() / 2) && (column == getColumnSize() / 2)) {
365          block.setColor(getColor().darker());
366        } else {
367          block.setColor(getColor());
```

[12]A **package** can be defined inside another **package**. There is a java **package** containing a `util` package. Objects defined in that package have **package** `java.util` as their package line. Further, there is, somewhere in the code, a directory called `java` that contains a directory called `util`.

```
368         }
369       addSprite(block);
370
371       // populate all four facings with the new block
372       for (int facingNdx = 0; facingNdx != 4; ++facingNdx) {
373         int facingRowNdx = blockPositions.get(facingNdx).getRow();
374         int facingColNdx = blockPositions.get(facingNdx).getColumn();
375         ArrayList<ArrayList<RectangleSprite>> facingBlocks
376             = blocksByFacing.get(facingNdx);
377         ArrayList<RectangleSprite> blocksRow =
378           facingBlocks.get(facingRowNdx);
379         blocksRow.set(facingColNdx, block);
380       }
381     }
382   }
```

Listing 13.17: Piece generateBlocks

The last line in J_Piece is a call to generateBlocks. generateBlocks is long because generating a piece requires two different representations, both the grid, which is described above, *and* the CompositeSprite, which displays the Piece on the Board.

The outer **for** loop loops over all of the blocks that make up the piece; the number of blocks is the number of entries in the blockPositionByFacing ArrayList. For all tetraminoes, this is four.

The block is located (inside the CompositeSprite) in its facing 0 location. That way we can use the regular rotateDegrees method to rotate the appearance when changing the facing. Lines 351–352 get the facing 0 row and column for our block. Lines 355–356 calculate the location corresponding to the position.

Remember that the center of a CompositeSprite is (0.0, 0.0). Each block, in internal screens, is 0.20 wide/high. This is so the whole grid is 1.0 screen in each dimension. That makes the scaling on the board work well.

Lines 359–369 create the new block and add it to the CompositeSprite. The color of the block is the color of the Piece unless the block is in the pivot position. The pivot block is colored darker. This adds some interest to the colors of the pieces and makes it easier to see how rotation is working.

The final loop, lines 372–380, processes each of the four facings. For each facing, the row and column where block belongs in the blocks grid is determined. The blocks grid, facingBlocks, is retrieved from blocksByFacing, the blocksRow is retrieved from facingBlocks, and, finally, the column position in blocksRow is set to refer to block. This last loop takes the blank grids built in the Piece constructor and populates them with the displayed blocks. Block 0 is put in at the appropriate positions according to Figure 13.4 (or, rather, according to blockPositionByFacing.get(0)).

When to Move a Piece

With two grids, one modeling the Board and the other modeling the Piece, how can we determine whether or not it is safe to move the piece down? This is necessary because advance calls moveDown when the move delay timer expires, and the method returns **true** if the piece was moved down one row and **false** if it could not be moved down and was, instead, frozen onto the board.

Before we look directly at when to freeze a piece, let's consider just how a piece moves. The previous section explained that we keep track of the position and facing of a Piece as it moves down the board.

Figure 13.5 shows a J piece at several points in its journey down from the top of the screen. Figure 13.5.a shows the piece with a facing of 0 positioned at the top of the board. The position of the piece is (-1, 3) (shown at the top of the figure). That is the Position of the upper-left grid square in the Piece grid (the one marked with the X) in the grid coordinates of the Board.

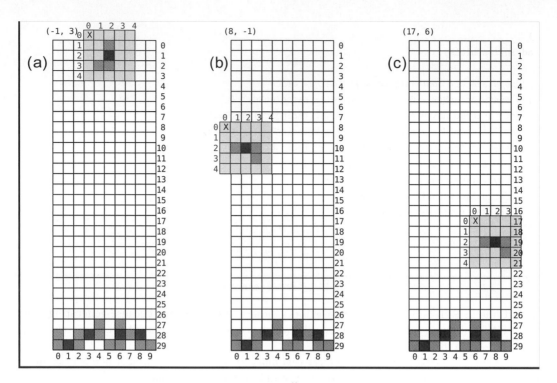

Figure 13.5: Falling Piece

That last bit is important: the Position of the Piece is expressed in the grid coordinates of the Board. Since we are tracking the upper-left corner of the Piece grid, the Position of that grid square is always (0, 0) *inside* the Piece. It is important to keep in mind the difference of the two coordinate systems.

Figure 13.5.b shows the same J piece later in its descent. It has been rotated to facing 3 (according to Figure 13.3) and moved to the left edge of the Board. The Piece is positioned at (8, -1). The piece cannot be moved farther to the left *in its current facing* because some of its blocks (to be differentiated from its grid squares) are off the board. The limitation to a column coordinate of -1 depends on the facing of 3. In facing 2, there are two blank columns on the left edge of the piece grid, so it could move farther left in that facing.

The core collision detection method is in Board. It is called canMoveTo and it takes a Piece and a board position (row, column, and facing). The board position is provided in parameters because that way we can test a piece in different positions before we decide to actually move it.

```
29   /** Constants for reporting whether a piece is in the wrong place */
30   public static final int CLEAR = 0;
31   public static final int HIT = 1;
32   public static final int HIGH = 2;
33   public static final int LOW = 3;
34   public static final int LEFT = 4;
35   public static final int RIGHT = 5;
142  public int canMoveTo(Piece piece, int row, int column, int facing) {
143    int canMove = CLEAR;
144    for (int r = 0; (canMove == CLEAR) && (r != piece.getRowSize());
145        ++r) {
146      int boardRow = row + r;
```

```
147     for (int c = 0;
148          (canMove == CLEAR) && (c != piece.getColumnSize()); ++c) {
149       int boardCol = column + c;
150       if (piece.hasBlock(r, c, facing)) {
151         canMove = positionOnBoard(boardRow, boardCol);
152         if (canMove == CLEAR) {
153           if (hasBlock(boardRow, boardCol)) {
154             canMove = HIT;
155           }
156         }
157       }
158     }
159   }
160   return canMove;
161 }
```

Listing 13.18: Board canMoveTo

canMoveTo returns an **int**; the list of constants in the listing (from the beginning of the .java file), lists the values it might return. CLEAR means that there were no problems: all piece blocks on the board, no piece blocks overlapping board blocks. The other five values indicate what kind of problem there was. LOW, for example, means that at least one piece block is past the bottom of the board.

Back to canMoveTo. It goes through each row in the piece (the **for** loop on lines 144–159). Note that the loop is both count-controlled and sentinel-controlled. The loop exits as soon as a block in piece is found to not be CLEAR. The inner loop (lines 148–158) loops through each column in the piece. Inside the loop a check is made whether there is a block at position (r, c). If not, then the empty grid cannot effect whether or not the Piece can go in the given position, so we jump over the rest of the body of the inner loop.

If position (r, c) *has* a block, then we need to check if the corresponding board position, (boardRow, boardCol), is on the board. positionOnBoard simply checks whether the (row, column) position it is passed as a parameter is on the board, or in the range [0-rows) for row and [0-columns) for column. Depending on which limit is violated, the method returns an appropriate non-CLEAR value.[13]

If the J piece in Figure 13.5.b were tested in the same facing and one column to the left, then the block at (2, 1) would be at board location (10, -1). If the *board* row or *board* column of a Piece block is off the board, then canMove is set to something other than CLEAR by positionOnBoard; the **if** statement at line 153 is **false**, so we go back to the top of the inner loop, then back to the top of the outer loop; and canMoveTo returns a non-CLEAR value.

If the board position of the block is on the board, it still might be on top of a block already in the game. Check that using the hasBlock method of the Board. One advantage of using the same model of the grid for both Piece and Board is the reuse of method names that do the same thing. Once you understand that hasBlock returns **true** if a position is occupied by a block (either in Board or in Piece), then it is easy to logically use the hasBlock method.

Figure 13.5.c shows the same piece farther down, now on the right side of the board. Now the piece cannot move to the right because it would have two blocks off of the board. How do we actually move a piece down?

```
204 public boolean moveDownIfPossible() {
205   if (currentPiece.canMoveDown() == CLEAR) {
206     currentPiece.moveDown();
207     return true;
208   } else if (contains(currentPiece)) {
```

---

[13] The method is not listed here for brevity.

```
209      freeze(currentPiece);
210      int moveScore = deleteAllFilledRows();
211      if (score != null) {
212        score.increment(moveScore);
213      }
214      return false;
215    }
216    return false;
217  }
```

Listing 13.19: `Board moveDownIfPossible`

The `moveDownIfPossible` method asks the piece if it can move down. `canMoveDown` is a wrapper method that just fills in the position and facing of the `Piece` and calls `canMoveTo`, returning the value it gets back.

```
117  public int canMoveDown() {
118    return board.canMoveTo(this, getRow() + 1, getColumn(),
119      getFacing());
120  }
253  public void moveDown() {
254    setRow(getRow() + 1);
255  }
```

Listing 13.20: `Piece moveDown and canMoveDown`

The `canMoveDown` method exists so that we don't mix the logic of making the current piece move (`Board.moveDownIfPossible`) with the arithmetic of figuring out the row number (`Piece.canMoveDown`). The `Piece` then uses its reference to the `Board` it is on to call `canMoveTo` with the right parameters.

If the piece *can* move down, `moveDownIfPossible` moves the piece, again by telling the piece to `moveDown`. It should be noted that `moveDown` does *no* error checking. If the piece is ordered down when `canMoveDown` returns **false**, the consistency of the game world is broken. It is safe to call in line `Board.java:206` (because of the surrounding **if** statement). `moveDownIfPossible` then returns **true** (the piece moved).

If the piece could not move down, then the method returns **false** but not until it freezes the piece, removes all full rows, and increments the score.

```
381  private void freeze(Piece piece) {
382    for (int r = 0; r != piece.getRowSize(); ++r) {
383      int boardRow = piece.getRow() + r;
384      for (int c = 0; c != piece.getColumnSize(); ++c) {
385        int boardCol = piece.getColumn() + c;
386        if ((piece.hasBlock(r, c)) &&
387            (positionOnBoard(boardRow, boardCol) == CLEAR)) {
388          RectangleSprite block = acquireBlock(piece.blockAt(r, c),
389              boardRow, boardCol);
390          blocks.get(boardRow).set(boardCol, block);
391          addSprite(block);
392        }
393      }
394    }
395    removeSprite(piece);// remove the CompositeSprite
396  }
```

Listing 13.21: `Board freeze`

The `freeze` method has a structure very similar to that found in `canMoveTo`. It has two nested loops that go over the grid of the piece passed in as a parameter. Here it uses the current position and facing of the block rather than providing one as a parameter. For each location in the piece grid, if it has a block and the corresponding board position is actually on the board,[14] then the `Board` steals the block from the `Piece`. The `RectangleSprite` representing the block is returned with the call `piece.blockAt`. The block is rescaled and relocated according to the board's size and the `boardRow` and `boardCol` where the block is going. It is inserted into `blocks` and added to the `Board`'s list of sprites to display.

Look at lines 388–391 again. The block is retrieved from the `Piece` and the reference to it is used (in `acquireBlock`) to recolor it and set its *location*. The grid model of the `Board` is updated with the addition of the block at the correct position. Finally, the visual model (the `CompositeSprite` model) of the `Board` is updated with a call to `addSprite`.

We hope you are a little bit concerned right now. Earlier we had four different grids, one for each facing, referring to each block in the `Piece`. Now we have not only the `Piece` but also the `Board` referring to the same `RectangleSprites`. Is this legal? Is it sound?

It is legal: recall that any number of references can refer to a single object, so references from different underlying objects are perfectly legal as far as Java is concerned. It is also sound *in this case*: line 395 removes the `Piece` from the `Board` so that there is no attempt to draw the block inside of the `Piece` ever again. It would still be sound even if the `Piece` remained on the `Board`, except for the fact that we rescaled and relocated the block. Comment out line 395 and see what happens.[15]

So, we transfer ownership of the blocks from the `Piece` and then stop paying attention to the `Piece`. Out in `moveDownIfPossible`, after freezing, the board clears out any filled rows. A row is filled if all positions in the row have a block in them; alternatively stated, a row is filled if it has no **null** references.

```
448   private boolean isRowFilled(int rowNdx) {
449     ArrayList<RectangleSprite> currRow = blocks.get(rowNdx);
450     int c = 0;
451     for (c = 0; c != columns; ++c) {
452       if (currRow.get(c) == null) {
453         break;// get out of the loop
454       }
455     }
456     return (c == columns);// did we finish the loop?
457   }
```

Listing 13.22: Board isRowFilled

Given a `rowNdx`, `isRowFilled` traverses across the row using a count-controlled/sentinel-controlled loop. This time, for variety (and ease of understanding the purpose of the code), the sentinel appears *inside* the loop. The **if** statement on line 452 is the sentinel condition stated positively. The **break** statement on line 453 "breaks out" of the innermost loop construct in the current scope. **break** stops execution of the **for** loop, continuing execution with the first line *after* the loop. This means that we can tell if the loop terminated by the count or by the sentinel by looking at the count-control variable. Since we want to check the value of c after leaving the loop, the variable must be declared *before* the loop. The row is filled if the **for** loop ended because c == columns.

---

[14]The move ... `IfPossible` and rotate ... `IfPossible` methods constrain movement; if they are the only ways the current piece was moved, this check is superfluous. The check for a position being on the board is not expensive either in running time for the program, or for programmers understanding why it is called, so it remains here.

[15]Little copies of the pieces begin to appear. They are scaled down because the `Board` has more blocks in its grid, so each block is smaller. They are offset from the piece on the screen because the position depends on where the piece last was on the `Board`. Commenting out a line of code is one way of trying to figure out what it does; you have to be careful not to randomly change things, though. Try to predict what the result is to check if you really understand the code.

To delete all filled rows, loop across all rows in the board and use `isRowFilled` to determine if it should be deleted.

```
345   private int deleteAllFilledRows() {
346     int rowsDeleted = 0;
347     for (int r = 0; r != rows; ++r) {
348       if (isRowFilled(r)) {
349         deleteRow(r);
350         ++rowsDeleted;
351       }
352     }
353     return rowsDeleted;
354   }
```

Listing 13.23: Board `deleteAllFilledRows`

The check of rows has to go from top to bottom. If it went the other way, `deleteRow` on row `r` would move the unchecked row `r -1` into the `r` row (all rows above `r` move down when the row is deleted; more just below). The increment in line 347 would move the index above the unchecked line. Moving from higher to lower indices this does not happen. Only already checked lines above the full line fall when the full line is removed and then the loop advances to the next lower line, the next *unchecked* line.

```
361   private void deleteRow(int deadRowNdx) {
362     removeRowOfSprites(blocks.get(deadRowNdx));
363     for (int r = deadRowNdx; r != 0; --r) {// counts backwards!
364       blocks.set(r, blocks.get(r - 1));// (r - 1) >= 0
365       ArrayList<RectangleSprite> currRow = blocks.get(r);
366       for (int c = 0; c != columns; ++c) {
367         if (currRow.get(c) != null) {
368           currRow.get(c).setLocation(locationFromRowColumn(r, c));
369         }
370       }
371     }
372     // add a new, empty row at the top.
373     blocks.set(0, initRow());
374   }
```

Listing 13.24: Board `deleteRow`

In `deleteRow`, all of the blocks in the dead row are removed from the `Board` (the `CompositeSprite` model) using `removeRowOfSprites`. While it is assumed that `deleteRow` is called only on filled rows, it is a good idea to check the blocks to make sure you don't try to remove **null** values. `removeRowOfSprites` shows how the curly braces after a **for** or **if** statement are optional. The **if** controls the execution of the next statement; if there is only one statement, the curly braces are optional, and if there are more than one, the curly braces make the multiple statements into a block that is treated as a single statement.

At line 363 the rows are taken from the dead row's index up to 0. This **for** loop counts backwards. Each time through the loop the row above (at index `r -1`) is moved down in `blocks` (line 364). That fixes up the grid model. The blocks in the row that moved must be relocated, too. That is what the loop in lines 366–369 does. Finally, after row 0 was moved down to row 1, make a new row 0. `initRow` was used in building the new, empty board grid and returns a new, empty row, just what we need at index 0.

`deleteAllFilledRows` returns the number of rows that are deleted; the `Board` adds that value to the score.

This section examined using two different models for a game simultaneously. While it might seem contrary to the DRY principle, two different models are not repeating one another but serving different purposes. In BlockDrop the two models are the grid and the CompositeSprite. Blocks (RectangleSprites) are kept in both models.

The simple, grid-based model is used to check for collisions and to keep track of the blocks. By having all facings of a given Piece take up the same space, rotating a piece does not require any fixing up of the position.

The CompositeSprite model, the screen model used by FANG since the beginning of the book, uses **double** values to keep track of locations. Blocks must be scaled so that they appear properly within the visual representation.

The next section looks at how another *factory* is used as a polymorphic constructor, how the high score list is implemented using a CompositeSprite with its own advance method, and a few other small finishing details for BlockDrop.

Review 13.3

(a) What is the type of the field Piece.blocksByFacing? What do each of the dimensions "mean"? How could you check if a there was a block in location [2,1] when a piece is in facing 1?

(b) What does the program do if rotating a piece puts part of the piece into the edge of the board? Would it make more sense to disallow the move? How would you do that?

(c) Could deleteAllFilledRows run its loop the opposite direction? What additional considerations would there have to be?

(d) How could you change the scoring to give a bonus for clearing more rows on any single drop?

13.4 Finishing BlockDrop

The whole BlockDrop program, with all of the pieces, the game, the board, and the high score handling, runs just about 35 pages. That means there is not enough room in this chapter to carefully examine every line. Earlier we looked at how a given Piece, the J_Piece is constructed. The other six pieces are the same except that the locations where the blocks go in the grid are specific to the given piece shape.

The ScoreSprite is simply a StringSprite with an **int** score field and a get and a set method for the score. When the score is set, the text of the StringSprite is updated to reflect the new score. The implementation details are so similar to other sprites from earlier chapters that detailed study of the code is left as an exercise for the reader.

BlockDrop implements a simple level mechanism: every 10 filled rows, the speed of the game goes up by 5%. The level is advanced whenever the tens digit of the score changes as a result of freezing a piece. The code for doing this is called from advance in BlockDrop; it is not explored further here.

The remainder of this section takes a look at the NextPieceBox, a sprite (for showing the next piece coming up in the game), *and* a factory for creating random Pieces; a look at creating a random *contrasting* color; and finally a look at the ScrollingMessageBox in the HighScoreLevel.

Another Factory

Part of the gameplay of BlockDrop is being able to see into the future. While maneuvering a piece as it falls, the play can see the next piece to be served up. In FANG terms, this means the next Piece, a Sprite, must be displayed on the screen. To keep the scale of the Piece consistent with the size it has on the Board, the new Piece is generated by a CompositeSprite-derived class called the NextPieceBox. The NextPieceBox is a square scaled to match the grid of one Piece. The scaling is accomplished by passing the blockSize determined by the Board into the NextPieceBox constructor.

The piece inside the box can be accessed through a getter method; that is necessary so that when the currentPiece is frozen in the Board, the piece in the NextPieceBox can be added to the game. The one other public method of NextPieceBox is nextPiece. Calling that method has the box create a random new Piece. Since there are seven different kinds of pieces, the code to do this is a factory.

```
70   public void nextPiece() {
71     // remove old piece from display
72     if (piece != null) {
73       removeSprite(piece);
74     }
75
76     // randomize piece, facing, and color
77     int randomPiece = Game.getCurrentGame().randomInt(
78         Piece.PIECE_COUNT);
79     int facing = Game.getCurrentGame().randomInt(4);
80     Color randomColor = getRandomContrastingColor(getColor());
81
82     // the factory code; call the right constructor
83     if (randomPiece == 0) {
84       piece = new I_Piece(facing, randomColor);
85     } else if (randomPiece == 1) {
86       piece = new L_Piece(facing, randomColor);
87     } else if (randomPiece == 2) {
88       piece = new J_Piece(facing, randomColor);
89     } else if (randomPiece == 3) {
90       piece = new Z_Piece(facing, randomColor);
91     } else if (randomPiece == 4) {
92       piece = new S_Piece(facing, randomColor);
93     } else if (randomPiece == 5) {
94       piece = new O_Piece(facing, randomColor);
95     } else if (randomPiece == 6) {
96       piece = new T_Piece(facing, randomColor);
97     }
98     addSprite(piece);
99   }
```

Listing 13.25: NextPieceBox nextPiece

The nextPiece method is broken into three parts: get rid of the old piece (if there was one); generate a random piece number, facing, and color contrasting with the board color; and finally call the right constructor to create the piece that was randomly selected.

Lines 71–75 are straightforward. The old Piece has probably been added to the Board so it should no longer be displayed.

Lines 76–80 are also understandable, so long as we accept that getRandomContrastingColor does what its name claims.

In TwentyQuestions the factory code used a String value found in a text file to determine what kind of AdventurePage to create (see Section 12.1 on page 381). Here, instead of encoding the class of the Piece as a String, we encode it as an int. Since there are seven possible pieces (the number is stored in the Piece.PIECE_COUNT constant), we generate a non-negative int less than seven and then use a multi-way if to call one of seven constructors. The result is stored in a reference to a Piece and the Piece is added to the NextPieceBox's display.

Contrasting Colors

How can `getRandomContrastingColor` work? First, what does it mean for two colors to be contrasting? For the our purposes here, all colors are either light or dark and opposites contrast. How can we tell a light from a dark color? Take the three *channels* of color information, red, green, and blue. Each is an `int` on the range [0–256). Average the three channels together. If the average is greater than or equal to half of the range (128), then the color is light; less than half and it is dark.

```
134  private Color getRandomContrastingColor(Color bgColor) {
135    int low = 128;// assume we want a light color
136    int high = 256;
137    int averageBrightness = (bgColor.getRed() + bgColor.getGreen() +
138      bgColor.getBlue()) / 3;
139
140    if (averageBrightness >= 128) {// bgColor is light
141      low = 0;// need dark color
142      high = 128;// range
143    }
144
145    Game curr = Game.getCurrentGame();
146    Color randomColor = Game.getColor(curr.randomInt(low, high),
147      curr.randomInt(low, high), curr.randomInt(low, high));
148    return randomColor;
149  }
```

Listing 13.26: NextPieceBox getRandomContrastingColor

If the parameter color, `bgColor`, is dark, we generate numbers in the upper half of the range for each color channel of the random color, and if `bgColor` is light, the lower half. Lines 135–136 assume we want a light color. If the average brightness of `bgColor` is in the light range, change the high and low limits for the random numbers. Finally, just generate a color from three random integers.

Scrolling List

When we show the high scores list, how can we make it interesting? Further, how can we show scores than would comfortably fit on the screen at one time? The answer is that we could scroll the names on the screen. Have a `CompositeSprite` positioned so that everything below a certain point is not visible on the screen and move items up the screen, wrapping them to the bottom of the list when they go off the top of the `CompositeSprite`.

Everything is stuff we have done before: the `StringSprites` in the list are sprites with velocity, moving a sprite until it hits some horizontal line is dealing with falling apples, even relocating the sprite as it crosses one horizontal line back at the beginning horizontal line is from `NewtonsApple`. Doing all of this with several sprites at the same time in an `ArrayList` extends what was done in previous games but we have moved groups of sprites before as in `RescueMission`.

The public protocol (not to be confused with a Java **interface**) for `ScrollingMessagBox` is a little like what we would have for a game because it contains other sprites and advances them.

```
class ScrollingMessageBox
  extends CompositeSprite {
  ScrollingMessageBox()...
  ScrollingMessageBox(ArrayList<String> msg, double velocity, int gap)...
```

```
    public void add(String newMsg)...
    public void advance(double dT)...

    // get/set for Gap, LineHeight, and Velocity

    public void setColor(Color color)...
}
```

We hope it is clear that the get/set comment expands into six methods. Further, we hope it is obvious how to write the six methods (or will be once you know the types of the values). setColor is necessary so that the color set to the sprite is propagated to the lines. The ScrollingMessageBox has no background or edges; those must be provided by the client code if they are required.

The primary ScrollingMessageBox constructor takes three parameters: the list of messages to scroll, the velocity to scroll the messages, and the gap between the last message and the repeat of the first message. The gap is expressed in blank lines between the last message and the starting over of the message list. It increases the length of the cycle as if there were gap blank messages at the end of the list. The default constructor passes in an empty list of String and default values set in the **public static final** constants of ScrollingMessageBox. The line height, in internal screen coordinates, is set to a default in the constructor. It can be changed with the appropriate get/set methods.

```
 92  public void advance(double dT) {
 93    scrollMessages(dT);
 94    wrapIfNecessary();
 95  }
190  private void scrollMessages(double dT) {
191    for (int i = 0; i != messages.size(); ++i) {
192      messages.get(i).translateY(dT * velocity);
193    }
194  }
201  private void wrapIfNecessary() {
202    StringSprite top = messages.get(indexOfTopLineOnScreen);
203    if (top.getMinY() < TOP_EDGE) {
204      int indexOfBottomLineOnScreen = (indexOfTopLineOnScreen +
205          (messages.size() - 1)) % messages.size();
206      StringSprite bottom = messages.get(indexOfBottomLineOnScreen);
207      top.setY(bottom.getY() + lineHeight);// top just below bottom
208
209      if ((indexOfTopLineOnScreen == 0) && (gap > 0)) {
210        top.translateY(lineHeight * gap);
211      }
212
213      indexOfTopLineOnScreen = (indexOfTopLineOnScreen + 1) %
214        messages.size();
215    }
216  }
```

Listing 13.27: ScrollingMessageBox advance

The primary public method is advance, which calls two implementation methods, one to move all of the lines according to the velocity and one to wrap. The movement is done in ScrollingMessageBox.scrollMessages rather than inside a StringSprite-extending sprite because all of the sprites share the same velocity.

The wrapIfNecessary method gets the StringSprite with the highest y-coordinate and checks if it is past the top edge of the "screen." If it is, the StringSprite is relocated to one line height below the line with the lowest y-coordinate. The scrolling is designed to work only going up the screen. If the line moved had index 0, then the gap is opened up between the last and first lines.

When we checked whether an apple hit the ground or if swimmers hit the edge of the screen, we checked *all* of the sprites. How does wrapIfNecessary find the StringSprite with the highest y-coordinate? Or the one with the lowest y-coordinate, for that matter?

One way it could work is to search the ArrayList<StringSprite> messages for the highest/lowest y-coordinate (just call getY() on each element). This sprite uses an alternative: it has a field called indexOfTopLineOnScreen. The field is initialized to 0 because lines are located from top to bottom of the sprite. Line 213 in wrapIfNecessary advances the field to the next highest line on the screen *after* the old top is wrapped.

Finding the other extreme, the lowest y-coordinate, just means finding the one before. Lines 204–205 do the arithmetic. The expression in those two lines should be read as

(indexOfTopLineOnScreen -1) % messages.size()

The problem with using that simple statement is that computer modular numbers are not the same as mathematical modular numbers. In mathematics, modulo 17 (just to pick a modulus), (0 -1) % 17 is 16; this makes sense because (16 + 1) % 17 is 0 and mod 17 arithmetic limits the values to [0–17).

In Java and most computer languages, modular arithmetic limits the values for mod 17 to (-17-17). -1 is a valid value and makes sense to be the value of the expression (0 -1) % 17. Unfortunately, -1 is not a good value to use as an index into an ArrayList. So, instead of subtracting one, in Java we add the modulus minus one. We evaluate (0 + (17 -1)) % 17. This expression evaluates to 16 in Java and to 16 in mathematics.

Since the modulus for the indexes of the messages list is the size of the list, on line 205 the size minus one is added to the index and then the modulus of that sum is taken. This makes sure that the value of indexOfBottomLineOnScreen is the index right before (in a cycle modulus messages.size()) indexOfTopLineOnScreen.

Review 13.4

(a) How does the game pick a *random* but *contrasting* color? How can you tell that a color is "light"? What about "dark"? Does the definition used in this section make sense?

(b) How is the *factory* pattern used in this project? How is the type required of the "polymorphic constructor" encoded? Where does that encoding come from?

(c) What type does HighScore.compare return? What do different values mean? How do HighScore objects compare?

(d) Put the following HighScoreLevel.HighScore objects in sorted order according to the compare method.

```
    name:   Slate
    score:  3


    name:   Ruby
    score:  21


    name:   Stone
    score:  8


    name:   Opal
    score:  5


    name:   Jade
    score:  10
```

13.5 Summary

Interfaces

Java supports only *single inheritance*: a class must extend exactly one parent class (exception: Object, the root of the tree). Some languages support *multiple inheritance*, the ability to have more than one parent class.

Instead, Java uses the idea of *interfaces*. An interface is a completely abstract class: all methods are just headers. A class **implements** an **interface** by importing the definition, including an **implements** clause naming the interface, and implementing all methods called for in the interface.

The HighScoreLevel.HighScore class (a class nested in HighScoreLevel) **implements** Comparable<HighScore>. This means two things: HighScore defines a **public int** compare(HighScore rhs) method to compare itself with another high score object, *and* a HighScore object *is-a* Comparable<HighScore>. In particular, Collections.sort can sort a collection of HighScore because the sort method requires that the elements of the collection be Comparables (same as saying: elements of the collection must implement the Comparable interface).

Nested Classes

A class definition can contain additional class definitions. This is done to hide the class from other classes. Details of HighScore, the entries put on the high-score screen, do not impact any class but HighScoreLevel. No other class need know anything about this implementation detail of the level.

The name of the Java file must match the top-level **public** class. A Java file must contain a top-level **public** class matching the name of the file. All other top-level class definitions in the Java file must be non-**public**. Nested class definitions can have any access level. If they are **public** they are considered part of the public protocol of the class; if they are **private** they are implementation details.

Packages

Separate class files partition the solution so that the programmer focuses on the details of one abstraction at a time. As projects get bigger, the number of classes grows unmanageable. Java supports the idea of *packages*.

Collision Detection

BlockDrop uses a grid to keep track of filled and unfilled locations. It is implemented as a list of lists. It mimics pixels (picture elements) on the screen, and the collision detection mimics pixel-perfect sprite collision (which was available on some sprite controllers in the 1980s).

Collision detection here is done *before* the piece is moved. This makes sure that the constituent blocks of the pieces never overlap on the screen. Predictive collision detection works well here because the speed of the falling object is fixed as is its distance from anything with which it might collide.

Even when FANG intersection tests are used, they are effectively done before pieces move (it is all undone if there is no way to make the move work).

Breaking Apart a Composite

The sprites in a composite remain there. This chapter takes advantage of that, pulling RectangleSprites out of a Piece and putting them directly into a Board.

Because Java collections hold references, this sharing of sprites between two different composites could lead to a tug-of-war as each container makes changes to the sprite to suit itself. In this case it is safe because the Piece is no longer in use after the squares are put on the board.

Java Templates

```
<classDeclaration> := <accessLevel> class <className>
                        [extends <parentClassName>]
                        [implements <interfaceName> [,<interfaceName>]*]


<classBody> := {
                    <definition>*
                 }

<definition> := <fieldDeclaration> |
                <methodDefinition> |
                <classDefinition>
```

```
<packageID> := <identifier>
<packageID> := package <packageName>;

<classFile> := [<packageID>]
                <imports>
                <classDefinition>
```

13.6 Chapter Review Exercises

Review Exercise 13.1 What is *multiple inheritance*? Does Java support multiple inheritance?

Review Exercise 13.2 What parameters does `Collections.sort` take? What are the limits on the types of elements in a sortable collection?

Review Exercise 13.3 What is a Java *package*?

Review Exercise 13.4 You are defining a package called `animals`.

    (a) What directory contains all `.java` files?

    (b) What is the first non-comment line of each `.java` files in the directory?

    (c) How is the file `Platypus.java` in the package `animals` compiled from the command line.

    (d) If `animals` has a main class (extends `Game` or contains its own `main` method), how is it run from the command line?

    (e) Your project also has another package, `entertainment`. In the class `Zoo` there is a collection of `Platypus` objects. What **import** statement (if any) is required at the top of `Zoo` to include the `Platypus` class from `animals`?

Review Exercise 13.5 What method must a class provide to `implement` `Comparable<T>` where `T` is the type of the class?

Review Exercise 13.6 How do you set the next level FANG starts? How do you end the current level and start another?

Review Exercise 13.7 Put the following `HighScoreLevel.HighScore` objects in sorted order according to the `compare` method.

```
   name:  Cliff
   score: 19


   name:  Muffy
```

```
score: 8

name:  Benton
score: 19

name:  Niel
score: 5

name:  Jimmy
score: 5
```

13.7   Programming Problems

Programming Problem 13.1   Go back to `TicTacToe` in Chapter 7. Add a new kind of level, one that shows which player won the last game and keeps track of win/lose statistics for an entire online gaming session. The level should display a button to start a new game.

The game itself must be modified to take the game statistics (so that it can pass them back to the next instance of the statistics screen).

Programming Problem 13.2   Modify the game to drop *pentaminoes*, pieces with 5 blocks.

(a) Assume all blocks must share an edge (not just a vertex) with at least one other block in the piece: how many pieces are there in the new game?

(b) Can all of the pentaminoes be fit in a 5×5 grid or must the grid be expanded?

(c) What parts of the game must be modified? How much of `Board` or `NextPieceBox` is aware of the number of blocks in a `Piece`? (Data hiding makes later modification much easier. The less one class depends on the implementation details of another, the better.)

(d) Make the changes. Is the game more fun than the original? Is there anything particularly satisfying about the pentominoe version of the game? Anything particularly unsatisfying?

Programming Problem 13.3   Modify the game so that, instead of moving a piece toward the center of the board when rotation would embed it in the wall, the game just ignores the attempt to rotate the piece. Require the player to explicitly move the piece away from the wall before it can rotate.

Does this improve the playability of the game? Why or why not? If you want, continue with Programming Problem 13.4

Programming Problem 13.4   Look at Programming Problem 13.3. Having completed the described modification, design a playtest experiment to determine whether or not your intuition on improving the game holds for other gamers.

Your playtest experiment should plan on recruiting about five–eight of your fellow students, and you can probably count on about half an hour of their time. The following things should be considered and answered in a written design of the playtest:

- Does your institution have in Institutional Research Board? Does your plan to use fellow students or friends in an experiment for which you might get a grade require any interaction with the IRB?

- Doe the ACM code of ethics have anything to say about such a user experiment? If so, how can you address the professional organization's concerns?

- How can you minimize bias in the playtesters for whatever they learned first? What model does the real Tetris follow?

- What happens if your sample is biased toward students who are very much into video games? How would you expect them to react?

14

String Processing: Interactive Fiction

This chapter brings together all of the topics presented so far while examining a *text adventure game*. A text adventure game is a game where the player explores a virtual world; the exact goal of the game depends on the contents. It is called a *text* adventure game because the world and everything in it is described in text and the user's interaction with the game is by typing commands.

Creating the game engine is only half of the effort in creating a text adventure game: every object in the world must be described in a data file. To support game authors, this chapter examines a flexible data file formatting what Jon Bentley calls a "self-describing data file" [Ben88].

Text adventure games require more sophisticated *string processing* than we have yet seen. User commands are short declarative sentences such as "get ticket" or "talk Dean of Students" or "move north." The last one can be shortened to "north" in most games. Taking apart a sentence like this involves *parsing* the string, breaking the whole thing up into syntactic units. Remember that syntax, when applied to programming languages, talks about structure. The same is true when writing a simple parser: the parser breaks the string into tokens, words and symbols defined as being significant. The sequence of tokens is then processed to figure out the meaning, the semantics, of the user command.

Similar parsing tasks are necessary when processing a self-describing file. Rather than having each record in a text file have exactly the same ordering, each field is identified by name. The value of a field might be just one line or multiple lines long so the syntax of the data file must indicate where the field values begin and end and the parser must be able to handle them. Finally, printing descriptions for the user requires *wrapping* the text so no lines are too long to display. Wrapping is frequently used in word processors and other text editors.

The scale of the text adventure game program lends itself to *incremental development*, the creation of increasingly complete and complex "versions" of the program. Incremental development permits the programmer to focus on one piece at a time and is one component in the currently popular development methodology known as *agile* development.

First, a quick introduction to what a text adventure game *is* and a high-level design of the game. The project is then broken into phases for incremental development, starting with reading the data files and then working with the commands in the game.

14.1 Back to the Future: Interactive Fiction

Text adventure games are games where the player interacts with a virtual world through text: the user's commands are entered as lines of text, typically imperative sentences, and the results are described to the user with text on the screen. This section gives a broad overview of how a text adventure game works and discusses the design of a game *engine* (it also defines the difference between a game and a game engine). Limited to text input and output, interactive fiction is well-suited to less powerful computing devices such as smart phones and MP3 players. They are also well-suited to our abilities to read and write from standard input and standard output.

Interactive Fiction

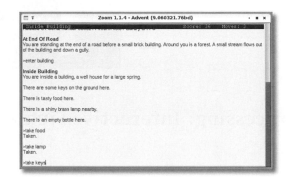

Figure 14.1: zoom running a z-machine port of *Advent*

Text adventure games or, in the more modern parlance, *interactive fiction* is a medium for gameplay and storytelling that came into being before there were computers to play the stories. It is related to hypertext and experimental fictions such as the French Oulipo movement. The genre came into full flower during the 1980s because the personal computers of the time were well suited to displaying text, perhaps in different colors, but they were not yet powerful enough to display *bit-mapped graphics*. (Bit-mapped graphics are computer controlled graphics where every pixel's color can be set.)

Experimental novels and poems from the late 1950s and early 1960s were sometimes printed in interesting, mixable ways permitting the reader to interact with the ordering of the story as well as with the story itself. Raymond Queneau, a French poet, wrote *Hundred Thousand Billion Poems*, a book of ten sonnets. Each sonnet, having fourteen lines, was cut into fourteen strips of paper. There were therefore 10^{14} different poems in the book because each strip could display the line from any of the ten sonnets. This same mechanism has been used by Ray Kurtzweil to have a computer generate poetry.

In Section 12.1 we saw that *Choose Your Own Adventure* books are also interactive fiction printed on paper. A paragraph or two atop each page offers the reader a choice. At the bottom of the page each choice planned by the author is listed along with a page number. The reader turns to the page number corresponding to her choice of action.

Computerized interactive fiction traces its history back to William Crowther's *Advent*, also known as *Colossal Cave Adventure* (file names had a limit of six characters in the operating system where the game was written). Crowther was an amateur spelunker as well as a systems programmer on the early ARPANet (predecessor to the Internet). He wanted to share his passion for exploring caves with his daughters, so in 1974 he wrote *Advent*. The original *Advent* was written in the FORTRAN programming language, one of the oldest compiled languages which focused on scientific/mathematical programming (the name is a contraction of *FORmula TRANSlator*).

Because he was a network programmer, he put his program source code out where other ARPANet programmers could find it. Many of them compiled it and passed it on. Others modified or extended it. In 1976 Don Woods expanded *Adventure*, adding many fantasy elements influenced by J.R.R. Tolkein. In 1978 Scott Adams wrote *Adventureland*, which he advertised and sold. This was the first commercial text adventure game. If you want more information on *Adventure*, visit http://www.rickadams.org/adventure/ (that is where the version shown in the figure was obtained).

The first wave of personal computers came on the market at about the same time as Adventureland. In 1979 Infocom, the most successful commercial interactive fiction vendor, was created. For a decade, Infocom produces amazing stories such as *Zork*, *Trinity*, and *The Hitchhiker's Guide to the Galaxy* (authored by Douglas Adams himself). They developed a bytecode machine designed for playing text adventure games known as a *z-machine*.

Interactive Fiction

It is interesting to look at the beginnings of the computer game industry around the world and trace it to former Infocom (or Level 9 in the UK) employees. Given that IF bloomed just about a working generation ago, most established game companies were founded by maker/players or players of interactive fiction.

The z-machine is a bytecode machine, just like Java. That means that the interpreter can be ported to new hardware and old byte-compiled files can be given a new life. Z-machines exist for iPhone, MS Windows, Mac OSX, and various flavors of Unix. Figure 14.1 shows a modern z-machine interpreter, zoom, running a ported version of *Colossal Cave Adventure* on a modern workstation.

While text adventure games were replaced by graphic adventure games in the commercial realm, they moved on to be a consuming hobby for many. They provide an interesting storytelling environment with low barriers to entry. Interactive fiction has even been studied academically (see Monfort, *Twisty Little Passages*, for a literary take on the genre along with history).

The Internet was part of the first adventure game being shared, and with the *Interactive Fiction Archive* (http://ifarchive.org), it is part of keeping the genre alive. The archive hosts the "Comp," the annual competition for best interactive fiction of the year. If you find yourself wondering how it is possible to build a "good," "fun" game with limited graphics capabilities, try one or more of the Comp finalists to see how it is done.

Text Adventure Games

The World

The world of a text adventure game is a collection of *locations* that are connected, one to another. In these locations there are *critters*, characters inhabiting the virtual world. Locations and critters can have *items* in their possession which can be picked up by, stolen by, or perhaps traded for by the player. The player is also a critter because he has an *inventory*, a collection of items.

This description is intentionally very general. Exactly *how* locations are connected to one another depends on the world being modeled. If the game world is on the surface of the Earth, it would make sense to discuss locations being laid out in a grid with locations laying to the "north," "south," "east," and "west" of a given location; it should be possible that a location has no location in a given direction so that the location is at the edge of the map in that direction. If the game world represents the interior of a submarine, "fore," "aft," "port," "starboard," "up," and "down" might all make sense. A space station, a system of deep caves, or a collection of airports might each have a connection scheme different than either of the above.

Critters and items differ primarily in how the player can interact with them. A critter is something to which the player can *speak* or with which the player can *fight* or *barter*. Note that any given game might have none, some, or all of these options. A critter might represent a talking garden gnome, a superhero in blue spandex, or a clanking robot. A critter might even be a vending machine *if* the interaction with the vending machine is more like that of interacting with other actors in the drama rather than in interacting with *things*.

Items can be *picked up* or *dropped*. Some might be able to be *eaten* or *drunk*, *read*, or, perhaps, even *combined* to make some new item. It is possible that the connections from one location to another might require the player to possess some particular item (generically a *key*) to pass or require the player to have met some particular critter.

Note that the last several examples show that text adventure games on a computer go well beyond what is possible in a choose-your-own-adventure book. In the book, no matter how you turned to page 57, the choices presented to you are the same. So if you got there after the second page you read or after bouncing through more than a hundred pages of epic combat; whatever happens on and after page 57 is the same.

In a text adventure the player critter has state which can be checked at any time. If the player must have visited the great elf before leaving the forest, this can be enforced. If killing the dragon precludes any happy ending, then lock the happy ending choices after the dragon dies. The key here is that the computerized game has *state*, which can be used to permit choices at one point in the game to have consequences in another part.

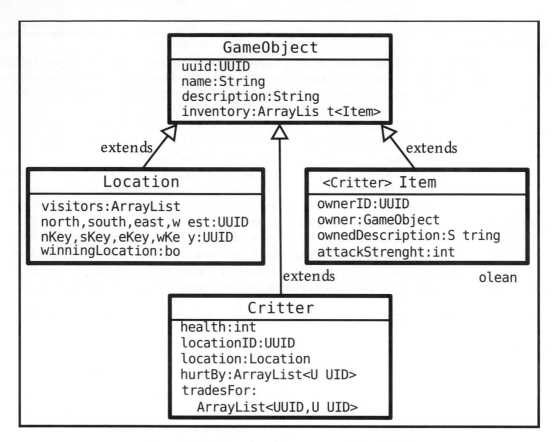

Figure 14.2: Hierarchy of GameObjects Listing Fields

What fields define a location, critter, or item? Figure 14.2 shows an inheritance diagram indicating the fields in each object.

Each game item has a *universally unique identifier* (UUID). A UUID is unique within the collection of all objects in a given game. Each field is followed by its type; the type UUID means whatever type we choose for UUIDs. The UUID, UUID is just a placeholder for a type to be defined later: it indicates that a critter will trade one item for another item.

Unique identifiers permit any object to refer to another by its UUID. This should sound familiar: the page number in TwentyQuestion served as a UUID for the AdventurePages. We could, again, use a serial number to identify each item; the UUID of an object would be implicit in its position in the data file, a record number counting from the beginning of the file.

Consider how difficult it was to write and read (as a human) the short data files for TwentyQuestions. With just eight entries, keeping track of the index number of each and having a given question refer to its yes and no children was not easy. Explicit UUIDs, included in each object's entry in the data file, make it much easier to refer from one object to another.

What *data type* should the UUIDs have? The choices seem to be int or String. The int would make it possible to use the UUID as an index into an ArrayList to make looking things up easier.

Did that last sentence make you uncomfortable? It insidiously mixes different levels of abstraction. When designing a class to hold associated information, it is not appropriate to worry about how a collection of instances of the class is structured. It is enough to assume that we can look up a game object in a collection of game objects and, based on the UUID, find the one we want.

So, one option for UUID remains `int`. Does `String` have any advantages over `int`? For the game author the answer is "Yes!"

Imagine that an item has a field, call it owner. The owner of an item is the critter or location where that item currently resides. The data file contains something indicating that the owner of the *Dagger of Ensidor* is either 1003452 or **GrummTheBarbarian**. Which would make the data file easier for the human being to read, write, and debug?

An item, a location, and a critter each have a UUID. They also each have a name (the *Dagger of Ensidor* or *Grimm the Barbarian*), and a description (the text displayed on the screen when the player enters the location or sees the critter or item). Working on designing the hierarchy showed that critter and location both needed an inventory, a list of items held by that object. Factoring the inventory and its routines out of those two classes and putting it in the game object shortened the code. It also made it possible to implement container objects (like a suitcase); the code to actually use container objects is not part of the engine.

A location has some number of links to other locations, the connections that let players move around. For our game engine, the fields are the four cardinal directions, and each records a UUID. There are also corresponding "key" fields. A key is some item or critter that must be present (or must *not* be present) to permit traveling to a neighboring location. Explicitly naming the directions in the data file as in `north = infirmary` makes writing a game data file much easier; there is no requirement to list *all* of the possible out directions, most saying "no such place." Labeling also removes the need to remember the exact order of the outgoing connections (does "nsew," "news," or "ensw" make more sense in ordering them?).

Critters have health, a list of items that hurt them, and a list of item pairs that they are willing to trade for. These exact features fit the "game" designed for this chapter. More importantly they provide an opportunity to look at how to read values from data files with different types: health is an integer, the hurt by is a list of strings, and the trade list is a list but the values are, themselves, structured (each contains two UUIDs).

Items have an owner (stored as an owner UUID in the data file). Each has an optional "owned description." The owned description is description text added to the description of any critter or location that owns the object — for example, the `CheddarCarp`, are originally owned by the `VendingMachine` adding the sentences "There is a single package of Ridge River brand Cheddar Cheese Carp, 'The cheese cracker that tastes like a fish.' It is marked $0.25." to the description of the vending machine when it is examined. The attack strength of an item is the amount of damage it does to critters hurt by it. The game engine is not designed around combat but there is a need, at times, to be able to remove a critter which is in the way.

These lists are minimal and focused on the game designed for this chapter, *Escape from T-Hall*. The next section presents the design for the game with emphasis on the interesting interactions (and data structures needed to make them work) such as "hurt by" and "trades for." The section after looks at reading self-describing data files and the section after that looks at the game code.

Review 14.1

(a) Why would it make more sense to have a *vending machine* be a `Critter` rather than an `Item`? Does the player need to be aware of this choice?

(b) What advantages would there be of enforcing a more structured UUID? All locations begin "LOC:," for example. Would there be any disadvantages?

(c) Why does it seem that all decisions are being made to make the life of the game author easier?

(d) Think about how you would store the *map*. It is a collection of `Location` objects. How would you find a particular location given its UUID? How long would that take on a large map?

14.2 *Escape from T-Hall*

The "game" for this chapter is very short. The player is a harried computer science major at the end of the semester and, quite possibly, at the end of his or her rope. They are in the fictional T-Hall, the computer science building on campus. They have not seen the sun, trees, or sky since midterms. Starting in room 101 they must figure out how to get out of the building to the quad.

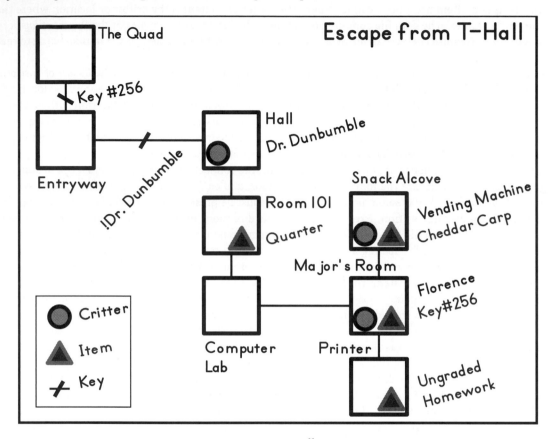

Figure 14.3: T-Hall Map

Figure 14.3 shows the map for the game. The squares are the locations. The directions between them are the obvious ones (north is to the top of the figure). The rooms contain critters and items. In the two rooms on the east with both a critter and an item, the critter actually has the item and you must trade for it. This design provides motivation for the data files read in the next section.

Notice the block marks on the two links in the northwest. These indicate that those links can be crossed only if key conditions are met. The game has "positive" and "negative" keys: some keys are items or critters that must be present before a link is available whereas others are items or critters that cannot be present for a link to be available. The "!" in front of "Dr. Dunbumble" on the link between the *Entryway* and the *Hallway* indicates that the professor blocks that connection. There is no "!" on "Key #256," so that item must be in the player's possession before he or she can get to *The Quad*.

14.3   Reading the Data

This section takes a bottom-up approach to design. Instead of dividing a problem into smaller and smaller pieces, this section builds up how a complex record could be stored. First, we review the requirements of a self-describing data file and then look at how to implement them.

A self-describing data file is a text file that describes what it contains. This is, in a data file sense, exactly how we try to write Java code. Choosing good names, using indentation to document inclusion, and writing comments that document the intention, these all can be applied to *data* files.

Why do we apply those techniques to Java programs? They make the code more *readable* and *maintainable*. Code is read many more times than it is written; it is worth the investment to make it as readable as possible. Maintenance of software is rewriting it to remove bugs or to accommodate any changed program requirements. Good programming style and documenting the programmer's intent make the code easier to follow and much easier to edit when it is necessary.

These same techniques can be applied to data files so that the data can be *read* and, more importantly, *written* by a human being using a text editor. This means that the programmer can develop a series of test files to test the file reading code. It means game designers can work on data files *before* the game engine is finished. One big win in separating data from the code is that data changes can be made quickly; this is only true if the data can be understood so the *appropriate* changes can be made quickly.

A self-describing data file should

- permit comments — ignored by the system;

- be free format — ignore most spaces;

- explicitly identify each object and each field;

- be order independent — with field identifiers, the fields can come in any order;

- permit multiline entries.

The Craft of Adventure

The Craft of Adventure by Graham Nelson [Nel97] weighs in at just under 40 pages and is the best introduction to thinking like a game designer, bar none. The following "guidelines" of what not to do come from the "Player's Bill of Rights" section. All good here is drawn directly from Graham Nelson; any mistakes or misunderstandings belong to the present authors.

The adventure game player is the protagonist, the star of the unfolding story. The world literally *does* revolve around them and whenever you describe something to them, they have every reason to expect that there is a reason and that they can *use* what you described.

In *Craft*, Nelson uses the example of a room described as having a banister running down a set of stairs and continuing down the opposite hallway. Because the banister (or is it "rail"?) plays in the description, players try to tie a rope to it, balance a ball on it, and come up with some way to use it. The most frustrating response is if the game says "I can't understand what you are trying to do." At the least it should have the response Nelson quotes: "That's not something you need to refer to in the course of this game." This means the game recognizes "banister" and the author recognizes that it is not unreasonable to try to use it in some way. And the response tells the player to move along; there is nothing to use here.

This is an example of making sure you have enough nouns. You want to make sure that the game recognizes reasonable synonyms. Failure to follow this rule means that playing the game becomes guessing the right word (in graphic adventure games there is a similar problem of "clicking on the right pixel" to activate something); guessing the right word is seldom fun in an adventure game (the amnesiac awakening with a headache as in the *Bourne Identity* is a cliche in adventure games; unless you are an interactive fiction Ludlum, let that one be).

Players should not die without warning. Going north from the winery and seeing, "You fall in a fermenting vat and drown" is unacceptable without some hint as to what will happen if you go north. Players should be able to win with some common sense (perhaps tuned to the setting of the game) and not need prior (game) life knowledge. If the bomb is hidden in one of the 99 rooms in the mansion and the player

---

The Craft of Adventure

has three guesses to find it, they are likely to find it only after hearing that the ballroom exploded and they died.

This applies to any action that makes the game unwinnable. If you can never go home again, don't let the player leave home without his or her credit card *if* the credit card is the only way to get a plane ticket to Dallas. Or rather, make sure the player knows that it seems like a bad idea to abandon the credit card. Make sure the hints are not too obscure. Make sure that outcomes are not too random.

Graham Nelson packed a lot more useful game design thinking into *The Craft of Adventure*. He is also the creator and programmer of *Inform*, a free Z-code (z-machine) byte-compiler. *Craft* was originally released as a companion for the *Inform* manual and found its way into the hard copy *Inform Designer's Manual* by Nelson and Rees [NR06]. *Inform* is on version 7 and can be found at `http://inform7.com`. Interestingly, the most current version of the manual is an interactive nonfiction programmed and read inside the *Inform* system itself.

Low-Level Reading

Back in Section 10.5, the `File` and `Scanner` classes were introduced. That section also looked at how to read a text file word by word and how to read a text file line by line; it is notable that we have not read a file or keyboard input *character by character*.

One of the greatest contributions of the original Unix operating system was the abstraction of all files (and devices like the network card) as streams of bytes. This uniform abstraction means a program can be written to work with a stream of bytes with no knowledge of the bytes' origin: the user could be typing them in, they could be the result of requesting a given URL from a Web server, or they could come from a file stored on the user's USB flash drive. This is an example of separating concerns: the code that *opens* a source interacts with the real source and that code is part of the operating system; the code that *uses* the stream of bytes is insulated from the details.

Similarly, in Java, we have been working with a high-level abstraction of input. Rather than working directly with streams of bytes or even streams of characters,[1] we have worked with the `Scanner` class. The `Scanner` reads a sequence of characters (insulated from the source of the characters) and groups the characters together into *tokens*. A token is a sequence of characters fitting some syntactic description. We work out the syntactic description used by `Scanner` by default and how to change it below.

Readers and Writers

Can we gain access to a stream of bytes like `Scanner`? If we can, what can we do with a stream of bytes that we could not do with the `Scanner`? Yes, we can, using the built-in family of classes known as `Reader` classes.[2]

There is a large number of `Reader` classes; they can be recognized by `Reader` ending their class names. We look at two: a `FileReader`, which can be constructed from a `File`, just like we have been constructing `Scanner`; and a `FilterReader`, which is constructed as a wrapper around another `Reader` possibly modifying the stream of characters before passing the characters on.

We start by writing a program, `CountCharacters`, modeled on our earlier `EchoFile` program, which reads a file named on the command line *character by character*, counting the total number of characters in the file; the listing shows only the `count` method that actually reads the file.

```
46   public void count() {
47      if (file.exists() && file.canRead()) {
```

---

[1]There is a distinction between the two: remember Unicode? Some characters take more than one byte to express.

[2]`Reader`- and `Writer`-derived classes work with streams of **char**; there are `InputStream` and `OutputStream` classes that permit direct access to the stream of *bytes*. We note their existence here and return to working with streams of **char**.

```
48    FileReader reader = null;
49    try {
50      reader = new FileReader(file);
51      int characterCount = 0;
52
53      int ch = reader.read();
54      while (ch != EOF) {
55        ++characterCount;
56        ch = reader.read();
57      }
58      System.out.println(file.getName() + ": " + characterCount);
59    } catch (FileNotFoundException e) {
60      System.err.println("PANIC: This should never happen!");
61      e.printStackTrace();
62    } catch (IOException e) {// file was opened before this exception
63      System.err.println("Problem while reading \"" + file.getName() +
64        "\".");
65      e.printStackTrace();
66    } finally {
67      try {
68        if (reader != null) {
69          reader.close();
70        }
71      } catch (IOException e1) {
72        System.err.println(
73          "Error closing Reader assciated with + \"" +
74          file.getName() + "\".");
75        e1.printStackTrace();
76      }
77    }
78  } else {
79    System.err.println("Unable to open \"" + file.getName() +
80      "\" for input");
81  }
82 }
```

Listing 14.1: CountCharacters: count

CountCharacters is structured just like ExistsFile (see Listing 10.10 on page 322) where the main method treats all command line arguments as file names, constructs an object of the right type (CountCharacters in this case) with the file name, and then calls the processing method, count. The field file is a File associated with the given file name.

count is twice as long as echo (Listing 10.11). Most of the code in count handles different kinds of *exceptions*.

Recall that when Java executes a **try** . . . **catch** statement, the code in the **try** block is executed (lines 49–59) and *if* an exception is thrown, the first **catch** block following the **try** that matches the type of exception thrown is executed.

Whether an exception was thrown or not, after finishing the **try** . . . **catch** block, the program executes the **finally** block (if any) associated with the **try**. This makes the **finally** block a great place to close files. If the **new** in line 50 succeeded, reader is non-**null** and should always be closed. It is in line 69, which is executed only if reader was assigned a value in line 50.

Back to the **try**: just like a Scanner a FileReader can be constructed from a File object. Assuming no exceptions, any open Reader provides a read() method that returns an **int**. The return type is **int** to accommodate Unicode characters. Each call to read() reads one character from the underlying stream, advancing the current position in the file, and returns the value. If the stream has been exhausted, read() returns -1. This class defines a constant, EOF, to make the loop on lines 54–57 easier to read.

If we run the program on its own Java source file, the following output is generated:

```
~/Chapter14% java core.CountCharacters core/CountCharacters.java
CountCharacters.java: 2330
```

Notice that the name of the class for Java to run is the package name, a dot, and the name of the class. The name of the *file*, which is a parameter to the program, is the name of the folder, a slash, and the full path to the file.

When constructing a Scanner, if we pass it a File, under the hood, the Scanner constructs an InputFileStream, the byte-reading version of a FileReader. We can provide the Scanner with a FileReader to use as its input source.

```
50   public void echo() {
51     if (file.exists() && file.canRead()) {
52       FileReader reader = null;
53       try {
54         reader = new FileReader(file);
55         Scanner echoScanner = new Scanner(reader);
56         String line;
57         while (echoScanner.hasNextLine()) {
58           line = echoScanner.nextLine();
59           System.out.println(line);
60         }
61       } catch (FileNotFoundException e) {
62         System.out.println("PANIC: This should never happen!");
63         e.printStackTrace();
64       } finally {
65         if (reader != null) {
66           try {
67             reader.close();
68           } catch (IOException e) {
69             System.err.println(
70               "Error closing Reader assciated with + \"" +
71               file.getName() + "\".");
72             e.printStackTrace();
73           }
74         }
75       }
76     } else {
77       System.out.println("Unable to open \"" + file.getName() +
78         "\" for input");
79     }
80   }
```

Listing 14.2: EchoFileWithReader: echo

EchoFileWithReader behaves just like Chapter 10's EchoFile. The File is used to construct an FileReader which is then used to construct the Scanner. The FileReader is what is closed in the **finally** block; it is possible the reader was initialized and echoScanner was *not*; to make sure the file is closed no matter what, we close the low-level FileReader if it is non-**null**.

FilterReader — Changing What Is Read

That is not very exciting. What if we wanted to *change* the value being echoed? What if we wanted to convert curly braces (both opening and closing braces) into vertical bars, |? We could write a FilterReader-derived class to do the work.

The "Filter" in FilterReader is meant to make you think of a water filter and the stream of characters as the water passing through. Just as a stream of water may carry many different things along with it, some of which you would rather not see in your drinking glass, so might a character stream have characters we do not want passed to our program. For our example we want the stream modified so that no curly braces make it to our program, and we want to introduce a different character at that same spot.

FilterReader is a Reader that takes a Reader as a parameter to its constructor. As written, every method defined in FilterReader just passes its parameters to the same method in the inside reader. These wrapper methods are provided so that child classes get all of the methods and can choose which ones they want to change. In the interest of space the listing omits most comments.

```
12  public class NoCurlyFilterReader
13    extends FilterReader {
14    /** state flag; have we already seen the end of the stream? */
15    private boolean endOfStream = false;
22    public NoCurlyFilterReader(Reader in) {
23      super(in);
24      this.endOfStream = false;
25    }
33    public int read() throws IOException {
34      int ch;// the character to return
35
36      ch = in.read();
37      if ((ch == '{') || (ch == '}')) {
38        ch = '|';
39      }
40      return ch;
41    }
53    public int read(char[] text, int offset, int length)
54      throws IOException {
55      if (endOfStream) {
56        return -1;// end already reached
57      }
58
59      int charCount = 0;
60      for (int i = offset; i < (offset + length); i++) {
61        int temp = this.read();
62        if (temp == -1) {
63          endOfStream = true;
64          break;
65        }
66        text[i] = (char) temp;
```

```
67      charCount++;
68    }
69    return charCount;
70  }
80  public long skip(long n) throws IOException {
81    char[] chArray = new char[(int) n];
82    int charCountSkipped = this.read(chArray);
83    return charCountSkipped;
84  }
85 }
```

Listing 14.3: NoCurlyFilterReader

The FilterReader has a **protected** constructor. This is so that no one can construct one (this is similar to writing an **abstract class**); it is possible to construct only some subclass of FilterReader that declares a **public** constructor. NoCurlyFilterReader does that. It takes a Reader as its parameter and passes the object to FilterReader's constructor. It also initializes a field that flags whether or not we have reached the end of the input stream. This is explained below.

Lines 33–41 override the read() method. You can see, at line 36, that we call read() on the internal Reader provided as a **protected** field in FilterReader. If we didn't want to make any changes to the characters we could just pass ch back. Instead, we check if the character is a curly brace. If it is, we set the value of ch to a vertical bar. Line 40 returns ch.

There is one other read method we must override because it calls in.read directly (so it would not have any changed characters). That method is read(**char**[] text, **int** offset, **int** length). The [] show that the first parameter is an *array*. length is the number of characters that should be read into the array and offset is the index where the first read character is to be stored. This is known as a *buffered read* where the array of characters is a buffer for holding some number of characters. This is the most general header of a buffered read and, while there are other buffered read methods, they are all defined in terms of this one. Another win for Do Not Repeat Yourself: because the most general version can do what all of the others do (with the right parameters), it is the only one that needs to be written or, in our case, overridden.

Looking at the comments in the *JavaDoc* for read, we find

```
read
public abstract int read(char[] text,
                          int offset,
                          int length)
            throws IOException


Reads characters into a portion of an array. This method
will block until some input is available, an I/O error
occurs, or the end of the stream is reached.

Parameters:
    text    - Destination buffer
    offset  - Offsetset at which to start storing characters
    length  - Maximum number of characters to read
Returns:
    The number of characters read, or -1 if the end of the
    stream has been reached
Throws:
    IOException - If an I/O error occurs
```

The characters must be read into the array starting at text[offset] and continuing until text[offset+length-1]. The return value is the number of characters actually read into the array or, if the end of the input stream has been reached, -1.

This is where endOfStream comes in. When reading the last bunch of characters from the input, the buffered version of read reads in fewer than the required number. If the first call to read() (line 62) returns -1, then the buffered method returns 0 for the character count read. If, instead, the tenth call returns -1, then the buffered call returns 9. In any case, when the call to read() returns -1, indicating the end of the input stream has been reached, endOfStream is set true. Any future call to the buffered read returns -1 (see line 55 following).

So long as read() does not return -1, then each entry in text, starting with text[offset], is set to the next character read. To set an element of an array, the array name, the square brackets, and an index appear on the left-hand side of an assignment operator, as in line 66. The character count, the value returned, is incremented each time a character is added to the array.

This buffered version of read makes use of read() in line 61; this is used to read *every* character put in the buffer. This is important because it keeps us from having to repeat character replacement logic in the buffered read method. This exact buffered read code can work with multiple read() implementations (as we shall see below).[3]

Line 80 begins the override of skip(int). The FilterReader version of the method just calls super.skip(n), returning the result. This method makes use of a buffered read method that eventually calls the one defined at line 33. Because this filter replaces a single character with a different single character, the number of characters read does not change so overriding skip is not, strictly speaking, necessary. Since read() could (and, later, will) read a different number of characters from the underlying stream than it returns to its client, it is good practice to override skip so that it counts returned characters rather than read characters.

Decorators

A FilterReader or a class that **extends** FilterReader is an example of a recurring pattern in computer science, one that has its own name. A class that serves as a wrapper around an object (or objects) of the same class that it extends is said to *decorate* the wrapped object; the wrapper class is a *decorator*.

One popular software design pattern book, *Head First Design Patterns*, by Freeman *et. al.* [FFBD04], discusses decorators in terms of coffee drinks. The following discussion is loosely based on theirs (but much less complete).

A coffee drink is something you can purchase at the café. An **abstract** class, CoffeeDrink, represents *all* drinks. Part of the public protocol of CoffeeDrink is getPrice() so that the system can determine what to charge customers.

When you order a drink you can request a flavor shot of chocolate, vanilla, or cinnamon. Any drink plus a flavor shot yields a *coffee drink*. The flavor shot is a *decorator*: it is both a coffee drink *and* a modifier of a coffee drink. It is possible that the coffee drink being decorated is another flavor shot.

Look at the inheritance diagram, Figure 14.4. The three coffee drinks, Coffee, Espresso, and FlavorShot, are shown, each extending the **abstract** class CoffeeDrink. Each box represents a class and each arrow represents the **extends** relationship, pointing at the parent class.

When ordering an Espresso, the system constructs a Espresso object. This situation is shown in Figure 14.5(a). What happens when you get a Coffee with a chocolate FlavorShot? Just like the barista makes the coffee and then augments it with the flavoring, the system constructs a Coffee object and passes that object into the constructor for a FlavorShot. The resulting composite object is seen in Figure 14.5(b). Finally, when a customer orders an espresso with vanilla and cinnamon, the result is seen in Figure 14.5(c).

When checking out, the system asks the CoffeeDrink object to getPrice() so it knows how much to charge. For object (a) in the figure, Espresso.getPrice() is called and returns 3.50. For object (b), FlavorShot.getPrice() is called. Notice that the first thing it does is call getPrice() for *whatever drink* the flavor shot was based on.

---

[3]In fact, the implementations of read(**char**[], **int**, **int**) and skip(**int**) are slight variations on versions written for a completely different FilterReader project in *Java I/O, 2E* by Harold [Har06].

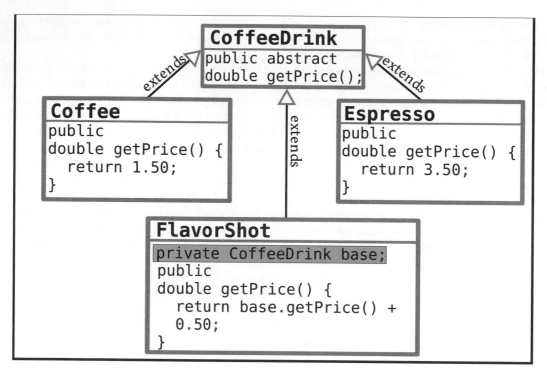

Figure 14.4: `CoffeeDrink` Class Hierarchy

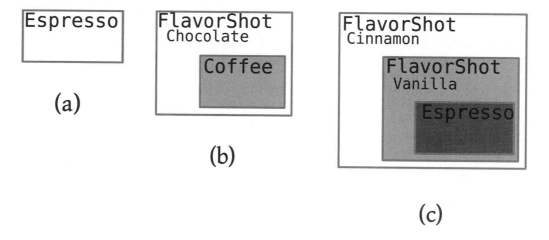

Figure 14.5: Decorated `CoffeeDrink` Objects

This calls `Coffee.getPrice()` which returns 1.50. When `Coffee.getPrice()` returns, `FlavorShot.getPrice()` adds 0.50 to the value and returns it for a price of 2.00.

The double-flavored espresso in (c) is handled similarly with the sequence of calls going from `FlavorShot.getPrice()` (cinnamon) to `FlavorShot.getPrice()` (vanilla) to `Espresso.getPrice()`. These return, in reverse order, 3.50, 4.00 (vanilla), and 4.50 (cinnamon). The flavors in parentheses are just to differentiate the two flavor shots (to show the last-in first-out nature of the calls).

Back to our `FilterReader`. Notice that `read()` does call the inner `Reader`'s `read()` method. This is a common aspect of a decorator: it wraps around some object, providing the same public protocol, and the routines implementing the protocol call into the wrapped object. The decorator does more than just forward calls, though. It also decorates the results or changes the values coming back. By implementing the same public protocol (either by extending the same object or literally implementing the same Java **interface**), the decorated object can be used in all of the same places the undecorated object could be used.

```java
53  public void echo() {
54    if (file.exists() && file.canRead()) {
55      Reader reader = null;
56      try {
57        reader = new NoCurlyFilterReader(new FileReader(file));
58        Scanner echoScanner = new Scanner(reader);
59        String line;
60        while (echoScanner.hasNextLine()) {
61          line = echoScanner.nextLine();
62          System.out.println(line);
63        }
64      } catch (FileNotFoundException e) {
65        System.out.println("PANIC: This should never happen!");
66        e.printStackTrace();
67      } finally {
68        if (reader != null) {
69          try {
70            reader.close();
71          } catch (IOException e) {
72            System.err.println(
73              "Error closing Reader assciated with + \"" +
74              file.getName() + "\".");
75            e.printStackTrace();
76          }
77        }
78      }
79    } else {
80      System.out.println("Unable to open \"" + file.getName() +
81        "\" for input");
82    }
83  }
```

Listing 14.4: `EchoFileWithFilterReader: echo`

The `echo` method of `EchoFileWithFilterReader` is, except for line numbers, identical to the `echo` method of `EchoFileWithReader` except for the line assigning a value to `reader` (line 57 here, line 54 there). Here the `reader` is a `NoCurlyFilterReader` *wrapped around* a `FileReader`. The `Scanner`, written to use the interface, does not care that the object type is different. It reads the file that is decorated by the `FilterReader` so that all curly braces are replaced with vertical bars.

It is possible to decorate something by *removing* something as well as by adding something. How would a `FilterReader` remove end-of-line comments from a text file as it reads it? Such a filter would help in writing a self-describing file reader.

Preprocessing Comments

The first step to compiling a Java program is to break it down into *tokens*. A token is a string that has meaning to Java: keywords, operators (+, ==, etc.), punctuation ({, }, ;, etc.), integer and double literals, and string literals. You should convince yourself that processing the stream of input characters to tokenize the source code is not a trivial task (consider how you would handle quoted strings with escape characters or even identifiers). Imagine that, while tokenizing, you also had to juggle comments: when you're inside a comment, the sequence "int" means nothing; when outside comments, "int" is a keyword.

The Java tokenizer would be much simpler to write if only programmers would leave out comments.[4] If comments are necessary, perhaps we could split the tokenizing task in two: first, process the stream of characters into another stream containing only those characters not in comments. *Filter out* the comment text. The tokenizer is then much easier to write and the two processes together, comment stripper and tokenizer, are probably simpler to write and understand than a comment-avoiding tokenizer.[5]

It is similarly easier to preprocess a data file to remove comments and then process the comment-free records rather than read information with a Scanner and have to worry about inside/outside comment. A FilterReader can process an incoming stream of characters into a different sequence of characters, filtering out all of the comments in the self-describing data file.

To further simplify the job of stripping comments we support only end-of-line comments. So, how can you filter *out* Java-style end-of-line comments?

Given a Reader reading the following character sequence:

```
Line one // beginning
// this whole line is blank
three/visible right here
//
Line five (blank above^)
```

we want to process it into the following character sequence:

```
Line one

three/visible right here

Line five (blank above^)
```

SansCommentFilterReader is-a FilterReader. It scans its input for the // sequence and skips over the characters from the first slash to the end of the current line. The characters are skipped by reading them from the input FileReader but *not* returning any of them as the result of calling read. End-of-line comments are "replaced" with the end-of-line marker.

Figure 14.6 shows our file on disk being read by a FileReader. The sequence of characters read is shown on the arrow going into the FilterReader. The sequence returned, one after the other, by FileReader.read() is shown on the arrow going into SansCommentFilterReader. The sequence in and the sequence out of FileReader are identical.

The arrow going from the SansCommentFilterReader to the Scanner shows the characters returned by SansCommentFilterReader.read(). The Scanner is performing next, nextLine, skip, and other methods reading the information. The sequence of characters it gets back from the sans comment filter is no longer (and, in this case, *shorter*) than the number of characters the sans comment filter gets back from the file reader.

SansCommentFilterReader is identical to NoCurlyFilterReader except for read() so we examine that method.

---

[4]Most students would be more than happy to oblige.

[5]This is how most programming languages are compiled. An early phase goes through and removes comments from the sequence of characters and only later is the sequence of characters changed into a sequence of tokens.

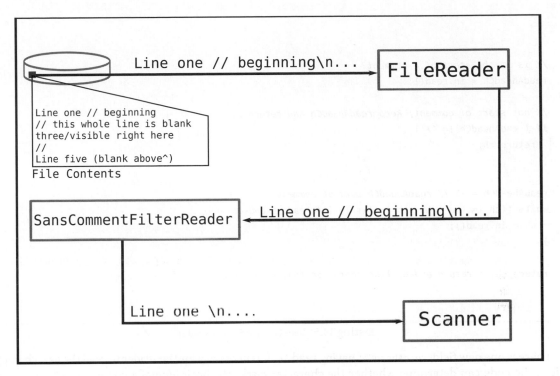

Figure 14.6: A sequence of FilterReaders.

```
20  public class SansCommentFilterReader
21    extends FilterReader {
22    /** /** state flag; have we already seen the end of the stream? */
23    private boolean endOfStream = false;
24
25    /** the extra, read-ahead character (-1 if not useful) */
26    private int readAheadCh;
48    public int read() throws IOException {
49      int ch;// the character to return
50
51      // was there already a character read ahead when dealing with a
52      // slash? If so, return that character
53      if (readAheadCh != -1) {
54        ch = readAheadCh;
55        readAheadCh = -1;
56        return ch;
57      }
58
59      ch = in.read();
60
61      // it can't start a comment so return it
62      if (ch != '/') {
63        return ch;
```

```
64      }
65
66      // is it the start of a comment?
67      readAheadCh = in.read();
68
69      // not start of comment; keep readAheadCh and return ch
70      if (readAheadCh != '/') {
71        return ch;
72      }
73
74      readAheadCh = -1;// readAheadCh part of comment
75      while ((ch != '\n') && (ch != '\r')) {// read to end-of-line
76        ch = in.read();
77      }
78
79      return ch;// return end-of-line character that terminated loop
80    }
130 }
```

Listing 14.5: SansCommentFilterReader

There is one new field, readAheadCh: having read '/' it is necessary for the reader to read the *next* character before the code can determine whether the character marks the beginning of a comment. When the next character *is* a '/', as in the first line of the data file, the read method goes into a loop to skip over the comment.

What if the next character is *not* a slash? In the second line of the data file read reads a '/' followed by a 'v'. read should return the slash (there is not an end-of-line comment here) but we have a problem.The method has already read the next character, the 'v'; it must remember the good character and return it the *next* time read() is called. readAheadCh stores the value of any character read accidentally. It is set to -1 (in the constructor and in read()) when it does not contain a useful character.

So, lines 53–57 handle returning the saved value (and resetting readAheadCh to -1) when necessary. When the method **returns** in line 56, execution of the method stops (so line 59 is never reached in that case).

If there is no read ahead character to return, we decorate the value returned by the Reader in line 59. If ch is anything other than a slash, then it is just returned. If it is a slash, we must read ahead. If the read ahead is *not* a slash, the slash is the right character to return and we save the read ahead.

If the read ahead was a second slash then we skip over the rest of the current line. A line is ended by a '\n' (newline), a '\r' (a carriage return), or a combination of the two characters. We don't have to worry about how the current line is terminated: just use a sentinel-controlled loop to read until one of the end-of-line characters is seen and return that character. This puts the end-of-line marker exactly where the first slash was (to anyone watching just the decorated output).

In the SansCommentFilterReader it is necessary to override skip because the number of characters read from in does not relate to the number of characters returned from read(). skip skips over characters that would have been returned to the user of the Reader.

Review 14.3

(a) What is a *decorator*? What does it have to do with coffee? What does it have to do with reading a file character by character?

(b) Why is CoffeeDrink **abstract**?

(c) How would a Coffee with a double shot of chocolate be represented using the coffee objects in Figure 14.4? How would its price be calculated?

(d) Why might the following comment be a problem if Java did not preprocess comments?

```
/**
 * class makes sure that cool stuff works.
 */
class CoolStuff {
...
}
```

(e) Why was such a big deal made of overriding `skip` in `SansCommentFilterReader`?

14.4 Attribute-Value Pairs

An *attribute-value pair* is an abstract way of encoding description information. An *attribute* is some aspect of a game object expressed as a `String` naming the attribute: `Age`, `Class-Number`, `CollegeIDNumber`. Each attribute has, associated with it, a *value*. The value is also expressed as a `String`, which we can, if necessary, interpret as a number or some other object: `29`, `CIS 201`, `P005-555-1212`. This is a flexible way of storing information that we can adapt to storing fields of objects. Each field is stored as an attribute with the name of the field and a value of the value intended for the field. It is also possible to use attribute-value pairs to store command aliases for the text adventure game.

Command Aliases

Consider processing the various commands the player types into a text adventure game. With compass directions as movement commands, a player would type "north" to go north. The next time the player wants to move he or she would, again, type "north". And so on. Think about the code you would use to process this. Assume there are **do**`<Direction>()` methods that handle movement.

```
if (command.equalsIgnoreCase("north")) {
  doNorth();
} else if (command.equalsIgnoreCase("south")) {
  doSouth();
} else if (command.equalsIgnoreCase("east")) {
  doEast();
} else if (command.equalsIgnoreCase("west")) {
  doWest();
} else {
  unknownCommand();
}
```

This snippet assumes the movement directions are the only possible commands; in the real game there are other commands such as "get" and "put," perhaps "attack" or "talk". Consider the user's experience typing the movement commands. "north" is only five characters, but typing it over and over is a waste of the player's time. It would be nice if "n" were enough.

So, how would you change the first Boolean expression in the snippet to handle either "n" or "north"?

```
if (command.equalsIgnoreCase("north") ||
    command.equalsIgnoreCase("n")) {...
```

That would then need to be repeated for each of the directions. But what if our game has a convention that the user is always facing north and we want "forward" and "f" to be *aliases* for "north" (or "n"). An alias is a different name for the same thing. We want to support an arbitrary number of aliases for each command.

Putting the aliases in the code violates the concept of separating program and data. Some number of basic commands have to be coded in the game but aliases are more flexible: it should be possible to add an alias for an existing command without having to recompile the code.

A file full of alias-command pairs (where the alias is the attribute and the command is the value) could be read into a dictionary. Instead of rewriting the `if` statement when we wanted new aliases, we can just update the alias file used to initialize the dictionary.

Assume the variable `dictionary` is a `Dictionary` that has been filled from the alias file. `Dictionary` has a `get` method which, given an attribute, returns the corresponding value. It returns `null` if there is no match. We could then rewrite the code snippet above to

```
String normalizedCommand = dictionary.get(command);
if (normalizedCommand.equalsIgnoreCase("north")) {
  doNorth();
} else if (normalizedCommand.equalsIgnoreCase("south")) {
  doSouth();
} else if (normalizedCommand.equalsIgnoreCase("east")) {
  doEast();
} else if (normalizedCommand.equalsIgnoreCase("west")) {
  doWest();
} else {
  unknownCommand();
}
```

The data file would look like this:

```
n=north
north= north
// more directions follow
s =south
south = south

e =<east>
east      =<
   east> // and so on
// western stuff here
west = <west  >
w = < west >
```

The odd spacing and ordering is on purpose: being able to read a file like this improves our confidence that the code works with free-form files. The object reading code counts on the free-form reading capabilities so it is good to give it a workout now.

Dictionary

The `Dictionary` class has the following public protocol:

```
public class Dictionary {
  public Dictionary()...
  public Dictionary(Scanner dictionaryFile)...
  public String get(String attribute)...
  pubic boolean hasKey(String attribute)...
  pubic String put(String attribute, String value)...
```

Another name for an attribute in a dictionary is the *key*, the special value used to look up an entry. This protocol is modeled on the Map **interface** provided in java.util; Map is part of the Java *Collections* package like List and ArrayList. That is why the method to test if a given attribute is in the Dictionary is called hasKey.

The first constructor builds an empty Dictionary. The second reads a file with lines of the form *<alias>=<command>*. The file can have comments if the Scanner is constructed with a SansCommentFilterReader and it can contain blank lines which are ignored. An extra blank space around the equal sign and at the beginning and ending of the lines is also ignored.

The get method looks up the entry in the Dictionary. If there is an entry, the value is returned. If no such entry exists, get returns **null**. hasKey returns **true** if there is an entry with the given attribute and **false** otherwise. put associates the given value with the given attribute; put returns the old value of the attribute or **null** if it had no previous value.

The entries in the Dictionary are AttributeValuePair objects stored in the allEntries ArrayList. The public protocol for AttributeValuePair is

```
public class AttributeValuePair
  implements Comparable<AttributeValuePair> {
  public AttributeValuePair(String attribute, String value)...
  public boolean compareTo(AttributeValuePair rhs)...
  public String getAttribute()...
  public String getValue()...
  public String setValue()...
  public String toString()...
```

The constructor takes two Strings, the attribute and the value, and initializes all the fields in the object. The getter/setter method are standard except that there is no setAttribute method. Once a pair is made, the attribute is *immutable*: it cannot be changed. It makes sense to keep it fixed because comparison is by attribute only (compareTo returns the result of comparing the attribute fields of the two AttributeValuePair objects). If the attribute could change, then the sorted order of a list of AttributeValuePair objects could be modified by assignment to one of the elements of the list.

```
20   public static void main(String[] args) {
21     if (args.length > 0) {
22       Scanner aliases = null;
23       try {
24         aliases = new Scanner(new SansCommentFilterReader(
25             new FileReader(new File(args[0])))));
26         Dictionary dictionary = new Dictionary(aliases);
27         System.out.println("====================");
28         System.out.println("dictionary = \n" + dictionary);
29         System.out.println("====================");
30       } catch (FileNotFoundException e) {
31         System.err.println("Unable to open " + args[0] + " for input.");
32       } finally {
33         if (aliases != null) {
34           aliases.close();
35         }
36       }
37     } else {
38       System.err.println("usage: java TestDictionary dictionaryFName");
39       System.err.println("       where dictanaryFName is a file");
40     }
```

```
41    }
```

Listing 14.6: `TestDictionary` main

`core.TestDictionary` constructs a `Dictionary` with a file name provided on the command line and then prints the contents of the dictionary to standard output. When it is run with the sample aliases given earlier, the output is

```
~/Chapter14% java core.TestDictionary aliases.txt
====================
dictionary =
e = east
east = east
n = north
north = north
s = south
south = south
w = west
west = west
====================
```

This is what we would expect because the `Dictionary` was described as being kept in sorted order. We look at how `Dictionary.get` takes advantage of this ordering in Section 14.6.

Reading Game Objects One Field at a Time

How could we use the comment stripping and attribute-value pairs reading to read a self-describing record of some class type? Comment stripping makes it possible to support commented files. Attribute-value pairs can be used to implement order independence: each field is stored with its name, an equal sign, and then the value. An object factory needs two pieces of information we have not yet accounted for: the type of the object to create and when the data for that object ends. The two are marked similarly: the name of the class appears on a line by itself, then any fields as attribute-value pairs, and then the name of the class with a slash (/) in front of it. A `Location` could be stored like this:

```
Location
UUID = Room101
Name = Lecture Room 101
Description = A large, cavernous room. This is where you took CS1. It still
north = Hall
south = ComputerLab
/Location
```

This self-describing file gives the names of the fields in the `Location`. The description (and, perhaps, other fields) are unduly constrained if we limited values to a single line. We need to be able to read a multiline value.

Parsing Multiline Values

A container, like a Java block, makes sense. If the first character in a value is the container opening character, then the value continues until the corresponding close character is seen; if the first character is anything else, then the value continues to the end of the current line. The only question now is what characters to use to set off our value *block*. For ease of processing do not permit blocks within blocks or escaped characters. These simplifications mean that a block ends at the first end of block character after a start of block character.

Using the new notation, a more complete `description` can be written:

```
Location
UUID = Room101
Name = Lecture Room 101
Description = <A large, cavernous room. This is where you took CS1. It
still causes a bit of a shiver when you remember sitting in the back
corner taking the final exam. Questions about ArrayList, searching,
and . . . it is all too much. There is a door at the back of the room
leading north. Another, less conspicuous doorway leads from the front
of the room to the south; that way lies the computer lab.>
north = Hall
south = ComputerLab
/Location
```

Much better: with an arbitrary length of description we can really capture the feel of the game. Attribute-value pairs must be broken into three pieces: attribute, equal sign, and value. The attribute is a run of non-whitespace characters terminated by a space *or* an equal sign. The equal sign is just that, the string "=" but it can appear following any amount of white space. Finally, the value is either any run of non-closing angle bracket characters enclosed between angle brackets, "<" and ">", *or* the remainder of the current line after the "=". Giving the author choices makes her life easier, but we must write code that can recognize the two different formats and respond accordingly.

The read* Helper Methods

The three helper functions for reading these parts of an attribute and value are more general than just reading an attribute-value pair. They are in a utility class, util.ReadAndWrite, along with some writing utilities (arbitrary length descriptions can cause some output problems, too). The methods are be **static** methods returning String read from a provided Scanner.

```
25  public static String readAttribute(Scanner in) {
26      String retval = "";
27      in.skip("\\s*");// unlimited whitespace
28      Pattern oldDelimiter = in.delimiter();
29      in.useDelimiter("[\\s=]");// stop at whitespace or =
30      retval = in.next();// next using new delimiter
31      in.useDelimiter(oldDelimiter);// reset delimiter
32      return retval;
33  }
```

Listing 14.7: ReadAndWrite readAttribute

readAttribute uses a *regular expression pattern* to skip over whitespace. A regular expression is a compact expression for a pattern of characters that can be interpreted by a regular expression matcher. The Java type java.util.regex.Pattern represents regular expressions in Java. The grammar of regular expressions is similar to what we have used in describing Java templates.[6]

Regular expressions, shortened as *regexes*, use a simple, formal language to express character sequences. The Scanner class has several methods with use regexes: findInLine, findInHorizon, and skip. Earlier we used

---

[6]EBNF, the Extended Backus-Naur Form, can actually describe patterns that are more complex than those a standard regular expression can describe. The theory of computation spends a good amount of time examining what can and cannot be recognized by the two types of grammars. Java "regular expressions" are actually more powerful than standard regular expressions; wait until you take theory and ask the professor about it.

the pattern string ".*"; the . is a regex matching any single character and the * modifies any preceding regex to match 0-or-more copies of itself.

What does the pattern string on line 22, "\\s*", match? \s is a pattern matching any whitespace character (a space, end-of-line marker, tab, or Unicode equivalents). The extra \ is necessary so that the string passed in to skip is \s (the backslash is an escape character in a String; to get a backslash character *in* a String, the escape must be escaped: "\\" is the single character String containing a backslash). As stated above, the * modifies the regex before it to match zero or more copies of itself. The pattern is any number of whitespace characters.

When Scanner.next is called, it skips over any number of copies of a pattern called the *delimiter*. The default delimiter is \s, any whitespace character. After finding a character not in the delimiter, next collects all of the characters until it finds another delimiter match. This more detailed view explains how next, with the default delimiter, skips over all whitespace and returns one word at a time. To a Scanner, a word is any contiguous sequence of non-whitespace characters.

It is possible to change the delimiter used by a Scanner. This can be useful for reading specially formatted input such as our attribute. The description above says an attribute ends with whitespace or an equal sign. The pattern string in line 29, "[\\s=]", is a pattern consisting of a whitespace or = character. The square brackets are a regular expression matching any character in the list of characters in the brackets. \s is the list of whitespace characters and = is that character; this delimiter matches whitespace or equals.

The call to next in line 29 stops where it should. In line 27 we skipped over *leading* space (delimiter), so when line 29 executes, the scanner is scanning a non-whitespace character. We save the old delimiter and restore it so that readAttribute does not change how the Scanner works in the rest of the program.

```
56  public static String readMatch(Scanner in, String match) {
57    return in.findInLine(match);
58  }
```

Listing 14.8: ReadAndWrite readMatch

readMatch takes a Scanner and a String to match. The findInLine method takes a pattern string and, ignoring the delimiter completely, searches for a match from the current read point. If a match is found before the end of the current line in the stream, then the matching string is returned and the current read point is moved past the match. No match means it returns null and the current read point is left where it was.

For finding the =, we just pass in the pattern string "=". This matches the equal sign and the Scanner skips over anything before it finds a match. Any whitespace to the left of = is skipped by this method.

```
77  public static String readValue(Scanner in) {
78    String retval = "";
79    String openMark = readMatch(in, "<");
80    if (openMark == null) {
81      retval = in.nextLine();
82    } else {
83      retval = in.findWithinHorizon("[^>]*", 0);
84      in.skip(">[\r\n]*");// consume end of line (and blank lines)
85    }
86    return retval.trim();
87  }
```

Listing 14.9: ReadAndWrite readValue

readValue uses matchString to figure out if it is looking at an angle brace or something else. This makes use of how Scanner.findInLine works when the pattern matches and when it fails to match. If "<" matches, then the current read point is just past the < character. That means it is at the beginning of the contained text, the value that should be read. If the pattern fails to match, the value returned is `null` (for the `if` statement) and the current read pointer remains *unchanged*.

If `openMark` is `null` (no match), then the return value is just the rest of the line as read with `nextLine`. If `openMark` is non-`null` (a match), then the return value is set using `findWithinHorizon`. `findWithinHorizon` is like `findInLine` except it searches across some number of characters rather than until an end-of-line marker.

The use of 0 for the horizon means search for the rest of the file. The pattern string, `"[^>]*"`, means 0-or-more characters which are *not* >. The `[^` as the opening of the list of characters means "all characters *except* those in this list", so the pattern `[^>]` is any one character that is not a closing angle bracket. The * means any number (including 0).

The `skip` in line 84 uses the pattern string to skip over the > and any end-of-line markers following it.

Each Tending to Its Own

A data file containing the name of each object and then, within the object, listing all of the fields (that need to be set) using an attribute name for the field name and the value for the value to read makes sense for the author of the data files. How does the code construct the right type of object and how does a `Location` know how to handle the "north" field and the "UUID" field?

The data file reading code cannot determine the type of class to construct until reading the first line of the record in the data file. This requires some sort of *polymorphic constructor*. But Java has no polymorphic constructors.

A factory method accomplishs what we want. A **static** method in `GameObject` to read the next non-blank line from a `Scanner` and call the right constructor based on the named class. The method would then return a `GameObject`, the parent class of all game objects. Rather than writing the general factory we use three different data files, one each for the game map, cast, and props. This is to avoid having to cast `GameObjects` down to `Locations` (or `Critters` or `Items`), which is required if the general factory returns references with the static type of `GameObject`. Each game object subclass provides its own static factory method.

This section examines the `Location` factory because the next phase of the game is to load the game map and move around the locations. The factory reads the name of the class and then, while it does not see the end-of-class marker, it handles each attribute-value pair.

How is "handle each attribute-value pair" done? The problem is, who knows how to handle the name (attribute) of all of the **private** fields in `Location`, `GameObject`, `Item`, and `Critter`? No one object has access to all of those fields. That is actually a good thing. We pass the attribute-value pair into the lowest element in the hierarchy and that object *first* passes the pair up to its **super** class. If the **super** recognizes the attribute, it handles it; if the **super** fails to recognize it, then the child tries to recognize it, returning **true** if it recognizes it and uses the associated value to set a field. The returning **true** is important because that is how a child of the child would know the field was handled.

```
68   public static Location readObjectFromFile(Scanner gameObjectScanner) {
69       String classID = gameObjectScanner.next();
70       if (!classID.equalsIgnoreCase("Location")) {
71           return null;// not the expected type of object; punt
72       }
73
74       String endClassID = "/" + classID;
75
76       Location lo = new Location();
77       GameObject.processAttributes(gameObjectScanner, endClassID, lo);
78       return lo;
79   }
```

Listing 14.10: Location `readObjectFromFile`

The method assumes it is called with the current read point somewhere before the opening `Location` line in a location record file. Line 69 reads the next word from the file; since the file is opened with a `SansCommentFileReader`, the next word should be the name of the class. This factory, rather than handling multiple different class names, validates that the class name found in the file matches "Location". If it doesn't match then there is no point in reading the record so we return `null`. If the `Location` constructor is called, then the `processAttributes` method is called.

```
40  protected static GameObject processAttributes(
41    Scanner gameObjectScanner, String endClassID, GameObject go) {
42    String attribute = ReadAndWrite.readAttribute(gameObjectScanner);
43    while (!attribute.equalsIgnoreCase(endClassID)) {
44      /* ignore */ ReadAndWrite.readMatch(gameObjectScanner, "=");
45      String value = ReadAndWrite.readValue(gameObjectScanner);
46      go.handleAttributeValuePair(attribute, value);
47
48      attribute = ReadAndWrite.readAttribute(gameObjectScanner);
49    }
50    return go;
51  }
```

Listing 14.11: `GameObject processAttributes`

In `processAttributes` the three reading helpers are used. The first reads the attribute and if the attribute is the end-of-record string, then the record is done, so the method returns. Otherwise the attribute and value are passed to the object's `handleAttributeValuePair`; this method is overridden in `Location` (and `Critter` and `Item`), so the call is *dynamically* made to `Location.handleAttributeValuePair`.

```
302  protected boolean handleAttributeValuePair(String attribute,
303    String value) {
304    if (super.handleAttributeValuePair(attribute, value)) {
305      return true;
306    }
307
308    value = value.toLowerCase(); // all of them need it
309    if (attribute.equalsIgnoreCase("nKey")) {
310      setNKey(value);
311      return true;
312    } else if (attribute.equalsIgnoreCase("eKey")) {
313      setEKey(value);
314      return true;
315    } else if (attribute.equalsIgnoreCase("nKey")) {
316      setNKey(value);
317      return true;
318    } else if (attribute.equalsIgnoreCase("sKey")) {
319      setSKey(value);
320      return true;
321    } else if (attribute.equalsIgnoreCase("wKey")) {
322      setWKey(value);
323      return true;
324    } else if (attribute.equalsIgnoreCase("east")) {
325      setEast(value);
```

```
326      return true;
327    } else if (attribute.equalsIgnoreCase("north")) {
328      setNorth(value);
329      return true;
330    } else if (attribute.equalsIgnoreCase("south")) {
331      setSouth(value);
332      return true;
333    } else if (attribute.equalsIgnoreCase("west")) {
334      setWest(value);
335      return true;
336    } else if (attribute.equalsIgnoreCase("winningLocation")) {
337      setWinningLocation(Boolean.parseBoolean(value));
338      return true;
339    }
340    return false;
341  }
```

Listing 14.12: Location handleAttributeValuePair

The first thing that happens, line 304, is that the GameObject version of this method is called. GameObject gets first shot at handling the given attribute name. If it does (we see the code below), it returns **true** and the Location version is done: it just returns **true** to signal that the field was consumed somewhere at or above Location.

If the method reaches line 309, this is a large if/else if structure. It checks the attribute string against the names of fields it knows. If there is a match, the value is interpreted (as the appropriate type) and the method returns **true**.

The code in GameObject.handleAttributeValuePair is very similar to that in Location, just without the call to the **super** version of the method (this is the base class of all game objects).

```
302  protected boolean handleAttributeValuePair(String attribute,
303    String value) {
304    if (attribute.equalsIgnoreCase("uuid")) {
305      setUUID(value.toLowerCase());
306      return true;
307    } else if (attribute.equalsIgnoreCase("name")) {
308      setName(value);
309      return true;
310    } else if (attribute.equalsIgnoreCase("description")) {
311      setDescription(value);
312      return true;
313    }
314    return false;
315  }
```

Listing 14.13: GameObject handleAttributeValuePair

The three fields that it "knows" are uuid, name, and description. If the attribute contains any of the three, the value is assigned to the right field. The return value of **true** tells Location.handleAttributeValuePair that the attribute has been handled.

Beyond `String`

How can a `GameObject` that expects a value other than a `String` for some field process the value in the file? Using the attribute-value code always gives back a string as the value. How can a `GameObject` get a different type?

This section draws code from the `Critter` object because the critter has a health field, a numeric field, a "hurt by" field that can appear multiple times with multiple values, and a "trades for" field, a field where the value is structured. The code snippets here are very short, showing only the one entry in the `handleAttributeValuePair` method of `Critter`.

An Integer

```
174    } else if (attribute.equalsIgnoreCase("health")) {
175        setHealth(Integer.parseInt(value));
176        return true;
```

Listing 14.14: `Critter` "health"

Handling the `health` attribute in the critter file is similar to handling any `String`-valued attribute except that the value, passed in from the file, is parsed as an integer by the `Integer` class. `parseInt` reads the string it is given as an `Integer`. Java automatically converts from the returned `Integer` to an **int** when that is what the parameter for `setHealth` expects. `Double.parseDouble` and `Boolean.parseBoolean` do just what you would expect (`Location` uses `parseBoolean` for the `winningLocation` field).

These methods can throw exceptions if you pass them strings containing ill-formed numbers (or Booleans).

Multiple Values

A `Critter` can be hurt by items it receives. That sounds kind of silly unless you imagine that the critter is *Superman* and the item is *kryptonite*. Any given critter can be susceptible to any number of items in the game. The `hurtBy` field is an `ArrayList` of UUID (`String`).

```
177    } else if (attribute.equalsIgnoreCase("hurtBy")) {
178        addHurtBy(value.toLowerCase());
179        return true;
```

Listing 14.15: `Critter` "hurtBy"

The `addHurtBy` method does what you would expect (calls `hurtBy.add`) to add the value to the list. This means that `hurtBy` can appear multiple times in any one critter's entry in the cast file. The UUID is converted to lowercase to permit the use of `.equals` rather than `.equalsIgnoreCase` for checking values in the list during the game.

Structured Values

A `Critter` might be willing to give the player something if it is given something. In the game if the player gives the vending machine a quarter, the vending machine will give the player the cheddar carp (assuming the player has not already gotten them; they are given only if they are held by the vending machine).

Because a given critter might have any number of trades it is willing to make, `tradesFor` is a list. What is it a list of? Trading involves two UUIDs: the UUID of what the critter *gets* and the UUID of what the critter *gives*. How can we store two UUIDs in one string? Or, barring that, how can we specify how two fields, one for gets and one for gives, go together?

```
180     } else if (attribute.equalsIgnoreCase("tradesFor")) {
181         String gets = value.substring(0, value.indexOf(':')).trim().toLowerCase();
182         String gives = value.substring(value.indexOf(':')+1).trim().toLowerCase();
183
184         addTradesFor(new TradesFor(gets, gives));
185         return true;
```

Listing 14.16: Critter "tradesFor"

The answer is to pick a character that marks the dividing point in the field and split the string on that value. This method uses the colon, :. The indexOf method returns the index (with the first location being 0) of the first matching character. The substring method in line 181 pulls out the characters from the beginning to the colon and puts them in gets. Line 182 does the same thing but with the characters after the colon. Both are trimmed and converted to lowercase (all UUID are forced to lowercase for using built-in search routines). A pair is made out of the two using a class called TradesFor. The class just associates the two UUIDs and has two getters: getGetsUUID and getGivesUUID. The list tradesFor is used when the player gives something to a critter; see Section 14.7.

Review 14.4

(a) What is an attribute-value pair? Why are we using them?

(b) What do angle brackets around a value mean? Should the angle brackets be "escapable" like quotes in Java? How would you begin to do that?

(c) Why is the factory pattern used? Your answer should say something about *polymorphism*, constructors, and at what time (compile-time, run-time) we know what kind of object to construct.

(d) What is a *regular expression*? What does the pattern string "\\S*" match (uppercase "S").

(e) What does the use of : as a separator in the tradesFor mean for what constitutes a usable UUID?

14.5 Incremental Development

This program has more packages than Tetris and a few more lines of code. When writing a program of more than trivial length, how should you approach development? What classes and methods should you write first?

This section talks briefly about a software engineering approach that has much currency as this book is going to press, the *agile* approach. The agile approach focuses on breaking the final project into units of value to the user of the system. The programmer then focuses on implementing units of value in an order determined by the intended customer (best return on investment first).

The *Agile* Approach

The agile approach is spelled out in the *Agile Manifesto* [Gro07] which cites a dozen principles. Many of them have more to do with team projects developed directly for a customer, things beyond the scope of this book. We focus on a four of them in this section; the following are paraphrased from the *Manifesto* itself.

- Simplicity is essential: maximize what is *not* done.

- Deliver working software frequently.

- Working software is the primary measure of success.

- Continuous attention to technical excellence enhances agility.

We hope the first item seems familiar to readers of this book. Simplification is one of the goals of the book, a theme underlying the idea of using the right level of abstraction.

The idea of delivering working code frequently is what motivated this section. We just spent a long, long section discussing how to read structured text files. While reading text files is necessary to make a text adventure game, a program that just reads structured text files is not very interesting.

The measure of success is delivering working code. The key is that the definition of *working* for our purposes is delivering a game. Perhaps a simple, not quite complete game, but a game all the same.

The agile approach, because of the focus on working code, is considered at odds with the *waterfall model*, a model where very complete documentation of the interfaces and implementations is done before coding. Some students who read that working code is the most important thing begin to wonder why they waste time on writing comments. Comments are not code!

But comments are necessary in excellent code. Agility requires delivering code in multiple phases. That means the code is read by the agile programmer over the course of development as it is enhanced in each phase. Comments are part of technical excellence and make the code maintainable (sustainable coding practices and pacing are another of the dozen principles).

This is a very cursory introduction to the idea of agile development. There are many books and Web sites devoted to different methodologies that support the agile approach. The next section looks at how to break our text adventure game into phases, phases that are, more or less, games.

Delivering Units of Work

What is the least functionality we could deliver and yet consider what we have a partial text adventure game? A dictionary test program? No, while the alias dictionary is a useful tool, it is not, by itself, a game.

What about a program that reads a file full of locations? That would test out the GameObject reading code. What does the program *do*? How about a program that reads the map file and permits the player to move around the map? That would let us test the reading code *and* deliver a program that is a step along the way to a text adventure game.

Loading the Whole Map

Given that we have looked at the code for reading a single record from a Location file, how does the game keep track of the whole map? We have one answer when it comes to storing a collection of objects: an ArrayList. The code to read the whole list can be broken into two methods, one to open the file and one to read it. The opening code is broken out because we can reuse it when reading the Critter and Item files.

```
162   private Scanner openFileForInput(String fname) {
163     Scanner opened = null;
164     try {
165       opened = new Scanner(new SansCommentFilterReader(
166             new FileReader(new File(fname))));
167     } catch (FileNotFoundException e) {
168       // do nothing (null will be returned which is what we want)
169     }
170     return opened;
171   }
206   private ArrayList<Location> readMapFile(String fname) {
207     ArrayList<Location> returnMap = null;
208     Scanner mapFile = openFileForInput(fname);
209     if (mapFile != null) {
210       returnMap = new ArrayList<Location>();
211       while (mapFile.hasNext()) {
```

```
212    Location location = Location.readObjectFromFile(mapFile);
213    if (location != null) {
214      returnMap.add(location);
215    }
216   }
217  }
218  return returnMap;
219 }
```

Listing 14.17: `GameWithMapOnly` Map Reading Routines

The `openFileForInput` takes the name of the file and returns a `Scanner` wrapped around a `SansCommentFilterReader`, which is, in turn, wrapped around a `FileReader` reading the given file. When `readMapFile` uses the `Scanner`, comments are automatically skipped (never to be seen). Because opening the file is more complex than just calling **new** `Scanner`, it makes sense to break it out into its own method. Further, notice that the method returns **null** if there is a problem (*i.e.*, an `Exception` is thrown). The read method can tell there was a problem and return **null** as the value for the list.

The read method uses an eof-controlled while loop: it checks if there is a next token (non-blank space) and if there is it tries to read a `Location`. If there was no problem reading the `Location`, then the new `Location` is added to the map. Finally the map is returned. In the constructor for a `GameWithMapOnly`, the `map` field is set to the result of the read method.

```
56  public GameWithMapOnly() {
57    aliases = new Dictionary(openFileForInput("school.aliases"));
58    map = readMapFile("school.map");
59    if (map != null) {
60      player = map.get(0).getUUID();
61    }
62  }
```

Listing 14.18: `GameWithMapOnly` Constructor

The `aliases` field is also initialized in the constructor. What is line 60 all about? We need some way to keep track of where the player is in the game. Since we have no `Critter` objects, we cannot use one to keep track of the player. So, we can keep track of the player by having a `String` field, a `player` that holds the `UUID` of the location where the player is. Line 60 makes the arbitrary decision that the player begins in the first location in the location file (the one put at index 0 in `map`). This is arbitrary but since we are just moving around in the map, it is as good a place to start as any other.

Moving

So, what does the game loop look like? It needs to show the current state of the game: this is just printing out the `Location` where the player is. It then needs to get input from the user: we define a `Keyboard` class that wraps a `Scanner` around `System.in` and provides `next`, `nextLine`, `nextWithPrompt`, and `nextLineWithPrompt`. It also has versions of the old `answeredYes` method. All of the methods are **static**. Finally, the state of the game must be updated: we use the multi-way **if** described to motivate the `Dictionary` adding just an `exit` command to permit the player to exit the game.

```
67  public void play() {
68    gameOver = false;
69    while (!gameOver) {
70      // show state
```

```
71      System.out.println(locationByUUID(player));
72      // get user input
73      String command = Keyboard.next();
74      // update state
75      processCommand(command);
76    }
77  }
```

Listing 14.19: GameWithMapOnly play

play is the main game loop. The location referred to by player is looked up (we see how it is looked up in the next section) and the whole thing is displayed. The toString method dumps all of the field values:

```
~/Chapter14% java core.GameWithMapOnly
Game Begins
gamestuff.Location [
uuid = thequad
name = The Quad
description = The fresh air, the trees, the odd, bright disk in the
sky. It must be, must be the "sun" you have heard tell of. You
remember that sound, too, the birds twittering (no, not Twittering) as
they cartwheel across the sky.
inventory = []

north = NO_SUCH_LOCATION
south = t-hallentrance
east = NO_SUCH_LOCATION
west = NO_SUCH_LOCATION
]
```

The values are those read in from school.map in the first position. The cursor is waiting on the line below the listing for a command to be typed.

```
181  private void processCommand(String command) {
182    String normalizedCommand = aliases.get(command);
183    if (normalizedCommand.equalsIgnoreCase("north")) {
184      doNorth();
185    } else if (normalizedCommand.equalsIgnoreCase("south")) {
186      doSouth();
187    } else if (normalizedCommand.equalsIgnoreCase("east")) {
188      doEast();
189    } else if (normalizedCommand.equalsIgnoreCase("west")) {
190      doWest();
191    } else if (normalizedCommand.equalsIgnoreCase("exit")) {
192      gameOver = true;
193    } else {
194      unknownCommand(command, normalizedCommand);
195    }
196  }
```

Listing 14.20: GameWithMapOnly processCommand

When the command is typed, it is passed in to processCommand which looks it up as an alias. So, if the player enters south, the alias for that command was also south. In processCommand, south matches in line 185 so doSouth is called.

```
112   private boolean doSouth() {
113     Location here = locationByUUID(player);
114     boolean canMove = (here.getSouth() != Location.NO_SUCH_LOCATION);
115     if (canMove) {
116       player = here.getSouth();
117     }
118     return canMove;
119   }
```

Listing 14.21: GameWithMapOnly doSouth

How can we move south? First, we check if it is safe to move south. If it is, then we do. Looking at the short doSouth method, do you see any problems? What, in particular, do you think of line 114? It looks like GameWithMapOnly has to reach quite deeply into Location and know a lot about what getSouth returns when there is no such place. This works for the current program but noticing the mixing of different levels of abstraction in the same method can give you some places where fixing up the code would make the next iteration better.

It would be better if we had a canMoveSouth method in Location so that doSouth could just call it to see if it was possible to move.

Besides that problem, all we do is get the Location from map with a call to findLocation with the UUID of the location. Find the UUID of the location to the south; if it is not the "null" UUID the player can move: update the player (UUID of where the player is) with the southern UUID.

Now, how does locationByUUID search map to find the current location? How long does such a search take? And do we care?

Review 14.5

(a) What does the word "agile" mean? Why do you think it was applied to the given software development approach?

(b) How do agile developers measure progress? How does that match with the grading rubric applied to your class programs? What causes any differences?

(c) Given what you know about the fields in Location, sketch the canMoveSouth method that would be part of Location. Would the method be **public** or **private**?

(d) Did the util.ReadAndWrite methods make the Location reading code in the game easier to follow? Why or why not?

14.6 Finding a Match

Sorting, presented in Chapter 11, is an important algorithm to know; you may find yourself needing to sort something in a way that the Collections sort method does not easily support — for example, if your objects do not implement the Comparable interface.

Another useful algorithm is *searching*, being able to find a particular object in a collection efficiently. One nice thing about searching is that it gives us some insight into how one determines what *efficient* means. It is possible to write two different versions of a search algorithm and then compare how much work each does. This is known as *algorithm analysis* and is a powerful tool in theoretical computer science, a tool with obvious practical applications. The "analysis" in this section consists of hand waving and assurances; real analysis requires rigor beyond the scope of the current argument.

Examine Each One: Sequential Search

Imagine that you had a notebook containing every single page of notes you have ever taken; each page is labeled with the date that it was written (we're imagining here). Unfortunately, someone dropped the notebook, everything fell out, and, in his hurry to get it cleaned up, he jammed in the pages in a random order. All of the pages are in the notebook but in no discernible order. How would you find your notes for the first Monday of last month? How would you even know if you *took* notes on that date?

The *only* viable approach to the unordered notebook is to look at each and every page, checking the date against the first Monday of last month. Any page you skipped *could* be just the page you were looking for, so you cannot skip any. We grant that there is at most one page for a given day, so if you do find the given date, you can stop searching.

Because you examine each page in the notebook in sequence, this is known as the *sequential search.* This is the same search used in findLocation in GameWithMapOnly.

```
144   private Location locationByUUID(String uuid) {
145     for (int i = 0; i != map.size(); ++i) {
146       if (map.get(i).getUUID().equalsIgnoreCase(uuid)) {
147         return map.get(i);
148       }
149     }
150     return null;
151   }
```

Listing 14.22: GameWithMapOnly locationByUUID

This code matches search code we have seen before. The count control variable runs across all of the index values for map. If a match is found, the matching Location is returned. If there is no match, then, after checking every single Location, the method returns null.

Consider how long it takes to search your notebook. Each page takes a certain amount of time to check. That time involves getting to the page, finding the date fields, interpreting the date field, and then comparing it. Note that that time depends on who is doing the search. If your dates are in cursive, then the deciphering stage would take much longer for Dr. Ladd's seven-year old son than it would for you, the author of the notes. So, saying that it takes one hour to search for the notes from the first Monday doesn't really tell us anything. How many notes were there in the book? Who was reading them?

How long does a sequential search of map take? Again, it depends on what computer you are running, what Java interpreter is used, what other programs are running, and how many locations are in map. Saying it took one quarter second does not tell us anything.

Computer scientists tend to talk about average times, and express time as a function of the size of the data on which the algorithm works. For map, the size of the data is the number of entries to be searched. What we are interested in is not how long it takes to find the MajorsRoom location but rather how long it takes to find *any* entry (on average) and what happens to that time as the size of map varies.

So, how many entries must be checked when we search for a given Location? We make a simplifying assumption: the map is completely random. There is no order in the list; searching for any given UUID from the front of the list has the same chance of ending on any given entry; also, each entry has the same chance of being searched for. How many entries must be checked if the UUID is not in the list? That is easy: map.size(). Let's call that value n. How about for an entry that is in the map? The random nature of the list means that any given entry is found, on average, halfway through. For every time we search for the last entry we also search for the first entry. Every long run, past halfway, is averaged together with a short run, less than half-way. Rest assured that the number of entries compared, on average, is $n/2$.

What happens if we double the size of map? Whatever amount of time the search took on a given machine is doubled. And if we multiply the size by 10? Ten times slower. This is known as a *linear* algorithm.

Dismissing Half at a Time: Binary Search

Let's consider a different situation. One author lives in a very small town with an equally small free library. The library is small enough that it would be practical to go through it in an hour, checking each and every book to see if it was *Sorting and Searching* by Donald Knuth. Starting at one end of the stacks and working down to the other, all 1024 books could be checked.

Is that a practical search technique for Knuth's book in your college library? Or, perhaps, in the United States Library of Congress? How *would* you search for the book in a large library? No card catalog permitted.

If the books are randomized you have a task 1000 or 10000 or 100000 times harder than the one in the free library and a sequential search of a long, long time in front of you. Fortunately, very few libraries are randomized. Let's say the books are ordered by author's last name.[7] How would you search the *sorted* library?

We hope you would go to the middle of the stacks and look at the author's name there. Seeing it is "Milton," what would you do? You would know that "Knuth" must come before "Milton," so you would dismiss all of the books after the middle one you checked. You could then check the middle of the first half. Seeing "Franklin" you would know that "Knuth" was in the upper half of the lower half. You could dismiss all books before "Franklin." And so on. How long would it take to search for "Knuth" in terms of the number of books?

In the free library, using the smart search algorithm, it would take no more than eleven comparisons. It could take fewer if "Knuth" were in the middle of any section you were searching. It could not take more than eleven; the proof is by looking at the number of books still to be considered. The sequence of search area sizes is

1024
512
256
128
64
32
16
8
4
2
1

You must check a book in each search area to dismiss half of the books. After checking the last book there is no where else to go. Either you found "Knuth" or it is not in the library.

The number of comparisons here is $lg(n)$, the logarithm of the size of the original search area.[8] If the number of books were doubled, the number of comparisons would go up by 1 rather than double. This search, the *binary search*, is faster than the sequential search.

But it requires that the entries be sorted by the field being search for. If the library were ordered on publication date and we had only the author of the book we wanted, it would be no better than a random ordering. To use this algorithm on a list, we need to maintain a sorted list. Recall that the `Dictionary` class keeps its list in order by `attribute`.

```
140    private int indexOfKey(String matchKey) {
141        int matchingNdx = -1;
142        int lowerNdx = 0;
143        int upperNdx = allEntries.size();
144        // invariant: if matchKey is in allEntries then
```

---

[7] The Library of Congress number or Dewey Decimal number serve the same purpose. Assume we know Knuth's book's number in the applicable system and the argument remains valid.

[8] Assume we are using logarithms base 2.

```
145    // matchNdx is on the range [lowerNdx, upperNdx).
146    while (rangeSize(lowerNdx, upperNdx) > 0) {// any remaining entries?
147      int midNdx = (lowerNdx + upperNdx) / 2;
148      int compareMidToMatch = allEntries.get(midNdx).getAttribute()
149        .compareTo(matchKey);
150      if (compareMidToMatch > 0) {
151        // allEntries[midNdx] < matchKey; search upper half of remaining
152        upperNdx = midNdx;
153      } else if (compareMidToMatch == 0) {
154        // allEntries[midNdx] == matchKey; return midNdx
155        matchingNdx = midNdx;
156        break;
157      } else {// if (compareMidToMatch > 0
158        // matchKey < allEntries[midNdx]; search lower half of remaining
159        lowerNdx = midNdx + 1;
160      }
161    }
162    return matchingNdx;
163  }
```

Listing 14.23: Dictionary indexOfKey

The search method uses a helper method, rangeSize, which just returns the number of entries in the index range [lowerNdx, upperNdx). The range is asymmetric, including lowerNdx but excluding upperNdx. This is how the indexes for an ArrayList are reported if we use 0 and allEntries.size(). This is how we have talked about index ranges through out the book.

Lines 141–143 initialize everything. The comment on lines 144–145 talks about an *invariant*. An invariant is a property of a loop that is always true at the top of the loop. The property holds when the loop begins and, going all the way through the body of the loop, makes sure the property is again true. In the body of the loop it is possible that the invariant is, momentarily, violated but the body of the loop must restore it.

If the invariant on 144–145 *is* invariant, then our search works. The if inside the loop either finds the match (it happens to be at midNdx) or it makes the range smaller. It closes in on the matching entry by throwing away half of the entries.

The comments explain where the matching entry must be after the comparison. The > and the < in the comments are used to make the ordering easier to read; they mean "later in the lexicographic order" and "earlier in the lexicographic order," respectively.

The tricky part of the code is the difference between lines 152 and 159. The important thing is that the size of the range being searched *must* get smaller each time through the loop. Since midNdx is between lowerNdx and upperNdx, it follows that making sure we exclude the entry at midNdx makes sure that at least one element is removed. Line 159 moves lowerNdx up *past* midNdx since that entry has already been checked. Similarly, line 152 does the same with upperNdx but without subtracting 1 because of the asymmetry of the range. By setting upperNdx to midNdx, midNdx is excluded from the range. So long as the range gets smaller each time, eventually we find the match or the range size is reduced to 0. We are done in either case.

So, why don't we always use binary search? Because the elements must be in sorted order by the search key. When you searched for your notes, the notebook would have had to be in sorted order by date for you to take advantage of binary search. If you did a lot of searches by date, it would be worth sorting it. If, however, you search by date only once in a very long while, it might be worth the cost of sequential search to avoid the task of sorting.

Similarly, if you search by date commonly, then sorting make sense. If you then occasionally search by course name, you would not want to have to resort the notebook twice (once into course name order and then back into date order when you perform the more common search).

Because the dictionary is searched for each command and the alias list might grow large, it was determined to sort it and use binary search.

Review 14.6

(a)

```
165   public Item itemByName(String itemName) {
166     Item retval = null;
167     int ndx = itemIndexByName(itemName);
168     if (ndx >= 0) {
169       retval = inventory.get(ndx);
170     }
171     return retval;
172   }
257   private int itemIndexByName(String itemName) {
258     for (int i = 0; i != inventory.size(); ++i) {
259       if (inventory.get(i).getName().equalsIgnoreCase(itemName)) {
260         return i;
261       }
262     }
263     return -1;
264   }
```

Listing 14.24: GameObject itemByName

In Listing 14.24, how long *does* itemByName take to find the matching item (or to determine that there is no match)? Identify n and then consider how much work is done, on average, to find an arbitrary entry.

(b) How many steps would it take to find a book (using the binary search approach) to find a book in a library with

(a) 256 books?

(b) 500 books? (Hint: It is no *worse* than the next bigger power of 2.)

(c) 100000 books?

(d) 1048576 books?

(c) Take a look at Dictionary.java. Where is the sort routine?

(d) Explain what could go wrong if going through the **while** loop in Dictionary.indexOf (Listing 14.23) failed to reduce the size of the range.

14.7 Making It a Real Game

So far we are well along to having a working game: the program can load game object (at least one kind) and we can move. No items or critters interacting, yet. This section focuses on the *code* for doing the interesting things. Game is about a thousand lines long; this section highlights it rather than listing all of it. Remember the code is sorted so that the line numbers are based on the names of the methods listed.

Finish Initialization

`GameWithMapOnly` had the name of the alias and map files hard-coded into it. It would be better (from a game-mod point of view) if those files could be specified without recompiling. `Game` hard-codes the name of the configuration file, `gameconfig.txt` and then uses the `processConfigurationFile` method:

```
656    private boolean processConfigurationFile(String configurationFName) {
657      aliasesFName = null;
658      castFName = null;
659      mapFName = null;
660      propsFName = null;
661
662      Scanner config = openFileForInput(configurationFName);
663      String attribute = ReadAndWrite.readAttribute(config);
664      while (config.hasNext()) {
665        /* ignore */ ReadAndWrite.readMatch(config, "=");
666        String value = ReadAndWrite.readValue(config);
667        if (attribute.equalsIgnoreCase("alias")) {
668          aliasesFName = value;
669        } else if (attribute.equalsIgnoreCase("cast")) {
670          castFName = value;
671        } else if (attribute.equalsIgnoreCase("map")) {
672          mapFName = value;
673        } else if (attribute.equalsIgnoreCase("props")) {
674          propsFName = value;
675        }
676        if (config.hasNext()) {
677          attribute = ReadAndWrite.readAttribute(config);
678        }
```

Listing 14.25: Game `processConfigurationFile`

The code is similar to the field handling code for game objects. The files can be named in any order. The method returns `true` if a name was provided for every file, `false` otherwise. The truth value is used in the constructor to determine whether or not to try reading the data files; if there is a missing data file name, just bail out.

How does the game know that the constructor bailed out? Constructors do not have a return type. One way to handle a problem in a constructor is to throw an exception but that takes more Java than we have. Instead, `Game` has a `ready` field and an `isReady` method. It is set to `false` unless all of the configuration completes. That way, `main` looks like this:

```
127    public static void main(String[] args) {
128      theGame = new Game();
129      if (theGame.isReady()) {
130        theGame.play();
131      } else {
132        System.err.println("Trouble initalizing game.");
133      }
134    }
```

Listing 14.26: Game main

Either the game is initialized or the player gets an error message (remember, System.err is the error output stream).

What is theGame and why is it not declared as a local variable? It must be a field but main is **static**: that means there is no **this** reference. So what *is* theGame? It is a **static** field. There is only one for the class Game.

Why is it a field? So that this Game class can offer a getCurrentGame method.[9]

```
116    public static Game getCurrentGame() {
117      return theGame;
118    }
```

Listing 14.27: Game getCurrentGame

The method is called with Game.getCurrentGame(), and it is used by the various game objects to set messages that are displayed the next time through the game loop.

Connecting Things Up

The methods to read the cast file and the props files (containing Critter and Item descriptions, respectively) are similar to the map-reading code. There are three ArrayLists in Game, one for each type of game object. After the three files are read, the data are not ready to use.

Looking back at Figure 14.2, you see that each Critter has its location UUID stored in it *but* the critter is not in the visitors list of the appropriate location. The interconnected structure of locations containing critters that contain items (that can also be in locations) has to be untangled for saving and loading. The use of UUID is one step in that direction.

After reading all of the information from the three files, the critters must all be placed in their locations (and the items given to their owners). The distributeCritters method does this by going through the cast list and placing each critter in the right location:

```
224    private void distributeCritters() {
225      for (int i = 0; i != cast.size(); ++i) {
226        Critter critter = cast.get(i);
227        Location location = locationByUUID(critter.getLocationID());
228        location.add(critter);
229      }
230    }
```

Listing 14.28: Game distributeCritters

The Location.add(Critter) method automatically fixes up the location field in the given critter, making moving a critter from one spot to another easier.

Finally, how do we find the player? In the map-only phase we just plunked them down in an arbitrary location. The player, now, is a Critter. That way they have an inventory, a health, whatever critters have. Which critter is the player? The one with the UUID of player, of course. So, after loading all of the files and fixing up the loot and the critters, the game sets the Critter field player to refer to the appropriate member of the cast.

---

[9]The code in main setting theGame is not the same as that found in FANG, but with the exception of the name of the field, getCurrentGame is identical.

Pickup/Drop

Movement is similar to that in the map-only phase except that the current location is part of a `Critter` rather than a field. The section on keys below covers movement in greater depth.

How can the player interact with the environment? In particular, how can she pick something up?

The normalized command is "pickup." So to pick up the quarter in *Room 101* at the beginning of the game is easy.

```
A large, cavernous room. This is where you took CS1. It still causes a
bit of a shiver when you remember sitting in the back corner taking the
final exam. Questions about ArrayList, searching, and . . . it is all too
much. There is a door at the back of the room leading north. Another,
less conspicuous doorway leads from the front of the room to the south;
that way lies the computer lab. There is some crud here! There is some
other crud here!
You see Quarter.
Game> pickup quarter
You picked up Quarter.
Game>
```

Imagine what happens internally: the user types something in, and in the main loop *commandLine* is set to `Keyboard.nextLine()`.[10] Inside `processCommand` the command line (passed in as a parameter) is taken apart. How?

It is possible to construct a `Scanner` that takes its input from a `String` rather than from a stream attached to a file; that permits us to parse a line using `next` (and, if we have to, `skip` and `setDelimiter`). The listing below shows the creation of the command line scanner and the first branch of the `if`. The middle branches of the `if` are elided down to the "pickup" case.

```java
595    private void processCommand(String commandLine) {
596      if (commandLine.length() == 0) {
597        return;
598      }
599      // Scan across the command line as entered by the user
600      Scanner lineProcessor = new Scanner(commandLine);
601      String command = lineProcessor.next();
602
603      String normalizedCommand = aliases.get(command);
604      if (normalizedCommand == null) {
605        normalizedCommand = command;
606      }
622      } else if (normalizedCommand.equalsIgnoreCase("pickup")) {
623        if (!doPickup(lineProcessor)) {
624          addMessage("Unable to find anything to pickup.");
625        }
```

Listing 14.29: Game `processCommand`

Line 600 constructs a new `Scanner` passing it a `String`. You might have wondered why various `Files` and streams could be constructed with a file name but `Scanner` could not. Now you know: pass a `String` to a `Scanner` constructor and scan the string.

---

[10]`Keyboard` wraps up a **static** `Scanner` wrapped around standard input; it looks like the `keyboard` field in `TwentyQuestions` from Chapter 12.

command and normalizedCommand are just like what they were in the map-only phase. The equalsIgnoreCase checks for the various commands. Line 623 calls doPickup. It passes in the whole scanner wrapped around the user's input line.

So, what happens in doPickup? Use next to pull the next word off the line, and check the current location for an Item with that name (GameObject.itemByName is just the ticket). All is well when the quarter is picked up.

There are two things we want to be able to support: picking up multiple things in one command *and* multi-word item names. Either one alone would be easy. Single-word names and multiple objects at once: loop over the words remaining in the command line and pickup each one. Multi-word names and one object at a time: pull the rest of the line in as the name and pick it up. Both together: not so easy.

```
382    private boolean doPickup(Scanner commandLine) {
383        Location curr = locationByUUID(player.getLocationID());
384        boolean gotOne = false;
385        String pickedup = "";
386        String separator = "";
387        while (commandLine.hasNext()) {
388            Item theItem = itemByCommandLine(curr, commandLine);
389            if (theItem != null) {
390                give(curr, player, theItem);
391                pickedup += separator + theItem.getName();
392                gotOne = true;
393            }
394        }
395        if (gotOne) {
396            addMessage("You picked up " + pickedup + ".");
397        }
398        return gotOne;
399    }
474    private Item itemByCommandLine(GameObject owner,
475        Scanner lineProcessor) {
476        String name = "";
477        String separator = "";
478        while (lineProcessor.hasNext()) {
479            name += separator + lineProcessor.next();
480            separator = " ";
481            Item theItem = owner.itemByName(name);
482            if (theItem != null) {
483                return theItem;
484            }
485        }
486        return null;
487    }
```

Listing 14.30: Game doPickup and itemByCommandLine

The code shows two methods. The real work is in itemByCommandLine. The name of an item is built up out of words. The first word is pulled off lineProcessor and the owner (current location) is checked for an item by that name. If there is not one, pull off another word, put it (after a space) after the name so far, and try again. If we run out of words before getting a match, return null. If we get a match before running out of words, return a reference to the match.

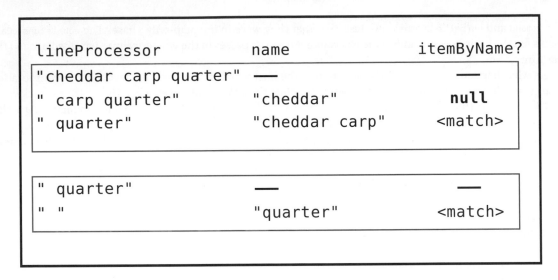

Figure 14.7: Values inside itemByCommandLine

What happens when the player types "pickup cheddar carp quarter" in a location where both "cheddar carp" and "quarter" are available?

Figure 14.7 shows the values of the variable lineProcessor and name inside itemByCommandLine when it is called from doPickup. The quotes are there so we, humans, can see what is going on. Remember that lineProcessor is a Scanner; the part that is showing is the part of the string remaining to be scanned.

When itemByCommandLine is called the first time, name has not yet been initialized and no call has been made to itemByName on the owner (the current location). The value in the scanner is all three words after "pickup." The while loop is entered; line 479 pulls the next word off lineProcessor and appends it on the end of name (after a copy of separator which is empty the first time through). Line 481 calls itemByName with the current name.

This is the second line in the first box in the figure. The call returns null, so the loop goes around again. Line 479 pulls off another word, it is appended (with a space this time), and the new name is looked up. This time there is a match and that reference is returned to doPickup.

Because Scanner is an object type, all variables are references to it. When it is passed into a method, a new reference is made but it refers to the original value. lineProcessor in doPickup has the same value it had at the end of itemByCommandLine.

doPickup does its thing (transfers the item returned from itemByCommandLine from the location's inventory to the player's inventory) and then it loops back, checking if lineProcessor.hasNext() is true. It is, so itemByCommandLine is called again, entering the second box in the figure.

On entry the value of lineProcessor is as shown. When execution enters the loop at line 478, the last word in lineProcessor is pulled out and the name is used to look up an Item; it matches so that reference is returned. In doPickup the quarter is transferred from the location to the player and the loop finishes (hasNext() is false), doPickup is done, and two items were transferred from the current location to the player's inventory.

Looking at doPickup, we notice that as each item went from the location to the user, a message was added. The next time through the game loop, the message is displayed (and the description of the location is suppressed for one cycle). This lets the actions send messages to the user but have them displayed by the main game loop (keeps every method from having a System.out.println in it).

You might be wondering why itemByCommandLine is broken out as its own routine. Think about what doDrop must look like. It looks for named items in the *player's inventory* (rather than the location's) and transfers matching items from the player *to* the location. Having a helper method to do the look up makes the methods a lot easier to write.

Trading

Trading is giving something to a critter. If you are in a location and there is a critter there, you can "give" some item to the critter. It is also possible that the critter might be willing to give something back for a specific item.

First, think about processing the command line. When the player types "give vending machine quarter", what must doGive do? Just like itemByCommandLine it must pull off words and check for matches to the name. Instead of checking the location's inventory, it checks the visitors list. When it finds a match, the rest of the line should be the name of an item in the player's inventory. Look it up and give the item to the critter if both were found.

But what if the player instead typed "give quarter vending machine"? It should have the same effect. This time we look up "quarter" in the player's inventory and then the rest of the line is the name of a critter in the current location.

How do we know which way to parse the command parameters? Without making an arbitrary decision and forcing players to conform, the program cannot tell the difference. It attempts both parses in parallel, choosing whichever works first.

```
314   private boolean doGive(Scanner commandLine) {
315       String firstName = commandLine.next();
316       Location curr = locationByUUID(player.getLocationID());
317       Item theItem = player.itemByName(firstName);
318       Critter theCritter = curr.critterByName(firstName);
319
320       while (commandLine.hasNext() && (theItem == null) &&
321           (theCritter == null)) {
322         firstName += " " + commandLine.next();
323         theItem = player.itemByName(firstName);
324         theCritter = curr.critterByName(firstName);
325       }
326
327       if (theItem != null) {
328         String critterName = restOfLine(commandLine);
329         theCritter = curr.critterByName(critterName);
330       } else if (theCritter != null) {
331         String itemName = restOfLine(commandLine);
332         theItem = player.itemByName(itemName);
333       }
334
335       if ((theCritter != null) && (theItem != null)) {
336         String trade = theCritter.willTradeFor(theItem.getUUID());
337         addMessage("You give the " + theItem.getName() + " to the " +
338           theCritter.getName());
339         give(player, theCritter, theItem);
340         if (trade != null) {
341           Item tradeItem = theCritter.itemByUUID(trade);
342           if (tradeItem != null) {
343             give(theCritter, player, tradeItem);
```

```
344       addMessage("The " + theCritter.getName() + " gives you a " +
345          tradeItem.getName());
346       }
347    }
348
349    if (theCritter.getHealth() <= 0) {
350      addMessage(theCritter.getName() + " has left.");
351      curr.removeCritterUUID(theCritter.getUUID());
352    }
353
354    return true;
355    }
356
357    return false;
358  }
```

Listing 14.31: Game doGive

Line 320 is a loop that keeps going until either an item in the player's inventory matches the name, a critter in the current location matches the name, or we run out of words to add to name. This is a slightly different programming style for building up a name. Here the first word is pulled off before the loop, and the itemByName and critterByName calls appear before the loop and in the loop.

This version does not need the separator variable to keep track of when to add a space between elements but it does have repeated code. This is a case where neither has any obvious superiority, so this code shows both.

The loop exits when either the item or critter matches. The rest of the line is used to look up a critter or an item (the if at 327 attempts to match the object that is still null). Line 335 ensures that both an item (in the player's inventory) and a critter (in the current location) have been matched. If both have, the player attempts to give the item to the critter. The code also checks if the critter will trade any item for the given item. If so *and* the critter has the item to trade, the transaction takes place.

Remember the game designer included a tradesfor entry in the critter's record in the cast file. It gave two UUIDs, the item it wanted and the item it would give. willTradeFor looks in the list of pairs for one beginning with the UUID the player is giving. The value of trade in line 336 is either null (no trade offered) or the UUID of the item the critter will give. If there is a UUID to give, see if the critter owns it and will give it to the player (if statement at 342).

Having written a give helper function to transfer items from one GameObject to another permitted focusing on the doGive level of abstraction (figuring out when and how to call give) rather than inventory handling.

Combat

It is hard to call it combat, really. The game mechanic for "hurting" a critter is to let the critter record specify items (by UUID) that can hurt the critter. When the critter is given an item on the list of items that hurts it, the critter's health is reduced by the attack strength of the item.

In the game, *Dr. Dunbumble* is hurt by the *Ungraded Homework*. Giving him the homework reduces his 1 health by 1, causing him to leave the game. (It might improve the game if a critter could specify a "leaving" description. See Programming Problem 14.6.)

Keys

It is good that *Dr. Dunbumble* leaves. He is an "anti-key" to getting to the *Entryway*. How does that work? Look at doWest (and compare it to the doSouth shown in Listing 14.21):

```
421   private boolean doWest() {
422     Location here = player.getLocation();
423     boolean canMove = (here.getWest() != Location.NO_SUCH_LOCATION) &&
424       unlocked(here.getWKey(), player, here);
425     if (canMove) {
426       moveTo(locationByUUID(here.getWest()));
427     }
428     return canMove;
429   }
885   private boolean unlocked(String key, Critter wantsToMove, Location here) {
886     boolean passable = true;
887     if (key != null) {
888       if (key.charAt(0) == '!') {// It is a "not" key
889         key = key.substring(1);// get rid of !
890         passable = (!wantsToMove.hasItemUUID(key) &&
891             (!here.hasCritterUUID(key)));
892       } else {
893         passable = (wantsToMove.hasItemUUID(key) ||
894             (here.hasCritterUUID(key)));
895       }
896     }
897     if (!passable) {
898       addMessage("Your way appears to be blocked.");
899     }
900     return passable;
901   }
```

Listing 14.32: Game doWest

The doWest routine is not too much longer than the previous version. It just adds a call to unlock. The unlock method is somewhat complicated (it is also the very last method in the Game.java source file and the last one we explore here).

unlocked is called with a key, the wKey value of the location. wKey holds the UUID of a key item or critter to go west from the current location. By default, all direction keys are null. That means that most of the time unlocked returns true because the if at line 887 is never entered.

When the key is non-null it is a UUID of an item *or* it is "!" followed by a UUID. The difference is that a UUID alone must be *present* for moving; a "!" UUID must be *absent* for moving.

To go west from *Hallway* has wKey of "!CrazyProfessor." Line 888 checks for the "!" using the charAt method of String. Like ArrayList.get, it takes an integer and the characters are numbered from 0. If the first one is an exclamation point, then strip it off and look for the critter with that UUID in the here location and the item with that UUID in the inventory of the wantsToMove critter. If neither is there, then passable is set true.

Alternatively, if there is no "!", then check for the item and critter and set passable to true if either is present.

Review 14.7

(a) Does the Game ever display the UUID of any GameObject? Why or why not?

(b) How would picking up and dropping items be different if the player typed in the UUIDs?

(c) Why is unlocked broken out into its own method? Would it make sense to move a copy of the code into each of the directional movement methods?

(d)   What character is used to indicate an "anti-key"? What impact, if any, does that have on the UUIDs thatgame authors can use?

(e)   What field in a `Critter` record is used to specify items that will be given for other items? What is the structure of the value?

14.8   Summary

Self-describing Data Files

Self-describing data are data written using plain text where the parts of the data file are labeled. The thought behind self-describing data is to permit editing of the data with a standard text editor and not require the human editor to have to memorize arcane formatting.

Field names along with the values permit reordering fields when editing. Comments and blank lines make it possible for the human editor to discuss the meaning of the file and structure the data.

Readers and Writers: Low-level I/O

`Scanner` is a high-level reading object: it produces a stream of tokens (e.g., words, lines, `int`). The Java file model treats files as streams of bytes (the `Stream` classes) or sequences of `char` (the `Reader` classes).

`FileReader` can be constructed with a `File` and opens the file, permitting the characters in it to be read using the overloaded `read` methods. All processing is done with characters.

The `FilterReader` and its subclasses are also readers. Filters are constructed with another reader passed as a parameter. Calls to `read` are forwarded to the wrapped reader, and the result is manipulated as the filter reader sees fit.

The Decorator Pattern

A class that serves as a wrapper around an object (or objects) of the same class it extends is said to *decorate* the wrapped object; the wrapper class is a *decorator*. A `FilterReader` is a decorator: whatever sequence of characters is produced by the wrapped reader can be arbitrarily modified by the wrapper.

Imagine wanting to let a program count the number of characters that were in a file but that the contents of the file were all of your financial records. A `BlindFilterReader` could replace every character read from the underlying reader with an underscore. Then the user of the reader could get the size of any underlying file without having access to the contents.

The decorator pattern is also discussed in terms of coffee drinks: a drink with a shot decorates some underlying coffee drink. The term decorator comes from the GUI field: a screen window can be decorated by wrapping a title bar and the like around it; the rectangle containing the title bar as well as the original window is, itself, a window. The wrapper decorates a window, producing a fancier window.

Binary Search

Binary search is a way to quickly search a sorted, random access data structure. The search is like searching for a book in the library: check the middle entry to find if the target is in the first or second half of the collection. Because the collection is sorted, this can be done with a single comparison: if the target value is less than the value of the middle entry, the target is in the first half; if the target value is more than the value of the middle entry, the target is in the last half.

A standard *sequential search*, on the other hand, means checking each book in turn to see if it is the target book. Sequential search dismisses one book per comparison; binary search dismisses half of the books remaining to be considered with each comparison.

14.9   Chapter Review Exercises

Review Exercise 14.1 Why are the three different GameObjects kept segregated in separate lists?

Review Exercise 14.2 What is a *UUID*? What type is the UUID field?

Review Exercise 14.3 What is a self-describing data file?

Review Exercise 14.4 What is the difference between constructing a Scanner with a File and constructing a FileReader with a File?

Review Exercise 14.5 What is a *regular expression*?

Review Exercise 14.6 What does each of the following *pattern strings* match?

(a) "\\S*" (uppercase "S").

(b) "[^a]*"

(c) "[abc]Taxi"

Review Exercise 14.7 Give an example of a sorted array that could cause an infinite loop if line 159 of Dictionary.indexOf was changed to read

```
159        lowerNdx = midNdx;
```

Review Exercise 14.8 Using Figure 14.4, explain how the cost of each of the following is evaluated and what is printed out.

(a) ```
     CoffeeDrink a = new Coffee();
     System.out.println(a.getPrice());
     ```

(b)  ```
     CoffeeDrink b = new FlavorShot(Cinnamon, new Coffee());
     System.out.println(b.getPrice());
     ```

(c) ```
     CoffeeDrink c = new FlavorShot(Cinnamon,
                         new FlavorShot(Vanilla, new Espresso()));
     System.out.println(c.getPrice());
     ```

(d)  ```
     CoffeeDrink d = new FlavorShot(Cinnamon,
                         new FlavorShot(Basil,
                           new FlavorShot(Anise, new Espresso()));
     System.out.println(d.getPrice());
     ```

14.10   Programming Problems

Programming Problem 14.1 Write your own text adventure game using the engine presented in the chapter. Your game should have 40 locations, and 10 each of critters and items.

You should design one "specialization," something that your game does that requires a small change to the engine. It could be something as simple as supporting container items (most of the code is there for this; you just have to define a command for taking things out of a container and how to look into the container). Alternatively, you could extend the I/O to work with the color capabilities of most terminals and have the output print in color.

If you need inspiration, play some games entered into the Comp or just read the *Inform* manual. Inform can certainly give you ideas for extending the engine.

Programming Problem 14.2 Go back to TwentyQuestions in Chapter 12. Modify the file format so that it is *self-describing* in the sense of this chapter. How could you make the format more friendly for an editor to figure out what number an entry is in the list?

Programming Problem 14.3 Go back to TwentyQuestions in Chapter 12. Modify the file format so that each page has a UUID. Modify the program so that instead of referring to other pages by their position, the program uses the UUID.

How much easier is a file with UUID to edit than one that depends on position from the beginning of the file?

Programming Problem 14.4 Write a program that reads a map file into an ArrayList, sorts the entries into ascending order by UUID, and then prints the map contents out to a file. Your program should "pretty print" the entries, indenting fields inside the Location and /Location lines. Make sure you wrap long descriptions and put them in appropriate delimiters.

What happens to user's comments in the file? How would you modify the reading of the file to capture the comments? How would you store comments in parallel with the Location objects? The difficulty of doing this for such a simple file makes one appreciate IDEs that support code sorting and movement, keeping all of the parts of a definition together.

Programming Problem 14.5 Extend the game to have combat. Combat involves:

- A new "attack" command.

- Some attribute to determine how successful an attack is.

- A way to determine the range of health reduction on a successful attack.

- Some way for critters to respond to being attacked (probably by attacking back).

Consider: **Can all critters be attacked?** Some games like *Fallout 3* marks some critters as "essential to the game" and does not let them die. Further, *Fallout 3* disallows targeting or hitting child critters (since most critters are human or humanoid, this avoids having to explain why they sell a child-murder simulator).

What happens when a critter dies? Where are the critter's items? Do they spill on the floor or must the critter be searched? Does a dead critter yield any items?

Are any items "weapons" or "armor"? A weapon would improve the chance to hit an enemy or increase the damage done when you hit. Armor would protect the owner. Then, are these items active or passive? Must the user specify what he or she is using and is there a limit on how many different items can be in use at the same time.

You might want to look at Programming Problem 14.6, too. It would be interesting to support some sort of "death scene" for critters. This would be a leaving message, in essence.

Programming Problem 14.6 What if we wanted to add a "leaving message" for a critter. When its health is reduced to 0, the critter will leave the game (as it does now), but if it specifies a leavingDescription, then instead of saying "critter-name has left", the leavingDescription would be displayed.

This would let the critter have some parting soliloquy or let some last description be imparted. Dr. Dunbumble could shout, "No, no, no more homework! The semester is over!" and run, screaming, from the building.

(a) What method(s) would have to be changed to add a leavingDescription field for Critter?

(b) What method(s) would have to be changed to display the message (if one is provided) when the critter leaves?

  i. Does the name of the method give any clue that it has to do with critters leaving the game?

  ii. Could you break the "leaving" functionality out into a more appropriately named method?

Java Language Keywords

The following table lists the reserved words in Java (as of version 6.0); none of these may be used as an identifier in your Java program. Note that, while not in the table, `true`, `false`, and `null` are also off limits (they are literals (of the `boolean` and reference types).

abstract	continue	for	new	switch
assert	default	goto	package	synchronized
boolean	do	if	private	this
break	double	implements	protected	throw
byte	else	import	public	throws
case	enum	instanceof	return	transient
catch	extends	int	short	try
char	final	interface	static	void
class	finally	long	strictfp	volatile
const	float	native	super	while

Appendix

B

References

[AHD00]   *The American Heritage Dictionary of English Language.*
           Houghton Mifflin Company, 4 edition, 2000.
           Updated 2003.

[Aug03]   Tony Augarde.
           Oxford Guide to Word Games.
           Oxford University Press, Oxford, England, 2 edition, 2003.

[Ben88]   Jon Bentley.
           More Programming Pearls: Confessions of a Coder.
           ACM, New York, NY, USA, 1988.

[Ben00]   Jon Bentley.
           Programming Pearls (2nd ed.).
           ACM Press/Addison-Wesley Publishing Co., New York, NY, USA, 2000.

[Bog07]   Ian Bogost.
           Persuasive Games: The Expressive Power of Videogames.
           The MIT Press, Cambridge, Massachusetts, USA, 2007.

[Bro09]   The first video game?
           Technical report, Brookhaven National Laboratory, 2009.
           On-line article, accessed April 2009, http://www.bnl.gov/bnlweb/history/higinbotham.asp.

[Bus96]   Nolan Bushnell.
           Relationships between fun and the computer business.
           Commun. ACM, 39(8):31–37, 1996.

[Cas05]   Edward Castranova.
           Synthetic Worlds: The Business and Culture of Online Games.
           Univerity of Chicago Press, Chicago, Illinois, USA, 2005.

[CCA86]   D N Card, V E Church, and W W Agresti.
          An empirical study of software design practices.
          IEEE Trans. Softw. Eng., 12(2):264–271, 1986.

[Con07]   Mia Consalvo.
          Cheating: Gaining Advantage in Videogames.
          The MIT Press, Cambridge, Massachusetts, USA, 2007.

[Cra84]   Chris Crawford.
          The Art of Computer Game Design: Reflections of a Master Game Designer.
          Osborne/McGraw-Hill, New York, New York, USA, 1984.
          Electronic version of text `http://www.vancouver.wsu.edu/fac/peabody/game-book/Coverpage.html`.

[Dar35]   Charles Darrow.
          Monopoly: Parker Brothers Real Estate Trading Game Rules.
          Parker Brothers, 1935.
          Retrieved from `http://www.hasbro.com/common/instruct/monins.pdf`.

[DW92]   Nell Dale and Chip Weems.
          Turbo Pascal.
          Houghton Mifflin, Boston, MA, 3 edition, 1992.

[FFBD04] Elisabeth Freeman, Eric Freeman, Bert Bates, and Kathy Dierra.
          Head First Design Patterns.
          O'Reilly Media, Inc., Sebastapol, CA, USA, 2004.

[Gee03]   James Paul Gee.
          What Video Games Have to Teach Us About Learning and Literacy.
          Palgrave MacMillan, New York, New York, USA, 2003.

[Gro07]   Agile Manifesto Group.
          The agile manifesto.
          Technical report, 2007.
          `http://www.agilemanifesto.org/principles.html`.

[Har06]   Elliote Rusty Harold.
          Java I/O.
          O'Reilly Media, Sebastapol, CA, USA, 2nd edition, 2006.

[Hop47]   Smithsonian image 92-13137: Grace hopper's computer bug.
          Museum specimen, National Museum of American History, Washington, DC, USA, 1947.
          Photo available: `http://americanhistory.si.edu/collections/comphist/objects/bug.htm`;
          2009-02-15.

[HT99]   Andrew Hunt and David Thomas.
          The Pragmatic Programmer: From Journeyman to Master.
          Addison-Wesley Professional, October 1999.

[Hui55]   Johan Huizinga.
          Homo Ludens: A Study of the Play Element in Culture.
          Beacon Press, Boston, MA, 1955.

[IMS76]   Item 102626678: Gandalf imsai 8800.
          Museum specimen, Computer History Museum, Mountain View, CA, USA, 1976.
          Photo available: `http://www.computerhistory.org/collections/accession/102626678`; 2009-02-21.

[Kni00]   Reiner Knizia.
          Dice Games Properly Explained.
          Elliot Right Way Books, London, England, November 2000.

[KO08]   Lawrence Kutner and Cheryl Olson.
          Grand Theft Childhood: The Surprising Truth About Violent Video Games.
          Simon and Schuster, New York, New York, USA, 2008.

[KR78]   Brian W. Kernighan and Dennis M. Ritchie.
          The C Programming Language.
          Prentice Hall, Englewood Cliffs, NJ, February 1978.

[Ló08]   Javier López.
          Tetris tutorial in c++ platform independent focused in game logic for beginners.
          Web published, December 2008.
          CC-Attribution Unported, `http://gametuto.com/tetris-tutorial-in-c-render-independent/`.

[MAM09]   Multiple arcade machine emulator official site.
          Retrieved 29 July 2009 from: `http://mamedev.org/`, 2009.

[McC04]   Scott McConnell.
          Code Complete: A Practical Handbook of Software Construction.
          Microsoft Press, 2nd edition, 2004.

[Nel97]   Graham Nelson.
          The craft of adventure.
          On-line archive, accessed July, 2009, `http://ifarchive.org/if-archive/info/Craft.Of.Adventure.pdf`, 1997.

[New04]   James Newman.
          Videogames.
          Routledge, London, England, 2004.

[NR06]   Graham Nelson and Gareth Rees.
          The Inform Designer's Manual.
          Dan Sanderson, 2006.

[OED71]   *The Compact Edition of the Oxford English Dictionary*.
          Oxford University Press, Oxford, England, 1 edition, 1971.

[OED89]   *Oxford English Dictionary Online*.
          Oxford University Press, Oxford, England, 2 edition, 1989.
          Accessed online, July 29, 2009.

[Pan70]   *PanzerBlitz*.
          Avalon Hill Games, 1970.

[Par99]   David Parlett.
          The Oxford History of Board Games.
          The Oxford Univesity Press, Oxford, England, 1999.

[Rad]   20q – radica games.
             On-line product information, accessed online, July, 2009, `http://www.radicagames.com/20q-cb.php`.

[RBC+06]   Eric Roberts, Kim Bruce, James H. Cross, II, Robb Cutler, Scott Grissom, Karl Klee, Susan Rodger, Fran Trees, Ian Utting, and Frank Yellin.
             The acm java task force: Final report.
             In *SIGCSE '06: Proceedings of the 37th SIGCSE technical symposium on Computer science education*, pages 131–132, New York, NY, USA, 2006. ACM.

[Ruc02]   Rudy Rucker.
             Software Engineering and Computer Games.
             Addison-Wesley, 2002.

[Sch08]   Jesse Schell.
             The Art of Game Design: A Book of Lenses.
             Morgan Kaufmann, Burlington, MA, 1 edition, 2008.

[Sha50]   Claude Shannon.
             Programming a computer for playing chess.
             Philosophical Magazine, 41(314), 1950.
             On-line Archive, accessed April 2009, `http://archive.computerhistory.org/projects/chess/related_materials/text/2-0%20and%202-1.Programming_a_computer_for_playing_chess.shannon/2-0%20and%202-1.Programming_a_computer_for_playing_chess.shannon.062303002.pdf`.

[Spi07]   Frank Spillers.
             What is design? (yes, all 10 definitions!).
             `http://experiencedynamics.blogs.com/site_search_usability/2007/10/what-is-design-.html`, October 30 2007.

[SZ04]   Kattie Salen and Eric Zimmerman.
             Rules of Play: Game Design Fundamentals.
             MIT Press, Cambridge, Massachusetts, USA, 2004.

[Tol54]   J. R. R. Tolkien.
             The Lord of the Rings.
             Houghton Mifflin, 1954.

[Wal82]   Mansfield Tracy Walsworth.
             Twenty Questions: A Short Treatise on the Game to Which Are Added a Code of Rules.
             Henry Holt and Company, New York, New York, 1882.
             Retrieved from Google Books July 2009, `http://books.google.com/books?id=VzoVAAAAYAAJ`.

[Whi92]   Jeff White, editor.
             TI International Users Network Converence. Texas Instruments, September 1992.
             Transcript of interview: `http://groups.google.com/group/comp.sys.ti/msg/73e2451bcae4d91a`, 2009-02-02.

Java Templates

Classes

```
<comment> := // <commentFromHereToEndOfLine>


<comment> := /*
             <anyNumberOfCommentLines>
             */
```

```
<identifier> := <letterOrUnderscore><letterOrDigitOrUnderscore>*

<definition> := <fieldDeclaration> |
                <methodDefinition> |
                <classDefinition>

<accessLevel> := <empty> |
                 public |
                 protected |
                 private

<className> := <identifier>

<parentClassName> := <identifier>

<classDeclaration> := <accessLevel> class <className>
                        [extends <parentClassName>]
                        [implements <interfaceName> [,<interfaceName>]*]
<classBody> := {
                  <definition>*
                }
```

Interfaces

```
<interfaceName> := <identifier>


<parentInterfaceName> := <identifier>


<interfaceDeclaration> :=
    <accessLevel> interface <interfaceName>
      [extends <parentInterfaceName> [, <parentInterfaceName>]*]


<interfaceBody> := {
                    [<methodDeclaration>;] *
                 }
```

Class, Interface Files

```
<packageID> := <identifier>


<packageID> := package <packageName>;


<import> := import <importClassPath>;


<classFile> := [<packageID>]
               <import>*
               <classDefinition>


<interfaceDefinition> := <interfaceDeclaration>
                         <interfaceBody>


<interfaceFile> := [<packageID>]
                   <imports>
                   <interfaceDefinition>
```

Expressions, Fields, Variables

```
<typeName> := <identifier>


<variableName> := <identifier>


<variableDeclaration> := <typeName> <variableName>


<localVariableDefinition> := <variableDeclaration> [= <expression>];


<fieldDeclaration> := <accessLevel> <variableDeclaration>;


<actualParameterList> := [<expression> [, <expression>]*]


<object> := <identifier> |
            <expression>
```

```
<methodName> := <identifier>

<methodCall> := [<object>.]<methodName>(<actualParameterList>)

<op> := + | - | * | / | \% |
        == | != | < | <= | >= | > |
        \&\& | '||' |
        =

<post-op> := ++ | --

<pre-op> := ++ | -- |
            + | - |
            !

<expression> := <literal> |
                new <typeName>(<actualParameterList>) |
                <methodCall> |
                <expression> <op> <expression> |
                <expression> <post-op> |
                <pre-op> <expression> |
                (<expression>)
                <methodCall>
```

Method Declarations

```
<block> := {
              <statement>*
          }

<returnType> := <typeName> |
                void

<methodName> := <identifier>

<formalParameter> := <variableDeclaration>

<formalParameterList> := [<formalParameter> [, <formalParameter>]*]

<methodDeclaration> :=
  <accessLevel> <returnType> <methodName>(<formalParameterList>)

<methodDefinition> := <methodDeclaration>
                          <block>

<constructorDeclaration> :=
    <access-level> <class-name>(<formalParameterList>)

<constructorDefinition> := <constructorDeclaration>
                              <block>
```

Statements

```
<thenStatement> := <statement>

<elseStatement> := <statement>

<ifStatement> := if (<booleanExpression>)
                    <thenStatement>
                 [else
                    <elseStatement>]

<returnStatement> := return <expression>; |
                     return;

<forStatement> ::= for (<init>; <continuation>; <nextStep>)
                      <statement>

<whileStatement> ::= while (<continuation>)
                        <statement>

<exceptionalStatements> := <statement>*

<tryCatchFinallyStatement> :=
    try {
        <exceptionalStatements>
        } catch (<exceptionType1> <identifier1>) {
        <statement>*
        } [ catch (<exceptionTypei> <identifieri>) {
        <statement>*
        } ]*
        [ finally {
        <statement>*
        } ]

<statement> := <localVariableDefinition> |
              <expression>; |
              <forStatement> |
              <whileStatement> |
              <ifStatement> |
              <tryCatchFinallyStatement> |
              <block>
```

Appendix **D**

FANG Color Names

The table on the following page lists all of the color names built into the FANG `Palette` class. The name is given with the "Web" color string specifying the red, green, and blue channels of the color. These names can be used directly in the **static** `getColor` method of `fang.attribute.Palette` or in the **static** `getColor` method of `fang.core.Game`. Note that both `getColor` methods are case-insensitive and they compress out all whitespace within the name string.

Alice Blue	#F0F8FF	Gold	#FFD700	Navajo White	#FFDEAD
Antique White	#FAEBD7	Goldenrod	#DAA520	Navy	#000080
Aqua	#00FFFF	Gray	#808080	Old Lace	#FDF5E6
Aquamarine	#7FFFD4	Grey	#808080	Olive	#808000
Azure	#F0FFFF	Green	#008000	Olive Drab	#6B8E23
Beige	#F5F5DC	Green Yellow	#ADFF2F	Orange	#FFA500
Bisque	#FFE4C4	Honey Dew	#F0FFF0	Orange Red	#FF4500
Black	#000000	Hot Pink	#FF69B4	Orchid	#DA70D6
Blanched Almond	#FFEBCD	Indian Red	#CD5C5C	Pale Goldenrod	#EEE8AA
Blue	#0000FF	Indigo	#4B0082	Pale Green	#98FB98
Blue Violet	#8A2BE2	Ivory	#FFFFF0	Pale Turquoise	#AFEEEE
Brown	#A52A2A	Khaki	#F0E68C	Pale Violet Red	#DB7093
Burlywood	#DEB887	Lavender	#E6E6FA	Papaya Whip	#FFEFD5
Cadetblue	#5F9EA0	Lavender Blush	#FFF0F5	Peachpuff	#FFDAB9
Chartreuse	#7FFF00	Lawn Green	#7CFC00	Peru	#CD853F
Chocolate	#D2691E	Lemon Chiffon	#FFFACD	Pink	#FFC0CB
Coral	#FF7F50	Light Blue	#ADD8E6	Plum	#DDA0DD
Cornflower Blue	#6495ED	Light Coral	#F08080	Powder Blue	#B0E0E6
Cornsilk	#FFF8DC	Light Cyan	#E0FFFF	Purple	#800080
Crimson	#DC143C	Light Goldenrod Yellow	#FAFAD2	Red	#FF0000
Cyan	#00FFFF	Light Green	#90EE90	Rosy Brown	#BC8F8F
Dark Blue	#00008B	Light Grey	#D3D3D3	Royal Blue	#4169E1
Dark Cyan	#008B8B	Light Gray	#D3D3D3	Saddle Brown	#8B4513
Dark Goldenrod	#B8860B	Light Pink	#FFB6C1	Salmon	#FA8072
Dark Gray	#A9A9A9	Light Salmon	#FFA07A	Sandy Brown	#F4A460
Dark Green	#006400	Light Sea Green	#20B2AA	Sea Green	#2E8B57
Dark Khaki	#BDB76B	Light Sky Blue	#87CEFA	Seashell	#FFF5EE
Dark Magenta	#8B008B	Light Slate Gray	#778899	Sienna	#A0522D
Dark Olive Green	#556B2F	Light Slate Grey	#778899	Silver	#C0C0C0
Dark Orange	#FF8C00	Light Steel Blue	#B0C4DE	Sky Blue	#87CEEB
Dark Orchid	#9932CC	Light Yellow	#FFFFE0	Slate Blue	#6A5ACD
Dark Red	#8B0000	Lime	#00FF00	Slate Gray	#708090
Dark Salmon	#E9967A	Lime Green	#32CD32	Slate Grey	#708090
Dark Sea Green	#8FBC8F	Linen	#FAF0E6	Snow	#FFFAFA
Dark Slate Blue	#483D8B	Magenta	#FF00FF	Spring Green	#00FF7F
Dark Slate Gray	#2F4F4F	Maroon	#800000	Steel Blue	#4682B4
Dark Turquoise	#00CED1	Medium Aquamarine	#66CDAA	Tan	#D2B48C
Dark Violet	#9400D3	Medium Blue	#0000CD	Teal	#008080
Deep Pink	#FF1493	Medium Orchid	#BA55D3	Thistle	#D8BFD8
Deep Sky Blue	#00BFFF	Medium Purple	#9370DB	Tomato	#FF6347
Dim Gray	#696969	Medium Sea Green	#3CB371	Turquoise	#40E0D0
Dim Grey	#696969	Medium Slate Blue	#7B68EE	Violet	#EE82EE
Dodger Blue	#1E90FF	Medium Spring Green	#00FA9A	Wheat	#F5DEB3
Fire Brick	#B22222	Medium Turquoise	#48D1CC	White	#FFFFFF
Floral White	#FFFAF0	Medium Violet Red	#C71585	White Smoke	#F5F5F5
Forest Green	#228B22	Midnight Blue	#191970	Yellow	#FFFF00
Fuchsia	#FF00FF	Mint Cream	#F5FFFA	Yellow Green	#9ACD32
Gainsboro	#DCDCDC	Misty Rose	#FFE4E1	FANG Blue	#6464FF
Ghost White	#F8F8FF	Moccasin	#FFE4B5	SCG Red	#A62126

Index